Visual Basic® 6 Bible

Visual Basic® 6 Bible

Eric A. Smith, Valor Whisler, and Hank Marquis

Hungry Minds™

Best-Selling Books • Digital Downloads • e-Books • Answer Networks • e-Newsletters • Branded Web Sites • e-Learning

New York, NY ◆ Cleveland, OH ◆ Indianapolis, IN

Visual Basic® 6 Bible

Published by
Hungry Minds, Inc.
909 Third Avenue
New York, NY 10022
www.hungryminds.com

Library of Congress Catalog Card Number: 98-71861

ISBN: 0-7645-3227-8

Printed in the United States of America

10 9 8 7 6

1B/QS/QY/QR/IN

Distributed in the United States by Hungry Minds, Inc.

Distributed by CDG Books Canada Inc. for Canada; by Transworld Publishers Limited in the United Kingdom; by IDG Norge Books for Norway; by IDG Sweden Books for Sweden; by IDG Books Australia Publishing Corporation Pty. Ltd. for Australia and New Zealand; by TransQuest Publishers Pte Ltd. for Singapore, Malaysia, Thailand, Indonesia, and Hong Kong; by Gotop Information Inc. for Taiwan; by ICG Muse, Inc. for Japan; by Intersoft for South Africa; by Eyrolles for France; by International Thomson Publishing for Germany, Austria and Switzerland; by Distribuidora Cuspide for Argentina; by LR International for Brazil; by Galileo Libros for Chile; by Ediciones ZETA S.C.R. Ltda. for Peru; by WS Computer Publishing Corporation, Inc., for the Philippines; by Contemporanea de Ediciones for Venezuela; by Express Computer Distributors for the Caribbean and West Indies; by Micronesia Media Distributor, Inc. for Micronesia; by Chips Computadoras S.A. de C.V. for Mexico; by Editorial Norma de Panama S.A. for Panama; by American Bookshops for Finland.

For general information on Hungry Minds' products and services please contact our Customer Care Department within the U.S. at 800-762-2974, outside the U.S. at 317-572-3993 or fax 317-572-4002.

For sales inquiries and reseller information, including discounts, premium and bulk quantity sales, and foreign-language translations, please contact our Customer Care Department at 800-434-3422, fax 317-572-4002, or write to Hungry Minds, Inc., Attn: Customer Care Department, 10475 Crosspoint Boulevard, Indianapolis, IN 46256.

For information on licensing foreign or domestic rights, please contact our Sub-Rights Customer Care Department at 212-884-5000.

For authorization to photocopy items for corporate, personal, or educational use, please contact Copyright Clearance Center, 222 Rosewood Drive, Danvers, MA 01923, or fax 978-750-4470.

For information on using Hungry Minds' products and services in the classroom or for ordering examination copies, please contact our Educational Sales Department at 800-434-2086 or fax 317-572-4005.

Please contact our Public Relations Department at 212-884-5163 for press review copies or 212-884-5000 for author interviews and other publicity information or fax 212-884-5400.

Hungry Minds™ is a trademark of Hungry Minds, Inc.

About the Authors

Eric A. Smith is a Microsoft Certified Professional at Information Strategies, a Washington, D.C.-based Solution Provider Partner. He is also the creator of Ask the VB Pro (http://www.inquiry.com/thevbpro), one of the most popular Visual Basic sites on the Internet. Eric is the author of *Visual Basic 6 One Step at a Time*, also for IDG Books Worldwide, and he is also a frequent contributor to *Visual Basic Programmer's Journal*. Eric can be reached at easmith@northcomp.com.

Valor Whisler, a software engineer with over 13 years of development experience, has been involved with Visual Basic since Version 1.0. He has written several commercial applications, including the first add-in for VB: VB AppFramework. Valor has also spoken at software development conferences, authored several white papers for Microsoft, and been involved in developing the browser for the Microsoft Repository. When Valor isn't programming, he heads out to the Colorado mountains near his home.

Hank Marquis is a senior software designer and developer with over 18 years of experience designing and developing tools for developers such as Modern GuardX, Modern DemoX, FailSafe, CodeReview, VB/Magic, Visual/db, and others. Hank writes the "Components" column for *BackOffice Magazine* and is a frequent contributor to *Visual Basic Programmer's Journal*. When Hank isn't programming or writing about programming, he works on his horse farm in rural Connecticut.

Credits

Acquisitions Editor
John Osborn

Development Editors
Matthew E. Lusher
D. F. Scott

Technical Editors
Sheila Davis
Laura McCarthy

Copy Editors
Barry Childs-Helton
Dennis Weaver
Nancy Crumpton

Project Coordinator
Susan Parini

Cover Design
Murder By Design

Graphics and Production Specialists
Linda Marousek
Hector Mendoza
Elsie Yim
Jude Levinson
Mary Penn

Quality Control Specialists
Mick Arellano
Mark Schumann

Illustrator
Donna Reynolds

Proofreader
C^2 Editorial Services

Indexer
Ann Norcross

For Jodi. — Eric Smith

For my wife Dawn, and my daughters, Danielle and Alison. — Valor Whisler

To my family, for putting up with me. — Hank Marquis

Preface

Ever since Visual Basic was introduced to the public in 1991, it has improved with every release. Users who expect it to be like the original Basic language will be shocked to find it barely resembles its now-distant ancestor. With each release, the product has gotten both better and more popular. By 1998, Visual Basic was the primary language used by more than half the developers in the United States. This certainly says a lot about the many improvements made to the language over the years.

As with previous versions, this new version of Visual Basic has a wealth of new features and improvements. Besides the numerous bug fixes added since Visual Basic 5, this version also includes new tools to enhance developer productivity. Many tools that were once third-party add-ons are now part of the development environment. You learn how to use these tools and features, as well as how to integrate them into your new and existing projects.

Because Visual Basic does have such a large user base, there is a wealth of knowledge and techniques you can adapt from other programmers. This book covers a wide variety of intermediate to advanced topics not normally covered in this type of book. This book is also designed to be a complete desk reference to the many techniques and tools related to Visual Basic. It is not simply a rewritten user manual. You find original applications and code snippets you can use in your own projects; these are mostly from real applications that have been written for various purposes. They're not simply "theoretical" techniques — we've been using them in the real world already, so you can be confident they work as advertised.

How to Use This Book

Visual Basic® 6 Bible is a comprehensive look at programming with Visual Basic 6. Because this book is fairly large, it is divided into seven parts.

Part I: Introduction to Visual Basic 6 – Chapters 1–2

These chapters describe the new features of Visual Studio and Visual Basic. This, for the most part, is a high-level introduction to the Microsoft development tools strategy. You see how Visual Basic fits into the Visual Studio suite of products and how it can interact with the other product family members.

Part II: Building Better Applications – Chapters 3–8

Beginning with a Visual Basic primer, these chapters cover some easy techniques for designing and developing your applications so they are both more reliable and expandable. You learn how to use object-oriented programming to make your code more modular and easier to distribute to other programmers. Object-oriented programming also makes your own coding easier to understand. In addition, you learn some techniques for making your applications easier to use from a user's point of view.

Part III: Database Programming – Chapters 9–13

These chapters cover database programming, but not always in the traditional way. Instead of having data access code spread throughout your application, several of these chapters show you how to embed this code into classes so changes can be more easily made and controlled. You also learn about the newest data access library, Active Data Objects (ADO). ADO is an integral part of Microsoft's long-term data access strategy. Using ADO in combination with OLE DB, you can access a wide variety of data sources, including ones not typically used with databases, such as Microsoft Index Server information. You also learn about the new data tools included in the Visual Basic development environment. These tools will save you from having to keep several applications open simultaneously — you can do most tasks from within the VB environment now.

Part IV: Expanding Your Applications – Chapters 14–18

Programmers don't just write standalone applications any longer. With the advent of the Internet, you need to think about writing applications that can work on a variety of platforms, including the strange, stateless environment of the Internet. Visual Basic now includes special features designed for the Internet. If you're interested in writing server-side applications, you can build WebClass modules that can be accessed like Web pages from a client's point of view. These modules and applications are compiled code and can run extremely quickly. Finally, you learn how to take advantage of resource files, a development feature previously restricted to applications built in languages like Visual C++. Resource files are also an efficient way to internationalize your applications.

Part V: ActiveX Development – Chapters 19–26

ActiveX covers Microsoft's strategy for developing for the Internet. From a slogan of "Activating the Internet," ActiveX has grown to cover a wide variety of features, not all of which have to be Internet-related. For instance, these chapters show you how to build ActiveX servers, which are simply reusable libraries of objects and functions you can deploy to a traditional client-server environment as easily as you can push them over the Web. You also learn how to build good ActiveX controls that can be used in both client-server and Web environments. Many pitfalls are involved in developing these controls and you learn how to avoid them and exploit the power of these controls. Finally, you learn how to build Add-ins for the Visual Basic environment. If you don't like how a feature works in VB, you can rewrite it and expand the functions to do just what you want.

Part VI: Windows API Programming — Chapters 27–32

Although Visual Basic hides much of the complexity of the Windows API, it doesn't restrict you from using it. With some simple guidelines under your belt, you can exploit the power of the Windows API to perform tasks simply unavailable or impractical to do through the Visual Basic language. You learn about API functions to work with the keyboard and mouse directly. You learn more about how to manipulate the user's display and how to get into the files and disk drives on a user's computer. You also learn how to retrieve vital system information from a user's system. This information can help your application adapt more quickly to the changing Windows environment.

Part VII: Reliable Programming — Chapters 33–34

One of the topics most books overlook is how to make programs more reliable. With the growing demand to have programs that don't need a fix or patch every other week, you must make sure your application is bulletproof before you let a single user see it. These chapters cover techniques for making both traditional and component-based applications more reliable. You learn how to build robust error handlers that can deal with every error reliably and efficiently. Only in some cases will you actually need to exit your application once you apply some of the techniques from these chapters. Although an error handler can't do everything, it can make a user's exit quick and painless without showing any ugly stop-sign dialog boxes.

Conventions and Features

Visual Basic 6 Bible uses several typographic conventions and includes several features designed to increase the readability and usability of the text.

Conventions

Throughout the text, examples of programming code have been typeset in a `monospace` font. Where code elements appear in the running text, they have also been typeset in monospace to distinguish them from the body of the text. Text the reader should type, as in step-by-step instructions, has been typeset in **boldface**.

Features

We have used icons in the text to call attention to certain features you may find useful.

Note icons call attention to useful pieces of information you may want to keep track of for later.

Tip icons point out helpful hints for increasing efficiency or productivity.

CD-ROM icons point out materials on the CD-ROM that accompanies this book.

Microsoft Certified Professional Program

The Microsoft Certified Professional Program has been growing in popularity since it was introduced several years ago. With the release of the Visual Studio 6.0 products, the Microsoft Certified Solution Developer requirements have changed dramatically. Under the new rules, every developer will have to pass two tests on Visual Basic 6.0 or Visual C++ 6.0. This book covers many of the topics included on these two exams. Appendix A lists all the requirements and where you can find them covered in this book. For more information on the MCP and MCSD programs, visit http://www.microsoft.com/mcp.

Acknowledgments

First and foremost, I thank God for the ability he has given me to do all things in my life.

Next, I thank my wife Jodi for her patience and prodding during the months in which I worked on this book. I'm not sure what I was thinking when I figured I could get married and write a book simultaneously, but it worked out okay in the end. Don't worry, sweetie, this is the last one for a while.

Many thanks are also due my two coauthors, Valor Whisler and Hank Marquis, both stellar developers and writers who have contributed greatly to this book.

Matt Lusher and John Osborn, both of IDG Books Worldwide, deserve a round of applause for their patience and enthusiasm for this book. Through all the missing beta products, late chapters, injuries, and illnesses, they kept encouraging all of us without seeming to nag. Thanks for all your help.

I'd also like to thank Jim Townsend and everyone else at Information Strategies for their support of this book and my publishing "career." Thanks for all the suggestions and comments on the material you saw, as well as a little writing time here or there between projects.

Thanks to Margot Maley and everyone else at Waterside Productions, I didn't have to deal with all the nasty details of writing books professionally. Through their help, everyone got paid and I could concentrate on my chapter-writing procrastination (just kidding).

Finally, thanks to everyone at Fawcette Technical Publications, publishers of *Visual Basic Programmer's Journal*, for their support of the Ask the VB Pro Web site (http://www.inquiry.com/thevbpro/index.html). They stepped up and purchased my previous employer's Web site and allowed the VB Pro site to live on. Without this Web site, I probably never would have gotten into publishing of any sort, print or electronic.

— Eric Smith

Contents at a Glance

Contents

Part V: ActiveX Development   533

Chapter 19: ActiveX Server Planning Strategies **535**

VII: Reliable Programming   867

Introduction to VB 6

Introduction to Visual Studio 6

✦ ✦ ✦ ✦

In This Chapter

Introducing Visual Studio

Getting used to the development environments

Understanding the enterprise application model

✦ ✦ ✦ ✦

Welcome to the *Visual Basic 6.0 Bible*. Interestingly enough, we begin this book not with an introduction of Visual Basic but with an introduction of Visual Studio. The development landscape has changed dramatically within the last two years, and today's developers require a mixed bag of tools to complete their tasks. Though we will be talking almost exclusively about Visual Basic in this book, it is important to understand the entire development framework—Visual Studio.

Introduction

Visual Studio, introduced at about the same time as Visual Basic 5.0, was at first a loose collection of programming tools and utilities—in truth, little more than a packaging exercise. Visual Studio 6.0 is now starting to show a tighter integration between these tools and utilities, and our guess is this integration will get even more seamless over time.

So, what is Visual Studio anyway? Visual Studio is a collection of Microsoft Visual development applications and related tools. This collection is intended to provide a single source and framework for all of the development needs of an enterprise development team. There is some overlap, but the tools are designed to complement each other while providing a complete design, development, and deployment environment.

Figure 1-1 shows some of the tools and utilities that are included with the Visual Studio Enterprise Edition. The most notable Visual tools are Visual Basic, Visual C++, Visual J++, and Visual InterDev. Visual FoxPro is also included for those die-hard FoxPro fans. In addition to the individual development applications, a number of components and tools are shared by (potentially) all of the applications. A partial list of these shared components is shown in Table 1-1. Finally, tools such as Visual SourceSafe and SQL Server Developer Edition round out the suite.

Table 1-1 Some Shared Components	
Component Name	**Description**
DAO	Data access objects.
Designers	Many of the designers used in Visual Basic are actually shared components within Visual Studio.
Repository	The Repository is used by many Visual Studio tools to store and retrieve information.
VBA	Visual Basic for Applications is shared not only by Visual Studio components but by other Microsoft applications such as Excel and Word.

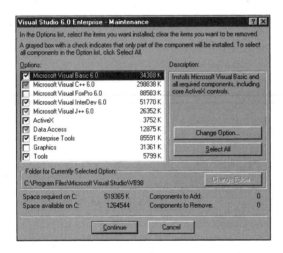

Figure 1-1: Visual Studio 6.0 Enterprise Edition Install screen, showing the available components of the development suite

The tools in this suite are designed to address the varying development needs of different types of developers, including Web developers, application developers, enterprise developers, and content developers.

A *Web developer* is one who is developing and deploying applications over the Web. Such a person might use Microsoft Internet Information Server (IIS) and Microsoft SQL Server along with Active Server Pages (ASP) on the back end, and Web pages containing VBScript, ActiveX controls, and Java applets on the front end.

An *application developer* is one who is developing and deploying standalone Windows applications and tools. They might use a combination of Visual Basic and Visual C++ to develop such programs, using Microsoft Access as their database.

An *enterprise developer* is one who is developing strategic business applications that help manage a company's enterprise resources. Enterprise developers are interested in using teams of developers to build business components that are scalable and can be distributed around the enterprise. These developers are interested in tools such as Microsoft's Visual Modeler, Visual SourceSafe, and Visual Component Manager. In addition, the Application Performance Explorer as well as other modeling tools will prove to be valuable. The common object model (ActiveX/COM) and common database model (OLEDB) are important considerations as the application becomes more complex and distributed.

Finally, tools such as Microsoft's Image Compose, Music Producer, Media Manager, and Visual InterDev help *content developers* produce multimedia content that can be used by other developers.

With this release of Visual Studio, a lot of emphasis is on database programming. Microsoft is having us move from former database connection models, such as DAO, RDO, ADO, and so forth, to OLE DB. Figure 1.2 shows several of these OLE DB components, most notably Oracle. OLE DB is discussed in detail later in this book.

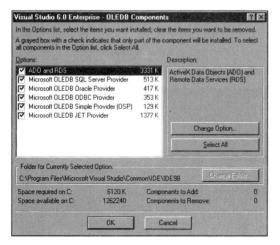

Figure 1-2: Visual Studio Install screen showing the wide variety of OLEDB components available in the developer suite

Cross-Reference

Figure 1-3 shows some of the enterprise development tools that are provided with Visual Studio. The Microsoft Visual Modeler, Repository, and Visual Component Manager are important to developers creating enterprise applications. These tools are fairly heady for casual development, but they become increasingly important as the scale and complexity of a project grows. We cover the Repository and the Visual Component Manager in Chapter 15.

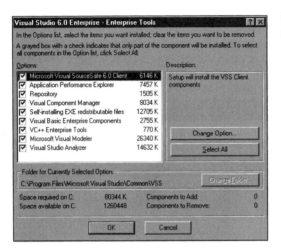

Figure 1-3: Visual Studio enterprise tools

Figure 1-4 shows the directory structure after an installation. Note that the directory structure is different from that of Visual Studio 5. The files are no longer located in DevStudio but are now in Microsoft Visual Studio. Note also, in the root of Visual Studio, there are a number of Readme files, stored in HTML format. This is another nice feature of Visual Studio 6.0 — integration of the Help system with Microsoft Developer Network (MSDN).

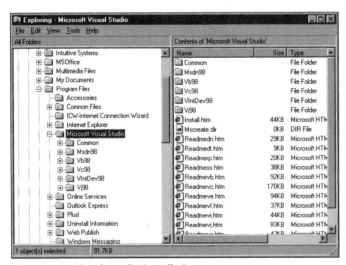

Figure 1-4: Visual Studio installation

The Development Environments

Whereas the first release of Visual Studio was more of a packaging exercise, some integration of the development environments is starting to appear in this 6.0 release. Unfortunately, this version only provides a partial integration — some of the integrated development environment (IDE) features are unavailable in all products. An example of this is the new IDE task list (Figure 1-5). We think this is a nice feature, but it is not available in Visual Basic.

Task List - 2 Comment tasks shown			☒
☑ Description	File	Line	
Click here to add a new task			
TODO: Add any constructor code after initForm call	C:\My Documents\...\Project1\Form1.java	25	
TODO: Add your property and event infos here	C:\My Documents\...\Project1\Form1.java	57	

Figure 1-5: The task list

The task list enables you to embed ToDo-type tasks directly into a working project. This is especially useful for a team of developers who want to define tasks for themselves or other members of the team. Once a task is defined in the Task List window, it can be located and reviewed using the View ➪ Show Tasks menu items (Figure 1-6).

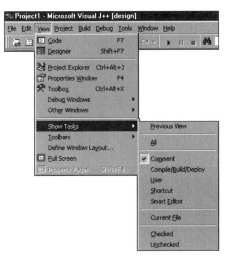

Figure 1-6: The Show Tasks menu in Visual J++

As far as IDE integration goes, there is a tight coupling between Visual J++ and Visual InterDev. These two environments are, in fact, one and the same; when you launch either application, the same IDE appears. The task list just shown is only available in these IDEs. One of the neat features of this IDE is the Window UI combo that appears on the right of the toolbar (Figure 1-7). This provides a quick way to change the window arrangements that show up in the IDE.

Figure 1-7: The Window UI list

Visual C++ and Visual Basic still have their older IDEs, although some integration is starting to show up — most notable is the integration of the Visual Component Manager. The Visual Component Manager (VCM) is an object library that sits on top of the Microsoft Repository. It provides a way to store, catalog, and retrieve resources that can be used by the various Visual tools (Figure 1-8). For this release of Visual Studio, the VCM is the main integration point of all of the tools. Due to this fact, and the power behind the VCM and the Repository, you should take the time to look thoroughly at this tool. The other integration point that is common to all the tools is the Microsoft Developer Network (MSDN) library.

Figure 1-8: The Visual Component Manager

The Enterprise Application Model

One of the new terms introduced in Visual Studio 6.0 is the solution. A *solution* is a metalevel above a standalone application — it is a system of applications. This term reflects the increasing complexity of systems development as well as the increasing potential to interconnect systems through a common communication medium — the Internet.

The *enterprise application model* is another term that is introduced in Visual Studio 6.0. This model is Microsoft's answer to building enterprise systems, or solutions. Here are some of the characteristics of an enterprise application:

✦ **Large-scale** — The system will consist of many components that will be physically deployed over multiple machines. Creation of the system will require multiple teams of developers. It has the capability to manipulate huge amounts of data and utilize many distributed network resources. Such a system will typically have a long life span.

✦ **Business-oriented** — The system is to be targeted toward a particular business domain or problem. It will encompass all aspects of this problem, including user interface, business processing, and database manipulation.

✦ **Mission-critical** — An enterprise application is designed to meet the continuous operational needs of the enterprise. To do so, it must be flexible, scalable, and maintainable. In addition, it must provide the capability to be monitored for availability and performance, as well as provide an administration facility.

Developing such an enterprise application in the past has been the exclusive domain of larger systems, such as minis and mainframes. In today's world of the incredibly powerful and networkable microcomputer, an enterprise application can be successfully deployed on microcomputers, or perhaps a mixture of micros and other networked devices. The enterprise application model is thus the programming model used to create such systems.

The enterprise application model is actually a set of models that are used together to create an enterprise system. An enterprise application is so large in scope and complexity that no individual can grasp all of the elements of the system. Therefore, the entire system is broken down into smaller submodels that are targeted towards different members of the enterprise development team. These submodels are listed in the following Table 1-2.

Table 1-2
Enterprise Application Submodels

Submodel	Description
Development model	This is the model used by the development teams to develop and test the application. Development practices and processes must be defined. Implementation strategies and source code control must be established.
Business model	This model pertains to the business processes, rules, policies, and constraints of the project. Business goals and time lines must be defined. Concerns for security, integration into existing infrastructures, and maintenance are considered.
User model	This model deals with the user's interaction with the system. Consistency with and integration to other applications must be considered. This also includes installation, training, documentation, and configuration.
Logical model	This model describes the logical makeup of the system. This includes the definition of objects, services, and interfaces.
Technology model	This model pertains to the technologies that will be utilized throughout the development process and for the life of the application. Development methodologies and tools must be chosen. Deployment options must be considered. Build, buy, or reuse decisions must be made.
Physical model	This comprises the physical makeup and interactions of the system. The actual machines that will be used are defined, as well as the network interconnections between components.

The enterprise application model is a sophisticated and thorough way of conceptualizing a large-scale and complex system. It helps you view the requirements of such a system from a number of different perspectives. It also provides a template, which helps you through the process of designing and developing such systems.

For Further Reading

IDG Books Worldwide publishes a number of books about the Microsoft Visual Studio development environments. Here are a few you might want to read:

> Harold Davis, *Visual Basic 6 Secrets* (ISBN 0-7645-3223-5)
>
> Rick Leinecker and Tom Archer, *Windows 98 Programming Bible* (ISBN 0-7645-3185-9)
>
> Clayton Walnum, *Windows 98 Programming Secrets* (ISBN 0-7645-3059-3)
>
> Rick Leinecker, *Visual C++ 6 Bible* (ISBN 0-7645-3228-6)
>
> Chuck Wood, *Visual J++ 6 Secrets* (ISBN 0-7645-3138-7)
>
> Richard Mansfield and Debbie Revette, *Visual InterDev 6 Bible* (ISBN 0-7645-3135-2)

You can look up these and more books at the IDG Books Web site, http://www.idgbooks.com/.

Summary

As systems become more complex and distributed, no single tool can address all of the needs of the system. Visual Studio provides the development environments with the raw tools needed to build small systems as well as components of large systems. It is also starting to introduce enterprise tools and methodologies, such as the enterprise application model.

If you look at all of the new features and functions added to the 6.0 release of Visual Studio, a couple of themes become evident: the Internet and the database. These two areas are strategic to both Microsoft and corporate America. Expect Visual Studio to further these themes in future revisions, as well as increase the amount of integration among all the tools.

✦   ✦   ✦

Introduction to Visual Basic 6.0

In this chapter, we introduce the newest version of Visual Basic — Visual Basic 6.0. It has been a relatively short time since the introduction of VB5, but that seems to be the way of things lately in this Internet-crazed world — the pace has quickened. We will, of course, provide our obligatory overview of new features. We'll then discuss the development environment, but not just from a VB perspective. We'll describe what's new in VB6 to support the all-important Internet. The development platform that was once an isolated VB is no more; we are now clearly part of a grandiose plan. Moreover, why does Microsoft make certain changes to VB? We'll also provide a perspective on the strategic direction of Visual Basic and compare it to Java.

Introduction

Somewhere within the Visual Basic 6.0 documentation, we found the phrase: "the Visual Basic programming environment." After briefly reflecting on this notion, we realized just how true that description is. Visual Basic is, of course, a language. Its roots extend back to earlier versions of the Basic programming language. However, Visual Basic varied greatly from Basic in that it provided a visual environment for your development activities. From the beginning, Visual Basic provided a way to extend this development environment with components such as VBXs, then OCXs, and so on. Unlike earlier Basic libraries, these components provided an interface and events so that they could be used to construct a visual interface.

As Visual Basic has evolved, the core language has been extended to add new functionality. However, when you compare the enhancements made to the language versus the enhancements made to the ability to construct applications, you will probably agree that the bulk of the enhancements have been made to the application programming environment. For example, Visual Basic can now use a large number of reference libraries and components, and the two original component types (form and module) have been expanded to a large array of component types. In addition, Visual Basic — the environment — now provides integration with a variety of other tools, including source code management (SourceSafe), component reuse tools (Visual Component Manager), and data manipulation (a variety of tools).

Visual Basic truly is much more of a "programming environment" than just a language. Using this environment, a single developer can quickly create a simple application; a team of developers can create a sophisticated, distributed application.

It used to be possible to be an expert in all aspects of Visual Basic's earlier versions. The development environment was such that a full-time VB programmer could put his or her arms around the entire product and be good at it. This is just not true anymore — the environment has ballooned, starting with VB4, then 5, and now 6. The product has many facets, and the numbers of tools that are included are tremendous. For example, the Enterprise tools, including Visual Component Manager, Visual Modeler, Remote Automation Connection Manager, and Application Performance Explorer, have all been updated. Many other tools previously known as Visual C++ tools are now installed as Visual Studio tools. These include such tools as a DataObject viewer, DocFile viewer, OLE viewer, as well as many other low-level tools. In today's Visual Basic, we are finding that in order to get *really* good in one area, you have to specialize.

New Features in Visual Basic 6.0

This chapter introduces a sampling of some of the new features in Visual Basic 6.0. Each of these features is covered in detail in the chapters to follow.

Data access

There has been a lot of work related to data in Visual Basic 6.0. ADO, or ActiveX Data Objects, features a simpler object model than DAO (Data Access Objects) or RDO (Remote Data Objects). ADO also provides more flexibility in working with other data sources and improved performance. ADO is now the native format, although VB still supports RDO and DAO. One of the more interesting features of ADO is its capability to abstract different types of data sources — not just databases. In addition to the new ADO object references, an ADO data control has been provided. In addition to ADO, VB also provides support for the emerging database connectivity standard: OLEDB.

The Data Environment, shown in Figure 2-1, is a new ActiveX designer that enables you to visually manage database connections and commands. This tool supercedes the ActiveX UserConnection designer (Visual Basic 5.0) and enables you to create ADO objects at design time. With the UserConnection designer, you could set up a data source as a "connection" and manipulate that connection by adding queries and code to it. This "connection" could then be used in a Visual Basic project. The new Data Environment provides all of the functionality of the UserConnection designer and adds the following functionality:

✦ **Multiple connections** — Creates multiple connection objects in a single data environment. Each connection object can access a different data source.

✦ **OLEDB** — Provides OLEDB as well as ODBC support.

✦ **Creates methods** — Command objects that you create in your Data Environment become methods that are usable at runtime. A *command object* is a definition of a specific type of command that can execute against a data source. It is a combination of properties and methods that can be used to do such things as query a data source.

✦ **Commands collection** — Related commands can be organized into collections.

✦ **Data binding** — You can bind fields from the Data Environment onto controls on a form or report.

✦ **Extensibility model** — As with other Visual Basic tools, the Data Environment provides an extensibility model so that you can create add-ins to manipulate it.

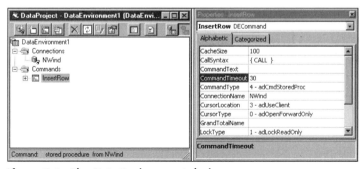

Figure 2-1: The Data Environment designer

Note

A *designer* is a tool that enables you to perform a complex task within the Visual Basic IDE. You might think of it as a complex component. Whereas a form or class component provides a simple set of functions, a designer is more like a mini-IDE.

Perhaps one of the coolest data-related features is *enhanced data binding*. Binding is the mechanism whereby a data source and a component are tied together. Once a component is bound, it has the capability to receive information directly from the data source. In earlier versions of Visual Basic, controls on a form (*data consumer*) could be bound to a data control (*data source*), which was connected to a database. In this version, you can bind any data consumer to any data source. This mechanism enables you to create abstract data sources such as a collection of files on a disk, and bind them to controls on a form. In fact, it is possible to create a single form that displays database information, file extractions, and proprietary data-file information using this new binding mechanism. You can also create classes that encapsulate data sources and consumers as needed. There is also the notion of *complex binding*, which is the capability to bind a number of user controls to an entire recordset — similar to how a data grid works.

Another great addition to Visual Basic is the *Data Report designer* (Figure 2-2). This is a data report generator that enables you to create banded, hierarchical reports. The designer uses a data source, such as one created with the Data Environment, to create these reports. In addition to providing a way to display and print these reports, the designer provides ways to export a report to HTML or a text file. Although the Data Report is not as feature-rich as Crystal Reports, we believe Data Report has a tighter integration with the programming environment.

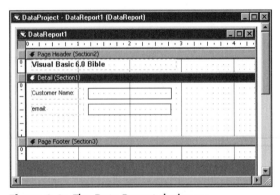

Figure 2-2: The Data Report designer

VB6 includes enhancements to the data controls. These controls include the Hierarchical Flexgrid control, the DataGrid control, and the DataList and DataCombo controls.

The new DataRepeater control (Figure 2-3) should become an immediate success. The DataRepeater enables you to assemble a number of controls together to represent a single row of data in a recordset. The control then provides a way to display multiple rows in a list fashion — like a data grid but with much more potential.

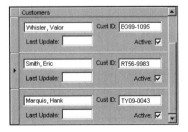

Figure 2-3: The DataRepeater control

Format objects provide a two-way conversion of data between a data source and a data consumer, or *bound control*. This conversion is similar to formatting that can be performed using the Format function, but the Format objects extend this functionality by providing the following:

✦ **Format and Unformat events** — These events provide a way to intercept a formatting operation and perform complex formatting, depending on the content of the data or other conditions. For example, you can apply the system format "long date" to data that is coming into the format event. Your bound control would then display the raw date, which is not necessarily how the data is being stored in the database. When the information is edited in the bound control, the unformat event would then convert the information back to the format that the database expects.

✦ **Design-time formatting** — Unlike the Format function, which is only available at runtime, the format objects work at designtime within the IDE.

A new set of *File System objects* is provided for manipulation of file systems. The File System objects are members of the Scripting type library. This collection of objects greatly enhances your ability to manipulate drives, folders (directories), and files. For example, file manipulation is now done using a `TextStream` object. To work on a file, you use the `OpenAsTextStream` method instead of the old `Open` method. Once you have a `TextStream`, you access its methods to read and write lines of text and get information about your location within the file. Similar methods and objects are provided to manipulate drives and folders.

As you can see, a large amount of work has been done to enhance data manipulation in Visual Basic. While many of these features have been added to provide a more robust and flexible way to manipulate traditional data sources, they also set the stage for the manipulation of nontraditional data sources such as distributed Internet data.

Internet features

A substantial amount of work has been done in this version of Visual Basic to enhance existing Internet capabilities and provide new ones. Most notable are DHTML support and the capability to create IIS (Internet Information Server) applications.

An *IIS application* is a combination of Visual Basic code and HTML in a browser-based application. An IIS application works in conjunction with Microsoft Internet Information Server. It is installed on an IIS Web server where it processes data requests using the Visual Basic code and serves up the associated HTML Web pages. Visual Basic even provides a project template to begin the creation of such an application: File⇨New Project (IIS Application).

Once the server hands the client request (via the browser) to the IIS application, the embedded code can manipulate data sources or other objects as required by the processing. This code can then dynamically generate HTML pages, adding appropriate content, before handing the page back to the server to be forwarded to the browser.

To a user, an IIS application appears as any other Web site—a collection of Web pages. To the developer, an IIS application uses WebClass and WebItem objects, which are designed with the Visual Basic IDE. A WebClass provides all of the application's services, including request processing and page creation. A WebItem is an HTML page or associated item that can be displayed in a browser. In the Visual Basic IDE, a WebClass appears in a designer that provides an Explorer-style interface (Figure 2-4).

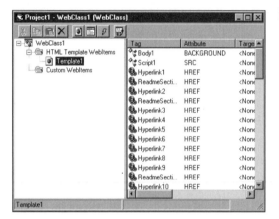

Figure 2-4: The WebClass designer

An IIS application might be thought of as the next evolution of the capabilities provided by Active Server Pages (ASP). To a user, an ASP-based Web site and an IIS application appear to be the same. However, the development model is very different. Active Server Pages are created by script developers who are typically interested in adding dynamic nature to their content. IIS applications are created by Visual Basic developers who are interested in building comprehensive and fully functional applications. An IIS application does not necessarily replace ASP—it can work in conjunction with this technology.

The user interface for an IIS application consists of HTML pages, rather than the forms interface in a traditional application. Because Visual Basic doesn't intend to be a feature-complete HTML editor, the pages can be created in any HTML editing tool. These pages can then be linked to a WebClass as a WebItem.

A *DHTML application* (Figure 2-5) is a Visual Basic application that combines Visual Basic code with Dynamic HTML to create a browser-based application. Unlike an IIS application, which resides on the server and provides HTML pages, a DHTML application resides entirely on the browser.

The purpose of a DHTML application is to interact with a user at the browser. Typically, any interaction with a Web page requires a complete round-trip to the server and back. First the original Web page prepares a request; then the request is sent to the server, which processes it; then a response is sent back to the browser, which redraws the page. These end-to-end interactions are time-consuming, expensive, and they hog resources. DHTML solves this problem by providing a way to interact locally with a user.

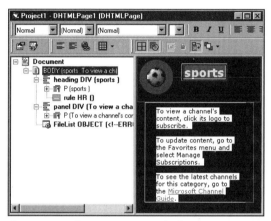

Figure 2-5: The DHTMLPage designer

A DHTML application and an IIS application are not exclusive — in fact, they complement each other. You can create an IIS application that provides the overall framework for your application and one or more DHTML applications to provide user interaction. When these two types of applications work together, the result will be a solution that is responsive to the user and requires fewer server resources.

Controls

New and enhanced data controls are in Visual Basic, such as the ADO Data control, DataGrid control, DataList control, DataCombo control, Hierarchical Flexgrid control, and DataRepeater control. These were mentioned in the data access section above.

The new Coolbar control enables you to create toolbars such as the ones you see in Microsoft Internet Explorer. While the buttons on these toolbars initially have a flat appearance, they transform to buttons as you move your mouse over them. The FlatScrollBar control gives you a standard Windows scroll bar with a flat look — matching well with the Coolbar. The DateTimePicker control, shown in Figure 2-6, provides a drop-down combo that reveals a calendar. The calendar can be used to select a date, which is returned to the combo. The calendar itself can be accessed using the MonthView control. With the ImageCombo control, you can add images to a standard ComboBox.

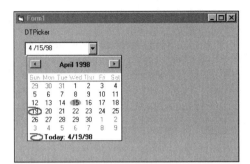

Figure 2-6: The DateTimePicker control

In addition to these new controls, a number of enhancements have been added to existing controls. The `Validate` event, `ValidateControls` method, and `CausesValidation` property help to facilitate more control over data validation. The `DataFormat` property contains a `StdDataFormat` object, which is used to format and unformat data between the data consumer and the data source. The `DataSource` and `DataMember` properties describe the data source that a particular data consumer will be using.

Finally, *dynamic control addition* is now available. You can programmatically add and remove controls to or from a form *without having to have an initial instance of a control!* This exciting new feature provides a way for you to build dynamic forms that can be shaped to match any data source. You just declare a new instance of any valid control and then set its properties.

Component creation

The most interesting enhancement to UserControl creation is the capability to create data sources and data consumers. A UserControl that is set up as a data source provides a user interface and a complete set of properties, events, and methods to manipulate the data within that source. With this capability, you could quickly create your own data control and customize it to your particular needs. You could not only customize the properties, events, and methods, but the user interface elements provided by the control as well. Any other bindable control can then bind to your custom data source, as it would to an intrinsic data control. You can also create UserControls that act like data consumers. Such a consumer can bind to any data source in the same way that intrinsic controls bind to sources.

It is now possible to create *lightweight* UserControls. A lightweight control does not have an `hWnd` property, which requires many Windows resources. This is not only advantageous within traditional applications but is especially needed when deploying distributed Internet applications over networks, where resources are precious. Lightweight controls can also be made transparent, with specific *hit regions* defined. This enables you to create irregularly shaped controls.

Language

Now we'll describe some of the additions and enhancements to the core language. It is now possible to have **user-defined types** (UDTs) as arguments to or returns of public functions and properties. We know many developers who have been crying for this capability. A new set of **File System objects** helps you manipulate drives, directories, and files in a more object-oriented way. An interesting new function, `CallByName()`, enables access to a method or property of an object by name. This alleviates the need for complicated `Select-Case` statements when you want to access a particular property or method. This feature, combined with the capability of creating controls on the fly, greatly enhances the capability of creating dynamic forms. The `CreateObject()` function now has a new argument: `ServerName()`. This enables you to easily create objects on remote machines.

The many new string functions include `Filter()`, `FormatCurrency()`, `FormatDateTime()`, `FormatNumber()`, `FormatPercent()`, `InstrRev()`, `Join()`, `Split()`, `StrReverse()`, and others. The `Filter()` function enables you to create a subset of a string array based on certain criteria. The `Join()` function quickly joins a number of substrings contained within a particular array. The corollary to this function, `Split()`, breaks a string into a number of substrings. These functions should come in handy for those parsing fanatics out there. An interesting function, `StrReverse()`, reverses the characters in a string—we haven't thought of a use for this one yet, but we're sure it was added for a reason.

Wizards

The Setup Wizard has been enhanced and renamed to reflect the increasing emphasis on Internet application development. It is now the Packaging and Deployment Wizard. This wizard helps you create application setup programs—including the deployment of CAB files to a Web server. The wizard can now be run from within the Visual Basic IDE and can be run in a silent mode as a batch process. The Data Object Wizard is used to create custom data sources and data consumers. It works in conjunction with connections that have been created in the Data Environment. The Data Form Wizard incorporates the capability to create controls dynamically and to create forms where the controls are not dependent on a data control to bind to. Enhancements have been added to some of the other wizards.

The Integrated Development Environment

The Visual Basic Integrated Development Environment (IDE) is provided when you launch the Visual Basic application (VB6.exe). This environment consists of a number of familiar elements including menu bars, context menus, toolbars, a toolbox, Project Explorer, and the properties window.

One of the first things you will notice when you launch Visual Basic are some new project templates (Figure 2-7). These include the Data Project, IIS Application, and DHTML Application templates. The Data Project template sets up your environment to create data connections and data reports. This template creates a project with three items: a single blank form, a DataEnvironment designer, and a DataReport designer. In addition, it sets up all of the appropriate references for data-related activities. The IIS Application template creates a single WebClass object/designer and the corresponding references. The DHTML Application template creates a DHTML designer (used to create a DHTML object) and a code module with some property stubs that are used by the DHTML object.

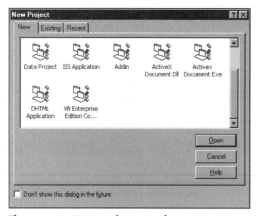

Figure 2-7: New project templates

A few new menus and several new menu items are related to the new data capabilities. The Query menu adds a number of query-related features directly into the IDE. The Diagram menu facilitates the diagramming of database relationships. The Publish Wizard, shown in Figure 2-8 (Tools ➪ Publish ➪ Source Files), is used to add components to the Microsoft Repository/Visual Component Manager. In addition to providing an enhanced Visual Component Manager where components can be published and retrieved, a feature has been added to create a new project from an existing project that is in SourceSafe (Tools➪ SourceSafe➪ Create Project from SourceSafe). This more robust integration with SourceSafe and the Repository has greatly enhanced Visual Basic's enterprise story.

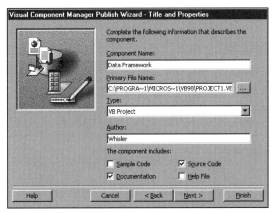

Figure 2-8: Publishing components to the Repository

The only other obvious changes to the Visual Basic IDE are two new toolbar buttons: Data View Window and Visual Component Manager. The Data View window (Figure 2-9) shows all of the connections that have been established within the project. For each connection, Tables and Views are shown. There is drag-and-drop support between the Data View window and other windows, such as the Data Environment designer. For example, you can drag a view into the Data Environment, which then appears as a command. This command can then be dragged onto a form—once the command is dropped, all of the fields in that view/command, along with appropriate labels, are added to the form.

Figure 2-9: The Data View window

Note   Some of the new IDE features were not complete at the time this book was submitted for publication.

We're Not Alone

One of the more interesting VB6 changes, which is outwardly subtle but has major implications, is the way that the Microsoft Visual Studio installation program lays out the Visual Basic directories. It is clear from looking at these directories that our Visual Basic development environment is not just about VB anymore — it's now a suite of tools shared by all Visual Studio components. These tools were briefly introduced in Chapter 1. In all likelihood, you will find yourself using some of the other Visual Studio tools as you tackle your programming problems.

About the Platform

Earlier in this chapter, we took a matter-of-fact look at Visual Basic 6.0 — the tool. Now we are going to step back a little and offer a number of different perspectives:

✦ Why use Visual Basic?

✦ What is the synergy between Visual Basic and other Microsoft development tools?

✦ How does Visual Basic compare to Java?

✦ What are the strategic motivations for the changes in VB6?

In this section, you get a lot of fact and some opinion, but the opinion is based on the experiences of the authors and their peers — a group that collectively has dozens of years of experience with Visual Basic and in software engineering as a whole. If you disagree on the opinions, that's okay; this section still makes interesting reading and fodder for conversation.

Why use Visual Basic?

Visual Basic has evolved to be much more than a language — it is an application-producing "machine." No other development environment on the planet provides as wide a variety of capabilities in the box as Visual Basic (and Visual Studio). With it, an individual can build a simple application in minutes, or an entire team can build a sophisticated, world-class application. Visual Basic enables you to be object oriented in your design, or you can just build applications as you did years ago. Many would argue that the language is not as object oriented or pure as other languages, but it is hard to argue that other tools offer any more productivity than VB.

A word of warning — because there is such a plethora of ways to build an application in Visual Basic, it is easy to piece something together that works but is a bad design. Even though Visual Basic is much more productive than other tools, it also requires more discipline to produce clean design. A key to improving your programming technique is to embrace the capability to create classes and ActiveX components in Visual Basic. These constructs force you to think in a more object-oriented way.

So, why use Visual Basic? Because we like to get stuff done!

The synergy between Visual Basic and other development tools

As stated earlier, Visual Basic is slowly evolving from a standalone development tool to one of the tools in Visual Studio. Is Visual Basic the center of the development universe, with the other Visual Studio tools being consumed by VB, or is Visual Studio the center of the universe, with Visual Basic being used for specific tasks? The answer to this, of course, depends on your perspective. If you are primarily creating applications that are either standalone or distributed on a network but do not involve an Internet browser, then Visual Basic is your central tool. If you are creating HTML-based applications with much of the work being done server-side, then you probably lean toward Visual InterDev tools as your central environment, with VB Script and ActiveX components complementing the Web pages. However, with Visual Basic 6.0's new data and Web capabilities, you may find yourself going back to Visual Basic as your primary tool for developing Web applications. In any case, the fact that you can purchase one package (Visual Studio) and have it address most, if not all, of your needs is a compelling story.

What about Java?

Java has *really* been scaring many developers lately. It scares those developers who have built their careers around Visual Basic. With thousands and thousands of hours invested in becoming a VB expert, along comes Java—and the prospect for cashing in on our investment is suddenly in jeopardy.

But we believe. We believe that Microsoft is not going to let us down and will make VB the coolest tool on the market. We believe that the Java promise is more fiction than fact and that corporate America will reject the hype and get back to work, building enterprise applications fast—with Visual Basic.

Java is a really cool language. This is a fact confirmed by developers around the country as well as developers found near Redmond. In level of complexity, Java sits somewhere between Visual Basic and C++. It is very object-oriented like C, shields you from many system internals like VB, and has a syntax that will be familiar to any C programmer. If you're a C programmer, then you will be comfortable with Java. If you are down on Microsoft or are a UNIX programmer, then Java is where it's at. If you are a typical VB programmer, then you won't like Java for the same reason you don't like C—its syntax is cryptic, and the tools are just not as cool or easy to use.

Java is also a platform—this is clearly how its creators are positioning it. Java is not only a replacement for VB and VC, it is also a replacement for Windows (if certain companies have their way). This may be good or bad depending on your perspective, but one thing is for sure—Java has made Microsoft get on its toes and work hard to combat this serious threat.

"Write once; run everywhere"—this seems to be more of a myth than a reality. Many articles have appeared recently explaining less-than-gratifying experiences when trying to run a single code base on multiple platforms. Many have also found that you give away a lot of operating system-specific functionality by trying to develop a product in this mode. Although there are currently many problems getting code to behave the same across all platforms, an objective thinker would have to believe that these problems can be solved over time.

Let's put all this in perspective and come up with a conclusion:

1. Java is a cool language—but it is also a platform.

2. Java development tools are in their infancy.

3. Tremendous interest in Java still exists, although some of the hype has subsided.

4. "Write once; run everywhere" is still a myth, although it stands to reason that this goal will be realized as time goes on.

5. Visual Basic is a mature, solid tool that provides an enormous tool suite combined with an integrated development platform. Visual Basic is a strategic part of Microsoft's development and COM strategies.

The conclusion is this: Although Java is not a bad choice, Visual Basic has clearly positioned itself as a strategic enterprise development tool for corporate America. If you think Java is going to win, then why are you reading this book? If you think Microsoft is going to win, then hang on for the ride!

Why is Visual Basic what it is?

At times, it is interesting and useful to try and understand why the changes to the new version of Visual Basic were made. The assumption is that the core changes made to any version are indicative of the strategic direction that Microsoft is taking with the product. If you believe that Microsoft is generally on target when predicting the future of software development (as we do), then it is important to understand these new and evolving features so that they can be exploited. When you look at the new feature sets, two areas really jump out at you: data, and the Web. A third area, to which a lot of time has been devoted, also emerges: enterprise development capabilities.

✦ **All About Data**—Wow! There are a lot of new features related to data manipulation. From the new Data objects, to new binding mechanisms, to new formatting objects, to DataRepeater controls, to new data designers, and so on. All of these new capabilities add up to the best data manipulation environment on the planet! As we all know, corporate America is all about data—and this new set of capabilities should knock its socks off.

✦ **All About the Web** — The Web is not only hot, it is the future of application development. This doesn't mean that all new applications are going to be browser based, but it does mean that all new applications will expect this ubiquitous communications pipeline (the Internet) to be available to them. A lot of new features — not only in Visual Basic, but also in other Visual Studio products — make Web development much easier.

✦ **Better Enterprise Development Capabilities** — Most development is shifting from monolithic applications to distributed ones. As the use of interdependent and distributed objects increases, the complexity of application development also increases. This new complexity requires new tools to manage projects. Microsoft is slowly assembling a great enterprise development story — tools are getting more integrated, the Repository is connecting more tools behind the scenes, the Visual Component Manager is really getting usable, and the Visual Modeler is getting better. We should expect continued improvement of overall enterprise capabilities with future versions.

Summary

Visual Basic continues to evolve with Version 6.0. As has been apparent with the last few releases, it is not so much the core language that is being perfected but the overall development capabilities that are being enhanced. In fact, when we refer to Visual Basic, we are not so much referring to the language at all, but rather to the application-building environment that it provides. There is no doubt that when you use Visual Basic, the emphasis is more on application construction than application programming.

In our opinion, most of the development effort for Visual Basic 6.0 has been targeted at two key areas: databases and the Internet. In doing so, Microsoft is "raising the bar" in its positioning of this tool. In the early days, Visual Basic was considered the premier prototyping tool. Microsoft is trying to position this release as the premier distributed enterprise application-development tool.

✦   ✦   ✦

Building Better Applications

Visual Basic Primer

This chapter is designed to give you an introduction to Visual Basic and how it differs from other programming languages you may have used. While this chapter does assume knowledge of programming techniques and concepts, it assumes no knowledge of Visual Basic. If you have already used Visual Basic, you may just want to skim this chapter to make sure you understand everything covered.

What Is Visual Basic?

Before you begin learning how to use Visual Basic 6, it's important that you understand a little bit about how the product developed. Before Microsoft Windows 3.0 was introduced in May 1990, application programming for IBM-compatible PCs was a very boring proposition — all text with no concept of a mouse or a window. Some enterprising programmers created toolkits to create window-like atmospheres using IBM's extended character set, which included graphical characters such as line segments and partially shaded characters. An example of this type of "window" is shown in Figure 3-1.

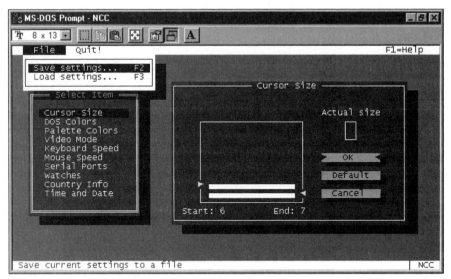

Figure 3-1: An early DOS-based "window"

However, after the introduction of Microsoft Windows for IBM-compatible PCs, PC programmers had a whole new world to explore. Application programs such as Microsoft Word and Excel gave programmers ideas for their own applications, including features such as the following:

✦ Toolbars

✦ Multiple windows within an application's window

✦ Basic support for multiple applications running simultaneously

Unfortunately, programming these features was time-consuming and confusing. The only languages that were available were traditional languages, such as Basic, COBOL, and C. Microsoft did have a product called QuickBasic, which was fairly popular among Basic programmers. QuickBasic could run old Basic programs that used line numbers and lots of GOTO statements, but it was better than Basic. It supported many additional language concepts, but it could not create Windows applications. It did not support the Windows API (application programming interface), which specified how to create windows, graphics, and the other components used in Windows applications.

Windows introduced the concept of a *message*. Every action you perform in Windows generates one or more messages. For instance, if the user moves the mouse across the screen, a series of messages are generated for each position the mouse occupies while it is being moved. If the user moves the mouse over the window for an application that is running, Windows sends these messages to that application. The application then has to determine if the user is doing something within itself, or if the user is just "passing through." Every application has to look at every message sent by Windows and make this determination. The code required to make this work is lengthy and complex, to say the least.

Besides having to handle simple messages such as mouse movements, a Windows application also has to handle complex actions, such as when the user moves a window from one place to another. Windows tells your program what the user is doing, but it doesn't do any of the work of handling the user's action for you. Your application has to repaint your windows in a new position, for instance. Even after you have dealt with all the Windows messages you *might* receive, you're still not done. Your program still has to have code to handle all of your application's features.

Visual Basic revolutionized all this tedious code. Instead of a programmer's having to write lengthy code to make a window respond to a mouse, Visual Basic handled all those actions and hid them from the programmer. To indicate to your program that the user clicked the mouse, Visual Basic provides an *event* instead of a series of messages. You then write code to respond to the event and not the message. This is an important distinction. An event, when translated into Windows messages, could consist of one or more messages. Even a simple action such as a mouse click actually consists of more than one Windows message.

With the introduction of the event, Visual Basic programmers could concentrate on writing the application's features and not worry about the low-level things such as why a button click worked. They could simply write the code to run when a button was clicked. The code that runs when the user clicks a button (or any other event, for that matter) is known as an *event handler.*

Besides hiding the complexities of Windows messaging, Visual Basic also provided a design environment in which the programmer could draw an application's windows instead of writing code to create them. Want a button on your form? Pick it from the Visual Basic Toolbox and draw it on your window. Button not quite in the right place? Grab it with your mouse and drag it to the correct position.

This ability to rapidly draw the interfaces of an application made Visual Basic into an excellent tool for creating *prototypes.* A prototype is a preliminary version of an application used for discussion among designers. For consultants, a prototype is an excellent way to show your client what the application might look like. With Visual Basic, you could even add simple code to cause one window to flow into the next. Speaking from personal experience, it is much easier to let your client interact with a real live application instead of one on paper. Besides being able to see how the windows work, the user might also suggest changes in functionality before you even start writing your application.

Since its introduction in 1991, Visual Basic has become the most popular programming language among professional programmers. Over half of the programmers in the United States report VB as their primary language. Besides its popularity among programmers, Visual Basic has also created an entire industry: the third-party component market. Components can be added to the Visual Basic environment to provide features not currently available in the Visual Basic product. Literally hundreds of components are available from third parties that provide features such as geographic mapping, complex mathematical processing, and more. By taking advantage of the reusability of component software, you can make your programs much quicker to build and maintain. You can leverage another company's investment and use their work in your own programs for a very small amount of money—most components are in the $100 – $200 range.

Learning the VB Development Environment

Before you can learn the features of Visual Basic 6, you need to be able to navigate through the Visual Basic integrated development environment (IDE). The exercises in this section will show you all the parts of the IDE and how to use each part.

Windows in the Visual Basic workspace

The first part of your tour will cover the windows that are on your screen. To begin your tour, follow these steps:

1. Start your copy of Visual Basic by selecting it from your Start menu.

2. When you start Visual Basic, the first screen you will see is called the *splash screen*. This type of window commonly shows the logo and version information while the program is loading.

3. After the splash screen disappears, you will be prompted to create a new *project*. A Visual Basic project consists of all the files required to create some sort of application. For now, select Standard EXE from the New Project window so that you can see the rest of the Visual Basic workspace.

4. There are eight parts to the Visual Basic workspace. These parts are shown in Figure 3-2, along with their names.

Toolbar   Properties window   Project Explorer

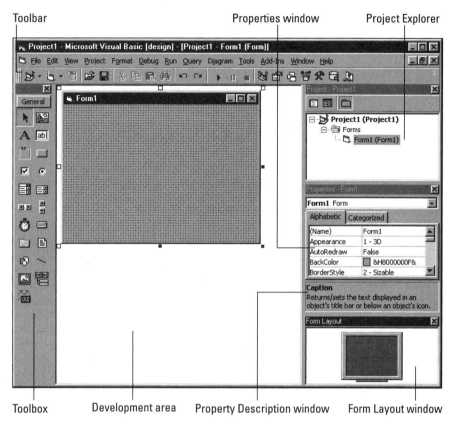

Toolbox   Development area   Property Description window   Form Layout window

Figure 3-2: The Visual Basic workspace

You'll be learning more about each of these windows as you work through this chapter.

Exploring the menu bar

The next stop on your tour is the menu bar. You can access every function in Visual Basic from the menu bar. There are many choices on each menu, and you learn about each one in this and other lessons of this book. For now, just look at the types of functions available on each menu. Follow these steps to start your tour of the menu bar:

1. Click File on the menu bar. The File menu is where you will find all the commands to let you add, save, and remove projects. You can also print individual files and entire projects from here, as well as create working

programs from your projects. Finally, the Exit command is on this menu. The File menu is shown in Figure 3-3.

Figure 3-3: The Visual Basic File menu

2. Click Edit on the menu bar. As in many other Windows applications, the Edit menu contains commands for cutting, copying, and pasting text and controls between windows in your application. In addition, the Edit menu of Visual Basic contains the Find and Replace features, as well as some text editing features. The Edit menu contains the commands to access the Quick Info features. These features will pop up useful information while you are writing your code. The complete Edit menu is shown in Figure 3-4.

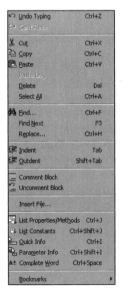

Figure 3-4: The Visual Basic Edit menu

To increase your productivity, most of the commands on the Edit menu have shortcut keys. Shortcut keys allow you to use menu commands without selecting them from the menus. The shortcut keys for the Edit menu are shown to the right of the command on the menu. Shortcut keys are also available for other functions on all the menus.

3. To continue your tour, select View from the menu bar. The main purpose of the View menu is to help you customize your Visual Basic workspace. This menu contains all the commands to show and hide the various windows on your desktop. You can also access and customize all the toolbars that Visual Basic has. As shown in Figure 3-4, the Comment Block and Uncomment Block options have been added to the menu. These are not on the menu by default; however, you can edit the menus and add more commands to them. You can also add completely new menus to the workspace. The customization features can be accessed by selecting View ➪ Toolbar ➪ Customize. The View menu also has several functions to help you navigate through your Visual Basic code. The complete View menu is shown in Figure 3-5.

Figure 3-5: The Visual Basic View menu

For instance, you may not always want to see the Form Layout window on your desktop. To remove it, simply click the Close box on that window or select Form Layout Window from the View menu. Either method will cause that window to disappear. Reselect the menu item to make the window appear once again. Feel free to experiment with the settings on your workspace.

4. Next, select Project from the menu bar. As you might guess, the Project menu is designed to help you add, change, and remove components to your project. From this menu, you can add components to your toolbox, add new files to your project, and add references to other applications such as Microsoft Office. You'll be using this menu extensively throughout this book, so we won't spend time on it now. However, the complete Project menu is shown in Figure 3-6.

Figure 3-6: The Visual Basic Project menu

5. The Format menu is the next stop on our tour, so select it from the menu bar. The Format menu, which is shown in Figure 3-7, provides functions to space, stack, size, and generally clean up messy windows.

Figure 3-7: The Visual Basic Format menu

6. Once you start writing programs, the Debug menu will come in very handy. Select it from the menu bar to see its features. This menu contains a number of commands to help you find errors in your programs. You can stop execution of your program, change both code and values on the fly, and even change the order in which lines of code are executed. All of these features make Visual Basic programs much easier to debug than most other languages. The Debug menu is shown in Figure 3-8.

Figure 3-8: The Visual Basic Debug menu

7. Select Run from the menu bar. Used in combination with the Debug menu, the Run menu and its associated keyboard shortcuts let you start, stop, and pause your programs. In addition, you can choose to compile your program before running it. Compilation involves a number of steps, the first of which is a complete check of your code for *syntax*, or language, errors. This check will find typos and any simple errors in your code. The Run menu is shown in Figure 3-9. Note that you will never have all of the menu choices available at the same time.

Figure 3-9: The Visual Basic Run menu

8. The Tools menu is our next stop, so select it from the menu bar. The Tools menu contains several features, including the Menu Editor and the Options dialog. The Options dialog lets you customize features about Visual Basic itself. This menu seems to be the one for orphaned functions that really didn't belong anywhere else. The Tools menu will vary widely from system to system, based on how your system is configured.

9. Select Add-Ins from the menu bar. The Visual Basic environment can be expanded with additional features through the use of *add-ins*. Visual Basic comes with several add-ins, which are preloaded on the Add-Ins menu. In addition, other programs designed to work with Visual Basic may be used as add-ins. Any add-ins that you load with the Add-in Manager will be listed on this menu.

Like the Tools menu, this menu can vary widely based on the add-ins you have loaded. You will be using some of Visual Basic's add-ins in later lessons. For instance, one of the add-ins helps you build windows that interact with databases. You'll be learning more about add-ins later in the book.

10. The Window menu, which is common to many Windows applications, helps you manage the windows in the Visual Basic workspace. You can rearrange your windows automatically using the menu choices available here.

11. A vital piece of any development tool, the Visual Basic Help menu lets you access the wealth of online documentation about Visual Basic. Besides the Help menu, you can press F1 for help at any time while you are using Visual Basic and get *context-sensitive* help. Context-sensitive help means that you will be shown documentation about the particular thing you are doing when you press F1. If you don't see exactly what you need, just use the search capabilities of Windows Help to find your answer. The complete Help menu is shown in Figure 3-10.

Figure 3-10: The Visual Basic Help menu

Touring the toolbars

As with most other Windows applications, Visual Basic has toolbars with the most commonly used functions. For quick reference, you can leave your mouse over a button to see a *ToolTip* that says what the button does. A ToolTip will appear as a yellow box next to whatever button your mouse is over.

Visual Basic has four toolbars that you can have on your workspace, which are detailed later in this lesson. To access these toolbars, follow these steps:

1. Select Toolbars from the View menu. Another menu opens that lists the four toolbars (Standard, Debug, View, Form Editor) that are available.

2. Click each toolbar's name to show it on the screen. If you want to remove a toolbar from the window, click its name again and it will disappear.

The Standard toolbar is normally visible in your workspace. It contains the most common functions that you will use while programming. These functions are located on several different menus. The Standard toolbar is shown in Figure 3-11.

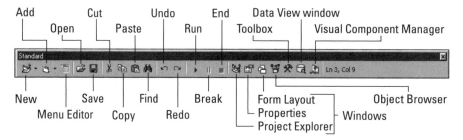

Figure 3-11: The Visual Basic Standard toolbar

The Debug toolbar, shown in Figure 3-12, mirrors many of the functions of the Debug and Run menus.

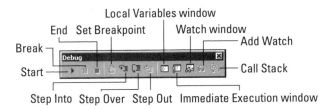

Figure 3-12: The Visual Basic Debug toolbar

The Edit toolbar (Figure 3-13) contains quick-use buttons for editing your code. These features are also available on either the Edit or View menus.

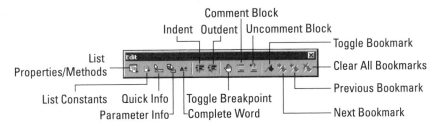

Figure 3-13: The Visual Basic Edit toolbar

The Form Editor toolbar's buttons (Figure 3-14) are the most commonly used items from the Format menu.

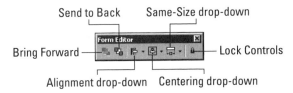

Figure 3-14: The Visual Basic Form Editor toolbar

Like the menus, buttons are only colored if they can be used. Colored buttons are said to be *enabled*; grayed-out buttons are said to be *disabled*. For instance, the Break button on the Standard toolbar will only be available if a program is running. In addition, some of the buttons are actually drop-down lists with multiple options. Those buttons are noted for your reference. You will be learning more about each of the functions provided by these buttons and the corresponding menu choices later in the book.

Using the Toolbox

The Toolbox window contains all the components that are available to use in your project. Each component you add to your project adds one or more new features to your palette. For instance, one component you'll add in a later chapter adds nine new items to the Toolbox, each of which provides a feature from the Windows 98 environment. Most components require additional files to run, which normally have OCX as an extension.

When you create a new project, Visual Basic automatically adds a group of controls for your use. These controls are known as the intrinsic controls because they do not require additional files to work. The intrinsic controls are shown in Figure 3-15 as they appear in the Toolbox.

Figure 3-15: The Visual Basic Toolbox

Of course, you may want to use other components besides those already shown in the Toolbox. To add more controls to the Toolbox, do the following:

1. Open the Components window by selecting Components from the Project menu. Alternatively, you can press Ctrl+T, or you can right-click on the Toolbox and select Components from the popup menu. Depending on the controls already installed on your system, the list of components will differ.

2. Scroll down the list to Microsoft Windows Common Controls 6.0.

3. Select the box next to Microsoft Windows Common Controls 6.0 and click Apply.

4. The new controls will appear in the Toolbox. Close the Components window by clicking Close.

If you are using a small screen, you will notice that the controls have expanded the Toolbox beyond the bottom edge of the screen. To correct this problem, you have a couple of options. The first is to resize the Toolbox window. Click the right-hand edge of the window and stretch it until all the controls are visible.

Note

You also should have noticed nine new controls added to your Toolbox. These are called the Windows Common Controls. You have already seen them in applications like Windows Explorer and other basic Windows applications. You'll be learning about all these controls in later chapters.

The other option for organizing your controls is to create tabs within the Toolbox. Once you have a new tab, you can drag controls into that tab to better organize them. Do the following:

1. Right-click on the Toolbox and select Add Tab from the popup menu.

2. Visual Basic will ask you for a name for the new tab. Type **Windows Ctls** and click OK. Your Toolbox will now look like the one shown in Figure 3-16.

Figure 3-16: The Visual Basic Toolbox with an additional tab

3. Click one of the controls you just added and drag it to the Windows Ctls button. The control will move from the General tab to the Windows Ctls tab.

While moving the controls may be tedious, this is a great feature for small screens. You can add any controls you need and keep adding tabs to organize the controls. For now, you can just leave the new controls in the General tab or move the newest controls to the new tab if you want more practice.

If you need to rename or remove a tab (other than the General tab), follow these steps:

1. Right-click on the tab you wish to remove.

2. From the popup menu that appears, select either Rename Tab or Delete Tab.

You can also reorganize the tabs using the Move Up and Move Down menu items on the popup menu.

Organizing with Project Explorer

As you start building Visual Basic projects, you will find that you have a lot of files. You may have files that have windows in them, some files that are just code, and still other files that may be special files for your program. Visual Basic provides the

Project Explorer window to help you manage the files in your project. The Project Explorer is shown in Figure 3-17.

View Circle   View Object

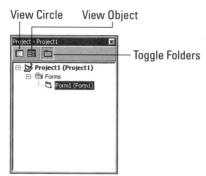

Toggle Folders

Figure 3-17: The Project Explorer window

This window will help you organize all the files in your project. Currently, since you just have a simple project of one form, only the Forms category is shown. For small projects, you may not want to categorize the files. In such a case, you can press the Toggle Folders button on the top of the Project Explorer window. The Toggle Folders button, which happens to have a picture of a folder on it, is already depressed. Pressing it again will cause the categories to disappear and show all the files listed under the project.

A relatively new feature of Visual Basic is its ability to work with multiple projects simultaneously. To see this feature in action, do the following:

1. Add a new project to the workspace by either selecting Standard EXE from the Add toolbar button drop-down list or by selecting Add Project from the File menu.

2. Your Project Explorer window will now show both projects together and will look like the one shown in Figure 3-18.

Figure 3-18: The Project Explorer window containing a project group

You just created a *project group.* This feature allows you to better manage all of the projects that interrelate. For instance, you may have one program that requires two other smaller programs. You can add all of those projects to a project group and always have them at your fingertips.

Once you have a project group, you will notice some changes on the File menu and on the toolbar. Instead of the File menu saying *Save Project,* it now says *Save Project Group.* The same is true for the Save button on the toolbar. Visual Basic is intelligent enough to recognize that instead of saving just one project, you will most likely want to save the entire project group.

Besides the Toggle Folders button on the Project Explorer window, you will also find two other buttons. The first is the View Code button, and the second is the View Object button. When you click a file in the Project Explorer, these buttons will be enabled or disabled based on the type of file you select. For instance, if you select a *form*, which is Visual Basic's term for a window design, both buttons will be enabled because a form also has code in it. However, if you click on a *module*, only the View Code button will be enabled. A module only has Visual Basic code in it.

One last feature: Like many other Windows applications, Visual Basic makes extensive use of popup menus that display when you right-click on a window. If you right-click on the Project Explorer window, you will see the menu shown in Figure 3-19.

Figure 3-19: The Project Explorer window popup menu

In the interest of making functions available where they are most likely to be used, you will find a duplicate of many toolbar and menu bar choices here. This feature is known as *context sensitivity*. You are always presented with the most appropriate choices for wherever your mouse happens to be. Visual Basic realizes when you have clicked on a form and presents you with the applicable choices for working with that form. You may want to save it under a different name, view it, or even print it. When in doubt, right-click and you will probably find a menu for that area of the workspace.

Working with the Properties window

As you will learn later, everything in Visual Basic is known as an *object*. Without going into too much detail now, we'll say an object can have characteristics (known as *properties*) and actions (known as *methods*) associated with it. Properties will be a major part of your development efforts. Everything from the controls you put on your forms to the project itself will have properties that need to be viewed and set.

The Properties window and the associated Description window are designed for this purpose. These two windows are shown in Figure 3-20.

Figure 3-20: The Property window and Property Description pane

Property Description pane

To see some of the properties you will be using, click on either copy of Form1 in the Project Explorer. (If you skipped the previous example, just start a new Standard EXE project and select Form1 when the project appears.) The Properties window will fill with the properties for the form itself. As you select properties from the Properties window, the Description window will give you an explanation of what that property is. If you are new to the Visual Basic environment, make use of this quick help. It will save you from having to look up what various properties mean. For instance, follow these steps:

1. Click on a property from the Properties window that you don't already know.

2. The description of the property appears in the lower pane of the window automatically.

As you can see, there are a large number of properties. However, many of them deal with similar topics. For instance, Form1 has properties for its height, width, top (vertical coordinate), and left (horizontal coordinate). All these properties really deal with the form's position. If you would rather work with categories of properties, click the Categorized tab at the top of the Properties window. The properties will then be organized into logical categories. This is also a feature introduced in Visual Basic 5. The following categories will be shown for Form1:

✦ **Appearance** — These properties deal with the form's color and other graphical features.

✦ **Behavior** — These properties control how this form will operate with the rest of the application.

✦ **DDE** — These properties deal with Dynamic Data Exchange, which is a means of interform communication.

✦ **Font** — This one-property category contains text font information.

✦ **Misc.** — These properties control various features of the form, including whether to show it in the Windows taskbar, the form's name within the program, and whether buttons should be shown in the upper-right corner of the window.

✦ **Position** — These properties control the form's size and position on the screen.

✦ **Scale** — These properties can be used to measure the interior of a form and to better position controls within it.

Depending on your preference, you may like having categorized or alphabetical properties. Try out both methods and see which one you like. Besides this customization, you can also change whether the description pane is shown. To try this out, do the following:

1. Right-click on the Properties window and select Description.

2. If the Description pane is currently visible, selecting Description will hide it. If you hid the Description pane, selecting Description will make it visible again.

Using the Form Layout window

One of the things you have to do for each form in your program is position it on the screen. While it is more reliable to do this in your code, you can position the form at design time and the form will remember its position when you run your program. Until version 5 of Visual Basic, you had to position your form within the development environment. If you moved the form to get it out of the way, that new position would be remembered and used when you ran the program. This "feature" was a major problem. However, Visual Basic 5 uses a new method for positioning forms on a user's desktop: the Form Layout window, which is shown in Figure 3-21.

Figure 3-21: The Form Layout window

This thumbnail picture of the desktop shows you where the form will appear. You can drag the small form within the picture of the monitor to pick a new position for it. As you will notice, the form in the workspace will not move. Similarly, if you move your form within your workspace, its position on the Form Layout window will not change. This is a great feature for those users who like to position their forms at design time instead of writing code to do it. Some of the options that are available, such as Center Screen, are perfect for login and other types of modal dialogs. Having this option available saves you the time it would take to write the centering code.

Besides being able to position the window anywhere on the user's screen, you can also select some predefined positions for the window. By right-clicking on the Form Layout window, you can access a popup menu with some interesting features on it. Here is a short explanation of each feature on the popup menu that appears when you right-click on the Form Layout window:

✦ **Resolution Guides**: If you are using a monitor larger than 640 × 480 resolution, you have to be careful not to make your windows larger than 640 × 480. If you make the window too large, it won't fit on the screen for a user who happens to have smaller screen than you do. Visual Basic will show you how big a 640 × 480 monitor is on the miniature screen in the Form Layout window, as seen in Figure 3-22.

To try out Resolution Guides, Right-click on the Form Layout window and select Resolution Guides from the popup menu. If the guides were already visible, they will disappear. If the guides were not yet shown, they will appear as shown in the figure.

Figure 3-22: The Form Layout window with Resolution Guides enabled

Note According to your monitor size, you will see guidelines for all standard resolutions down to 640 × 480. In the figure, the screen was set at 1,024 × 768, so both the 800 × 600 and 640 × 480 guidelines are shown.

✦ **Startup Position**: Another feature introduced in Visual Basic 5 is the ability to put a window in the center of the screen or the center of its parent automatically without having to write any code. The Startup Position menu offers four choices:

• **Manual** — The form is positioned via the Form Layout window or via user-written code.

• **Center Owner** — The form is positioned in the center of the form that owns it. Whenever a form is shown, it is normally shown either through code that is not part of a form or through code that is in a form. If the code in a form opens another form, Center Owner will cause the second form to be centered over the first.

- **Center Screen** — The form is positioned in the center of the user's screen. Splash screens should always use this setting, as should most dialog boxes.

- **Windows Default** — Windows can automatically position your window on the screen. This choice tells Windows to pick the next position that is available and put your window there. Typically, Windows starts at the upper-left corner of the screen and places successive windows diagonally to the lower-right corner of the screen.

Note that the Startup Position choice is only available if you right-click on a form in the Form Layout window. Otherwise, the preceding four choices will be disabled. You can, however, use the StartupPosition property of the form to access all four choices for window positioning.

The other two choices on the popup menu, Dockable and Hide, refer to the Form Layout window itself. If you toggle the Dockable choice, the Form Layout window will detach and attach itself to the edge of your VB workspace. The Hide choice will cause the Form Layout window to disappear altogether.

Surveying the development area

Depending on the size of your screen, you may have little room left with all of the utility windows visible. The rest of the dark gray area is left open for you to develop your forms and other code modules. As you dismiss the utility windows that you just learned about, the rest of the space becomes available for spreading out your work and all of the windows you will need to write your Visual Basic programs.

Unlike the other windows in the workspace, right-clicking in the development area will not bring up a popup menu. However, if you right-click any of the forms or other modules in the development area, a popup menu will be displayed with appropriate choices for that type of module. For instance, if you right-click on a form, the menu will have choices appropriate to editing a form. In general, Visual Basic sticks to a doctrine of making all applicable choices available everywhere it possibly can.

As you have more and more open windows, you will want to organize them. The Window menu provides several commands for better organizing the windows in the development area:

- **Tile Horizontally** — The open windows (excluding the special windows, such as the Properties and Toolbox windows) will stack themselves horizontally to fill the development area.

- **Tile Vertically** — Any open windows will line themselves up, side by side, to fill the development area.

- **Cascade** — Any open windows will be stacked on top of each other so that the title bar of each window is visible.

✦ **Arrange Icons**—If you have minimized any of the windows in the development area, Arrange Icons will cause all of the minimized windows to align themselves to the bottom of the development area.

As with all Windows applications, the Window menu also contains a list of all the open windows in the development area, as shown.

Final notes

This section was designed to give you a good introduction to the Visual Basic IDE and all the windows available to you. The IDE has steadily improved since VB was first released, and many of the features were added for the power developer that you want to become. As you use Visual Basic, you'll learn to take advantage of all of these features.

Elements of Visual Basic Syntax

Every program, no matter how simple, uses a number of basic building blocks. These elements will be in every program you write in one way or another:

✦ Literals

✦ Constants

✦ Data types

✦ Variables

✦ Operators

Using literals

A *literal* is the simplest building block you will use in your Visual Basic programs. A literal is either a piece of text or a number that you use in your programs. Every program will have some literals in it. Text literals are known as *strings*, and are always surrounded with double quotes when used in a program. Here is an example of a string:

```
Print "This is a test."
```

In this example, "This is a test." is a string. Numeric literals do not require double quotes within your programs. Here are a few examples of numeric literals in use:

```
Print 5
Print 3.1415926
Print -619
```

All these numbers are literals and can be used in your programs. To help you understand how to use literals, you are going to follow the steps below to write some simple code that uses literals.

1. Start Visual Basic and create a new Standard EXE project.

2. At the bottom of the screen, look at the window labeled Immediate. You can type code directly into this window at any time and run it immediately. If you cannot see the window, select View ➪ Immediate Window or press Ctrl+G.

3. Type the following into the Immediate window:

```
Debug.Print "Welcome to Visual Basic."
```

4. Press Enter and your literal is printed directly under the line of code you just typed.

Congratulations! You just used your first literal (the printed message) and used your first function (Debug.Print()) all in just a single line of code. Visual Basic printed the literal you gave it. Note that the double quotes at the beginning and end of your literal are not part of the literal itself. If you need to print the double quote character, type it as follows:

```
Debug.Print "Double quote character: "" Cool, eh?"
```

By putting two double quote characters in your literal, you tell Visual Basic that you actually want to print the double quote character as part of your literal.

To help simplify the learning process, you can enter almost any code into the Immediate window and have it run right there without any other work. For these first examples, you used the Debug.Print() function to immediately print a result. This function puts its output in the Immediate window. As the name implies, this function is useful for debugging your programs. It only works within the Visual Basic development environment. If you create a running program with Visual Basic and run it directly, Debug.Print() statements will not print any output.

Now that you've gotten your feet wet with string literals, try some numeric literals. Type the following lines of code in the Immediate window:

```
Debug.Print 5
Debug.Print 3.1415926
Debug.Print -150
Debug.Print $15.00
```

Did you get the results you expected? The first three lines of code should have presented no hassle and given you the results you expected. The fourth line, while it looks like a number, is not really a number. If you put that line into the Immediate window, you should see an error message display, as shown in Figure 3-23.

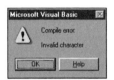

Figure 3-23: An error occurs if you try to print a currency value with a dollar sign preceding it

This is known as a *runtime* error. Visual Basic checks each line before it attempts to run it. In this case, it found an error while it was attempting to run this line of code. This is a simple error, but perhaps you want more information about it. Just click the Help button on the error message box.

Tip   If you can't find what is wrong with your code, look at the help document for the error you are getting. The help text might suggest a possible solution. In this case, the help document says that you probably used an invalid character, which you did (the dollar sign). When you are done looking at the document, close the help window and press the OK button on the error message box.

At this point, you probably have a lot of lines in your Immediate window. To empty the window, select Edit ⇨ Select All or press Ctrl+A. Press the Delete key to delete all of the text in the Immediate window.

Declaring and using constants

Literals are useful for using numbers and text directly in your programs without any other code. But what if you need to use the same number in many places? For instance, you write a cash register program and need to calculate sales tax in five or ten places in your code. If you put the sales tax rate directly into your program, you would have to put that number directly in five or ten times. Your program would work fine, but what if the politicians get greedy and raise the sales tax rate? (You never thought politics would affect your programming, did you?) You would have to go to each place in your code where you put the numeric sales tax rate and change each one. You hope that you won't make an error in changing it, but there is always that chance.

Visual Basic provides a solution for this problem: the *constant*. A constant can be used to replace a literal that is directly in your code. By using a constant, you can change the value of the constant, and all of the uses of that constant will use the correct value. In the previous example, you could use a constant that represented the sales tax rate instead of the actual sales tax percentage. Constants are treated just like literals by Visual Basic, so it is best to think of them just like any other literal.

In order to use a constant, you must *declare* it. Declaring a constant simply means that you are telling Visual Basic about it. To declare your first constant, do the following:

1. Constants cannot be used in the Immediate window, so you will have to put your code into the project you have loaded in Visual Basic.

2. In the Project Explorer window, click on Form1 and then press the View Code button at the top of the Project Explorer window.

3. You are currently viewing Form1's *Declarations* area. This is where you will define your constant. After the line that says Option Explicit, type the following:

```
Const MyConstant = "Hi"
```

The `Const` keyword is used to declare a constant. As this example shows, the name of the constant follows the `Const` keyword. You then follow the name with the equal sign and then the value the constant should hold. As was mentioned before, any strings must be enclosed in double quotes. If you happen to add or omit spaces around the equal sign, VB will automatically adjust them for you.

Note

The line with the Option Explicit keywords forces you to declare every variable and constant that you use in your program. If you don't use the Option Explicit keywords, Visual Basic automatically declares each variable for you. This may seem easier, but if you have a typo in your variable name, you'll never know it since Visual Basic will create a new variable with the misspelled name. In order to have Option Explicit added to every new module and form in your project, select Tools ⇨ Options and check Require Variable Declaration. For any files you already created, you'll have to add Option Explicit to each of them yourself.

4. You just declared your first constant, and now you can use it. From the drop-down list box labeled (General), select Form. Your window should now resemble Figure 3-24.

Select from this drop-down menu

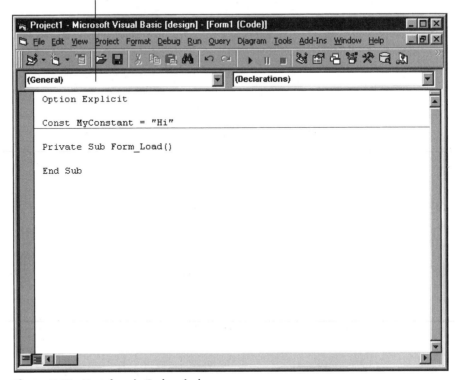

Figure 3-24: Your form's Code window

5. The new lines that were just added to your Code window are the start and end of the Form_Load *subroutine*. As the name implies, this piece of code runs before the form is first shown by your program. A subroutine is simply a piece of code stored in a manageable unit. You will learn more about subroutines later in this chapter.

6. Add this line between the first and last lines of the Form_Load subroutine:

```
Debug.Print MyConstant
```

7. Run your program by pressing the Start button or selecting Run ➪ Start.

Once you run your program, you should see the following line printed in the Immediate window:

```
Hi
```

If you see it, great! You just wrote your first Visual Basic program! If you didn't see the line printed, check the following things:

✦ Is your Debug.Print statement after the line starting with the words Private Sub and before the line that says End Sub?

✦ Did you spell everything correctly?

✦ Did Visual Basic give you any error messages?

Remember to stop your program by pressing the End button on the toolbar or by selecting Run ⇨ End.

Tip

For more practice, try changing the value of your constant and then running your program again. The new value will print in the Immediate window. Constants can hold either numeric or text data.

Data types

Until now, you have been using text and numeric data as literals and constants. However, Visual Basic is a bit more specific than just calling data "numeric." Each kind of data you use in Visual Basic is known as a *data type*. Each data type has limits to the kind of information and the minimum and maximum values it can hold. In addition, some types can interchange with some other types. Table 3-1 provides a list of Visual Basic's simple data types.

Table 3-1 Visual Basic Data Types	
Type Name	**Value Range**
Byte	0 to 255
Boolean	True or False
Integer	-32,768 to 32,767
Long	-2,147,483,648 to 2,147,483,647
Single	-3.402823 × 10^3 to -1.401298 × 10^{45} for negative values
	1.401298 × 10^{-45} to 3.402823 × 10^{38} for positive values
Double	-1.79 × 10^{308} to -4.94 × 10^{-324} for negative values
	4.94 × 10^{-324} to 1.79 × 10^{308} for positive values
Currency	-922,337,203,685,477.5808 to 922,337,203,685,477.5807
Decimal	+/-79,228,162,514,264,337,593,543,950,335 with no decimal point
	+/-7.9228162514264337593543950335 with 28 places to the right of the decimal
	Smallest nonzero number is +/- 10^{-28}
Date	January 1, 100, to December 31, 9999
String	0 to approximately 2 billion characters

As you can see from the table, Visual Basic supports a vast array of data types and sizes. The trick to managing your data types is picking the correct type to use. Some are obvious: the `Boolean` data type should only be used for values that are either `True` or `False`. Some of the other data types are not so easy, such as picking an `Integer` versus picking a `Long`.

For the most part, pick a data type that will accommodate the largest value you expect to use in your program. If in doubt, pick the bigger data type. For instance, if you think that a number might be close to 32,000 (the upper end of the `Integer` data type), use a `Long` instead of an `Integer`. If the value were to pass the upper end of the `Integer`'s range, Visual Basic will give you an error and your program would stop.

You will use Visual Basic's data types for every program you write, so you need to learn the capabilities of each. If you are coding and can't remember what a particular data type supports, look for a particular type in Visual Basic's online help file. Then select Data Type Summary from the See Also choice at the top of each help page to retrieve a list of all the data types that Visual Basic supports.

Declaring and using variables

Variables are the mechanisms by which a computer program saves you countless hours of hand calculations. Variables are pieces of memory in which the computer stores values that are used in calculations that it performs. Imagine if you had to add 1,000 numbers together by hand. You would probably add the first two, and then add the next, and so on until you got through the entire list. Variables serve a similar purpose. You can create a variable to hold the running total, just as you would do yourself. You add the first two numbers and put the result into a variable. You then add the third value to that variable, and then the fourth, and so on. This type of variable is known as an *accumulator*, since it is used to accumulate a result.

The other main use for variables is like an organizer tray that you might have on your desk. You can put things into it for storage and then later retrieve them. This type of variable is commonly called a *storage variable*.

You will use both types of variables at different times in your programs. Variables can be used just like literals and constants. When your program runs, it treats a variable or a constant just as if the variable or constant's value were right there in the code.

To create your first variable, you must *declare* it, just as you declared your constant in the previous section. Follow these steps to declare and use a variable in your program:

1. If your program from the previous section is still running, end it by pressing the End button on the toolbar.

2. Type the following line in the Declarations section of Form1 following your constant's declaration line:

```
Dim MyVariable As String
```

The `Dim` keyword is used to declare variables. You follow the `Dim` keyword with the name of the variable; in this case, the name is `MyVariable`. The keyword `As` follows the variable name, and then you have to pick a data type.

3. Now that you have declared your variable, you can use it. As in the previous example, select Form from the left-hand drop-down list box. In the `Form_Load()` subroutine, type the following lines of code:

```
MyVariable = MyConstant
Debug.Print MyVariable
```

4. Run your program by pressing the Run button on the toolbar and see what is displayed in the Immediate window.

The word "Hi" was printed twice in the Immediate window. This is because the first new line of code you added did an *assignment* of the constant to your variable. You are using `MyVariable` as a storage variable to hold the value of your constant. The next line prints the value of the variable. That accounts for the first "Hi" on the output. The second came from the line of code that printed the value of `MyConstant`. As you can see, the variable assignment worked fine, since both the constant and the variable have the same value.

Using the operators

When you assigned the value of `MyConstant` to `MyVariable`, you used one of Visual Basic's *operators*. Operators are, in many cases, the same as the operators you use to do math and other similar operations. Visual Basic has a number of operators to work with numeric, Boolean, and text data. This section will show you what these operators are and how to use them.

You are already familiar with the simplest operator: the assignment operator. The equal sign (=) is used to assign the value of a constant, literal, or variable to another variable. Note that you cannot reverse the process; that is, a literal or constant cannot be on the left side of the assignment operator.

Arithmetic operators

As their name suggests, these arithmetic operators are designed to work with numeric literals, constants, and variables. You are already familiar with most of them from doing basic arithmetic. However, a few new operators are thrown in, so look at the operators' symbols carefully to be sure you pick the right one.

Addition operator +

The *addition operator* is the plus sign commonly used for doing addition. To try this operator, use the Break button to access the Immediate window while you are running your project. Perform the following steps to try your hand at computerized addition:

1. Enter the following lines in the Immediate window:

```
Debug.Print 1 + 2
Debug.Print 3 + 4.5
```

2. Results of 3 and 7.5 should be displayed, respectively.

One note about the second line of code in Step 1: Visual Basic performed something known as *type conversion*. While you may not think of 3 and 4.5 as different types of data, Visual Basic does. In this case, it converts 3 (an Integer) to 3.0 (a Single) internally so that it can be added to 4.5. Two values' data types must be the same to use an operator on them. Even if you don't see it, Visual Basic is performing the type conversion for you.

Subtraction operator -

The *subtraction operator* is the same as the one you use for subtraction—the minus sign. This is, incidentally, the same character used to show that a number is negative.

1. Try out some subtraction in your Immediate window:

```
Debug.Print 5 - 3
Debug.Print 10 - 10.5
```

2. You should get the results 2 and -0.5, respectively.

Again, Visual Basic is converting 10 in the second example to 10.0 so that it can subtract 10.5 from it. Both values must be of the same type before Visual Basic can perform the subtraction.

Multiplication operator *

The asterisk is used to multiply two variables, constants, or literals and produce a result. Note that using an x will not perform multiplication—it will give you an error.

Division operator /

The forward slash is used to divide two variables, constants, or literals. Be careful not to divide a quantity by zero or you will get an error.

Integer division operator \

Integer division rounds the two numbers (which need not be integers) to integer values and produces the result as an integer. Standard decimal division does not round or truncate the operands or the result. An example of the difference follows:

1. Enter this statement in the Debug window:

```
Debug.Print 5.6 / 2
```

2. This example uses standard decimal division, and its expected result is 2.8.

3. Enter this statement in the Debug window:

```
Debug.Print 5.6 \ 2
```

4. In this example, integer division produces a result of 3. The process rounds 5.6 to 6, and division produces the result of 3.

As an example of integer division in practical usage, you can calculate the number of pages filled by a certain number of lines. Use integer division to divide the number of lines by the number of lines per page. The result is the number of full pages produced.

In general, integer division should only be used when you are dividing other integers. Using integer division with nonintegers can produce unexpected results, as in the previous examples.

Exponent operator ^

The *exponent operator* is used to raise a number to a power.

1. Try this example in the Immediate window:

```
Debug.Print 2 ^ 3
```

2. This will print the result of 2 cubed, which is 8. You can raise any number, whole or decimal, to any power, whole or decimal.

Modulus operator mod

Using the previous example for a basis, imagine that you need to know how many lines the last page of the document holds. The *modulus* function calculates this value by producing the remainder left when dividing the two integers. Because the modulus function deals with remainders not logically associated with decimal point numbers, you should avoid using the function with noninteger values. When used with nonintegers, the function rounds both operands before processing the result.

The following is an example of the modulus function:

1. Enter this statement in the Debug window:

```
Debug.Print 8 Mod 3
```

2. This statement produces the value 2, which is the remainder of dividing 8 by 3.

3. Enter this statement in the Debug window:

```
Debug.Print 8 Mod 2
```

4. This statement produces the value 0, which is the remainder of dividing 8 by 2.

Comparison operators

Visual Basic provides a number of operators to use for comparisons of numbers and strings. Using one of these operators with two variables, constants, or literals creates a *logical expression*. Logical expressions can be used with several *control structures,* which you learn about later in this chapter. These expressions can help direct the flow of your program. The operators listed in Table 3-2 can be used to compare two quantities.

Table 3-2 Comparison Operators	
Operator	**Meaning**
=	Is equal to
<>	Is not equal to
>	Is greater than
<	Is less than
>=	Is greater than or equal to
<=	Is less than or equal to

In the Immediate window, you can print the result of logical expressions. Try these in the Immediate window and see what you get.

1. Enter this statement in the Debug window:

```
Debug.Print 3 > 4
```

This statement displays False in the Immediate window.

2. Enter this statement in the Debug window:

```
Debug.Print 4 >= 5
```

This statement displays False in the Immediate window.

3. Enter this statement in the Debug window:

```
Debug.Print 6 < 7
```

This statement displays True in the Immediate window.

4. Enter this statement in the Debug window:

```
Debug.Print 10.0 = 10
```

This statement displays True in the Immediate window.

As in the other examples, Visual Basic converts 10 to 10.0 before it performs the comparison.

Concatenation operator

Concatenation is the process of putting two strings together. Concatenation is a very useful feature, and you will use it a lot in your programs. To concatenate two strings, you use the ampersand (&) operator.

1. Enter this statement in the Immediate window:

```
Debug.Print "This" & "is" & "a" & "test"
```

You should see "Thisisatest" printed on the output window.

2. If you wanted spaces between the words, you would have had to include them. The concatenation operator does not add them for you.

Logical operators

Logical operators are used to perform operations between values or expressions that result in either `True` or `False`. You can use logical operators to combine multiple expressions, as the examples that follow will demonstrate.

Not operator

The `Not` operator simply reverses a `True` to `False`, and vice versa.

1. Enter this statement in the Debug window:

```
Debug.Print Not(3 > 4)
```

This example displays `True`, which is the opposite of the result of 3 > 4 (evaluates to `False`).

2. Enter this statement in the Debug window:

```
Debug.Print Not(10 = 10)
```

This example displays `False`. This expression is the same as the following:

```
Debug.Print 10 <> 10
```

It is important to learn how to reverse logical expressions. It is a skill that can help simplify complicated expressions. Table 3-3 provides a quick reference to reversing the logical operators you learned about.

Table 3-3 Reversing Logical Operators	
Original Operator	*Reversed*
=	<>
<>	=
>	<=
<	>=
>=	<
<=	>

Use this table to help you reverse the following conditions and thus simplify them.

```
Debug.Print Not(3 > 4)
```

becomes

```
Debug.Print 3 <= 4
```

Consider this case, however:

```
Debug.Print Not(Not(4 = 5))
```

the two Not operators cancel each other, so the condition becomes

```
Debug.Print 4 = 5
```

And operator

The And operator is used to combine two logical expressions and produce a result. When you use the And operator, both expressions must be True in order to get a True result.

1. Enter this statement in the Debug window:

   ```
   Debug.Print (3 = 4) And (4 > 3)
   ```

   This produces False because the first expression is false.

2. Enter this statement in the Debug window:

   ```
   Debug.Print Not(3 = 4) And (4 > 3)
   ```

   Note that you can combine the Not operator as part of the overall condition. In this case, the Not reverses the result of the first comparison but not the overall result. This condition produces True, but if it were written like the following, the result would also be True:

   ```
   Debug.Print Not((3 = 4) And (4 > 3))
   ```

   In this case, the Not reverses the result of the And operation, which is False. Parentheses are used to group the expressions so that the operators work on the correct part of the expression. If the parentheses were removed from this expression, the result would not be easy to ascertain or verify.

Or operator

The Or operator will produce a True result if either condition is True. If both conditions are False, that is the only time the Or operator will produce a False result.

1. Enter this statement in the Debug window:

   ```
   Debug.Print True Or False
   ```

   This produces a result of True.

2. Enter this statement in the Debug window:

```
Debug.Print Not(True) Or False
```

This produces a result of `False`, because the `Not` changes the `True` to `False`. However, the following condition produces `False` as well, because the outermost `Not` reverses the result of the `Or` operation:

```
Debug.Print Not(True Or False)
```

Like the logical operators, the `And` and `Or` operators can be reversed to make them easier to read. These conversions can get tricky, so watch closely:

```
Debug.Print (3 >= 4) Or (5 < 4)
```

If you wished to reverse this condition, it would become

```
Debug.Print (3 < 4) And (5 >= 4)
```

This is still the same condition as the previous one. To reverse a condition like this, reverse each half of the expression and then change `And` to `Or`, or vice versa. When you learn about the control structures, this skill will come in handy since different structures require different types of conditions to work correctly.

There are three other logical operators that Visual Basic provides: `XOr`, `Eqv`, and `Imp`. For more information, search for *operators* in your Visual Basic help file. You will use the `Not`, `And`, and `Or` operators most often in your programming.

Subroutines and functions

All of the programs you have written to this point have been very short and simple. However, your programs will not stay that way for long. You may find that you need to perform the same block of code numerous times in various locations in your program. For this reason, Visual Basic allows you to build *subroutines* and *functions*. Both allow you to create reusable blocks of code that are like self-contained programs. You can give them some input and they can produce some output, just as a regular program does.

The only functional difference between a subroutine and a function is that a function always returns a value, whereas a subroutine does not. When you declare a function, you have to give it a specific return data type. If you do not declare the return data type, the function will default to the *variant* data type. Other than this feature, subroutines and functions are functionally the same.

Note

Variants are special data types that can adapt to hold any type of data. Unfortunately, the fact that they can adapt in this way makes it tough to track down data calculation errors. For this reason, stick to the simple data types introduced earlier in the chapter. You'll find that you get better results in your coding.

You have already used a subroutine: `Form_Load()` is actually a special type of subroutine called an *event handler*. In all respects, `Form_Load()` is just another subroutine. However, it is one that is called by Visual Basic when a form is loaded in your program. If you remember the code for the subroutine, it looked like this:

```
Private Sub Form_Load()
    ' statements that you added
End Sub
```

Note

The single apostrophe indicates a *comment* in the code. Comments are used to document code, and are used here in place of real code.

Every subroutine begins with the `Sub` keyword, which is followed by the name of the subroutine. The parentheses following the name contain the subroutine's *parameters*, which are a special type of variable. As was mentioned before, a subroutine is really a self-contained program that can accept and return data. Parameters are the method by which data is sent into and received from subroutines. Analyze the following subroutine designed to create a message with a value supplied by the caller of the subroutine:

```
Private Sub BuildMessage(Value as Integer)
    MsgBox "The value is " & Value & "."
End Sub
```

As with the `Form_Load()` subroutine, the subroutine first starts with the `Private Sub` keywords, followed by the name of the subroutine, which in this case is `BuildMessage()`. Within the parentheses is what looks like a variable declaration without the `Dim` keyword. In fact, you are declaring the parameter to this subroutine must be an integer. Within the subroutine, parameters are treated exactly like other variables that you might declare within the subroutine. In this case, the `Value` variable is concatenated with a string to produce the complete message.

Cross-Reference

One other thing to note is that we call another subroutine from within the `BuildMessage()` subroutine. The `MsgBox()` subroutine is actually a *built-in function* that is provided by the Visual Basic language itself. There are many other built-in functions that do everything from returning the square root of a number to finding characters within a string. You will learn about many other built-in functions in Chapter 5.

Creating a function is very similar to creating a subroutine. For instance, you can modify the `BuildMessage()` subroutine to return the message it created, instead of calling the `MsgBox()` function to show it. That code would look like this:

```
Private Function BuildMessage(Value as Integer) As String
    BuildMessage = "The value is " & Value & "."
End Function
```

Can you find the differences? Here they are:

✦ The keywords `Function` and `End Function` are used in place of `Sub` and `End Sub`.

✦ The keywords `As String` follow the parameter list. These keywords define the return data type of the function.

✦ When you build the message, you set the name of the function equal to the value that should be returned.

Other than these changes, everything else about a function is the same. Parameters are treated the same in functions as they are in subroutines.

Now that you know how to create subroutines and functions, you need to know how to use them in your code. Create a brand-new project and remove any old ones from your workspace. Instead of using the form to store your code, you will be putting your code in a *module*. A code module is a file that only has Visual Basic code in it. Since the little application you are building does not have a window, it does not make sense to have any forms in it. Do the following to get ready for writing your subroutine:

1. Right-click on Form1 in the Project Explorer and select Remove Form1. If Visual Basic asks you to save the file, do not save the file.

2. Right-click on Project1 in the Project Explorer, select Add and then select Module from the menu that shows under the Add menu choice.

3. Select Module from the dialog shown in Figure 3-25. This will add Module1 to your project and open the window so you can see the code.

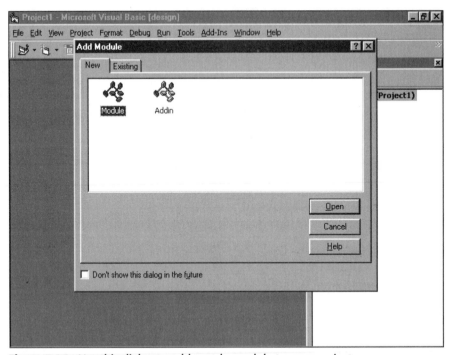

Figure 3-25: Use this dialog to add a code module to your project.

If you do not see `Option Explicit` at the top of the module, type it in. This will prevent any unexpected errors from variables being declared automatically. (See the section on variables in this chapter for more information on this problem.)

Like the `Form_Load()` subroutine, Visual Basic has another special subroutine that can be used when a program starts. The subroutine named `Main()` is a special name that Visual Basic can look for when a program starts. You will use this subroutine from which to call your own subroutine, so follow these steps to create `Sub Main()`:

1. Type `Sub Main()` after `Option Explicit` in the Code window for Module1 and then press Enter. Visual Basic recognizes that you are creating a subroutine and makes the appropriate changes to the code you typed.

2. So that Visual Basic knows to run this subroutine first, you have to tell it to do so. Right-click Project1 in the Project Explorer and select Project1 Properties from the popup menu.

3. When you see the dialog box that follows (Figure 3-26), make sure that Startup Object says `Sub Main()`. Since there are no other forms in the project, Visual Basic will default to running `Sub Main()` when the program starts. If you do add more forms, this dialog will let you pick a form to start with instead of `Sub Main()`, just as the first project you created did.

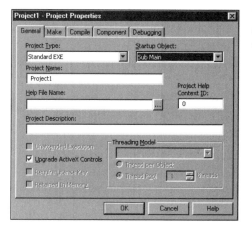

Figure 3-26: Select Sub Main from the Startup Object drop-down list box.

4. Close the dialog box and return to your code module.

Now add this code to the `Sub Main()` subroutine:

```
Dim Message as String
Message = BuildMessage(10)
Debug.Print Message
```

Don't run the project now — if you do, you will get an error. This is because the `BuildMessage()` function has not yet been created. That is the next step you will perform. To add the subroutine, you can put the cursor after the `End Sub` for `Sub Main()` and type

```
Function BuildMessage(Value As Integer) as String
```

When you press the Enter key, VB will automatically add `End Function` to your code to mark the end of the function.

If you don't want to type all that, Visual Basic provides a dialog for adding subroutines and functions. Follow these steps to use this tool:

1. Select Tools ⇨ Add Procedure.

2. Fill in the fields in the dialog box with the values shown in Figure 3-27.

Figure 3-27: Add your new procedure with the options shown in this dialog.

3. Visual Basic will add this code to your module:

```
Private Function BuildMessage()

End Function
```

4. The Add Procedure dialog does not add the return data type or your parameters. For this reason, modify the definition of the function to look like this:

```
Private Function BuildMessage(Value as Integer) As String
```

Because the Add Procedure dialog is fairly limited, you may find it easier just to type the function name into your code module. Either way, once the function is created, add this code to it:

```
BuildMessage = "The value is " & Value & "."
```

Now that your function has been defined, you can run your project. In the Immediate window, you should see this output:

```
The value is 10.
```

Did the program window flicker on your screen and then stop? This is normal. To see the output of the program, view the Immediate window by pressing Ctrl+G or select Immediate Window from the View menu. Try changing the value that you are passing to the `BuildMessage()` function and watch the change in the output on the Immediate window.

Looping and decision control structures

Now that you have a handle on the basic building blocks of programs, you have to learn how to control the flow of your program. If left to their own devices, your program lines would simply execute just as they did in your sample programs from the last section. The program would run the lines and then finish. However, most programs require *conditional logic* to handle all sorts of tasks while the program is running. Conditional logic looks at various program values and determines what to do next.

Besides the conditional logic, you may need to use *control structures* in your code to control the program flow. These control structures allow your program to loop for a specified number of times or continue until a condition is met. This section will show you how to use these structures and conditional logic in your program to modify the flow of your programs.

If/Then/Else structure

The If/Then/Else structure is the simplest conditional logic structure, since it actually mimics the chips in your computer. In your computer's central processing unit (CPU), there are millions of *gates* (not Bill) that switch one way if the input is True and switch another if the input is False. The If/Then structure works the same way. Look at this example:

```
If 4 > 5 Then Debug.Print "Something is really wrong."
```

This statement can be read out loud: If 4 is greater than 5, then print the message. Obviously, 4 is not greater than 5, so the message will not be printed in this case. In some cases, this condition will suffice for your programming needs. However, if you need to do more than one statement if the condition is True, you should use the If/Then block shown here in a subroutine or function — you can't put this code into the Debug window.

```
If 4 > 5 Then
    Debug.Print "Something is really wrong."
    MsgBox "I found an error."
End If
```

In this case, if 4 is greater than 5 the code prints a message to the Immediate window and displays a *message box* to the program's user with the message, "I found an error." The End If keyword closes the If/Then block.

The last way you can use the If/Then block is shown here:

```
If 4 > 5 Then
Debug.Print "Something is really wrong."
Else
    Debug.Print "That's what I thought."
End If
```

In this case, you need to perform some code if the condition (4 > 5) is False. That code follows the Else keyword. This structure is just like this sentence:

If it is sunny, I will go to the park. Otherwise, I will read my book.

You can lay these sentences out like the If/Then/Else block above:

```
If (it is raining) Then
    I will go to the park
```

```
Else
    I will read my book
End If
```

The parentheses around the condition after the If keyword are optional, but they help to set the condition apart from the surrounding keywords. The logical mapping of the If/Then conditions to common language makes them easy to understand.

1. Try writing the code to test this condition:

   If X is greater than 5 and Y is less than 10, then print "Condition is True"; otherwise, print "Condition is False."

2. You should have code that looks like this:

```
If (X > 5) And (Y < 10) Then
    Debug.Print "Condition is True"
Else
    Debug.Print "Condition is False"
End If
```

Did you get it right? Always make sure you have the closing End If keyword at the end of your block. One handy tip is to type the End If at the same time you type the If keyword. Just insert the rest of the code between the two keywords, and you will never forget your End If at the end! You can also use spaces and tabs to indent your code, as is done in these examples. Each time you start an If statement, indent all the lines beneath it until you reach the End If, which should be indented to the same level as the If statement. This makes it easier to find the beginning and end of each block of code.

1. How about the following statement, which is slightly different from the last one:

   If X is greater than 5 and Y is less than 10, then print "Both parts are True." If this isn't the case, if X is greater than 5, then print "First half is True." If this isn't True either, if Y is less than 10, then print "Second half is True." If even this fails, print "Both are False."

2. This is a slightly different condition. Besides checking to see if both parts of the condition are True, you are also interested in whether each half is True. If both of those checks fail, you print a final message. Using the keywords you know, this condition would look like this:

```
If X > 5 And Y < 10 Then
    Print "Both parts are True."
Else
    If X > 5 Then
        Print "First half is True."
    Else
        If Y < 10 Then
            Print "Second half is True."
```

```
      Else
         Print "Both are False."
      End If
   End If
End If
```

As you can see, If/Then blocks can be *nested* as parts of other If/Then blocks. However, this type of structure could get to be many levels deep and be essentially unreadable. For this reason, Visual Basic provides the ElseIf keyword. Using this keyword, the previous block of code would become much simpler and look like this:

```
If X > 5 And Y < 10 Then
   Print "Both parts are True."
ElseIf X > 5 Then
   Print "First half is True."
ElseIf Y < 10 Then
   Print "Second half is True."
Else
   Print "Both are False."
End If
```

Note that you now only need one End If at the end of the entire block. This condition is functionally identical to the last one, but is much easier to read and sounds much more like the original statement.

Select structure

Suppose you are writing code to do different things based on five possible values of a variable. If you only had the If/Then structure, you would probably have code that looks like this:

```
If X = 1 Then
   ' do something
ElseIf X = 2 Then
   ' do something else
ElseIf X = 3 Then
   ' do a third thing
ElseIf X = 4 Then
   ' do the fourth option
ElseIf X = 5 Then
   ' do the last option
End If
```

When there were a large number of lines to perform for each case, this would become a very messy piece of code. Even the ElseIf keyword does not help clean it up in this case. For this reason, Visual Basic provides the Select structure. The previous piece of code, rewritten using the Select structure, would look like this:

```
Select Case X
   Case 1
   ' do something
   Case 2
   ' do something else
   Case 3
   ' do a third thing
   Case 4
   ' do the fourth option
   Case 5
   ' do the last option
End Select
```

This still has the same structure but with far fewer keywords, which means far less chance for typos and other errors. Each *case*, or possible value for X, begins with the Case keyword. You can have any number of statements, any keywords, or even more Select statements between the Case keywords. A particular case is done when Visual Basic finds the next Case keyword. The entire structure is enclosed between Select and End Select keywords.

One other benefit of using the Select structure is the fact that you can put an expression in place of X. Each case simply checks the result of the expression and does not have to reevaluate it each time. For instance, the following Select structure would be very messy as an If/Then block:

```
Select Case ((-1 * b) + (4 * a * b))/(2 * a)
   Case 1
   ' do something
   Case 2
   ' do something else
etc.
```

This statement, converted to an If/Then block, would look like this:

```
If ((-1 * b) + (4 * a * b))/(2 * a) = 1 Then
   ' do something
ElseIf ((-1 * b) + (4 * a * b))/(2 * a) = 2 Then
' do something else
etc.
```

Imagine what would happen if you needed to change the condition. You would have to go to each part of the If/Then block and change each expression and hope you don't introduce any errors. In addition, the computer will reevaluate the condition each time it sees it —it doesn't remember the results. This can be very time-consuming for a large complex calculation.

One last feature of the Select statement is its ability to process groups of possible values at the same time. Look at the following example:

```
Select Case X
   Case 1 To 4, 6 To 8, Is > 10:
   ' do something for this group
   Case Else:
   ' do something for all other values
End Select
```

This example introduces several special features. The first is that the first case is checking for three different ranges:

✦ 1 through 4, inclusive

✦ 6 through 8, inclusive

✦ If X > 10

Each range is separated by commas. The `Is` keyword essentially creates a sentence with the variable following the initial `Select Case` keywords. In this case, `Is > 10` checks to see if X is greater than 10. This is a powerful feature that many people overlook. You can create a very capable and thorough block of code for checking numeric values with these features.

The last feature introduced here is the `Case Else` keyword. Just like the final `Else` keyword in an `If/Then` block, `Case Else` will apply to every value that did not fall into any other range specified by a previous `Case` keyword. Unless you are absolutely sure what values you will be testing for, it is always a good idea to have a `Case Else` block to catch any unexpected values.

For/Next structure

One of the many things that computers do well is repetitive tasks. However, you need a structure to repeat a block of lines. Otherwise, you would have to make multiple copies of the lines within your program, which is obviously not a good solution. The `For/Next` structure lets you specify a block of lines to repeat for a certain number of times, as shown in this example:

```
Dim i as Integer
For i = 1 To 50
   Debug.Print "Current Value of i: " & i
Next i
```

This block of code will print the following lines in the Immediate window. (The lines must be put in your program, however. You cannot create loops in the Immediate window.)

```
Current Value of i: 1
Current Value of i: 2
Current Value of i: 3
... etc ...
Current Value of i: 50
```

The loop will repeat until the value of *i* passes the ending value, which is shown after the To keyword. By default, the For loop will continue to increment the value stored in the *i* variable. If you were to print the value after the loop terminates, its value will be 51. This is important to remember if you are using that value in other lines of code.

Another feature of the For/Next structure is that you can reverse or change the increment value of the For/Next loop by using the Step keyword. In this example, the loop will count backwards.

1. Enter this code into a subroutine in your program:

```
Dim i as Integer
For i = 50 To 1 Step -1
    Debug.Print "Current Value of i: " & i
Next i
```

2. The value after the Step keyword will be used as the increment (or decrement) value for the variable following the For keyword.

You can also use values other than 1, as in this example.

1. Enter this code into a subroutine in your program:

```
Dim i as Integer
For i = 50 To 1 Step -5
    Debug.Print "Current Value of i: " & i
Next i
```

2. This particular block of code will produce the following values:

```
Current Value of i: 50
Current Value of i: 45
Current Value of i: 40
... etc ...
Current Value of i: 5
```

Even though the ending value of the loop is 1, the loop will never reach that value. When *i* is equal to 0, the loop exits immediately. If you were to print the value of *i* after the loop, the value will be zero.

Do/Loop structure

Although the For/Next structure is good for cases in which you know how long a loop should run, most times you will simply need to loop until a condition is met. The Do/Loop structure is the most flexible structure of all the available ones. There are four different ways this loop can be used:

```
Do While condition
    ' statements run while
    ' condition is true
Loop
```

```
Do Until condition
    ' statements run until
    ' condition is true
Loop

Do
    ' statements will run
    ' once and then continue
    ' while the condition at
    ' the end is true
While condition

Do
    ' statements will run
    ' once and then continue
    ' until the condition at
    ' the end is true
Until condition
```

The first two variations will run the statement block zero or more times, while the second two variations will run the statement block at least once. The difference between the Until and the While keywords is much like the difference between the And and Or keywords. By reversing the condition, you use the other keyword.

   1. Look at the following block of code:

```
Do While X <= 5
    ' statements
Loop
```

   Most programmers prefer to use the simpler operators; that is, < and > instead of <= and =>. This condition is really saying "run until X is greater than 5."

   2. Since that's what it really means, make the code reflect that:

```
Do Until X > 5
    ' statements
Loop
```

Follow the same rules for reversing the condition that you used in the last section to convert a condition with the And keyword into a condition using the Or keyword.

   1. The same rules apply to the second two variations on the Do/Loop structure, as shown here:

```
Do
    ' statements
While X <= 5
```

2. The statements above are identical to these:

```
Do
    ' statements
Until X > 5
```

Basically, the choice between the two variations comes down to either personal preference or your company/project standards. With the simple rules presented in the previous section, you can switch back and forth at will.

While/Wend structure

The While/Wend structure is structurally identical to one variation of the Do/Loop structure. This block of code:

```
Do While X <= 5
    ' statements
Loop
```

can be rewritten as such:

```
While X <= 5
    ' statements
Wend
```

The Wend keyword takes the place of the Loop keyword. In addition to this difference, the While/Wend does not have a way to exit prematurely, as in the Exit For or Exit Do statements. Because the Do/Loop structure is more flexible, most programmers prefer to always use it instead of using the While/Wend structure.

Using the Intrinsic Controls

So far, your programs have been very simple ones that printed output to the Debug window. While this is useful for learning simple concepts, it is time to learn about the real power of Visual Basic: *component-based development*. Component-based development is a major concept behind the success of Visual Basic. It meant that a component, now more commonly known as a *control*, could be purchased at relatively low cost and added to a program to enhance its functionality. Now, development teams could concentrate on the business functions and not worry about, for instance, how a grid worked. For managers, purchasing a $100 control might save hundreds of hours of development time and at the same time allow developers to use support facilities provided by the control manufacturer.

Component-based development has now spread to the Internet. In 1996, Microsoft unveiled its ActiveX strategy, which allows these same components to be put on Web pages and downloaded just like graphics or text. This strategy allowed developers to simultaneously build applications for the desktop and the Web using the same components. Unfortunately, Web designers have to develop pages for the lowest common feature set between Netscape's Navigator and Internet Explorer; thus, ActiveX controls are in a holding pattern until Netscape agrees to support them in its browser. Netscape has announced support for it, so this will be a boon to developers when the feature is available.

For now, you will learn how to use the power of components in your Visual Basic applications. In the development environment, all components are stored in the Toolbox. When you start a new project, Visual Basic always provides you with a default set of controls, which are called *intrinsic controls*. These controls are built into the Visual Basic environment and are always available to your programs without adding any other files. The controls cover a wide variety of features. The controls' proper names are shown in Figure 3-28. These names will be used throughout this and other lessons in this book.

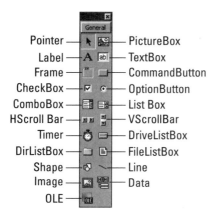

Figure 3-28: Visual Basic starts you off with a series of intrinsic controls.

Like the other toolbar buttons used in Visual Basic, each Toolbox component has ToolTips. Just leave your mouse over a control to determine its name. To better introduce you to each control, the following sections describe each control and its function. In your programs, you will always use at least a few of the intrinsic controls, since they cover the basic features nearly every program provides.

Pointer

This Toolbox entry is not really a component; rather, it is the default item. If you want to draw a control on your form, you do the following:

1. Pick the control in the Toolbox by clicking it.

2. Draw it on the form.

3. When you release your mouse after drawing the control, the Pointer control will be selected again.

Label

The Label control is just that: a way to label controls and other parts of your form. Labels let you provide information to the user about the purpose of your form. In general, every piece of text on every form you build will be a Label control.

Frame

In cases where forms have a lot of information, the Frame control can be used to divide the controls into logical groups. For instance, look at the form shown in Figure 3-29.

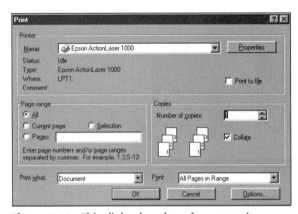

Figure 3-29: This dialog has three frames on it.

This form has three frames: Printer, Page range, and Copies. These Frame controls are used to help the user understand all of the options on this form. Frame controls serve a valuable purpose; without them, the form would look like Figure 3-30.

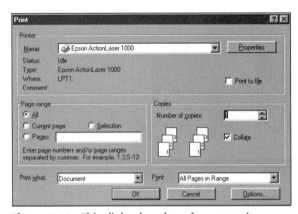

Figure 3-30: This dialog would be very confusing with no frames on it.

As you can see, the rest of the controls have little meaning without the Frame controls in which they were originally placed.

In Visual Basic, controls can be placed into a Frame control. You can then manipulate the Frame control and all the controls inside retain their size and position. This feature causes the Frame control to be known as a *container control*. There are several other controls that can be used as containers, including the PictureBox control. You will learn how to use these controls as containers later in the chapter.

CheckBox

The CheckBox control is used to provide the user a Yes or No choice for a particular question. In Figures 3-29 and 3-30, CheckBox controls are used to ask the user whether he or she wishes to print to a file and/or collate the output from the print job.

ComboBox

The ComboBox control is a very flexible control. It is known as the ComboBox since it combines a drop-down ListBox and a TextBox control into one control. The user can, based on the style selected, select an item from a list or type one into the TextBox portion of the control. You can create three different styles of ComboBox:

✦ **Dropdown List**: This style of ComboBox allows the user to pick from a list but not type into the text portion of the control. This is useful when you have a limited set of choices from which the user must pick.

✦ **Simple Combo:** In this style, the user can type a choice, but the list does drop down beneath the text box. This style is rarely used because it can be confusing to users, who might not understand exactly what is going on when they type.

✦ **Dropdown Combo:** This style provides both features: a drop-down list as well as a text portion where the users can type their choices.

HScrollBar

As you might guess, HScrollBar is a horizontal scroll bar. This control can be used in a variety of ways, including allowing a user to select a value from a range of values, such as a color or similar setting. This type of control is intuitive for the user because, as the user drags the control, another change on the form (such as a color or text/numeric value) also changes.

In most cases, you won't have to use this control with the other controls, such as the TextBox, directly. Most other controls will, if necessary, provide their own scroll bars for the user to use.

Timer

The Timer control allows you to react to elapsed or passing time while an application is running. The Timer can be programmed to notify you after a number of *milliseconds* have elapsed. A millisecond is 1/1000th of a second; thus, 1,000 milliseconds equals 1 second. However, the Timer control's maximum interval is just slightly larger than a minute. For this reason, you will often need additional code to perform an action after 5 minutes, for instance.

DirListBox

This control serves one purpose: to give a list of directories in the current directory on the user's computer. This control is aware of long filenames, so it can be used in Windows 98. In most cases, you will want to use the Common Dialog provided by Visual Basic. The Common Dialog allows you to present dialog boxes that are common across all Windows applications, such as Print or Open File. However, you may not always be able to get the features you need in the Common Dialog. For this reason, the DirListBox can be used to build a custom file/directory dialog. This control works together with the DriveListBox and FileListBox controls.

Shape

Since Windows is a graphical environment, you may need to draw shapes on your forms. For this reason, the Shape control is able to create many shapes, including rectangles, circles, and ovals, as well as rounded rectangles and squares. The one shape it does not create is a simple line. Use the Line control for this, instead.

Image

You may wonder why there is both a PictureBox and an Image control. The Image control provides a much smaller set of features than the PictureBox does and thus uses less memory and other system resources (controls of this type are called *lightweight controls*). The Image control is able to display a variety of image formats, including Windows Bitmap (BMP), Windows icons (ICO), Windows Metafile (WMF), and now the CompuServe GIF (Graphics Interchange Format) and JPEG (Joint Photographic Experts Group) formats, commonly used on the Internet. Unlike the PictureBox control, the Image control cannot contain other controls, and therefore should primarily be used only to display pictures.

OLE

Besides the standard controls, Visual Basic also has the ability to have other applications *embedded* on forms. For instance, you might want to have a PowerPoint presentation or an Excel spreadsheet as part of your application. The OLE control allows you to embed any object on your form that complies with the Object Linking and Embedding protocols. As you will see, when you add this control to your form, you get a list of the available OLE types you can use.

PictureBox

The PictureBox has several features that the simpler Image control lacks. The first is that it can be used as a *container control,* like the Frame. In order to use the TabStrip, controls have to be placed in PictureBox controls because the TabStrip control is not a container control. You then shuffle the PictureBox controls like flash cards to show the correct set of controls.

Besides being a container control, the PictureBox control will respond to a number of events. The Image control will respond to a smaller set of events. In addition, when you finally do get into some advanced programming that requires the use of the Windows API, you must use the PictureBox for any API-related work.

Finally, like the Image control, the PictureBox supports Windows Bitmap, GIF, and JPEG graphic file formats, among others. In general, if you need a picture control to contain other controls or to be used in conjunction with the Windows API, use the PictureBox control. Otherwise, use an Image control.

TextBox

As you write Visual Basic programs, you will come to know and love the TextBox control. Well, you may just get tired of it since you will be using it so much. The TextBox can be used in a variety of configurations, including a multiline version that can hold a virtually unlimited amount of text. The TextBox can also add its own scroll bars if the amount of text is larger than the visible size of the box. If you're wondering about the difference between the TextBox and the Label controls, it's this: Text in a TextBox can be edited, and text in a Label can't be edited.

CommandButton

CommandButton controls are used to let the user select a course of action. In the dialog box in Figure 3-31, the user can press OK to continue, Cancel to forget the action, or Help to get more information about the dialog box. Later in this chapter, you will learn about some of the commonly accepted uses of CommandButton controls so that your applications will resemble others running in the Windows environment.

OptionButton

More commonly known as *radio buttons,* OptionButton controls allow the user to select one of a group of options. They are known as radio buttons because they suggest the way older car radios worked. Typically, there were five buttons on the radio, only one of which could be pressed at a time. If you selected the first button, any button that was depressed would pop back out. The OptionButton works the same way and is illustrated in Figure 3-31.

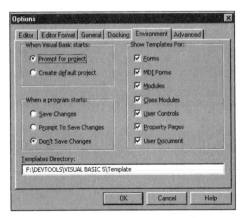

Figure 3-31: This dialog has two sets of OptionButton controls.

On this dialog box, there are actually two sets of OptionButton controls; one in the Frame labeled "When Visual Basic starts," and another group in the Frame is labeled "When a program starts." Frames allow you to create multiple groups of OptionButtons on the same Form. If the Frames were missing, all five OptionButtons would behave as if they were in the same group; that is, only one could be selected at a time.

In general, you should only use OptionButtons when you have five or fewer choices. If you have more choices than that, use a ComboBox with a list of choices.

ListBox

Until Version 5.0 of Visual Basic, the ListBox did basically what its name suggested: provide a list of items in a box. Besides the basic version, you can create a ListBox that provides a CheckBox next to each list item by changing the Style property.

VScrollBar

Similar to its horizontal counterpart, the VScrollBar control produces a vertical scroll bar. You can use it with the horizontal scroll bar to create more usable dialog boxes. Later in the book, you will learn about the Slider control, which is similar but provides a more useful interface for the user.

DriveListBox

The DriveListBox control produces a drop-down list box of the floppy, hard, network, and CD-ROM drives on your system. You can use this control with or without the DirListBox and FileListBox controls to create custom file dialog boxes. Once you learn about it, you may find that the Common Dialog provides much more professional-looking dialog boxes; however, these other controls are provided to give you the most flexibility in your development.

FileListBox

The FileListBox control provides a list of files in a directory, from which the user can pick a file. This control is able to handle long filenames and can be used in Windows 98 and NT 4.0. You can also use this control with the DriveListBox and DirListBox controls to create a custom dialog.

Line

The Line control performs one function: drawing a line on the screen. You can use lines to create graphical effects on forms.

Data

The Data control allows you to access external databases. Other controls can then use the Data control database links to automatically fill in their values (these are called *data-aware controls*).

Building Your First Form

Now that you've learned what controls are, you can learn how to use them in your programs. This is the fun part, if you haven't guessed already. Building forms and interfaces can be both challenging and interesting. Maybe you will come up with the next interface revolution in your development!

This section will show you how to create a project, add a form, and add controls to the form. When you're done, you'll run your project and interact with your form. You'll also be learning about the properties associated with the basic controls and how to use them to customize the appearance and features of each. You'll also be learning some object-oriented technology, since Visual Basic is partially object-oriented. Object-oriented means that instead of thinking of your data and subroutines as separate, you think of them together and associated with each other. Real-world objects and concepts translate into computer objects that you create and manipulate. You will be learning more about object-oriented programming (OOP) in the next and several other chapters in the book.

If you've not already done so, start Visual Basic and create a new Standard EXE project. As usual, Visual Basic will create a new project and add Form1 to it. Remember that a form is Visual Basic's name for a window design. We'll be adding controls to Form1. When it is done, your form will look like Figure 3-32.

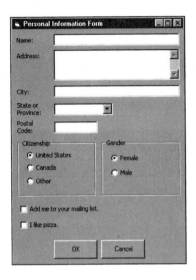

Figure 3-32: The completed data entry form you'll be building

Even though it is a simple data entry form, this form makes use of all of these controls:

✦ TextBox, both single and multiline

✦ Label

✦ OptionButton in two different groups

✦ ComboBox

✦ CheckBox

✦ Frame

✦ CommandButton

This exercise will first show you how to place and align the controls, change *properties* of each control, and even let you run your project and interact with this form.

Adding the TextBox controls

Since there are mainly TextBox controls on this form, you will add them first. They also will help align the Label controls. Begin by selecting the TextBox control from the Toolbox. To add a control to your form, you can either draw it on the form or double-click the TextBox icon on the Toolbox. To draw the control, follow these steps:

1. Select the TextBox control from the Toolbox.

2. Select the left-hand corner of the area where the TextBox should go.

3. Press the left mouse button and hold it.

4. Drag the mouse to the lower-right corner of where the TextBox should go.

5. Release the mouse button and the TextBox will appear.

Once the TextBox is placed, you can resize it by grabbing the *handles* on the control and resizing the control. The handles of the control are the small squares around the border of the control that are shown when the control is selected. When the control is selected, you can move it by pressing your left mouse button while the cursor is positioned over the center of the control. Drag the control to the position that you want it.

For now, there are four TextBox controls that you need to add to your form. As a guide, you can use Figure 3-32 as a guide to laying out the controls. However, the important thing to learn from this exercise is how to use the interface to build your form. In addition, Visual Basic provides a number of tools to help you align and size your controls so that they have a uniform appearance.

Adding Label controls

Label controls can be added in the same manner as TextBox controls; that is, either draw them on the form or double-click the Label control icon on the Toolbox. Do the following:

1. Click the Label control in the Toolbox, and draw a label on the form next to a TextBox control you drew in the last exercise.

2. Repeat step 1 for each of the other TextBox controls on the form.

3. Moving from top to bottom, change the Caption property of each to be the following values:

Name:

Address:

City:

State or Province:

Postal Code:

There are other pieces of text on the form, but you do not have to use Label controls to create that text. Those *captions* are added by the controls they accompany. One other thing to note: In this form, the labels all are followed by colons. Microsoft, in its infinite wisdom, has waffled back and forth on whether labels should have colons after them. In the last two versions of Microsoft Office, they have finally standardized having a colon after a label that is before another control, as in our example. As a rule, if you use the same standards that Microsoft Office uses, your applications will fit in very well with other Windows applications. What is also important is that whatever you decide (colons or not), you need to be consistent throughout your whole program.

Adding the Frame and OptionButton controls

OptionButton controls are a little trickier to use than other controls. In our example, we have two separate groups of OptionButton controls. These groups need to function independently of each other. In order to do this, all the controls in a group must be in the same container. If you remember from earlier in this lesson, a frame is a container. For this reason, you will be putting your OptionButton controls *inside* the frame and not just on top. You may need to enlarge your form to fit all the controls on it. To do this, follow these steps:

1. Draw your two Frame controls on the form just as you have drawn the other controls on the form.

2. Draw each OptionButton within the confines of the Frame control just as you have drawn other controls on the form. You can't double-click a control in the Toolbox to make it show up in a frame — you actually have to draw it in there.

3. To test that the control is inside, try dragging it out of the frame. The control will stop when it hits the edge of the frame, which means you created it correctly. When the controls are in correctly, you should be able to move the frame and see all the controls move as part of the frame. If you see a control not moving, select the control and then select Edit ⇨ Cut to remove the control from the form. Click on the frame and select Edit ⇨ Paste to put the control into the frame.

4. You might also notice that none of the OptionButtons is selected; that is, none of them has a black dot in the circle area. It is a generally accepted practice to always have one OptionButton selected. Therefore, set the `Value` property of the first OptionButton control to `True`.

Adding the ComboBox

The ComboBox is simple to add, so just draw it on your form next to the Label control that says State or Province. Under Visual Basic 6.0, you have the option to add your data at design time, but you can also do it through code. In this example, you will add your data through a few lines of Visual Basic code later in this chapter. You'll also set the properties for this control in a later exercise in this chapter.

Adding CheckBox Controls

The CheckBox controls are simple to add — just draw them on your form. Do the following:

1. Draw two CheckBox controls on your form.

2. Position the controls so they are at the left-hand side of the form, lined up with the other controls. Don't worry — the controls don't have to be lined up exactly.

You'll set the rest of the properties for these controls in a later exercise.

Adding the CommandButton controls

Like the other controls, the CommandButton control also has a `Caption` property that sets the text that should show on the button itself. The CommandButton also has two additional properties: `Default` and `Cancel`. If a CommandButton's `Cancel` property is set to `True`, then if the user presses the Esc key, that particular button will be pressed automatically. This property should only be set on buttons intended to close the window. To try this feature, set the `Cancel` property on your Cancel button. Then, open the window and try pressing the Esc key. The window should exit.

The `Default` button is similar, but it responds to the Enter key. In cases where you are entering large amounts of data, having a `Default` property set is a bad idea. This is because the Enter key might be used for adding multiline text into a TextBox. If the `Default` property is set to `True`, the button will press and the user won't get to enter all of his data.

To add your CommandButton controls, do the following:

1. Draw two CommandButton controls at the bottom of the form.

2. Resize the buttons so that they are the same size. You can use the choices on the Format menu to do this automatically. Click the first button, press the Shift key, and then click the second button. You can then select Format ➪ Make Same Size ➪ Both to make them the same size.

3. Center the two buttons at the bottom of the form. You can select Format ➪ Center in Form ➪ Horizontally to do this.

You'll set the rest of the properties of these controls in the next exercise.

Learning the basic properties

When you draw your TextBox controls on the form, Visual Basic sets several properties on each control to some default values. For instance, the `Text` property is set to be the same as the control's `Name` property. Before this form can be shown to a user, several of these properties' values need to be changed so that the form will look correct. To get ready to change properties, be sure the Properties window is visible. If you haven't moved it, it should be located at the lower-right corner of the Visual Basic workspace. You can also resize the window and detach it from the side of the desktop by dragging it away from the edge.

Many of the property names, shown on the left side of the window, are self-explanatory. However, some of the names may seem simple but in fact have a slightly different purpose. Here is a quick description of some of the key properties in this window. Once you see what the properties mean, you will set the properties of each of your TextBox controls. You'll be learning about other properties of this and other controls throughout the rest of the book.

✦ (Name): This property is listed in parentheses so that it appears at the top of the list at all times. The Name property is how you will access this control in your Visual Basic code.

✦ Alignment: This property controls how text will be displayed in the TextBox. It has three preset values: Left-Justified, Centered, and Right-Justified. You can choose any of these from the drop-down ListBox available for this property.

✦ Appearance: This property allows you to control whether the control is shown in 3D or shown flat. Windows 98 uses 3D controls by default, as does the Office 97 suite.

✦ BackColor: This is the background color that should be shown behind your text. Visual Basic provides some preset system colors that you should use so that your application can use the colors set in the Control Panel by the user.

In order to make your application look like other Windows applications, you should normally leave the BackColor property at its default setting. However, having this property available gives you the flexibility to adapt your application to special needs.

By using colors from the System portion of the drop-down box, your application will automatically use colors that the user has specified in the Control Panel on his or her computer. If the user has decided to use a neon green and day-glow orange scheme, your application will look like that, too. For this reason, be careful when mixing and matching System and Palette colors. You may pick a color from the Palette that will not work when used with a particular System color. For instance, if you force text in your control to be red and allow the background to be the system background color, you may end up in a situation in which the user has changed all the backgrounds to also be red, thus making your text unreadable.

Color should be used to highlight important details only, and should not be used as an interface component. Because some people are color blind, they may not be able to use an interface that relies chiefly on color differences.

✦ BorderStyle: This property lets you add or remove a border around your control.

✦ Enabled: If a control is enabled, the user can enter text into it. If it is disabled, the text within the control is shown in gray. If you wish to show text but not allow the user to change it, use the Locked property instead. In addition, the background color of the TextBox should be changed to gray (or to the background color of the form) so that the user gets a visual clue that the text is being displayed only and cannot be edited.

✦ Font: From the dialog box that appears (shown in Figure 3-33), you can select the font used in this control. Until the introduction of Visual Basic 5.0 and Office 97, the standard font was MS Sans Serif, 8.25-point. However, VB 5.0 and Office 97 introduced a new font: Tahoma. To make your application look like Office 97, use Tahoma 8-point for all text except the text on CommandButton controls.

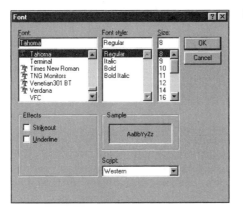

Figure 3-33: The Font Selection dialog

Unlike the BackColor property, you cannot simply tell your application to use the default fonts used on the system. When selecting fonts, you do need to remember that not every system has every font. However, you can always use certain fonts that are installed with Windows. These fonts are listed here for reference:

✦ Times New Roman

✦ Arial (including all variations, such as Narrow and Black)

✦ Courier New

If you specify a font that is not on the computer where your program is running, Windows will choose another font to use.

Several other fonts are now included with various packages; however, by sticking to the three installed fonts, you will be able to support a wide range of computer configurations.

✦ ForeColor: This is the foreground color for the control. Any text in the control will be shown in this color. The same rules apply to picking foreground colors as they do to background colors for the BackColor property.

✦ Height, Width: These are self-explanatory and should not need to be set by hand. By default, the Height and Width are given in *twips*, which is a unit of measurement that helps to ensure that controls will retain their proportions on different screens. A twip is 1/20th of a PostScript laser printer point. Since a point is 1/72nd of an inch, there are 1,440 twips per inch.

While you are resizing your control, a ToolTip will pop up (if you pause briefly) displaying the height and width of the control. The same will occur when you move the control; however, the numbers will then be the position of the upper-left corner of the control on the form. The dimensions and position also appear at the far-right end of the standard VB toolbar.

✦ Index: In large interface forms, you may have 30 or more controls, and having to come up with unique names for all your Label controls, for instance, can be tedious. In addition, you may have a number of TextBox controls that contain a series of data relying heavily on a numerical order. For this reason, Visual Basic provides a feature known as a *control array*. A control array lets you give a group of identical controls the same name but be able to access them by number. The Index property holds a number for a control in a control array.

✦ Left, Top: The Left and Top properties are the horizontal and vertical positions respectively of the upper-left point of the control. Like the Height and Width properties, you will probably never need to hand-enter these values. Just drag the control to where you want it. While you are dragging a control, pause briefly and a ToolTip will appear with the current values of the Left and Top properties.

✦ Locked: When a control is locked, it appears to be usable, but data in it cannot be changed. This is, unfortunately, confusing for the user. However, if you combine the Locked property with a background color change, you can effectively use one window for two purposes; that is, viewing and editing. In View mode, all controls are set to Locked and any white backgrounds are changed to gray. In Edit mode, you unlock all the controls and change the background colors back to white. This lets you get double use from a single window and thus saves you coding time.

✦ MaxLength: This property sets the maximum amount of text the TextBox is allowed to hold. If this value is set to zero, the TextBox is not limited.

✦ MouseIcon: If you wish to show a custom icon while the cursor is over a control, set the MouseIcon property to that picture.

✦ MultiLine: For the TextBox you will be using for the address, the MultiLine property allows you to have multiple lines of text. By default, this property is set to False, which means that you will only see and be able to enter one line of text. When using the MultiLine property, be sure to also use the ScrollBars property (described later) to add at least a vertical scroll bar. The scroll bar will allow the user to see more text than can be displayed on the window. Note that this property works in conjunction with the Alignment property, which is not applied unless the MultiLine property is set to True. When you set the MultiLine property to True, the Enter key can be used to add a new line to the TextBox.

✦ RightToLeft: For languages such as Hebrew and Arabic, characters are displayed from right to left instead of left to right. Visual Basic now supports this for these languages. Just set this property to True and the characters will scroll from right to left instead of the default left to right.

✦ ScrollBars: This property lets you select horizontal, vertical, or both scroll bars for this control.

✦ TabIndex: Even though Windows is primarily a point-and-click environment, it is often faster to be able to use the Tab key to move between fields on the screen. For this reason, you should always use the TabIndex property to determine the order in which the user moves through the screen. In general, you should move the cursor left to right, and then top to bottom. Starting with zero in the upper-left corner control, change each control's TabIndex to the next value in sequence to set the tab order correctly.

✦ TabStop: If the TabStop property is set to False, the user cannot reach the control by pressing the Tab key. You should use this property for controls such as PictureBox controls being used as containers, which you do not want the user to accidentally Tab into.

✦ Text: This property contains the text displayed in the TextBox control. As a default, Visual Basic always puts the name of the control into the Text property. You will remove this value before running your project, since the user won't understand what Text20 means. However, you can set this value at design time so that a default value is shown to the user when the form loads.

✦ ToolTipText: This property lets you provide quick, helpful information about what a control does by putting it in the ToolTipText property. If the user pauses over a control, the ToolTip will appear, with your text describing the control. This often saves the user a trip to the online help to find out what your control does. Although this feature is most often used with toolbars, you could add it to every control on your form to help provide more information to the user.

✦ Visible: This property indicates whether the control should be visible to the user.

If this list of properties looks menacing, don't worry. In most cases, you will only be using a few of the properties provided in a control. To see them more easily, you can organize the properties categorically if it makes it easier to see them all. Just click the Categorized tab of the Properties window to see the properties divided by function.

In addition, many of these properties will be used in all of the other controls, so once you learn the basic set, you can easily put new ones in your controls. That is the method you'll be using here — new properties for the other controls you use will be introduced individually as needed.

Finally, you can always get a complete list of properties for any control by following these steps:

1. From the Help menu, select Microsoft Visual Basic Help Topics.

2. Enter the proper name of the control in the box at the top of the window. Pick the entry that has the word *control* after the name of the control. This will generally take you to the general help page for that control.

3. The general help page will appear for the control. At the top of the screen, click Properties.

4. You will see a list of properties for the selected control. Click on any of them for more information. You can also select a property in the Properties window and press F1 for more information.

Setting the TextBox properties

Now that you have a little more knowledge about all the properties you *can* use, let's look at the properties you *will* use in this example. These properties are divided into two groups:

✦ **Mandatory:** Must be set for control to function correctly in this example.

✦ **Optional:** Can be set to add or change the appearance, but does not change the functionality.

Even though some properties are mandatory (listed next), you may not have to change them. The default values for some of the properties will already be visible. However, you need to understand that you may have to change these properties in some cases, so it is important to build a mental checklist of things to do.

Mandatory properties

These properties must be set in order for the form to work correctly:

✦ Name: Each control on the form must have a unique name so that you can use it correctly in your code. Visual Basic automatically creates a new name for each control; however, these names are not particularly well chosen. Text5, for instance, does not adequately describe a control since it is not meaningful. For this reason, you should start using a *naming standard* for your controls. A naming standard specifies a way to describe everything you use in Visual Basic. Having a standard that is easy to learn and use makes you more likely to use it.

For this example, the TextBox controls will be named txtName, txtAddress, txtCity, and txtPostalCode. You can name the controls anything you like, but make them meaningful and relatively short. You can use any length you wish, but you have to use that same name every time you wish to use it. By making it shorter, you save yourself some typing later. Of course, if you have code referring to a control and the control is renamed, you'll have to change your code. For this reason, pick names for your controls and stick with them.

✦ Enabled: All controls must have the Enabled property set to True.

✦ Locked: All controls must have the Locked property set to False.

✦ MaxLength: This should be set to zero for each TextBox control to allow an unlimited length of text.

✦ MultiLine: In all TextBox controls except the Address box, this property should be set to False. For the Address box, this property should be set to True.

✦ ScrollBars: In all TextBox controls except the Address box, this property should be set to None. For the Address box, this property should be set to Vertical.

✦ Text: You should set the value of all the TextBox's `Text` properties to nothing. Highlight the text in the Properties window and press Delete to remove it. If you've already set the `MultiLine` property to `True`, you will have to set the `MultiLine` property back to `False` in order to delete the text.

✦ `Visible`: All controls must have the Visible property set to `True`.

Optional properties

As mentioned before, you can use the `Font` property on the TextBox and other controls to make your form look like Office 97. Just use the Tahoma font if it is available on your system. Otherwise, stick to the standard MS Sans Serif, which is commonly used throughout Windows and applications written for it.

You can also experiment with the `ForeColor` and `BackColor` properties if you wish. Since they are not required, no exercise is provided for that purpose.

Setting other controls' properties

Now that you are familiar with how properties are set, you can zip through the other controls' properties so you can get on with this exercise and even write a little bit of code. The rest of the controls and the properties that need to be set are listed here. Step through each control and set the appropriate properties. If a property is not listed, then it should be left at its default value.

ComboBox (next to label State or Province)

```
Name:    cboStateProvince
Sorted:  True
Style:   2 - Drop-down List
```

Frame (contains three OptionButton controls for citizenship information)

```
Name:    fraCitizenship
Caption: Citizenship
```

OptionButton (labeled United States)

```
Name:    optCitizenUS
Caption: United States
Value:   True
```

OptionButton (labeled Canada)

```
Name:    optCitizenCanada
Caption: Canada
Value:   False
```

OptionButton (labeled Other)

```
Name:    optCitizenOther
Caption: Other
Value:   False
```

Frame (contains gender information)

```
Name:    fraGender
Caption: Gender
```

OptionButton (labeled Female)

```
Name:    optGenderFemale
Caption: Female
Value:   True
```

OptionButton (labeled Male)

```
Name:    optGenderMale
Caption: Male
Value:   False
```

CheckBox (labeled with mailing list information)

```
Name:    chkMailingList
Caption: Add me to your mailing list.
Value:   0 - Unchecked
```

CheckBox (pizza preference)

```
Name:    chkPizza
Caption: I like pizza.
Value:   0 - Unchecked
```

CommandButton (labeled OK)

```
Name:    cmdOK
Cancel:  False
Caption: OK
Default: False
```

CommandButton (labeled Cancel)

```
Name:    cmdCancel
Cancel:  True
Caption: Cancel
Default: False
```

Running and testing your form

To test your program, do the following:

1. Save your project files by pressing the Save button on the toolbar. For ease of finding your files later, you should probably create a new folder for each project you build.

2. Run your program by pressing the Run button on the toolbar.

3. Try typing data into the TextBox controls.

4. Change the value of one group of OptionButton controls. The data won't change in the second group. If the data does change, go back to the step where you added your OptionButton controls and make sure you drew the control *inside* the frame.

5. Click the CheckBox controls and then close the window by clicking the Close button (X button in upper-right corner).

You might notice that the title on the window is still showing Form1 or something similar. This is because we did not set the properties of the form itself. The form, just like a control, has properties and events. The next section of this example shows you how to use one of those events to populate the State or Province ComboBox control.

Using the form properties

Just like any other control, the form itself can have properties set to make it more appropriate to what your application needs. Many of the properties are similar to ones you have already learned. However, there are a few special properties indigenous to the form alone that are worth mentioning:

✦ BorderStyle: Forms can have a variety of types of borders. Some of the available settings can cause other form properties to be ignored. The borders that are available are as follows:

• None: No border is shown. In addition, the Minimize button, Maximize button, the title bar, and Close buttons are hidden from view.

• Fixed Single: A single-pixel-width border is shown around the form.

• Sizable: This is the default setting. The border around the window is left so that it can be resized by the user. Note that the controls on the form will not automatically change position or size without code.

• Fixed Double: A double-pixel-width border is shown around the form.

• Fixed ToolWindow: This type of border is used for toolbars that might be floating in the workspace. Only the title bar and Close box are visible, but in a reduced size.

• Sizable ToolWindow: Same as Fixed ToolWindow, but borders are resizable.

✦ `Caption:` The title for the window is stored in the `Caption` property.

✦ `ControlBox:` This property determines whether the Control box, available by clicking the upper-left corner/icon of a window, will be shown.

✦ `Icon:` This specifies the icon for the window. This icon will be shown in the Windows 98 taskbar, as well as the upper-left corner of the window.

✦ `MaxButton:` This property indicates whether the Maximize button should be shown and the Maximize choice made available in the Control Box menu.

✦ `MDIChild:` This property specifies if this window must be shown within a multiple document interface (MDI) window.

✦ `MinButton:` This property indicates whether the Minimize button should be shown and the Minimize choice made available in the Control Box menu.

✦ `Moveable:` This is a property introduced with Visual Basic 5.0. By setting it to `False,` you can prevent the user from moving the window manually. This is useful for splash screens and other informational dialog boxes that are shown and dismissed quickly.

✦ `ShowInTaskbar:` In some cases, you may not want every window in your application to be shown in the Windows 98 taskbar. For the most part, there should be only one entry in the taskbar per application, so any forms other than the main form should have this property set to `False`.

✦ `StartUpPosition:` This is a property introduced with Visual Basic 5.0. Instead of having to write code to position your window, you can pick a starting position from this drop-down menu. Here are the available choices:

  • `Manual:` Any positioning must be done in the Layout window. (See Lesson 2 for more information on the Layout window.)

  • `CenterOwner:` The form should be shown in the center of the form that owns it.

  • `CenterScreen:` The form should be shown in the center of the user's screen.

  • `WindowsDefault:` Let Windows decide where the form should be shown.

✦ `WindowState:` The `WindowState` indicates whether the window is shown normally, maximized, or minimized. You can pick a starting state for your form at design time so that when you show the window, it comes up in that state.

For the program you've built in this chapter, you do not have to set any form properties to make the program work correctly. However, you may want to set the `Caption` property to a new title for your form, pick the `StartUpPosition` of the window, and change the `BorderStyle` to a fixed border instead of a sizeable one. Finally, you may want to change the name of the form. In this example, it is not really necessary, but you may want to start naming your forms to get into a good habit. Experiment on your own with these settings. The rest of this lesson will refer to that name.

Using the Form_Load event

When a Visual Basic form loads, it goes through several steps before it is actually visible to the user of your program. By understanding this sequence, you can learn where code should go to perform various actions.

1. After a call to show the window is made (by the operating system or by other program code), the window is loaded into memory.

2. At this time, the Load event is triggered in the form. The Load event signifies that the window is being prepared to be shown to the user, so any initialization that needs to be done should be done immediately.

3. The form is shown to the user.

There are several other events that occur during a form's load that you'll learn about later in the book.

In this example, you are going to load the ComboBox with data during the Load event. To add your code, follow these steps:

1. In the Project Explorer window, make sure that frmPersInfo is highlighted.

2. Press the View Code button to open up a code window.

3. From the drop-down list on the left, select Form.

4. The Load event code will automatically be added to your code.

   This subroutine is known as an *event handler*, since it is designed to run when an event is triggered. In this case, the event handler will run only when the form is being loaded by the operating system.

5. To load the ComboBox's data, you need to add the following code to your Form_Load event handler. Since having a postal code lookup list is a common feature of many forms, feel free to keep this code and reuse it in your own projects.

```
'
' Add US States and codes
'
CboStateProvince.AddItem "AL - Alabama"
CboStateProvince.AddItem "AK - Alaska"
CboStateProvince.AddItem "AZ - Arizona"
'
'  more lines to add states and their codes
'
CboStateProvince.AddItem "WV - West Virginia"
CboStateProvince.AddItem "WI - Wisconsin"
CboStateProvince.AddItem "WY - Wyoming"
'
' Add Canadian provinces and codes
'
```

```
CboStateProvince.AddItem "AB - Alberta"
CboStateProvince.AddItem "BC - British Columbia"
CboStateProvince.AddItem "MB - Manitoba"
CboStateProvince.AddItem "NB - New Brunswick"
CboStateProvince.AddItem "NF - Newfoundland"
CboStateProvince.AddItem "NT - Northwest Territories"
CboStateProvince.AddItem "NS - Nova Scotia"
CboStateProvince.AddItem "ON - Ontario"
CboStateProvince.AddItem "PE - Prince Edward Island"
CboStateProvince.AddItem "QC - Quebec"
CboStateProvince.AddItem "SK - Saskatchewan"
CboStateProvince.AddItem "YT - Yukon Territory"
```

Note that even though we do not add all the states and provinces in alphabetical order, they will display in order on the form. This is because we set the Sorted property of the ComboBox to True. It will sort all these words and display them to you sorted. This way, if Canada or the United States were to add another state or province, you could just list it at the end instead of in between. Maybe that is stretching just a bit for an example, but you get the idea.

One other note about the internationalization of this form. When you are designing an application, always remember that a user might not be familiar with what a ZIP code is, or might not have a state code. For this reason, applications you design must be done with some flexibility. In this application, for instance, we designed it to deal with both U.S. and Canadian addresses. If you were designing for an even larger market, you would definitely want to have a country TextBox as well as additional address space. Always remember your target audience and their needs when you are designing your forms.

6. Once you have added the code to your application, go ahead and run it.

The once empty ComboBox will now be filled with the list of states and provinces that your code told it to add.

In the code you added, you performed your first object-oriented programming. You invoked a method on an object. You didn't mean to, you say? Don't worry about it. You will be doing a lot of it in Visual Basic. *Invoking a method on an object* simply means that you told a control or other object to do something. In this example, you instructed the ComboBox object to perform an action, known as a method. In this case, you told it to add an item to its list. Because the action is being performed on the ComboBox object, a dot is added between the name of the object (cboStateProvince) and the method you are invoking (AddItem).

Apart from the differing notation, a method is just like a subroutine in that it can accept parameters for input. In this case, you pass a single parameter to the AddItem method: the text you wish to add. It is placed after the name of the method without any parentheses or other punctuation. If a method is designed to return a value, you call it just as you would a function. Any parameters you pass to it are surrounded by parentheses.

Just like the property listings for each control, you can find a complete list of the methods and events for an object in the online help file. At the top of the page, just click the appropriate hyperlink to see a list of methods or events for the object or control.

Exploiting the events

Besides the Load event that you just learned about, the Form object has a number of other events that you can use in your programs. Two of these events, QueryUnload and Unload, are best demonstrated in an application like Microsoft Word. Whenever you make changes to a document and then attempt to exit, Word catches that you haven't saved your work and asks you to save or not.

The QueryUnload event and Unload event work in concert. When a window is told to exit by the user or the operating system, a QueryUnload event is first triggered. This event lets you check to see if anything has to be done before the window exits. For simple windows with no data entry, you won't have any code in this event. However, if you are allowing your user to enter data, the QueryUnload event is where you will want to ask the user to save. This is accomplished with a couple of pieces of code. Make sure your program is stopped and then do the following:

1. The first piece of code you need is a Boolean variable that indicates whether the data on the form has been changed or not. A common name for this is *dirty*, which is a term originally from electronics and operating systems. "Dirty" flags are stored with data to indicate that the value has recently been changed.

   To create this code, add the following line to the Declarations section of your form. To open the Declarations section, pick Declarations from the left-hand drop-down list box in the Code Window for your form. Because all of the code in your form will need access to this variable, it must be declared at the form level. Adding the variable to the Declarations section instead of just declaring it in an event handler makes this possible.

   ```
   Private bDirty As Boolean
   ```

   In this case, the variable will be a Boolean (True or False) data type, so the variable name is prefixed with a lowercase *b*. Finally, since this variable will be used only by this form, the keyword Private is used to declare the variable. Variables declared with the Public keyword can be accessed by other forms.

2. Next, you must set the dirty bit every time some piece of data changes. To do this, you will use the Change event of the controls on the form. The Change event is triggered every time the data in the control changes. Add the following code into the Change events of all the controls that have Change events on this form:

   ```
   bDirty = True
   ```

   The Change events of the following controls are affected:

   ```
   txtName
   ```

```
txtAddress
txtCity
txtPostalCode
```

3. The CheckBox and OptionButton controls do not have `Change` events; rather, they have `Click` events. In addition, the ComboBox uses its `Change` event only in a few circumstances. Put the code from the steps above (`bDirty-True`) in each of these controls' `Click` events.

```
cboStateProvince
optCitizenUS
optCitizenCanada
optCitizenOther
optGenderFemale
optGenderMale
chkMailingList
chkPizza
```

This code will cause any data change to make the form "dirty," which means that the changes need to be saved to a file or database.

4. The `QueryUnload` event is triggered in direct response to a request to unload the form. For that reason, add the following line to the `Click` event of the btnCancel control. This code will, as the name suggests, be run when the user clicks the Cancel button:

```
Unload Me
```

Since we are writing the code within the form, the keyword `Me` refers to the current form. The `Unload` statement causes Visual Basic to request that the form named be unloaded. This immediately causes the `QueryUnload` event to be triggered.

5. Add this code to the `QueryUnload` event of the form:

```
Dim iReturnValue As Integer

If Not bDirty Then Exit Sub

iReturnValue = MsgBox("Save changes?", _
   vbYesNoCancel + _
 vbExclamation)
Select Case iReturnValue
Case vbYes:
'
' Code to save data would go here
'
   MsgBox "Saving Data now."
Case vbNo:
'
' User does not want to save changes, so
' no code is necessary.
'
```

```
    MsgBox "Exiting without saving the data."
Case vbCancel:
'
' If the user presses the Cancel button, we have
' to stop the form from exiting.  Setting the
' Cancel parameter of the QueryUnload event to
' True will cause the Unload request to stop.
'
 Cancel = True
End Select
```

The first thing your code does is check to see if the form is actually dirty and needs to be saved. Using the logical Not operator, you check the bDirty variable to see if it is True. If it is not, you use the Exit Sub statement to exit this subroutine immediately. When it is used properly, Exit Sub can help simplify your code. As you program larger and larger programs, you may have code *nested* three or more levels deep. Nested code is shown in the previous example—the If/Then block contains code, which also contains code. The more levels of nesting, the more likely you will have an error. By eliminating certain conditions at the beginning, you can simplify your code.

The next piece of code creates a message box, which is shown in Figure 3-34.

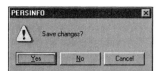

Figure 3-34: The message box your program will create

You can use a variety of button combinations by adding values together as we have done. For more information on the other choices, use your online help to search for the MsgBox() function.

In this code, the MsgBox() function returns a value that indicates which button the user pressed. The response has to be interpreted as a response to the question, "Do you wish to save your changes?" Whenever you use MsgBox() in this manner, be sure that the answers and their implications are clear to the user. Sometimes message boxes are very unclear, and pressing one button does something unexpected. For this example, these are the choices and the expected results:

✦ **Yes:** Save changes before exiting.

✦ **No:** Abandon changes and exit.

✦ **Cancel:** Don't save and don't abandon; go back to where you were before.

The code that follows the function call implements these results. The first, which handles the Yes case, would typically have code to save the data the user entered.

You have not added that code, but there is a space there that you will be filling in as an exercise in a later lesson.

The next case handles the No choice, which actually requires no code. If you do nothing, the QueryUnload event handler will exit and the form will be unloaded. For completeness, you should always list all of the possibilities, even if no code is required. In this exercise, there are three possible outcomes, and all of them have at least a comment indicating that yes, you did think about that outcome. This is helpful to other programmers, and to yourself if you have to go back later and change the code. You won't have to remember what you were thinking at the time.

The final case handles the Cancel choice, which means that the user simply wants to continue with what he or she was doing. The QueryUnload event provides the Cancel parameter, which is an *output* parameter. No data is passed to the event handler through it, but you pass data back to the operating system through it. By setting this parameter to True, you tell the operating system that the Unload request should be canceled. This will stop even a request to exit Windows. You can observe this behavior, too, in Microsoft Word by following these steps:

1. Start Microsoft Word and enter some data in the document.

2. From the Start menu, choose Shutdown so that you can exit Windows.

3. Word will ask you to save your data. In the dialog that appears, click the Cancel button.

4. Because you clicked the Cancel button, Word informed the operating system that it could not exit. Nothing more will happen and you can continue working on your document.

Now that you've added all the code, save and run your project. Make some changes to any of the fields and then press the Cancel button. Try out all three choices to make sure they do what you expect:

✦ **Yes:** Window will close, simulating the data being saved.

✦ **No:** Window will close without saving the data.

✦ **Cancel:** Message box will disappear, leaving you back in your form.

Summary

This chapter was designed to give you an introduction to Visual Basic. The rest of this book will build heavily on the concepts and techniques introduced in this chapter. Remember to rely on the online help for information on anything dealing with Visual Basic.

✦   ✦   ✦

Using MDI Forms

Many Visual Basic programs are nothing more than a string of windows, each of which causes the next to be displayed. In such a case, often the programmer gives no thought to whether the user can see more than one window at a time. Each form may have its own menus, toolbars, and other controls, all of which take resources to display and time to code and manage.

The Multiple Document Interface (MDI) was originally designed for applications such as Microsoft Word and Microsoft Excel, which are designed to show more than one document simultaneously. The user can arrange multiple windows within Microsoft Word's workspace, switching back and forth effortlessly between windows. The toolbars and menus are shared by all open documents, but the user always sees the appropriate menu choices for whatever can be done with the active document.

This chapter shows you how principles developed for traditional MDI applications such as Word and Excel can be used in your own applications, which probably have nothing to do with word processing. Many of the features available in the Word interface have real-world business applications, as well.

The databases being used in some of this chapter's examples are in the Access 97 format. You'll need to build queries in the format used in an Access database. You can do so by using Access (if you have it installed on your machine) or by using the Visual Data Manager included with Visual Basic. The Visual Data Manager can perform all the same functions as Access, so you can still use the exercises even without Access installed. You can start the Visual Data Manager by selecting Add-Ins ➪ Visual Data Manager.

In addition, you will probably have to change the pathname to the database being used in the examples in this chapter. Make sure you use the appropriate directory and filename to point to the database located on your own system.

All files used in this chapter are located in the \SAMPLES\CH04 directory on the CD-ROM.

MDI Form Basics

This section will show you some of the main features of MDI windows. You'll also see how normal windows interact with MDI windows. You'll also see some of the restrictions and other quirks of MDI windows that set them apart from regular windows.

Standard MDI form features

In Visual Basic, the central window that may contain other windows is treated as the *MDI form*. The primary noticeable difference between an MDI form and an ordinary form is the darker background color that Windows uses to fill the MDI form. You can see this background color in Microsoft Word by either closing or minimizing all the documents you have open. The dark color within the MDI form is not the same gray shown on the menu and toolbars. This gray area is known by a number of different names; this book calls it the *child form area*. Child forms are windows managed within the child form area. In Microsoft Word, each document is considered a child window.

Most MDI windows have menu bars and many also have toolbars. MDI windows often have status bars, similar to those found in the Microsoft Office suite. These status bars vary from the complex one included with Word to the simpler version found in Access. Status bars, in general, are designed to give information that could be needed at any time. A message shown in a message box is important only at that point in time. For instance, Word displays the current page, section, and cursor information, as well as the status of the special keys on your keyboard, such as the Caps Lock key. It also has some animated icons dealing with spelling/grammar checking; these animate when the check is going on. Although many MDI windows do have toolbars and status bars, such extra features are not part of the MDI form itself. The MDI form simply allows you to add them.

In order for the user to manage the windows within the MDI child form area, all MDI windows have a Window menu. This menu contains, at a minimum, methods for arranging the child windows, plus a list of currently open child windows.

There are a number of variations of the Window menu, but the most common choices are listed and described here:

✦ **Tile Horizontally** — Arrange the windows so that each one extends from the left edge of the form to the right. The windows are essentially stacked within the child form area, and each window is visible in its entirety, even if it has to be made smaller to fit. If you have a large number of open child windows, such a choice is probably not wise; you won't be able to see much of anything in each one.

✦ **Tile Vertically** — Each window extends from the top of the child form area to the bottom, and stands next to the others in a line-up. The same caution applies to this method as in Tile Horizontally — limit the number of open windows before performing this action.

✦ **Cascade** — Starting in the upper-left corner of the window, each window is placed slightly below and to the right of the previous window. The windows are fanned out like a hand of cards, with just the title bars sticking out revealing their titles, but with the active window out in front.

✦ **Arrange Icons** — Although not as popular under Windows 95, this choice lines all the minimized icons up neatly. In Windows 3.*x*, minimized documents looked like the now-familiar icons on the Windows 95 desktop. Arranging them made sense. Windows 95 minimized icons are not really icons any more but are simply miniature copies of the title bars of each window. In addition, they automatically arrange themselves under Windows 95. If you are only programming 32-bit Windows, you can leave this choice out of your Window menu.

Using MDI forms in Visual Basic

Visual Basic fully supports MDI forms but treats them differently from regular forms. The reason is, an MDI form is a different type of form and is not simply a property that you need to set. The MDI form is designed to maintain other forms (or documents) within its client area. VB doesn't use an MDI form by default, so if you want one, you have to request it specifically. You cannot change an MDI form to a regular form, or vice versa.

Visual Basic restricts you to a single MDI form for your entire application. Because an MDI form is meant to be a way to collect the elements belonging to the entire application, it really doesn't make sense to have more than one MDI form in an application. If you find the need for more than one, you either have a design problem or you need two separate applications.

When you have an MDI form in your application, the other regular forms in the application can be of two different types:

✦ A standard form, which operates outside the MDI child form area. Options, dialogs, and other modal windows should remain standard forms.

✦ MDI child forms, which remain within the child form area. The user should be able to switch between child forms without having to close one and open a new one. In addition, you may need to support having more than one copy of a particular type of form open at once. For instance, Microsoft Word can have any number of document windows open simultaneously. Each document window is based on the same design but may contain different data. Each window is known as an *instance*.

The property of a form that switches its behavior is the `MDIChild` property. *This property can only be set at design time.* There is no way to switch a form from an MDI child to a regular form at runtime. This restriction comes from the underlying Windows architecture and is not a Visual Basic feature.

An MDI child form should always be shown non modally. Whenever you want to show an MDI child form, you should use code such as the following to do it:

```
frmMDIChildForm.Show
```

No arguments are necessary for the Show method, since the default is to show the window non modally. Because of the way MDI child forms are supposed to work, there isn't any other logical way to show a child form.

Using menus with MDI forms

As with Microsoft Word, most MDI applications have only a single set of menus. These menus reside in the MDI form and not on the child forms. This is because the logic for dealing with each of the child forms will, in most cases, reside with the MDI container form itself. For instance, each of the documents in Word has the same available features and really has no need for its own menus.

If you do decide to use menus on child forms, you see the rest of your menus disappear when your child form has the focus. This is a feature of MDI forms and by no means a bug. This is the reason that menus should be kept at the MDI parent form level only. There are a variety of methods for communicating between the MDI parent form and the child forms so that if the user selects Cut from the Edit menu, the correct text is cut from the active child form. You'll see how to do this later in the chapter.

Designing an MDI-Based Application

Now that you know some things about MDI forms, you need to know a bit about designing MDI form-based applications. They are quite a bit different from the ones you may have built using a series of standard forms. They are also quite a bit more flexible than those previous applications because you have the ability to see multiple forms simultaneously.

Starting your design

The first question to ask yourself when designing your application is whether or not you need the features (and some of the hassles) of using an MDI-based application. In several cases, you may want an MDI-based application instead of another type. Those reasons include:

◆ The need to view multiple documents simultaneously, as is the case with financial applications

◆ The need for multiple windows containing separate data, but which share similar functions, such as Add Record, Edit Record, or Delete Record. These windows can share the same menu choices but change the word "Record" to "Customer" or "Order" as appropriate for the application.

◆ The ability to use a common toolbar between multiple MDI child forms, as in Microsoft Word or Excel.

All of these are indicators of the need for an MDI form-based application. As you'll see, there are a number of benefits that may convince you that MDI form-based applications fit in many other cases besides these.

When you've decided to build an MDI form-based application, you may need to make some modifications to your system design. Although these changes aren't required, they simplify your application and make it fit better within the MDI structure.

Genericizing your windows

The first change you need to consider making is to translate the specific functions your window performs into more generic versions. For instance, you may have one window that displays invoices in a particular format and another that displays purchase orders in a different format. However, you want to sort each window's data by a set of criteria. Both of these functions deal with sorting; therefore, Sort should be a generic action supported by your application. This means that you might have a Sort menu choice that shows a list of options by which the data in the window can be sorted. Using this method is an alternative to having many different menu items, each being specific to a particular window. Another example of this would be an Add Record function. Each window adds a different type of record; however, all windows are performing an Add function. This means that Add Record should be a shared function that is changed at runtime to show "Add Customer" so the user knows what data is be added by picking the menu choice.

Identifying common actions

Next, identify any places on your forms where common actions, such as cut/copy/paste, are allowed. Most of these places are standard TextBox controls, but you may have some other controls, such as grids or drop-down list boxes, which allow users to enter text. These controls, for consistency's sake, should also support cut/copy/paste operations. You'll need to know what types of controls you wish to support before proceeding to the development of the MDI form. Although some cut/copy/paste operations are supported automatically, the Windows standards specify that the Cut, Copy, and Paste menu choices should be available if you support the actions.

Identifying commonly used controls

As every VB programmer knows, the more controls you add to your form, the slower it will be. There is really no need to have multiple instances of controls such as the Common Dialog, the Crystal Reports control, and others. Instead, the MDI form can be the receptacle for all of these controls. Each of the child forms, as well as the parent form, can simply retrieve a reference to the single instance of a control on the parent form to use it during execution. Identify any other controls that you use frequently and in which you have to set properties to make actions happen. Obviously, you can't have a single TextBox control that you share, but controls such as the Common Dialog can easily be shared among all the forms in the application. Any of your controls can be shared on the MDI form; however, only a few can be placed directly in the child form area. If you can't draw your control in the child form area, draw a PictureBox control on the MDI form and put your control into it. The key is that the control you put on the MDI form has to have an Align property. Some controls, such as the Common Dialog, don't have an `Align` property but can be placed on the form because they are not shown at runtime.

When you have all these questions and items answered, you're ready to get down to the business of building the application.

Building the MDI Form

The application you're going to build in this chapter is going to be a high-tech version of the BIBLIO database included with Visual Basic. Even though it uses a simple database, the application you're going to build incorporates a wide range of features:

✦ A single menu on the MDI form that all child forms use

✦ A single form that reconfigures itself to view each of the tables in the database

✦ Centralized Common Dialog and Status Bar controls for child windows to use

✦ A graphical toolbar

All of these features are implemented in a way you can use in your own applications. In most cases, the code is generic enough that you can implement it anywhere.

Creating and configuring the MDI form

For now, do the following to get started:

1. Start a new Standard EXE project.

2. Remove the existing form (named Form1) by right-clicking on it in the Project Explorer window and selecting Remove Form1 from the popup menu that appears.

3. Add an empty MDI form by selecting Project ➪ Add MDI Form and then picking MDI Form from the dialog shown in Figure 4-1.

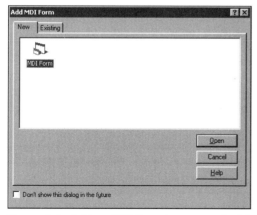

Figure 4-1: Add an MDI Form to your project from this dialog.

4. From the Properties window, name your MDI form **frmMDI**.

Visual Basic automatically loads the startup form when your application starts. Before continuing, you need to tell Visual Basic to use frmMDI as the startup form. To do this, follow these steps:

1. Select Project ➪ Project1 Properties.

2. From the dialog shown in Figure 4-2, select frmMDI from the Startup Object drop-down list. Click the OK button when you're done.

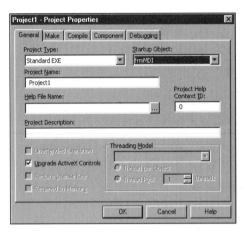

Figure 4-2: Select frmMDI from the list to make it the startup form.

If you don't select the MDI parent form as the startup form and instead use a child form, both the MDI form and the child form are shown. The best way to start an MDI-based application is by first showing the MDI form and allowing the user to open up any subsequent windows.

Now that you have the important things set, you can take care of some of the less important properties, such as the window caption or the icon.

Tip   If you don't have icons of your own to use, there are hundreds shipped with Visual Basic. These icons, bitmaps, and even movie files are installed when you install Visual Basic. Be sure to include the graphics files during the installation if you wish to use them.

While you're looking at and modifying the form's properties, make sure you don't change the `BorderStyle`, `ControlBox`, `MinButton`, or `MaxButton` properties. MDI forms are *always* sizeable, which means minimizing and maximizing are also allowed. You also don't need to add any menus yet — you'll do those later in the chapter.

Adding controls to the MDI form

As mentioned in the introduction, the MDI parent form is responsible for holding the Common Dialog control and a Status Bar control. If the user wanted to run reports with Crystal Reports, you could add a Crystal Reports control to the MDI form as well. Unlike previous versions of Visual Basic, the current version enables you to put the Common Dialog control directly on the child form area. To do this, do the following:

1. Make sure the Common Dialog control is in your Toolbox. If you don't see it, right-click the Toolbox and select Components from the popup menu that appears.

2. From the dialog shown in Figure 4-3, check the box next to Microsoft Common Dialog Control and click on the OK button.

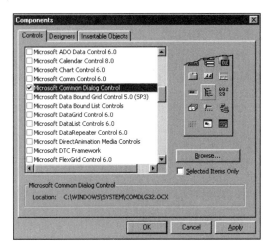

Figure 4-3: Select Microsoft Common Dialog Control to add it to your Toolbox.

3. In the Toolbox, double-click the Common Dialog control to add it to your MDI form. It places itself somewhere near the middle of your MDI form. Since it won't display at run time, drag the control up to the upper-left corner of the MDI form so that it won't get lost if you shrink the window at design time.

4. In the Properties window, name the Common Dialog control **ctlComDlg**. No other properties need be set for the Common Dialog; your program sets them all at runtime.

When you have the Common Dialog control on the form, you can add the Status Bar control. The Status Bar is part of the Windows Common Controls; if they are not in your Toolbox, repeat steps 1 and 2 just given, and then add Microsoft Windows Common Controls 6.0 to your Toolbox. Add the StatusBar to the window and name it **ctlStatusBar**. Your form should resemble the one in Figure 4-4 when you run your project.

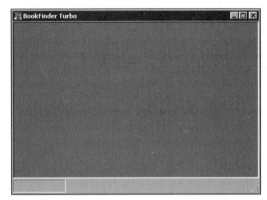

Figure 4-4: The BookFinder Turbo's MDI form so far

Building control accessors

Since we are making both the MDI form and its controls available to the child forms within it, you need to manage access to those controls. First of all, you don't want to hard-code the name of the MDI form or any of the controls within your child forms. In addition, you wouldn't want to access the controls directly with code that looks like this:

```
frmMDI!ctlComDlg.DialogTitle = "Open File"
```

If either the Common Dialog name or the MDI form's name were to change, your code would break.

The alternative to this method of coding is for you to create *accessors* that return references to each control on the MDI form. In addition, when a child form is opened, a parameter gives it a reference to its parent MDI form. The child form simply references that form whenever it needs to communicate or use one of the controls.

To make all this happen, add the following code to your MDI form:

```
Public Property Get GetCommonDialog() As CommonDialog
    Set GetCommonDialog = ctlComDlg
End Property
```

```
Public Property Get GetStatusBar() As StatusBar
   Set GetStatusBar = ctlStatusBar
End Property
```

These properties can be used by a child form in the following manner:

```
frmMyParent.GetCommonDialog.DialogTitle = "Open File"
```

In this code, frmMyParent is a *reference* to the main MDI form and the name of any form in your application. This reference will be set by the child form when the child is told to show itself. You'll see how that code works later in this chapter. GetCommonDialog returns a CommonDialog object. It makes all properties and methods of the dialog accessible to the child form, almost as if they belonged to the form itself.

Note that there are no Property Let procedures to go along with the above Property Set procedures. Since Property Let procedures are used to let a caller set an object reference, those property procedures have been omitted. It doesn't make sense to let a child form make changes to the Common Dialog control.

If you're using other controls like Common Dialog on the MDI form, simply build accessors for them using the same format as above. Don't use a control's type as the name of any subroutine or function — you'll probably get errors in addition to your headache.

Creating MDI Child Forms

Now that you have the outer MDI framework set up, you can start building MDI child forms. In this section, you build two different child forms: one to view entries from each of the tables in the database, and another to edit entries from the tables in the database. Each of these forms — and the ideas used in each — can be used in your own applications because the view window is very generic.

Building the view window

The view window for this application is designed to show users the data in a table without making them load and view an entire record. For this example, you can use either the ListView control or a DBGrid bound to the database. Since more users are familiar with the ListView control from Windows Explorer, this example uses it as the primary control on the form.

To get started, add a new blank form to your project. Set the Name property of this new form to **frmViewList**.

Next, add a ListView control to the form and name that control **ctlListView**. Place the ListView control in the upper-left corner of the window and add a small margin around the edge, as shown in Figure 4-5. You can add an icon if you wish, as well as a title. Your code generates a default title at runtime, so it doesn't really matter what title you put in at design time.

Figure 4-5: The beginnings of the list view window

Next, to make the form automatically resize its ListView control, add the following code to the Form_Resize event:

```
Private Sub Form_Resize()
    '
    ' If we hit a negative property value,
    ' just continue out of the event
    ' handler.
    '
    On Error Resume Next
    ctlListView.Height = Me.ScaleHeight - _
        (2 * ctlListView.Top)
    ctlListView.Width = Me.ScaleWidth - _
        (2 * ctlListView.Left)
End Sub
```

This code will automatically make the ListView control fill the form and leave a border around the edge. The error handler instruction, On Error Resume Next, takes care of cases in which the user has sized the window so that the calculation would result in a negative number. That error can simply be ignored.

To complete your MDI child form, you need to set its MDIChild property to True. You should notice that the icon in the Project Explorer window will change, as shown in Figure 4-6.

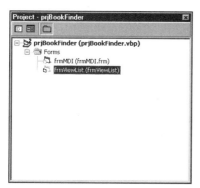

Figure 4-6: MDI and MDI child forms have slightly different icons in Project Explorer.

Now that you've built your form, you can try it out. Save and run your project and you'll see the MDI form appear. Since there are no menus yet, you can show your list window by typing the following line into the Immediate window after first selecting Run ➪ Break:

```
frmViewList.Show
```

You'll probably have to switch back to your application, but when you do, you'll see something resembling Figure 4-7.

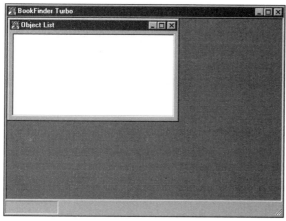

Figure 4-7: The BookFinder MDI form with a child form visible

As you can see, the MDI child form has resized itself automatically. This is because you haven't set the border style to a fixed style. VB/Windows will resize child windows within the child form area automatically. In addition, the forms are, by default, cascaded from the upper-left corner toward the lower right. Notice the Resize event code worked just as designed, and there is a uniform margin around the ListView control. Try resizing the form to see how the other controls expand to fill the window.

Since the basics are working, it's time to add some more code to hook into the database and fill up the list with some records. Regardless of the database your own application will eventually use, you'll need code similar to what you're going to write here. Some of the code that follows for opening the database will be replaced by code that uses the Registry and the Common Dialog to get the database filename.

To start building the database module, first add this line of code to the Declarations section of frmMDI:

```
Private dbBooks as Database
```

Note   After you type the word as in the instruction given here, if the Database type is not listed in the drop-down list box that automatically pops up, you don't have the Microsoft DAO 3.5 Object Library loaded. Select Project⇨References to add this library to your project.

Next, add the following code to frmMDI. Make sure that you use the correct filename for the database file included with Visual Basic.

```
Private Sub MDIForm_Load()
    Set dbBooks = _
        OpenDatabase("C:\Visual Studio\VB98\Biblio97.MDB")
End Sub

Private Sub MDIForm_Unload(Cancel As Integer)
    dbBooks.Close
    Set dbBooks = Nothing
End Sub
```

The MDIForm_Load event handler will open the database, and MDIForm_Unload will close the database and clean up before exiting. You will be adding more code to the MDI form shortly. You now need to add code to the frmViewList form so that it will work with the MDI form. Add the code shown in Listing 4-1 to frmViewList.

Listing 4-1: **Code for the frmViewList Form**

```
Option Explicit
Private dbPrimary As Database
Private rsListData As Recordset
Private frmMDIRef As MDIForm


' Public Sub Display
'
' This procedure is called by the parent MDI form
' to show a list of data. The particular type of
' data is stored in the sDataType parameter. There
' needs to be a matching query in the database
' corresponding to each type of data.
'
Public Sub Display(dbInput As Database, _
    frmParent As MDIForm, _
    sDataType As String)

    Dim itemReturned As ListItem
    Dim fldLoop As Field
    Dim i As Integer

    '
    ' Store references to global objects
    '
    Set dbPrimary = dbInput
    Set frmMDIRef = frmParent
    Me.Caption = sDataType
    Set rsListData = dbPrimary.OpenRecordset( _
        "qryList" & fnRemoveSpaces(sDataType), _
        dbOpenDynaset, _
        dbSeeChanges)


    ' Field layout for List queries:
    '
    ' Field 0: Unique ID value - stored in Key
    ' Field 1: Name - stored in Text of ListItem
    ' Fields 2 - n-1: Column Headers
    '
    ctlListView.View = lvwReport
    ctlListView.Sorted = True
    For i = 1 To rsListData.Fields.Count - 1
        ctlListView.ColumnHeaders.Add _
            ' _
```

(continued)

Listing 4-1 *(continued)*

```
             "Column" & i, _
             rsListData.Fields(i).Name
        Next i

        Do While Not rsListData.EOF
           Set itemReturned = ctlListView.ListItems.Add( _
             , _
             "Item" & rsListData.Fields(0), _
             rsListData.Fields(1))
           For i = 2 To rsListData.Fields.Count - 1
              '
              ' In case field is Null, appending an
              ' empty string prevents errors.
              '
              itemReturned.SubItems(i - 1) = _
                 rsListData.Fields(i) & ""
           Next i

           rsListData.MoveNext
        Loop


End Sub


'
' Private Function fnRemoveSpaces
'
'
' This function removes spaces from a string. This
' lets the MDI form send in a name like "Book Authors"
' and the code will look for a query named
' "qryListBookAuthors".
'
Private Function fnRemoveSpaces(sInput As String) _
    As String
    Dim sTmp As String
    Dim i As Integer
    For i = 1 To Len(sInput)
       If Mid$(sInput, i, 1) <> " " Then
          sTmp = sTmp & Mid$(sInput, i, 1)
       End If
    Next i
    fnRemoveSpaces = sTmp
End Function
```

The Display procedure, which is part of the code you just added, has several key features:

✦ It is called by the MDI form, and accepts several object parameters that are quickly stored in local variables. This eliminates the need to refer to objects or controls not on the current form.

✦ It uses a predefined query (which you'll define next) to retrieve the data for the window. With this feature, you can use the display form as a prototype for the display of all types of data without having to alter its controls for each data type. Just add a new query to your database and the form will work fine.

✦ When the data has been retrieved from the database, the Display procedure automatically adds column headers to the ListView control for each of the columns that were in the query.

✦ The procedure also adds each row from the query to the ListView control. It also sets the SubItems properties of the ListItem so that all fields are shown in the ListView control.

To make your ListView control work similarly to the left pane of Windows Explorer, you need to add code to make the control sort its data in ascending order when a user clicks on a column header. That code is listed here:

```
Private Sub ctlListView_ColumnClick( _
   ByVal ColumnHeader As ComctlLib.ColumnHeader)
   ctlListView.SortKey = ColumnHeader.Index - 1
End Sub
```

If you wanted to make this code smarter — and allow the user to click a column header twice to reverse the sort direction — you could use the following code instead:

```
Private Sub ctlListView_ColumnClick( _
   ByVal ColumnHeader As ComctlLib.ColumnHeader)

   If ctlListView.SortKey = ColumnHeader.Index - 1 Then
      If ctlListView.SortOrder = lvwAscending Then
         ctlListView.SortOrder = lvwDescending
      Else
         ctlListView.SortOrder = lvwAscending
      End If
   Else
      ctlListView.SortOrder = lvwAscending
      ctlListView.SortKey = ColumnHeader.Index - 1
   End If

End Sub
```

This code checks to see if the current `SortKey` represents the same header as the one the user just clicked on. If so, it then checks the `SortOrder` property to determine which order is visible. If it's ascending, the new order should be descending, and vice versa.

The form is now ready to be tested; however, the query in the database has not yet been built. Before you build the query, you need to know how the `Display` procedure assumes the database fields will be listed. You have three choices:

✦ **Field 0:** Unique ID of the record.

✦ **Field 1:** "Name" of the record. For a Title, this would be the title of the book.

✦ **Fields 2–n:** Any other fields you wish to display. If you want to show the ID to the user, add it in again.

The `Display` procedure will show the fields in the ListView control in the order you add them to the query. Since the ListView control is automatically sorting by the "name" of the record, you don't have to sort your query.

To build the Microsoft Access query, do the following:

1. Start Microsoft Access and open the BIBLIO database.

2. Click the Queries tab and then click the New button.

3. Select Design View from the dialog shown in Figure 4-8.

Figure 4-8: To build a new query from scratch in Access, select Design View.

4. The next dialog that appears lists all the tables in the database. As shown in Figure 4-9, select Publishers and click the Add button. Since this is the only table you need, click the Close button.

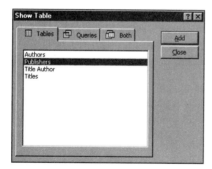

Figure 4-9: Add the Publishers table from this dialog.

5. Drag the PubID field to the first column in the grid at the bottom of the Select Query dialog. After you drag the field there, your window should look like the one shown in Figure 4-10.

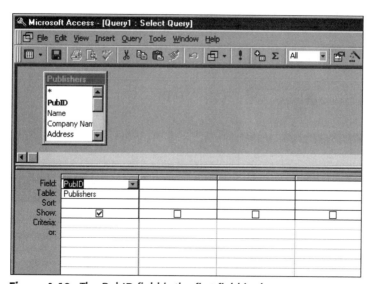

Figure 4-10: The PubID field is the first field in the query.

6. Next, add the Company Name field by dragging it to the next column in the grid. This is the name that will show in the first column of the ListView control.

7. Add any other fields you want to see by repeating the same procedure. You are only adding fields to view in the ListView control. The editor window will load and edit all of the fields in the table.

8. When you are done, click the Save icon on the toolbar or select File ↔ Save. Save the query as **qryListPublishers**.

9. Close Access when you are done.

Now that both the form and query are built, you can use the list window. To do this, you will have to tell the MDI form to open it. Normally, this would be done by way of a menu. There are no menus yet, so you have to add the line of code to `MDIForm_Load`. The whole procedure should look like the following:

```
Private Sub MDIForm_Load()
    Set dbBooks = _
        OpenDatabase("D:\Samples\Chapter04\Biblio97.MDB")
    frmViewList.Display dbBooks, Me, "Publishers"

End Sub
```

This code calls the Display method of `frmViewList` and tells it to load data about Publishers. The Display method opens the query you just built, loads all the data into `frmViewList`, configures all the column headers, and gives you the resulting dialog shown in Figure 4-11.

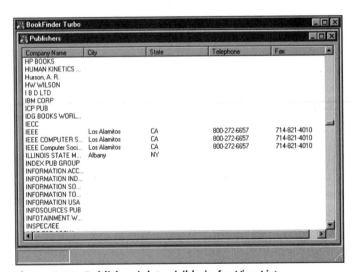

Figure 4-11: Publishers' data visible in frmViewList.

Note   Many of the publisher records do not have complete address information, so the resulting columns are empty. Don't worry—your code is working correctly.

Try resizing the child window and clicking on the column headers. Both of these features should work fine; if not, make sure you added all the code to both `frmMDI` and `frmViewList`.

To show other types of data, all you have to do is create a query for the table(s), then call the Display method of `frmViewList` with the "base name" of the query. For instance, if you create an Authors query, name the query `qryListAuthors` and call the Display method with the string `"Authors"` as the method's third argument.

If you really want to test this, try doing the above steps with a completely different database. As long as you follow the rules used by the Display procedure, you can use this window with any table in any database.

You may notice, however, that if you load large tables, your program will slow or even crash. For instance, the Titles table is too large to load in the ListView control. In this and other cases, you need to use a data-bound DBGrid control. The DBGrid control does not load all the data at once; rather, it loads data as it is requested by the user. This lets the DBGrid control represent a virtually unlimited amount of data.

Since the list window is essentially self-contained, no code changes are required in frmMDI. The list window will be smart enough to reconfigure itself based on the amount of data in the query selected. To make this enhancement, follow these steps:

1. Select Project ➪ Components and add the Microsoft Data Bound Grid Control 6.0 to your Toolbox.

2. While viewing frmViewList, draw a DBGrid control over the ListView control that is already on the form. Be sure to keep a margin at the upper-left corner as you did with the ListView control.

3. Set the properties for the DBGrid control as shown in Table 4-1.

4. The DBGrid control requires a Data control to work correctly, so draw one somewhere on frmViewList. Name the Data control ctlDataCtrl and set its Visible property to False. The user won't actually need to use the Data control to access data in the DBGrid, so there is no reason to show the control.

5. Set the DataSource property of the DBGrid control to ctlDataCtrl. This sets up the link between the DBGrid control and the Data control.

Table 4-1
Properties for the DBGrid Control

Property	Value
(Name)	ctlGrid
AllowAddNew	False
AllowDelete	False
AllowUpdate	False
BackColor	Button Face (on System tab)

Don't worry about the DBGrid control obscuring the ListView control. The new and modified code for the list window will correctly position the controls when necessary.

There are several places you need to either add or modify code. First, change the frmViewList_Resize procedure to read as follows:

```
Private Sub Form_Resize()
    '
    ' If we hit a negative property value,
    ' just continue out of the event
    ' handler.
    '
    On Error Resume Next
    '
    ' Resize ListView control
    '
    ctlListView.Height = Me.ScaleHeight - _
        (2 * ctlListView.Top)
    ctlListView.Width = Me.ScaleWidth - _
     (2 * ctlListView.Left)
    '
    ' Resize Grid control
    '
    ctlGrid.Height = Me.ScaleHeight - (2 * ctlGrid.Top)
    ctlGrid.Width = Me.ScaleWidth - (2 * ctlGrid.Left)
End Sub
```

This will resize the DBGrid in the same way that you resized the ListView control. This code does not care which control is visible to the user — both are resized simultaneously. The rest of the code goes into the Display procedure of the frmViewList form. Next, add the code in Listing 4-2 just after the call to OpenRecordset and before this instruction: ctlListView.View = lvwReport

Listing 4-2: **Code to Load Databound DBGrid Control**

```
rsListData.MoveLast
rsListData.MoveFirst
If rsListData.RecordCount <= 1000 Then
    ctlGrid.Visible = False
    ctlGrid.ZOrder 1
    ctlListView.ZOrder 0
    ctlListView.Visible = True
Else
    ctlGrid.Visible = True
    ctlGrid.ZOrder 0
    ctlListView.ZOrder 1
    ctlListView.Visible = False

    Set ctlDataCtrl.Recordset = rsListData
```

```
            ctlDataCtrl.Refresh
            Exit Sub
        End If
```

If there are more there 1,000 rows, this code will bring the DBGrid to the top and store the recordset in the Data Control's `Recordset` property. Calling the `Refresh` method of the Data Control will cause it to load records, which will subsequently be loaded into the Grid automatically. When the DBGrid and Data control have been initialized, no further code is required and the procedure ends when `Exit Sub` is reached.

When you run this form and load one of the large tables (for example, Titles or Authors) the DBGrid will show the data as in Figure 4-12.

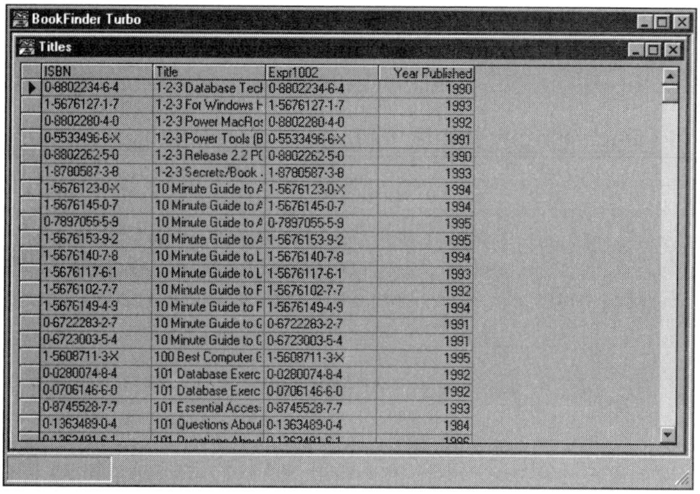

Figure 4-12: Title data visible in DBGrid on frmViewList.

In the case of Titles, the ISBN field is duplicated because, in addition to being the unique ID for the row, it was also useful information to show the user. Note that although the third column in the DBGrid is showing the ISBN number, the column header is not labeled correctly. This is because the Jet engine does not allow two copies of the same field to be named the same in a query. The best solution is to alias the column to a name other than ISBN. For instance, you could use "ISBNNumber" as the alias for the field name.

In general, you're likely to know in advance how many records a table will have; you can build your queries accordingly. If you're not sure how large a table will be, plan for the worst-case situation and design the query to be shown in the DBGrid. This advance planning will help you make the most appropriate use of this generic list window. In addition, queries shown in DBGrid controls will not have the automatic sorting available in the ListView control. If you want to sort your data, you need to do it in the actual query.

For now, you have all the code required for the list form. The next task you have is to create a form for the user to edit data stored in the table currently being viewed. This window will necessitate some changes to both the list window and the MDI window to make communication between them possible.

Building the edit window

Unless your display form allows both editing and viewing at the same time, you'll normally want a separate editing window. This is also because you can't show or edit every piece of information in a DBGrid or ListView control—not efficiently.

The edit window you'll be building is used to edit author information. Even though there are a just a few fields in the Author table, the techniques used for this window are identical to those you'll use in other edit windows. Figure 4-13 shows the form you'll be building. You might notice that the caption of the form is "*xxx* Author" instead of something like "Edit Author" or "Add Author." This is because the form will be used for both and will reconfigure itself on the fly, in much the same way that the list window did.

Figure 4-13: The completed Author Edit window, used for both additions and edits

To build this window, do the following:

1. Add a new form to your project. Table 4-2 shows the properties you need to set for the form.

Table 4-2
Properties for the Author Editor

Property	Value
(Name)	frmEditAuthor
BorderStyle	3 - Fixed Dialog
Caption	xxx Author **(will be set at runtime)**

Property	Value
Icon	Pick one from the Graphics directory.
MaxButton	False
MinButton	False
MDIChild	True

2. Add Label, TextBox, and CommandButton controls to the form in the positions shown in Figure 4-14.

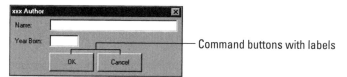

Figure 4-14: Create controls on the form with the names marked here.

3. Set the TextBox and CommandButton control properties as shown in Table 4-3. Name both of your Label controls lblLabel. Visual Basic prompts you to create a control array, which is fine in this case. A control array consolidates these Label controls under one entry so you can find them all in one place when you look at your code.

Table 4-3
Author Editor Form Controls' Properties

Control Name	Property	Value
cmdCancel	Cancel	True
txtName	MaxLength	50
	Text	(No text value; delete what is there.)
txtYear	MaxLength	4
	Text	(No text value; delete what is there.)

Now that the form is built, you can start adding code to it. Several form-level variables need to be declared to make the form work correctly. The lines of code shown in Listing 4-3 are these declarations; they go into the form's Declarations area.

Listing 4-3: **frmEditAuthor Declarations Section**

```
Option Explicit
Private Const EDIT_MODE = 1
Private Const ADD_MODE = 2
Private Const OBJECT_TYPE = "Author"
Private iMode As Integer
Private dbLocal As Database
Private rsLocal As Recordset
Private frmParent As MDIForm
Private iRecordID As Long
```

The edit form uses the first two constants to determine which function it is performing; some database actions differ on the basis of whether a record is being added or edited. The edit form uses the OBJECT_TYPE variable to fill the form's caption and select a database table. The other variables are shared throughout the form and thus need to be defined in the form's Declarations section. You'll see what all the variables are for shortly.

The code shown in Listing 4-4 creates a public method called Edit used to edit an existing record. This method takes care of configuring and loading the window with data.

Listing 4-4: **frmEditAuthor Edit Method Code**

```
Public Sub Edit(dbInput As Database, _
    frmMDIInput As MDIForm, _
    iID As Long)

    iMode = EDIT_MODE
    Set dbLocal = dbInput
    Set frmParent = frmMDIInput
    iRecordID = iID
    Me.Caption = "Edit " & OBJECT_TYPE
    Set rsLocal = dbLocal.OpenRecordset( _
        "SELECT * FROM Authors WHERE Au_ID = " _
        & iRecordID, _
        dbOpenDynaset)
    txtName = rsLocal("Author") & ""
    If Not IsNull(rsLocal("Year Born")) Then
        txtYear = rsLocal("Year Born")
    End If
    Me.Show

End Sub
```

When a record needs to be edited, other forms can call the Edit method instead of directly calling the Show method. Thus the caller can pass all the required parameters to the form; the form then loads the appropriate data from the database.

You also need a separate method for adding a new record. The code for this method is shown in Listing 4-5.

Listing 4-5: **frmEditAuthor Add Method Code**

```
Public Sub Add(dbInput As Database, _
    frmMDIInput As MDIForm)

    iMode = ADD_MODE
    Set dbLocal = dbInput
    Set frmParent = frmMDIInput
    Me.Caption = "Add " & OBJECT_TYPE
    Set rsLocal = _
        dbLocal.OpenRecordset("Authors", dbOpenDynaset)
    txtName = ""
    txtYear = ""
    Me.Show

End Sub
```

In this code, the controls are emptied instead of filled with data from the database. The recordset is still opened; however, a particular record is not selected.

When the data has been loaded into the form, you need to determine whether the user should change any data. If that is the case, you'll need to remind the user to save the data back to the database. That code requires a new variable declaration to be added to the Declarations section of the form:

```
Private bDirty As Boolean
```

(This technique was introduced in Chapter 2.) Next, add the code in Listing 4-6 to your form:

Listing 4-6: **Event Handlers That Mark a Form as "Dirty"**

```
Private Sub txtName_Change()
    bDirty = True
End Sub
```

(continued)

Listing 4-6 *(continued)*

```
Private Sub txtYear_Change()
    bDirty = True
End Sub
```

Listing 4-7 shows the Edit and Add subroutines. Add the highlighted code to the existing subroutines.

Listing 4-7: **Marking a Form as "Dirty" — Edit and Add Subroutines**

```
Public Sub Edit(dbInput As Database, _
    frmMDIInput As MDIForm, _
    iID As Long)

    iMode = EDIT_MODE
    Set dbLocal = dbInput
    Set frmParent = frmMDIInput
    iRecordID = iID
    Me.Caption = "Edit " & OBJECT_TYPE
    Set rsLocal = dbLocal.OpenRecordset( _
        "SELECT * FROM Authors " _
& "WHERE Au_ID = " & iRecordID, _
        dbOpenDynaset)
    txtName = rsLocal("Author") & ""
    If Not IsNull(rsLocal("Year Born")) Then
        txtYear = rsLocal("Year Born")
    End If
    bDirty = False
    Me.Show

End Sub

Public Sub Add(dbInput As Database, _
    frmMDIInput As MDIForm)

    iMode = ADD_MODE
    Set dbLocal = dbInput
    Set frmParent = frmMDIInput
    Me.Caption = "Add " & OBJECT_TYPE
    Set rsLocal = _
        dbLocal.OpenRecordset("Authors", dbOpenDynaset)
    txtName = ""
```

```
    txtYear = ""
    bDirty = False
    Me.Show

End Sub
```

The code has to be in the Edit and Add subroutines so that the flag is reset whenever a new record is being edited. In addition, we have to reset the flag manually since whenever the TextBox's value is changed, a Change event is generated by Visual Basic just as if a user had typed data into the box.

The last code you need to add is shown in Listing 4-8. This code handles database changes that need to be saved.

Listing 4-8: **Save Subroutine**

```
Private Sub Save()

    If iMode = ADD_MODE Then
        rsLocal.AddNew
    ElseIf iMode = EDIT_MODE Then
        rsLocal.Edit
    End If

    rsLocal("Author") = txtName
    rsLocal("Year Born") = CInt(txtYear)
    rsLocal.Update

    bDirty = False

End Sub
```

This subroutine has to be smart enough to distinguish whether a new record is being added or a current record is being edited. The constant you set when the form first loaded takes care of that for you — you simply check it and know which mode you're in.

The Save code is called from several places. The code for all the places is shown in Listing 4-9.

Listing 4-9: **Event Handlers That Call the Save Subroutine**

```
Private Sub cmdCancel_Click()
    Unload Me
End Sub

Private Sub cmdOK_Click()
    Save
    Unload Me
End Sub


Private Sub Form_QueryUnload(Cancel As Integer, _
    UnloadMode As Integer)

    Dim iRetValue As Integer
    If bDirty Then
        iRetValue = MsgBox("Save changes?", _
            vbYesNoCancel + vbQuestion, _
            "Save Changes")
        Select Case iRetValue
        Case vbYes:
            Save
            Cancel = False
        Case vbNo:
            ' Do nothing but allow form to close
            Cancel = False
        Case vbCancel:
            Cancel = True
        End Select
    End If
End Sub
```

Both OK and Cancel tell the form to unload, which first causes the QueryUnload event to fire. If the form is still "dirty," the user is prompted to save changes (as in Word's or Excel's functionality). If the user selects Cancel, the Cancel parameter of the QueryUnload event is set to True, which causes the form to stop unloading itself. This is a handy technique that you should adapt for every editable form you may build.

That's all the code required for the data entry/editor form. You would want to add additional features such as data validation (don't let the user save until the data is valid) and Cut/Copy/Paste functionality, which you'll see later in the chapter.

Using Menus

Now that you've built both a data viewing form and an editor form, you have to build some menus to show these windows in your application. MDI applications make extensive use of menus. Due to the restrictions in the way MDI menus work, you will always want to have menus on the MDI form and not on the individual forms. This makes dealing with menus slightly more complicated. For instance, only one list window is active at a time; the menus need show only the choices relevant to that window. All the author editing choices need not be visible at the same time as those used to edit publishers. For this reason, you will want to build a generic menu structure that can be modified at runtime by the windows themselves. If a list window is currently showing a list of authors, show the choices that are relevant to viewing and editing authors. Using the available events, you can guarantee that the visible menus will always show the relevant choices.

Designing your menus

As does an application, your menu structure needs an overall design. Although using the standard Windows menu choices (File, Edit, etc.) does not always make sense, in this application it does make sense. You need the following functions:

File Menu	Edit Menu	View Menu	Window Menu
Open a database file	Cut/Copy/Paste data between fields	View each type of data (for example, Publishers and Authors)	Tile horizontally and vertically
Close a database file	Add a record (of varying types)		Cascade windows
Exit the application	Modify a record		Show list of open windows
	Delete a record		

Of course, there are many more options that a full-scale application would have, but you can add those options as you see fit. Even though this application will be showing all types of data from the database, you should notice that there is only one set of record editing features: add, edit, and delete. Through inter-window communication, the child windows will inform the parent MDI window what type of data is being edited, added, or deleted so that the menu choices are always correct.

Building the menus

Use the built-in Menu Editor (select Tools ➪ Menu Editor) to add the menus to your MDI form. The structure of the menus is shown here:

File	Edit	View	Window
Open Database	Cut Ctrl+X	Authors	Tile Horizontally
Close Database	Copy Ctrl+C	Publishers	Tile Vertically
(Separator bar)	Paste Ctrl+V	Titles	Cascade
Exit	(Separator bar)	(Separator bar)	(Window List follows)
	Add Item Ctrl+A	Sort Option 1	
	Modify Item Ctrl+M	Sort Option 2	
	Delete Item	Sort Option 3	

Table 4-4 lists all the properties that you need to set for each menu choice. First, however, a few notes:

✦ Placing an ampersand before a letter tells Windows that you want that letter underlined. This allows for users to select menu options by letter quickly.

✦ Submenus of the top-level menus (File, Edit, View, Window) need to be indented using the Menu Editor, as shown in Figure 4-15. Use the button with the right arrow on it to indent a menu item.

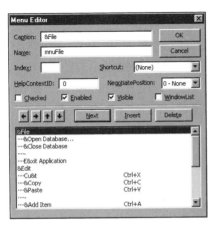

Figure 4-15: Submenus need to be indented under their top-level menu.

✦ Separator bars are created by making the caption of a menu choice a single dash. You then name the control as you would any other.

Table 4-4
frmMDI Menu Choices and Properties

Menu Choice	Property	Value
File	Caption	&File
	Name	mnuFile
Open Database	Caption	&Open Database…
	Name	mnuFileOpen
Close Database	Caption	&Close Database
	Name	mnuFileClose
(separator bar)	Caption	- (single dash)
	Name	mnuFileSeparator
Exit	Caption	E&xit
	Name	mnuFileExit
Edit	Caption	&Edit
	Name	mnuEdit
Cut	Caption	Cu&t
	Name	mnuEditCut
	Shortcut	Ctrl+X
Copy	Caption	&Copy
	Name	mnuEditCopy
	Shortcut	Ctrl+C
Paste	Caption	&Paste
	Name	mnuEditPaste
	Shortcut	Ctrl+V
(separator bar)	Caption	-
	Name	mnuEditSeparator
Add Item	Caption	&Add Item
	Name	mnuEditAdd
	Shortcut	Ctrl+A
Modify Item	Caption	&Modify Item
	Name	mnuEditModify
	Shortcut	Ctrl+E

(continued)

Table 4-4 *(continued)*		
Menu Choice	**Property**	**Value**
Delete Item	Caption	Delete Item
	Name	mnuEditDelete
View	Caption	&View
	Name	mnuView
Authors	Caption	&Authors
	Name	mnuViewAuthors
Publishers	Caption	&Publishers
	Name	mnuViewPublishers
Titles	Caption	&Titles
	Name	mnuViewTitles
Window	Caption	&Window
	Name	mnuWindow
	WindowList	Checked
&Horizontally	Caption	Tile Horizontally
	Name	mnuWindowHorizontal
&Vertically	Caption	Tile Vertically
	Name	mnuWindowVertical
&Cascade	Caption	Cascade
	Name	mnuWindowCascade

Adding the basic menu code

When you have the menus built, you can start adding code to make all the options work correctly. Some of the code you will be adding will replace the temporary code you added earlier. The temporary code was designed to let you try out the windows you've built to date.

First, remove all the code from the MDIForm_Load and MDIForm_Unload event handlers. This code was designed to be temporary. Replace it with the code in Listing 4-10.

Listing 4-10: **MDI Form Subroutines and Code**

```
Private Sub MDIForm_Load()
    mnuFileClose.Enabled = False
    mnuEdit.Visible = False
    mnuView.Visible = False
    mnuWindow.Visible = False
End Sub

Private Sub MDIForm_Unload()
    On Error Resume Next
    dbBooks.Close
    Set dbBooks = Nothing
    End
End Sub
```

This code will hide all menus that are not available until a database file has been opened. The Unload event procedure will close the database if it's open and terminate the program with the End statement. Next, you'll add the File menu code, shown in Listing 4-11.

Listing 4-11: **File Menu Subroutines and Code**

```
Private Sub mnuFileOpen_Click()
    On Error GoTo EH

    ctlComDlg.DialogTitle = "Open Database File"
    ctlComDlg.CancelError = True
    ctlComDlg.Filter = _
        "Database Files (*.mdb)|*.mdb|All Files (*.*)|*.*"
    ctlComDlg.FilterIndex = 1
    ctlComDlg.Flags = cdlOFNHideReadOnly _
        + cdlOFNExplorer _
        + cdlOFNLongNames
    ctlComDlg.ShowOpen
    Set dbBooks = OpenDatabase(ctlComDlg.filename)

    mnuFileOpen.Enabled = False
    mnuFileClose.Enabled = True
    mnuEdit.Visible = True
    mnuView.Visible = True
    mnuWindow.Visible = True
    Exit Sub
```

(continued)

Listing 4-11 *(continued)*

```
EH:
    If Err.Number = cdlCancel Then
        '
        ' If the Cancel button was clicked,
        ' exit quietly.
        '
        Err.Clear
    Else
        '
        ' All other errors need to be handled
        ' with your own error handler. This
        ' code should be replaced with your own.
        '
        Err.Raise Err.Number, Err.Source, Err.Description
    End If
End Sub

Private Sub mnuFileClose_Click()
    dbBooks.Close
    Set dbBooks = Nothing
    mnuFileOpen.Enabled = True
    mnuFileClose.Enabled = False
    mnuEdit.Visible = False
    mnuView.Visible = False
    mnuWindow.Visible = False
End Sub

Private Sub mnuFileExit_Click()
    Unload Me
End Sub
```

Next, add the code for the Edit menu, shown in Listing 4-12. This code provides for automatic cut, copy, and paste between controls on the child forms.

Listing 4-12: **Edit Menu Subroutines and Code**

```
Private Sub mnuEditCopy_Click()
    If TypeOf ActiveForm.ActiveControl Is TextBox Then
        Clipboard.SetText ActiveForm.ActiveControl.SelText
    End If
End Sub

Private Sub mnuEditCut_Click()
    If TypeOf ActiveForm.ActiveControl Is TextBox Then
        Clipboard.SetText ActiveForm.ActiveControl.SelText
```

```
        ActiveForm.ActiveControl.SelText = ""
    End If
End Sub

Private Sub mnuEditPaste_Click()
    If TypeOf ActiveForm.ActiveControl Is TextBox Then
        ActiveForm.ActiveControl.SelText = _
            Clipboard.GetText
    End If
End Sub
```

The Cut/Copy/Paste code is flexible enough to allow other controls to be used, assuming they support the SelText property or something similar. For instance, you could cut and copy from a grid cell. You just have to determine what the user has highlighted to be copied or cut. ActiveForm.ActiveControl always returns a reference to the control currently in use, so you don't have to change this part of the code when you expand your application. All you need do is add specific code that specifies using other types of controls with the same cut/copy/paste functionality. (For instance, you might want to use data in the current DBGrid cell.)

Next, add the View menu's code, shown in Listing 4-13. For now, you'll just be adding the code to show each type of data.

Listing 4-13: **View Menu Subroutines and Code**

```
Private Sub mnuViewAuthors_Click()
    Dim frmNew As New frmViewList
    frmNew.Display dbBooks, Me, "Authors"
End Sub

Private Sub mnuViewPublishers_Click()
    Dim frmNew As New frmViewList
    frmNew.Display dbBooks, Me, "Publishers"
End Sub

Private Sub mnuViewTitles_Click()
    Dim frmNew As New frmViewList
    frmNew.Display dbBooks, Me, "Titles"
End Sub
```

Notice that you have to create new instances of frmViewList since you can have multiple copies of the form open simultaneously. Omitting the New keyword would cause the single copy to overwrite itself with new data each time you called the Display procedure.

The last menu you need to build is the Window menu. This code is fairly simple since the arrangement feature is built into the MDI form. Listing 4-14 shows the code for the three Window menu choices.

Listing 4-14: **Window Menu Subroutines and Code**

```
Private Sub mnuWindowCascade_Click()
    Me.Arrange vbCascade
End Sub

Private Sub mnuWindowHorizontal_Click()
    Me.Arrange vbHorizontal
End Sub

Private Sub mnuWindowVertical_Click()
    Me.Arrange vbVertical
End Sub
```

At this point, you can run your program and try out these features:

✦ Opening a database

✦ Opening each of the windows under the View menu

✦ Trying out the features of the Window menu to arrange the list windows

Implementing the advanced menu code

With the basic menu structure and features in place, you can start adding the more advanced features of this application, which include context-sensitive Edit menus, as well as a capability to switch between windows and have only the relevant menu choices available.

As you will see, these features are fairly simple to implement with a good structure such as the one you just built. The first new feature you'll be building is the mechanism that keeps the MDI menus updated based on the list window that is visible. For instance, when the Authors list window is visible, the Edit menu choices should say Add Author, Modify Author, and Delete Author.

Here's how you make it work: First, using the Menu Editor, change the following menu choices' Visible flag to False or Unchecked:

```
mnuEditAdd

mnuEditModify

mnuEditDelete

mnuEditSeparator
```

These menu choices need to start hidden; they are not immediately available. Next, add the following code to `frmViewList`:

```
Public Property Get MenuItem() As String
    MenuItem = sMenuDescription
End Property
```

You'll also need to add this line to the Declarations section of the form:

```
Private sMenuDescription As String
```

This variable will hold the name of the data elements being shown, such as `Authors`. This variable will be used by the MDI form to change the Edit menu dynamically.

Currently, the `Display` method of the form contains a parameter that specifies the type of data to show. You now need to modify that method so that it accepts a description of the individual menu item. For instance, when you are showing Authors, the individual item would be Author. This feature allows for cases in which you may have a plural that doesn't end in *s*. Modify the `Display` method where marked in Listing 4-15.

Listing 4-15: **Display Method Modified to Accept Another Parameter**

```
Public Sub Display(dbInput As Database, _
    frmParent As MDIForm, _
    sDataType As String, _
    sMenuItemDesc As String)

    Dim itemReturned As ListItem
    Dim fldLoop As Field
    Dim i As Integer

    '
```

(continued)

Listing 4-15 *(continued)*

```
' Store references to global objects
'
Set dbPrimary = dbInput
Set frmMDIRef = frmParent
sMenuDescription = sMenuItemDesc
Me.Caption = sDataType
Set rsListData = dbPrimary.OpenRecordset( _
    "qryList" & fnRemoveSpaces(sDataType), _
    dbOpenDynaset, _
    dbSeeChanges)

... rest of the code is the same ...
```

You now need code to signal the MDI form that the list window has the focus. The Activate event fires whenever a child window opens or comes to the top of the child window stack. Add the code in Listing 4-16 to frmViewList:

Listing 4-16: **Activate and Deactivate Event Code**

```
Private Sub Form_Activate()
    frmMDIRef.ActivateEditMenu
End Sub

Private Sub Form_Deactivate()
    frmMDIRef.DeactivateEditMenu
End Sub
```

Next, add the code in Listing 4-17 to your MDI form:

Listing 4-17: **Activate and Deactivate MDI Form Code**

```
Public Sub ActivateEditMenu()
    mnuEditSeparator.Visible = True

    mnuEditAdd.Caption = _
        "Add " & ActiveForm.MenuItem
    mnuEditAdd.Visible = True

    mnuEditModify.Caption = _
        "Modify " & ActiveForm.MenuItem
```

```
   mnuEditModify.Visible = True

   mnuEditDelete.Caption = _
      "Delete " & ActiveForm.MenuItem
   mnuEditDelete.Visible = True
End Sub

Public Sub DeactivateEditMenu()
   mnuEditSeparator.Visible = False
   mnuEditAdd.Visible = False
   mnuEditModify.Visible = False
   mnuEditDelete.Visible = False
End Sub

Private Sub Form_Unload(Cancel As Integer)
   frmMDIRef.DeactivateEditMenu
End Sub
```

These methods are called only by `frmViewList`; you can safely use the `MenuItem` property that you added to determine what to add to your menu.

The last change to your code required to test this new feature is in the View menu choices on the MDI form. Modify the code shown in Listing 4-18 where marked:

Listing 4-18: **Modified View Menu Code**

```
Private Sub mnuViewAuthors_Click()
   Dim frmNew As New frmViewList
   frmNew.Display dbBooks, Me, "Authors", "Author"
End Sub

Private Sub mnuViewPublishers_Click()
   Dim frmNew As New frmViewList
   frmNew.Display dbBooks, Me, "Publishers", "Publisher"
End Sub

Private Sub mnuViewTitles_Click()
   Dim frmNew As New frmViewList
   frmNew.Display dbBooks, Me, "Titles", "Title"
End Sub
```

With all of those changes made, you can run your program. Open up two of the types of data, switch back and forth, and watch the Edit menu change automatically. Notice that if you close the last list window, the `Deactivate` event does not fire. That's why you added duplicate code to the `Unload` event.

Now that the Edit menu choices are available, you need to add code to cause the specific editing windows to open. There are several ways to do this, but since you've already made efforts to keep the "smart" code in the MDI form, that's the premise you'll use for the next part of the code as well. The user will select an option from the menu, the MDI form will determine what item needs to be edited by "asking" the active list window, and the appropriate editing window will be opened by the MDI form.

To manage how the editing windows are opened, first add this line of code to the Declarations section of `frmViewList`:

```
Private sEditID As String
```

This variable will hold the currently selected record's ID for the MDI form to retrieve. Next, add the code in Listing 4-19 to `frmViewList`:

Listing 4-19: **New Property Procedure for frmViewList**

```
Public Property Get EditID() As String
    EditID = sEditID
End Property
```

You now need to set the ID whenever the user clicks on a record. Because the list window has both a DBGrid and a ListView control, put this code in two places, as shown in Listing 4-20.

Listing 4-20: **Code to Store Record ID When the User Clicks a Control**

```
Private Sub ctlGrid_RowColChange( _
    LastRow As Variant, ByVal LastCol As Integer)
    sEditID = ctlGrid.Columns(0).Text
End Sub

Private Sub ctlListView_ItemClick(ByVal _
    Item As ComctlLib.ListItem)

    sEditID = Mid$(Item.Key, 5)
End Sub
```

If the user clicks on a grid row, the ID is always in the first column. Using the `Bookmark` property immediately moves the Data control to the correct record, and the ID is in field 0 of the `Recordset` object. For the ListView control, the ID is concatenated to the end of the word `Item`. The `Mid$` function simply returns everything from the fifth character to the end of the string.

Since the form needs to have a valid editable record ID at all times, you also need to add code to the `Display` subroutine of the list window. Add the code highlighted in Listing 4-21.

Listing 4-21: Code to Store Record ID When the Form Is Loaded

```
Public Sub Display(dbInput As Database, _
    frmParent As MDIForm, _
    sDataType As String, _
    sMenuItemDesc As String)

    Dim itemReturned As ListItem
    Dim fldLoop As Field
    Dim i As Integer

    '
    ' Store references to global objects
    '
    Set dbPrimary = dbInput
    Set frmMDIRef = frmParent
    sMenuDescription = sMenuItemDesc
    Me.Caption = sDataType
    Set rsListData = dbPrimary.OpenRecordset( _
        "qryList" & fnRemoveSpaces(sDataType), _
        dbOpenDynaset, _
        dbSeeChanges)

    rsListData.MoveLast
    rsListData.MoveFirst
    If rsListData.RecordCount <= 1000 Then
        ctlGrid.Visible = False
        ctlGrid.ZOrder 1
        ctlListView.ZOrder 0
        ctlListView.Visible = True
    Else
        ctlGrid.Visible = True
        ctlGrid.ZOrder 0
        ctlListView.ZOrder 1
        ctlListView.Visible = False
```

(continued)

Listing 4-21 *(continued)*

```
        Set ctlDataCtrl.Recordset = rsListData
        ctlDataCtrl.Refresh
        sEditID = ctlGrid.Columns(0).Text
        Exit Sub
    End If


    '
    ' Field layout for List queries:
    '
    ' Field 0: Unique ID value - stored in Key of ListItem
    ' Field 1: Name - stored in Text of ListItem
    ' Fields 2 - n-1: Column Headers
    '
    ctlListView.View = lvwReport
    ctlListView.Sorted = True
    For i = 1 To rsListData.Fields.Count - 1
        ctlListView.ColumnHeaders.Add _
            , _
            "Column" & i, _
            rsListData.Fields(i).Name
    Next i

    If Not rsListData.EOF Then
        sEditID = rsListData.Fields(0)
    End If

    Do While Not rsListData.EOF
... rest of the code is the same ...
```

Now that the current ID is known, it's a simple task to bring up the correct editing window. Add the code in Listing 4-22 to the MDI form.

Listing 4-22: Code to Open Editing Window

```
Private Sub mnuEditAdd_Click()
    Dim frmNew As Form

    Select Case ActiveForm.MenuItem
    Case "Author"
        Set frmNew = New frmEditAuthor
    Case "Publisher"
        'Set frmNew = New frmEditPublisher
```

```
        Case "Title"
            'Set frmNew = New frmEditTitle
        End Select

        If frmNew Is Nothing Then Exit Sub
        frmNew.Add dbBooks, Me

    End Sub

    Private Sub mnuEditModify_Click()

        Dim frmNew As Form

        Select Case ActiveForm.MenuItem
        Case "Author"
            Set frmNew = New frmEditAuthor
        Case "Publisher"
            'Set frmNew = New frmEditPublisher
        Case "Title"
            'Set frmNew = New frmEditTitle
        End Select

        If frmNew Is Nothing Then Exit Sub
        frmNew.Edit dbBooks, Me, ActiveForm.EditID

    End Sub
```

As you build more editing windows, you can uncomment the code for the currently non existent windows. However, the Author editing window is available and will work fine now. Run your project and try it out. As you click a row in the DBGrid or ListView control, the record's ID will be quietly put away just in case you decide to edit the record. When you select Edit ➪ Modify Author, the MDI form checks the active form, determines what window to use, and opens the window while passing the record ID to it. Neither the list nor the edit window know anything about each other, which means that you can add and remove types of forms without a lot of work. All you have to ensure is that you have Add and Edit methods on each of your editor forms.

There are many things you can do with the framework introduced in this chapter. For instance, you could sort by any column by simply adding more communication between the list window and the MDI form. The framework introduced here is flexible enough to support toolbars and other similar controls, such as the graphical list bar made popular by Microsoft Outlook. By keeping the functionality in the MDI form, you make it much more flexible than it would be otherwise.

Summary

This chapter was designed to show you how to build an MDI form that can both control and be controlled by MDI child forms.

✦ By sharing common resources such as menus and toolbars, you can save quite a bit of programming time.

✦ You can design more independent forms if they all use the same means to communicate with the parent MDI form.

✦ You also saw how to build generic windows that can be reconfigured based on the database query you are using.

✦ You'll see more of this throughout the book and even build an edit form that can reconfigure itself.

✦　　✦　　✦

Using Forms as Objects

One of Visual Basic's strengths is its capability to let a new programmer build an application quickly. The programmer doesn't have to worry about how the underlying VB engine works; rather, he or she just has to draw a window, put some controls on it, and write a little bit of code.

Unfortunately, many experienced programmers are still doing the same thing. They spend weeks doing database designs, and at least as much time reviewing windows with users, but then they build rudimentary forms that barely function without lots of extra code modules.

What if you started thinking about each window as a self-aware component of the application? What if each window knew everything about opening and populating itself — making its data available to other parts of the application — and could save its data in whatever format was required? This chapter is designed to show you how to do just that with some fairly commonly used dialogs: the About Box and the Login form. Each of these windows will be transformed into living, breathing entities that you can reuse in other applications as well.

The About Box

Even if you've never heard it called an About box, you've probably seen it before. Examples are shown in Figures 5-1 and 5-2.

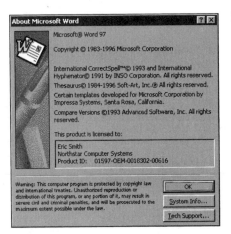

Figure 5-1: The About box from Microsoft Word

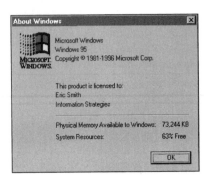

Figure 5-2: The About box from Windows Explorer

This window typically contains information about the application, its designers, and copyright and serial number information. It is normally listed on the bottom of the Help menu, as shown in Figure 5-3.

Figure 5-3: The About box is normally listed at the end of the Help menu.

Many About boxes also have *Easter eggs*, which are hidden bits of functionality added by the developers of the application. Typically, Easter eggs are triggered by some obscure key and/or mouse button combinations. Although Easter eggs are somewhat amusing, they really don't belong in a professional business application, especially if you are being paid by the hour as a consultant or contractor.

This window needs to perform a number of tasks to provide all the necessary information about itself:

✦ Retrieve information about itself, such as the registered user and/or serial number of the application.

✦ Provide any necessary information regarding trademarks and copyrights required by law.

✦ Provide the user access to pieces of system information that may be relevant to a technical support issue.

✦ Provide technical support contact information and other company information, as this is the first place experienced users look. You may also want to link to a Web site automatically.

As you can see, even a simple window like the About box can contain a great deal of functionality. Depending on your application, you may or may not want to include all of the features that were listed. Some of the features may be overkill, and may not be necessary. On the other hand, you may have need for additional features in the About box that aren't even listed. In this section, you'll be developing all of the features listed above for our About box.

The code for this example can be found on the CD-ROM: Copy the contents of the folder D:\Samples\Chapter05\ to your hard drive.

Creating the basic elements

The first features you'll build into this window handle some of the basics, such as setting the window title correctly and loading other application-specific information. These features will be implemented by using some of the built-in features of Visual Basic.

You'll be creating an About box that looks similar to the one used in Word. To get started, do the following:

1. In either a new or existing project, add a new form. Don't add the prebuilt About Dialog template, which is shown in Figure 5-4. You'll be building your own, and it is tedious to remove all the existing code first.

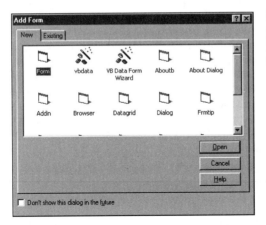

Figure 5-4: Visual Basic provides a prebuilt About Dialog template, which is shown in the Add Form dialog.

2. Use the values shown in Table 5-1 to set the properties of your form. Feel free to use different names for your form; however, you'll need to change your code appropriately.

Table 5-1 Properties of the About Box	
Property	**Value**
(Name)	frmAbout
BorderStyle	3 - Fixed Dialog
Caption	About xxx
ControlBox	False
Icon	(none)
StartUpPosition	2 - CenterScreen

To clear the value of the Icon property (or any property that uses a filename), simply select the property and then press the Delete key to clear the box.

3. Since this is a generic About box, you need to provide places for the following pieces of information:

- Application name
- Version number
- Copyright information

There are some other pieces of text on the form that are static and do not
need to loaded at runtime. These will be simple labels. Add the labels marked
in Figure 5-5, and use the values in Table 5-2 to set the `Caption` and `Name`
properties correctly.

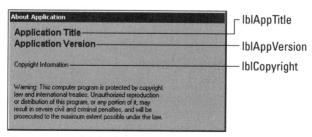

Figure 5-5: Add the labels to the About
window in the places shown here.

Your window, with all the elements discussed here, will eventually look like
Figure 5-6.

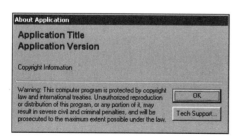

Figure 5-6: The About box with all
the controls correctly placed on it

Table 5-2
Label Properties for the About Box

Control	Caption
lblAppTitle	Application Title
lblAppVersion	Application Version
lblCopyright	Copyright Information

The other label used for the warning message can be named whatever you wish; it
will not be used in code. You can also choose your own fonts; however, remember
that not everyone has every font that you might have. Stick to Arial, Times New
Roman, or the default of MS Sans Serif. Tahoma was introduced with Office 97, so if

you know your users have it, you can use that font also. The example shown was done using MS Sans Serif font.

Next, you need to add several buttons. The first is the OK button, which will always be available. Name it `cmdOK` and place it in the lower-right portion of the window. The other button to add is labeled **Tech Support...** and should be placed below the OK button. Name it `cmdTechSupport`. Depending on the application's needs, this button may or may not be visible, but you can set the default as visible.

The last piece to add to this window is the separator line between the top and bottom sections of the window. To get the three-dimensional effect used in Word's About box, do the following:

1. Draw a frame on the form and set its `Height` property to 135.

2. Delete the value in the `Caption` property.

Adding code to the form

Now that the form is built, you can add the necessary code. The code needs to support the following functions:

✦ Setting of the three visible fields; that is, application name, application version, and copyright information

✦ Providing information for the Tech Support... button

Most of these features can be handled easily; however, the form can be a bit smarter and take care of some of the details automatically, as you'll see.

The simple version of the code consists of three `Property Let()` procedures, each of which sets one of the three labels you drew on the form. That code is listed here:

```
Option Explicit

Public Property Let AppTitle(sTitle As String)
    Me.Caption = "About " & sTitle
    lblAppTitle = sTitle
End Property

Public Property Let AppVersion(sVersion As String)
    lblAppVersion = "Version " & sVersion
End Property

Public Property Let Copyright(sInfo As String)
    lblCopyright = sInfo
End Property
```

The `AppTitle` property has to set both the `Caption` of the form and the `AppTitle` label that is actually on the form itself. The other two `Property Let()` procedures set their labels and finish. The `Version` property also adds the word "Version" in front of the value.

The only other code required is in the OK button's `Click` event, to hide the window. That code is listed here:

```
Private Sub cmdOK_Click()
    Unload Me
End Sub
```

The `Unload Me()` will remove the About box's form from memory and return control to the code that called the form initially. To test the form, add the following code to a module:

```
Sub Main()
    frmAbout.AppTitle = "Testing Application"
    frmAbout.AppVersion = "1.0"
    frmAbout.Copyright = "Copyright 1998 by Eric Smith"
    frmAbout.Show vbModal
End Sub
```

To run the project, set the project's Startup object to Sub Main. Do this by selecting Project ⇨ Properties and selecting Sub Main from the drop-down list. When you run it, this code will produce the window shown in Figure 5-7.

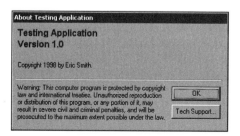

Figure 5-7: The About Box after being called from Sub Main()

The OK button will unload the window and return control to `Sub Main()`, which promptly exits as it should.

Although there's not a lot of code yet, you should already see how using the properties of the About Box form is a lot easier than trying to remember the names of the controls on the form. It's also more reliable, since control names change every so often. The `Property Let()` procedures will have to be updated, but any code calling those `Property Let()` procedures will still work fine. You've isolated the control names from the external code that uses them. This is one type of encapsulation about which you'll learn more in this and other chapters.

Building a smarter About box

Of course, the code you just wrote is only the beginning for this form. One of the first things you want to do is to create a method that the calling code uses to show the window, instead of calling Show 1. The form itself should be responsible for showing and hiding itself when necessary. That code, which should be added to the About Box form, is shown here:

```
Public Sub Display()
    Me.Show vbModal
End Sub
```

The calling code in Sub Main() now becomes

```
Sub Main()
    frmAbout.AppTitle = "Testing Application"
    frmAbout.AppVersion = "1.0"
    frmAbout.Copyright = "Copyright 1998 by Eric Smith"
    frmAbout.Display
End Sub
```

The caller now doesn't have to worry whether the About form is being shown modally or not—it leaves that up to the About form itself. This allows every About box to be shown exactly the same way: modal to the application.

Another feature the code needs to support is an easier way to set all three form label captions. If you're not aware of it, the App object contains a number of properties that contain information you can set when you build your executable. To see all the possible settings, do the following:

1. Select File ➪ Make prjAboutBox.

2. On the dialog that appears, press the Options button. The window shown in Figure 5-8 will appear.

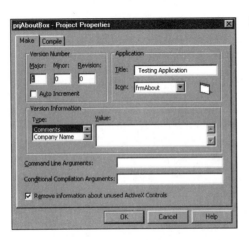

Figure 5-8: The Make Options dialog

Each of the items in the list box in the Version Information frame has a corresponding property in the App object, as shown in Table 5-3.

<table>
<tr><td colspan="2" align="center">Table 5-3
App Object Properties</td></tr>
<tr><td>*Version Information Type*</td><td>*Corresponding Property*</td></tr>
<tr><td>Comments</td><td>App.Comments</td></tr>
<tr><td>Company Name</td><td>App.CompanyName</td></tr>
<tr><td>File Description</td><td>App.FileDescription</td></tr>
<tr><td>Legal Copyright</td><td>App.LegalCopyright</td></tr>
<tr><td>Legal Trademarks</td><td>App.LegalTrademarks</td></tr>
<tr><td>Product Name</td><td>App.ProductName</td></tr>
</table>

To set one of these properties, you pick it from the list on the left and fill in your contents in the box on the right. You can switch between properties on the left without losing your work.

Besides these properties, you can also use the version and revision numbers. Version numbers (for example, MS-DOS 3.3) are normally broken into two sections: the major version on the left of the dot, and the minor version on the right. The App.Major and App.Minor properties correspond to the halves of the version number. In addition, you can keep track of revision numbers if you wish by using the App.Revision property, which can be set to autoincrement every time you rebuild your executable.

The idea of having these App properties available is to use them to store information such as the application name, version numbers, and so on, so that you don't have to hard-code them in your source code. Those properties can be used with the About form in several ways. The first way is to pass those values to the About form from the calling code — in this case, Sub Main(). The code below uses this method to populate the About form:

```
Sub Main()
    frmAbout.AppTitle = App.Title
    frmAbout.AppVersion = App.Major & "." & App.Minor
    frmAbout.Copyright = App.LegalCopyright
    frmAbout.Display
End Sub
```

Note If you want to insert the copyright character (©) in the Value box, hold down your Alt key and enter **0169** on the numeric keypad. It's a bit tedious to do it this way, but you can then use any of the characters shown in the Character Map program, which is normally accessed by clicking Windows Start Menu ⇨ Programs ⇨ Accessories ⇨ Character Map. The character map will show you the numeric value for any character. You then use the number in combination with the Alt key to produce the character. This will work in DOS mode also.

The resulting form, once the appropriate data has been entered in the Options dialog, is shown in Figure 5-9. The main change you should see here is the addition of the copyright character in the copyright notice on the form.

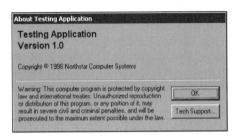

Figure 5-9: The About box being populated from the App object

Now that you've tried your hand at using the App object, why not make your About box be smarter about using the object itself? An easy way to do this is to load all the data from the App object whenever the About form loads:

```
Private Sub Form_Load()
    Me.Caption = "About " & App.Title
    lblAppTitle = App.Title
    lblAppVersion = "Version " _
        & App.Major & "." & App.Minor
    lblCopyright = App.LegalCopyright
End Sub
```

The calling code in Sub Main() then becomes fairly simple:

```
Sub Main()
    frmAbout.Display
End Sub
```

This produces exactly the same window as before, but with slightly less code on the caller's part. Since we now have similar code in two places on the About form, it is time to consolidate it. The form should have private variables to store the application information and should have a method that fills the form from that stored information. This makes the code much easier to maintain. The new code for the About form is shown in Listing 5-1.

Listing 5-1: **The Code for the About Form**

```
Option Explicit

Public Property Let AppTitle(sTitle As String)
    lblAppTitle = sTitle
    Me.Caption = "About " & sTitle
End Property

Public Property Let AppVersion(sVersion As String)
    lblAppVersion = sVersion
End Property

Public Property Let Copyright(sInfo As String)
    lblCopyright = sInfo
End Property

Public Sub Display()
    Me.Show vbModal
End Sub

Private Sub cmdOK_Click()
    Unload Me
End Sub

Private Sub Form_Load()
    '
    ' Start out by loading the default values
    ' into the locations on the form.
    '
    lblAppTitle = App.Title
    Me.Caption = "About " & App.Title
    lblAppVersion = App.Major & "." & App.Minor
    lblCopyright = App.LegalCopyright

End Sub
```

The major changes are summarized here:

The default values are loaded into the window when the form is loaded, and then are shown with the public Display() method.

Notice that this code stores the version information as a string and not numbers. This is to provide flexibility to other programs that may use version numbers consisting of more than two parts, as in many of Oracle's product numbers. The Property Let() routines will still work correctly if the calling code needs to set each value manually, as well. Since each of the values has a corresponding Property Let() procedure, you can change any of the values that are in the App object. This feature gives you more flexibility in this window.

Adding advanced features

There are several other features that the About form can have to make it even more useful, the first of which is to support Web access to a company's Web site. To do this, we need two things:

✦ The URL of the Web site

✦ The user's browser location

The first is easy and can be set with a new `Property` procedure. The second involves reading the computer's Registry. Finding the user's browser is actually not as hard as it might seem, as you'll see shortly.

The new `Property Let()` procedure is listed below:

```
Property Let WebSite(sWebSite As String)
   m_sWebSite = sWebSite
End Property
```

You also need to add this line to the Declarations section of the form:

```
Private m_sWebSite As String
```

Since this information is not stored in the `App` object, the calling code will need to set this property before using the form.

The second half of this task is to retrieve the user's browser. To do this, we need the API call to access the Registry. The Registry is where most key information about Windows and applications running in Windows is stored. The code in Listing 5-2 can be used to do this. This code, since it will be used in other sections of this chapter, should be placed in a separate code module. This will allow you to share the function throughout your application.

Listing 5-2: Code for Function fnGetRegistryKey()

```
Public Function fnGetRegistryKey(sKey As String, _
   sEntry As String, _
   Optional bHKeyClassesRoot As Boolean = False, _
   Optional bHKeyCurrentConfig As Boolean = False, _
   Optional bHKeyCurrentUser As Boolean = True, _
   Optional bHKeyDynamicData As Boolean = False, _
   Optional bHKeyLocalMachine As Boolean = False, _
   Optional bHKeyPerformanceData As Boolean = False, _
   Optional bHKeyUsers As Boolean = False, _
   Optional bDirectory As Boolean = False) As String

   Const BUFFER_LENGTH = 255

   Dim sKeyName As String
```

```
Dim sReturnBuffer As String
Dim lBufLen As Long
Dim lReturn As Long
Dim hKeyHandle As Long
Dim lKeyType As Long
'
' Set up return buffer
'
sReturnBuffer = Space(BUFFER_LENGTH)
lBufLen = BUFFER_LENGTH

lKeyType = fnDetermineKeyType(bHKeyClassesRoot, _
    bHKeyCurrentConfig, _
    bHKeyCurrentUser, _
    bHKeyDynamicData, _
    bHKeyLocalMachine, _
    bHKeyPerformanceData, _
    bHKeyUsers)

lReturn = RegOpenKeyEx(lKeyType, sKey, _
    0, KEY_ALL_ACCESS, hKeyHandle)
If lReturn = ERROR_SUCCESS Then
    lReturn = RegQueryValueExString(hKeyHandle, _
        sEntry, 0, 0, sReturnBuffer, lBufLen)
    If lReturn = ERROR_SUCCESS Then
        '
        ' Have to remove the null terminator from string
        '
        sReturnBuffer = Trim$(Left$(sReturnBuffer, _
            lBufLen - 1))
        '
        ' Add a backslash if one isn't already on a
        ' directory entry.
        '
        If bDirectory Then
            If Right$(sReturnBuffer, 1) <> "\" Then
                sReturnBuffer = sReturnBuffer & "\"
            End If
        End If
        fnGetRegistryKey = sReturnBuffer

    Else
        fnGetRegistryKey = ""
    End If
Else
    fnGetRegistryKey = ""
End If
'
' Close the key
'
RegCloseKey hKeyHandle

End Function
```

The main purpose of this code is to retrieve a particular set of data from the Windows Registry. First the section of the Registry is found. The Windows 95 Registry is broken into six major sections, called *hives*. The caller of this subroutine specifies which hive to use. Next, the key is found with the RegOpenKeyEx() API call. A key contains values related to that key. For instance, you'll be looking for the program used to start the default browser. That information is a value within a key. After the key is found, a value is retrieved using the RegQueryValueString() API call. Finally, the key is closed and you're all done!

For this code to work properly, you need to add a number of items to the Declarations section of your form. These are listed here (see Listing 5-3) and are also included on the form on the CD-ROM, as is all the code for this form.

Listing 5-3: **Registry API Declarations for Visual Basic**

```
Private Declare Function RegCloseKey Lib "advapi32.dll" _
    (ByVal hKey As Long) As Long

Private Declare Function RegCreateKeyEx _
    Lib "advapi32.dll" _
    Alias "RegCreateKeyExA" _
    (ByVal hKey As Long, ByVal lpSubKey As String, _
    ByVal Reserved As Long, ByVal lpClass As String, _
    ByVal dwOptions As Long, ByVal samDesired As Long, _
    lpSecurityAttributes As Any, _
    hKeyHandle As Long, _
    lpdwDisposition As Long) As Long

Private Declare Function RegQueryValueExString Lib _
    "advapi32.dll" Alias "RegQueryValueExA" _
    (ByVal hKey As Long, ByVal lpValueName As String, _
    ByVal lpReserved As Long, lpType As Long, _
    ByVal lpData As String, _
    lpcbData As Long) As Long

Private Declare Function RegOpenKeyEx _
    Lib "advapi32.dll" _
    Alias "RegOpenKeyExA" _
    (ByVal hKey As Long, _
    ByVal lpSubKey As String, ByVal ulOptions As Long, _
    ByVal samDesired As Long, hKeyHandle As Long) As Long

Private Declare Function RegSetValueEx _
    Lib "advapi32.dll" _
    Alias "RegSetValueExA" _
    (ByVal hKey As Long, ByVal lpValueName As String, _
    ByVal Reserved As Long, ByVal dwType As Long, _
    lpData As Any, ByVal cbData As Long) As Long

Private Const ERROR_SUCCESS = 0&
```

```
Private Const HKEY_CLASSES_ROOT = &H80000000
Private Const HKEY_CURRENT_CONFIG = &H80000005
Private Const HKEY_CURRENT_USER = &H80000001
Private Const HKEY_DYN_DATA = &H80000006
Private Const HKEY_LOCAL_MACHINE = &H80000002
Private Const HKEY_PERFORMANCE_DATA = &H80000004
Private Const HKEY_USERS = &H80000003

Private Const KEY_CREATE_SUB_KEY = &H4
Private Const KEY_ENUMERATE_SUB_KEYS = &H8
Private Const KEY_QUERY_VALUE = &H1
Private Const KEY_SET_VALUE = &H2
Private Const KEY_NOTIFY = &H10
Private Const KEY_CREATE_LINK = &H20
Private Const REG_OPTION_NON_VOLATILE = 0
Private Const REG_SZ = 1
Private Const STANDARD_RIGHTS_ALL = &H1F0000
Private Const SYNCHRONIZE = &H100000

Private Const KEY_ALL_ACCESS = ((STANDARD_RIGHTS_ALL Or _
    KEY_QUERY_VALUE Or _
    KEY_SET_VALUE Or _
    KEY_CREATE_SUB_KEY Or _
    KEY_ENUMERATE_SUB_KEYS Or _
    KEY_NOTIFY Or _
    KEY_CREATE_LINK) And (Not SYNCHRONIZE))
```

Finally, because the `fnGetRegistryKey()` function makes extensive use of optional arguments, the support subroutine shown in Listing 5-4 is also required in the About form to make it self-sufficient. Put this code into the code module you created for the other Registry function.

Listing 5-4: **Code for Function fnDetermineKeyType()**

```
Private Function fnDetermineKeyType(bHKeyClassesRoot _
    As Boolean, _
    bHKeyCurrentConfig As Boolean, _
    bHKeyCurrentUser As Boolean, _
    bHKeyDynamicData As Boolean, _
    bHKeyLocalMachine As Boolean, _
    bHKeyPerformanceData As Boolean, _
    bHKeyUsers As Boolean) As Long

    Dim lResult As Long

    If bHKeyClassesRoot Then
        lResult = HKEY_CLASSES_ROOT
```

(continued)

Listing 5-4 *(continued)*

```
    ElseIf bHKeyCurrentConfig Then
        lResult = HKEY_CURRENT_CONFIG
    ElseIf bHKeyCurrentUser Then
        lResult = HKEY_CURRENT_USER
    ElseIf bHKeyDynamicData Then
        lResult = HKEY_DYN_DATA
    ElseIf bHKeyLocalMachine Then
        lResult = HKEY_LOCAL_MACHINE
    ElseIf bHKeyPerformanceData Then
        lResult = HKEY_PERFORMANCE_DATA
    ElseIf bHKeyUsers Then
        lResult = HKEY_USERS
    End If

    fnDetermineKeyType = lResult
End Function
```

Now that the Registry reading code is in place, you can add the code for the Tech Support button, which is listed below:

```
Private Sub cmdTechSupport_Click()
    Shell fnGetRegistryKey("htmlfile\shell\open\command", _
        "", bHKeyClassesRoot:=True) & " " & m_sWebSite, _
        vbNormalFocus
End Sub
```

If you look in your Registry, you can see the entry that this code will retrieve by opening the HKEY_CLASSES_ROOT tree, and then drilling down to HTMLFile\Shell\ Open\Command. If you are using Internet Explorer, you will see something that looks like this value:

```
"F:\COMMUN~1\INTERN~1\iexplore.exe" -nohome
```

This string will reference the current location of the default Web browser that is installed on your machine. Although the string is a bit messy to look at, luckily that entire string can be passed directly to the `Shell` command to start the appropriate browser. However, if the Web site address is not set, this code really shouldn't be allowed to execute; it would cause the Web browser to open and not go to a Web site. To enforce this, the Tech Support button can simply be hidden if no Web site has been specified. The code to do this goes into the `Display()` subroutine, making the whole subroutine look like this:

```
Private Sub Display()
    cmdTechSupport.Visible = (m_sWebSite <> "")
    Me.Show vbModal
End Sub
```

If you run your existing `Sub Main()`, you will see a window resembling Figure 5-10, and no Tech Support button will be visible.

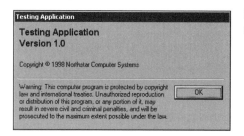

Figure 5-10: The About box without a WebSite property

If you modify your `Sub Main()` code to set the `WebSite` property of the form, the Tech Support button will show up. Click it and watch your browser launch immediately to the designated Web site.

About Box notes

As you can see, even a simple window like the About box can be souped up so that the calling code really doesn't have to do much to make it work. Adding appropriate properties and other methods to the form can make your colleagues' lives (and yours) much easier.

One feature not demonstrated here is the idea of keeping the form in memory. If the About box is being launched from an MDI window, that MDI window can keep a variable to refer to the instance of the About box. The window never has to be reinitialized; it is always in memory, ready to show. Depending on the size of your application, this may or may not be an option for you. Large applications require more memory, which may preclude keeping some of your forms in memory during the life of the application. If you do want to do it, simply change the code in the OK button to say `Me.Hide` instead of `Unload Me`.

The Login Form

Now that you've got your feet wet with the About form, the Login form is the next one to tackle. The Login form is shown in Figure 5-11.

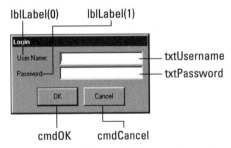

Figure 5-11: The Login form you're going to build

This form has fewer controls than the About form; however, it does incorporate some new functionality. Its primary feature is its capability to both store and retrieve information from the Registry. In this way, the form is able to retrieve the last user ID used to log in. This saves the user some typing in most cases.

Building the Login form

To get started, create a new form in your project. Table 5-4 shows the properties you need to set on the form so that it works properly.

Table 5-4 Login Form Properties	
Property	**Value**
(Name)	frmLogin
BorderStyle	3 - Fixed Dialog
Caption	Login
ControlBox	False
Icon	(none)
ShowInTaskbar	False
StartUpPosition	2 - CenterScreen

The other controls on the form, marked in Figure 5-11, are listed in Table 5-5 with the properties that you need to set for each. The PasswordChar property causes any text in the txtPassword box to be replaced (visually only) with whatever character you specify. The real text value is still in the Text property, just as the user typed it.

Table 5-5
Control Properties

Control	Property	Value
lblLabel(0)	Caption	User Name:
lblLabel(1)	Caption	Password:
txtUsername	Text	(empty string)
txtPassword	Text	(empty string)
PasswordChar		* - asterisk

Adding code to the form

The first code you need to add to this form will take care of setting and retrieval of username and password information. In addition, the calling code will need to set the *root registry key* of the application so that the Login form knows where to look for previous user information. The root registry key is the topmost key used by the application in the Registry. In Figure 5-12, the highlighted key is the root registry key for Visual Basic. The key is HKEY_CURRENT_USER\Software\Microsoft \Visual Basic. The application calling the Login form simply sends the section of the registry (HKEY_CURRENT_USER) as well as the root key, and the Login form can take it from there.

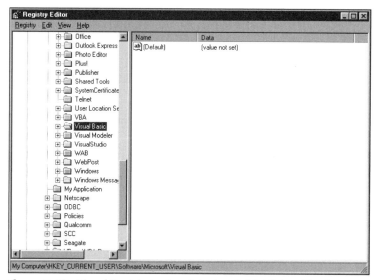

Figure 5-12: Visual Basic's root registry key is highlighted in the Registry Editor.

To get started, add this code to the Login form:

```
Option Explicit

Private m_bUserLoggedIn As Boolean
Private Const m_sRegKey = _
   "Software\My Company\My Application\Login Information"

Property Get UserName() As String
   UserName = txtUserName
End Property

Property Let UserName(sInput As String)
   txtUserName = sInput
End Property

Property Get Password() As String
   Password = txtPassword
End Property

Property Let Password(sInput As String)
   txtPassword = sInput
End Property
```

These `Property Get()` and `Property Let()` procedures are the only ones required for this form, unless you decide to add something more to it.

Like the About form, the Login form will have a `Display()` routine. In this case, however, it needs to be a function so that it can return a value for whether or not the user actually logged in. Listing 5-5 shows the code for the OK button, Cancel button, and `Display()` method so that you can see how they interact.

Listing 5-5: Event Subroutines for Login Form

```
Public Function Display() As Boolean

   txtUserName = fnGetRegistryKey(m_sRegKey, _
      "User Name", _
      bHKeyCurrentUser:=True)

   Me.Show vbModal
   Display = m_bUserLoggedIn
End Function

Private Sub cmdOK_Click()
   m_bUserLoggedIn = True
   subSaveRegistryKey m_sRegKey, _
      "User Name", _
```

```
        txtUserName, _
        bHKeyCurrentUser:=True
    Me.Hide
End Sub

Private Sub cmdCancel_Click()
    m_bUserLoggedIn = False
    Me.Hide
End Sub
```

A new variable, m_bUserLoggedIn, is located in the Declarations section of the form and is defined as shown here:

```
Private m_bUserLoggedIn As Boolean
```

The caller of this form can use the following code to determine if the application actually needs to start:

```
Sub Main()
    frmLogin.UserName = "EricS"

    If frmLogin.Display Then
        MsgBox "Login completed."
    Else
        MsgBox "Login aborted."
    End If

    End
End Sub
```

The resulting window from this code is shown in Figure 5-13. The calling code presets the username, which is loaded into the box before the window is shown.

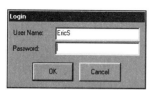

Figure 5-13: The Login form in action

The calling code then can validate the user ID against whatever scheme is in place. Security schemes are too customized in most cases to try to generalize the process. The calling code can simply retrieve the user ID and password and continue on its way.

Adding advanced features

As mentioned earlier, this Login form is going to be smart enough to read and write to the Registry so that the last user's name shows up in the box automatically. Since you already have the fnGetRegistryKey() function in your code module that you built in the previous section, we'll just use that function. The subSave RegistryKey() subroutine is also fairly simple, and is shown in Listing 5-6.

Listing 5-6: **Code for subSaveRegistryKey() Subroutine**

```
Public Sub subSaveRegistryKey(sKey As String, _
    sEntry As String, _
    sValue As String, _
    Optional bHKeyClassesRoot As Boolean = False, _
    Optional bHKeyCurrentConfig As Boolean = False, _
    Optional bHKeyCurrentUser As Boolean = True, _
    Optional bHKeyDynamicData As Boolean = False, _
    Optional bHKeyLocalMachine As Boolean = False, _
    Optional bHKeyPerformanceData As Boolean = False, _
    Optional bHKeyUsers As Boolean = False, _
    Optional bDirectory As Boolean = False)


    Dim lReturn As Long
    Dim hKeyHandle As Long
    Dim lKeyType As Long

    lKeyType = fnDetermineKeyType(bHKeyClassesRoot, _
        bHKeyCurrentConfig, _
        bHKeyCurrentUser, _
        bHKeyDynamicData, _
        bHKeyLocalMachine, _
        bHKeyPerformanceData, _
        bHKeyUsers)

    '
    ' RegCreateKeyEx will open the named key if
    ' it exists, and create a new one if it doesn't.
    '
    lReturn = RegCreateKeyEx(lKeyType, sKey, 0&, _
        vbNullString, REG_OPTION_NON_VOLATILE, _
        KEY_ALL_ACCESS, 0&, hKeyHandle, lReturn)


    '
    ' RegSetValueEx saves the value to the string
    ' within the key that was just opened.
    '
```

```
lReturn = RegSetValueEx(hKeyHandle, sEntry, _
    0&, REG_SZ, ByVal sValue, Len(sValue))

'
' Close the key
'
RegCloseKey hKeyHandle

End Sub
```

Like the `fnGetRegistryKey()` function, `subSaveRegistryKey()` determines which Registry hive to store the key in first. It then opens the appropriate key and writes the value to the Registry. This subroutine, in combination with the other Registry functions you've built, will be a handy one to keep in your programmer's toolkit.

After you've got the required Registry functions into the module, add the following code to your form:

```
Public Function Display() As Boolean

    txtUserName = fnGetRegistryKey(m_sRegKey, _
        "User Name", _
        bHKeyCurrentUser:=True)

    Me.Show vbModal
    Display = m_bUserLoggedIn
End Function
```

The primary change in this code is to call the `fnGetRegistryKey()` function to retrieve the `User Name` value from the Login Information key beneath the root registry key that was stored in the Login window. The calling code in `Sub Main()` looks like the following:

```
Sub Main
If frmLogin.Display Then
    MsgBox "Login completed."
Else
    MsgBox "Login aborted."
End If

    End
End Sub
```

To show you that the code works, look at Figure 5-14. It shows the Login Information key with the `User Name` value filled with "Jodi Smith."

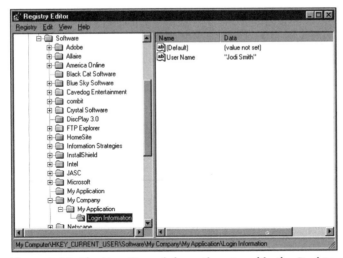

Figure 5-14: The User Name information stored in the Registry

When you run the program, the code correctly retrieves the last user's name from the Registry and shows it in the Login window, as shown in Figure 5-15.

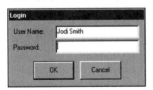

Figure 5-15: The username displays correctly in the Login window.

The last feature to add is the code to save the last user ID after it has been entered. That code goes in the cmdOK_Click() event, as shown here:

```
Private Sub cmdOK_Click()
    m_bUserLoggedIn = True
    subSaveRegistryKey m_sRegKey, _
        "User Name", _
        txtUserName, _
        bHKeyCurrentUser:=True
    Me.Hide
End Sub
```

If you now run your program, even if you haven't created any keys, there will be a key created beneath the key that you pass in to the form.

In addition, if you run your program a second time after having "logged in" successfully, the Login dialog will be automatically populated with the last username you used. Finally, if you want to see how to retrieve information from the Login dialog, use the following code in your Sub Main() subroutine:

```
If frmLogin.Display Then
    MsgBox "Login completed. " _
        & frmLogin.UserName _
        & " logged in successfully."
Else
    MsgBox "Login aborted."
End If
```

When it runs, you should see a dialog box similar to that shown in Figure 5-16.

Figure 5-16: The username is retrieved successfully from the Login window.

Final notes

Of course, the code in the Login form has not been properly commented, and error handlers need to be added; however, the point of this example is to show how to make your form smarter than it used to be.

Summary

In this chapter, you've learned how to build forms that go beyond the simple ones that every VB programmer starts out building.

✦ Forms, once thought of as objects, take on a more powerful role.

✦ Instead of keeping lots of variables to remember what options have been set, for instance, you could create an Options dialog with some of the same techniques used here.

✦ Once loaded, a form can simply stay in memory, available for any application to access.

✦ What can you do with your forms? The sky is really the limit.

✦   ✦   ✦

Developing with TreeView and ListView Controls

◆   ◆   ◆   ◆

In This Chapter

When to use the
TreeView and
ListView controls

Using ImageList
controls

Reviewing TreeView
control basics

Using the ListView
control with the
TreeView

◆   ◆   ◆   ◆

Windows 95, when it was first released, introduced a number of new controls into the Visual Basic developer's repository. The TreeView control, most commonly known as the left side of Windows Explorer, created a number of new options for displaying hierarchical data. In addition, the ListView control, which was the right side of Windows Explorer, provided a way to list data complete with multiple views and the capability to use more fields than a typical list box or other control. Although there are some limitations to using these controls, this chapter shows you ways to code around those limitations and provide a really intuitive interface for your user.

The application you build in this chapter is shown later in Figure 6-1. It is a fairly simple application that demonstrates all the major features of three controls: TreeView, ListView, and ImageList.

On the CD-ROM

All files used in this chapter are located in the \SAMPLES\ CH06 directory on the CD-ROM.

When to Use TreeView and ListView Controls

The TreeView and ListView controls are a great way for you to provide intuitive interface features. Because users of Windows 95 are already familiar with both controls, you don't have to teach the user how to use them.

On the basis of the way TreeView is used in Windows Explorer, users assume that the data it shows is hierarchical. For instance, files are shown in folders, which are themselves in folders or on a drive. There is a definite logical structure in place. Any time you have data in categories, you can use a TreeView control to show it. The examples used later in the chapter use the Northwinds Trader database included with Visual Basic. This database has a hierarchy of products arranged in categories. There are other examples in the same database, such as order detail lines associated with orders, and customers associated with orders.

Even if data isn't in a category, there are cases in which you can create categories on the fly. For instance, although customers might not be categorized, they could be grouped by the first letter of their last names. Your groups would then be A – Z, and the customer records would be in these groups. This method is an option if you don't have a lot (more than 10 to 20 per letter) of records. If you have more, you may want to use a combination of the TreeView and ListView controls together. As the user selects a category on the left (TreeView control), the list of items in the category shows up on the right in the ListView control. This method expands the number of items you can show, since the ListView control can handle approximately 1000 items without a problem.

Note

If you want to see how the ListView handles a particular number of items, use the example from Chapter 4. There is code in the list viewer that controls how many items should be loaded into the ListView control. You'll see that as you add many more than 1000 items, the ListView control gets much slower and may even crash if you have too many items.

If you have more than 1000 items in a category, you can replace the ListView control with a high-volume data control such as a DBGrid control. The DBGrid control can display more data because it doesn't really keep the data in memory — it is linked to a database recordset.

The overriding rule is not to add a large number of items into either a TreeView or ListView control. The reason is that these controls have to allocate more memory per item than a control like a ListBox might. Later in this chapter, you'll see how to load data into these controls dynamically during the program's run, so that you don't have to load all the data initially, when the control is first shown to the user.

Using ImageList Controls

Both the TreeView and ListView controls can show a couple of types of graphics. The TreeView control uses 16x16-pixel graphics for each item on the tree, and the ListView control uses 16x16, 32x32, and 48x48-pixel graphics for its various views. The ImageList control can only hold one size of graphics at a time. If you need two sizes of graphics, you need separate ImageList controls.

Note   You can see the different views available in a ListView control by running Windows Explorer and selecting View ⇨ Arrange Icons. Try out the other settings and you'll see all the different sizes of icons.

Figure 6-1 shows a TreeView control using 16x16 icons. Two different graphics are in use: one for the category and one for the product. The TreeView control supports the use of two graphics per item: one for when the item is selected, another for when the item is not selected. This feature lets you have open and closed folders, just as you would in Windows Explorer.

Figure 6-1: A TreeView control that uses two graphics from an ImageList control

This simple form uses both a TreeView control and an ImageList control. To re-create the form shown in Figure 6-1, first create the form and add the ImageList control to it. Follow these steps:

1. In a new Standard EXE project, name the form **frmProductViewer.**

2. If the Microsoft Windows Common Controls 6.0 are not already on your Toolbox, add them by selecting Tools ⇨ Components and selecting Microsoft Windows Common Controls 6.0 from the dialog box that appears.

3. Add an ImageList control to your form and name it **ctlTreeImages.**

4. Set the `MaskColor` property to &H00000080&, which is a dark red color. A *mask color* is a color in each graphic that Visual Basic assumes to be transparent. The graphics provided on the CD-ROM use a dark red as the mask since that color does not appear in the graphics.

5. Verify that the `UseMaskColor` property is set to `True`.

6. In the Properties window, click the `Custom` property. The property page for the ImageList control appears. Make sure the options you see for your control's General tab match those shown in Figure 6-2.

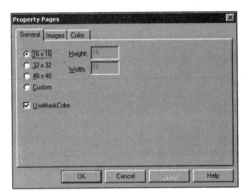

Figure 6-2: The property values on your General tab should match the ones shown here.

7. In the property page, click the Images tab. To add an image, click the Insert Picture button and select the file to add. You can add images in any order because you retrieve them via the `Key` property. Add the `product.bmp` file and set its `Key` property to `Product`.

8. Repeat step 7 to add the `category.bmp` file with a `Key` property value of `Category`. When you are done adding these pictures, your Images tab should resemble Figure 6-3.

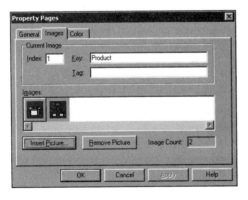

Figure 6-3: Each picture you add is displayed on the Images tab.

9. You don't need to make any changes to the Color tab, so click the OK button.

That's all you need to do for the ImageList control. The next exercise shows you how to add basic code for the TreeView control.

TreeView Control Basics

The next part of this mini-application to be built is the TreeView section of the form. The TreeView holds a basic two-tier structure of data: categories and products. The code you write here loads data from a database, creates items in theTreeView control, and arranges them in the correct hierarchy.

Before you get started, you need a few definitions. Each item in a tree is called a *node*. Nodes in a tree are related to each other with familial definitions. Using Figure 6-4 as an example, look at how the folders relate to each other.

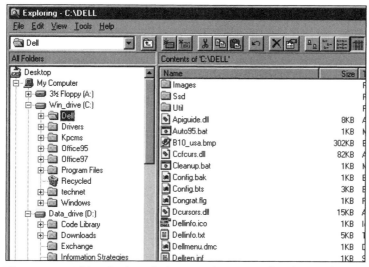

Figure 6-4: Folders in the Windows Explorer are related to each other.

✦ Desktop is called the *root* of this tree. Just as real trees have roots in the ground, all nodes in a TreeView can be linked to a root node. You can also have multiple nodes at the root level if you don't want to have just a single root node. The example you'll be building uses multiple nodes at the root level.

✦ The Dell folder is represented by a *child* node of the node representing the Win_drive (C:) disk. Node Win_drive (C:) is the *parent* of node Dell.

✦ All nodes that are subordinate to node Win_drive (C:) are *sibling* nodes to one another.

Now that the definitions are out of the way, it's time to add your TreeView control and the appropriate code. First, add a TreeView control to your form and change its Name property to ctlTreeView. Place it in the upper-left corner of the form you built.

Next, the TreeView control needs to be instructed as to how to retrieve images. So open the `Custom` property of the TreeView control, which brings up the property page shown in Figure 6-5. Set the `ImageList` property to `ctlTreeImages` and click the OK button.

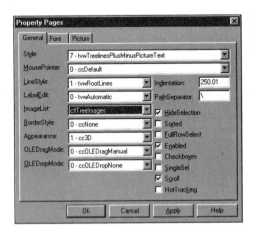

Figure 6-5: Set the ImageList property on the TreeView control so images can be displayed.

Next, add the code in Listing 6-1 to the `Form_Resize` event handler.

Listing 6-1: **Form_Resize Event Handler**

```
Private Sub Form_Resize()
    On Error Resume Next
    ctlTreeView.Height = Me.ScaleHeight - _
        (ctlTreeView.Top * 2)
    ctlTreeView.Width = Me.ScaleWidth - _
        (ctlTreeView.Left * 2)
End Sub
```

The procedure given in Listing 6-1 takes care of resizing the TreeView control to fill the form.

To use the database functions in this example, select Project ➪ References and add a reference to the Microsoft DAO 3.5 Object Library. Next, add these instructions to the Declarations section of the form:

```
Option Explicit
Dim dbStore As Database
Dim rsCategories As Recordset
Dim rsProducts As Recordset
```

These variables will hold object references for the database you'll be using.

If you haven't done any database coding, some of the techniques embodied in the instructions you're about to add may be new to you. However, they are very simple, as you'll soon see. Taking this code apart piece by piece, you'll see how the database records become TreeView nodes in the proper locations. Follow along and type in the following instructions as I explain to you what they mean and how they work. The Set statement opens the Northwind Traders database, which is located in the main Visual Basic directory on your computer.

```
Private Sub Form_Load()
Set dbStore = OpenDatabase("C:\VB\NWind.MDB")
```

Note   Be sure to change the filename to match your system configuration.

The next two instructions (shown in Listing 6-2) retrieve all the categories and all the products. Both sets of records are already sorted alphabetically by name, so that they show up sorted in the TreeView control. Although the TreeView control is able to sort nodes, it does not sort nodes any lower than the root level.

Listing 6-2: **Retrieving All Categories and All Products**

```
otherthose at     Set rsCategories = dbStore.OpenRecordset( _
        "SELECT * FROM Categories ORDER BY CategoryName",_
    dbOpenSnapshot)
    Set rsProducts = dbStore.OpenRecordset( _
        "SELECT * FROM Products ORDER BY ProductName", _
    dbOpenSnapshot)
```

Now that you have the categories, your code adds them to the TreeView control with the code shown here:

```
Do While Not rsCategories.EOF
    ctlTreeView.Nodes.Add _
        , _
        , _
        "Cat" & rsCategories("CategoryID"), _
        rsCategories("CategoryName"), _
        "Category", _
        "Category"

    rsCategories.MoveNext
Loop
```

The Do loop traverses all the category records and processes each one in turn. The key statement in the code is the Add method of the Nodes collection. Note that this Add method is not on the TreeView control itself. This is because TreeView uses the Nodes collection to hold its data.

The first argument to the Nodes.Add method is missing; the category record should be added as a root node. This argument would have been a reference to the relative node to which the new node should be attached. You'll see how that works in the next code segment. The second argument, which is also missing, would specify how a new node should be added with respect to the relative node listed.

The third argument provides a unique key for the new node. A key is similar to an index in that it lets you specify a particular item quickly. One restriction is that the key cannot be simply numeric. For that reason, the prefix "Cat" is added before the unique ID associated with that category (the data from the rsCategories ("CategoryID") field). You'll see how that prefix is used when you add products to your TreeView control.

The fourth argument specifies the text that should be shown in the TreeView control for the new node. In this case, the logical text to show is the category name.

The last two arguments are used to access the ImageList control's images. The first name refers to the icon that should be shown when the node is not selected. The second name specifies the icon to be shown when the node is selected. In this case, the images to be shown are the same. This is because the images in question are not folders or other graphics that can logically be animated. If you were dealing with nodes that were in folders, the first graphic would be a closed folder, and the second would be an open folder.

With the new node added, the MoveNext goes to the next record and the code repeats for each record in the recordset.

The next section of code is nearly identical to the first. It traverses the products and adds each to the TreeView's Nodes collection. However, the arguments used with the Add method are slightly different.

```
ctlTreeView.Nodes.Add _
        "Cat" & rsProducts("CategoryID"), _
        tvwChild, _
        "Prod" & rsProducts("ProductID"), _
        rsProducts("ProductName"), _
        "Product", _
        "Product"
```

For the Nodes.Add method here, the first two arguments have values in them. The first value specifies that the new product node should be related to the node representing the product's category. Remember the key you created for each category? This is where it comes into play. By specifying the key of the category node, you tell the TreeView control which node is related to the new product node.

The second argument, `tvwChild`, indicates that the new node should be a child node of the one you specified in the first argument. This sets up a parent-child relationship so that the product is listed under the category's node.

That's all the code you need to make this basic TreeView control work properly. Save your work and run your project to see everything in action. Experiment with the settings of the TreeView control to change the appearance of the nodes shown. The `Indentation`, `LineStyle`, and `Style` properties can be used to adjust the look of the TreeView control. Using the values shown in Table 6-1, your TreeView control should look like the one shown in Figure 6-6.

Table 6-1		
TreeView Control Properties		
Property	*Value*	
Indentation	250	
LineStyle	1 - tvwRootLines	
Style	7 - tvwTreeLinesPlusMinusPictureText	

Figure 6-6: The TreeView control, complete with data from the Northwind Traders database

ListView Control Basics

Although the TreeView control is great for displaying hierarchical information, it has some practical limits on how much information it should store. For instance, you wouldn't want to see every file in your computer listed beneath each folder in Windows Explorer. Besides the fact that a lot of useful information can't be shown, the TreeView control can only hold about 1000 items without slowing significantly.

In many cases, you'll want to add a ListView control to your form. Figure 6-7 shows an example of a ListView control.

Figure 6-7: The ListView control is the right-hand side of Windows Explorer.

In this section, you'll take the form you built with the TreeView control and modify it to use both a TreeView and ListView control. To get started, if the TreeView project from a few paragraphs back isn't currently in your VB workspace, then open that project. Next, add a ListView control to the form and resize the form so that it resembles Figure 6-8. Don't worry that the TreeView and ListView don't fill up the whole form — you'll write code to resize them on the fly. You just have to make sure the TreeView is positioned in the upper-left corner of the window. The code you'll write uses the distance from the upper-left corner to the TreeView control as the margin that should be used all around the form.

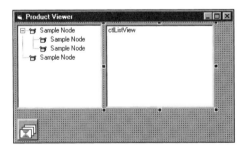

Figure 6-8: Your form now has both a TreeView and a ListView control.

Name the ListView control **ctlListView**. With your controls drawn, you need to make some adjustments to your code. The first code that needs to be changed is shown in Listing 6-3, which entirely replaces the procedure of the same name from Listing 6-1. This new code handles the resizing of the TreeView and ListView controls in response to the form being resized.

Listing 6-3: **Form_Resize Event Handler**

```
Private Sub Form_Resize()
    On Error Resume Next
    ctlTreeView.Height = _
        Me.ScaleHeight - (ctlTreeView.Top * 2)
    ctlListView.Height = _
        Me.ScaleHeight - (ctlTreeView.Top * 2)
    ctlListView.Width = _
        Me.ScaleWidth - ctlListView.Left - ctlTreeView.Left
End Sub
```

The first two lines after On Error Resume Next adjust the heights of the two controls to the height of the form, less a small margin. The third line changes the width of the ListView control to fill all the way to the right edge of the form, less the same margin that is to the left of the TreeView control. Note that this code does not support a "splitter," as is common with Windows Explorer. There are third-party splitter controls available to make this task easier than it would be to do by hand.

You now need to make some changes to the controls on your form. First, add another ImageList control. Because the ListView control can show different sizes of graphics, you need a separate ImageList control for the 32x32 graphics. The ImageList control you have — which is loaded with 16x16 graphics — can be shared between the ListView and TreeView controls. Name the second ImageList control ctlListImages and set its graphic size to 32x32.

The ListView control should show only product entries; you need add only one image to the new ImageList control. Add the file named lrg_product.bmp and give it the key value of Product. Next, with the ImageList control selected, select the Custom property of the ListView control from the Properties window. Set the values on the Image Lists tab as shown in Figure 6-9. Normal icons are those that are 32x32, and the small icons are 16x16. On the basis of the view you are using, the ListView control shows the icon of the correct size.

Figure 6-9: Set the Image Lists to point to the two ImageList controls on your form.

With the controls configured, you can turn your attention back to the code. The Form_Load procedure will need to change since you won't automatically be loading the product data into the TreeView control. Replace the Form_Load procedure entirely with the code in Listing 6-4.

Listing 6-4: **Form_Load Event Handler**

```
Private Sub Form_Load()

    Set dbStore = _
        OpenDatabase("E:\DevStudio\VB\NWind.MDB")
    Set rsCategories = dbStore.OpenRecordset( _
        "SELECT * FROM Categories ORDER BY CategoryName", _
        dbOpenSnapshot)
    Set rsProducts = dbStore.OpenRecordset( _
        "SELECT * FROM Products ORDER BY ProductName", _
        dbOpenSnapshot)
    Do While Not rsCategories.EOF
        ctlTreeView.Nodes.Add _

            , _

            , _
            "Cat" & rsCategories("CategoryID"), _
            rsCategories("CategoryName"), _
            "Category", _
            "Category"
        rsCategories.MoveNext
    Loop

End Sub
```

Because the ListView should show the items in the category selected in the TreeView, add the code shown in Listing 6-5 to your form.

Listing 6-5: **ctlTreeView_NodeClick Event Handler**

```
Private Sub ctlTreeView_NodeClick(ByVal Node As ComctlLib.Node)
    Dim rsFiltered As Recordset

    ctlListView.ListItems.Clear

    rsProducts.Filter = _
        "CategoryID = " & Mid$(Node.Key, 4)
    Set rsFiltered = rsProducts.OpenRecordset()
    Do While Not rsFiltered.EOF
        ctlListView.ListItems.Add , _
            "Prod" & rsFiltered("ProductID"), _
            rsFiltered("ProductName"), _
            "Product", _
            "Product"
        rsFiltered.MoveNext
    Loop
    rsFiltered.Close
    Set rsFiltered = Nothing

End Sub
```

This code will load the ListView on the basis of the node you click in the TreeView control. An easy enhancement would be to automatically select an item in the TreeView when the form loads and then populate the ListView appropriately.

The last change for you to make is to set the View property of the ListView control. This feature changes how data is displayed in the control. For now, be sure the setting is 0 - lvwIcon. This view will show large icons in the ListView section.

With all those changes done, save your project and run it. After you click an item in the TreeView, your window should resemble Figure 6-10.

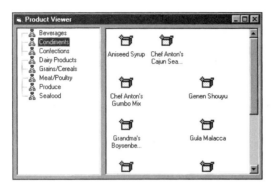

Figure 6-10: The window as it appears after you click an item in TreeView

Enhanced ListView Features

One major reason to use a ListView is its capability to display a number of additional fields besides just the name of the list item. Making this feature work is not very difficult. In this section, you also add a popup menu to change which view is current on the ListView control. Because the ListView must be in Report view before you can see additional information, adding the popup menu is important to making this feature work properly. When these changes are complete, your window should look like Figure 6-11.

Product Name	Units In Stock	Unit Price
Chocolade	15	$12.75
Gumbär Gummibärchen	15	$31.23
Maxilaku	10	$20.00
NuNuCa Nuß-Nougat-Creme	76	$14.00
Pavlova	29	$17.45
Schoggi Schokolade	49	$43.90
Scottish Longbreads	6	$12.50
Sir Rodney's Marmalade	40	$81.00
Sir Rodney's Scones	3	$10.00
Tarte au sucre	17	$49.30
Teatime Chocolate Biscuits	25	$9.20
Valkoinen suklaa	65	$16.25
Zaanse koeken	36	$9.50

Figure 6-11: The Enhanced Product Viewer, complete with additional information fields for each product listed

To get started on these modifications, make the changes marked in Listing 6-6 to the Form_Load event handler.

Listing 6-6: Enhanced Form_Load Event Handler

```
Private Sub Form_Load()

    Set dbStore = _
        OpenDatabase("E:\DevStudio\VB\NWind.MDB")
    Set rsCategories = dbStore.OpenRecordset( _
        "SELECT * FROM Categories ORDER BY CategoryName", _
        dbOpenSnapshot)
    Set rsProducts = dbStore.OpenRecordset( _
        "SELECT * FROM Products ORDER BY ProductName", _
        dbOpenSnapshot)
    Do While Not rsCategories.EOF
        ctlTreeView.Nodes.Add _

            , _

            , _
            "Cat" & rsCategories("CategoryID"), _
            rsCategories("CategoryName"), _
            "Category", _
            "Category"
        rsCategories.MoveNext
    Loop

    ctlListView.ColumnHeaders.Add _
        , "Col1", "Product Name"
    ctlListView.ColumnHeaders.Add _
        , "Col2", "Units In Stock"
    ctlListView.ColumnHeaders.Add _
        , "Col3", "Unit Price"

End Sub
```

These new instructions add three column headers to the report view of the ListView control. You'll only see these headers when the ListView control is in report view; otherwise, there will be no headers.

The next changes are to the code that adds items to the ListView control, shown as highlighted additions in Listing 6-7.

Listing 6-7: **Revised ctlTreeView_NodeClick Event Handler**

```
Private Sub _
    ctlTreeView_NodeClick(ByVal Node As ComctlLib.Node)

    Dim rsFiltered As Recordset
    Dim itemReturn As ListItem
    ctlListView.ListItems.Clear

    rsProducts.Filter = _
        "CategoryID = " & Mid$(Node.Key, 4)
    Set rsFiltered = rsProducts.OpenRecordset()
    Do While Not rsFiltered.EOF
        Set itemReturn = ctlListView.ListItems.Add(, _
            "Prod" & rsFiltered("ProductID"), _
            rsFiltered("ProductName"), _
            "Product", _
            "Product")
        itemReturn.SubItems(1) = rsFiltered("UnitsInStock")
        itemReturn.SubItems(2) = _
            Format$(rsFiltered("UnitPrice"), "Currency")
        rsFiltered.MoveNext
    Loop
    rsFiltered.Close
    Set rsFiltered = Nothing

End Sub
```

The ListItems.Add method returns the newly created ListItem. You can then set the SubItems property for each subitem you wish to add to the ListItem. In this case, the stock count and the retail price are added as two additional subitems.

Because you want to be able to switch the ListView's View property at runtime, you need to add a menu to your form that will be shown as a popup menu. The menu structure is shown in Figure 6-12 as it appears in the Menu Editor. Table 6-2 provides the other property values to set.

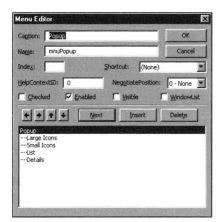

Figure 6-12: The structure for the ListView view-mode popup menu, shown in the Menu Editor.

Table 6-2
Popup Menu Properties

Menu Item	Property	Value
Popup	Name	mnuPopup
	Visible	False
Large Icons	Name	mnuPopupLarge
Small Icons	Name	mnuPopupSmall
List	Name	mnuPopupList
Details	Name	mnuPopupDetails

The code to make the popup menu comes next. First, you need to display the popup menu whenever the user right-clicks on the ListView control. That code is shown in Listing 6-8.

Listing 6-8: **Popup Menu Activation Code**

```
Private Sub ctlListView_MouseDown(Button As Integer, _
    Shift As Integer, _
    x As Single, _
    y As Single)
```

(continued)

Listing 6-8 *(continued)*

```
      If Button = vbRightButton Then
         PopupMenu mnuPopup, _
            0, _
            x + ctlListView.Left, _
            y + ctlListView.Top, _
            mnuPopupDetails
      End If
End Sub
```

This code has to make some adjustments to the *x* and *y* coordinates passed to the PopupMenu function, since the function works on the basis of an overall *x* and *y* position from the entire screen. The MouseDown event gives an *x/y* pair based on the control and not this form or the screen. By adding the Left and Top property values to the *x* and *y*, respectively, the PopupMenu function gets the correct values.

You now need to add code to make the menu functions work. That code is fairly simple and is shown in Listing 6-9. When you change the value of the View property, the ListView shows a different arrangement of icons and text.

Listing 6-9: Popup Menu Code

```
Private Sub mnuPopupDetails_Click()
   ctlListView.View = lvwReport
End Sub

Private Sub mnuPopupLarge_Click()
   ctlListView.View = lvwIcon
End Sub

Private Sub mnuPopupList_Click()
   ctlListView.View = lvwList
End Sub

Private Sub mnuPopupSmall_Click()
   ctlListView.View = lvwSmallIcon
End Sub
```

The last piece of code causes a click on a column header to sort by that column. That code is shown in Listing 6-10.

Listing 6-10: **Column-Header Click Handler**

```
Private Sub ctlListView_ColumnClick(ByVal ColumnHeader _
    As ComctlLib.ColumnHeader)
    ctlListView.SortKey = ColumnHeader.Index - 1
End Sub
```

For this procedure to work, you need to set the Sorted property of the ListView control to True at design time. If you want to perform the same task programmatically, you can add an appropriate line of code to Form_Load.

If you want a second click to cause the sort order to reverse, use the code in Listing 6-11 instead of that in Listing 6-10.

Listing 6-11: **Revised ctlListView_ColumnClick Event Handler**

```
Private Sub ctlListView_ColumnClick( _
    ByVal ColumnHeader As ComctlLib.ColumnHeader)

    '
    ' Use this code to reverse the sort on a second click
    ' on a column header.
    If ctlListView.SortKey = ColumnHeader.Index - 1 Then
        If ctlListView.SortOrder = lvwAscending Then
            ctlListView.SortOrder = lvwDescending
        Else
            ctlListView.SortOrder = lvwAscending
        End If
    Else
        ctlListView.SortOrder = lvwAscending
        ctlListView.SortKey = ColumnHeader.Index - 1
    End If

End Sub
```

At this point, the enhancements are done and you can try out all the new features of your enhanced product viewer. Try out the popup menu. Click a column and watch the data sort. Did you notice that sorting on the quantity or price fields does not work correctly? This is because the ListView control is sorting the numbers alphabetically and not numerically. This is a bit of a bug; there is no way to override the alphabetical sort.

Summary

The TreeView and ListView controls are a powerful pair and can help create very useful user interfaces.

✦ Because users are familiar with these types of controls already, you need not teach them how to use the controls. They simply point and click without any instruction.

✦ Although the controls do have some limitations, good design can help you avoid them and create powerful, visually interesting interfaces.

✦ When you use these controls, make sure you program for all the features they have in common (such as clicking column headers, allowing for different views, and so on).

✦ With the techniques described in this chapter, you'll be able to use these controls in your own applications.

✦   ✦   ✦

Enhancing the User Experience

◆ ◆ ◆ ◆

In This Chapter

Learn how to enhance basic controls with just a few lines of code

Provide better data integrity with smarter data entry forms

Learn how to build a wizard to assist the user in completing complex tasks

◆ ◆ ◆ ◆

With the proliferation of good Windows applications on the market today, there are always new features being introduced that other applications quickly acquire. For instance, toolbars, tabbed dialog controls, and the quick-find drop-down list — which automatically scrolls to items that partially match the string you typed — have been around in many other applications, making them popular additions to new applications being created. Numerous products started adding wizards to do various tasks, and so on.

Each of these features provides a useful service, some of which you can take advantage of in your own applications. This chapter will show you how to implement some of the most commonly used features so that you can use them yourself.

Enhancing Basic Controls

Although hundreds of third-party controls are available for you to purchase to add various pieces of functionality to your application, many of them are simply basic controls with a few extra lines of code added to them. This section will show you how to replicate the features of several popular controls without having to add a third-party control to your project.

Another feature you'll learn about in this chapter is enforcement of data integrity. Whenever you can restrict the type of data a user is entering, you can enforce better data integrity. For instance, there are a number of calendar controls on the market that force users to enter valid dates. If you don't need the calendar drop-down feature, a date control is very easy to build using basic controls; in fact, you're going to build one right now!

This control will support the following features:

✦ Capability to validate a date entered by a user

✦ Support a variety of formats, which you can specify

✦ Support plus- and minus-key operations to move the date ahead or backward, respectively

This date control is convenient because it is based on a standard TextBox control and requires no additional OCXs or DLLs. In this age of 10MB installation packages for 100K applications, the more space-conscious you can be, the better.

This example is built on a plain form. Start a new Standard EXE project, then on Form1 (the default form added to the project) add a TextBox control and name it **txtStartDate**. Delete the text in the Text property so that the box is empty. Add a Label control next to the TextBox, if you like.

In order to allow you to test the code that activates when you change focus, add a CommandButton to your form, name it **cmdOK**, and label the button **OK**. You need the other control on the form so that you can use the Tab key to change the input focus away from the TextBox control. Your form should resemble the one shown in Figure 7-1.

Figure 7-1: Your test form as it should appear, so far

The first piece of code you need to add will load the form with the current date. Start by adding these lines to the Declarations section of the form:

```
Option Explicit
Const DATEFORMAT = "MM/DD/YY"
```

The DATEFORMAT constant provides the overall date format for this string. This particular case uses a two-digit year, which may not be sufficient for your needs. If you need to use a four-digit year, use the following line of code:

```
Const DATEFORMAT = "MM/DD/YYYY"
```

You can refer to the online help to see the available date formats. Next, add the lines in Listing 7-1 to the Form_Load event handler:

Listing 7-1: **Form_Load Code**

```
Private Sub Form_Load()
    txtStartDate = Format$(Date$, DATEFORMAT)
End Sub
```

This code loads the initial date into the box. Most programs which use this type of control use the current date as the default. Although you can't store a formula in the Text property, preloading the TextBox in Form_Load accomplishes the same purpose.

To cause the data to be updated after the user makes a change, add the code in Listing 7-2 to your form.

Listing 7-2: **TextBox Update Code**

```
Private Sub txtStartDate_LostFocus()
    txtStartDate = _
        Format$(CDate(txtStartDate), DATEFORMAT)
End Sub
```

At this point, you can try out your code by running your project, entering a date in any format, and then pressing the Tab key to leave the field. The Change event is triggered whenever you make changes to the data, and the LostFocus event only happens when you use your mouse or keyboard to move out of the TextBox.

To further enhance this form, you can add code to process plus and minus keys being entered while the box has focus. This code increments or decrements the date, as many products do. Add the code in Listing 7-3 to your form to make this work.

Listing 7-3: **KeyPress Code**

```
Private Sub txtStartDate_KeyPress(KeyAscii As Integer)
    If Chr$(KeyAscii) = "+" Then
        txtStartDate = _
            Format$(DateAdd("d", 1, CDate(txtStartDate)), _
                DATEFORMAT)
        KeyAscii = 0
```

(continued)

Listing 7-3 *(continued)*

```
    ElseIf Chr$(KeyAscii) = "-" Then
        txtStartDate = _
            Format$(DateAdd("d", -1, CDate(txtStartDate)), _
                DATEFORMAT)
        KeyAscii = 0
    End If
End Sub
```

You'll now be able to enter plus and minus keys to increment and decrement the date. Setting the `KeyAscii` to 0 causes the key to be ignored and not added to the TextBox.

You could further enhance this control by adding a SpinButton control to provide additional functionality to the user.

Finally, the techniques used in the `LostFocus` event procedure can be applied to any type of data whose format you need to enforce. For instance, you can enforce a numeric value by converting the text to a number and then back to a piece of text. You can also make your `KeyPress` event smarter by only allowing numeric characters. All of these techniques are easy to implement; you'll see some of them later in the chapter.

Ensuring Data Integrity

Although controls can help to restrict what data a user enters on a form, you can't rely on them alone to provide every restriction you may require. Users have a knack for uncovering every possible flaw in your data integrity schemes. Because of this, you have to make your forms bulletproof enough to prevent a bad record from ever being saved to a database or a file. This section demonstrates some simple techniques to keep users from breaking your system and causing all sorts of problems in your database or data files.

The form you build in this section is designed to accept input about a group of files to be processed in one way or another. The point of the form is to gather information in such a way that all of the necessary criteria are collected, no matter what options the user chooses, so you don't have to do much validation thereafter. The form you'll be building is shown in Figure 7-2.

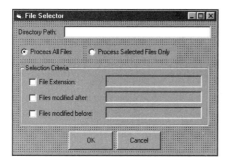

Figure 7-2: The completed File Selector form in Design view

Working from left to right and top to bottom, each of the controls appears with its properties in Table 7-1. Add these controls to a form in a new Standard EXE project.

Table 7-1
File Selector Form and Control Properties

Control	Property	Value
lblLabel (Label Control)	Caption	Directory Path:
txtPath (TextBox Control)	Text	(no value — should be empty)
optAllFiles (OptionButton Control)	Caption	Process All Files
	Value	True
optSelectedFiles (OptionButton Control)	Caption	Process Selected Files Only
	Value	False
fraCriteria (Frame Control)	Caption	Selection Criteria
	Enabled	False

(continued)

Table 7-1 *(continued)*

Control	Property	Value
chkExtension (CheckBox Control)	Caption	File Extension:
	Enabled	False
txtExtension (TextBox Control)	Text	(no value – should be empty)
	BackColor	Button Face (from System portion of color palette)
	Enabled	False
chkAfterDate (CheckBox Control)	Caption	Files modified after:
	Enabled	False
txtAfterDate (TextBox Control)	Text	(no value – should be empty)
	BackColor	Button Face (from System portion of color palette)
	Enabled	False
chkBeforeDate (CheckBox Control)	Caption	Files modified before:
	Enabled	False
txtBeforeDate (TextBox Control)	Text	(no value – should be empty)
	BackColor	Button Face (from System portion of color palette)
	Enabled	False
cmdOK (CommandButton Control)	Caption	OK
	Enabled	False
cmdCancel (CommandButton Control)	Caption	Cancel
	Cancel	True

Once you have all the controls drawn and configured, you can save your project files. If you run your project now, the form looks like Figure 7-3.

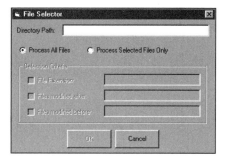

Figure 7-3: Your form should look like this when you run it without any additional code.

Since the OptionButton next to Process All Files is marked, the Selection Criteria frame is disabled, as are all the controls within it. The TextBox controls are both disabled and set with a gray BackColor property. This provides a visual clue to the user that the boxes are unavailable. Simply disabling the control does not change the appearance of the control when there is no text in it.

Building the code to make all the controls work together is fairly straightforward. The first code you add is designed to enable or disable the frame control on the basis of the setting of the OptionButton controls on the form. Add the code in Listing 7-4 to your form.

Listing 7-4: **Code for OptionButton Controls**

```
Private Sub optAllFiles_Click()
    fraCriteria.Enabled = False
    chkExtension.Enabled = False
    chkAfterDate.Enabled = False
    chkBeforeDate.Enabled = False
End Sub

Private Sub optSelectedFiles_Click()
    fraCriteria.Enabled = True
    chkExtension.Enabled = True
    chkAfterDate.Enabled = True
    chkBeforeDate.Enabled = True
End Sub
```

Next, you need code to enable and disable the TextBox controls within the Selection Criteria frame. The Enabled property can be used for this purpose; when set to False, it makes a control appear unavailable by coloring its text gray. One approach to this problem is shown in Listing 7-5.

Listing 7-5: Standard Instructions for Handling CheckBox Controls

```
Private Sub chkExtension_Click()
    If chkExtension.Value Then
        txtExtension.BackColor = vbWindowBackground
        txtExtension.Enabled = True
    Else
        txtExtension.BackColor = vbButtonFace
        txtExtension.Enabled = False
    End If
End Sub

Private Sub chkAfterDate_Click()
    If chkAfterDate.Value Then
        txtAfterDate.BackColor = vbWindowBackground
        txtAfterDate.Enabled = True
    Else
        txtAfterDate.BackColor = vbButtonFace
        txtAfterDate.Enabled = False
    End If
End Sub

Private Sub chkBeforeDate_Click()
    If chkBeforeDate.Value Then
        txtBeforeDate.BackColor = vbWindowBackground
        txtBeforeDate.Enabled = True
    Else
        txtBeforeDate.BackColor = vbButtonFace
        txtBeforeDate.Enabled = False
    End If
End Sub
```

This code works fine for your form. However, a more efficient process — especially if you have more than just a few controls — is shown in Listing 7-6.

Listing 7-6: Revised Code for Selection Criteria

```
Private Sub ConfigureControl(ctlFlag As Control, ctlRelated As
Control)
    If ctlFlag.Value Then
        ctlRelated.BackColor = vbWindowBackground
        ctlRelated.Enabled = True
    Else
        ctlRelated.BackColor = vbButtonFace
        ctlRelated.Enabled = False
```

```
    End If
End Sub

Private Sub chkExtension_Click()
    ConfigureControl chkExtension, txtExtension
End Sub

Private Sub chkAfterDate_Click()
    ConfigureControl chkAfterDate, txtAfterDate
End Sub

Private Sub chkBeforeDate_Click()
    ConfigureControl chkBeforeDate, txtBeforeDate
End Sub
```

By creating the ConfigureControl procedure, you've eliminated several redundant pieces of code and encapsulated the functionality into a single procedure. You can use this procedure with any controls that support the BackColor and Enabled properties, which are used by the TextBox control in this particular example.

Now that the controls are properly synchronized, you can add code to validate the input the user has entered. This code is shown in Listing 7-7.

Listing 7-7: **Validation Code for Form**

```
Private Sub ValidateInput()
    Dim bValid As Boolean
    bValid = True
    bValid = bValid And txtPath <> ""
    If optSelectedFiles.Value Then
        bValid = bValid And _
            (chkExtension.Value Or _
            chkAfterDate.Value Or _
            chkBeforeDate.Value)
        If chkExtension.Value Then
            bValid = bValid And txtExtension <> ""
        End If
        If chkAfterDate.Value Then
            bValid = bValid And txtAfterDate <> ""
        End If
        If chkBeforeDate.Value Then
            bValid = bValid And txtBeforeDate <> ""
        End If
    End If
    cmdOK.Enabled = bValid
End Sub
```

This code uses a Boolean variable `bValid`, which becomes `False` if any of the conditions are `False`. The first condition ensures that there is a value in the Directory Path box. Next, the procedure determines if any of the selection criteria are required. The first condition verifies that at least one of the criteria CheckBox controls was marked. Once this has been determined, you then check each CheckBox control and its associated TextBox control. Once all these checks are complete, the result of the check is stored in the `Enabled` property of the `cmdOK` button. If all the required criteria check out correctly, the OK button is enabled and the data can be processed or stored.

Finally, you need to revalidate the data any time it changes. The `ValidateInput` procedure needs to be called from a number of places. The changes to the code are marked in Listing 7-8.

Listing 7-8: **ValidateInput Procedure Calls**

```
Private Sub chkExtension_Click()
    ConfigureControl chkExtension, txtExtension
    ValidateInput
End Sub

Private Sub chkAfterDate_Click()
    ConfigureControl chkAfterDate, txtAfterDate
    ValidateInput
End Sub

Private Sub chkBeforeDate_Click()
    ConfigureControl chkBeforeDate, txtBeforeDate
    ValidateInput
End Sub

Private Sub optAllFiles_Click()
    fraCriteria.Enabled = False
    chkExtension.Enabled = False
    chkAfterDate.Enabled = False
    chkBeforeDate.Enabled = False
    ValidateInput
End Sub

Private Sub optSelectedFiles_Click()
    fraCriteria.Enabled = True
    chkExtension.Enabled = True
    chkAfterDate.Enabled = True
    chkBeforeDate.Enabled = True
    ValidateInput
End Sub

Private Sub txtAfterDate_Change()
    ValidateInput
End Sub
```

```
Private Sub txtBeforeDate_Change()
    ValidateInput
End Sub

Private Sub txtExtension_Change()
    ValidateInput
End Sub

Private Sub txtPath_Change()
    ValidateInput
End Sub
```

The last pieces of code you'll need are in the OK and Cancel buttons. The prototypes for these event handlers are shown here:

```
Private Sub cmdOK_Click()
    '
    ' Since the OK button won't be enabled if the data is not
    ' valid, no additional checks are required here.
    '
    ' Save your data to the database or file here. Code will
    ' vary based on your implementation.
    '
    Unload Me

End Sub

Private Sub cmdCancel_Click()
    If Not bValid Then Unload Me
End Sub
```

This code varies on the basis of what you need to do with this form. However, the validation logic may be able to be reused in a variety of forms. The main point is to avoid a situation where you could have bad data saved to a form or database.

Building a Wizard

Ever since their introduction, wizards have provided an excellent way to break up a complex task into manageable steps. For instance, the Microsoft Word Fax Wizard asks all the appropriate questions required to build a fax document without the user having to do everything by hand. In this section, you build a wizard that gathers all the information required to schedule a program you intend to run at a certain time.

Introduction to wizards

Before you start building your wizard, you need to pick a design for it. Most wizards resemble the one shown in Figure 7-4.

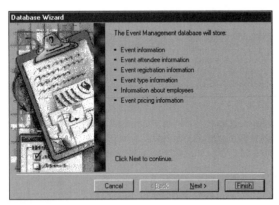

Figure 7-4: Many wizards look similar to the one shown here.

The window's title bar gives the name of the wizard. In many cases, it gives the step number so that you can tell how far you are through the process. There is often a graphic appropriate to the wizard's task. The right side of the window contains the data entry area, which provides a great deal of instruction per step. That's the whole purpose of using a wizard — to explain the process to the user in each step.

The bottom of the form contains the navigation buttons. A Cancel button provides a way out for the user. The Cancel button is always preceded by a confirmation dialog box to make sure the user wanted to exit the wizard. This is especially important if the wizard is long and involved.

The Back and Next buttons allow navigation between the steps of the wizard. At the beginning of the sequence, the Back button should be disabled, as should the Next button at the end of the sequence. The Finish button should only be enabled when the user can actually quit. If the wizard hasn't collected all the information yet, don't enable the Finish button.

The main design technique used in building a wizard is one you can't really see. As the user moves through the wizard's sequence, all of the controls are being shown on the same form. Essentially, the computer is flipping a series of flash cards, each of which has controls on it. Each time you hit the Next button, the next page is brought to the top of the form. This is the technique you'll be using for your wizard.

Building the storyboards

An author who writes a book (this very one, for instance) follows an outline for its chapters and subjects. When a movie director is creating a movie, the process analogous to outlining a book is known as *storyboarding*. This involves building a sequence of scenes on which to make the entire movie. To build your wizard, you need to do much the same thing. You need to determine what information is required at what points in the process. You also need to know if information from one step is dependent on an answer from a previous step in the wizard. Designing the entire sequence before you start can save you a great deal of time and effort later.

The sequence you'll be building for this wizard is fairly straightforward and is shown here. Each step corresponds to another "flash card" that you'll build for the wizard form.

1. **Welcome panel** — This is the description of the wizard, which is shown to the user when the wizard starts. In many cases, the user can choose not to see this panel.

2. **Application Selection panel** — This panel allows the user to select the program to run. This panel contains a box in which to enter a program name as well as a button to browse the user's system.

3. **Interval Selection panel** — This panel is used to select whether the program should be run once or multiple times. If the user selects to run it once, the wizard goes to the next page. If the user wants to run the program multiple times, the wizard goes to Step 5.

4. **Single Run Time Selection panel** — If the user chose to run the program just once, only the date and time for the run are required. After those two pieces of information are collected on this panel, the Finish button is available.

5. **Multiple Run Time Selection panel** — If the user chose to run the program more than once, the interval information needs to be collected. For instance, the user needs to select a start time and the frequency of runs after that. Once that information has been collected, the Finish button is available.

6. **Finish panel** — This panel is shown whenever the user presses the Finish button. It shows a quick summary of how often the program will run — and gives the user a final chance to bail out before scheduling the program.

That's the storyboard for this wizard. Depending on your needs, you may need to create multiple branches — or even looping subroutines in which a panel collects several copies of the same information. There's really no restriction on what you can do with your wizards.

Building the wizard framework

Now that your storyboard is done, you can build the framework for your wizard. This framework includes the navigation buttons on the bottom of the form, a graphic appropriate for this wizard, and the other properties required for this form to be configured correctly.

To get started, in a new Standard EXE project, add four buttons to the default Form1 that VB creates for you automatically. These buttons will provide the navigational tools for this wizard. The buttons and their properties are shown in Table 7-2.

Table 7-2		
Wizard CommandButton Properties		
Control	*Property*	*Value*
cmdCancel	Caption	Cancel
	Cancel	True
cmdBack	Caption	< &Back
	Enabled	False
cmdNext	Caption	&Next >
cmdFinish	Caption	Finish
	Enabled	False

You can position these buttons as you see fit, but the most common layout is shown in Figure 7-5.

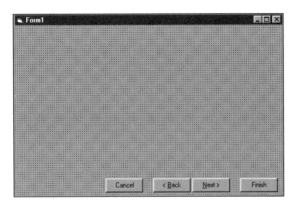

Figure 7-5: Position the navigational buttons as shown on this form.

Next, you can add a graphic to the left hand side of the form. Be sure to use an Image control as you won't be writing any code involving the graphic you add. Image controls require less resources than PictureBox controls do. Name the Image control `imgLogo` or another appropriate name. For a graphic, you can use any graphic you wish. If you happen to have Microsoft Access , there are some graphics included that are used in the Access Database Wizards, but they are free for use. The graphics are located in the Bitmaps\DBWiz directory under the main Office 97 directory. Using that graphic, you can either resize it or simply let VB crop it. You can also set the `BorderStyle` property to `3 Fixed Dialog`. Your form will resemble Figure 7-6 after the graphic has been added. The example shows the graphic named `MONYTRAK.GIF`.

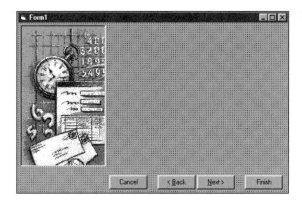

Figure 7-6: The wizard form as it appears with a graphic on it

The last boilerplate visual item to add is the separator bar that is placed just above the navigational buttons. This bar provides a visual separator between the buttons and the rest of the form. Add a Frame control that is only high enough to show the top edge of it. Delete the value of the `Caption` property and stretch the frame to fill the form. Your form should resemble Figure 7-7 when you get done adding this control.

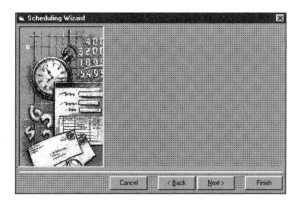

Figure 7-7: The wizard form with the separator bar on it

With the boilerplate controls inserted, it comes time for you to configure the form. The options you need to set are shown in Table 7-3. The only really critical option you need to set is the `Name` property; it will be used throughout the rest of the code.

Table 7-3 Form Properties	
Property	**Value**
Name	frmScheduleWizard
BorderStyle	3 - Fixed Dialog
Caption	Scheduling Wizard
Icon	(none)

Building the wizard's panels

With the wizard's framework complete, you can now start building each of the panels that will be displayed in the sequence you designed in your storyboard. Each panel consists of a container control, such as a Frame, and the controls used for data entry in that step. Since it can be difficult to sort out these overlapping controls during design time, a good technique to use is to put a border around each one, which is eliminated at run time through code. You'll also find the Bring to Front (Ctrl+J) and Send to Back (Ctrl+K) keyboard shortcuts handy as you switch back and forth between panels as you build the wizard.

Creating the Welcome panel

The Welcome panel is the easiest one to build. It simply consists of several Label controls on top of a Frame. To build it, start by drawing a Frame control on your wizard form. Size it so that it nearly fills up the right side. Set the properties on the Frame as shown in Table 7-4.

Table 7-4
Welcome Panel Frame Properties

Property	Value
Name	fraWelcomePanel
BorderStyle	0 - None
Caption	no caption

Next, add two Label controls to the form. These controls display messages to the user, explaining the purpose of this wizard. Figure 7-8 shows the messages and the placement of these Label controls. Be sure that the Label controls are actually part of the Frame control. If you move the Frame but the Label controls don't move, cut the Label controls and paste them into the Frame control.

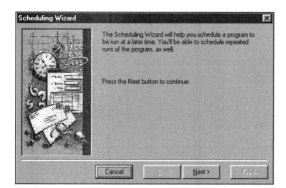

Figure 7-8: The Welcome panel of the Scheduling Wizard

You'll want to put the Label controls into a control array because they won't have any code attached to them. Once you have the controls placed, you're done with the Welcome panel for your wizard. A popular feature that you'll find in many such wizards is a CheckBox control labeled *Don't show this screen again*. This lets experienced users skip the Welcome panel and get right into the main features of the wizard. This setting can be stored with the rest of the application's settings in the Registry.

Creating the Application Selection panel

The Application Selection panel is next on the list. Add another Frame to your wizard and name it `fraAppSelPanel`. Set the same properties as you did for the previous Panel. This panel has three controls: a Label control, a TextBox control, and a CommandButton. These controls are shown in Figure 7-9 in a suggested layout. Add these controls to your form and set the properties as shown in Table 7-5.

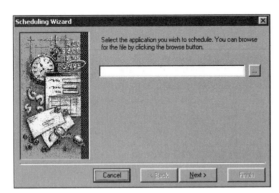

Figure 7-9: The Application Selection panel of the Scheduling Wizard

Table 7-5
Application Selection Panel Control Properties

Control	Property	Value
TextBox	Name	txtApplicationName
	Text	empty
CommandButton	Name	cmdBrowse
	Caption	... (three periods)

In order for the code on this panel to work, you'll also need a CommonDialog control on the form. If you don't have one elsewhere in your application, add one to this form (not to the Frame control). The name used in the sample code is `ctlComDlg`. No other properties are required to be set on this control.

Creating the Interval Selection panel

The Interval Selection panel is used to specify whether the program should be run once or multiple times. This is a very simple panel and only requires a pair of OptionButton controls and a Label control. The panel is shown in Figure 7-10.

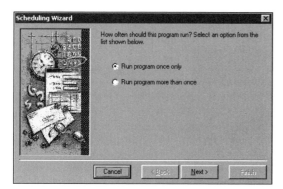

Figure 7-10: The Interval Selection Panel of the Scheduling Wizard

Set the controls' properties as shown in Table 7-6.

Table 7-6		
Interval Selection Panel Controls		
Control	*Property*	*Value*
Frame	Name	fraIntervalSelPanel
	BorderStyle	0 - None
OptionButton	Name	optSingleRun
	Caption	Run program once only
	Value	True
OptionButton	Name	optMultipleRun
	Caption	Run program more than once

Creating the Single Run panel

The Single Run panel is shown if the user chooses to run the selected program only once. This panel has fewer controls than the one shown for multiple runs of the program. Although this example uses plain TextBox controls, this would be a perfect location for a more specialized date and/or time control. This example will use some of the same techniques introduced in Chapter 6 to help validate data entered by the user — without using a masked edit box, which tends to be difficult for most users to understand.

The layout of the controls is shown in Figure 7-11, and the controls' properties are listed in Table 7-7.

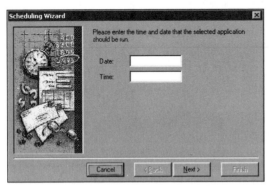

Figure 7-11: The Single Run Panel of the Scheduling Wizard

Table 7-7 Single Run Panel Controls		
Control	**Property**	**Value**
Frame	Name	fraSingleRunPanel
	BorderStyle	0 - None
TextBox	Name	txtSingleTime
	Value	no value — box should be empty
TextBox	Name	txtSingleDate
	Value	no value — box should be empty

Creating the Multiple Run panel

The Multiple Run panel is shown if the user wants to run a program more than once. This panel allows the user to pick a starting date and time and then an interval for the scheduler program to wait before running the program again. The panel is shown in Figure 7-12.

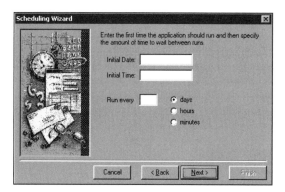

Figure 7-12: The Multiple Run Panel of the Scheduling Wizard

This panel has a few more controls than others, but they are all straightforward to build. Add the controls and set the properties shown in Table 7-8.

	Table 7-8	
	Multiple Run Panel Controls	
Control	**Property**	**Value**
Frame	Name	fraMultipleRunPanel
	BorderStyle	0 - None
TextBox	Name	txtMultipleTime
	Value	no value — box should be empty
TextBox	Name	txtMultipleDate
	Value	no value — box should be empty
TextBox	Name	txtMultipleInterval
	Value	no value — box should be empty
OptionButton	Name	optMultipleDays
	Caption	days
	Value	True
OptionButton	Name	optMultipleHours
	Caption	hours
	Value	False
OptionButton	Name	optMultipleMinutes
	Caption	minutes
	Value	False

Creating the Finish panel

The Finish panel is shown to users when they have completed either the Single Run or Multiple Run panels. At this point, you can be sure that the wizard has collected all the necessary information for your program to continue running. The message shown in Figure 7-13 is a common way to end wizards. To some users, it may sound somewhat condescending, but since wizards often exist to help inexperienced users, the content of the message should be friendly and congratulatory.

Figure 7-13: The Finish Panel of the Scheduling Wizard

The Label control in the middle needs to be given a unique name, such as `lblScheduleSummary`. Part of your code will create a simplified version of the schedule that the user requested. This lets them confirm the information before exiting the wizard.

Coding the wizard

Because of the way a wizard forces the user to enter valid data at every step, you'll find that the code required to make a wizard work is fairly minimal. The code normally deals with navigation and some validations at each step in the process. When the wizard is near completion, all it needs to do is retrieve all the data from the controls on each panel, and then gracefully exit.

Creating the navigation code

The navigation code is responsible for these features of the wizard:

✦ Showing the correct panel when the user presses the Next or Back buttons

✦ Making the directional buttons active or inactive on the basis of the user's current position in the wizard

✦ Triggering the validation code to check data before proceeding

To get started building the code, you first need a series of constants, each of which represents a panel in the wizard. These constants will be used throughout the navigation and validation code to determine what data needs to be validated and what step is next or previous to the current one. The integer variable declared at the end will hold the current stage so that all subroutines can use it. Add the code in Listing 7-9 to your wizard form's Declarations section.

Listing 7-9: **Wizard Stage Constants**

```
Private Const WZ_START = 1
Private Const WZ_APPSEL = 2
Private Const WZ_INTERVAL = 3
Private Const WZ_SINGLE = 4
Private Const WZ_MULTIPLE = 5
Private Const WZ_FINISH = 6

Private iStage As Integer
```

Before you start building the procedures that the wizard will run, take a look at the pseudocode shown here. This explains how elements of the wizard's navigation will work:

Next Button

Validate current panel's data

If data is valid, determine what panel is next

If at the end, disable Next and enable Finish

Clear fields on panel

Show panel to user

Back Button

Determine what panel came before current one

If at the beginning, disable Back

Don't clear fields on panel

Show panel to user

Much of the functionality of such code is used by more than one feature of the wizard; building general procedures where possible can help you expand or change the flow of the wizard.

The easiest code to write is the code behind the Next button, which is shown in Listing 7-10. You'll be adding some instructions to this later, but this is the bulk of what you need.

Listing 7-10: Code for Next Button

```
Private Sub cmdNext_Click()
    Select Case iStage
        Case WZ_START
            iStage = WZ_APPSEL
        Case WZ_APPSEL
            iStage = WZ_INTERVAL
        Case WZ_INTERVAL
            If optRunOnce.Value Then
                iStage = WZ_SINGLE
            ElseIf optRunMultiple.Value Then
                iStage = WZ_MULTIPLE
            End If
        Case WZ_SINGLE, WZ_MULTIPLE
            iStage = WZ_FINISH
        Case WZ_FINISH
            '
            ' Next button won't be enabled
            ' on Finish panel. This code
            ' makes sure that the code does not
            ' go past the last panel.
            '
            iStage = WZ_FINISH
    End Select

    ChangePanel
End Sub
```

The Select Case statement is primarily responsible for determining which panel should be shown after the current one. When the user is on the Interval Selection panel, the choice of path is really up to the user. On the basis of the choices represented by the option buttons on the panel, the path goes either to the Single Run or the Multiple Run panel. However, both of those panels go to the Finish panel next. The call to ChangePanel causes the new panel to be shown to the user.

The next block of code is the ChangePanel procedure, shown in Listing 7-11.

Listing 7-11: **ChangePanel Subroutine**

```
Private Sub ChangePanel()
    Dim fraPanelToShow As Frame

    Select Case iStage
        Case WZ_START
            Set fraPanelToShow = fraWelcomePanel
            cmdBack.Enabled = False
            cmdNext.Enabled = True
        Case WZ_APPSEL
            Set fraPanelToShow = fraAppSelPanel
            cmdBack.Enabled = True
        Case WZ_INTERVAL
            Set fraPanelToShow = fraIntervalSelPanel
        Case WZ_SINGLE
            Set fraPanelToShow = fraSingleRunPanel
            cmdNext.Enabled = True
        Case WZ_MULTIPLE
            Set fraPanelToShow = fraMultipleRunPanel
            cmdNext.Enabled = True
        Case WZ_FINISH
            Set fraPanelToShow = fraFinishPanel
            cmdNext.Enabled = False
            cmdFinish.Enabled = True
    End Select

    fraPanelToShow.ZOrder 0
End Sub
```

At each step, the correct panel is stored in the temporary variable fraPanelToShow, so that only one call needs to be made at the end of the subroutine. In addition, each stage changes the command buttons to their correct states. Notice that the cmdNext button is re-enabled in both the Single Run and Multiple Run stages. This is because this procedure will be used for the Back button as well, and pressing Back from the Finish panel will take the user to one of those panels. Since the Finish panel disables the Next button, it needs to be re-enabled after the user presses Back.

The next piece of code, shown in Listing 7-12, is for the Back button.

Listing 7-12: **Code for Back Button**

```
Private Sub cmdBack_Click()
    Select Case iStage
        Case WZ_START
            '
            ' Back button won't be enabled
            ' on Welcome panel. This code
            ' makes sure that the code does not
            ' go past the first panel.
            '
            iStage = WZ_START
        Case WZ_APPSEL
            iStage = WZ_START
        Case WZ_INTERVAL
            iStage = WZ_APPSEL
        Case WZ_SINGLE, WZ_MULTIPLE
            iStage = WZ_INTERVAL
        Case WZ_FINISH
            If optRunOnce.Value Then
                iStage = WZ_SINGLE
            ElseIf optRunMultiple.Value Then
                iStage = WZ_MULTIPLE
            End If
    End Select

    ChangePanel
End Sub
```

Notice that the code that runs when the iStage variable is equal to the WZ_FINISH constant, is the same as that which runs for the Next button when the iStage variable is WZ_INTERVAL. This allows the Back button to be context-sensitive on the basis of what the user entered.

The last piece of code you need to get the form started is shown in Listing 7-13. This brings the Welcome panel up when the form first starts.

Listing 7-13: **Form_Load Event Handler**

```
Private Sub Form_Load()
    iStage = WZ_START
    ChangePanel
End Sub
```

The last piece of navigation code, shown in Listing 7-14, is for the Cancel button. If the user is on a panel other than the Welcome panel, a confirmation dialog box appears. This lets the user have one last chance before bailing out of the wizard.

Listing 7-14: **Cancel Button Code**

```
Private Sub cmdCancel_Click()
    If iStage = WZ_START Then Unload Me

  If MsgBox("Are you sure?", _
     vbYesNo + vbExclamation, _
     "Exit Scheduling Wizard") = vbYes Then Unload Me
End Sub
```

At this point, save your project and give it a try. You should be able to navigate forward and backward. Try changing the option buttons and watch how the Next and Back buttons function differently.

Creating the validation code

The validation code you add will ensure that the user has entered valid data on each panel of the wizard. Data validation only needs to occur when the user moves forward in the wizard—not backward. This is because the user couldn't have moved forward if the previous data were not already valid.

Before you get started with the specific validation code for each panel, you need to make a few changes to the Next button's event handler. The changes are marked in Listing 7-15.

Listing 7-15: **Next Button's Event Handler with Validation**

```
Private Sub cmdNext_Click()

  If Not IsDataValid() Then Exit Sub

  Select Case iStage
     Case WZ_START
        iStage = WZ_APPSEL
     Case WZ_APPSEL
        iStage = WZ_INTERVAL
     Case WZ_INTERVAL
        If optRunOnce.Value Then
           iStage = WZ_SINGLE
```

(continued)

Listing 7-15 *(continued)*

```
        ElseIf optRunMultiple.Value Then
            iStage = WZ_MULTIPLE
        End If
    Case WZ_SINGLE, WZ_MULTIPLE
        iStage = WZ_FINISH
    Case WZ_FINISH
        '
        ' Next button won't be enabled
        ' on Finish panel. This code
        ' makes sure that the code does not
        ' go past the last panel.
        '
        iStage = WZ_FINISH
    End Select

    ChangePanel bSaveData:=False

End Sub
```

The first call will cancel the Next button's action if the data is not valid. The IsDataValid function will return True if the data was valid. The change to the ChangePanel call will allow ChangePanel to clear each box as the boxes are displayed. You'll be making some more changes to ChangePanel later to make this feature work.

Listing 7-16 shows the validation function you call from the Next button's event handler.

Listing 7-16: **IsDataValid Function**

```
Private Function IsDataValid() As Boolean
    Dim bReturn As Boolean
    Dim sErrorMsg As String

    bReturn = True

    Select Case iStage
        Case WZ_START
            ' No validation - bReturn remains True
        Case WZ_APPSEL
            If txtApplication = "" Then
```

```
                    sErrorMsg = "Please enter a filename."
                    bReturn = False
                End If
            Case WZ_INTERVAL
                ' No validation - one OptionButton
                ' is always marked
            Case WZ_SINGLE
                If Not IsDate(txtSingleDate) Then
                    sErrorMsg = "Please enter a valid date."
                    bReturn = False
                ElseIf Not IsDate(txtSingleTime) Then
                    sErrorMsg = "Please enter a valid time."
                    bReturn = False
                End If
            Case WZ_MULTIPLE
                If Not IsDate(txtMultipleDate) Then
                    sErrorMsg = "Please enter a valid date."
                    bReturn = False
                ElseIf Not IsDate(txtMultipleTime) Then
                    sErrorMsg = "Please enter a valid time."
                    bReturn = False
                ElseIf Val(txtMultipleInterval) <= 0 Then
                    sErrorMsg = "Please enter a valid interval."
                    bReturn = False
                End If
            Case WZ_FINISH
                ' No validation - bReturn remains True
        End Select

        If Not bReturn Then
            MsgBox sErrorMsg, vbExclamation, "Data Entry Error"
        End If

        IsDataValid = bReturn
    End Function
```

Since there are many types of data errors that could occur, the MsgBox call is kept at the bottom instead of being replicated throughout the Select Case statement. This keeps the code a bit simpler than it would be otherwise. As you can see, there really isn't much validation that needs to be done. Best of all, the wizard simply won't continue until the data is valid.

The last changes for validation that need to be made are in the ChangePanel procedure. These changes are shown in Listing 7-17.

Listing 7-17: Revised ChangePanel Subroutine

```
Private Sub ChangePanel _
   (Optional bSaveData As Boolean = True)

   Dim fraPanelToShow As Frame

   Select Case iStage
      Case WZ_START
         Set fraPanelToShow = fraWelcomePanel
         cmdBack.Enabled = False
      Case WZ_APPSEL
         If Not bSaveData Then txtApplication = ""
         Set fraPanelToShow = fraAppSelPanel
         cmdBack.Enabled = True
      Case WZ_INTERVAL
         Set fraPanelToShow = fraIntervalSelPanel
      Case WZ_SINGLE
         If Not bSaveData Then
            txtSingleDate = Format$(Date$, "MM-DD-YYYY")
            txtSingleTime = Format$(Time$, "HH:MM")
         End If
         Set fraPanelToShow = fraSingleRunPanel
         cmdNext.Enabled = True
      Case WZ_MULTIPLE
         If Not bSaveData Then
            txtMultipleDate = _
               Format$(Date$, "MM-DD-YYYY")
            txtMultipleTime = Format$(Time$, "HH:MM")
            txtMultipleInterval = "1"
         End If
         Set fraPanelToShow = fraMultipleRunPanel
         cmdNext.Enabled = True
      Case WZ_FINISH
         Set fraPanelToShow = fraFinishPanel
         cmdBack.Enabled = True
         cmdNext.Enabled = False
         cmdFinish.Enabled = True
   End Select

   fraPanelToShow.ZOrder 0

End Sub
```

The instructions you just added will clean out any old values in the boxes as the user moves forward through the wizard. For the date-and-time related boxes, it fills in the current date and time as a default.

The final piece of code, shown in Listing 7-18, wires up the Browse button next to the application pathname box on the second panel. This code uses the Common Dialog control you added to the form.

Listing 7-18: **Browse Button Event Handler**

```
Private Sub cmdBrowse_Click()
    ctlComDlg.DialogTitle = "Select Application"
    ctlComDlg.DefaultExt = "*.exe"
    ctlComDlg.Filter = _
        "Applications (*.exe)|*.exe" & _
        "|Batch Files (*.bat)|*.bat" & _
        "|All Files (*.*)|*.*"
    ctlComDlg.FilterIndex = 1
    ctlComDlg.Flags = _
        cdlOFNFileMustExist + _
        cdlOFNHideReadOnly + _
        cdlOFNPathMustExist
    ctlComDlg.ShowOpen
    txtApplication = ctlComDlg.FileName
End Sub
```

This code enables the Open File dialog box to appear when the user clicks the Browse button, as shown in Figure 7-14.

Figure 7-14: The Select Application dialog of the Scheduling Wizard

Final touches

The only other code you need to add is the code behind the Finish button. This code would execute whatever action the wizard was preparing data for; in this case, a program would need to be scheduled. The wizard form could also have a public method on it that would return the data collected from the user in the wizard. This means any code that calls the wizard need not worry about how the wizard works and simply get the data it collected. A sample prototype function is shown here:

```
Private Sub cmdFinish_Click()
    '
    ' Since the Finish button is only available
    ' after all data has been validated, this
    ' code can simply run without any further
    ' validation.

    ' Schedule the program using whatever tool
    ' the wizard works with.

    Unload Me
End Sub
```

Summary

This chapter was designed to give you ideas on how to make a user's experience in your application better. Using the tips and techniques presented in this chapter can help make a user's experience in your application more productive and enjoyable.

✦ Wizards provide a step-by-step way to guide an inexperienced user through a complicated set of questions.

✦ A wizard's sequential structure alleviates the confusion caused by having too many controls on a form, especially if the controls change as the user enters data.

✦ By restricting what the user can enter, you help save yourself time in data validation later. If the user shouldn't put letters into a box, don't allow it. If the box should only contain a date, make sure it does before letting the user leave it.

✦ No one likes using applications that are inflexible or hard to navigate. The features shown in this chapter can help your applications work better on both counts.

✦   ✦   ✦

Building Classes and Collections

In This Chapter

Learning the basics of object-oriented programming

Learning how to build a class

Learning how to use classes in your code and forms

Learning how to build collections

◆ ◆ ◆ ◆

Although object-oriented programming (OOP) is nothing new, only now are the mainstream tools such as Visual Basic really integrating its concepts. OOP is really nothing more than translating real-world business concepts into logical entities the computer can understand. Instead of an invoice being thought of as a series of rows in a table, it is treated as a complete entity within the computer program.

This chapter shows you how to put the myriad of OOP features supported by Visual Basic to work in building useful business applications. Although you won't always want to use every feature, many options exist for making your applications more modular and object-based.

OOP Primer

The first thing you'll learn in this chapter is the basic object-oriented programming terminology. Most of these terms may already be familiar to you; they are the same words used to talk about objects in everyday language.

In Visual Basic, objects have three major components:

- ✦ **Properties** — Properties are like the fields of a user-defined type. They contain data about the object. Property procedures provide controlled access to data stored within an object.

- ✦ **Methods** — These are actions that are associated with the object. You may have a Print or Save method, for instance. Methods operate on the data in an object.

- ✦ **Events** — You can define and trigger events on objects, in much the same way controls and forms receive events as the user does various operations.

These major components can also be further subdivided into two groups:

✦ **Public** — The entire application can access the property, method, or event.

✦ **Private** — Only the object itself can access the property, method, or event.

Besides having single objects, you can also create groups of objects. These groups are called *collections*. A number of collections are built into the Visual Basic language and object model, such as the Controls and Forms collections. Collection names are usually the same as their component object's name made into a plural.

Object-oriented programming also provides a number of advantages over regular programming. The first is that business logic can be *encapsulated* within an object. For instance, if you decide that a variety of validations need to be done on data, you can put that validation code within the object. The object can cause an error to occur if the data is invalid.

Encapsulation is also sometimes called *data hiding*. Because objects control access to the data within themselves, the data in each object is essentially hidden from other code. Normally, each class has a series of *Property procedures*, which are pieces of code used to retrieve and modify the hidden values in an object, accordingly. If a value in an object is not meant to be modified, it is defined as *private* and no modifier is provided. Accessors can be designed to return different types of data. For instance, a value stored as a date variable could be returned as a formatted text string or even in another unit, such as days or hours.

Another feature of OOP is *polymorphism*. It's a fancy word for a really simple concept. Both a car and a truck can be driven, parked, and repaired. As a programmer, you don't have to worry about whether the object is a car or a truck — you just have to know it is a vehicle that supports the drive, park, and repair methods.

One common OOP feature not supported in Visual Basic is *inheritance*. Inheritance allows you to set up parent-child relationships between classes. A child class contains all the same properties, methods, and events of its parent. It can add or modify those class members as it sees fit. Inheritance may eventually find its way into Visual Basic; however, it has not yet been included.

Building a Simple Class

To help you learn how to use object-oriented programming, your first task is to create a simple class. This Customer class represents a business customer; it includes the customer's name, address, and other relevant information. You use this class in combination with another class later in the chapter.

The class you build here is included on the CD-ROM in the prjBusinessObjects.vbp project in the \Samples\Ch08 directory.

This class has the properties shown in Table 8-1. Each property represents an attribute of a customer.

Table 8-1		
Customer Class Properties		
Property Name	**Data Type**	**Description**
ID	Long	Unique ID associated with this customer — could be provided by database
LastName	String	Customer's last name
FirstName	String	Customer's first name
MidInitial	String	Customer's middle initial
Company	String	Company name
Address	String	Mailing address for customer
City	String	City portion of mailing address
State	String	State portion of mailing address
PostalCode	String	ZIP/Postal code portion of mailing address
Country	String	Country portion of mailing address
PhoneNumber	String	Primary phone number
FaxNumber	String	Primary fax number
EMail	String	Primary e-mail address

There are more fields you may want to add, such as sales representative information, credit limit, and so forth. As you decide on other fields to add, you can follow the model given in this class to add them.

To start building your class, follow these steps:

1. In a new Standard EXE project, add a new Class module. Even though Visual Basic has the Class Builder Wizard, knowing how to build classes by hand helps you understand what the wizard actually does.

2. Set the name of the class to CCustomer. Class names are normally prefixed with a C to help distinguish them from other data types. Set a class name by selecting View ➪ Properties Window and changing the Name property of the class.

3. The first item to add to the Class module are the variables that represent each of the properties of the class. These are the private variables that are hidden from view by the class. Add the code from Listing 8-1 to the Declaration section of your Class module.

Listing 8-1: **CCustomer Declarations Section.**

```
Option Explicit

Private mvarID As Long
Private mvarLastName As String
Private mvarFirstName As String
Private mvarCompany As String
Private mvarMidInitial As String
Private mvarAddress As String
Private mvarCity As String
Private mvarState As String
Private mvarPostalCode As String
Private mvarCountry As String
Private mvarPhoneNumber As String
Private mvarFaxNumber As String
Private mvarEMail As String
```

Note Each variable in Listing 8-1 is prefixed with `mvar`, which stands for *m*ember *var*iable. Member variables store the values within a class.

Each member variable is designed to be retrieved and modified using Property procedures. The exception would be the ID variable. Typically, unique IDs are generated by the database and would only be read-only. For now, you can just build Property procedures corresponding to each variable. An accessor and a modifier are shown in Listing 8-2.

Listing 8-2: **CCustomer Accessor and Modifier**

```
Public Property Get ID() As Long
    ID = mvarID
End Property

Public Property Let ID(iInput As Long)
    mvarID = iInput
End Property
```

The `Property Get` and `Property Let` subroutines are specially built for handling property access and modification. If you follow the pattern shown here, you can create all the accessors and modifiers that you need. Listing 8-3 shows all the accessors and modifiers that the `CCustomer` class requires.

Listing 8-3: **CCustomer Accessors and Modifiers**

```
Public Property Let Company(ByVal sInput As String)
    mvarCompany = sInput
End Property

Public Property Get Company() As String
    Company = mvarCompany
End Property

Public Property Let EMail(ByVal sInput As String)
    mvarEMail = sInput
End Property

Public Property Get EMail() As String
    EMail = mvarEMail
End Property

Public Property Let FaxNumber(ByVal sInput As String)
    mvarFaxNumber = sInput
End Property

Public Property Get FaxNumber() As String
    FaxNumber = mvarFaxNumber
End Property

Public Property Let PhoneNumber(ByVal sInput As String)
    mvarPhoneNumber = sInput
End Property

Public Property Get PhoneNumber() As String
    PhoneNumber = mvarPhoneNumber
End Property

Public Property Let Country(ByVal sInput As String)
    mvarCountry = sInput
End Property

Public Property Get Country() As String
    Country = mvarCountry
End Property

Public Property Let PostalCode(ByVal sInput As String)
    mvarPostalCode = sInput
End Property

Public Property Get PostalCode() As String
    PostalCode = mvarPostalCode
End Property
```

(continued)

Listing 8-3 *(continued)*

```
Public Property Let State(ByVal sInput As String)
    mvarState = sInput
End Property

Public Property Get State() As String
    State = mvarState
End Property

Public Property Let City(ByVal sInput As String)
    mvarCity = sInput
End Property

Public Property Get City() As String
    City = mvarCity
End Property

Public Property Let Address(ByVal sInput As String)
    mvarAddress = sInput
End Property

Public Property Get Address() As String
    Address = mvarAddress
End Property

Public Property Let MidInitial(ByVal sInput As String)
    mvarMidInitial = sInput
End Property

Public Property Get MidInitial() As String
    MidInitial = mvarMidInitial
End Property

Public Property Let FirstName(ByVal sInput As String)
    mvarFirstName = sInput
End Property

Public Property Get FirstName() As String
    FirstName = mvarFirstName
End Property

Public Property Let LastName(ByVal sInput As String)
    mvarLastName = sInput
End Property

Public Property Get LastName() As String
    LastName = mvarLastName
End Property
```

```
Public Property Let ID(iInput As Long)
    mvarID = iInput
End Property

Public Property Get ID() As Long
    ID = mvarID
End Property
```

Now that you have a way to modify the object's data, you can add additional methods to provide more services. These methods are essentially identical to Property procedures. The method returns True if all the required values have been set. This method is shown in Listing 8-4.

Listing 8-4: **The IsValid() Function**

```
Public Function IsValid() As Boolean
    Dim bValid As Boolean

    bValid = True
    bValid = bValid And mvarLastName <> ""
    bValid = bValid And mvarFirstName <> ""
    bValid = bValid And mvarAddress <> ""
    bValid = bValid And mvarCity <> ""
    bValid = bValid And mvarPostalCode <> ""
    bValid = bValid And mvarCountry <> ""
    bValid = bValid And mvarPhoneNumber <> ""
    bValid = bValid And mvarEMail <> ""
    IsValid = bValid
End Function
```

This function could have been written as a Property Get procedure. This Boolean variation is shown in Listing 8-5 with the changes shown in boldface.

Listing 8-5: **Public Property Get IsValid() as Boolean**

```
Public Property Get IsValid() As Boolean
    Dim bValid As Boolean

    bValid = True
    bValid = bValid And mvarLastName <> ""
    bValid = bValid And mvarFirstName <> ""
```

(continued)

Listing 8-5 *(continued)*

```
      bValid = bValid And mvarAddress <> ""
      bValid = bValid And mvarCity <> ""
      bValid = bValid And mvarPostalCode <> ""
      bValid = bValid And mvarCountry <> ""
      bValid = bValid And mvarPhoneNumber <> ""
      bValid = bValid And mvarEMail <> ""
      IsValid = bValid
End Property
```

These two versions work the same way and are both called as follows:

```
If Customer.IsValid Then MsgBox "Data is valid."
```

Typically, Property procedures are only used for accessing and modifying member variables. In addition, Property procedures cannot accept additional arguments. For instance, `Property Let` procedures are designed to be called as follows:

```
Customer.FirstName = "Eric"
```

This code calls the `Property Let` procedure called `FirstName`. In this call, no logical place is available for additional parameters. If you need more parameters, you have to use subroutines and functions; they can accept any number of parameters.

Using Classes in Code and Forms

As with the other objects you've used in Visual Basic, creating your own objects is very simple—and using them is just as easy. Although code is not yet included in the object to save data (you'll add that in a later chapter), you can still use objects to store data and manipulate it as a unit.

This project will show you how to use your Customer object with a form designed to manipulate it. You'll use the object to do some form data validation using the `IsValid()` method you built. This feature demonstrates encapsulation of business logic within the Customer object. Instead of putting the logic in the form, you let the object determine if its data is valid.

This class is included on the CD-ROM in the prjBusinessObjects.vbp project in the \Samples\Ch08 directory.

To get started, you'll build the simple form shown in Figure 8-1.

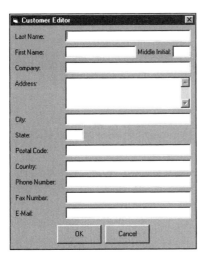

Figure 8-1: Customer Editor window

You're probably fairly well versed in building forms like this one, so we won't provide a lot of information about how to build this form. Table 8-2 describes the controls from the top of the form to the bottom, with the relevant properties listed. All TextBox controls should have their Text properties cleared so that no data is shown in them. Draw and configure these controls on your form.

Table 8-2
Customer Editor Controls and Properties

Control	Property	Value
Form	Name	frmEditCustomer
	BorderStyle	3 — Fixed Dialog
TextBox	Name	txtLastName
TextBox	Name	txtFirstName
TextBox	Name	txtMidInitial
TextBox	Name	txtCompany
TextBox	Name	txtAddress
TextBox	Name	txtCity
TextBox	Name	txtState
TextBox	Name	txtPostalCode

(continued)

Table 8-2 *(continued)*

Control	Property	Value
TextBox	Name	txtCountry
TextBox	Name	txtPhoneNumber
TextBox	Name	txtFaxNumber
TextBox	Name	txtEMail
CommandButton	Name	cmdOK
	Caption	OK
CommandButton	Name	cmdCancel
	Caption	Cancel
	Cancel	True

Cross-Reference

Using the techniques you learned in Chapter 5, you need to build both an Add() and an Edit() method for this form. The code for both is shown in Listing 8-5. You'll also need to declare the objCurrentCustomer object in the Declarations section of the form.

Listing 8-5: **Customer Editor Form Code**

```
Option Explicit
Dim objCurrentCustomer As CCustomer

Public Function Add() As CCustomer
    Set objCurrentCustomer = New CCustomer
    Me.Show vbModal
    Set Add = objCurrentCustomer
    Unload Me
End Function

Public Function Edit(objCustomer As CCustomer)
    Set objCurrentCustomer = objCustomer

    txtLastName = objCurrentCustomer.LastName
    txtFirstName = objCurrentCustomer.FirstName
    txtMidInitial = objCurrentCustomer.MidInitial
    txtCompany = objCurrentCustomer.Company
    txtAddress = objCurrentCustomer.Address
    txtCity = objCurrentCustomer.City
    txtState = objCurrentCustomer.State
    txtPostalCode = objCurrentCustomer.PostalCode
    txtCountry = objCurrentCustomer.Country
    txtPhoneNumber = objCurrentCustomer.PhoneNumber
```

```
txtFaxNumber = objCurrentCustomer.FaxNumber
txtEMail = objCurrentCustomer.EMail

Me.Show vbModal
Unload Me

End Function
```

This code will either create a new object or load the data from an existing object into the fields on the form.

The next code you need to add takes care of updating each of the object's properties as the user changes data on the form. Each TextBox's Change event also calls a new subroutine that checks to see if the data can be saved yet. The code you need to add is shown in Listing 8-6.

Listing 8-6: **Object Updating Code**

```
Private Sub CheckOKButton()
    cmdOK.Enabled = objCurrentCustomer.IsValid
End Sub

Private Sub txtAddress_Change()
    objCurrentCustomer.Address = txtAddress
    CheckOKButton
End Sub

Private Sub txtCity_Change()
    objCurrentCustomer.City = txtCity
    CheckOKButton
End Sub

Private Sub txtCompany_Change()
    objCurrentCustomer.Company = txtCompany
    CheckOKButton
End Sub

Private Sub txtCountry_Change()
    objCurrentCustomer.Country = txtCountry
    CheckOKButton
End Sub

Private Sub txtEMail_Change()
    objCurrentCustomer.EMail = txtEMail
    CheckOKButton
End Sub
```

(continued)

Listing 8-6 *(continued)*

```
Private Sub txtFaxNumber_Change()
    objCurrentCustomer.FaxNumber = txtFaxNumber
    CheckOKButton
End Sub

Private Sub txtFirstName_Change()
    objCurrentCustomer.FirstName = txtFirstName
    CheckOKButton
End Sub

Private Sub txtLastName_Change()
    objCurrentCustomer.LastName = txtLastName
    CheckOKButton
End Sub

Private Sub txtMidInitial_Change()
    objCurrentCustomer.MidInitial = txtMidInitial
    CheckOKButton
End Sub

Private Sub txtPhoneNumber_Change()
    objCurrentCustomer.PhoneNumber = txtPhoneNumber
    CheckOKButton
End Sub

Private Sub txtPostalCode_Change()
    objCurrentCustomer.PostalCode = txtPostalCode
    CheckOKButton
End Sub

Private Sub txtState_Change()
    objCurrentCustomer.State = txtState
    CheckOKButton
End Sub
```

The only other code required to make this form work is a subroutine that calls either the Add() or Edit() method of the form. This is, of course, just for testing, but you need a way to try out your work. Add a new form to your project and add two CommandButton controls to it, as shown in Figure 8-2.

Figure 8-2: Customer Tester window

Add the code in Listing 8-7 to your tester form. You'll also have to designate this form as your startup form by right-clicking on the project and selecting the new test form as the startup form. The code in Listing 8-7 will cause the editor form to be shown.

Listing 8-7: **Customer Tester Window Code**

```
Option Explicit
Dim objCustomer As CCustomer

Private Sub cmdAdd_Click()
    Set objCustomer = frmEditCustomer.Add
End Sub

Private Sub cmdEdit_Click()
    frmEditCustomer.Edit objCustomer
End Sub
```

At this point, you can run your tester form and try adding and editing your object contents. A logical extension of your class would be to add capabilities to it to save data to a disk file or database. You'll learn more about this in a later chapter. Because you'll be changing each object's data as the changes are made on the form, you'll want to program both a Save and a Revert method, which would be used to modify the data in the file or database.

Building Collections

As with most computer programs and databases, very few cases occur in which you'll be dealing with a single object or record. In most cases, you'll need to work with a group of objects together as a unit. Although you could create an array of a particular class, arrays cannot have code associated with them. However, by building a collection class, you can combine your objects with associated code. For instance, you may have code to add a new object to the collection or to retrieve the number of objects currently being stored.

A collection class is built using a regular class module — no special collection class exists. As you'll soon see, the collection's power is in its properties and methods. To demonstrate how collections interact with classes, Listing 8-8 shows the code for a new class named CContact, which contains address information about a particular person.

Listing 8-8: **CContact Class Code**

```
Option Explicit

Private m_sCustName As String
Private m_sAddress As String
Private m_sCity As String
Private m_sState As String
Private m_sZIP As String

Public Property Let CustName(ByVal vData As String)
    m_sCustName = vData
End Property

Public Property Get CustName() As String
    CustName = m_sCustName
End Property

Public Property Let Address(ByVal vData As String)
    m_sAddress = vData
End Property

Public Property Get Address() As String
    Address = m_sAddress
End Property

Public Property Let City(ByVal vData As String)
    m_sCity = vData
End Property

Public Property Get City() As String
    City = m_sCity
End Property

Public Property Let State(ByVal vData As String)
    m_sState = vData
End Property

Public Property Get State() As String
    State = m_sState
End Property

Public Property Let ZIP(ByVal vData As String)
    m_sZIP = vData
End Property

Public Property Get ZIP() As String
    ZIP = m_sZIP
End Property
```

This is a fairly simple class with a few string properties and the associated accessors/modifiers to read and modify the data in the object. Although the code for this class can be built with the Class Builder included with Visual Basic, the code shown has a few modifications. First of all, the comments have been removed; they are fairly irrelevant. Secondly, the variables are prefixed with m_s, standing for member variable, string. The Class Builder uses mvar for the prefix for member variables, regardless of the data type of the variable. The default prefix does not provide information about what data type is being used for the variable. Each collection class needs to support several standard properties and methods. These properties and methods are shown in Table 8-3.

Table 8-3
Collection Properties and Methods

Name	Type	Description
Add	Method	Adds a new object to the collection
Count	Property	Returns the number of objects in the collection
Item	Property	Returns an object from the collection, based on a number or a key value
NewEnum	Property	Allows code to iterate through a collection using a For Each statement
Remove	Method	Removes a selected item from the collection

All this code will be automatically added and customized when you create a collection class based on a simple class like CContact. Standard naming conventions suggest that collection classes should be named with the plural of the simple class. For instance, the collection class for CContact would be CContacts. The code the Class Builder built for the CContacts collection class is shown in Listing 8-9.

Listing 8-9: **CContacts Collection Class Code**

```
Option Explicit

Private mCol As Collection

Public Function Add(ZIP As String, State As String, _
    City As String, Address As String, _
    CustName As String, Optional sKey As String) _
    As CContact
```

(continued)

Listing 8-9 *(continued)*

```
    Dim objNewMember As CContact
    Set objNewMember = New CContact

    objNewMember.ZIP = ZIP
    objNewMember.State = State
    objNewMember.City = City
    objNewMember.Address = Address
    objNewMember.CustName = CustName
    If Len(sKey) = 0 Then
        mCol.Add objNewMember
    Else
        mCol.Add objNewMember, sKey
    End If

    Set Add = objNewMember
    Set objNewMember = Nothing

End Function

Public Property Get Item(vntIndexKey As Variant) As CContact
  Set Item = mCol(vntIndexKey)
End Property

Public Property Get Count() As Long
    Count = mCol.Count
End Property

Public Sub Remove(vntIndexKey As Variant)
    mCol.Remove vntIndexKey
End Sub

Public Property Get NewEnum() As IUnknown
    Set NewEnum = mCol.[_NewEnum]
End Property

Private Sub Class_Initialize()
    Set mCol = New Collection
End Sub

Private Sub Class_Terminate()
    Set mCol = Nothing
End Sub
```

Although this code is good for starters, it doesn't provide for a way to load data from a database or other file. Instead of creating every object, VB provides ways to let each object load its own data. The functionality is built into the simple class instead of the collection. The collection is responsible for informing the object how to load its data. It then simply adds the object to the collection instead of actually filling each object itself.

The Add() method is designed to accept all the property values for a new CContact object. It creates a new CContact object by using the New keyword. Incidentally, using the New keyword causes the CContact's Initialize event to fire. That code will be discussed shortly. Once the new object has been created, each of the properties is set.

Once the object has been created and filled, it is then added to the collection. Objects added to a collection can have a key value set for quick retrieval. The code provided only adds a key if one was provided to the Add() method. As you'll see when you build a collection based on a database, the key value should always be added to enable quick retrieval of the item from the collection later. Keys cannot be strictly numeric values, so if you wish to use some unique ID as the basis for the key value, you'll need to add some text to it as well. For instance, you can't have a Key of 15, but you can have a Key of Item15. This is simply a requirement of the collection object.

Finally, the new object is returned to the calling code. This allows the caller to use the object in whatever way is required. That's really all there is to the code. The rest of the code is simply returning properties of the collection or reimplementing methods of the collection, such as the Remove() method. The only tricky code is in the NewEnum property. This code should basically be left as is. This code allows the For Each feature to work correctly. As each object in the collection is seen, For Each creates an enumeration code that the collection can interpret. This code provides this functionality for you. Keep a copy of it somewhere, or let the Class Builder add it for you; the code must be kept exactly as it is.

Cross-Reference You'll see how to use collection classes in many other chapters in the book, including Chapter 12 and Chapter 14.

Summary

This chapter was designed to give you an introduction to object-oriented programming in Visual Basic.

✦ A number of other features and techniques will be introduced in later chapters.

✦ Although an object is not really complete without a way to make it persist, in a number of cases you'll have objects that are never saved permanently.

✦ Objects provide a great way to aggregate related data and their related methods.

✦ Although creating a good object model can take time and effort, it is an excellent exercise in system design.

✦ By encapsulating logic into objects instead of interfaces, you simplify the process of building windows.

✦ Instead of having to replicate validation logic throughout an application, you can put it in the class once and let the class do the work for you.

✦   ✦   ✦

Database Programming

Visual Basic's New Data Tools

In This Chapter

Learn about the new data tools included with Visual Basic

Use the new Data Environment Designer to connect to a database

Add a new query into a database

Build a form to show data directly from a query or table

Build a class to load and save data to and from a database table

In previous versions of Visual Basic, a typical programmer would need to have at least two applications open simultaneously: Visual Basic and a database manager, such as Access. Finally, many of the common tasks you need to do as a database designer have been integrated into the Visual Basic environment. Many of the VB tools, in fact, are even better than what the database managers themselves provide. This chapter will introduce some of these tools and explain how you can use them with Visual Basic. The examples will use an Access database already on your system; however, because you have to build an ODBC connection to it, you can use any ODBC-compliant database you have with these tools.

On the CD-ROM
The code built in this section is located on the CD-ROM in the \Samples\Ch09\DataEnvTester.vbp project.

Introducing the New Data Tools

Before you get started, a round of introductions are required so that you know what tools are included with Visual Basic and what their general purposes are. None of these tools are included with the Learning Edition of Visual Basic; however, they are included with both the Professional and Enterprise Editions of Visual Basic.

Data View window

The first addition to the VB workspace is the Data View window. This window, like the Properties window and the Toolbox, can attach itself to the sides of the VB workspace and is shown in Figure 9-1.

Figure 9-1: The Data View window within the Visual Basic workspace

This window shows all the current connections you've built to databases, as well as any Data Environment connections that you may have added. In the figure, the connection to the Northwind Traders database was created using a Data Environment. From this view, you can see all the tables and views (predefined queries in Access). When you start using the other tools provided with Visual Basic, you'll see how to easily drag fields from this view onto the Query Designer and Report Designer windows.

Query Designer

The Quer Designer enables you to design queries and save them in your database. The bonus in doing this instead of just writing plain SQL is that the database can essentially compile your query so it runs faster at runtime. Queries can be designed with parameters for which you can fill in data values at runtime. This enables you to create generic queries to retrieve a single record, for instance, without having to create a separate query for each possible record ID value. The Query Designer is shown in Figure 9-2.

Data Report Designer

This is one of the most exciting new features of Visual Basic. Instead of needing a third-party utility to build simple reports, you can now do it within Visual Basic. The resulting report object can then be called programmatically and used within your program. An example of a Data Report is shown in Figure 9-3.

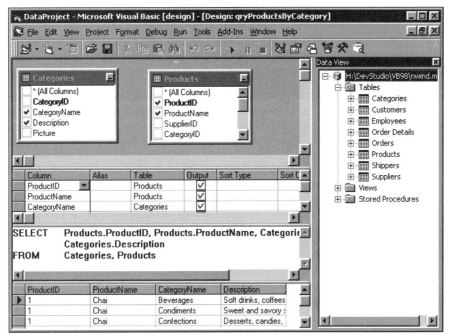

Figure 9-2: The Query Designer within the Visual Basic workspace

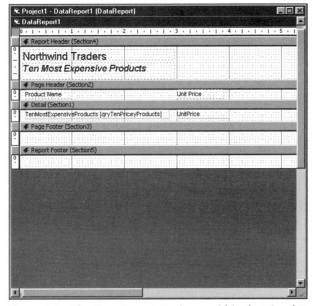

Figure 9-3: The Data Report Designer within the Visual Basic workspace

If you're familiar with Access's report designer, you will find the Data Report Designer just as powerful and easy to use. It supports both page and report headers, detail lines, and many other common features, including a wide variety of graphics and font features. The Data Report is not designed to replace all the third-party report writers on the market, but it will help get you started without your having to leave Visual Basic.

Data Environment Designer

A concept new to this version of Visual Basic is that of the Data Environment. Instead of having to worry about ten different places where you reference your database file, you now simply have to make one change, and it can be propagated throughout your application. Think of a Data Environment as a universal Data control. It's always available, but instead of just linking to a single query or table, you can link to all your databases, tables, and queries with a single object. The Data Environment Designer has a simple dialog (that provides a series of wizards), as shown in Figure 9-4.

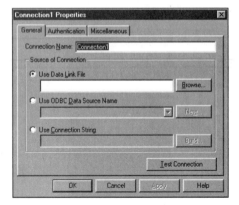

Figure 9-4: The Data Environment Designer

All of the new data tools in Visual Basic take advantage of the Data Environment; in fact, it is required. If you're getting worried about all the new features, don't — the wizards are better than ever and guide you through the process.

Data Form Wizard

The Data Form Wizard, which was available in VB5, is much smarter now. Instead of only providing the simple Data control interface, the Data Form Wizard can actually write real ADO code that is designed to browse records the same way the old Data control could. You can still use that control, as well as the new ADO Data control, with this wizard. The wizard is available by following these steps:

1. Click Add-In ➪ Add-In Manager.

2. From the dialog shown in Figure 9-5, scroll down to VB6 Data Form Wizard.

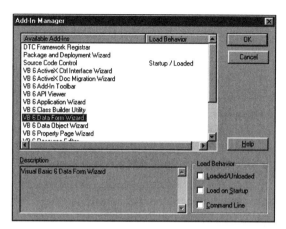

Figure 9-5: The new Add-In Manager, with the VB6 Data Form Wizard selected

3. A new feature of the Add-in Manager is to load an Add-In for either this instance alone of VB or for every time you start VB. Make your choice, and click the check box controls in the lower right-hand corner of this dialog. If you plan to use the wizard often, mark the choice to load it every time, which will save you time in the future.

4. Click the OK button to close the dialog. The Data Form Wizard will now be listed on your Add-Ins menu.

With its new capabilities, the Data Form Wizard is actually a good way to learn the basics of ADO code, and how to use the new objects, methods, and properties.

Data Object Wizard

With heavy emphasis on object-oriented programming, Visual Basic finally includes a utility that builds class modules based on database tables. By embedding the data access code in your classes, you make your objects capable of "taking care of themselves" when it comes to loading and saving database data. This is similar functionality, just with different code, to what you see later in the book. You can add the Data Object Wizard in the same way you added the Data Form Wizard. This chapter will show you how this wizard works and the code that it generates.

Creating a Data Environment

As mentioned, the Data Environment consolidates many of what used to be separate objects and controls into a single, unified entity. Once you create your Data Environment, you can access any database, query, or stored procedure that you added to the Data Environment. You no longer have to worry about keeping track of lots of individual objects throughout the life of a program. Just initialize the Data Environment, and you're ready to go.

In this section, you'll create a Data Environment to access the Northwind Traders database that is included in the Visual Basic directory. You use this Data Environment throughout this chapter, so be sure to save it often. The Data Environment is actually saved as part of your project with the filename extension .DSR, which stands for designer.

To create the Northwind Traders Data Environment, follow these steps:

1. In a new Standard EXE project, select Project ➪ More ActiveX Designers ➪ Data Environment. The Data Environment designer dialog will appear.

2. This dialog enables you to add a new connection to the Data Environment. A connection defines how you will access a particular set of data, whether it is over ODBC, OLE DB, or another method. The fastest connection that we can use for this Access database is to create an OLE DB connection. Click the OptionButton next to Use Connection String, and then click the newly enabled Build button.

3. Once you click the Build button, the dialog shown in Figure 9-6 appears. Visual Basic comes with a number of OLE DB providers, including one for the Jet engine (used with Access databases). Click Microsoft Jet 3.51 OLE DB Provider, and click the Next button to continue.

How Far Can Jet Take You?

The Jet engine discussed here is the real brain behind Microsoft Access and the built-in database support provided by Visual Basic. Jet is an all-purpose relational database engine that can handle most small-to-medium databases. Larger databases that require more capabilities will need to move up to Microsoft SQL Server, Oracle, or another enterprise-level database.

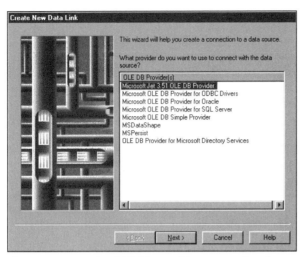

Figure 9-6: Use the OLE DB provider appropriate for your database.

4. The next dialog, shown in Figure 9-7, prompts you for a pathname to your database. Type in the directory and filename of your Northwind Traders database, and click the Next button. The Northwind Traders database is located in the main Visual Basic installation directory.

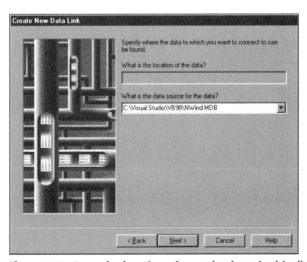

Figure 9-7: Enter the location of your database in this dialog.

5. The dialog shown in Figure 9-8 may seem unnecessary; however, you always need a username for your database. Even if you haven't created one manually, Access provides the Admin username for every database. There is no password (unless you've created one) for this username. If you did create usernames and passwords, you'll have to set this information at runtime. For now, use a username and password that has the most privileges to read your data. Click Next when you're done.

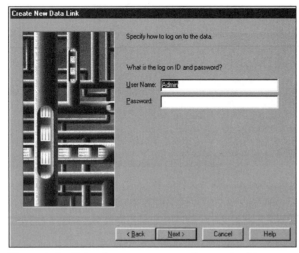

Figure 9-8: Enter the username and password to access your database.

6. The last step of building a connection is to test the connection. In the dialog shown in Figure 9-9, you can click the Test Connection button to attempt a connection to the data source you specified. If you don't get a PASSED result (as shown in Figure 9-9), go back through the wizard, and make sure all the information is correct. The most common error when making a Jet connection is to omit a username, even if it is Admin.

7. If you click the Advanced button on this dialog, you can manually set more options. The dialog shown in Figure 9-10 lists all available options. You can double-click an option to change its value. For this example, no changes are needed, so close the Advanced Properties window, and then press the Finish button in the wizard.

As shown in Figure 9-11, Visual Basic has generated an OLE DB connection string for you and placed it in the appropriate place on the window.

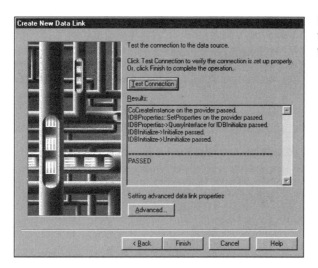

Figure 9-9: Before exiting this wizard, be sure to test your connection.

Figure 9-10: Any database connection option can be set from the Advanced Properties window.

Figure 9-11: The OLE DB connection string is now visible in the Connection Properties window.

If you don't want to go through the wizard every time, you can simply type in the connection string, as shown here:

```
Provider=Microsoft.Jet.OLEDB.3.51;

    Data Source=C:\Visual Studio\VB98\NWind.MDB
```

Before you go on, give this connection a name such as dcnNorthwind. You need to use this name in the rest of this chapter. Click the OK button, and you'll see the connection shown in the Data Environment window, similar to the one seen in Figure 9-12.

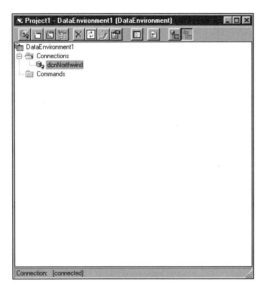

Figure 9-12: Your Northwind Traders data connection is now part of the Data Environment.

If you need to, you can change the properties of the connection by right-clicking it and selecting Properties from the popup menu. Before you go on, you should also rename the Data Environment to something more appropriate. Click the Properties button on the VB toolbar, select the Data Environment from the list, and change the name to something like envApplication.

To see your Data Environment in action, you can bring up the Data View window by selecting View ➪ Data View Window. As shown in Figure 9-13, you can see all the tables, views, and any action queries (called *stored procedures* in VB) that are part of the database.

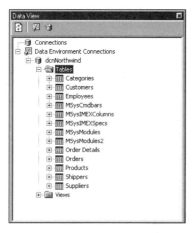

Figure 9-13: The Data View window shows all members of any databases with which you made connections.

You may notice a few "new" tables listed in the Tables tree. These are system tables that Access typically hides from you. As shown in Figure 9-13, all the tables prefixed with MSys are system-level tables and should not be used or modified directly. These tables are maintained automatically by the Jet engine and do not provide useful information if you try to use them directly. In this window, you'll also see that queries you will build are actually divided into either Views or Stored Procedures. Views are queries that simply retrieve data and do not modify any data. Stored Procedures are known as action queries in Access and can update, delete, or append data to one or more tables. Because Views and Stored Procedures are common names across most databases, VB shows the objects in this fashion. Once you know these terms, you'll always be able to find the objects you've built.

Adding Queries to a Data Environment

In addition to the queries you may have had in your database, you can add new queries to the Data Environment. The benefit of adding a query to the Data Environment is that you can join multiple databases without having to link tables within your database.

In this section, you'll see how to add a new query to the Data Environment. You're going to build a query to retrieve a list of customer's names and addresses, sorted by country, state/region, and city. This is a fairly simple query, but it introduces the Query Designer feature of VB. This query will be added to the Data Environment and thus is available to any module within the application.

To get started, do the following:

1. Open the Data Environment window. Right-click Commands, and select Add Command from the popup menu that appears.

2. The dialog shown in Figure 9-14 will appear. Enter qryListCustomers as the name of the new command, and select dcnNorthwind as the connection to use.

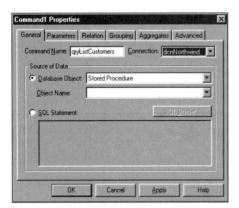

Figure 9-14: This dialog enables you to specify the Command object's options.

3. When you select the dcnNorthwind connection, you may see the warning shown in Figure 9-15. Because there is no code in this command yet, the warning is fairly meaningless. However, if you change your database connection, your SQL code will no longer be valid because the table names in the new database probably won't match the old database. Click Yes to continue.

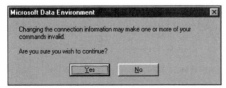

Figure 9-15: If you change the database connection you're using, more than likely you'll have to change your SQL code, too.

4. Now that the name and the connection are specified, you can build the query itself. Click the radio button next to SQL Statement and then click the SQL Builder button to open the Query Designer, which is shown in Figure 9-16.

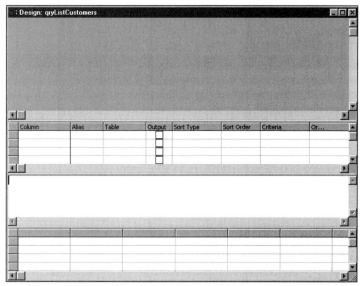

Figure 9-16: The Query Designer is similar to the one found in Microsoft Access.

5. If it is not open already, open the Data View window by selecting View ➪ Data View Window. Click the plus sign next to dcnNorthwind, and then click the plus sign next to Tables to show all the tables in the database.

6. Click the Customers item, and drag it to the uppermost gray area on the design window. This tells the designer you want to use that table in the query. Your design window should now look like the one in Figure 9-17.

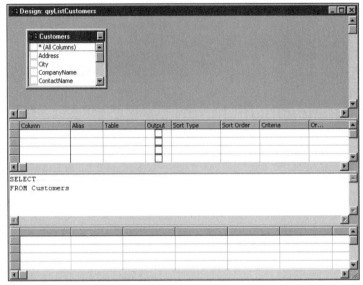

Figure 9-17: Add tables to the Query Designer by dragging them from the Data View window.

7. You can now select each field you want to view by simply checking the box next to the field in the Query window. In this query, you only need `City`, `CompanyName`, `Country`, and `Region`. As you mark each box, the fields will show up in the second pane and also in the SQL string that is generated as you go, as shown in Figure 9-18. Note that the fields are added to the SQL string in the order you click them.

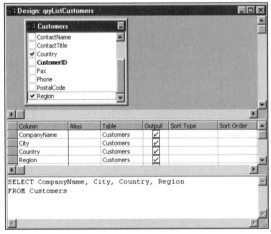

Figure 9-18: Adding fields to the query makes them show up in the grid and in the actual SQL string.

8. You now need to specify the order in which the fields are sorted. Click once to highlight the row. Holding down the left mouse button, drag each row to arrange them in the following order: Country, Region, City, and CompanyName. Then, click Ascending from the drop-down combo box on the Sort Type column for each row. The Sort Order column will automatically be generated based on the order in which you specify the Sort Type. If these do not match, you can switch the field order by picking a different numerical value from the Sort Order list. When you're done rearranging the rows, your window should look like the one in Figure 9-19.

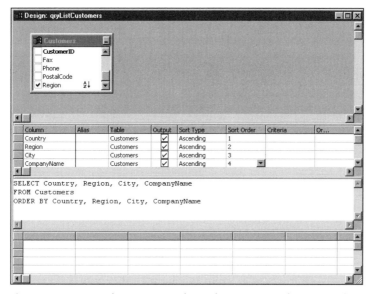

Figure 9-19: Drag the rows into the order you want them sorted.

9. Finally, before exiting the designer, you can test your query in the bottom pane. Right-click the bottom pane, and select Run from the popup menu. You should see the data that will be returned from the query when you run it, as shown in Figure 9-20.

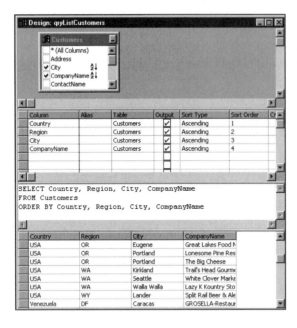

Figure 9-20: The bottom pane is used to test your query against the live database.

As you use the Query Designer, you can show and hide panes as you need to, simply by using the menu under View ➪ Show Panes. This will help you conserve space if you have a small monitor.

That's all the SQL you need, so close the design window. Be sure to save your changes when you are prompted to do so. Those changes are saved to the Data Environment and not the actual database. And with that, you just created a query within your Data Environment. Be sure to save your project, which will save the query you just built. While the designer prompts you to save your query, it simply means it will update your Data Environment with the changes you made. You still have to save the entire Data Environment for the changes to be written to disk. You use this query in the next chapter to build your report, so be sure to keep track of it.

Using the Data Form Wizard

Just as in previous versions of VB, the Data Form Wizard builds a simple form designed to read and modify data in a single table. This version of VB's Wizard is significantly smarter, in that it doesn't always have to use the Data control to do its work. Because ADO is the long-term direction for Microsoft's Universal Data Access strategy, this wizard helps the process by actually writing real ADO code in the form. To see this in action, do the following:

1. If you haven't already loaded it, add the Data Form Wizard to the VB environment by selecting Add-Ins ➪ Add-In Manager.

2. The first step in the wizard, shown in Figure 9-21, enables you to load settings for the wizard. If you use the wizard often, this will save you time because you won't be asked the same questions over and over. In this case, there won't be any profiles, so just press the Next button.

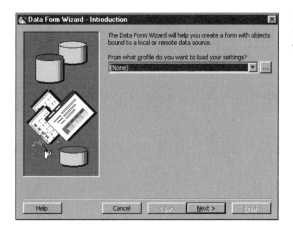

Figure 9-21: Wizard profiles save you time if you use the wizard repeatedly.

3. Next, you need to select the database type from the dialog shown in Figure 9-22. Because we're using an Access database, pick Access from the list shown in this dialog. Click Next to continue.

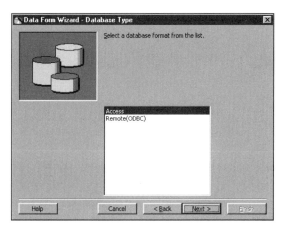

Figure 9-22: Select the type of database you want to use from this dialog.

4. You can pick the location of your database in the dialog shown in Figure 9-23. Use the Browse button to find the Northwind Traders database, and then press Next to continue.

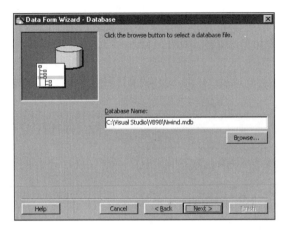

Figure 9-23: This dialog prompts you for the filename of your database.

5. The next dialog in the wizard is shown in Figure 9-24. You can experiment with quite a few of the options here. For now, enter **frmCustomers** as the name of the form, select a Single Record form layout, and select ADO Code as the Binding Type. Click Next when you've set all these options.

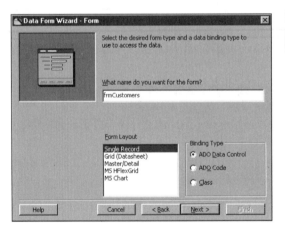

Figure 9-24: This dialog provides a variety of data forms you can use.

6. The next dialog, shown in Figure 9-25, gets down to the real point of this form: the data fields. Select the Customers table as the source of the records, and then add a number of fields to the Selected Fields list — you don't have to have the same as those in the dialog. Pick a column to sort your records, such as the CompanyName column, and then press the Next button. The order that you add the columns to the list will determine the order that they are shown on the form, so make sure you have them in the order you want. You can use the buttons on the right to move the columns up and down the list.

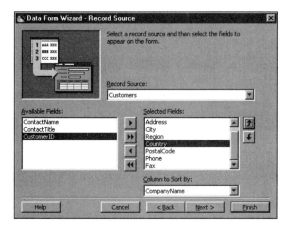

Figure 9-25: Use the Record Source dialog to pick your data source and fields for the form.

7. Because this form can be used to perform all database functions, Figure 9-26 shows you the dialog that lets you pick the functions you want to support. If you want a view-only form, keep only the Close Button marked. Otherwise, pick the features you want, and then press the Next button.

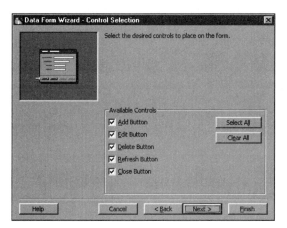

Figure 9-26: Select the database functions you want to support in this dialog.

8. If you see the checkered flag, you're all done. Press the Finish button to let VB create your form, which is shown in Figure 9-27. Yours may vary based on the fields and functions you selected, but it should resemble the form shown here.

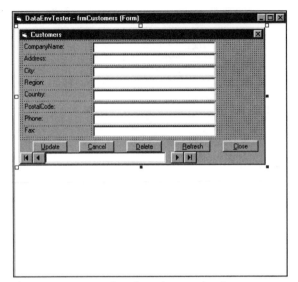

Figure 9-27: Your data form is complete!

As with any wizard-generated form, you'll probably want to adjust the sizes and locations of controls and other graphical elements. The code, which is included on the CD-ROM, is fairly straightforward and is actually a good ADO primer. This form, instead of using a Data control, simulates the functions of the Data control with a few CommandButton controls. If you can understand the functions of this form, writing your own will be a piece of cake.

Summary

This chapter was designed to provide an introduction to the new tools included with Visual Basic to deal with all sorts of databases. All of these tools and objects are interrelated: the Data Object Wizard uses the Data Environment, the Query Designer uses the Data View window, and so on. Visual Basic's designers did a great job of integrating the tools, so you may n≈ever have to write SQL in your code — just build a new Command!

The wizards, while limited, can help you get a good start in programming with these new data features. Use them to build a basic class or form, and then add your own code inside or in place of the code that is generated. Let VB do the tedious work, and save your strength for the real coding.

✦   ✦   ✦

Migration to Active Data Objects

CHAPTER

10

◆ ◆ ◆ ◆

In This Chapter

Learn about Active
Data Objects (ADO)

Learn how the ADO
object model differs
from DAO

Learn how to change
a form using a Data
control to use ADO

Learn how to modify
existing code to use
ADOs

Find out where to get
more information
about Universal Data
Access

◆ ◆ ◆ ◆

One of the more daunting tasks in programming is
creating functionality to read a variety of types of data.
For instance, reading Access databases is easy with the use of
the Data Access Objects library, but what about a file from
Intuit's Quicken product? You may be able to get Microsoft
SQL Server data with a built-in feature, but you won't be able
to read plaintext files in the same way.

In early 1998, Microsoft launched Universal Data Access,
which is Microsoft's strategy for providing access to all types
of information, whether that data is stored locally or remotely
(that is, on the same machine or on a different machine
accessible through a network). This specification is based on
open industry standards (such as ODBC and the Distributed
Component Object Model), which helps to further the
pervasiveness of it. There are a number of components
that enable Universal Data Access, one of which is Active
Data Objects (ADO). ADO replaces both the Data Access
Objects (DAO) and Remote Data Objects (RDO) technologies.
One benefit of ADO is that it can be used both in Visual Basic
programs and in Web sites built using Active Server Pages.
This lets you leverage your knowledge in ADO for both
technologies.

This chapter will describe the ADO object model and how it
differs from the previous types of data access. You'll see how
to take existing code that uses DAO or Data controls and
convert it to use ADO. Given Microsoft's support for ADO
and their plan to make it the primary data access mechanism,
changing your code and your designs now makes a lot of
sense. Performance is already matching current software
and will only improve over time.

ADO and OLE DB Primer

Universal Data Access's goal is to let you build enterprise-wide applications that can access a variety of both relational and nonrelational data across any type of network. Three major components interact in the Universal Data Access platform:

✦ **Data providers** make a particular type of data available. For instance, there are currently providers available for ODBC, Microsoft SQL Server (Microsoft's enterprise database system), and Index Server, and more are on the way. These providers know how to retrieve data from a particular data source and how to make it available within the Universal Data Access framework.

Note   Microsoft Index Server, which is part of Microsoft's Internet Information Server Web server, allows content on a single machine or group of machines to be searched rapidly. This is helpful for Web sites with large amounts of content. ADO allows programs to access the indexes generated by Index Server to search content. The best part is that the programming interface is always Active Data Objects. When you learn ADO, you can read any data source that has an OLE DB provider.

✦ **Data consumers** use various types of data from a variety of sources. These consumers are typically applications running as either traditional clients (Visual Basic programs, Microsoft Office applications, and so on) or as Web clients (Internet Explorer, Netscape). Either way, these applications are using data and presenting or manipulating it.

✦ **Service components** are the glue that ties consumers and providers together. These components are able to transform data from one type to another without relying on either end of the connection for help. Query processors, such as Visual Basic's Visual Data Tools, are an example of service components.

The service components in the Universal Data Access platform provide four distinct services that handle tasks crucial to keeping the providers and consumers talking to each other:

✦ A **cursor service** provides a way to cache data on the client machine and to provide local scrolling, filtering, and sorting capabilities. Having a client-side cache helps eliminate much of the network traffic typically involved with remote data access.

✦ A **synchronization service** allows batches of data that are cached on the client to be updated on the server. It also allows data to be synchronized between the client and the server. Having a current copy of data on the client saves time in saving the program from having to request data across the network each time it needs new data.

✦ A **shape service** allows hierarchical data to be used without any other special features. For instance, you can design a data structure that represents a company's invoices. Invoices contain line items, which contain references to products. That hierarchy can be represented using the shape service.

✦ A **data service** allows data to be moved between client and server, regardless of whether they are connected or not. This enhances users who are working over the Internet, an inherently "disconnected" environment. The data service will help keep track of the data in between connection sessions to a central server.

All of the interaction between the components and the services can happen over common network protocols, such as HTTP or Distributed COM (DCOM). Microsoft's Transaction Server (MTS) can be used to coordinate the interactions between the services. MTS provides the reliability and guaranteed data integrity needed for transaction processing.

What are OLE DB and ADO?

OLE DB is a low-level programming interface designed to access a wide variety of data sources. It can support both relational and nonrelational data sources, including messaging, file system, and other nontraditional data sources. OLE DB specifies a set of Component Object Model (COM) interfaces that are used to hide the implementation details required for building data access services. Building OLE DB interfaces is not a task for the meek; you must be extremely skilled in COM development to even attempt this task. Luckily for us mere mortals, a number of OLE DB interfaces are already available, and more are on the way.

The programs you'll write will never be using OLE DB directly. Just as you use DAO or RDO to talk to the Open Database Connectivity (ODBC) layer, you'll be using Active Data Objects (ADO) within your programs to talk to the OLE DB layer. ADO provides a set of programmable objects that represent the data being provided by the OLE DB provider you're using.

ADO Object Model

ADO consists of seven objects, three of which are independent and four of which are dependent objects. Independent objects can exist by themselves; dependent objects must exist in connection with an independent object.

✦ **Connection** — This object represents a single session with the selected data source. This is equivalent to the type of connection a Data control makes directly to the database. The Connection object can be shared throughout an entire instance of an application, just as you might do using the DAO Database object.

✦ **Command** — This object specifies the data definition or data manipulation statement to be executed. Since ADO supports both data definition and manipulation, you'll still be able to create databases on the fly using ADO. You simply give the correct statement, such as CREATE TABLE, and you've got a new table in your database.

✦ **Recordset** — This object represents a set of rows returned from a command given to the database. You can control what type of cursor is used on the records, how they should be sorted and filtered, as well as look at the definitions of each field in the Recordset. This is similar to the DAO Recordset object.

✦ **Field** — This object is dependent and always exists as part of a Recordset. Just as you can do with DAO, you can traverse the Fields collection to retrieve information about each field in the Recordset. This is great if you're building forms on the fly. Simply look at the data type and provide the correct type of control for viewing and editing the data in the field.

✦ **Parameter** — These objects are part of the Command object and allow you to fill in values in a query. This is similar to the QueryDef object, which also has a Parameters collection. By using Parameter objects with your Command objects, you can take advantage of the database's precompiling of your query. This greatly improves speed and efficiency, since the SQL statement is already evaluated within the DBMS.

✦ **Property** — The Connection, Command, Field, and Recordset objects all contain collections of Property objects. Properties allow you to look at the important information about a particular object. For instance, every object has a Name property.

✦ **Error** — The Error object is dependent on the Connection object. As errors occur during data access operation, the errors are stored in the Errors collection, which is part of the Connection object. You can use this collection to determine if any errors occurred during an operation. This is helpful if you're doing a large number of actions and don't necessarily want to stop midstream.

Although this looks like a lot of new objects to learn, if you've done any DAO or RDO programming, the changes are very minimal to use this new feature. Since Microsoft is really pushing developers toward the Universal Data Access platform, you'd be wise to convert your programs now and reap the improvements as they occur.

Converting DAO Code to Use ADO

As with any new technology, there is always work in converting older code. ADO is no exception. This section is designed to show you how to convert some common DAO code snippets into the new ADO format. You can think of this section as your toolchest for working with ADO.

Before you can use any of this code, you have to reference all of the necessary libraries by selecting Project ⇨ References. If you want to use ADO, pick the Microsoft Active Data Objects 2.0 Library; all the objects will be available within VB.

Connecting to the database

The first thing every database program needs to do is to connect to the database. In DAO, this is fairly simple:

```
Dim DB As Database
Set DB = OpenDatabase("C:\VB\NWind.MDB")
```

This, by default, opens the database as multiuser and in Read/Write mode. If you need to supply a password to open the database, that can be added to the OpenDatabase call as well:

```
Dim DB As Database
Set DB = OpenDatabase("C:\VB\NWind.MDB", False, False, _
    ";PWD=chubbybunny")
```

Connections to ODBC data sources are similar except in the final string, which varies by database.

ADO uses the idea of a Connection instead of a database. This is because a Connection can be to any OLE DB data source, which includes nondatabase types. The code to create a Connection to an Access database goes as follows:

```
Dim dcnNWind as New ADODB.Connection
dcnNWind.CursorLocation = adUseClient
dcnNWind.Open "PROVIDER=Microsoft.Jet.OLEDB.3.51;" _
    & "Data Source=C:\Visual Studio\VB98\NWind.MDB;"
```

Because ADO will be accessing the Access database through an OLE DB provider, that provider has to be specified in the Open() method. The string that follows the Open() method can also be stored in the ConnectionString property.

If you need to use a user ID and/or a password to access your database, they can be added to the ConnectionString as follows:

```
Dim dcnNWind as New ADODB.Connection
dcnNWind.CursorLocation = adUseClient
dcnNWind.Open "PROVIDER=Microsoft.Jet.OLEDB.3.51;" _
    & "Data Source=C:\Visual Studio\VB98\NWind.MDB;" _
    & "User ID=fluffy;Password=chubbybunny"
```

Since you may be accepting a user ID and password at runtime, this format makes it very easy to simply add those values to the `ConnectionString`.

Retrieving a recordset

The next thing you'll probably want to do is to retrieve some records from your open `Connection`. Under DAO, this typically would have been done with the `OpenRecordset()` method, as in the following:

```
Dim rs As Recordset
Set rs = db.OpenRecordset("Customers", dbOpenDynaset)
```

This particular piece of code creates an editable recordset known as a *dynaset*. You could also create a static snapshot of the data or open a table-based recordset when you were simply opening a table.

ADO provides similar features but uses the `Command` object to actually do the work. To open the Customers table using the `dcnNWind` connection, the code would be as follows:

```
Dim rs As ADODB.Recordset
Set rs = New ADODB.Recordset
rs.CursorType = adOpenKeyset
rs.LockType = adLockOptimistic
rs.Open "Customers", dcnNWind, , adCmdTable
```

This will create a table-type recordset based on the Customers table and store it in the `rs` variable. If you wanted to use a SQL strings, the changes are only in the call to the `Open()` method:

```
rs.Open "SELECT * FROM Customers " _
    & "ORDER BY CompanyName",_
    dcnNWind, , adCmdText
```

The `adCmdText` flag tells ADO to evaluate the statement and not simply use it directly to retrieve a database object.

In cases where you want a forward-only view of your data (for loading controls or doing reports, for instance), you can still create that type of recordset with the following code:

```
Dim rs As ADODB.Recordset
Set rs = New ADODB.Recordset
rs.CursorType = adOpenForwardOnly
rs.LockType = adLockReadOnly
rs.Open "Customers", dcnNWind, , adCmdTable
```

Forward-only recordsets are best when you are only viewing data. ADO needs to return less data as part of the recordset. It doesn't have to keep nearly as much navigation information as it might in another recordset.

Creating a query dynamically

Depending on the way your input form works, you may not always be able to use the same query; you may need to build SQL queries dynamically. For instance, a Query form that has five boxes on it can potentially have a different SQL query each time a user uses it. Typically, if the box is empty, there are no additional criteria to be included in the query.

As an example of this, If you had a form with five TextBox controls, they might be named as follows:

```
txtCustID    TextBox    (Numeric)
txtName      TextBox    (Text)
txtCity      TextBox    (Text)
txtState     TextBox    (Text)
txtAccount   TextBox    (Text)
```

The code to use when you build a query based on the contents of these boxes might be something like Listing 10-1.

Note

Note: The SQL generated by Listing 10-1 is not part of the Northwind Traders database. It is simply used for demonstration purposes.

Listing 10-1: **Dynamic SQL Query Builder**

```
Dim sSQL As String
Dim sWhereClause As String

'
' Build the where clause based on the
' values in the boxes on the form.
'
If txtCustID <> "" Then
    sWhereClause = "CustomerID = " & txtCustID
End If
        "Name = '" & txtName & "'"
End If

If txtCity <> "" Then
    If sWhereClause <> "" Then
        sWhereClause = sWhereClause & " AND "
    End If
    sWhereClause = sWhereClause & _
        "City = '" & txtCity & "'"
End If
```

(continued)

Listing 10-1 *(continued)*

```
If txtName <> "" Then
    If sWhereClause <> "" Then
        sWhereClause = sWhereClause & " AND "
    End If
    sWhereClause = sWhereClause & _

If txtState <> "" Then
    If sWhereClause <> "" Then
        sWhereClause = sWhereClause & " AND "
    End If
    sWhereClause = sWhereClause & _
        "State = '" & txtState & "'"
End If

If txtAccount <> "" Then
    If sWhereClause <> "" Then
        sWhereClause = sWhereClause & " AND "
    End If
    sWhereClause = sWhereClause & _
        "Account = '" & txtAccount & "'"
End If

sSQL = "SELECT * FROM Customers"
If sWhereClause <> "" Then
    sSQL = sSQL & " WHERE " & sWhereClause
End If
sSQL = sSQL & " ORDER BY Name"
```

At this point, the sSQL variable has a complete SQL query in it. If you need to sort the records or add additional criteria, they can be placed where the ORDER BY Name line is now. You can use this SQL statement just like any other query. This technique, by the way, can be used with any database language and any data access library. If you do this, make sure your users know to leave the boxes blank if no criteria should be used from that field. Other than that, this makes for a very easy way to build a dynamic query on the basis of a Query form.

Using a parameterized query

One of the most efficient ways to improve your database code's speed is to use stored procedures and queries saved in the database. The queries are already optimized and compiled by the database, which saves time when it comes time to run them. In addition, keeping the SQL within the database prevents inadvertent changes to valuable SQL code. Further, under the three-tier architecture that has become popular in the industry, using stored procedures and queries isolates the data access to the data tier that sits behind the application layer and business rule layer.

Cross-Reference

For more information on three-tier architecture, refer to Chapter 14.

Depending on the tool you use, adding a parameter to the query will involve different steps. For now, assume that the query, named qryGetCustomerByID, looks at the Customers table and accepts a Customer ID as a single Long parameter called paramCustomerID. To use this parameter in a query, you first create a Parameter object that is added to a Command object. The code shown in Listing 10-2 demonstrates how to create the Parameter and Command objects.

Listing 10-2: Using Parameter Object with Command Object

```
Dim dcnNorthwind As ADODB.Connection
Dim cmdCustomers As ADODB.Command
Dim paramCustomerID As ADODB.Parameter
Dim rsCustomers As ADODB.Recordset

Set cmdCustomers = New ADODB.Command
cmdCustomers.CommandText = "qryGetCustomerByID"
cmdCustomers.CommandType = adCmdText

Set paramCustomerID = _
    cmdCustomers.CreateParameter("paramCustomerID")
paramCustomerID.Type = adInteger
paramCustomerID.Direction = adParamInput
paramCustomerID.Value = 10   ' any Customer ID value
cmdCustomers.Parameters.Append paramCustomerID

Set rsCustomers = New ADODB.Recordset
rsCustomers.Open cmdCustomers
```

Using action queries

Action queries, more commonly known as *stored procedures*, perform an action on the database without returning a recordset. These queries are typically used to delete records, but can also be used to insert or update records. Stored procedures are just as easy to build as ones that return recordsets.

You can build a simple action query with just a SQL statement, as shown here:

```
Dim dcnNorthwind As ADODB.Connection
Dim cmdCustomers As ADODB.Command

Set cmdCustomers = New ADODB.Command
cmdCustomers.CommandText = _
    "DELETE FROM Customers WHERE CustomerID = 5"
cmdCustomers.CommandType = adCmdText
Set cmdCustomers.ActiveConnection = dcnNorthwind
cmdCustomers.Execute
```

You can also use the techniques shown earlier to add parameters to this query. As before, you want to keep as many of the SQL queries in the database as possible. This normally means that the queries need to be fairly flexible.

Adding records

One feature that didn't change in the transition to ADO is the method by which you add records to a recordset. The AddNew() method is still your friend and works as it always has. The constants used to open the recordset are fairly important. The documentation on these constants lists what features are supported by each constant.

To add a record into a Recordset, use the code shown here:

```
Dim dcnNorthwind As ADODB.Connection
Dim rsCustomers As ADODB.Recordset

Set rsCustomers = New ADODB.Recordset
rsCustomers.Open "Customers", dcnNorthwind, _
    adOpenStatic, adLockOptimistic
rsCustomers.AddNew
rsCustomers("CompanyName") = "Customer Name"
. . .
rsCustomers.Update
```

Editing records

A change you may or may not like in ADO is the fact that you no longer have to explicitly start the editing procedure. Unlike DAO, which requires you to call the Edit() method, ADO has no such method. This little omission will cause you many headaches until you remember that you don't have to use it any more. Although this change saves a method call, it does make the process inconsistent with the Add() process, which still requires a call to AddNew().

To edit a record in a Recordset, use the code shown here:

```
Dim dcnNorthwind As ADODB.Connection
Dim rsCustomers As ADODB.Recordset

Set rsCustomers = New ADODB.Recordset
rsCustomers.Open "SELECT * FROM Customers WHERE CustomerID =
5", dcnNorthwind, _
    adOpenStatic, adLockOptimistic

rsCustomers("CompanyName") = "Customer Name"
. . .
rsCustomers.Update
```

Closing the database connection

Closing the database connection is very simple in both DAO and ADO. In both variations, the code goes just like this:

```
dcnNWind.Close
Set dcnNWind = Nothing
```

Always remember to set your objects equal to `Nothing`. This informs VB that you're done using the object. If there are no other references to that particular `Connection` object, VB will release the memory and resources being used by it. Doing this on a regular basis helps make your programs good neighbors to other programs on your system.

Universal Data Access Resources

There are several main sites that concentrate on Universal Data Access and the products that go along with the strategy. These Web sites are always going to have the latest information and product releases, as well as bug reports and workaround information.

http://www.microsoft.com/data

This is the official Microsoft site that discusses Universal Data Access. It contains several extensive white papers on each of the related technologies, including OLE DB, ADO, Remote Data Services, and ODBC. Microsoft also makes all related product releases available on this site, so check it often.

http://www.devx.com

This Web site, produced by Fawcette Technical Publications, is devoted to technologies related to programming in Visual Basic. You have a wide variety of resources available here, including Ask the VB Pro (`http://www.inquiry.com/thevbpro`), where you can get answers to questions about all things Visual Basic. There are also libraries of product and book reviews, as well as helpful how-to articles.

http://www.oledb.com

This site, sponsored by Intersolv, is devoted to discussions about OLE DB and the latest advances in this powerful technology. You can read news articles related to the technology, including news from the latest holy war between Microsoft and some other company. There are also links to related sites, as well as a guided tour of all the related technologies.

In addition to these Web sites, there are a number of Usenet newsgroups devoted to Universal Data Access. As with all newsgroups, these groups are subject to change or removal over time, but in all likelihood they will expand into subgroups as the technologies mature.

```
microsoft.public.ado
microsoft.public.odbc
microsoft.public.odbc.sdk
```

You can also find help in the Visual Basic-specific database groups:

```
microsoft.public.vb.database
microsoft.public.vb.database.dao
microsoft.public.vb.database.odbc
microsoft.public.vb.database.rdo
```

If you don't have a newsreader and just want to search for articles, visit DejaNews (http://www.dejanews.com), which maintains an archive of several years' worth of Usenet news articles.

Summary

In this chapter, you saw the new ADO object model and how it differs from the older DAO and RDO models. Although the object names have stayed the same in some cases, their functions may have changed.

✦   ✦   ✦

Building Interfaces from the Database

♦ ♦ ♦ ♦

In This Chapter

Learning how to read the structure of a database through code

Using the database structure to build a form dynamically

Creating code to use a single form with multiple tables, views, or queries

♦ ♦ ♦ ♦

One of the most tedious tasks in a large application is building all the miscellaneous windows required to keep validation tables updated. Things like shipping codes, payment methods, and so on are basically all the same: a unique ID with some other descriptive attributes. The problem comes when you create a new feature that makes one form more intelligent or better in some way. You then have to make sure you propagate that change to every single form. In a business development environment, you then have to incur additional testing time to recheck every single window you added the change to.

Wouldn't it be nice if you could have a single form that was smart enough to redesign itself based on the type of data you gave it? Any changes to the database would be immediately reflected in the input and list forms without having to change a line of code.

This chapter uses this premise as a basis for building two different types of forms. The first is designed to list out a table's data. This type of window is typically shown before a full Edit window just to make sure the user really wants to edit a particular record. The second window you'll build in this chapter is even more intelligent. It is an Edit window that is able to reconfigure itself to the data structure of a particular table. While it won't be able to handle every type of data, it can at least take care of simple tables like the ones mentioned before.

The IntelliList Window

The form you're going to build in this section is shown in Figure 11-1 with some sample customer data from the Northwind Traders database.

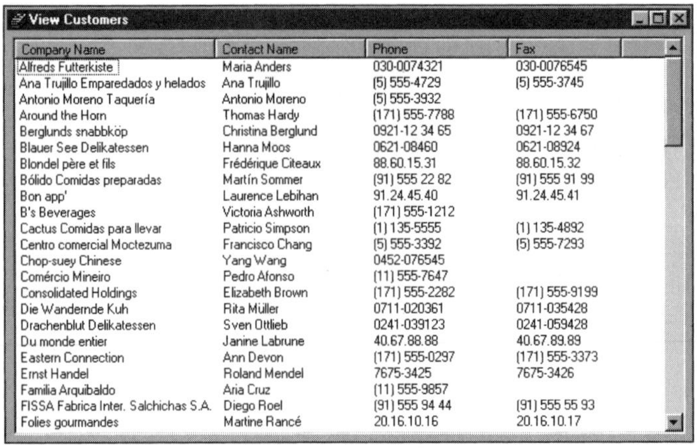

View Customers

Company Name	Contact Name	Phone	Fax
Alfreds Futterkiste	Maria Anders	030-0074321	030-0076545
Ana Trujillo Emparedados y helados	Ana Trujillo	(5) 555-4729	(5) 555-3745
Antonio Moreno Taquería	Antonio Moreno	(5) 555-3932	
Around the Horn	Thomas Hardy	(171) 555-7788	(171) 555-6750
Berglunds snabbköp	Christina Berglund	0921-12 34 65	0921-12 34 67
Blauer See Delikatessen	Hanna Moos	0621-08460	0621-08924
Blondel père et fils	Frédérique Citeaux	88.60.15.31	88.60.15.32
Bólido Comidas preparadas	Martín Sommer	(91) 555 22 82	(91) 555 91 99
Bon app'	Laurence Lebihan	91.24.45.40	91.24.45.41
B's Beverages	Victoria Ashworth	(171) 555-1212	
Cactus Comidas para llevar	Patricio Simpson	(1) 135-5555	(1) 135-4892
Centro comercial Moctezuma	Francisco Chang	(5) 555-3392	(5) 555-7293
Chop-suey Chinese	Yang Wang	0452-076545	
Comércio Mineiro	Pedro Afonso	(11) 555-7647	
Consolidated Holdings	Elizabeth Brown	(171) 555-2282	(171) 555-9199
Die Wandernde Kuh	Rita Müller	0711-020361	0711-035428
Drachenblut Delikatessen	Sven Ottlieb	0241-039123	0241-059428
Du monde entier	Janine Labrune	40.67.88.88	40.67.89.89
Eastern Connection	Ann Devon	(171) 555-0297	(171) 555-3373
Ernst Handel	Roland Mendel	7675-3425	7675-3426
Familia Arquibaldo	Aria Cruz	(11) 555-9857	
FISSA Fabrica Inter. Salchichas S.A.	Diego Roel	(91) 555 94 44	(91) 555 55 93
Folies gourmandes	Martine Rancé	20.16.10.16	20.16.10.17

Figure 11-1: A copy of the IntelliList window is currently showing a list of customers.

This window provides a number of features:

- ✦ Column headings are automatically assigned and widths are automatically calculated.
- ✦ Each entry in the ListView control has a unique ID stored in the `Key` property. This allows for easy retrieval later.
- ✦ A popup menu is available when you click on an item in the ListView. The menu is context-sensitive and will provide choices such as Modify Status instead of something generic.
- ✦ Multiple instances of this window can be created in an MDI environment (which is what you'll be using in this chapter).

The main feature of this window is that it builds itself based on the database behind the scenes. All the programmer needs to do is tell the window which kind of data to show; the IntelliList window takes it from there. For this chapter, you'll be designing your windows around the Northwind Traders database. This database has several types of data that will put your generic window through its paces.

Design assumptions

To make a generic window like this one work properly, you have to stick with several design decisions. The first decision is how the database should send data to the form. Each table you show will need to have a query that follows these rules:

- ✦ The first field is the unique ID for the record. This field's name should have an underscore in it to indicate that it should not be shown in the list.

✦ All other fields can be of any type of data. You can join any number of tables to create just the data set you want. Any fields you want to show should be named without using spaces. If a field should be titled "Company Name," the field should be named `CompanyName`. Most databases cannot alias columns to names with spaces. You'll write some code to add spaces at the appropriate places in the names.

✦ The name of the query does not have to be anything special, because you have to provide the query name whenever you create a new copy of the IntelliList window.

Several more assumptions are involved in building the edit windows, which you see later.

Building the view query

First, you need to design the query that will show the customer data from the database. The process is similar for any type of data you want to show. Follow these steps to build the query, which will be built with Access in this example. You can do the same thing in any database tool, of course.

1. Start Microsoft Access and open the Northwind Traders database, which should be in your Visual Basic installation directory. Click the Queries tab and then click the New button to start designing a new query.

2. From the dialog shown in Figure 11-2, select Design View to design your query.

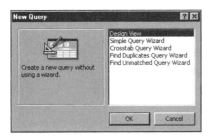

Figure 11-2: Click Design View to design your data list query.

3. From the dialog shown in Figure 11-3, select Customers to add the Customers table as part of your query. Close the Show Table dialog to continue.

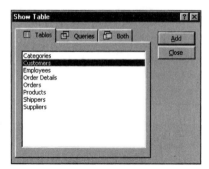

Figure 11-3: Add the Customers table to your query.

4. Drag the CustomerID field to the grid area of the query. To satisfy one of the design assumptions, the field needs to be aliased. Aliasing a field provides a different name with which you retrieve data from that field. To do this in Access, change the name of the field to the following:

```
_ID:CustomerID
```

5. Add other fields you wish to see in your data viewer. Your query should resemble Figure 11-4. If any of the fields have underscores in them, remove the underscores and used mixed case in the names.

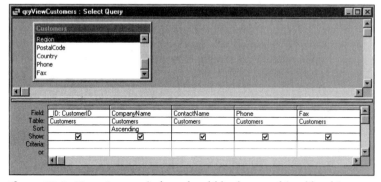

Figure 11-4: Your Query window should look something like this one.

6. Pick a field by which to sort the data. The example here sorts by CustomerName. You'll add code to enable users to sort by any column, but the column you select here will be the default. You should select columns for sorting based on the logical way the data should be shown. For instance, orders could be sorted by date, shippers could be sorted by name, and so on. The window enables the user to select a different field to sort by, so this is not overly important.

7. Save your query. For the example discussed later, the query here is named qryViewCustomers.

Designing the window

The window itself is really simple to build. Follow these steps to set up the window:

1. Start a new Standard EXE project. Name the form that is automatically added to the project `frmViewList` or another useful name. Because the window's title will be changed at runtime, you don't have to set the window's `Caption` property. However, you might want to change it to `View Data` so you know what the form does.

2. Add the Microsoft Windows Common Controls 6.0 component to your project by selecting Project ➪ Components.

3. Add a ListView control to the form. Give the control a useful name such as `ctlListView`, which is the name used in this example. Position the control in the upper-left hand corner of the window, but leave a small margin at the top and left edges. You'll be adding code that sizes the control automatically to fill the form whenever the form is resized. The resize code will leave a margin around the control based on the upper-left hand corner's position.

4. Set the `View` property of `ctlListView` to `3 - lvwReport`. This will allow the control to have column headings and to be sorted by those headings. Also, set the `LabelEdit` property of `ctlListView` to `1 - lvwManual`. Like the TreeView control, if the user clicks and then hovers over an item shown in the ListView control, the text will automatically be made available for editing. This is a view-only form; there is no need to provide this capability.

5. Set the form's `MDIChild` property to `True`, because this form will be shown within the MDI form you create in the next section.

There aren't any other controls you need to add to your form. A design view of your window is shown in Figure 11-5.

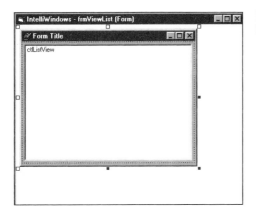

Figure 11-5: The IntelliList window in design view

Adding code to the form

The next step in building this form is adding the code to it. Follow these steps to add all the necessary code:

1. Add the code shown in Listing 11-1 to your form. This code will handle resizing the ListView control as the form is resized.

Listing 11-1: **Form_Resize Event Handler**

```
Private Sub Form_Resize()
    ctlListView.Height = _
        Me.ScaleHeight - (2 * ctlListView.Top)
    ctlListView.Width = _
        Me.ScaleWidth - (2 * ctlListView.Left)
End Sub
```

Note

The ScaleHeight and ScaleWidth properties specify the size of the usable form area. The usable form area is space within the borders and beneath the title bar (and menu bar, if there is one). Because you can't really do anything outside of this area, ScaleHeight and ScaleWidth give you the size of the space you can work with in the form. If you need the size of the entire form, use the Height and Width properties.

2. The next piece of code, shown in Listing 11-2, enables users to click a column header to sort data by that column.

Listing 11-2: **ColumnClick Event Handler**

```
Private Sub ctlListView_ColumnClick( _
    ByVal ColumnHeader As ComctlLib.ColumnHeader)

    ctlListView.SortKey = ColumnHeader.Index - 1
End Sub
```

To make this work, be sure the Sorted property of the ListView control is set to True.

3. The next piece of code you need is shown in Listing 11-3. This code is the main public method you need to show data in the form.

Listing 11-3: **ShowData Public Subroutine**

```
Public Sub ShowData(objDB As Database, _
    sTable As String, _
    sViewQuery As String, _
    sWindowTitle As String, _
    sMenuItem As String)

    '
    ' Store parameters in member variables
    '

    Set m_DB = objDB
    m_sTableName = sTable
    m_sViewQuery = sViewQuery
    m_sWindowTitle = "View " & sWindowTitle
    m_sMenuItem = sMenuItem

    '
    ' Reconfigure window to show data
    ' for the selected table/query.
    '
    RefreshData

End Sub
```

This code is primarily responsible for storing all the values that are passed to it in member variables of the form. These variables are used later in the code. Table 11-1 shows the parameters and their meanings.

Table 11-1
ShowData Parameters

Parameter	Description
objDB	Reference to the currently open database.
sTable	Primary table from which the data is acquired. This name is supplied so records can be deleted from that table.
sViewQuery	This is the name of the query you just built to show the customer data.
sWindowTitle	This is the title on the window, which will be prefixed with the word "View," as in "View Customers."
sMenuItem	This is the text substituted into the Edit menu so a user can select "Add Customer," for instance.

4. You need to add the declarations shown in Listing 11-4 to your form.

Listing 11-4: **Declarations for frmViewList Window**

```
Option Explicit

Private Const LISTITEM_KEY = "Item"
Private Const LISTITEM_LEN = 4
Private Const COLUMN_KEY = "Column"
Private Const COLUMN_LEN = 6

Private m_sTableName As String
Private m_sViewQuery As String
Private m_sWindowTitle As String
Private m_sMenuItem As String

Private m_DB As Database
Private m_rsData As Recordset
```

You also need to add a reference to the Microsoft DAO 3.5 Object Library. Select Project ⇨ References to add this reference.

5. The major piece of code you need to add is shown in Listing 11-5. Following the listing is an explanation of each major section of code.

Listing 11-5: **RefreshData Subroutine**

```
Public Sub RefreshData()
    Dim objItem As ListItem
    Dim loopHeader As ColumnHeader

    Dim sTmpName As String
    Dim i As Integer
    Dim iNextSubitem As Integer
    Dim iHeaderLength As Integer

    Dim a_iFieldLength() As Long
    Dim iRecordCount As Long

    '
    ' Set up window for this type of data
    '
    Me.Caption = m_sWindowTitle

    '
    ' Empty out old data and layout
    '
    ctlListView.ColumnHeaders.Clear
```

```
ctlListView.ListItems.Clear

Set m_rsData = m_DB.OpenRecordset(m_sViewQuery, _
   dbOpenSnapshot)

'
' Resize array which will be used
' to determine average lengths
' of each column, based on the
' length of the data stored in the
' column.
'
ReDim a_iFieldLength(0 To m_rsData.Fields.Count - 1)
iRecordCount = 0


For i = 0 To m_rsData.Fields.Count - 1
   '
   ' Only add columns to list that do not have
   ' underscores in their name. Column width will
   ' be resized later. Any mixed case caps are
   ' prefixed with spaces by the AddSpacesToName
   ' function.
   '
   If InStr(1, _
      m_rsData.Fields(i).Name, _
      "_", _
      vbTextCompare) = 0 Then
      ctlListView.ColumnHeaders.Add , _
         COLUMN_KEY & i, _
         AddSpacesToName(m_rsData.Fields(i).Name), _
         3000
   End If
Next i


'
' Add all the items to the ListView control.
'
Do While Not m_rsData.EOF
   Set objItem = ctlListView.ListItems.Add(, _
      LISTITEM_KEY & m_rsData.Fields(0), _
      m_rsData.Fields(1))
   iNextSubitem = 1
   '
   ' First field is unique ID and is stored in key.
   ' Second field's value is in Name property
   '
   For i = 2 To m_rsData.Fields.Count - 1
      If InStr(1, m_rsData.Fields(i).Name, _
         "_", vbTextCompare) = 0 Then
```

(continued)

Listing 11-5 *(continued)*

```vb
            objItem.SubItems(iNextSubitem) _
                = CStr(m_rsData.Fields(i) & "")
            iNextSubitem = iNextSubitem + 1
        End If
    Next i

    For i = 0 To m_rsData.Fields.Count - 1
        a_iFieldLength(i) = a_iFieldLength(i) _
            + Len(m_rsData.Fields(i) & "")
    Next i
    iRecordCount = iRecordCount + 1

    m_rsData.MoveNext
Loop

'
' Prevent division by zero errors. Formatting
' code will automatically adjust column width
' to width of header, even if no records are
' shown.
'
If iRecordCount = 0 Then iRecordCount = 1

For i = 0 To m_rsData.Fields.Count - 1
    '
    ' Determine average width of data in column
    ' and store in array location.
    '
    a_iFieldLength(i) = _
        a_iFieldLength(i) \ iRecordCount
    '
    ' For columns with short or missing data, the width
    ' will be wide enough to see the column name.
    '
    If a_iFieldLength(i) < _
        Len(m_rsData.Fields(i).Name) Then
        a_iFieldLength(i) = Len(m_rsData.Fields(i).Name)
    End If
    '
    ' Determine width of field in twips and use
    '
    a_iFieldLength(i) = _
        Me.TextWidth(String(a_iFieldLength(i), "M"))
Next i
```

```
' Change each column's width to be the calculated
' length for that column. Since only visible
' columns need to be adjusted, use the key of
' each column header to access the correct
' average width.
'
For Each loopHeader In ctlListView.ColumnHeaders
   loopHeader.Width = _
      a_iFieldLength(CInt( _
         Mid$(loopHeader.Key, COLUMN_LEN + 1) _
      ))
Next loopHeader

End Sub
```

The main tasks accomplished by this code are as follows:

✦ Clear existing headers and data.

✦ Load data from the specified query.

✦ Add each field that needs a column header to the ListView control. This code uses a default width to start.

✦ Add all the data from the query to the ListView control.

✦ Based on the average length of the data in each field, change the width of each column to fit that much text.

One tricky part of the code is in the array that keeps track of the length of each record's field. This array is resized as soon as the number of fields is known. As each item is added to the ListView control, each field's width is added to the array entry for that column.

Another piece of code is involved in setting the subitems' values in each ListItem. The first field in the query, as determined by the design assumptions, becomes part of the unique key for the ListItem. The second field is stored in the Text property of the ListItem. Once those two fields are accounted for, the rest become subitems of the ListItem object.

6. The last piece of code you need is shown in Listing 11-6. This code allows the field name to have spaces embedded wherever a capital letter is found in the middle of a name.

Listing 11-6: **AddSpacesToName Subroutine**

```
Private Function AddSpacesToName(sInput As String) _
   As String

   Dim iPos As Integer
   Dim sTmpName As String

   sTmpName = Left$(sInput, 1)

   For iPos = 2 To Len(sInput)
      If Mid$(sInput, iPos, 1) <= "Z" Then
         sTmpName = sTmpName & " "
      End If
      sTmpName = sTmpName & Mid$(sInput, iPos, 1)
   Next iPos

   AddSpacesToName = sTmpName

End Function
```

That's all the code you need for now. To use this form, you need to build an MDI form to cause the child form to show itself.

Creating the MDI form

This form was designed from the start to be used in a multiple document interface (MDI) environment. There can be multiple instances of this form, all of which can be arranged within the MDI form through some simple menu choices. In addition, you can have multiple editing windows open simultaneously, as you see in the second half of this chapter. The form you'll build looks like the one shown in Figure 11-6.

To build the MDI form, follow these steps:

1. Add an MDI form to your project by selecting Project ➪ Add MDI Form. Give the form a useful name like frmMDIForm. You also need to select this form as the Startup Object. Select Project ➪ Properties to do this.

2. You next need to build the two menus needed for this part of the chapter. These menus and the related properties are shown in Table 11-2.

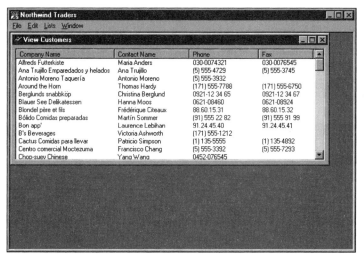

Figure 11-6: The MDI form with a single IntelliList window visible

Table 11-2		
MDI Form Menus		
Top-Level Menu	**Subitem**	**Menu Name**
&Lists		mnuList
	&Categories	mnuListCategories
	&Customers	mnuListCustomers
	&Employees	mnuListEmployees
	&Orders	mnuListOrders
	&Products	mnuListProducts
	&Shippers	mnuListShippers
	S&uppliers	mnuListSuppliers
&Window		mnuWindow
	Tile &Horizontally	mnuWindowHoriz
	Tile &Vertically	mnuWindowVertical
	&Cascade	mnuWindowCascade

3. Set the `WindowList` property to `True` on the top-level Window menu. This causes a list of the currently open MDI child windows to be appended to the Window menu. This setting is shown in Figure 11-7.

Figure 11-7: Mark the top-level Window menu's WindowList property to have a list of open windows added to the menu.

4. For now, the database will be opened automatically with a hard-coded name. Add the code in Listing 11-7 to your MDI form. Be sure to change the pathname to point to your Northwind Traders database. The first two lines of Listing 11-7 should go in the Declarations section of your form.

Listing 11-7: **Database Open/Close Code**

```
Option Explicit
Private g_DB As Database

Private Sub MDIForm_Load()
    Set g_DB = OpenDatabase("E:\DevStudio\VB\NWind.MDB")
End Sub

Private Sub MDIForm_Unload(Cancel As Integer)
    g_DB.Close
    Set g_DB = Nothing
End Sub
```

5. Next, you need to add code to make the Window menu items function correctly. The *list* of windows works automatically without any code. However, the first three choices (Tile Horizontally, Tile Vertically, and Cascade) need a few lines of code, shown in Listing 11-8.

Listing 11-8: **Window Menu Code**

```
Private Sub mnuWindowCascade_Click()
    Arrange vbCascade
End Sub

Private Sub mnuWindowHoriz_Click()
    Arrange vbTileHorizontal
End Sub

Private Sub mnuWindowVertical_Click()
    Arrange vbTileVertical
End Sub
```

There will be more code to add to the MDI form in the next section and later in the chapter. Save your file if you haven't done so already.

Linking the IntelliList with the MDI form

The last task you must complete is to link the MDI form's menu choices to your IntelliList window. This is actually easy to do. To display the Customers window, add the code in Listing 11-9 to your MDI form.

Listing 11-9: **Customers Menu Choice Code**

```
Private Sub mnuListCustomers_Click()

    Dim frmNew As New frmViewList
    frmNew.ShowData objDB:=g_DB, _
        sTable:="Customers", _
        sViewQuery:="qryViewCustomers", _
        sWindowTitle:="Customers", _
        sMenuItem:="Customer"

End Sub
```

All you're doing is telling the IntelliList window how to configure itself. Here are all the tasks you're accomplishing with these two lines of code:

✦ You pass in the database object so the window does not have to create a new connection to the database.

✦ You then tell the window what the general table name is. This allows the window to delete a record from the table when the time comes for that action.

✦ You tell the window what query to use to show records from that particular table. In this case, the customer-viewing query you built earlier is what you want to use.

✦ You also need to tell the window what type of data you are showing so that the title of the window can be "View Customers."

✦ The final parameter will be used to reconfigure menus, so when a user selects the Edit menu, he or she will see Add Customer instead of just a generic Add Item menu choice. You see how this is done later in the chapter.

At this point, save your work and give it a try. You can create multiple instances of your window because you are creating a new instance in the menu choice's code. If you want to try your hand a bit more, try adding the code and query to display data from the Products table. Follow the steps outlined in this chapter, and you'll have no problems.

Limitations of this window

The primary limitation of this window is in the use of the ListView control. Because all the items in the ListView control are actually objects kept in memory, they take more memory than simple text strings might. While the window can easily handle several hundred rows of data, the window's performance will degrade as you add more rows and/or more columns of data. However, by using another window or filter to limit the records you are viewing, you can get quite a bit more use out of this window.

The IntelliEdit Window

Now that you have a generic window to show various types of data, you need a window that is smart enough to be able to edit various types of data. This form can be used for simple tables that do not need to be joined with other tables. While this does restrict what you can do, remember: Every table that can use this form is one less form you have to create, test, and maintain. That translates to less debugging for you, and fewer errors for your end user. In addition, by simplifying the user interface, it is more intuitive for your users, especially when the same user interface is employed over and over again for this type of editing.

Designing the IntelliEdit window

The IntelliEdit window has few controls on it — four to be exact. However, the code underneath the form can produce a window that looks like the one in Figure 11-8.

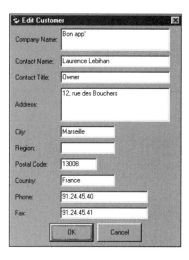

Figure 11-8: This form has automatically configured itself to the layout of the Customers table.

Each field in the table has space allocated for it, as well as a caption next to each TextBox control describing the data within the box. In addition, the unique ID of the record is hidden. This is because a unique ID like the ones used in this system should not be edited. Though the Customers table is currently using a text-based ID instead of a numerical one, the rule still stands. The ID can be entered when a user is adding a record and hidden when the record is being edited. This prevents a number of data integrity problems from occurring.

Figure 11-9 shows a view of the IntelliEdit window in design view.

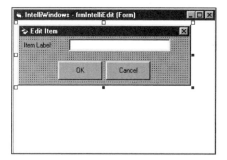

Figure 11-9: Design view of the IntelliEdit window

Table 11-3 lists the properties you need to set on a new form and its controls. As you can see, there are few controls and properties you need to set. However, the ones that do need to be set are critical to the operation of the window.

Table 11-3
IntelliEdit Properties

Control	Property	Value
Form	(Name)	frmIntelliEdit
	BorderStyle	3 - Fixed Dialog
	Caption	Edit Item
	Icon	(Pick a relevant icon to use)
	MDIChild	True
Label	(Name)	lblFieldName
	AutoSize	True
	Caption	Item Label:
	Index	0
	WordWrap	True
TextBox	(Name)	txtFieldData
	Index	0
	MultiLine	True
	ScrollBars	0 - None
CommandButton	(Name)	cmdOK
	Caption	OK
	Enabled	False
CommandButton	(Name)	cmdCancel
	Caption	Cancel
	Cancel	True
	Enabled	True

When you position the Label and TextBox controls, remember the two controls you draw will be the starting position for all the other controls. This means all the TextBox controls will be left-aligned with the edge of the form, as will the Label controls. This feature, which you code later in this section, enables you to change the starting position and margins without changing the code.

Adding public interfaces

Before this window can automatically configure itself to a particular data table, it will need to be called with a particular set of arguments. This call will actually come from the MDI form, but you'll see how that link is made later in the chapter.

Each time an IntelliEdit window is shown, it can be in either Add or Edit mode. Add mode shows an empty window, ready to accept data. Edit mode shows all the fields from an existing record and enables a user to make changes to that record. To get started, you need to add the code in Listing 11-10 to your Declarations section and then add the code in Listing 11-11 to your form.

Listing 11-10: **Declarations for the IntelliEdit Window**

```
Option Explicit
Private m_DB As Database
Private m_RS As Recordset

Private m_sTableName As String
Private m_sItemName As String
Private m_sIDField As String
Private m_vRecordID As Variant
Private m_iMode As Integer

Private Const MODE_ADD = 1
Private Const MODE_EDIT = 2
```

Listing 11-11: **Add Method for the IntelliEdit Window**

```
Public Sub Add(objDB As Database, _
   sTableName As String, _
   sItemSingular As String, _
   sIDField As String)

   Dim iField As Long
   '
   ' Make form invisible so
   ' that controls can paint
   ' without the user seeing
   ' it.
   '
   Me.Visible = False
   '
   ' Store input parameters
   ' in private variables for
   ' later use.
```

(continued)

Listing 11-11 *(continued)*

```
'
' m_DB:          Private reference to database
'                that is already open.
' m_sTableName:  Table in which data resides;
'                i.e. tblCustomers, tblCategories
' m_sItemName:   What an item in this table
'                is called, ie Customer, Category
' m_sIDField:    Which field in table is unique ID
' m_vRecordID:   Unique ID for the record being
'                edited. Stored as a variant to
'                accommodate both numeric
'                and text IDs.
'
Set m_DB = objDB
m_sTableName = sTableName
m_sItemName = sItemSingular
m_sIDField = sIDField

m_iMode = MODE_ADD
Me.Caption = "Add " & m_sItemName

'
' Open the table without picking a
' particular record.
'
Set m_RS = _
    m_DB.OpenRecordset(sTableName, dbOpenDynaset)

ConfigureForm
'
' No data needs to be loaded
' since the form should be
' empty initially.
'

Me.Visible = True

End Sub
```

Each of the parameters specified is key to the operation of this window. Although you could write code to imply the name of the object being edited (that is, tblCategories would have Add Category as a caption), this code would be too filled with exception cases to be useful.

The next piece of code has more lines than Add, but it is basically the same other than that. The changes are marked in Listing 11-12. Add this code to your form.

Listing 11-12: **Edit Method for IntelliEdit Window**

```
Public Sub Edit(objDB As Database, _
    sTableName As String, _
    sItemSingular As String, _
    sIDField As String, _
    vRecordID As Variant)

    Dim iField As Long
    '
    ' Make form invisible so that controls can paint
    ' without the user seeing it.
    '
    Me.Visible = False
    '
    ' Store input parameters
    ' in private variables for
    ' later use.
    '
    ' m_DB:          Private reference to database
    '                that is already open.
    ' m_sTableName:  Table in which data resides;
    '                i.e., tblCustomers, tblCategories
    ' m_sItemName:   What an item in this table
    '                is called, ie Customer, Category
    ' m_sIDField:    Which field in table is unique ID
    ' m_vRecordID:   Unique ID for the record being
    '                edited. Stored as a variant to
    '                accommodate both numeric
    '                and text IDs.
    '
    '
    Set m_DB = objDB
    m_sTableName = sTableName
    m_sItemName = sItemSingular
    m_sIDField = sIDField
    m_vRecordID = vRecordID

    m_iMode = MODE_EDIT
    Me.Caption = "Edit " & m_sItemName
    Set m_RS = _
        m_DB.OpenRecordset(sTableName, dbOpenDynaset)
    '
    ' Since this is an edit operation, filter
    ' the recordset down to just the entry we
    ' care about.
    '
    m_RS.Filter = m_sIDField & " = "
    If IsNumeric(m_vRecordID) Then
        m_RS.Filter = m_RS.Filter & m_vRecordID
    Else
```

(continued)

Listing 11-12 *(continued)*

```
        m_RS.Filter = _
            m_RS.Filter & "'" & m_vRecordID & "'"
    End If
    Set m_RS = m_RS.OpenRecordset()

    ConfigureForm

    '
    ' Load data from recordset
    ' into the form.
    '
    For iField = 0 To m_RS.Fields.Count - 1
        If IsNull(m_RS.Fields(iField)) Then
            txtFieldData(iField).Text = ""
        Else
            txtFieldData(iField).Text = m_RS.Fields(iField)
        End If
    Next iField
    Me.Visible = True

End Sub
```

The first change is in how the record to be edited is retrieved. First, the recordset is opened as in the Add() method. Then, based on the data type of the ID field, the filter criteria are built. String values need to have single quotes around them. One possibility for a bug would be to have a single quote in the value itself. If you do have this problem, you'll need a piece of code to replace each single quote with two single quotes *(not* a double quote). The database will then interpret the filter correctly and actually look for a single-quote character as part of the ID.

Note   Because the ID field variable is actually a variant, it can hold both text and numeric data. Variants are not good to use everywhere because they require much more memory than other data types like Integer and Long, but in cases like this, they are invaluable.

The second major change is the loading of data from the recordset into the form. The ConfigureForm subroutine, which you see shortly, takes care of drawing all the controls on the form so they are ready to be used. Using the Fields collection of the recordset lets the form not have to worry about field names or other considerations. It simply takes whatever data is in the field and puts it into the TextBox control.

Configuring the form

As mentioned previously, the ConfigureForm subroutine is the heart of how this form works. The code for it is shown in Listing 11-13.

Listing 11-13: **ConfigureForm Method for the IntelliEdit Window**

```
Private Sub ConfigureForm()
    Dim iField As Long
    Dim iWidthLoop As Long
    Dim iMaxWidth As Long
    Dim iMaxHeight As Long

    For iField = 0 To m_RS.Fields.Count - 1
        '
        ' First control array item is
        ' already on form; don't add it
        ' again.
        '
        If iField > FIRSTITEM Then
            AddTextBoxControl iField, iMaxWidth
            AddLabelControl iField, iMaxWidth
        End If
        '
        ' The unique ID cannot be edited
        ' in this form. If the ID field is
        ' not an AutoNumber field, however,
        ' it can be edited in Add mode only.
        ' The code below actually
        ' moves the box out of sight and
        ' hides it.
        '
        If m_RS.Fields(iField).Name = m_sIDField Then
            ConfigureIDField iField
        Else
            ConfigureTextBox iField
            '
            ' Use the widest text box as the width
            ' to adjust the form width with.
            '
            With txtFieldData(iField)
                If .Width > iMaxWidth Then
                    iMaxWidth = .Width
                End If
                If .Top + .Height > iMaxHeight Then
                    iMaxHeight = .Top _
                    + .Height
                End If
            End With
        End If

        '
        ' Set up Label control
        '
```

(continued)

Listing 11-13 *(continued)*

```
        lblFieldName(iField).Caption = _
            AddSpacesToName(m_RS.Fields(iField).Name) & ":"
        lblFieldName(iField).Top = _
            txtFieldData(iField).Top _
            + (txtFieldData(iField).Height _
            - lblFieldName(iField).Height) / 2

    Next iField

    '
    ' Move OK and Cancel buttons so that
    ' they are centered in the bottom of
    ' the form.
    '
    cmdOK.Top = iMaxHeight + TEXTSPACING
    cmdCancel.Top = cmdOK.Top

    '
    ' Adjust form size to fit all
    ' the controls. Since this
    ' calculation involves the
    ' OK and Cancel buttons, this
    ' code has to be after the
    ' button adjustment code.
    '
    Me.Height = Me.Height _
        - Me.ScaleHeight _
        + cmdOK.Top _
        + cmdOK.Height _
        + BUTTONSPACING
    Me.Width = (Me.Width - Me.ScaleWidth) _
        + lblFieldName(FIRSTITEM).Left * 2 _
        + txtFieldData(iField - 1).Left _
        + iMaxWidth


    cmdOK.Left = 0.5 _
        * (Me.ScaleWidth _
        - (2 * cmdOK.Width) _
        - BUTTONSPACING)

    cmdCancel.Left = _
        cmdOK.Left _
        + cmdOK.Width _
        + BUTTONSPACING

End Sub
```

Although all the Listing 11-13 code is commented, there is quite a bit of window-sizing "theory" going on in this code that may not make sense. The first code you encounter checks to see whether the first field is being processed. Since there is already a Label control and a TextBox control on the form, it is not necessary to add new ones.

The next action (for both the first and all subsequent controls) is to configure the control to show data. If the control happens to be the field holding the unique ID, it is configured slightly differently than the rest of the controls. This is because IDs can be edited only in certain cases. If the field is an AutoNumber or a sequence field, it can't be edited at all. Other types of IDs can only be edited in Add mode. This prevents referential integrity errors in which related data gets out of sync because the key value is changed. While this can be assisted through the use of constraints in the database, this form simply won't allow the problem to occur.

Once the TextBox has been configured, a check is made to see how wide the control is. Because other controls need to know where to find the right-hand edge of the column of TextBox controls, the maximum width is tracked in the `iMaxWidth` variable. In addition, total height of all the controls together is tracked in `iMaxHeight`. These two variables will be used to place the OK and Cancel buttons at the end of this subroutine, as well as to adjust the height and width of the window.

The last chunk of code configures the Label control next to each TextBox control. The Label is placed in a column so that it is centered between the top and bottom of each TextBox.

A number of support subroutines are invoked in this code. They are shown in Listing 11-14 and should be added to your form.

Listing 11-14: **ConfigureForm Support Subroutines**

```
Private Function AddSpacesToName(sInput As String) _
   As String

   Dim iPos As Integer
   Dim sTmpName As String

   sTmpName = Left$(sInput, 1)

   For iPos = 2 To Len(sInput)
      If Mid$(sInput, iPos, 2) = "ID" Then
         iPos = iPos + 2
         sTmpName = sTmpName & " ID"
      Else
         If Mid$(sInput, iPos, 1) <= "Z" Then
            sTmpName = sTmpName & " "
         End If
```

(continued)

Listing 11-14 *(continued)*

```
            sTmpName = sTmpName & Mid$(sInput, iPos, 1)
        End If
    Next iPos

    AddSpacesToName = sTmpName

End Function

Private Sub AddTextBoxControl(iField As Long, _
    iMaxWidth As Long)
    Dim iPixelPosition As Long
    '
    ' Add a new TextBox control
    ' and position it properly.
    ' Each TextBox control is based
    ' on the horizontal position
    ' of the first TextBox control.
    '
    Load txtFieldData(iField)
    '
    ' Determine how big the window
    ' is so far. If it exceeds
    ' MAXWINDOWHEIGHTINPIXELS
    ' then make a new column of
    ' controls. The new column
    ' of TextBox controls will be
    ' placed in such a way as to
    ' leave room for all the label
    ' controls.
    '
    iPixelPosition = (txtFieldData(iField - 1).Top _
        + txtFieldData(iField - 1).Height) _
        / Screen.TwipsPerPixelY

    If iPixelPosition > MAXWINDOWHEIGHTINPIXELS Then
        '
        ' Shift this TextBox into a new column.
        ' Use the maximum width found so far
        ' to make sure there is enough room for all
        ' the fields in the previous column.
        '
        txtFieldData(iField).Left = _
            (txtFieldData(FIRSTITEM).Left * 2) _
            + iMaxWidth
        txtFieldData(iField).Top = _
            txtFieldData(FIRSTITEM).Top
    Else
        txtFieldData(iField).Left = _
            txtFieldData(iField - 1).Left
        txtFieldData(iField).Top = _
            txtFieldData(iField - 1).Top _
```

```
            + txtFieldData(iField - 1).Height _
            + TEXTSPACING
    End If

End Sub

Private Sub AddLabelControl(iField As Long, _
    iMaxWidth As Long)
    '
    ' Add a new label control
    ' and begin positioning it.
    ' Each label control is based
    ' on the horizontal position
    ' of the first Label control.
    ' The Top property will be set
    ' when we know how big the
    ' TextBox will be. This lets the
    ' Label be approximately centered
    ' between the top and bottom
    ' of the box.
    '
    Load lblFieldName(iField)
    '
    ' Determine if multiple columns
    ' were built for the controls
    ' on the form.
    '
    If txtFieldData(iField).Left <> _
       txtFieldData(FIRSTITEM).Left Then

        lblFieldName(iField).Left = _
            txtFieldData(FIRSTITEM).Left + _
            iMaxWidth + _
            TEXTSPACING
    Else
        lblFieldName(iField).Left = _
            lblFieldName(iField - 1).Left
    End If
    lblFieldName(iField).Visible = True

End Sub

Private Sub ConfigureTextBox(iField As Long)
    '
    ' properties from the first control,
    ' fix the coloring and text for
    ' each control. This is because
    ' the first box could be an ID field
    ' with different attributes than the
    ' rest of the controls will have.
    '
```

(continued)

Listing 11-14 *(continued)*

```vb
    ' Since controls acquire their
    txtFieldData(iField).Locked = False
    txtFieldData(iField).BackColor = vbWhite
    txtFieldData(iField).Visible = True
    txtFieldData(iField).Text = ""
    txtFieldData(iField).MaxLength = _
        m_RS.Fields(iField).Size
    '
    ' Memo data types don't give
    ' correct Size values. Give a
    ' Memo some space to use.
    '
    If m_RS.Fields(iField).Type = dbMemo Then
        txtFieldData(iField).Height = _
            LINEHEIGHT * MEMOLENGTH
        txtFieldData(iField).Width = _
            CHARWIDTH * MAXTEXTLENGTH
    ElseIf m_RS.Fields(iField).Size > MAXTEXTLENGTH Then
        '
        ' Break large fields into multiple
        ' lines of reasonable size. (set by
        ' constant in declarations section
        ' of this form)
        '
        txtFieldData(iField).Height = _
            LINEHEIGHT * _
            ((m_RS.Fields(iField).Size \ MAXTEXTLENGTH) + 1)
        txtFieldData(iField).Width = _
            CHARWIDTH * MAXTEXTLENGTH
    Else
        '
        ' Everything less than a full line is
        ' sized appropriately.
        '
        txtFieldData(iField).Width = _
            CHARWIDTH * m_RS.Fields(iField).Size
    End If
End Sub

Private Sub ConfigureIDField(iField As Long)
    '
    ' Set default values first
    ' so that only exceptions need
    ' to be set in this procedure. This
    ' subroutine essentially overrides
    ' certain properties set in
    ' ConfigureTextBox.
    '
    ConfigureTextBox iField

    If m_iMode = MODE_EDIT Then
```

```
                         '
            ' Unique User IDs can not
            ' be edited through this form.
            '
            txtFieldData(iField).Locked = True
            txtFieldData(iField).BackColor = vbButtonFace
            '
            ' Adjust the width of the ID field so that
            ' the entire ID can be seen.
            '
            txtFieldData(iField).Width = _
             TextWidth(String$(m_RS.Fields(iField).Size, "M"))

      ElseIf m_iMode = MODE_ADD Then
         If m_RS.Fields(iField).Attributes _
            And dbAutoIncrField = dbAutoIncrField Then

               '
               ' Auto increment user IDs should
               ' not be edited manually by the
               ' user.
               '
               txtFieldData(iField).Text = "AutoNumber ID"
               txtFieldData(iField).Width = _
                  Me.TextWidth("AutoNumber ID")
               txtFieldData(iField).Locked = True
               txtFieldData(iField).BackColor = vbButtonFace
         End If
         '
         ' There is no Else statement since
         ' other types of user IDs can be
         ' edited in Add mode.
         '
      End If

End Sub
```

Each of these functions has its job:

✦ AddSpacesToName — This function takes a field name like CompanyName and
changes it to "Company Name." This routine assumes that fields are named
using mixed case. If your situation or naming scheme is different, you'll need
to modify this routine accordingly.

✦ AddTextBoxControl — This routine creates a new TextBox control and places
it either beneath the previous one or in a new column if the window has
become too tall.

✦ AddLabelControl — This routine creates a new Label control and places it
beside its corresponding TextBox control. It also checks to see whether it
needs to be put at the left-hand side or in the new column, if one was created.

✦ ConfigureTextBox — Because each newly created TextBox control takes its properties from the first TextBox control on the form, all the properties need to be reset through code. This is because the first control probably won't have the same properties you need for each of the other TextBox controls on the form. This routine also checks for fields that are long text fields, called *memos*, and gives them a reasonably sized field to use. Memo fields can hold up to 2 billion characters, but a reasonable number of lines is all that is really required. That change is made through the MEMO_LENGTH constant defined in the Declarations section.

✦ ConfigureIDField — This routine essentially overrides some of the settings made in ConfigureTextBox. For AutoNumber fields, no editing is ever allowed. In Add mode, non-AutoNumber fields can be edited. This routine checks for all those cases. If you have additional types of IDs that should not be edited, you can make your changes here.

Finally, you need to add the constants shown in Listing 11-15 to your form's Declarations section. Each of these constants is defined here so you know what to change, if necessary.

Listing 11-15: **Additional Constants for IntelliEdit Window**

```
Private Const TEXTSPACING = 120
Private Const BUTTONSPACING = 120
Private Const FIRSTITEM = 0
Private Const MAXTEXTLENGTH = 30
Private Const LINEHEIGHT = 300
Private Const CHARWIDTH = 100
Private Const MEMOLENGTH = 5
Private Const MAXWINDOWHEIGHTINPIXELS = 300
```

The definitions for these constants follows:

✦ TEXTSPACING — This is the default vertical space that should be maintained between each TextBox control.

✦ BUTTONSPACING — This is the default horizontal space that should be maintained between the CommandButton controls at the bottom of the window.

✦ FIRSTITEM — Because many of the calculations in this form rely on the attributes of the first TextBox or Label control, that control's index is kept in a constant. This makes it clearer in your code that you want the values of the first control on the form.

✦ MAXTEXTLENGTH—This value is an arbitrary number of characters that should be shown in a line for a TextBox control. You can adjust this as you see fit, based on the data you're going to be showing.

✦ LINEHEIGHT—This is an approximate height of a line of text in a TextBox control. This value is used in building multiline TextBox controls so that there is enough space to show a good part of the data.

✦ CHARWIDTH—This is the average width of a character in twips. This value is used to determine how wide each TextBox should be to show a certain number of characters.

✦ MEMOLENGTH—This constant indicates how many lines of text should be shown for a Memo field.

✦ MAXWINDOWHEIGHTINPIXELS—To prevent a window from being too long, this constant indicates how high a window can be, in pixels, before a new column is built for subsequent controls. Adjust this value based on your users' machine configurations. If, for instance, you know your users all have 800 × 600 resolution on their monitors, you could make the value larger to show more items per column.

Experiment with these constants to change the appearance of your form. These numbers will produce a fairly good-looking window, but you may want to make changes to it.

Saving data changes

Now that you have the code to load the data into the form, you need to respond to and save changes back to the database. The first part of this is fairly straightforward. By looking at the database structure, you can determine which fields are required and which are not. This will let you enable or disable the OK button based on whether enough fields are filled in on the form.

To make this happen, first add the code in Listing 11-16 to your form. This code will run whenever data is changed in the form.

Listing 11-16: **Change Event Handler**

```
Private Sub txtFieldData_Change(Index As Integer)
    ValidateData
End Sub
```

Because all the TextBox controls have the same name, they will all use the same event handler. The code for the ValidateData() subroutine is shown in Listing 11-17.

Listing 11-17: **ValidateData Subroutine Code**

```
Private Sub ValidateData()
    Dim bValid As Boolean
    Dim i As Long

    If bConfiguringForm Then Exit Sub
    bValid = True
    With m_RS.Fields
        For i = 0 To .Count - 1
            If .Item(i).Required _
                Or Not (.Item(i).AllowZeroLength) Then
                bValid = bValid And txtFieldData(i) <> ""
            End If
        Next i
    End With
    cmdOK.Enabled = bValid

End Sub
```

The primary function of this code is to check each TextBox control on the form. If the corresponding field in the database is marked either as required or not to allow zero length data, the OK button is not enabled. You might wonder, if a field is not required, why can't it be zero length? Well, this is sort of a design bug with Access. You can have fields that are not required but also do not allow zero-length data. Instead of trying to fix the bug, our recommendation is to either make fields in each table Required and not AllowZeroLength, or make them *not* Required and to AllowZeroLength data in the field. If you look at any of the tables in the Northwind Traders database, you'll notice that most of the data breaks the validation rules. For instance, the HomePage field is blank for most of the suppliers, even though the AllowZeroLength attribute is set to No.

The other check performed initially in this code is to determine whether the form is currently being configured. Because this subroutine looks at the number of fields in the table instead of the number of controls, it will cause an error if all the controls are not in place. The easiest way to check this is to make the changes shown in Listings 11-18 and 11-19 to your Declarations section and ConfigureForm subroutine, respectively.

Listing 11-18: **Changes to Declarations Section**

```
Option Explicit
Private m_DB As Database
Private m_RS As Recordset

Private m_sTableName As String
Private m_sItemName As String
```

```
Private m_sIDField As String
Private m_vRecordID As Variant
Private m_iMode As Integer

Private Const MODE_ADD = 1
Private Const MODE_EDIT = 2

Private Const TEXTSPACING = 120
Private Const BUTTONSPACING = 120
Private Const FIRSTITEM = 0
Private Const MAXTEXTLENGTH = 30
Private Const LINEHEIGHT = 300
Private Const CHARWIDTH = 100
Private Const MEMOLENGTH = 5
Private Const MAXWINDOWHEIGHTINPIXELS = 300

Private bDirty As Boolean
Private bConfiguringForm As Boolean
```

Listing 11-19: **Changes to ConfigureForm Subroutine**

```
Private Sub ConfigureForm()
    Dim iField As Long
    Dim iWidthLoop As Long
    Dim iMaxWidth As Long
    Dim iMaxHeight As Long

    bConfiguringForm = True
    For iField = 0 To m_RS.Fields.Count - 1
        '
        ' First control array item is
        ' already on form; don't add it
        ' again.
        '
        If iField > FIRSTITEM Then
            AddTextBoxControl iField, iMaxWidth
            AddLabelControl iField, iMaxWidth
        End If
        '
        ' The unique ID cannot be edited
        ' in this form. If the ID field is
        ' not an AutoNumber field, however,
        ' it can be edited in Add mode only.
        ' The code below actually
        ' moves the box out of sight and
        ' hides it.
        '
```

(continued)

Listing 11-19 *(continued)*

```
            If m_RS.Fields(iField).Name = m_sIDField Then
                ConfigureIDField iField
            Else
                ConfigureTextBox iField
                '
                ' Use the widest text box as the width
                ' to adjust the form width with.
                '
                With txtFieldData(iField)
                    If .Width > iMaxWidth Then
                        iMaxWidth = .Width
                    End If
                    If .Top + .Height > iMaxHeight Then
                        iMaxHeight = .Top _
                        + .Height
                    End If
                End With
            End If


            '
            ' Set up Label control
            '
            lblFieldName(iField).Caption = _
                AddSpacesToName(m_RS.Fields(iField).Name) & ":"
            lblFieldName(iField).Top = _
                txtFieldData(iField).Top _
                + (txtFieldData(iField).Height _
                - lblFieldName(iField).Height) / 2

        Next iField

        '
        ' Move OK and Cancel buttons so that
        ' they are centered in the bottom of
        ' the form.
        '
        cmdOK.Top = iMaxHeight + TEXTSPACING
        cmdCancel.Top = cmdOK.Top


        '
        ' Adjust form size to fit all
        ' the controls. Since this
        ' calculation involves the
        ' OK and Cancel buttons, this
        ' code has to be after the
        ' button adjustment code.
        '
        Me.Height = Me.Height _
            - Me.ScaleHeight _
            + cmdOK.Top _
            + cmdOK.Height _
```

```
        + BUTTONSPACING
    Me.Width = (Me.Width - Me.ScaleWidth) _
        + lblFieldName(FIRSTITEM).Left * 2 _
        + txtFieldData(iField - 1).Left _
        + iMaxWidth


    cmdOK.Left = 0.5 _
        * (Me.ScaleWidth _
        - (2 * cmdOK.Width) _
        - BUTTONSPACING)

    cmdCancel.Left = _
        cmdOK.Left _
        + cmdOK.Width _
        + BUTTONSPACING

    bConfiguringForm = False
End Sub

Private Sub ValidateData()
    Dim bValid As Boolean
    Dim i As Long

    If bConfiguringForm Then Exit Sub
    bValid = True
    With m_RS.Fields
        For i = 0 To .Count - 1
            If .Item(i).Required _
                Or Not (.Item(i).AllowZeroLength) Then
                bValid = bValid And txtFieldData(i) <> ""
            End If
        Next i
    End With
    bDirty = True
    cmdOK.Enabled = bValid

End Sub
```

These changes will cause the event handler for the `txtFieldData_Change()` event to ignore any changes until the form is done being configured.

There are a few other changes required now that the Change event handler is in place. The Change event is triggered by any change to the contents of the control, including those done through code. In order to disable the OK button until a change is made, you need to make the following changes:

1. Listing 11-20 illustrates the new variable you need to declare in your form's Declarations section.

Listing 11-20: **Change to Declarations Section of Form**

```
Option Explicit
Private m_DB As Database
Private m_RS As Recordset

Private m_sTableName As String
Private m_sItemName As String
Private m_sIDField As String
Private m_vRecordID As Variant
Private m_iMode As Integer

Private Const MODE_ADD = 1
Private Const MODE_EDIT = 2

Private Const TEXTSPACING = 120
Private Const BUTTONSPACING = 120
Private Const FIRSTITEM = 0
Private Const MAXTEXTLENGTH = 30
Private Const LINEHEIGHT = 300
Private Const CHARWIDTH = 100
Private Const MEMOLENGTH = 5
Private Const MAXWINDOWHEIGHTINPIXELS = 300
```

This variable will track whether the data on the form is dirty; that is, whether the data has been changed since the last time it was loaded into the form.

2. Listing 11-21 shows a change required in the Add method of the form. This change resets the OK button after the boxes have been drawn and cleared of their data.

Listing 11-21: **Add Method with Changes Marked**

```
Public Sub Add(objDB As Database, _
    sTableName As String, _
    sItemSingular As String, _
    sIDField As String)

    Dim iField As Long
    '
    ' Make form invisible so
    ' that controls can paint
    ' without the user seeing
    ' it.
    '
```

```
    Me.Visible = False
    '
    ' Store input parameters
    ' in private variables for
    ' later use.
    '
    ' m_DB:          Private reference to database
    '                that is already open.
    ' m_sTableName:  Table in which data resides
    '                i.e., tblCustomers, tblCategories
    ' m_sItemName:   What an item in this table
    '                is called, i.e., Customer, Category
    ' m_sIDField:    What field in table is unique ID
    ' m_vRecordID:   Unique ID for the record being
    '                edited. Stored as a variant to
    '                accomodate text IDs.
    '
    Set m_DB = objDB
    m_sTableName = sTableName
    m_sItemName = sItemSingular
    m_sIDField = sIDField

    m_iMode = MODE_ADD
    Me.Caption = "Add " & m_sItemName

    '
    ' Open the table without picking a
    ' particular record.
    '
    Set m_RS = _
        m_DB.OpenRecordset(sTableName, dbOpenDynaset)

    ConfigureForm

    '
    ' No data needs to be loaded
    ' since the form should be
    ' empty initially.
    '

    Me.Visible = True
    bDirty = False
    cmdOK.Enabled = False

End Sub
```

3. A similar change is required in the Edit method, shown in Listing 11-22.

Listing 11-22: **Edit Method with Changes Marked**

```
Public Sub Edit(objDB As Database, _
    sTableName As String, _
    sItemSingular As String, _
    sIDField As String, _
    vRecordID As Variant)

    Dim iField As Long
    Me.Visible = False
    '
    ' Store input parameters
    ' in private variables for
    ' later use.
    '
    ' m_DB:          Private reference to database
    '                that is already open.
    ' m_sTableName: Table in which data resides
    '                i.e., tblCustomers, tblCategories
    ' m_sItemName:  What an item in this table
    '                is called, i.e., Customer, Category
    ' m_sIDField:   What field in table is unique ID
    ' m_vRecordID:  Unique ID for the record being
    '                edited. Stored as a variant to
    '                accomodate text IDs.
    '
    Set m_DB = objDB
    m_sTableName = sTableName
    m_sItemName = sItemSingular
    m_sIDField = sIDField
    m_vRecordID = vRecordID

    m_iMode = MODE_EDIT
    Me.Caption = "Edit " & m_sItemName
    Set m_RS = _
        m_DB.OpenRecordset(sTableName, dbOpenDynaset)
    '
    ' Since this is an edit operation, filter
    ' the recordset down to just the entry we
    ' care about.
    '
    m_RS.Filter = m_sIDField & " = "
    If IsNumeric(m_vRecordID) Then
        m_RS.Filter = m_RS.Filter & m_vRecordID
    Else
        m_RS.Filter = _
            m_RS.Filter & "'" & m_vRecordID & "'"
    End If
    Set m_RS = m_RS.OpenRecordset()

    ConfigureForm

    '
```

```
' Load data from recordset
' into the form.
'
For iField = 0 To m_RS.Fields.Count - 1
   If IsNull(m_RS.Fields(iField)) Then
      txtFieldData(iField).Text = ""
   Else
      txtFieldData(iField).Text = m_RS.Fields(iField)
   End If
Next iField

bDirty = False
cmdOK.Enabled = False

Me.Visible = True

End Sub
```

With all those changes in, your form will now respond correctly to changes to the data. If you delete the data in a required field, the OK button will be disabled until you fix the missing data. As was mentioned before, make sure that the Required and AllowZeroLength attributes of each field are marked correctly.

Before you write the code to save a record to the database, you need to take care of unsaved data. This entails a confirmation dialog whenever the data has changed and the user is trying to close the form. The code to do this is shown in Listing 11-23.

Listing 11-23: **Exit Confirmation Code**

```
Private Sub cmdCancel_Click()
   Unload Me
End Sub

Private Sub Form_QueryUnload(Cancel As Integer, _
   UnloadMode As Integer)

   Dim iRet As Integer
   '
   ' Only want to ask if the data has been
   ' changed and is currently valid. The
   ' Enabled property of the OK button
   ' indicates if the data is valid to be
   ' saved.
   '
   If bDirty And cmdOK.Enabled Then
      iRet = MsgBox("Save changes?", _
```

(continued)

Listing 11-23 *(continued)*

```
            vbYesNoCancel + vbQuestion)
        Select Case iRet
        Case vbYes
            SaveData
        Case vbNo
            '
            ' No code required; listed for completeness
            '
        Case vbCancel
            Cancel = True
        End Select
    End If

End Sub
```

Because we want to catch the user's hitting the Cancel button and/or pressing the Close button on the window, the correct place for the code is the form's QueryUnload event. This event will also be triggered if the user decides to shut down the entire application or Windows itself. The only assumption made here is that the user should only be prompted to save data if changes were made and the data is currently valid to be saved. If either one of these conditions is False, the window is closed without any confirmation.

The final piece of code required is that needed to save the data. This code needs to be flexible enough to handle either the creation of a new record or the modification of an existing record. The code is shown in Listing 11-24.

Listing 11-24: **SaveData Subroutine**

```
Private Sub SaveData()

    Dim iField As Long
    Dim iStart As Long

    If m_iMode = MODE_ADD Then
        m_RS.AddNew
    ElseIf m_iMode = MODE_EDIT Then
        m_RS.Edit
    End If

    For iField = 0 To m_RS.Fields.Count - 1
        If m_RS.Fields(iField).Name = m_sIDField _
            And m_iMode = MODE_EDIT Then
            '
            ' Don't edit primary key in edit mode
```

```
        '
        ElseIf (m_RS.Fields(iField).Attributes _
            And dbAutoIncrField) = dbAutoIncrField Then
            '
            ' Don't edit field if field is auto increment
            '
        Else
            m_RS.Fields(iField) = txtFieldData(iField).Text
        End If
    Next iField

    m_RS.Update
    bDirty = False

End Sub
```

Using the mode flag we set earlier, data is saved to fields where it is legal to save the data. AutoNumber fields and unique IDs are never edited, unless it is a non-AutoNumber field in Add mode.

To call this subroutine from the OK button, add the code shown in Listing 11-25 to your form.

Listing 11-25: **OK Button Event Handler**

```
Private Sub cmdOK_Click()
    SaveData
    Unload Me
End Sub
```

The form can now add data. Unfortunately, you don't yet have a way to call the form to tell it what to do. That code is shown in the next section. For now, save your Visual Basic project.

Creating context-sensitive Edit menus

To make the MDI form be responsive to changes in the list windows, you need to set up some simple means of communication between the forms. You've already taken the first step in making common public methods available on both the IntelliList and IntelliEdit windows. Now you need to add the code to enable use of those interfaces.

To begin, make the MDI form's Edit menu reflect the contents of each IntelliList window. To do this, add the code in Listing 11-26 to the IntelliList window.

Listing 11-26: **IntelliList Form Code**

```
Private Sub Form_Activate()
    '
    ' Event fires whenever this window is brought
    ' forward in the MDI child form stack.
    '
    frmMDIMain.EnableItemMenus m_sItemSingular
End Sub

Private Sub Form_Deactivate()
    '
    ' Event fires whenever this window is sent
    ' backward in the MDI child form stack.
    '
    frmMDIMain.DisableItemMenus
End Sub

Private Sub Form_Load()
    '
    ' Event fires whenever this window is created
    '
    frmMDIMain.EnableItemMenus m_sItemSingular
End Sub

Private Sub Form_Unload(Cancel As Integer)
    '
    ' Event fires whenever window is destroyed.
    ' This code cleans up the menu so that no
    ' choices are displayed when no windows are
    ' visible.
    frmMDIMain.DisableItemMenus
End Sub
```

Listing 11-27 shows the corresponding code needed in the MDI form.

Listing 11-27: **MDI Form Menu Modification Code**

```
Public Sub EnableItemMenus(sItemSingular As String)
    mnuEditAdd.Caption = "Add " & sItemSingular
    mnuEditModify.Caption = "Modify " & sItemSingular
    mnuEditDelete.Caption = "Delete " & sItemSingular

    mnuPopupAdd.Caption = mnuEditAdd.Caption
    mnuPopupModify.Caption = mnuEditModify.Caption
    mnuPopupDelete.Caption = mnuEditDelete.Caption

    mnuEditSep.Visible = True
```

```
      mnuEditAdd.Visible = True
      mnuEditModify.Visible = True
      mnuEditDelete.Visible = True
   End Sub

   Public Sub DisableItemMenus()
      mnuEditSep.Visible = False
      mnuEditAdd.Visible = False
      mnuEditModify.Visible = False
      mnuEditDelete.Visible = False
   End Sub
```

The first subroutine takes care of changing the captions of both the visible Edit menu and the invisible popup menu. This code ensures that the user sees "Edit Category" instead of "Edit Item." This makes the menu choices more relevant to the task at hand.

Listing 11-28 shows the simple code required to make each of the menu choices work properly.

Listing 11-28: **Menu Choice Code**

```
Private Sub mnuEditAdd_Click()
   If TypeOf Me.ActiveForm Is frmIntelliList Then
      Me.ActiveForm.AddItem
   End If
End Sub

Private Sub mnuEditDelete_Click()
   If TypeOf Me.ActiveForm Is frmIntelliList Then
      Me.ActiveForm.DeleteItem
   End If
End Sub

Private Sub mnuEditModify_Click()
   If TypeOf Me.ActiveForm Is frmIntelliList Then
      Me.ActiveForm.ModifyItem
   End If
End Sub

Private Sub mnuPopupAdd_Click()
   If TypeOf Me.ActiveForm Is frmIntelliList Then
      Me.ActiveForm.AddItem
   End If
End Sub
```

(continued)

```
Private Sub mnuPopupDelete_Click()
    If TypeOf Me.ActiveForm Is frmIntelliList Then
        Me.ActiveForm.DeleteItem
    End If
End Sub

Private Sub mnuPopupModify_Click()
    If TypeOf Me.ActiveForm Is frmIntelliList Then
        Me.ActiveForm.ModifyItem
    End If
End Sub
```

Because this code needs to be flexible for all the windows in your application, be sure you check the type of the `ActiveForm`, which is a property of the MDI form. This property enables you to determine what type of form is on the top of the child form stack.

Adding the DeleteItem method

You've already written the `AddItem` and `ModifyItem` subroutines for the IntelliList window. The `DeleteItem` subroutine is shown in Listing 11-29.

Listing 11-29: **DeleteItem Method in IntelliList Window**

```
Public Sub DeleteItem()
    Dim sSQL As String

    If MsgBox("Delete this item?", vbYesNo + _
        vbExclamation, "Delete Item") = vbYes Then

        sSQL = "DELETE FROM " _
            & m_sTableName & " WHERE " & m_sIDField & " = "

        If m_rsData.Fields(0).Type = dbText Then
            sSQL = sSQL & "'"
        End If

        sSQL = sSQL & _
            Mid$(ctlListView.SelectedItem.Key, _
                Len(LISTITEM_KEY) + 1)

        If m_rsData.Fields(0).Type = dbText Then
            sSQL = sSQL & "'"
        End If

        m_DB.Execute sSQL
        RefreshData
```

```
        End If

    End Sub
```

This is fairly simple code, but it can end up causing problems. For instance, if you try to delete a record that is being used by another table, the referenced record will no longer be available. Your database can do some error checking on deletions. For instance, you shouldn't delete an item from a table that is being used in another table. Depending on your situation, you may want to eliminate the `Delete` function altogether, or make it a configurable property of the IntelliList window. Either way, this code will determine the correct code to use to delete the selected record.

Displaying the popup menu

The next change enables the user to right-click an item in the IntelliList window and see a relevant popup menu appear. That code is shown in Listing 11-30.

Listing 11-30: **Popup Menu Code in IntelliList Window**

```
Private Sub ctlListView_MouseDown(Button As Integer, _
    Shift As Integer, x As Single, y As Single)

    If Button = vbRightButton Then
        Set ctlListView.SelectedItem =
            ctlListView.HitTest(x, y)

        If ctlListView.SelectedItem Is Nothing Then
            Exit Sub
        End If

        PopupMenu frmMDIMain!mnuPopup, _
            vbPopupMenuLeftAlign, _
            x, y, _
            m_frmCaller!mnuPopupModify
    End If
End Sub
```

This routine makes sure the user presses the right-hand mouse button and then displays the MDI form's popup menu in the appropriate place. Notice that this code references a member variable that is set when the IntelliList window was created. This change helps enforce the proper use of objects so one object does not directly depend on another object's being named a certain way. To make this change complete, add this declaration to the Declarations section of the IntelliList window:

```
Private m_frmCaller As MDIForm
```

You also need to make the changes marked in Listing 11-31.

Listing 11-31: **ShowData Subroutine Changes**

```
Public Sub ShowData(objDB As Database, _
    frmCaller As MDIForm, _
    sTableName As String, _
    sItemSingular As String, _
    sItemPlural As String, _
    sViewQuery As String, _
    sIDField As String)

    '
    ' Store parameters in member variables
    '

    Set m_DB = objDB
    Set m_frmCaller = frmCaller
    m_sTableName = sTableName
    m_sViewQuery = sViewQuery
    m_sItemSingular = sItemSingular
    m_sItemPlural = sItemPlural
    m_sIDField = sIDField

    '
    ' Reconfigure window to show data
    ' for the selected table/query.
    '
    RefreshData

End Sub
```

The call to this window in the MDI form will resemble the one shown in Listing 11-32.

Listing 11-32: **Call to IntelliList Window**

```
Private Sub mnuListCategories_Click()
    Dim frmNew As New frmIntelliList
    frmNew.ShowData objDB:=g_DB, _
        frmCaller:=Me, _
        sTableName:="Categories", _
        sItemSingular:="Category", _
```

```
        sItemPlural:="Categories", _
        sViewQuery:="qryViewCategories", _
        sIDField:="CategoryID"

End Sub
```

Refreshing the list from IntelliEdit

The last piece of code you need to build will tell the IntelliList window to refresh after a change has been successfully saved in the IntelliEdit window. Because the two windows are not in a modal relationship, there has to be a specific way to send a message. For simplicity, the IntelliList window will tell the IntelliEdit window what window to signal when the data has been saved. The Edit window will actually signal the IntelliList window's RefreshData subroutine.

The first change you need to make is in the IntelliEdit window. After adding the following variable declaration to the form, make the changes marked in Listings 11-33 and 11-34.

```
Private m_frmCaller As frmIntelliList
```

Listing 11-33: **IntelliList AddItem Method Changes**

```
Public Sub Add(objDB As Database, _
    frmCaller As frmIntelliList, _
    sTableName As String, _
    sItemSingular As String, _
    sIDField As String)

    Dim iField As Long
    '
    ' Make form invisible so
    ' that controls can paint
    ' without the user seeing
    ' it.
    '
    Me.Visible = False
    '
    ' Store input parameters
    ' in private variables for
    ' later use.
    '
    ' m_DB:        Private reference to database
    '              that is already open.
    ' m_sTableName: Table in which data resides
    '              i.e., tblCustomers, tblCategories
```

(continued)

Listing 11-33 *(continued)*

```
' m_sItemName:   What an item in this table
'                is called, i.e., Customer, Category
' m_sIDField:    What field in table is unique ID
' m_vRecordID:   Unique ID for the record being
'                edited. Stored as a variant to
'                accommodate text IDs.
'
Set m_DB = objDB
Set m_frmCaller = frmCaller
m_sTableName = sTableName
m_sItemName = sItemSingular
m_sIDField = sIDField

m_iMode = MODE_ADD
Me.Caption = "Add " & m_sItemName

'
' Open the table without picking a
' particular record.
'
Set m_RS = _
    m_DB.OpenRecordset(sTableName, dbOpenDynaset)

ConfigureForm

'
' No data needs to be loaded
' since the form should be
' empty initially.
'

Me.Visible = True
bDirty = False
cmdOK.Enabled = False

End Sub
```

Listing 11-34: IntelliList Edit Method Changes

```
Public Sub Edit(objDB As Database, _
    frmCaller As frmIntelliList, _
    sTableName As String, _
    sItemSingular As String, _
    sIDField As String, _
    vRecordID As Variant)

    Dim iField As Long
```

```
Me.Visible = False
'
' Store input parameters
' in private variables for
' later use.
'
' m_DB:         Private reference to database
'               that is already open.
' m_sTableName: Table in which data resides
'               i.e., tblCustomers, tblCategories
' m_sItemName:  What an item in this table
'               is called, i.e., Customer, Category
' m_sIDField:   What field in table is unique ID
' m_vRecordID:  Unique ID for the record being
'               edited. Stored as a variant to
'               accommodate text IDs.
'
Set m_DB = objDB
Set m_frmCaller = frmCaller
m_sTableName = sTableName
m_sItemName = sItemSingular
m_sIDField = sIDField
m_vRecordID = vRecordID

m_iMode = MODE_EDIT
Me.Caption = "Edit " & m_sItemName
Set m_RS = _
   m_DB.OpenRecordset(sTableName, dbOpenDynaset)
'
' Since this is an edit operation, filter
' the recordset down to just the entry we
' care about.
'
m_RS.Filter = m_sIDField & " = "
If IsNumeric(m_vRecordID) Then
  m_RS.Filter = m_RS.Filter & m_vRecordID
Else
  m_RS.Filter = m_RS.Filter & "'" & m_vRecordID & "'"
End If
Set m_RS = m_RS.OpenRecordset()

ConfigureForm

'
' Load data from recordset
' into the form.
'
For iField = 0 To m_RS.Fields.Count - 1
   If IsNull(m_RS.Fields(iField)) Then
      txtFieldData(iField).Text = ""
   Else
      txtFieldData(iField).Text = m_RS.Fields(iField)
```

(continued)

Listing 11-34 *(continued)*

```
        End If
    Next iField

    bDirty = False
    cmdOK.Enabled = False

    Me.Visible = True

End Sub
```

You also need to change the AddItem and ModifyItem calls in the
frmIntelliList window. Those changes are shown in Listing 11-35.

Listing 11-35: AddItem/ModifyItem Subroutine Changes

```
Public Sub AddItem()
    Dim frmNew As New frmIntelliEdit
    frmNew.Add objDB:=m_DB, _
        frmCaller:=Me, _
        sTableName:=m_sTableName, _
        sItemSingular:=m_sItemSingular, _
        sIDField:=m_sIDField

End Sub

Public Sub ModifyItem()
    Dim frmNew As New frmIntelliEdit
    frmNew.Edit objDB:=m_DB, _
        frmCaller:=Me, _
        sTableName:=m_sTableName, _
        sItemSingular:=m_sItemSingular, _
        sIDField:=m_sIDField, _
        vRecordID:=Mid$(ctlListView.SelectedItem.Key,_
            Len(LISTITEM_KEY) + 1)

End Sub
```

The last change you need to make is to call the IntelliList's RefreshData
subroutine from the end of the SaveData subroutine. That change is shown in
Listing 11-36.

Listing 11-36: SaveData Subroutine Changes

```
Private Sub SaveData()

    Dim iField As Long
    Dim iStart As Long

    If m_iMode = MODE_ADD Then
       m_RS.AddNew
    ElseIf m_iMode = MODE_EDIT Then
       m_RS.Edit
    End If

    For iField = 0 To m_RS.Fields.Count - 1
       If m_RS.Fields(iField).Name = m_sIDField _
          And m_iMode = MODE_EDIT Then
          '
          ' Don't edit primary key in edit mode
          '
       ElseIf (m_RS.Fields(iField).Attributes _
          And dbAutoIncrField) = dbAutoIncrField Then
          '
          ' Don't edit field if field is auto increment
          '
       Else
          m_RS.Fields(iField) = txtFieldData(iField).Text
       End If
    Next iField

    m_RS.Update
    m_frmCaller.RefreshData
    bDirty = False

End Sub
```

With all that code in place, you can save your project and run it. Pick a list of data (like Shippers) and add a record. You'll see the new record appear in the list. You can then modify it and even delete it. The code you wrote will also work for any similar table. Just add the code to the MDI form to show the IntelliList window for that type of data, and you're all set!

Limitations of this window

Obviously, this type of form should not be used if you have data being stored in more than one table. The form is designed to handle data that only requires one table and no joins. In large applications, this could account for 15 or 20 validation tables. If you do the math on that, that's up to 40 windows you don't have to code; you just make the IntelliList and IntelliEdit windows work correctly and you're done with a good chunk of the tedious work.

In addition, this form should not be used with tables with a lot of fields. The display logic is fairly sound, but you will start running out of room with more than 15 fields or so. (The number of fields is based on the size of the field, so you can obviously get more of the shorter fields.)

Summary

As you can see from the examples presented in this chapter, analyzing the structure of a database can be more than just an academic exercise. By keeping your database functionality isolated, you can create windows that rely on the database for things like data validation, sizing, and so on. Having a single source for any information like this is always valuable, even if you don't take it to the level shown in this chapter.

You learned how to make windows that are intelligent enough to look at a database table and/or query and adjust their controls to fit the data being shown. This type of window won't work in every case, but it is an excellent solution for simple tables for which you wish to provide a simple viewer and editor.

You also learned how to use the form and control properties dealing with size to place controls dynamically. As your forms become more complicated, this will be an important skill. For example, you won't always have all the information available to completely configure a form until the user has made some preference choices.

✦   ✦   ✦

Encapsulating Database Functionality – Part 1

✦ ✦ ✦ ✦

In This Chapter

Designing classes
that are database
aware

Integrating a
database-aware class
with a Data Entry
form

Learning how to use
user-defined events to
communicate among
your windows

✦ ✦ ✦ ✦

Although object-oriented programming is a great idea
and provides substantial flexibility, objects without
permanent storage are not much better than simple variables.
However, if you take the power of OOP and classes and match
it up with database programming, you can create some
powerful classes. These classes can be designed to instantiate
themselves automatically as needed, which helps in memory
conservation. Each object can be told to perform saves; the
complex database code can be embedded in the class module.
This is especially valuable if you are building a complex
application in which the classes are built by a system architect
and then distributed to the other members of the team.

This chapter shows you some of the design techniques that go
into a database-aware class. You see how to load, populate,
and save an object from the database. You also see how you
can integrate your objects with your windows.

Chapter Project Overview

Before you start designing and coding, you need to know what
the finished product of this chapter will be. The List window
you'll be building is shown in Figure 12-1.

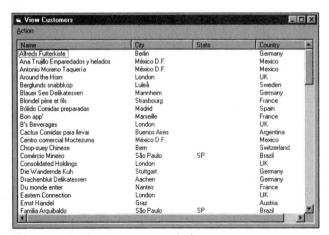

Figure 12-1: View Customers window

This window shows all the customers in the Northwind Traders database. If it looks familiar, it is similar to the window you built in the last chapter. This window is also equipped with a menu that has several action choices on it. The previous window used an MDI form and menus; however, the result is the same. When you choose to add or edit a customer record, the window shown in Figure 12-2 will appear.

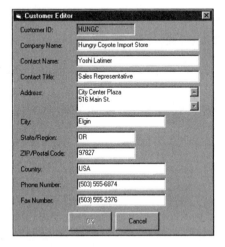

Figure 12-2: Edit Customer window

This window, after being given a `Customer` object, populates itself, detects and handles data changes, and signals the List window when a permanent change has been made. You learn how to build both windows in this chapter.

Building the CCustomer Class

Because the database has already been designed, creating a class is somewhat easier. However, if you were starting from scratch on an application, you'd need to follow the object design steps outlined earlier in Chapter 8. Instead of focusing on building the class, here in this chapter we will focus on how to integrate your class design with your database design. Because an object without a permanent storage location is fairly useless, this code can be helpful in getting your objects to become persistent.

Designing the class

Just like the class built in Chapter 8, your CCustomer class will need a series of accessors and modifiers, each of which maps to a particular attribute of the class. With the database aspect in this design, each attribute maps to a particular field in the Customers table. The accessors and modifiers are listed in Table 12-1, along with their corresponding fields.

Table 12-1	
CCustomer Class Accessors and Modifiers	
Accessor/Modifier Name	*Database Field*
ID	CustomerID
Name	CompanyName
ContactName	ContactName
ContactTitle	ContactTitle
Address	Address
City	City
Region	Region
PostalCode	PostalCode
Country	Country
PhoneNumber	Phone
FaxNumber	Fax

Although the names of the accessors and modifiers are not really important, you can see that a few of them are different from the fields in the database. The class will encapsulate all the database code without a problem.

Besides the accessors and modifiers, the `CCustomer` class will need several additional methods to interact with the database successfully:

✦ `Init`—This method takes care of loading data into the instance of the `CCustomer` class object. It might seem that you could use the `Class_Initialize` event for this function, but that event cannot take any parameters. The event fires automatically whenever you create a new object instance, and does not interact with the rest of the VB application as much as with the Windows event queue. The `Init` method handles anything that requires "outside assistance."

✦ `ValidateData`—This method checks to see if the data in the object is valid. The results of this check are announced to the caller through a custom event, `DataValidated`. This information can then be used to enable or disable action buttons. The event could be expanded to pass along a message indicating why the data is not yet valid. You'll see how to do that later in the chapter.

✦ `Save`—This method is used to store the data held in the object back to the database. The method is smart enough to either add or edit a record based on the way the object was created and initialized. This method can be called as many times as is required by your object. This allows a window to have an object behind it and to let the user save data as he or she proceeds through the window, just as Word or Excel might.

All the database functionality is in the `Init` and `Save` methods. `ValidateData` encapsulates your *business rules*. These rules can be used to make sure all fields are filled, state codes are two letters long, and so on. Because you want to prevent bad data from ever entering your database, the `ValidateData` subroutine is the place to check the data. You'll see how this works shortly.

Note

We are going to suggest some of these business rules, but you might notice the sample database does not follow all of them. For instance, the Region field in the database is not always populated. Based on the data you use, you will have to choose an appropriate set of validation and business rules.

These three—`Init`, `ValidateData`, and `Save`—are the key methods every database-aware class needs. By sticking to a common naming scheme, you can also take advantage of *polymorphism*. This means no matter what object you are editing, you know that you can always call the `Save` method. This is similar to the way that editable controls, for the most part, all have `Text` properties. You may not know specifically what control you are looking at, but because of the way controls were designed, you know you can access the `Text` property to retrieve the contents.

Coding the CCustomer class

To start building the class, you can use the Class Builder to build the accessors and modifiers. Because all the fields in the `CCustomer` class are strings of varying lengths, all your accessors and modifiers should accept and return string values.

Listing 12-1 shows the accessors and modifiers, as well as the private member variables, for the CCustomer class.

Listing 12-1: **CCustomer Accessors and Modifiers**

```
Option Explicit

Private m_sID As String
Private m_sCustomerName As String
Private m_sContactName As String
Private m_sContactTitle As String
Private m_sAddress As String
Private m_sCity As String
Private m_sState As String
Private m_sPostalCode As String
Private m_sCountry As String
Private m_sPhoneNumber As String
Private m_sFaxNumber As String

Public Property Let FaxNumber(ByVal vData As String)
    m_sFaxNumber = vData
    ValidateData
End Property

Public Property Get FaxNumber() As String
    FaxNumber = m_sFaxNumber
End Property

Public Property Let PhoneNumber(ByVal vData As String)
    m_sPhoneNumber = vData
    ValidateData
End Property

Public Property Get PhoneNumber() As String
    PhoneNumber = m_sPhoneNumber
End Property

Public Property Let ContactTitle(ByVal vData As String)
    m_sContactTitle = vData
    ValidateData
End Property
Public Property Get ContactTitle() As String
    ContactTitle = m_sContactTitle

End Property
Public Property Let ContactName(ByVal vData As String)
    m_sContactName = vData
    ValidateData
End Property
```

(continued)

Listing 12-1 *(continued)*

```
Public Property Get ContactName() As String
    ContactName = m_sContactName
End Property

Public Property Let ID(ByVal vData As String)
    m_sID = vData
    ValidateData
End Property

Public Property Get ID() As String
    ID = m_sID
End Property

Public Property Let Country(ByVal vData As String)
    m_sCountry = vData
    ValidateData
End Property

Public Property Get Country() As String
    Country = m_sCountry
End Property

Public Property Let PostalCode(ByVal vData As String)
    m_sPostalCode = vData
    ValidateData
End Property

Public Property Get PostalCode() As String
    PostalCode = m_sPostalCode
End Property

Public Property Let State(ByVal vData As String)
    m_sState = vData
    ValidateData
End Property

Public Property Get State() As String
    State = m_sState
End Property

Public Property Let City(ByVal vData As String)
    m_sCity = vData
    ValidateData
End Property

Public Property Get City() As String
    City = m_sCity
End Property
```

```
Public Property Let Address(ByVal vData As String)
    m_sAddress = vData
    ValidateData
End Property

Public Property Get Address() As String
    Address = m_sAddress
End Property

Public Property Let CustomerName(ByVal sData As String)
    m_sCustomerName = sData
    ValidateData
End Property

Public Property Get CustomerName() As String
    CustomerName = m_sCustomerName
End Property
```

Note that the names of the variables have been changed from the default Class Builder code. Instead of always using mvar as the prefix, the code shown here uses m_ to indicate a member variable, followed by a one-character prefix indicating the data type. Instead of mvarContactName, this code uses m_sContactName, because ContactName is a string data type.

The other change in this code from what the Class Builder creates is that each modifier (the Property Let procedures) calls the ValidateData method immediately after making the data change. The call is made after each change because each change could potentially make the data either valid or invalid. Instead of waiting until the end to check all the data, this lets us check the data as we get the changes.

The Init method is next on the checklist, and its code is shown in Listing 12-2. Make sure you also add the new declarations shown in Listing 12-3 to your class module.

Listing 12-2: **CCustomer Init Method**

```
Public Sub Init(objDB As Database, _
    Optional objRS As Recordset, _
    Optional sID As String = "")

    Dim qdData As QueryDef

    Set m_DB = objDB
```

(continued)

Listing 12-2 *(continued)*

```
' If the ID is missing, the object
' is being instantiated to be filled
' with new data.
'
If sID = "" And objRS Is Nothing Then
   m_bIsNewRecord = True
   Exit Sub
End If

If objRS Is Nothing Then
   '
   ' If no recordset was passed in, open
   ' one up to the correct record. Use a
   ' snapshot since no editing is required.
   '
   Set qdData = objDB.QueryDefs("qryGetCustomer")
   qdData.Parameters("paramCustomerID") = sID
   Set m_RS = qdData.OpenRecordset(dbOpenSnapshot, _
      dbForwardOnly)
Else
   '
   ' If one was passed in, store a reference
   ' to it in the object for use in loading
   ' the object.
   '
   Set m_RS = objRS
End If


' Load each of the private member
' variables with the corresponding
' data from the database.
'
m_sID = m_RS("CustomerID")
m_sCustomerName = m_RS("CompanyName") & ""
m_sContactName = m_RS("ContactName") & ""
m_sContactTitle = m_RS("ContactTitle") & ""
m_sAddress = m_RS("Address") & ""
m_sCity = m_RS("City") & ""
m_sRegion = m_RS("Region") & ""
m_sPostalCode = m_RS("PostalCode") & ""
m_sCountry = m_RS("Country") & ""
m_sPhoneNumber = m_RS("Phone") & ""
m_sFaxNumber = m_RS("Fax") & ""


' Clean up
'
```

```
    m_RS.Close
    Set m_RS = Nothing

End Sub
```

Listing 12-3: **Additional Declarations for CCustomer Class**

```
Private m_bIsNewRecord As Boolean
Private m_DB As Database
Private m_RS As Recordset
```

As you can see from the declaration, the Init() method is pretty flexible. The only parameter it has to have is a valid database object, which is created by the application using the CCustomer class. Using the same database object eliminates the need to open another connection to the database. This saves both time and connection count, which is important if you're dealing with a database that counts the number of connections. Using one database object means one connection.

The Init method is also smart enough to take a preexisting Recordset object. This is especially helpful if you are creating a number of Customer objects, and some outside code is using a recordset to loop through all the customers matching some criteria. This code assumes if a recordset is passed in, it is already positioned at the record that is to be shown.

Because you don't have to pass in a recordset, the object is smart enough to open up its own recordset to load data. The data from each field is loaded into the corresponding member variable. You might notice each field is suffixed with two double-quote characters. Because database fields can be Null, adding an empty string to the contents of the field prevents Invalid Use of Null errors that would occur otherwise.

In cases where an existing record is being edited, the ID parameter is filled in. However, if a new record is being added, the ID field will be blank. In these cases, the m_bIsNewRecord flag is set to True so the Save method can properly save the data to the database.

The Save method is the reverse of Init, and is shown in Listing 12-4.

Listing 12-4: **CCustomer Save Method**

```
Public Sub Save()

    Dim qdData As QueryDef

    '
    ' New records have to be added with
    ' the AddNew method instead of Edit.
    ' The m_bIsNewRecord flag is set in
    ' the Init method.
    '
    If m_bIsNewRecord Then
        Set m_RS = m_DB.OpenRecordset("Customers", _
            dbOpenDynaset, _
            dbSeeChanges, _
            dbPessimistic)
        m_RS.AddNew
    Else
        Set qdData = m_DB.QueryDefs("qryGetCustomer")
        qdData.Parameters("paramCustomerID") = m_sID
        Set m_RS = qdData.OpenRecordset(dbOpenDynaset, _
            dbSeeChanges, dbPessimistic)

        m_RS.Edit
    End If

    '
    ' Update data in each field. If you
    ' are using an AutoNumber field, never
    ' attempt to add/edit data in it. You
    ' will get an error.
    '
    m_RS("CustomerID") = m_sID
    m_RS("CompanyName") = m_sCustomerName
    m_RS("ContactName") = m_sContactName
    m_RS("ContactTitle") = m_sContactTitle
    m_RS("Address") = m_sAddress
    m_RS("City") = m_sCity
    m_RS("Region") = m_sRegion
    m_RS("PostalCode") = m_sPostalCode
    m_RS("Country") = m_sCountry
    m_RS("Phone") = m_sPhoneNumber
    m_RS("Fax") = m_sFaxNumber

    m_RS.Update

    '
    ' Any further changes will only be Edits
    ' and will not require the use of the
    ' AddNew method.
    '
    m_bIsNewRecord = False
```

```
'
' Clean up
'
m_RS.Close
Set m_RS = Nothing

End Sub
```

Note

You'll notice some of the data validation rules have been commented out. This is because the data in the database does not warrant checking these rules. Because some of the data deals with international addresses, the use of a state is not necessary. Also, some businesses do not have fax machines, so that rule has also been commented out. The end result of this check is either True or False, indicating whether or not the data in the object is valid yet.

Based on the m_bIsNewRecord flag, the record is either added or edited in the database. Each of the member variables is stored in its corresponding field, and the data is updated. Notice, once the Save is complete, the m_bIsNewRecord is cleared and set to False. This allows data to be saved again and again without creating a new record every time.

The last method you need to build is the ValidateData method, which is shown in Listing 12-5.

Listing 12-5: **CCustomer ValidateData Method**

```
Private Sub ValidateData()
    Dim bValid As Boolean
    bValid = True

    bValid = bValid And m_sID <> ""
    bValid = bValid And m_sCustomerName <> ""
    bValid = bValid And m_sContactName <> ""

    '
    ' Depending on your situation,
    ' the contact's title may or may not
    ' be required. For now, it's not.
    '
    'bValid = bValid And m_sContactTitle <> ""
    bValid = bValid And m_sAddress <> ""
    bValid = bValid And m_sCity <> ""
    '
    ' Depending on your situation,
    ' the state may or may not
    ' be required. For now, it's not.
```

(continued)

Listing 12-5 *(continued)*

```
'
'bValid = bValid And m_sState <> ""
' US States must be two letters long
'bValid = bValid And Len(m_sState) = 2

bValid = bValid And m_sPostalCode <> ""
bValid = bValid And m_sCountry <> ""
bValid = bValid And m_sPhoneNumber <> ""
'
' Depending on your situation,
' the fax number may or may not
' be required. For now, it's not.
'
'bValid = bValid And m_sFaxNumber <> ""


    RaiseEvent DataValidated(bValid)
End Sub
```

The validation result is used in the DataValidated event to indicate whether the data can be saved yet. DataValidated is a custom event defined in the CCustomer class. Other objects, such as forms where there are CCustomer objects, can listen for this event and respond appropriately. Custom events can be declared in any object module, which is basically any file except one that only has VB code in it. The same rule applies to modules that can listen for these custom events. You'll see how to use this and other events later in this chapter.

For now, add the line shown in Listing 12-6 to the Declarations section of your CCustomer class module.

Listing 12-6: DataValidated Event Declaration in CCustomer Class

```
Public Event DataValidated(bValid As Boolean)
```

That's all the code required for the CCustomer class to work. Of course, your needs will vary when you design your own classes. However, the features shown so far in this chapter will always need to be in every class you design, in one way or another.

Creating the List Window

The List window is fairly simple to create. Follow these steps to build the window:

1. Add a ListView control to your form and set the control's properties as shown in Table 12-2.

Table 12-2 ListView Control Properties	
Property	**Value**
(Name)	ctlListView
FullRowSelect	True
HideColumnHeaders	False
LabelEdit	1 - lvwManual
Sorted	True
SortKey	0
SortOrder	0 - lvwAscending
View	3 - lvwReport

2. Using the Menu Editor, add the menu items listed in Table 12-3 to your form.

Table 12-3 Menu Items	
Caption	**Name**
&Action	mnuAction (top-level menu)
&Add Customer	mnuActionAdd (beneath Action)
&Modify Customer	mnuActionModify (beneath Action)
- (hyphen)	mnuActionDash (beneath Action)
&Exit	mnuExit

The first code you need to add in your form is the Form_Load() event handler, shown in Listing 12-7. Also, add the variable and constant declarations shown in Listing 12-8 to the form.

Listing 12-7: **Form_Load Event Handler**

```
Private Sub Form_Load()

    '
    ' Open the database and load the
    ' records into the window.
    '
    Set m_DB = OpenDatabase("C:\DevStudio\VB\NWind.MDB")
    RefreshData

End Sub
```

Listing 12-8: **Variable Declarations for Form**

```
Option Explicit
Private m_DB As Database
Private Const ITEMPREFIX = "Item"
```

After opening the database object (be sure to adjust the pathname for your system), data needs to be loaded into the window. This task is done by the RefreshData subroutine that should be added to the form. It is shown in Listing 12-9.

Listing 12-9: **RefreshData Subroutine**

```
Public Sub RefreshData()

    Dim rsData As Recordset

    ctlListView.ListItems.Clear

    Set rsData = m_DB.OpenRecordset("Customers", _
        dbOpenSnapshot, dbForwardOnly)
    Do While Not rsData.EOF

        ctlListView.ListItems.Add , _
            ITEMPREFIX & rsData("CustomerID"), _
            rsData("CompanyName")

        With ctlListView.ListItems(ITEMPREFIX _
            & rsData("CustomerID"))
            .SubItems(1) = rsData("City") & ""
            .SubItems(2) = rsData("Region") & ""
```

```
        .SubItems(3) = rsData("Country") & ""
      End With
      rsData.MoveNext
    Loop
    rsData.Close
    Set rsData = Nothing

End Sub
```

This routine loads data from the Customers table and quickly adds each item to the ListView control. Each item's Key property consists of the word "Item" followed by the unique key for the record. In this form, the customer name, city, state/region, and country are listed. You can show whatever fields you like—just be sure to add column headers on the ListView control for whatever headers you wish to use. Once all the records are loaded, the recordset is closed and the form is shown.

While the form is in its event loop, there are several miscellaneous actions that can take place: The window can be resized, or the user can click a column header to re-sort the data. The code for those two actions is shown in Listing 12-10.

Listing 12-10: **Resize and Sort Code**

```
Private Sub ctlListView_ColumnClick _
   (ByVal ColumnHeader As ComctlLib.ColumnHeader)
   '
   ' This code causes the ListView control
   ' to be sorted by the column that was
   ' clicked by the user.
   '
   ctlListView.SortKey = ColumnHeader.Index - 1
   ctlListView.Sorted = True
End Sub

Private Sub Form_Resize()
   On Error Resume Next
   ctlListView.Height = _
      Me.ScaleHeight - (2 * ctlListView.Top)
   ctlListView.Width = _
      Me.ScaleWidth - (2 * ctlListView.Left)

End Sub
```

The ColumnClick event handler enables the user to click a column and have the data sorted by that column. The Resize event handler causes the ListView control to be enlarged to fill the form, less a margin around all the sides.

Now comes the nitty-gritty of this code: adding and editing records. First, add the code in Listing 12-11 to your form. This code calls the appropriate method (which you'll build shortly) when an action is selected from the menu.

Listing 12-11: **Action Menu Code**

```
Private Sub mnuActionAdd_Click()
   Add
End Sub

Private Sub mnuActionModify_Click()
   Edit
End Sub

Private Sub mnuExit_Click()
   Unload Me
End Sub
```

You also need to support the user being able to double-click a row to edit the record underneath. That code is shown in Listing 12-12.

Listing 12-12: **Double-Click Code**

```
Private Sub ctlListView_DblClick()
   '
   ' A double-clicked row is the
   ' same as having Edit picked
   ' from the application's menu.
   '
   Edit
End Sub
```

Now that the triggers are in place, you can write the Add and Edit methods, which are shown in Listing 12-13.

Listing 12-13: **Add and Edit Code**

```
Private Sub Add()
   '
   ' Create a new instance of the Customer
   ' editor window to create a new object.
   '
```

```
        Dim frmEdit As New frmEditCustomer
        frmEdit.Add objDB:=m_DB, frmCaller:=Me

    End Sub

    Private Sub Edit()
        '
        ' Create a new instance of the Customer
        ' editor window and call it with the
        ' existing object.
        '
        Dim frmEdit As New frmEditCustomer
        Dim objCust As New CCustomer
        objCust.Init objDB:=m_DB, _
            sID:=Mid$(ctlListView.SelectedItem.Key, _
          Len(ITEMPREFIX) + 1)
        frmEdit.Edit frmCaller:=Me, objCustomer:=objCust
    End Sub
```

The main task of these two subroutines is to create a new Editor window and to pass the appropriate arguments. For Add mode, the only items that need to be passed are the current database object and a reference to the List window itself. You'll see the need for that reference when you build the Editor window. In Edit mode, the current record's unique ID must also be determined. Because each item's key contains the unique ID, it's just a matter of removing the prefix and sending the rest into the Editor window.

That's all the code required for right now in the List window. You can now move on to the Customer Editor window.

Creating the Customer Editor

The Customer Editor form is pretty simple, and we won't go through each step individually. The main point is to get all the controls on the form and name them properly so that the code presented later makes sense to you. Figure 12-3 shows the Customer Editor, and Table 12-4 lists the controls and the names used in this section's code.

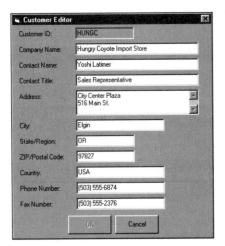

Figure 12-3: Edit Customer window

Table 12-4
Customer Editor Controls

Control Name	Caption (on Control or Next to It)
txtCustomerID	Customer ID:
txtName	Company Name:
txtContactName	Contact Name:
txtContactTitle	Contact Title:
txtAddress	Address:
txtCity	City:
txtState	State/Region:
txtPostalCode	ZIP/Postal Code:
txtCountry	Country:
txtPhoneNumber	Phone Number:
txtFaxNumber	Fax Number:
cmdOK	OK
cmdCancel	Cancel

The only control that needs additional properties set is the txtAddress control, which needs to be set to MultiLine. The rest of the controls' default property values are fine, other than to have their Text properties all cleared (so no text is visible).

With the form built, you can start adding code. The first code you need is the Add method, used to create a new record. Listing 12-14 shows this method along with the declarations needed for this form.

Listing 12-14: **Add Method and Form Declarations**

```
Option Explicit
Private m_DB As Database
Private m_frmCalledBy As frmListCustomers
Private m_iMode As Integer
Private m_bDirty As Boolean
Private Const MODE_ADD = 1
Private WithEvents m_objCust As CCustomer

Public Sub Add(objDB As Database, frmCaller As Form)
    Set m_DB = objDB
    Set m_frmCalledBy = frmCaller
    Set m_objCust = New CCustomer
    m_objCust.Init objDB:=m_DB
    m_iMode = MODE_ADD
    RefreshData
    Me.Show
End Sub
```

After saving the references to the database and the calling form, the preceding code creates a new Customer object and stores a constant to indicate that the form is in Add mode. This is important when data is saved in this window, because it signals the List window to update itself. There is an alternate way to write this form, which will be presented at the end, that uses a custom event on the form to signal the calling window that data needs to be updated. Both techniques are equally valid and require about the same amount of coding.

The next method you can add is the Edit method. This code is shown in Listing 12-15.

Listing 12-15: **Edit Method Code**

```
Public Sub Edit(frmCaller As Form, _
    objCustomer As CCustomer)

    Set m_frmCalledBy = frmCaller
    Set m_objCust = objCustomer
    RefreshData
    '
    ' In Edit mode, customer ID is
    ' not editable.
    '
    txtCustomerID.Locked = True
    txtCustomerID.BackColor = vbButtonFace
    txtCustomerID.TabStop = False

    Me.Show
End Sub
```

This technique does basically the same thing as the code in Listing 12-14, but because we made the decision that the customer IDs are not editable, this method locks the customer ID field so that the data cannot be changed.

The RefreshData subroutine takes care of loading the contents of a Customer object into the form. That code is shown in Listing 12-16.

Listing 12-16: **RefreshData Method Code**

```
Private Sub RefreshData()
    txtCustomerID = m_objCust.ID
    txtName = m_objCust.CustomerName
    txtContactName = m_objCust.ContactName
    txtContactTitle = m_objCust.ContactTitle
    txtAddress = m_objCust.Address
    txtCity = m_objCust.City
    txtState = m_objCust.State
    txtPostalCode = m_objCust.PostalCode
    txtCountry = m_objCust.Country
    txtPhoneNumber = m_objCust.PhoneNumber
    txtFaxNumber = m_objCust.FaxNumber

    cmdOK.Enabled = False
    m_bDirty = False

End Sub
```

Now that the data has been loaded into the form, you need to add code to detect and store changes to that data. Listing 12-17 shows this code for each of the controls on the form.

Listing 12-17: **Change Event Code**

```
Private Sub txtCustomerID_Change()
    m_objCust.ID = txtCustomerID
End Sub

Private Sub txtName_Change()
    m_objCust.CustomerName = txtName
End Sub

Private Sub txtContactName_Change()
    m_objCust.ContactName = txtContactName
End Sub

Private Sub txtContactTitle_Change()
    m_objCust.ContactTitle = txtContactTitle
End Sub

Private Sub txtAddress_Change()
    m_objCust.Address = txtAddress
End Sub

Private Sub txtCity_Change()
    m_objCust.City = txtCity
End Sub

Private Sub txtState_Change()
    m_objCust.State = txtState
End Sub

Private Sub txtPostalCode_Change()
    m_objCust.PostalCode = txtPostalCode
End Sub

Private Sub txtCountry_Change()
    m_objCust.Country = txtCountry
End Sub

Private Sub txtPhoneNumber_Change()
    m_objCust.PhoneNumber = txtPhoneNumber
End Sub

Private Sub txtFaxNumber_Change()
    m_objCust.FaxNumber = txFaxNumber
End Sub
```

As each box changes, the changes are immediately stored in the Customer object. Remember that, in the code from the Customer object modifiers, the data is immediately validated and an event is generated indicating whether the data is valid. To receive that event in this form, the m_objCust variable was declared using the WithEvents keyword, as shown in this excerpt from the Declarations section of the form:

```
Private WithEvents m_objCust As CCustomer
```

You should see in the left-hand drop-down list box on the Code window for the form an entry for m_objCust. Because you told VB the object could have events, VB has made it available for you to write code for it. Add the code in Listing 12-18 to your form.

Listing 12-18: **DataValidated Event Code**

```
Private Sub m_objCust_DataValidated(bValid As Boolean)
    cmdOK.Enabled = bValid
    m_bDirty = True
End Sub
```

As data is validated, the OK button is enabled or disabled, as appropriate. In addition, since data is being changed, the m_bDirty flag is set to True so that changes can be saved when the window is closed, which happens to be the code shown in Listing 12-19.

Listing 12-19: **CommandButton Code**

```
Private Sub cmdOK_Click()
    Save
    Unload Me
End Sub

Private Sub cmdCancel_Click()
    Unload Me
End Sub

Private Sub Save()
    m_objCust.Save
    If m_iMode = MODE_ADD Then
        m_frmCalledBy.AddListItem m_objCust
    Else
        m_frmCalledBy.EditListItem m_objCust
    End If
    m_bDirty = False
End Sub

Private Sub Form_QueryUnload _
    (Cancel As Integer, UnloadMode As Integer)
```

```
        Dim iRet As Integer
        If m_bDirty Then
           iRet = MsgBox("Save changes?", _
              vbQuestion + vbYesNoCancel)
           Select Case iRet
           Case vbYes
              Save
           Case vbCancel
              Cancel = True
           End Select
        End If

    End Sub

    Private Sub Form_Unload(Cancel As Integer)
       Set m_frmEdit = Nothing
    End Sub
```

The Save subroutine determines if the current record is being added or edited and, after saving the data, calls the appropriate method on the List window that spawned this window to open. To make this work, however, you need to add the code in Listing 12-20 *to the List window*.

Listing 12-20: **List Window Public Methods**

```
Public Sub AddListItem(objCust As CCustomer)
    '
    ' This public method is called after a
    ' new record has been successfully added.
    ' It creates a new ListItem object and
    ' then updates the other columns of the
    ' ListItem.
    '
    ctlListView.ListItems.Add , _
        ITEMPREFIX & objCust.ID, _
        objCust.CustomerName
    EditListItem objCust
End Sub

Public Sub EditListItem(objCust As CCustomer)
    '
    ' This public method is called by forms
    ' that are editing the contents of the
    ' form. This method is also called
    ' internally to fill the listitem with
    ' the other attributes of the object.
```

(continued)

Listing 12-20 *(continued)*

```
    '
    With ctlListView.ListItems(ITEMPREFIX & objCust.ID)
        .Text = objCust.CustomerName
        .SubItems(1) = objCust.City
        .SubItems(2) = objCust.State
        .SubItems(3) = objCust.Country
    End With
End Sub
```

These two methods take care of adding or updating an item on the ListView window.

Having two methods does help to divide up the logic, but there are several other options for handling this function. The first option is to combine these two methods into a single method that is called by the Customer Editor window. The code for the List window is shown in Listing 12-21.

Listing 12-21: Combined UpdateListItem() Method

```
Public Sub UpdateListItem(objCust As CCustomer)
    Dim objCurrItem As ListItem

    '
    ' Since accessing an item that doesn't
    ' exist will cause an error, "disable"
    ' the error handler temporarily.
    '
    On Error Resume Next
    Set objCurrItem = _
        ctlListView.ListItems(ITEMPREFIX & objCust.ID)
    If objCurrItem Is Nothing Then
        Set objCurrItem = _
            ctlListView.ListItems.Add(, _
            ITEMPREFIX & objCust.ID, _
            objCust.CustomerName)
    End If

    With objCurrItem
        .Text = objCust.CustomerName
        .SubItems(1) = objCust.City
        .SubItems(2) = objCust.State
        .SubItems(3) = objCust.Country
    End With

End Sub
```

This code takes advantage of the fact that an error will occur if the code attempts to access a ListItem that doesn't exist (when a new record is added). It then adds that item and proceeds to change the SubItem values. Existing items simply have their fields updated.

The code changes required in the Edit window to make this code work are shown in Listing 12-22.

Listing 12-22: **Modified Save Code for Edit Window**

```
Private Sub Save()
    m_objCust.Save
    m_frmCalledBy.UpdateListItem m_objCust
    m_bDirty = False
End Sub
```

The final way to simplify this code is to employ a user-defined event on the Edit form that the List form can listen for. The event is used to signal when data has been changed in an Edit window. Several changes are required to make this work — among them, changes to the Add and Edit methods on the List window. Those changes are shown in Listing 12-23.

Listing 12-23: **Modified Add and Edit Methods on List Window**

```
Private Sub Add()
    '
    ' Create a new instance of the Customer
    ' editor window.
    '
    Set m_frmEdit = New frmEditCustomer
    m_frmEdit.Add objDB:=m_DB

End Sub

Private Sub Edit()
    Dim objCust As New CCustomer
    Set m_frmEdit = New frmEditCustomer
    objCust.Init objDB:=m_DB, _
        sID:=Mid$(ctlListView.SelectedItem.Key, _
        Len(ITEMPREFIX) + 1)
    m_frmEdit.Edit objCustomer:=objCust
End Sub
```

The first difference is that frmEdit needs to be declared in the Declarations section as follows:

```
Private WithEvents m_frmEdit As frmEditCustomer
```

Any objects that have user-defined events must be declared as object-level variables in order for VB to recognize the events. The other difference is that all references to frmCaller have been eliminated. Because the Edit window will be signaling the List window with an event, no reference to the List window is needed.

The changes to the Edit window are somewhat more extensive, but similar. First of all, add the following line to the Declarations section of the Edit window.

```
Public Event DataSaved(objCust As CCustomer)
```

This will be the event the List window will listen for. Next, change the Add and Edit methods to resemble the code in Listing 12-24.

Listing 12-24: **Edit Window Methods**

```
Public Sub Add(objDB As Database)
    Set m_DB = objDB
    Set m_objCust = New CCustomer
    m_objCust.Init objDB:=m_DB
    RefreshData
    Me.Show
End Sub

Public Sub Edit(objCustomer As CCustomer)
    Set m_objCust = objCustomer
    RefreshData
    '
    ' In Edit mode, customer ID is
    ' not editable.
    '
    txtCustomerID.Locked = True
    txtCustomerID.BackColor = vbButtonFace
    txtCustomerID.TabStop = False

    Me.Show
End Sub
```

The frmCaller parameter has been removed, as have the references to which mode the form is in. The last change required to the Edit window is shown in Listing 12-25. Instead of calling the UpdateListItem method, you raise the DataSaved event.

Listing 12-25: **Save Method for Edit Window**

```
Private Sub Save()
   m_objCust.Save
   RaiseEvent DataSaved(m_objCust)
   m_bDirty = False
End Sub
```

To respond to this event, add the code in Listing 12-26 to the List window.

Listing 12-26: **DataSaved Event Handler for List Window**

```
Private Sub m_frmEdit_DataSaved(objCust As CCustomer)
   UpdateListItem objCust
End Sub
```

Your form works exactly the same way, except now the Editor does not talk directly to the List window. Depending on your own preference, you may like one version over the other. VB gives you the flexibility to use either method with the same results.

Final Notes

A number of things done in this example were design choices. For instance, the validation is done for every character. The benefit of this method is that every change can potentially alter the state of the OK button on the Edit window. This choice entails running a simple validation each time the user enters data. However, if you have complicated validation rules, this could be time-consuming. One option would be to split validation into two stages. The first stage handles the simple things, like whether the data is there. The second stage could handle the more complicated validations, such as checking whether a selected item is part of a database validation table. You'll have to make these types of choices based on the validation you'll be doing in your own application.

Some other choices were made regarding the level of object-oriented programming used. The List window read directly from the database; the Edit window used an object for dealing with customer records. This choice was made because it is inefficient to create objects for every item in a large list. An alternative to reading directly from the database would be to build a class that knows how to populate a List window. In that way, the database activity could be contained in a class module and not be directly in a form. The choice to use either direct access, classes, or a hybrid approach is really up to you.

Summary

Because many of the applications built with Visual Basic involve a database of some sort, it's important to learn how to combine your object-oriented programming with your database programming. By combining the two technologies, you can make your code easier to use and easier to maintain.

On multideveloper project teams, encapsulation of database logic becomes even more important. Because new programmers aren't going to understand how to access Oracle stored procedures, for instance, that logic should be buried in your class so that the new programmers can't modify or break the pretested code.

Encapsulation also provides you with the ability to change the underlying logic without breaking all the code that uses the object. As long as the external methods stay the same, you can change the underlying code to your heart's delight and no one will know the difference.

✦   ✦   ✦

Encapsulating Database Functionality – Part 2

◆ ◆ ◆ ◆

In This Chapter

Designing collection classes

Designing complex classes that use other classes

Building database design features into your classes

◆ ◆ ◆ ◆

As you saw in the last chapter, you can do quite a bit, even with a simple class, when you hook your class up with a permanent storage facility such as a database. This chapter will build on that knowledge and show you how to take your more-complex classes and integrate them with the database. You'll also see how to build collections of objects that are also database aware.

This chapter shows you how to build a series of classes to represent the data stored in the Northwind Traders database. Most of the classes are fairly simple; however, you will see how to expand the functionality you've already observed to make the classes work with collection objects that you can also build. You also see how to add features to your collection classes to make them more intelligent and easier to use.

Designing Collection Classes

Collections are essentially bags into which you can place objects. Visual Basic itself includes many collections, such as the Fields and Controls collections. Objects in a collection are not ordered as they are in an array. You can immediately access any member of a collection just by using a key, as you did with the TreeView and ListView controls in previous chapters. You can also iterate through all the objects in a collection with the For Each/Next syntax provided by Visual Basic.

This section shows you how to build a collection class that can be loaded from a database in the same way that a singular class (like the CCustomer class from the last chapter) is. You'll be building a collection of COrderDetail objects, which will be part of the complete COrder object you'll build later in the chapter. You will actually need to build a number of objects in order to create a single COrderDetail object. This is because the COrderDetail object refers to a CProduct, which then refers to a CSupplier and a Category. These classes are fairly simple to build, and implement many of the same features from the previous chapters.

When designing a series of classes, it is easiest to design from the top down but to implement from the bottom up. The structure of the data is as shown in Figure 13-1.

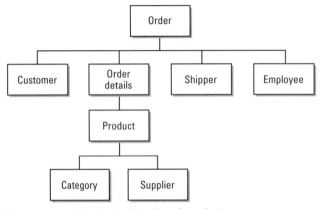

Figure 13-1: Northwind Traders data design

Building the simple classes

Before you can build the complex classes, such as the COrder and COrderDetail classes, you need to build the simple ones that are used by those complex ones. According to the design, there are five simple classes:

- ✦ CCustomer
- ✦ CSupplier
- ✦ CCategory
- ✦ CShipper
- ✦ CEmployee

Each of these classes follows the same pattern as those you built in previous chapters. Each class, besides its accessors and modifiers, will need the following subroutines and functions:

✦ Init()

✦ Save()

✦ ValidateData()

✦ IsValid() **property**

✦ DataValidated() **event**

In addition, these variables need to be declared for each class:

```
Private m_bIsNewRecord As Boolean
Private m_bIsDataValid As Boolean
Private m_DB As Database
Private m_RS As Recordset
```

Creating the CCustomer class

With the laundry list out of the way, let's look at the CCustomer class. This class code is slightly different from that in previous chapters. However, the code is easy to understand. The declarations and standard Property procedures are listed in Listing 13-1.

Listing 13-1: **CCustomer Class Declarations and Property Procedures**

```
Option Explicit

Private m_sID As String
Private m_sCustomerName As String
Private m_sContactName As String
Private m_sContactTitle As String
Private m_sAddress As String
Private m_sCity As String
Private m_sRegion As String
Private m_sPostalCode As String
Private m_sCountry As String
Private m_sPhoneNumber As String
Private m_sFaxNumber As String

Private m_bIsNewRecord As Boolean
Private m_bIsDataValid As Boolean
Private m_DB As Database
Private m_RS As Recordset

Public Event DataValidated(bValid As Boolean)
```

(continued)

Listing 13-1 *(continued)*

```vb
Public Property Let FaxNumber(ByVal vData As String)
    m_sFaxNumber = vData
    ValidateData
End Property

Public Property Get FaxNumber() As String
    FaxNumber = m_sFaxNumber
End Property

Public Property Let PhoneNumber(ByVal vData As String)
    m_sPhoneNumber = vData
    ValidateData
End Property

Public Property Get PhoneNumber() As String
    PhoneNumber = m_sPhoneNumber
End Property

Public Property Let ContactTitle(ByVal vData As String)
    m_sContactTitle = vData
    ValidateData
End Property

Public Property Get ContactTitle() As String
    ContactTitle = m_sContactTitle
End Property

Public Property Let ContactName(ByVal vData As String)
    m_sContactName = vData
    ValidateData
End Property

Public Property Get ContactName() As String
    ContactName = m_sContactName
End Property

Public Property Let ID(ByVal vData As String)
    m_sID = vData
    ValidateData
End Property

Public Property Get ID() As String
    ID = m_sID
End Property

Public Property Let Country(ByVal vData As String)
    m_sCountry = vData
    ValidateData
End Property
```

```
Public Property Get Country() As String
    Country = m_sCountry
End Property

Public Property Let PostalCode(ByVal vData As String)
    m_sPostalCode = vData
    ValidateData
End Property

Public Property Get PostalCode() As String
    PostalCode = m_sPostalCode
End Property

Public Property Let Region(ByVal vData As String)
    m_sRegion = vData
    ValidateData
End Property

Public Property Get Region() As String
    Region = m_sRegion
End Property

Public Property Let City(ByVal vData As String)
    m_sCity = vData
    ValidateData
End Property

Public Property Get City() As String
    City = m_sCity
End Property

Public Property Let Address(ByVal vData As String)
    m_sAddress = vData
    ValidateData
End Property

Public Property Get Address() As String
    Address = m_sAddress
End Property

Public Property Let CustomerName(ByVal sData As String)
    m_sCustomerName = sData
    ValidateData
End Property

Public Property Get CustomerName() As String
    Name = m_sCustomerName
End Property
```

As before, each `Property Let` procedure calls the `ValidateData` subroutine to check the data for validity. You should also notice that the private member variables are prefixed differently than in the code the Class Builder creates. The new naming convention makes it easier to determine the data type of the variable. For the `CCustomer` class, all variables are strings, so it doesn't help much. However, `mvar` is just not descriptive.

The subroutine and `Property` procedure used to validate the data are shown in Listing 13-2.

Listing 13-2: **ValidateData and IsValid**

```
Public Property Get IsValid() As Boolean
    '
    ' This property is available when having
    ' an event trigger is not always helpful.
    ' It can also be used within objects that
    ' contain this one. This object can be
    ' queried as part of the other object's
    ' validation routines.
    '
    IsValid = m_bIsDataValid
End Property

Private Sub ValidateData()
    Dim bValid As Boolean
    bValid = True

    bValid = bValid And m_sCustomerID <> ""
    bValid = bValid And m_sCustomerName <> ""
    bValid = bValid And m_sContactName <> ""

    '
    ' Depending on your situation,
    ' the contact's title may or may not
    ' be required. For now, it's not.
    '
    'bValid = bValid And m_sContactTitle <> ""
    bValid = bValid And m_sAddress <> ""
    bValid = bValid And m_sCity <> ""
    '
    ' Depending on your situation,
    ' the Region may or may not
    ' be required. For now, it's not.
    '
    'bValid = bValid And m_sRegion <> ""
    ' US States must be two letters long
    'bValid = bValid And Len(m_sRegion) = 2

    bValid = bValid And m_sPostalCode <> ""
```

```
    bValid = bValid And m_sCountry <> ""
    bValid = bValid And m_sPhoneNumber <> ""
    '
    ' Depending on your situation,
    ' the fax number may or may not
    ' be required. For now, it's not.
    '
    'bValid = bValid And m_sFaxNumber <> ""

    m_bIsDataValid = bValid
    RaiseEvent DataValidated(bValid)
End Sub
```

The IsValid property allows the object to be checked for validity on demand instead of just via the event. This allows other objects, as part of their validation routines, to check the Customer object to make sure it is valid. The ValidateData subroutine is the same as before. The result of the validation check is stored in the m_bIsDataValid variable for later use.

The object initialization code and Init method are shown in Listing 13-3.

Listing 13-3: **Init Method and Class_Initialize Event Handler**

```
Private Sub Class_Initialize()
    ValidateData
End Sub

Public Sub Init(objDB As Database, _
    Optional objRS As Recordset, _
    Optional sID As String = "")

    Dim qdData As QueryDef

    Set m_DB = objDB

    '
    ' If the ID is missing, the object
    ' is being instantiated to be filled
    ' with new data.
    '
    If sID = "" And objRS Is Nothing Then
        m_bIsNewRecord = True
        Exit Sub
    End If
```

(continued)

Listing 13-3 *(continued)*

```
If objRS Is Nothing Then
    '
    ' If no recordset was passed in, open
    ' one up to the correct record. Use a
    ' snapshot since no editing is required.
    '
    Set qdData = m_DB.QueryDefs("qryGetCustomer")
    qdData.Parameters("paramCustomerID") = sID
    Set m_RS = qdData.OpenRecordset(dbOpenSnapshot, _
        dbForwardOnly)
Else
    '
    ' If one was passed in, store a reference
    ' to it in the object for use in loading
    ' the object.
    '
    Set m_RS = objRS
End If

'
' Load each of the private member
' variables with the corresponding
' data from the database.
'
m_sID = m_RS("CustomerID")
m_sCustomerName = m_RS("CompanyName") & ""
m_sContactName = m_RS("ContactName") & ""
m_sContactTitle = m_RS("ContactTitle") & ""
m_sAddress = m_RS("Address") & ""
m_sCity = m_RS("City") & ""
m_sRegion = m_RS("Region") & ""
m_sPostalCode = m_RS("PostalCode") & ""
m_sCountry = m_RS("Country") & ""
m_sPhoneNumber = m_RS("Phone") & ""
m_sFaxNumber = m_RS("Fax") & ""

'
' Clean up
'
m_RS.Close
Set m_RS = Nothing

End Sub
```

The `ValidateData` subroutine is immediately called to check any existing data when the object is created. This will have the effect of signaling an Edit window not to allow a `Save` until more data is added to the object.

`Init` is the same as in the preceding chapter, but here's a refresher on its functions. First, if no unique record ID was passed in, the assertion is made that this object is going to be filled later in the program. In this case, the `m_bIsNewRecord` flag is set and the `Init` method ends. Using the `Exit Sub` statement makes the logic simpler to follow later in the subroutine because you needn't worry about where the `End If` statements are.

Once the `Init` method has determined an ID was passed in, it has to determine whether a recordset object was passed in. When you build your collection of `COrderDetail` objects, you will use this feature to speed the process of creating objects. The `CCustomer` class will probably not be a part of a collection; however, it is always good to plan ahead and make your classes consistent.

If no recordset was passed in, one needs to be created. Because the data is being read, the `dbForwardOnly` flag makes the snapshot load more quickly. The query is built using a predefined query in Access. You can use a similar procedure for Oracle or SQL Server stored procedures. (You could also opt to use as an SQL statement and omit the parameter creation.) The Query Definition window, which is part of Access 97, is shown in Figure 13-2.

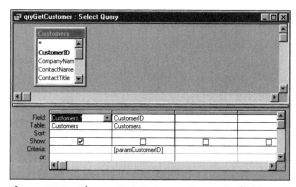

Figure 13-2: The qryGetCustomer Query Definition window in Access

This query accepts one parameter: `paramCustomerID`. After filling that in and creating a recordset, the data is loaded into each of the fields in the object. Because this object does not contain other objects, this process is fairly simple. As you can see in the more-complex objects, you actually have to create new objects as part of the `Init` method.

You might be wondering why a query was created in Access instead of just using an SQL string. As you've probably seen, SQL strings are fairly ugly to break into multiple lines in VB. Predefined queries have two benefits: (1) You don't have to deal with the actual SQL; and (2) They run faster because the database has already compiled them. This is especially true in cases where you are joining multiple tables together.

The last method to cover is the Save method, which is shown in Listing 13-4.

Listing 13-4: **Save Method for CCustomer Class**

```
Public Sub Save()

   Dim qdData As QueryDef

   '
   ' New records have to be added with
   ' the AddNew method instead of Edit.
   ' The m_bIsNewRecord flag is set in
   ' the Init method.
   '
   If m_bIsNewRecord Then
      Set m_RS = m_DB.OpenRecordset("Customers", _
         dbOpenDynaset, _
         dbSeeChanges, _
         dbPessimistic)
      m_RS.AddNew
   Else
      Set qdData = m_DB.QueryDefs("qryGetCustomer")
      qdData.Parameters("paramCustomerID") = m_sID
      Set m_RS = qdData.OpenRecordset(dbOpenDynaset, _
         dbSeeChanges, _
         dbPessimistic)

      m_RS.Edit
   End If


   '
   ' Update data in each field. If you
   ' are using an AutoNumber field, never
   ' attempt to add/edit data in it. You
   ' will get an error.
   '
   m_RS("CustomerID") = m_sID
   m_RS("CompanyName") = m_sCustomerName
   m_RS("ContactName") = m_sContactName
   m_RS("ContactTitle") = m_sContactTitle
   m_RS("Address") = m_sAddress
   m_RS("City") = m_sCity
   m_RS("Region") = m_sRegion
   m_RS("PostalCode") = m_sPostalCode
```

```
    m_RS("Country") = m_sCountry
    m_RS("Phone") = m_sPhoneNumber
    m_RS("Fax") = m_sFaxNumber

    m_RS.Update

    '
    ' Any further changes will only be Edits
    ' and will not require the use of the
    ' AddNew method.
    '
    m_bIsNewRecord = False
    '
    ' Clean up
    '
    m_RS.Close
    Set m_RS = Nothing

End Sub
```

This Save method is similar to the previous one you built, except that this one uses the same predefined query to retrieve the record to be edited. For new records, the table is opened and the AddNew method is used to add a new record. Each of the fields is copied from the private member variables of the object, the record is updated, and the recordset is closed.

One thing this class does not do that you might want to do is to refresh the data from the database after the record has been saved. This enables you to have default and autofilled values in the database and have them show up in the object. This is important if you plan to keep your object around. In this case, because the Customer ID is text and supplied by the user, this code is not necessary.

That's all the code you need for the CCustomer object. If you want to test it, add a module to your project and use the code shown in Listing 13-5.

Listing 13-5: **CCustomer Test Code**

```
Sub Main()
    Dim db As Database
    Dim objCust As New CCustomer

    Set db = OpenDatabase("E:\DevStudio\VB\NWind.MDB")
    objCust.Init objDB:=db, sID:="CHOPS"
    Debug.Print "Before changing ContactName"
    Debug.Print objCust.CustomerName
    Debug.Print objCust.ContactName
```

(continued)

Listing 13-5: **CCustomer Test Code**

```
Debug.Print objCust.ContactTitle
objCust.ContactName = "Eric Smith"
objCust.Save
Set objCust = Nothing


Set objCust = New CCustomer
objCust.Init objDB:=db, sID:="CHOPS"
Debug.Print "After changing ContactName"
Debug.Print objCust.CustomerName
Debug.Print objCust.ContactName
Debug.Print objCust.ContactTitle
Set objCust = Nothing
db.Close
Set db = Nothing

End Sub
```

This code first opens the database and instantiates a CCustomer object to represent *Chop-suey Chinese*. It prints out a few lines, makes a change to the ContactName and saves the object. Just to make sure it works, the CCustomer instance is erased and re-created before reprinting the same information. The results of this should show the change to the object's data, as shown in the following results:

Before changing ContactName

    Chop-suey Chinese

    Yang Wang

    Owner

After changing ContactName

    Chop-suey Chinese

    Eric Smith

    Owner

As you can see, the ContactName property was successfully changed in the database. By re-creating the object, you can make sure the data is saved correctly. This type of test code is great to use when you're first building your objects, so you don't have to build windows or other GUI objects to test them.

Creating the CSupplier class

The CSupplier class is fairly similar to the CCustomer class, so Listing 13-6 shows only the declarations and the nonstandard subroutines and functions. Be sure to add the call to ValidateData in each Property Let statement.

Listing 13-6: **CSupplier Class Subroutines and Functions**

```
Option Explicit

Private m_lngID As Long
Private m_sSupplierName As String
Private m_sContactName As String
Private m_sContactTitle As String
Private m_sAddress As String
Private m_sCity As String
Private m_sPostalCode As String
Private m_sCountry As String
Private m_sPhoneNumber As String
Private m_sFaxNumber As String
Private m_sRegion As String
Private m_sHomepage As String

Private m_bIsNewRecord As Boolean
Private m_bIsDataValid As Boolean
Private m_DB As Database
Private m_RS As Recordset

Public Event DataValidated(bValid As Boolean)

Public Property Get IsValid() As Boolean
    '
    ' This property is available when having
    ' an event trigger is not always helpful.
    ' It can also be used within objects that
    ' contain this one. This object can be
    ' queried as part of the other object's
    ' validation routines.
    '
    IsValid = m_bIsDataValid
End Property

Private Sub ValidateData()
    Dim bValid As Boolean
    bValid = True

    bValid = bValid And m_sSupplierName <> ""
    bValid = bValid And m_sContactName <> ""

    '
```

(continued)

Listing 13-6 *(continued)*

```vb
      ' Depending on your situation,
      ' the contact's title may or may not
      ' be required. For now, it's not.
      '
      'bValid = bValid And m_sContactTitle <> ""
      bValid = bValid And m_sAddress <> ""
      bValid = bValid And m_sCity <> ""
      '
      ' Depending on your situation,
      ' the Region may or may not
      ' be required. For now, it's not.
      '
      'bValid = bValid And m_sRegion <> ""
      ' US States must be two letters long
      'bValid = bValid And Len(m_sRegion) = 2

      bValid = bValid And m_sPostalCode <> ""
      bValid = bValid And m_sCountry <> ""
      bValid = bValid And m_sPhoneNumber <> ""
      '
      ' Depending on your situation,
      ' the fax number may or may not
      ' be required. For now, it's not.
      '
      'bValid = bValid And m_sFaxNumber <> ""

   m_bIsDataValid = bValid
   RaiseEvent DataValidated(bValid)
End Sub

Private Sub Class_Initialize()
   ValidateData
End Sub

Public Sub Init(objDB As Database, _
   Optional objRS As Recordset, _
   Optional lngID As Long = -1)

   Dim qdData As QueryDef

   Set m_DB = objDB

   '
   ' If the ID is missing, the object
   ' is being instantiated to be filled
   ' with new data.
   '
   If lngID = -1 And objRS Is Nothing Then
      m_bIsNewRecord = True
      Exit Sub
   End If
```

```
    If objRS Is Nothing Then
        '
        ' If no recordset was passed in, open
        ' one up to the correct record. Use a
        ' snapshot since no editing is required.
        '
        Set qdData = objDB.QueryDefs("qryGetSupplier")
        qdData.Parameters("paramSupplierID") = lngID
        Set m_RS = qdData.OpenRecordset(dbOpenSnapshot, _
            dbForwardOnly)
    Else
        '
        ' If one was passed in, store a reference
        ' to it in the object for use in loading
        ' the object.
        '
        Set m_RS = objRS
    End If

    '
    ' Load each of the private member
    ' variables with the corresponding
    ' data from the database.
    '
    m_lngID = m_RS("SupplierID")
    m_sSupplierName = m_RS("CompanyName") & ""
    m_sContactName = m_RS("ContactName") & ""
    m_sContactTitle = m_RS("ContactTitle") & ""
    m_sAddress = m_RS("Address") & ""
    m_sCity = m_RS("City") & ""
    m_sRegion = m_RS("Region") & ""
    m_sPostalCode = m_RS("PostalCode") & ""
    m_sCountry = m_RS("Country") & ""
    m_sPhoneNumber = m_RS("Phone") & ""
    m_sFaxNumber = m_RS("Fax") & ""
    m_sHomepage = m_RS("HomePage") & ""


    '
    ' Clean up
    '
    m_RS.Close
    Set m_RS = Nothing

End Sub

Public Sub Save()

    Dim qdData As QueryDef

    '
    ' New records have to be added with
```

(continued)

Listing 13-6 *(continued)*

```
' the AddNew method instead of Edit.
' The m_bIsNewRecord flag is set in
' the Init method.
'
If m_bIsNewRecord Then
   Set m_RS = m_DB.OpenRecordset("Suppliers", _
       dbOpenDynaset, _
       dbSeeChanges, _
       dbPessimistic)
   m_RS.AddNew
Else
   Set qdData = m_DB.QueryDefs("qryGetSupplier")
   qdData.Parameters("paramSupplierID") = m_lngID
   Set m_RS = qdData.OpenRecordset(dbOpenDynaset, _
       dbSeeChanges, dbPessimistic)

   m_RS.Edit
End If


' Update data in each field. If you
' are using an AutoNumber field, never
' attempt to add/edit data in it. You
' will get an error.
'
'm_RS("SupplierID") = m_lngID
m_RS("CompanyName") = m_sSupplierName
m_RS("ContactName") = m_sContactName
m_RS("ContactTitle") = m_sContactTitle
m_RS("Address") = m_sAddress
m_RS("City") = m_sCity
m_RS("Region") = m_sRegion
m_RS("PostalCode") = m_sPostalCode
m_RS("Country") = m_sCountry
m_RS("Phone") = m_sPhoneNumber
m_RS("Fax") = m_sFaxNumber
m_RS("HomePage") = m_sHomepage
m_RS.Update


' Any further changes will only be Edits
' and will not require the use of the
' AddNew method.
'
m_bIsNewRecord = False
'
' Clean up
'
m_RS.Close
```

```
        Set m_RS = Nothing

End Sub
```

The main difference between the CCustomer and CSupplier classes is that the SupplierID field is an AutoNumber field that is filled when the record is created. This field cannot be edited and is left out of the Save method. In addition, there is no Property Let procedure to modify the record's ID. Other than that, the code is similar. The same method for retrieving supplier information (a predefined query) was used, and this new query was added to the database. Also, because some of the fields are optional, make sure you set the AllowZeroLength fields on any database fields that are optional.

Creating the CCategory class

The CCategory class is one of the simplest in the database. It also follows the same pattern as the other classes so far, so again only the nonstandard code is shown in Listing 13-7.

Listing 13-7: **CCategory Declarations and Code**

```
Option Explicit

Private m_lngID As Long
Private m_sCategoryName As String
Private m_sDescription As String

Private m_bIsNewRecord As Boolean
Private m_bIsDataValid As Boolean
Private m_DB As Database
Private m_RS As Recordset

Public Event DataValidated(bValid As Boolean)

Public Property Get IsValid() As Boolean
    '
    ' This property is available when having
    ' an event trigger is not always helpful.
    ' It can also be used within objects that
    ' contain this one. This object can be
    ' queried as part of the other object's
    ' validation routines.
    '
    IsValid = m_bIsDataValid
End Property
```

(continued)

Listing 13-7 *(continued)*

```vb
Private Sub ValidateData()
    Dim bValid As Boolean
    bValid = True

    bValid = bValid And m_sCategoryName <> ""
    bValid = bValid And m_sDescription <> ""

    m_bIsDataValid = bValid
    RaiseEvent DataValidated(bValid)

End Sub

Private Sub Class_Initialize()
    ValidateData
End Sub

Public Sub Init(objDB As Database, _
    Optional objRS As Recordset, _
    Optional lngID As Long = -1)

    Dim qdData As QueryDef

    Set m_DB = objDB

    '
    ' If the ID is missing, the object
    ' is being instantiated to be filled
    ' with new data.
    '
    If lngID = -1 And objRS Is Nothing Then
        m_bIsNewRecord = True
        Exit Sub
    End If

    If objRS Is Nothing Then
        '
        ' If no recordset was passed in, open
        ' one up to the correct record. Use a
        ' snapshot since no editing is required.
        '
        Set qdData = objDB.QueryDefs("qryGetCategory")
        qdData.Parameters("paramCategoryID") = lngID
        Set m_RS = qdData.OpenRecordset(dbOpenSnapshot, _
            dbForwardOnly)
    Else
        '
        ' If one was passed in, store a reference
        ' to it in the object for use in loading
        ' the object.
        '
```

```vb
        Set m_RS = objRS
    End If

    '
    ' Load each of the private member
    ' variables with the corresponding
    ' data from the database.
    '
    m_lngID = m_RS("CategoryID")
    m_sCategoryName = m_RS("CategoryName") & ""
    m_sDescription = m_RS("Description") & ""

    '
    ' Clean up
    '
    m_RS.Close
    Set m_RS = Nothing

End Sub

Public Sub Save()

    Dim qdData As QueryDef

    '
    ' New records have to be added with
    ' the AddNew method instead of Edit.
    ' The m_bIsNewRecord flag is set in
    ' the Init method.
    '
    If m_bIsNewRecord Then
        Set m_RS = m_DB.OpenRecordset("Categories", _
            dbOpenDynaset, _
            dbSeeChanges, _
            dbPessimistic)
        m_RS.AddNew
    Else
        Set qdData = m_DB.QueryDefs("qryGetCategory")
        qdData.Parameters("paramCategoryID") = m_lngID
        Set m_RS = qdData.OpenRecordset(dbOpenDynaset, _
            dbSeeChanges, dbPessimistic)

        m_RS.Edit
    End If

    '
    ' Update data in each field. If you
    ' are using an AutoNumber field, never
    ' attempt to add/edit data in it. You
    ' will get an error.
    '
```

(continued)

Listing 13-7 *(continued)*

```
    m_RS("CategoryName") = m_sCategoryName
    m_RS("Description") = m_sDescription

    m_RS.Update

    '
    ' Any further changes will only be Edits
    ' and will not require the use of the
    ' AddNew method.
    '
    m_bIsNewRecord = False
    '
    ' Clean up
    '
    m_RS.Close
    Set m_RS = Nothing

End Sub
```

This class is basically the same as CSupplier except in the number of fields it uses. Again, there is an AutoNumber field for the ID, so no editing of the field is required. The query definition is similar to the qryGetSupplier one but is used with the Category table.

Building the Shipper class

The CShipper class is identical to the CCategory class except for the names of the fields and corresponding property procedures. The code for the class is shown in Listing 13-8.

Listing 13-8: CShipper Class Declarations and Subroutines/Functions

```
Option Explicit

Private m_lngID As Long
Private m_sCompanyName As String
Private m_sPhoneNumber As String

Private m_bIsNewRecord As Boolean
Private m_bIsDataValid As Boolean
Private m_DB As Database
Private m_RS As Recordset

Public Event DataValidated(bValid As Boolean)
```

```
Public Property Get IsValid() As Boolean
    '
    ' This property is available when having
    ' an event trigger is not always helpful.
    ' It can also be used within objects that
    ' contain this one. This object can be
    ' queried as part of the other object's
    ' validation routines.
    '
    IsValid = m_bIsDataValid
End Property

Private Sub ValidateData()
    Dim bValid As Boolean
    bValid = True

    bValid = bValid And m_sCompanyName <> ""
    bValid = bValid And m_sPhoneNumber <> ""

    m_bIsDataValid = bValid
    RaiseEvent DataValidated(bValid)

End Sub

Private Sub Class_Initialize()
    ValidateData
End Sub

Public Sub Init(objDB As Database, _
    Optional objRS As Recordset, _
    Optional lngID As Long = -1)

    Dim qdData As QueryDef

    Set m_DB = objDB

    '
    ' If the ID is missing, the object
    ' is being instantiated to be filled
    ' with new data.
    '
    If lngID = -1 And objRS Is Nothing Then
        m_bIsNewRecord = True
        Exit Sub
    End If

    If objRS Is Nothing Then
        '
        ' If no recordset was passed in, open
        ' one up to the correct record. Use a
        ' snapshot since no editing is required.
```

(continued)

Listing 13-8 *(continued)*

```
    '
    Set qdData = objDB.QueryDefs("qryGetShipper")
    qdData.Parameters("paramShipperID") = lngID
    Set m_RS = qdData.OpenRecordset(dbOpenSnapshot, _
        dbForwardOnly)
Else
    '
    ' If one was passed in, store a reference
    ' to it in the object for use in loading
    ' the object.
    '
    Set m_RS = objRS
End If


'
' Load each of the private member
' variables with the corresponding
' data from the database.
'
m_lngID = m_RS("ShipperID")
m_sCompanyName = m_RS("CompanyName") & ""
m_sPhoneNumber = m_RS("Phone") & ""


'
' Clean up
'
m_RS.Close
Set m_RS = Nothing

End Sub

Public Sub Save()

    Dim qdData As QueryDef

    '
    ' New records have to be added with
    ' the AddNew method instead of Edit.
    ' The m_bIsNewRecord flag is set in
    ' the Init method.
    '
    If m_bIsNewRecord Then
        Set m_RS = m_DB.OpenRecordset("Shippers", _
            dbOpenDynaset, _
            dbSeeChanges, _
            dbPessimistic)
        m_RS.AddNew
    Else
        Set qdData = m_DB.QueryDefs("qryGetShipper")
        qdData.Parameters("paramShipperID") = m_lngID
        Set m_RS = qdData.OpenRecordset(dbOpenDynaset, _
```

```
            dbSeeChanges, dbPessimistic)

        m_RS.Edit
    End If

    '
    ' Update data in each field. If you
    ' are using an AutoNumber field, never
    ' attempt to add/edit data in it. You
    ' will get an error.
    '
    m_RS("CompanyName") = m_sCompanyName
    m_RS("Phone") = m_sPhoneNumber

    m_RS.Update

    '
    ' Any further changes will only be Edits
    ' and will not require the use of the
    ' AddNew method.
    '
    m_bIsNewRecord = False
    '
    ' Clean up
    '
    m_RS.Close
    Set m_RS = Nothing

End Sub
```

Building the CEmployee class

The CEmployee class has quite a bit more data in it. It also has the feature of being able to point back to itself. The employee's supervisor, which is referenced by the ReportsTo field, can be used to retrieve another CEmployee object. That code is shown in the Supervisor property, which is shown with the rest of the class code (except for the standard accessors and modifiers) in Listing 13-9.

Listing 13-9: **CEmployee Class Declarations and Functions/Subroutines**

```
Option Explicit

Private m_lngID As Long
Private m_sLastName As String
Private m_sFirstName As String
Private m_sTitle As String
```

(continued)

Listing 13-9 *(continued)*

```
Private m_sTitleOfCourtesy As String
Private m_vBirthdate As Date
Private m_vHiredate As Date
Private m_sAddress As String
Private m_sCity As String
Private m_sRegion As String
Private m_sPostalCode As String
Private m_sCountry As String
Private m_sHomePhone As String
Private m_sExtension As String
Private m_sNotes As String
Private m_lngReportsToEmployeeID As Long

Private m_bIsNewRecord As Boolean
Private m_bIsDataValid As Boolean
Private m_DB As Database
Private m_RS As Recordset

Public Event DataValidated(bValid As Boolean)


Public Property Get Supervisor() As CEmployee
    Dim objSupervisor As CEmployee

    If m_lngReportsToEmployeeID <> 0 Then
        Set objSupervisor = New CEmployee
        objSupervisor.Init objDB:=m_DB, _
            lngID:=m_lngReportsToEmployeeID
        Set Supervisor = objSupervisor
    Else
        Set Supervisor = Nothing
    End If
End Property

Public Property Get IsValid() As Boolean
    '
    ' This property is available when having
    ' an event trigger is not always helpful.
    ' It can also be used within objects that
    ' contain this one. This object can be
    ' queried as part of the other object's
    ' validation routines.
    '
    IsValid = m_bIsDataValid
End Property

Private Sub ValidateData()
    Dim bValid As Boolean
    bValid = True

    bValid = bValid And m_sLastName <> ""
```

```vb
      bValid = bValid And m_sFirstName <> ""
      bValid = bValid And m_sAddress <> ""
      bValid = bValid And m_sCity <> ""
      bValid = bValid And m_sPostalCode <> ""
      bValid = bValid And m_sCountry <> ""
      bValid = bValid And m_sHomePhone <> ""
      bValid = bValid And m_sExtension <> ""

      m_bIsDataValid = bValid
      RaiseEvent DataValidated(bValid)

End Sub

Private Sub Class_Initialize()
   ValidateData
End Sub

Public Sub Init(objDB As Database, _
   Optional objRS As Recordset, _
   Optional lngID As Long = -1)

   Dim qdData As QueryDef

   Set m_DB = objDB

   '
   ' If the ID is missing, the object
   ' is being instantiated to be filled
   ' with new data.
   '
   If lngID = -1 And objRS Is Nothing Then
      m_bIsNewRecord = True
      Exit Sub
   End If

   If objRS Is Nothing Then
      '
      ' If no recordset was passed in, open
      ' one up to the correct record. Use a
      ' snapshot since no editing is required.
      '
      Set qdData = objDB.QueryDefs("qryGetEmployee")
      qdData.Parameters("paramEmployeeID") = lngID
      Set m_RS = qdData.OpenRecordset(dbOpenSnapshot, _
         dbForwardOnly)
   Else
      '
      ' If one was passed in, store a reference
      ' to it in the object for use in loading
      ' the object.
      '
```

(continued)

Listing 13-9 *(continued)*

```
        Set m_RS = objRS
    End If

    '
    ' Load each of the private member
    ' variables with the corresponding
    ' data from the database.
    '
    m_lngID = m_RS("EmployeeID")
    m_sLastName = m_RS("LastName") & ""
    m_sFirstName = m_RS("FirstName") & ""
    m_sTitle = m_RS("Title") & ""
    m_sTitleOfCourtesy = m_RS("TitleOfCourtesy") & ""
    m_vBirthdate = m_RS("Birthdate")
    m_vHiredate = m_RS("HireDate")
    m_sAddress = m_RS("Address") & ""
    m_sCity = m_RS("City") & ""
    m_sRegion = m_RS("Region") & ""
    m_sPostalCode = m_RS("PostalCode") & ""
    m_sCountry = m_RS("Country") & ""
    m_sHomePhone = m_RS("HomePhone") & ""
    m_sExtension = m_RS("Extension") & ""
    m_sNotes = m_RS("Notes") & ""
    m_lngReportsToEmployeeID = m_RS("ReportsTo")

    '
    ' Clean up
    '
    m_RS.Close
    Set m_RS = Nothing

End Sub

Public Sub Save()

    Dim qdData As QueryDef

    '
    ' New records have to be added with
    ' the AddNew method instead of Edit.
    ' The m_bIsNewRecord flag is set in
    ' the Init method.
    '
    If m_bIsNewRecord Then
        Set m_RS = m_DB.OpenRecordset("Employees", _
            dbOpenDynaset, _
            dbSeeChanges, _
            dbPessimistic)
        m_RS.AddNew
    Else
        Set qdData = m_DB.QueryDefs("qryGetEmployee")
```

```
        qdData.Parameters("paramEmployeeID") = m_lngID
        Set m_RS = qdData.OpenRecordset(dbOpenDynaset, _
            dbSeeChanges, dbPessimistic)

        m_RS.Edit
    End If

    '
    ' Update data in each field. If you
    ' are using an AutoNumber field, never
    ' attempt to add/edit data in it. You
    ' will get an error.
    '
    m_RS("LastName") = m_sLastName
    m_RS("FirstName") = m_sFirstName
    m_RS("Title") = m_sTitle
    m_RS("TitleOfCourtesy") = m_sTitleOfCourtesy
    m_RS("Birthdate") = m_vBirthdate
    m_RS("HireDate") = m_vHiredate
    m_RS("Address") = m_sAddress
    m_RS("City") = m_sCity
    m_RS("Region") = m_sRegion
    m_RS("PostalCode") = m_sPostalCode
    m_RS("Country") = m_sCountry
    m_RS("HomePhone") = m_sHomePhone
    m_RS("Extension") = m_sExtension
    m_RS("Notes") = m_sNotes
    m_RS("ReportsTo") = m_lngReportsToEmployeeID

    m_RS.Update

    '
    ' Any further changes will only be Edits
    ' and will not require the use of the
    ' AddNew method.
    '
    m_bIsNewRecord = False
    '
    ' Clean up
    '
    m_RS.Close
    Set m_RS = Nothing

End Sub
```

The new Supervisor property can be used as shown in Listing 13-10. The code can be used in your Sub_Main subroutine to test the class's functionality.

Listing 13-10: **CEmployee Test Code**

```
Dim objEmp As New CEmployee

Set db = OpenDatabase("E:\DevStudio\VB\NWind.MDB")
objEmp.Init objDB:=db, lngID:=6
Debug.Print "Employee:   " _
    & objEmp.FirstName & " " & objEmp.LastName
Debug.Print "Supervisor: " _
    & objEmp.Supervisor.FirstName & " " _
    & objEmp.Supervisor.LastName
```

This will produce the results shown in Listing 13-11.

Listing 13-11: **Results of CEmployee Test Code**

```
Employee:   Michael Suyama
Supervisor: Steven Buchanan
```

Of course, you can set the result of the Supervisor property to a new CEmployee object. Other than that change, the CEmployee class works in the same way as the others. Based on your data integrity requirements, the ValidateData procedure may need to be modified to have a different set of validation rules.

Building the Product class

The CProduct class is the first one that will actually contain references to other objects. This fact makes the Init and Save processes of the CProduct object slightly more complex, but it still is easy to do because you've already built the classes used in the CProduct class.

The declarations for the CProduct class are shown in Listing 13-12. You'll notice declarations for the CCategory and CSupplier classes, which are used by the CProduct class.

Listing 13-12: **CProduct Class Declarations**

```
Option Explicit

Private m_lngID As Long
Private m_sProductName As String
Private m_objSupplier As CSupplier
```

```
Private m_objCategory As CCategory
Private m_sQuantityPerUnit As String
Private m_cUnitPrice As Currency
Private m_iUnitsInStock As Integer
Private m_iUnitsOnOrder As Integer
Private m_iReorderLevel As Integer
Private m_bDiscontinued As Boolean

Private m_bIsNewRecord As Boolean
Private m_bIsDataValid As Boolean
Private m_DB As Database
Private m_RS As Recordset

Public Event DataValidated(bValid As Boolean)
```

The first change is that the `Class_Initialize` event handler actually needs
to initialize the two object variables. This prevents errors about invalid object
references when you go to initialize the fields and objects of the `CProduct` class. In
addition, the `Class_Terminate` event handler needs to clear out the references to
these objects when the `CProduct` object is set to `Nothing`. Those two event
handlers are shown in Listing 13-13.

Listing 13-13: **Class Event Handlers**

```
Private Sub Class_Initialize()
    Set m_objSupplier = New CSupplier
    Set m_objCategory = New CCategory
    ValidateData
End Sub

Private Sub Class_Terminate()
    Set m_objSupplier = Nothing
    Set m_objCategory = Nothing
End Sub
```

The `Init` method, shown in Listing 13-14, has a few new lines of code over the last
ones you built. Instead of filling each value of the `CCategory` and `CSupplier`
object, the `Init` method lets each object fill itself. Because each of the objects
knows how to load data from the database, the `CProduct` object simply points each
object to the right record and doesn't interfere.

Listing 13-14: **Init Method of CProduct Class**

```
Public Sub Init(objDB As Database, _
    Optional objRS As Recordset, _
    Optional lngID As Long = -1)

    Dim qdData As QueryDef

    Set m_DB = objDB

    '
    ' If the ID is missing, the object
    ' is being instantiated to be filled
    ' with new data.
    '
    If lngID = -1 And objRS Is Nothing Then
        m_bIsNewRecord = True
        Exit Sub
    End If

    If objRS Is Nothing Then
        '
        ' If no recordset was passed in, open
        ' one up to the correct record. Use a
        ' snapshot since no editing is required.
        '
        Set qdData = objDB.QueryDefs("qryGetProduct")
        qdData.Parameters("paramProductID") = lngID
        Set m_RS = qdData.OpenRecordset(dbOpenSnapshot, _
            dbForwardOnly)
    Else
        '
        ' If one was passed in, store a reference
        ' to it in the object for use in loading
        ' the object.
        '
        Set m_RS = objRS
    End If

    '
    ' Load each of the private member
    ' variables with the corresponding
    ' data from the database.
    '
    m_lngID = m_RS("ProductID")
    m_sProductName = m_RS("ProductName") & ""

    m_objSupplier.Init objDB:=m_DB, _
        lngID:=m_RS("SupplierID")
    m_objCategory.Init objDB:=m_DB, _
        lngID:=m_RS("CategoryID")

    m_sQuantityPerUnit = m_RS("QuantityPerUnit")
```

```
   m_cUnitPrice = m_RS("UnitPrice")
   m_iUnitsInStock = m_RS("UnitsInStock")
   m_iUnitsOnOrder = m_RS("UnitsOnOrder")
   m_iReorderLevel = m_RS("ReorderLevel")
   m_bDiscontinued = m_RS("Discontinued")

   '
   ' Clean up
   '
   m_RS.Close
   Set m_RS = Nothing

End Sub
```

The boldfaced instructions in the previous code listing show how the objects that are part of the CProduct class are initialized. You can't get away from storing the SupplierID and CategoryID in the Product table, however. This is simply a way to map a flat database table to an object that can have multiple levels of data.

The next method that requires some changes is the Save method. This method, shown in Listing 13-15, takes the ID values stored in each of the objects and puts them back into the CProduct table. These IDs that link the two tables, called foreign keys, are crucial to maintaining the relationships between the tables.

Listing 13-15: **Save Method of CProduct Table**

```
Public Sub Save()

   Dim qdData As QueryDef

   '
   ' New records have to be added with
   ' the AddNew method instead of Edit.
   ' The m_bIsNewRecord flag is set in
   ' the Init method.
   '
   If m_bIsNewRecord Then
      Set m_RS = m_DB.OpenRecordset("Products", _
         dbOpenDynaset, _
         dbSeeChanges, _
         dbPessimistic)
      m_RS.AddNew
   Else
      Set qdData = m_DB.QueryDefs("qryGetProduct")
      qdData.Parameters("paramProductID") = m_lngID
      Set m_RS = qdData.OpenRecordset(dbOpenDynaset, _
```

(continued)

Listing 13-15 *(continued)*

```
            dbSeeChanges, dbPessimistic)

        m_RS.Edit
    End If

    '
    ' Update data in each field. If you
    ' are using an AutoNumber field, never
    ' attempt to add/edit data in it. You
    ' will get an error.
    '
    m_RS("ProductName") = m_sProductName
    m_RS("SupplierID") = m_objSupplier.ID
    m_RS("CategoryID") = m_objCategory.ID
    m_RS("QuantityPerUnit") = m_sQuantityPerUnit
    m_RS("UnitPrice") = m_cUnitPrice
    m_RS("UnitsInStock") = m_iUnitsInStock
    m_RS("UnitsOnOrder") = m_iUnitsOnOrder
    m_RS("ReorderLevel") = m_iReorderLevel
    m_RS("Discontinued") = m_bDiscontinued

    m_RS.Update

    '
    ' Any further changes will only be Edits
    ' and will not require the use of the
    ' AddNew method.
    '
    m_bIsNewRecord = False
    '
    ' Clean up
    '
    m_RS.Close
    Set m_RS = Nothing

End Sub
```

There are several pieces of code, shown in Listing 13-16, to allow external code to refer to the CSupplier and CCategory objects used by this Product class. These two properties are supported by very small Property Get procedures, as there is never a need to change the reference to a particular CSupplier or CCategory object — only to change the values within each object. Both Property Get procedures shown below return references to their respective object variables, which can be used later to access the properties within the instances they represent. Because the objects involved will not need to be set externally, the Property Set procedures are omitted. All the properties of the CCategory and CSupplier objects can be set, though.

Listing 13-16: **Object Property Get Procedures**

```
Public Property Get Category() As CCategory
    Set Category = m_objCategory
End Property

Public Property Get Supplier() As CSupplier
    Set Supplier = m_objSupplier
End Property
End Listing 13-16
```

The final bits of code, shown in Listing 13-17, handle data validation. For checking the CSupplier and CCategory objects, all that is necessary is to check the IsValid property of each object. Because this property indicates whether the data is valid or not, the CProduct object can simply rely on each object to return its current status.

Listing 13-17: **Data Validation Code for CProduct Class**

```
Public Property Get IsValid() As Boolean
    '
    ' This property is available when having
    ' an event trigger is not always helpful.
    ' It can also be used within objects that
    ' contain this one. This object can be
    ' queried as part of the other object's
    ' validation routines.
    '
    IsValid = m_bIsDataValid
End Property
Private Sub ValidateData()
    Dim bValid As Boolean
    bValid = True

    bValid = bValid And m_sProductName <> ""
    bValid = bValid And m_objSupplier.IsValid
    bValid = bValid And m_objCategory.IsValid
    bValid = bValid And m_sQuantityPerUnit <> ""
    bValid = bValid And m_cUnitPrice <> 0

    m_bIsDataValid = bValid
    RaiseEvent DataValidated(bValid)

End Sub
```

That's all there is to the CProduct class. Some test code you can use is shown in Listing 13-18, with the results shown in Listing 13-19.

Listing 13-18: CProduct Test Code

```
objProd.Init objDB:=db, lngID:=23
Debug.Print objProd.Category.CategoryName
Debug.Print objProd.Supplier.SupplierName
Debug.Print objProd.UnitPrice
objProd.UnitPrice = 42
objProd.Save
Set objProd = Nothing
```

Listing 13-19: CProduct Test Code Results

```
Grains/Cereals
PB Knäckebröd AB
 21
```

When you run the program again, the unit price of the item will show the new value of 42.

Building the COrderDetail class

The COrderDetail class is going to be somewhat different from the other classes you've built in this chapter. First of all, the COrderDetail object really can't exist on its own without an associated COrder object and its COrderDetails collection of COrderDetail objects. This fact actually makes your job easier because you can design the COrderDetail object to work specifically with the collection. Secondly, because the COrderDetails collection has to delete all the individual details each time it saves the data, the COrderDetail object will never use the Edit() method to change its permanent data. The details are deleted and saved each time because it is much easier to do than to track the changes, additions, and deletions of COrderDetail objects to a COrder.

With that out of the way, Listing 13-20 shows the declarations for the COrderDetail class.

Listing 13-20: **COrderDetail Declarations**

```
Option Explicit

Private m_lngOrderID As Long
Private m_cUnitPrice As Currency
Private m_iQuantity As Integer
Private m_fDiscount As Single
Private m_objProduct As CProduct

Private m_bIsDataValid As Boolean
Private m_DB As Database
Private m_RS As Recordset

Public Event DataValidated(bValid As Boolean)
```

Notice the m_bIsNewRecord variable is gone because we don't have to worry about editing an existing record. In addition, you see an object representing the CProduct associated with this detail record.

You should also notice an ID field does not exist for this object. This is because this COrderDetail object does not make sense if it is not associated with a COrder. For this reason, the COrder's ID is stored in the COrderDetail object.

In the Class_Initialize event handler, you must instantiate the CProduct object. Similarly, you have to destroy the object whenever the COrderDetail object is being destroyed. This code is shown in Listing 13-21.

Listing 13-21: **Class_Initialize and Class_Terminate Event Handlers**

```
Private Sub Class_Initialize()
    Set m_objProduct = New CProduct
    ValidateData
End Sub

Private Sub Class_Terminate()
    Set m_objProduct = Nothing
End Sub
```

Next, you have to initialize the COrderDetail object. That code is shown in Listing 13-22.

Listing 13-22: **Init Method for COrderDetail Class**

```
Public Sub Init(objDB As Database, _
    Optional objRS As Recordset, _
    Optional lngOrderID As Long = -1, _
    Optional lngProductID As Long = -1)

    Dim qdData As QueryDef

    Set m_DB = objDB

    '
    ' New COrderDetail objects need
    ' no further initialization
    '
    If lngOrderID = -1 And objRS Is Nothing Then
        Exit Sub
    End If

    If objRS Is Nothing Then
        '
        ' If no recordset was passed in, open
        ' one up to the correct record. Use a
        ' snapshot since no editing is required.
        '
        Set qdData = objDB.QueryDefs("qryGetOrderDetail")
        qdData.Parameters("paramOrderID") = lngOrderID
        qdData.Parameters("paramProductID") = lngProductID
        Set m_RS = qdData.OpenRecordset(dbOpenSnapshot, _
            dbForwardOnly)
    Else
        '
        ' If one was passed in, store a reference
        ' to it in the object for use in loading
        ' the object.
        '
        Set m_RS = objRS
    End If

    '
    ' Load each of the private member
    ' variables with the corresponding
    ' data from the database.
    '
    m_lngOrderID = m_RS("OrderID")
    m_cUnitPrice = m_RS("UnitPrice")
    m_iQuantity = m_RS("Quantity")
    m_fDiscount = m_RS("Discount")
    m_objProduct.Init objDB:=m_DB, _
        lngID:=m_RS("ProductID")
```

```
   '
   ' Clean up, if we created the
   ' recordset here. Otherwise, the
   ' recordset came in open and needs
   ' to return the same way.
   '
   If objRS Is Nothing Then
      m_RS.Close
      Set m_RS = Nothing
   End If

End Sub
```

The main difference with this method is the query actually has to take two
different parameters to identify the row for this COrderDetail object. Once
the data is retrieved, it is filled into the member variables, and the associated
CProduct object is instantiated as well.

Data validation and a Total property are shown in Listing 13-23. These properties
and methods work in a similar fashion to previous objects and take advantage of
the CProduct object's IsValid property.

Listing 13-23: **Data Validation and Total Property**

```
Public Property Get Total() As Currency

   '
   ' In order for the calculation to work
   ' correctly, the discount value has to
   ' be subtracted from 1 so that for a 15%
   ' discount, the price is 85% of normal.
   '
   Total = m_iQuantity * m_cUnitPrice * (1 - m_fDiscount)
End Property

Public Property Get IsValid() As Boolean
   '
   ' This property is available when having
   ' an event trigger is not always helpful.
   ' It can also be used within objects that
   ' contain this one. This object can be
   ' queried as part of the other object's
   ' validation routines.
   '
   IsValid = m_bIsDataValid
End Property
```

(continued)

Listing 13-23 *(continued)*

```
Private Sub ValidateData()
    Dim bValid As Boolean

    bValid = True
    bValid = bValid And m_lngOrderID <> 0
    bValid = bValid And m_cUnitPrice <> 0
    bValid = bValid And m_iQuantity <> 0
    bValid = bValid And _
        (m_fDiscount >= 0 And m_fDiscount <= 1)
    bValid = bValid And m_objProduct.IsValid

    m_bIsDataValid = bValid
    RaiseEvent DataValidated(bValid)

End Sub
```

The last method is the Save method. This method is significantly simpler because
the COrderDetail is always added as a new record to the table. This does make
the assumption the COrderDetails collection is deleting all the existing rows, so
make sure you implement that when the time comes. The Save method is shown in
Listing 13-24.

Listing 13-24: Save Method for COrderDetail Class

```
Public Sub Save()

    '
    ' Because the COrderDetails collection
    ' will always remove all the COrderDetail
    ' objects for an order, we always want
    ' to add an COrderDetail record as a new
    ' record to the table. A COrderDetail
    ' object does not make sense to exist
    ' without a corresponding COrderDetails
    ' collection, so this is a valid way
    ' to implement the Save method.
    '
    Set m_RS = m_DB.OpenRecordset("Order Details", _
        dbOpenDynaset)
    m_RS.AddNew

m_RS("OrderID") = m_lngOrderID
    m_RS("ProductID") = m_objProduct.ID
    m_RS("UnitPrice") = m_cUnitPrice
    m_RS("Quantity") = m_iQuantity
    m_RS("Discount") = m_fDiscount
```

```
      m_RS.Update
      m_RS.Close
      Set m_RS = Nothing

   End Sub
```

Just as in the `CProduct` class, only the ID of the associated product is recorded in the Order Details table. That will be enough information to later retrieve the appropriate product record and create a Product object to represent it. With that method, you have all the code for the `COrderDetail` class. Because this object can't logically exist by itself, we'll skip the test code and go right into the associated collection, `COrderDetails`.

Building the COrderDetails collection class

Now that you've created a single `COrderDetail` class, you can build the collection class that can contain multiple `COrderDetail` objects. This collection will then be part of the `COrder` object you'll build shortly.

The key point to remember is you're not building a unique `Collection` object — Visual Basic already provides that object. What you're doing is wrapping the generic `Collection` object with logic to interact with the singular `COrderDetail` objects for a `COrder`. This logic provides various functions, including adding and removing records, providing totals for the objects in the collection, and so on. While building a collection of objects is not always a good use of resources, in cases like the `COrder` object, a collection is the only structure that makes sense.

The name of this collection class will be `COrderDetails`. The first code you need is shown in Listing 13-25 and handles the initialization of the objects and the data in them.

Listing 13-25: **COrderDetails Collection Initialization Code**

```
Private Sub Class_Initialize()
   Set m_Col = New Collection
End Sub

Public Sub Init(objDB As Database, lngOrderID As Long)

   Dim qdDetails As QueryDef
   Dim objDetail As COrderDetail
   Set m_DB = objDB
   m_lngOrderID = lngOrderID
   '
```

(continued)

Listing 13-25 *(continued)*

```
' Loop through all the order details for the
' specified order and create an object for
' each.
'
Set qdDetails = _
    objDB.QueryDefs("qryGetOrderDetailsByOrder")
qdDetails.Parameters("paramOrderID") = lngOrderID
Set m_RS = qdDetails.OpenRecordset(dbOpenSnapshot, _
    dbForwardOnly)

Do While Not m_RS.EOF
    Set objDetail = New COrderDetail
    objDetail.Init m_DB, m_RS
    Add objDetail
    m_RS.MoveNext
Loop

m_RS.Close
Set m_RS = Nothing

End Sub
```

The query used here, qryGetOrderDetailsByOrder, can be built in Access using the structure shown in Figure 13-3.

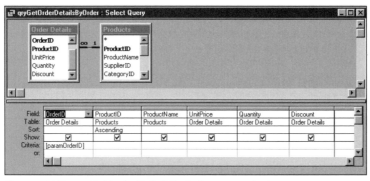

Figure 13-3: qryGetOrderDetailsByOrder query design

You should also add the following lines to the Declarations section of the COrderDetails class:

```
Option Explicit
```

```
Private m_Col As Collection
Private m_DB As Database
Private m_RS As Recordset

Private m_lngOrderID As Long
Private Const ITEMPREFIX = "Item"
```

After the `Class_Initialize` event handler instantiates the generic `Collection` object, the main body of code that instantiated the class would call the `Init` method with the database object and the order ID. The collection then retrieves each `COrderDetail` object in the `COrderDetails` collection and creates an object for each one by calling the `Init` method. This is where the optional recordset variable comes into play, being one of the inputs declared `Optional` in the `Init` method for the `COrderDetail` class module. Instead of making each `COrderDetail` object open a separate recordset independently of all the other members of the collection (however many there may be), all the `COrderDetail` objects share the same recordset and simply read their data from it. Each `COrderDetail` object is added to the generic `Collection` object after it has been formally initialized through its own native `Init` method.

Now that there is data in the `Collection` object, the `COrderDetails` class can provide information about it to any interested code. Listing 13-26 shows some utility functions you need to add.

Listing 13-26: **COrderDetails Utility Functions**

```
Public Property Get Item(vntIndexKey As Variant) As _
    COrderDetail

    Set Item = m_Col(vntIndexKey)
End Property

Public Property Get Count() As Long
    Count = m_Col.Count
End Property

Public Property Get NewEnum() As IUnknown
    Set NewEnum = m_Col.[_NewEnum]
End Property

Public Sub Add(objNewMember As COrderDetail)

    '
    ' The ProductID is not necessarily unique
    ' in the Northwind Traders database. This
    ' will cause a problem if you have multiple
    ' items in the Order Details table that have
    ' the same ProductID. This is more a problem
    ' with the database design instead of the object
```

(continued)

Listing 13-26 *(continued)*

```
    ' design.
    '
    m_Col.Add objNewMember, _
        ITEMPREFIX & objNewMember.Product.ID

End Sub
Public Sub Remove(iProductID As Long)

    '
    ' This method only removes the detail
    ' from the collection. It does not actually
    ' delete the detail from disk. The Save
    ' method takes care of that.
    '
    m_Col.Remove ITEMPREFIX & iProductID

End Sub
```

The first function, Item, returns a particular item from the collection. This property is also called when calling code requests OrderDetails("Item5"), for instance. This code is equivalent to saying OrderDetails.Item("Item5").

The next function, Count, returns the number of items currently in the collection. The next function, NewEnum, has to be written exactly as shown. This function interacts with the Visual Basic language to enable callers to write code as follows:

```
For Each objDetail In OrderDetails
    ... some code ...
Next objDetail
```

In addition, if you don't use the Class Builder, you have to set the *Procedure ID* to -4. This is to enable Visual Basic to know which procedure to use to support the For Each/Next syntax. To set the Procedure ID, do the following:

1. Put your cursor on the line that defines the NewEnum property.

2. Select Tools ➪ Procedure Attributes.

3. In the dialog shown in Figure 13-3, click the Advanced button and enter **-4** in the Procedure ID box.

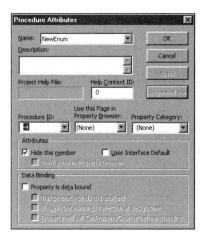

Figure 13-4: Procedure Attributes dialog

The last two utility functions in Listing 13-26 are used to add and remove
COrderDetail objects from the collection. These functions do not permanently
remove the data; that action is performed by the Save method, which is shown in
Listing 13-27.

Listing 13-27: COrderDetails Save Method

```
Public Sub Save()

    Dim objDetail As COrderDetail
    Dim qdDelete As QueryDef

    '
    ' Delete all the old details from the
    ' database table.
    '
    Set qdDelete = m_DB.QueryDefs("qryDeleteOrderDetails")
    qdDelete.Parameters("paramOrderID") = m_lngOrderID
    qdDelete.Execute
    '
    ' This object's parent can simply call
    ' Save on the collection instead of
    ' calling Save on each individual item.
    '
    For Each objDetail In m_Col
        objDetail.Save
    Next objDetail

End Sub
```

First, all existing COrderDetail records are eliminated. Because we have all the COrderDetail data in memory, this deletion is fairly safe. Each COrderDetail is saved to the database using the Save method on the COrderDetail object. The Delete query's Design window (from Access) is shown in Figure 13-4. To create a Delete query, you need to select it from the Access QueryType toolbar button or by selecting Query ⇨ Delete Query.

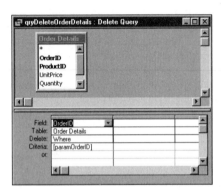

Figure 13-5: qryDeleteOrderDetails Query Definition in Access

The last property to add to the COrderDetails collection is the Total property. This property, shown in Listing 13-28, sums up the totals from each COrderDetail and returns the total to the caller. The listing shows how you can take advantage of the data stored in the collection to simplify calculations outside of the object. Encapsulation helps to reduce the amount of code required to do common tasks that can be handled by the objects themselves. Instead of making the calling code do all the total calculations, that same code simply asks the object to give a total for the order details.

Listing 13-28: **Total Property for COrderDetails Collection**

```
Public Property Get Total() As Currency
    '
    ' This property returns the total amount
    ' of all the Order Detail objects. This
    ' property does not format the total, as
    ' the currency format could be different
    ' per installation.
    '
    Dim cTemp As Currency
    Dim objDetail As COrderDetail
    cTemp = 0
    For Each objDetail In m_Col
        cTemp = cTemp + objDetail.Total
    Next objDetail
```

```
    Total = cTemp

End Property
```

This code uses the `Total` property of the `COrderDetail` object, which is where the real logic is housed. The `Total` property of the `COrderDetail` class actually does the calculation of discount, quantity, and unit price and returns the result. The `Total` property of the `COrderDetails` collection, shown in Listing 13-28 above, only accumulates all the results.

Building the COrder class

Now that all the underlying work is done, building the `COrder` class is just like the `CProduct` class. It simply involves instantiating and initializing more objects than in other cases. The declarations and nonstandard code are shown in Listing 13-29.

Listing 13-29: **COrder Class Code**

```
Option Explicit

Private m_objCustomer As CCustomer
Private m_objShipper As CShipper
Private m_objEmployee As CEmployee
Private m_objOrderDetails As COrderDetails
Private m_lngID As Long
Private m_dOrderDate As Date
Private m_dRequiredDate As Date
Private m_dShippedDate As Date
Private m_cFreightTotal As Currency
Private m_sShipToName As String
Private m_sShipToAddress As String
Private m_sShipToCity As String
Private m_sShipToRegion As String
Private m_sShipToPostalCode As String
Private m_sShipToCountry As String

Private m_bIsNewRecord As Boolean
Private m_bIsDataValid As Boolean
Private m_DB As Database
Private m_RS As Recordset

Public Event DataValidated(bValid As Boolean)

Public Property Get IsValid() As Boolean
```

(continued)

Listing 13-29 *(continued)*

```vb
    ' This property is available when having
    ' an event trigger is not always helpful.
    ' It can also be used within objects that
    ' contain this one. This object can be
    ' queried as part of the other object's
    ' validation routines.
    '
    Dim bValid As Boolean
    bValid = True

    bValid = bValid And m_objCustomer.IsValid
    bValid = bValid And m_objShipper.IsValid
    bValid = bValid And m_objEmployee.IsValid
    bValid = bValid And m_objOrderDetails.Count > 0
    bValid = bValid And m_dRequiredDate >= Date
    bValid = bValid And m_dShippedDate >= Date
    bValid = bValid And m_cFreightTotal >= 0
    bValid = bValid And m_sShipToName <> ""
    bValid = bValid And m_sShipToAddress <> ""
    bValid = bValid And m_sShipToCity <> ""
    bValid = bValid And m_sShipToRegion <> ""
    bValid = bValid And m_sShipToPostalCode <> ""
    bValid = bValid And m_sShipToCountry <> ""

    m_bIsDataValid = bValid
    IsValid = bValid
    RaiseEvent DataValidated(bValid)
End Property

Private Sub ValidateData()
    Dim bValid As Boolean
    bValid = True

    '
    ' Currently, no unique data is being
    ' validated. The function is here for
    ' completeness.
    '
    m_bIsDataValid = bValid
    RaiseEvent DataValidated(bValid)

End Sub

Private Sub Class_Initialize()
    Set m_objCustomer = New CCustomer
    Set m_objEmployee = New CEmployee
    Set m_objShipper = New CShipper
    Set m_objOrderDetails = New COrderDetails

    ValidateData
End Sub
```

```
Public Sub Init(objDB As Database, _
   Optional objRS As Recordset, _
   Optional lngID As Long = -1)

   Dim qdData As QueryDef

   Set m_DB = objDB

   '
   ' If the ID is missing, the object
   ' is being instantiated to be filled
   ' with new data.
   '
   If lngID = -1 And objRS Is Nothing Then
      m_bIsNewRecord = True
      Exit Sub
   End If

   If objRS Is Nothing Then
      '
      ' If no recordset was passed in, open
      ' one up to the correct record. Use a
      ' snapshot since no editing is required.
      '
      Set qdData = objDB.QueryDefs("qryGetOrder")
      qdData.Parameters("paramOrderID") = lngID
      Set m_RS = qdData.OpenRecordset(dbOpenSnapshot, _
         dbForwardOnly)
   Else
      '
      ' If one was passed in, store a reference
      ' to it in the object for use in loading
      ' the object.
      '
      Set m_RS = objRS
   End If

   '
   ' Load each of the private member
   ' variables with the corresponding
   ' data from the database.
   '
   m_objCustomer.Init objDB:=m_DB, _
      sID:=m_RS("CustomerID")
   m_objShipper.Init objDB:=m_DB, lngID:=m_RS("ShipVia")
   m_objEmployee.Init objDB:=m_DB, _
      lngID:=m_RS("EmployeeID")
   m_objOrderDetails.Init objDB:=m_DB, _
      lngOrderID:=m_RS("OrderID")
```

(continued)

Listing 13-29 *(continued)*

```vb
    m_lngID = m_RS("OrderID")
    m_dOrderDate = m_RS("OrderDate")
    m_dRequiredDate = m_RS("RequiredDate")
    m_dShippedDate = m_RS("ShippedDate")
    m_cFreightTotal = m_RS("Freight")
    m_sShipToName = m_RS("ShipName") & ""
    m_sShipToAddress = m_RS("ShipAddress") & ""
    m_sShipToCity = m_RS("ShipCity") & ""
    m_sShipToRegion = m_RS("ShipRegion") & ""
    m_sShipToPostalCode = m_RS("ShipPostalCode") & ""
    m_sShipToCountry = m_RS("ShipCountry") & ""


    '
    ' Clean up
    '
    m_RS.Close
    Set m_RS = Nothing

End Sub

Public Sub Save()

    Dim qdData As QueryDef


    '
    ' New records have to be added with
    ' the AddNew method instead of Edit.
    ' The m_bIsNewRecord flag is set in
    ' the Init method.
    '
    If m_bIsNewRecord Then
        Set m_RS = m_DB.OpenRecordset("Orders", _
            dbOpenDynaset, _
            dbSeeChanges, _
            dbPessimistic)
        m_RS.AddNew
    Else
        Set qdData = m_DB.QueryDefs("qryGetOrder")
        qdData.Parameters("paramOrderID") = m_lngID
        Set m_RS = qdData.OpenRecordset(dbOpenDynaset, _
            dbSeeChanges, dbPessimistic)

        m_RS.Edit
    End If


    '
    ' Update data in each field. If you
    ' are using an AutoNumber field, never
    ' attempt to add/edit data in it. You
    ' will get an error.
    '
```

```
m_RS("CustomerID") = m_objCustomer.ID
m_RS("ShipVia") = m_objShipper.ID
m_RS("EmployeeID") = m_objEmployee.ID
m_RS("OrderID") = m_lngID
m_RS("OrderDate") = m_dOrderDate
m_RS("RequiredDate") = m_dRequiredDate
m_RS("ShippedDate") = m_dShippedDate
m_RS("FreightTotal") = m_cFreightTotal
m_RS("ShipName") = m_sShipToName
m_RS("ShipAddress") = m_sShipToAddress
m_RS("ShipCity") = m_sShipToCity
m_RS("ShipRegion") = m_sShipToRegion
m_RS("ShipPostalCode") = m_sShipToPostalCode
m_RS("ShipCountry") = m_sShipToCountry

m_RS.Update

'
' Any further changes will only be Edits
' and will not require the use of the
' AddNew method.
'
m_bIsNewRecord = False
'
' Clean up
'
m_RS.Close
Set m_RS = Nothing

End Sub
```

The COrder object basically takes advantage of all the simple objects that you've
been creating throughout this chapter. It initializes the CEmployee, CCustomer,
CShipper, and COrderDetails objects and has a few extra fields besides. You can
now write the following lines of code and have a fully populated COrder class
object that you can use in a form:

```
Dim db As Database
Dim objOrder As New COrder

Set db = OpenDatabase("E:\DevStudio\VB\NWind.MDB")
objOrder.Init objDB:=db, lngID:=10314
```

While it seems like a lot of work to reduce your work to one line, imagine the
savings in development time if your programmers didn't have to worry about how
the data was loaded into the objects. They could simply concentrate on using the
data in whatever form was being used at the time.

Summary

This chapter was designed to show you how a common business application's database could be translated into a series of classes that are database-aware.

✦ With a single line of code, you can create a fully populated object to represent a particular order in the database.

✦ You saw how to build both simple data-bound classes and how to use those classes in combination with others to produce complex classes.

✦ By using a bit of Visual Basic's dot notation, you should be able to get any piece of data from any object that you create, even if that object is just a small part of a larger object.

✦   ✦   ✦

Expanding Your Applications

Planning Your Application

Now that you've had the opportunity to dive in and build some Visual Basic applications, it's time to stop, take a breath, and step back. It's time to do a little planning. This includes formulating an idea of what the app will do, how it will look, who will be using it, and what tools you will be using to develop it. Regarding this toolset, we discuss application frameworks and how they can increase your productivity through component reuse. We also talk about the Microsoft Repository—what it is and why it is important to you. Finally, we discuss an integrated reuse tool that sits on top of the Repository: the Microsoft Visual Component Manager.

Establishing Requirements

The process of going from a set of requirements to a spec to a product, and all the peripheral processes around this, is known as *software engineering*. Many smart people have spent years pontificating about software engineering approaches and development methodologies. Regardless of who you believe or what approach you decide to implement, any project can benefit from applying some sound engineering principles to the development of an application. The first of these principles is this: Define a workable set of functional requirements for your application.

Functional requirements are descriptions of the features and functions that your application provides. Typically, these are stated in a functional requirements document. These requirements are used to create a technical specification that is ultimately used to develop the application.

It is probably true that small projects need little or no formal documentation and big projects most definitely do, but it never hurts to formalize your requirements regardless of the project size. A requirements document has the obvious benefit of setting the expectations of the application and communicating to all interested parties just what your application will do. An additional benefit is that the *process* of producing a requirements document results in some deep thought about the application. In either case — developing a formal requirements document or merely jotting down ideas on a napkin — establishing a set of requirements is the first step in developing your application.

The functional requirements state what the system will do, not necessarily how it will do it. The how-it-is-done documentation is provided with the technical spec. For example, a functional requirement might be "The system shall provide a way for a user to store and retrieve configuration options," or "The system will provide an options dialog for maintaining configuration settings." The technical spec would then provide more granularity to this requirement by describing the implementation: "An options dialog will be created to read/write information to the system registry...It will be available from the Tools ➪ Options menu and provide public properties that can be called from anywhere within the program."

Now that you've got a good idea of what your system will do, you might think it's time to start coding — or is it? We recommend a couple more steps in the process before your fingers actually hit the keyboard.

Targeting the Customer

It is important to understand your intended audience — the customer — when developing an application. Knowing the customer may help create new functional requirements or refine existing ones. Knowledge of the customer's wants and likes will help to mold architectural decisions. This knowledge will also help you make implementation choices more intelligently. Although there are many ways to target your customer, we'll be discussing two such aspects: establishing a profile of your customer and describing some scenarios for how the system will be used.

Customer profile

What is the level of expertise of your customer as related to your system? Is your customer a seasoned veteran or a novice user? Is your customer a schooled adult or an elementary school child? The answers to these questions will be very important in driving the design of your application. Obviously a very simple, user-friendly interface would be almost mandatory in software for children. But other decisions regarding the customer's profile may not be so obvious. Although it may be true that your target customers may be considered an expert in the kinds of things your application provides, it may also be true that they only use your system once a month — in this case, a simpler interface might be desirable. As you can see, it is not just the profile of your customer that you need to know; it is also the profile of their usage of the system. For this reason, it is helpful to develop scenarios that describe usage patterns of your system as well as outline a typical session in front of your application.

Usage scenarios

When you are considering your customer, it may be useful to consider not only the overall profile of the customer but also some of the ways in which they will use the application. There may be several scenarios, depending on the various possible *roles* of users. For example, let's consider a database management system. Here are some likely roles for users of such a system:

> ✦ **Administrator** — This person is the overall administrator of the system. They have the maximum amount of *privileges* (permission to perform tasks and access data) related to accessing system functions, setting up systems, and defining roles of other users.

> ✦ **Manager** — This person has a moderate amount of system privileges. They can define other users, but not other managers or administrators.

> ✦ **User** — This person has the minimum amount of privileges when using the system. They only have rights to areas that have been assigned to them by managers or administrators. Many of the areas are read-only — data can be viewed but not changed.

As you can see, the process of defining roles may lead to other sets of requirements. For example, the database system described above will need a way to define the various roles and assign system privileges to each role.

The development of usage scenarios is a powerful way of exploring the ways a customer will use a system. These scenarios describe a situation in which a user uses the system. These are meant to be written in plain English and should be as real-life as possible. Following is a scenario for a fictional intelligent Web system.

Intelligent Web Scenario: Danielle, a political science major at the University of Denver, awakens at 5:30 a.m. — getting up a little early to try and finish an assignment before class. She needs to write a paper on the political climate of Brazil in 1960s. Her intelligent browser, sensing she is awake, lights up the screen for her and says "Good morning, Danielle." Danielle informs her personal agent about her dilemma and then proceeds to issue some instructions: "Go out and get some information about Brazil in the '60s. I am interested in the political structure of Brazil at that time, and particularly interested in the struggle between the core political structures and any of the right-wing extremist factions. Get some newspaper and magazine articles with lots of pictures, and assemble a report for me. Also, see if you can include some video footage. I'll check back with you after I've had my coffee."

The system creates a number of special agents to perform the task. It also contacts some agents it knows down in South America to dig deeper into this subject. While many of the agents are collecting the text and pictures, another agent is talking to the political science professor's agents to find out the desired format for the report. Once all the pieces are in place, an agent assembles the report to a minidisk. While the report is being prepared, a video agent is working with the local video disk recorder's agent to prepare the minidisk with the footage. Danielle grabs the minidisk and heads off to class.

Sure, this scenario seems a little far-fetched right now, but just you wait. The important point is that by developing the scenario, it is possible to get an idea of the usage of the system in the context of a real-life situation. This technique, combined with other solid engineering practices, allows you to get a pretty good understanding of what your system will do.

Software Architecture

It's finally time to architect your product. The word *architecture*, as it relates to software, can be a very nebulous term. One of the authors remembers a day when he was interviewing for a job with a high-profile software company. As he was talking to several people that day and the term *architecture* came up, each of the interviewers said the same thing: "What do you mean by software architecture?" Each had their own opinion of what it meant, but each also understood that the word in the realm of software engineering means a lot of different things to a lot of different people. Having said that, we will try and come up with a definition of software architecture that we can live with:

> Software architecture describes the overall way in which a system is constructed. It does this by describing the functional entities, or services, of the system and how they relate to and interact with one another. Furthermore, software architecture not only describes how the system is constructed, it oftentimes describes the construction process itself.

The important point here is that it is probably important that a system has some type of architecture to it. Some architectures that have received a lot of attention lately are client/server and three-tiered architectures. Each of these types of systems employs a different type of architecture. Most recently, Web-based systems are getting all the press. This type of architecture is very different from that of systems developed in the early '90s.

The choice of one architecture over another is never based purely on functionality, nor is it entirely objective. It is often based on compatibility or integration with existing systems, customer demands, or other strategic reasons. For example, which is the hotter product: a client/server application or a Web-based application? Go figure.

The actual choice, or recommendation, of one architecture over another is beyond the scope of this book. There are many good books on software architecture that delve deeply into this subject. Oftentimes, the best approach is a blend of various architectural models.

Using Application Frameworks

The use of application frameworks allows you to increase productivity by reusing components. The reuse of such components also helps promote consistency throughout an entire set of products. This section will discuss exactly what a framework is, how you can create one, how you can maintain one, and how you can share it in a group setting.

What is an application framework?

The term *framework* brings to mind such things as a "skeleton" or a "foundation," and that is exactly what it is. The term is very generic; a framework can be many different things to many different users. In general, it is a set of items that are used as the basis to develop an application. When you think of a framework, visualize the construction of a house. In the early stages of such construction the house only has a foundation and some two-by-fours that are visible. Ignoring the fact that foundations and layouts of houses vary, this basic set of things are common to all home building. As with the house, you will find that there is indeed a set of things common to all applications you develop as well.

Valor Whisler, the author of an early Visual Basic tool (VB AppFramework) and coauthor of this book, defines a framework as follows:

> A *framework* is a collection of items that provide the basis for the development of a particular type of new application. These items include such Visual Basic components as code modules, class modules, forms, and other VB intrinsic building blocks. In addition, external items such as ActiveX controls, OLE servers, and DLLs may be included.

Many of the discrete items that make up the framework are known as *templates*. As with the framework, a template is built to be generic so that it has maximum potential for reusability. For example, a framework that is used to build an MDI application might have the following templates: an MDI form, a child form, and an About box form.

Visual Basic frameworks

Typically, a developer or team of developers would create a number of frameworks, each of which serves as the starting point for a particular type of application. Visual Basic ships with several frameworks built into it. VB calls such frameworks *project templates*. These frameworks can be seen when you select File ⇨ New Project. The New Project dialog is shown in Figure 14-1.

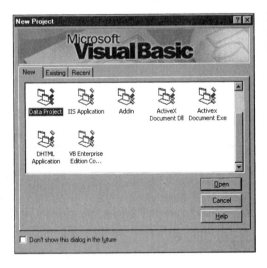

Figure 14-1: Visual Basic frameworks, or project templates, shown in the New Project dialog box.

The items that are displayed in this dialog include some intrinsic project frameworks, project (*.VBP) files that are found in the Templates directory, and Visual Basic wizards that are found in the Templates directory. We will take a look at a couple of these project frameworks later in this chapter. In addition, we will be showing you how to add your own frameworks to this dialog.

The Template directory

In order to have your frameworks and templates show up within the Visual Basic development environment, they must be placed in the Template directory. The location of this directory is specified in the Environment tab of the Options dialog (Figure 14-2), which is found on the Tools menu (Tools ➪ Options).

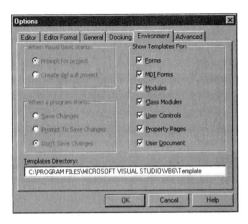

Figure 14-2: The Environment tab in the Options dialog box

Using Regedit

You can view and modify registry settings with the tool Regedit.exe. This can be found in your Windows directory. When you open the registry, you will see all information organized under six major keys. Be very careful when modifying or deleting data from the registry — such changes can have dire effects, including causing programs to no longer operate.

The Environment tab provides two options related to templates. The first allows you to specify which templates will appear when you add components using the Project menu (the use of such templates is explained in the following section). The second Environments option specifies the path and directory where Visual Basic will look for all its templates. The options in this dialog are stored in the registry under the following key:

```
HKEY_CURRENT_USER\Software\Microsoft\Visual Basic\6.0.
```

By the way, it is interesting to look at this key to see what other types of information pertaining to your development environment that Visual Basic stores in the Registry.

Note   The default location of the Template directory has changed from VB5 to VB6.

Within the main Template directory (as specified in the Options dialog) there are subdirectories where the actual templates reside. Although you can set the path and name of the Template directory itself, the names and organization of these subdirectories are not negotiable (Figure 14-3).

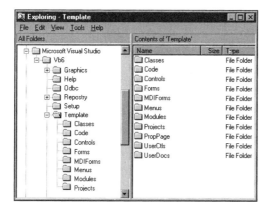

Figure 14-3: The Template directory

Using Visual Basic templates

Any form, module, class, or any other component that you place in a template subfolder will show up in the Visual Basic Add *Component* dialog (where *Component* corresponds to the particular type of component you are adding).

Figure 14-4 shows the Add Form dialog (Project ⇨ Add Form) with all the intrinsic types of forms that ship with Visual Basic, as well as two additional form templates we have developed for this book: VBB Options and VBB Status. These particular templates will be discussed later in this chapter.

Note

If you check "Don't show this dialog in the future" in the Add Form dialog box, it's like unchecking the corresponding box under the Show Templates For: frame (which is in the Environment tab in the Options dialog – see Figure 14-2). If you have turned off this dialog, just recheck that same box to get it back.

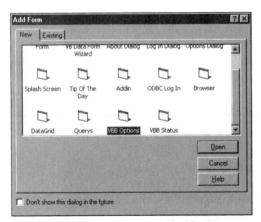

Figure 14-4: The Add Form dialog box

Sharing Visual Basic templates

There are a number of aspects of team development related to the use of frameworks, including shared resources, version control, configuration management, and cataloging and retrieval mechanisms. The inherent Visual Basic capability we have been discussing so far really only addresses the cataloging and retrieval mechanisms. However, if all the templates were moved to a shared directory on a network drive, it would be possible to share these template resources. To make this work, do the following:

1. Create a shared network resource.

2. Have each member of the development team map to that resource — preferably using the same drive letter.

3. Move some Master Template directory and all its subdirectories to this shared resource.

4. Have each member of the development team change the path in their Options dialog Environment tab to this new location.

It should also be easy to place the items in this shared directory under version control. Using this technique, you can achieve an initial level of reusability. Although such a system is lacking some of the sophisticated features we might want, it comes free with Visual Basic and is simple to implement. Later in this chapter we will be discussing two emerging technologies related to reusability: the Microsoft Repository and the Microsoft Visual Component Manager. These combined systems offer not only a greater level of sophistication but reusability throughout our different development tools (Visual C++, Visual J++) — not just within Visual Basic.

Sharing Templates

Sharing of templates requires access to network file servers — whether directly connected or dialing in. A *shared resource* is one that is accessible over a network. *Version control* is a way of saving the incremental changes that are made to the source code for an application — and a way of checking in and checking out code from a shared library to control who is editing any given source module. Visual SourceSafe is the version control system that ships with some of the editions of Visual Basic. *Configuration management* is the discipline of organizing information in a particular manner. This is important for team development. *Cataloging and retrieval mechanisms* are ways to organize, store, and retrieve source code into some type of library. One such system is SourceSafe. A complementary mechanism is the Visual Component Manager and the Microsoft Repository.

Visual Basic wizards

Wizards are special Visual Basic add-ins that are used to automate a particular task. An *add-in* is an application that uses Visual Basic's extensibility model to programmatically modify the development environment. Several add-ins and wizards are included with Visual Basic. We're going to just talk about the wizards in this section — those special add-ins that are referenced in the Template directory.

Figure 14-5 shows the *Application Wizard*, which is included with VB. To access this wizard, create a new project (File ➪ New Project) and select the VB Application Wizard template from the New Project dialog. This wizard walks you through a step-by-step process for the purposes of creating the framework of a new application. This particular wizard collects information as to the style of application, the menus you would like to include, what optional dialogs you would like, as well as other attributes of your target app. Once you have made your choices, it generates a number of forms, code modules, class modules, and even a resource file. These files are now the framework for your new application.

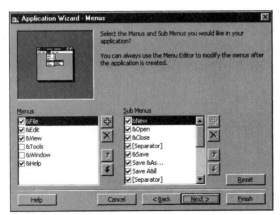

Figure 14-5: The Visual Basic Application Wizard

Fortunately, you don't have to learn a lot about VB's rather complex extensibility model to make a wizard of your own. There is a tool for doing this — it is VB's *Wizard Manager*. To use the Wizard Manager, you must first make the add-in available to your project. Do this as follows:

1. Select Add-Ins ➪ Add-In Manager.

2. From the Available Add-Ins list, select VB 6 Wizard Manager.

3. Click OK.

The add-in will now appear on the Add-Ins menu and is available for use. Select Add-Ins ➪ Wizard Manager to start this add-in. Follow the steps within this Wizards Wizard to produce your own wizard. Once your wizard is complete, compile it (File ➪ Make MyWizard.dll), and proceed as follows to make it available in the templates dialog:

1. A designer is provided to help you through the process of defining your wizard. Use this designer to name and describe your wizard.

2. Create a text file with the name you would like to appear in the Templates dialog; use the file extension .VBZ.

3. This file should have the following two lines of text in it:

```
VBWIZARD 6.0
Wizard=WizardTemplate.Wizard
```

This process will allow you to create your own wizards and hook them into the development environment as template dialogs. In order to make powerful wizards, you will have to spend some time and learn all about Visual Basic's extensibility model — you will need to know this to effectively manipulate the development environment.

Creating a framework

In this section, we will be discussing the creation of frameworks. As a framework is in itself the first step in building a system, it must be carefully thought out and constructed in order to realize its full potential. Thus, we will first be discussing some strategies for the development of the framework, followed by some discussions of the discrete pieces that make it up.

There are several ways to develop frameworks. One way would be to create a new framework from scratch. This technique will require a lot of thought when considering all the core services and functions that will be required. You have to be careful not to step over the bounds of creating a particular application—the goal is to create a starting place that can be reused as often as possible. The more specific features that you add to your framework, the less generically reusable it becomes. You must only add those components that are found in all applications of the generic application type you are targeting. Table 14-1 lists some of the templates that we like to add to every new application we create. These are part of a very generic framework we use that we call "Common Framework."

Table 14-1 The Common Framework	
Template	**Comment**
WinAPI.bas	Contains commonly used Windows API declarations and wrapper functions.
FunctionLib.bas	Contains some simple functions, such as a message to indicate that a function has not yet been implemented and a function to select all the text in a TextBox when it gets focus.
State.bas	Contains functions to save and retrieve state information related to the application. For example, there is a function that will save the size and position of a form, and a corollary function that will retrieve this information.
About.frm	An About box constructed so that the messages that are displayed can be constructed at runtime.

Another way to build a new framework is to branch, or enhance, an existing framework. A similar technique would be to create a number of primitive *template collections* and group those together as a framework. Although any template collection might be considered a framework, we are differentiating it here to illustrate the primitive nature of such a collection. One final technique would be to identify reusable components as you are developing—this is the technique we like best. The reason this technique is preferable is twofold: you will have a better understanding of the required functionality of a particular application type while you are in the midst of developing it, and the underlying thought process of making generic components will help result in a tighter, more encapsulated design in the current application. This results in a win-win situation — your current application benefits from better object-oriented design, and you get reusable frameworks that will help you next time around.

Creating a new framework

When you select File ➪ New, or when you first launch Visual Basic, the new project dialog is displayed (Figure 14-1). If you then select Standard EXE, a project will be started with a blank form, no additional controls in the toolbox, and no special references added in the References dialog. This is the same basic configuration that you would get for a new project in Visual Basic versions 1 through 4. This really isn't much of a framework, so let's go ahead and make one that is a little more useful. Proceed to create the example framework as follows:

1. Start out with a new EXE project by selecting the Standard EXE project from the New dialog.

2. Rename the form **frmMain** or any other name that you would like to call your main form. Set the properties of the form to conform with other standards you have. We will change the following:

   a. BorderStyle to 3 – Fixed Dialog.

   b. Caption to Main.

   c. Add an icon from the ones provided with Visual Basic.

   d. Change the StartUpPosition to 2 – Center Screen.

3. Add an About box form. Select Project ➪ Add Form and then select the About Dialog from the Add Form dialog.

4. Add some components that we typically use in a project. Select Project ➪ Components. Within that dialog, add the Microsoft Windows Common Controls 6.0 component and press OK.

Cross-Reference This step will add the Windows controls such as the ListView and TreeView (see Chapter 6), as well as others.

5. Save this new framework, making sure all the templates you have just created get back in the appropriate subdirectories where Visual Basic stores its templates. In this way, they will show up in the desired dialogs.

   a. Save the About box into the Forms subdirectory. We will call this form VBB About Box.frm.

   b. Save the main form into the Forms subdirectory. We will call this form VBB Main.frm.

   c. Save the project into the Projects subdirectory. We will call this project VBB SDI Frame.vbp.

With these simple steps we have created a basic framework that we can now reuse. When you use this framework and then save it, Visual Basic will treat the first save as a Save As and prompt you for names for the forms and project.

This example created a very simplistic framework, with just a few differences from a clean project. In an actual fast-paced, hard-core development setting, one could envision a lot of fairly sophisticated frameworks. The examples that follow later in this chapter explore two fairly complete frameworks: an MDI framework and an SDI framework.

Templates

How does a template differ from a framework? Within this book, we refer to templates as discrete items that provide the basis for the building of a particular item. For example, a form template for an About box would have just enough information in it to allow the creation of a generic About box dialog. The template would be added to a project, modified, and then saved under a different name — maintaining the generic nature of the template itself. A collection of templates becomes a framework.

ActiveX control components

ActiveX controls, formerly OCXs, formerly VBXs (collectively, *custom controls*) are certainly an important part of your framework. The trick is to pick and choose the controls that are right for you. Any seasoned Visual Basic developer will be able to tell you hours of "war stories" about experiences with custom controls. There will be the stories of incorrect documentation, features that don't work right, GPFs, and control-making vendors going out of business. There will also be a lot of great stories about the neat things made possible by these custom controls. So, custom controls should be considered a good thing, but the choice of the controls must be carefully made. Although we don't have any specific recommendations (being politically correct), we like to stick with the big vendors who have been around for awhile — chances are they have been there for a reason, have worked out their bugs, and will be around for a while longer. Of course, you can always create your own controls with the built-in ActiveX control creation abilities of Visual Basic.

ActiveX server components

Earlier in this chapter, we discussed the inherent Visual Basic capability to use frameworks and templates. These frameworks primarily exploited the use of Visual Basic components such as forms, code modules, and class modules as templates. In addition, a project template can be used as the basis for a new project. The project template would also load all the controls and references that it had listed, thus creating a fairly complete development environment.

An entirely different way to produce a framework is by using a collection of primitive ActiveX servers and adding them to your project. Unlike an ActiveX control, which is designed to be used within another program, an ActiveX server is designed to run as a standalone application. This server provides a particular set of functionality (known as a *service*) that is made accessible through properties, events, and methods. ActiveX servers will be covered in detail in Chapters 22 and 23. The use of ActiveX servers offers a lot of substantial benefits versus the use of templates. ActiveX Servers also have some disadvantages. Tables 14-2 and 14-3 outline some of these advantages and disadvantages.

Table 14-2
Advantages of ActiveX Servers

Item	Comment
Supports team development	The fact that an ActiveX server is a physically separate component makes it easy to manage by a small team. This helps to segregate the workload and allows the assignment of servers to teams with the appropriate expertise.
Scaleable	ActiveX servers can be easily scaled to match the deployment requirements of your application.
Reusable	Due to their physical encapsulation, ActiveX servers have a very high reusability potential. The trick is to make them generic enough to be reusable, but not so generic as to have little value. In addition, ActiveX servers have the added benefit of being able to be used by other OLE-enabled applications, including Microsoft Excel, Microsoft C++, and other similar tools.

Table 14-3
Disadvantages of ActiveX Servers

Item	Comment
Performance	ActiveX servers can be compiled as an out-of-process EXE or in-process DLL. The DLL will perform pretty well, but still not as well as if it were compiled within the project.
Modifiable	These servers are physically isolated components; they cannot be modified. This is both an advantage and a disadvantage. Use of templates allows for the basic code to be modified as needed.

For a detailed discussion on ActiveX servers, read Chapters 19–26. These chapters provide detailed insight into designing and building ActiveX servers.

An MDI framework

There are many times when an application is best suited to an MDI architecture. The fact that an MDI application has a centralized menu and toolbar system as well as internal window management, is useful when you want to provide a system that is completely standalone or when the free-form management of windows is not desirable. Two very popular examples of MDI applications are Microsoft Word and Microsoft Excel.

The MDI framework is designed to provide just enough of a skeleton to facilitate rapid development of an MDI application without providing any application-specific features. In this example, the framework would produce an MDI template that provides the interface shown in Figure 14-6.

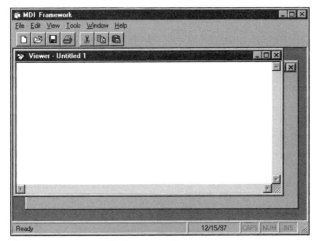

Figure 14-6: An MDI framework

Note that a standard menu, toolbar, and status bar have been provided. In addition, there are two types of MDI child document templates. Two different child types are provided to help easily facilitate the support of different types of child documents — as in the earlier versions of Excel, which supported worksheet and chart document types.

This framework is produced by adding a number of forms and code modules to a project, along with all the custom controls and references these items are dependent upon. These forms and modules are shown in Figure 14-7.

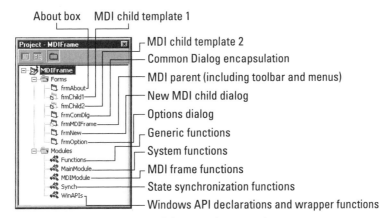

Figure 14-7: Components of the MDI framework

It is important that the components of this framework be extremely generic. The framework would lose its value if one had to spend a lot of time stripping out specific functions that were not required by the target application. For example, the MDIModule only contains the functions shown in Table 14-4.

Table 14-4
MDIModule Functions

Function Name	Purpose
NewChild()	Creates a new instance of a child form. Has the ability to create either child type and to limit the number of instances of a particular type that it will create.
RecentFile()	Creates the recent file menu and provides hooks to utilize it. The same function also persists the items in this menu to an INI file or registry.
ShowStatus()	Provides a central place to manage the information displayed in the status bar at the bottom of the MDI frame. Provides some generic status messages to implement specific messages.

Let's take a closer look at the RecentFile function. This function has been designed to manage a recent file menu system on any form. It requires a certain menu structure in the form, as mentioned in the <Required> tag. The information is written to and retrieved from the system registry using the VB intrinsic registry functions. This function is an example of how a function can be made generic and thus useful as part of a framework, as well as being useful as a standalone function that can be added to any project. This type of encapsulation of functionality is a desirable goal towards building reusable code. The code in Listing 14-1 retrieves entries from the system registry and builds a recent file list on a form. The same function also saves the current menu state to the registry. To make this work, you would create a form with a menu array named mnuFileRecent. This array would have four menu items (elements 1–4). This function can be placed in a central location in your project, such as a code module.

Listing 14-1: **A Generic Most Recently-Used Menu Function**

```
'_____
'<Purpose> Generates the recent file list in the File menu
' and also saves information to the system registry.
'<Required> The form "MenuForm" must have a menu array
' of 4 elements (1-4) named "mnuFileRecent", and a menu
' separator named "mnuFileSeparator4"
'_____

Public Sub RecentFile(Action As Integer, FileName As String, _
    MenuForm As VB.Form, AppName As String)
        Dim AlreadyInList        As Boolean
```

```
Dim i                      As Integer
Dim IsInList               As Integer
Dim SectionKey             As String
Dim ThisFileName           As String
Dim TempFiles()            As String
Static TheseFiles(1 To 4) As String

Select Case Action
    Case 1  '— add a file to the menu
        '— find out if the file is in the list
        For i = 1 To 4
            If (TheseFiles(i) = FileName) Then
                AlreadyInList = True

                '— if file is at position 1 then exit
                If (i = 1) Then Exit Sub

                '— else cascade the recent list down
                ThisFileName = TheseFiles(1)
                If (i = 3) Then
                    TheseFiles(3) = TheseFiles(2)
                ElseIf (i = 4) Then
                    TheseFiles(4) = TheseFiles(3)
                    TheseFiles(3) = TheseFiles(2)
                End If

                TheseFiles(2) = ThisFileName
                Exit For
            End If
        Next i

        '— move all items down, add new file to top
        If (Not AlreadyInList) Then
            ReDim TempFiles(1 To 5)
            For i = 1 To 4
                TempFiles(i + 1) = TheseFiles(i)
            Next

            For i = 1 To 4
                TheseFiles(i) = TempFiles(i)
            Next
        End If

        TheseFiles(1) = FileName
        For i = 1 To 4
            If (TheseFiles(i) = "") Then
                MenuForm.mnuFileRecent(i).Visible = False
            Else
                IsInList = IsInList + 1
                MenuForm.mnuFileRecent(i).Visible = True
                MenuForm.mnuFileRecent(i).Caption = "&" & _
                    Format(i, "0") & " " & TheseFiles(i)
```

(continued)

Listing 14-1 *(continued)*

```
                End If
        Next

        '— save recent file list to registry
        For i = 1 To 4
            SectionKey = "File" & Format(i, "0")
            Call SaveSetting(AppName, "MRU", SectionKey, _
                TheseFiles(i))
        Next

    Case 2   '— get the list from the registry
        For i = 1 To 4
            SectionKey = "File" & Format(i, "0")
            TheseFiles(i) = GetSetting(AppName, "MRU", _
                SectionKey)
            If (TheseFiles(i) = "") Then
                MenuForm.mnuFileRecent(i).Visible = False
            Else
                IsInList = IsInList + 1
                MenuForm.mnuFileRecent(i).Visible = True
                MenuForm.mnuFileRecent(i).Caption = "&" & _
                    Format(i, "0") & " " & TheseFiles(i)
            End If
        Next

End Select

'— show, or hide the separator preceeding the list
MenuForm.mnuFileSeparator4.Visible = (IsInList > 0)

End Sub
```

Let's take a look at a couple of other functions, described in Table 14-5, and how they have been created to be generic and reusable.

Table 14-5
More Reusable Functions

Function Name	Purpose
SelectText	Selects all the text in a TextBox — called when the control gets focus.
GetINIString	Wrapper for the Windows API GetPrivateProfileString.
IsFile	Checks for the existence of a file.
NotDone	Displays the message "This function is not yet implemented."

The SelectText function given in Listing 14-2 is a great example of a simple, generic function that is highly useful. It provides a way to select all of the text in a TextBox when the control gets focus; Listing 14-3 shows an example of using the function. This technique is often employed by Windows applications. It is a good idea to create a collection of these types of functions, organize them into appropriate code modules, and make them part of your framework.

Listing 14-2: **A Generic Function to Select All the Text in a TextBox**

```
'_____

'<Purpose> selects all text in a TextBox
'<WhereUsed> within _GotFocus event
'_____
Public Sub SelectText(ThisTextBox As TextBox)
    ThisTextBox.SelStart = 0
    ThisTextBox.SelLength = Len(ThisTextBox)
End Sub
```

Listing 14-3: **Calling the SelectText Function in the GotFocus Event**

```
Private Sub txtView_GotFocus()
    Call SelectText(txtView)
End Sub
```

An SDI framework

An SDI architecture is much more free-form than that of an MDI. For this reason, it may be harder for novice or casual users to use. It does, however, offer the major benefit of being much better suited to software reuse initiatives, object-oriented designs, and encapsulation. This is due to the fact that there need not be any centralized management metaphor — each window can be designed to be self-sufficient.

The SDI framework shown in Figure 14-8, like the MDI framework, provides a standard set of menus, toolbars, and a status bar. The difference is that there is no notion of a child window in an SDI application. If you needed more than one window, you would just create another instance of the entire application to support this additional need.

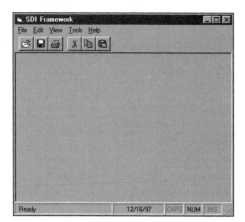

Figure 14-8: An SDI framework

This framework is produced by adding a number of forms and code modules to a project, along with all the custom controls and references these items are dependent upon. These forms and modules are shown in Figure 14-9.

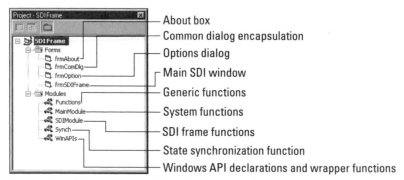

Figure 14-9: Components of the SDI framework

Of particular interest is the fact that several of the components found within the SDI frame are not only similar to some of the components in the MDI frame — they are in fact the same components! This is an example of how you can build new frameworks by assembling a number of primitive pieces.

The Microsoft Repository

The Microsoft Repository is an *enabling technology* for use with all Microsoft development tools and other related BackOffice products. The term *enabling technology* describes a core technology that enables other products to do something. In other words, you probably won't use the Repository directly, but you will definitely use tools that are built on top of it — tools such as the Microsoft Visual Component Manager mentioned in the next section.

The Repository was developed in order to deliver improved support in the following strategic areas:

✦ **Reuse** — Facilities for cataloging and locating relevant designs, code, and services

✦ **Dependency tracking** — Facilities for establishing and querying relationships between objects

✦ **Tool interoperability** — Facilities to publish standardized descriptions of systems, which allows independent tools to exchange data

✦ **Data resource management** — Global metadata for an enterprise data warehouse, and a resource library of available services and components

✦ **Team development** — Facilities to help manage concurrent activity on different versions and configurations of application design and development

The Repository has two basic classes of data: *tool information models* and *instance data*. Tool information models (TIMs) are descriptions of systems or processes that are published in a repository. A repository can contain any number of TIMs, each describing a different system or process. Each TIM defines the objects, interfaces, relationships, and properties that make up a system. You may also think of a TIM as a *template* for a particular type of system. Standardized TIMs allow for independent tools to interact with a common set of Repository data. For example, the MdoTypeLib TIM was created to describe Visual Basic projects. An instance of an MdoTypeLib would be the Repository equivalent of a framework.

Figure 14-10 shows the Repository Browser. This application is provided primarily as a means to view the contents of a repository. If you installed Visual Basic in the default path, this browser can be found in C:\Program Files\Common Files\ Microsoft Shared\Repository.

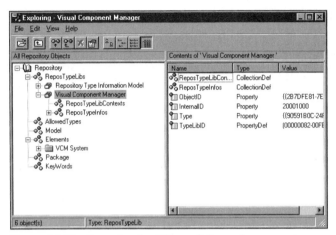

Figure 14-10: Browsing the Microsoft Repository

The model of a system in the Repository can get quite complex, and its representation in the browser may seem very different from the physical system it is designed to model. This is due to the fact that the Repository requires you to think of objects in the context of how their interfaces relate to other objects, and, furthermore, that objects exist only in that they support one or more interfaces. This type of representation provides a very powerful way to think of systems, yet may be too abstract for everyday use. For this reason, we suspect that use of the Repository will be primarily indirect — restricted to tools that utilize the underlying Repository capabilities. These tools will have already handled that abstraction for us, and will have translated the Repository representation of an information model to one that is more comfortable to us.

There is no doubt that the Repository serves as the foundation for Microsoft's reuse strategy for the foreseeable future. For this reason, it makes sense to get a better understanding of what it and its strategic partners offer. For more information on the Repository, visit the Microsoft Repository Web site at `http://www.microsoft.com/repository`. If you are into software engineering and software reuse, you should find the content of this Web site absolutely fascinating.

Microsoft Visual Component Manager

The Visual Component Manager (VCM) is an add-in that is provided with the Professional and Enterprise versions of Visual Basic. It is a replacement for the Component Manager provided in version 4.0, and is better suited to enterprise-wide application development because it is based on the open and scaleable Microsoft Repository. It facilitates code reuse and productivity through categorization, publishing, and retrieval of reusable components.

The VCM is available from the toolbar or the menus (View ⇨ Visual Component Manager). From within the Visual Component Manager, shown in Figure 14-11, a programmer can find and insert pieces of code, load a project template, launch a wizard, or add an ActiveX control to a project. The VCM can also provide a common and centralized location for documentation such as programming standards, functional specifications, or architectural diagrams.

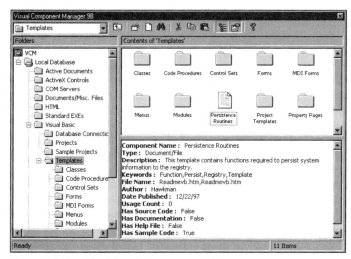

Figure 14-11: The Visual Component Manager.

The Visual Component Manager main dialog has an Explorer-style interface, except that there are three panes instead of two. The left pane has a tree control that is used to navigate the repositories that are currently opened. You can open additional repositories by right-clicking on a node in the tree. The right side of the VCM is divided into top-right and bottom-right panes. The top-right pane displays the current tree selection in more detail, in the same way that the Windows Explorer works. The bottom-right pane continues with the technique of displaying more granularity as it further describes the component that is selected in the top-right pane.

We think that this version of the VCM is now ready for prime time. Many early versions of Microsoft tools are just intended to "set the stage" for things to come. This was probably true for the VB5 version of the VCM — it was a somewhat useful tool that was buried away in obscurity within the product. Not true for this version, however — it is now an integral part of the Visual Basic development environment. More importantly, it is an integral part of Visual Studio. This is *the* tool that is the primary portal into the Microsoft Repository — and it is *the* tool to facilitate software and object reuse within all Microsoft development platforms.

The Visual Component Manager has four major functions:

✦ Provide a single place to store and retrieve reusable Visual Basic components including objects, code, and project-related documents

✦ Provide a way to categorize and catalog these components so that they may be easily located with the VCM search mechanisms

✦ Provide a way to make components you are working on available to other team members through the use of a publishing mechanism

✦ Provide a way to share Visual Basic components with other development tools and use the components published by these other tools — resulting in a deeper integration across development domains

Note Remember that since the VCM is built on top of the Microsoft Repository, the potential is there to not only share information between Microsoft development tools but also to share information between any tools that utilize the Repository.

This capability is starting to get very interesting. Microsoft is obviously doing a lot more than providing you with a development language. They are providing you with a suite of cross-domain tools that are integrated into a development platform.

Publishing a component

Let's take a look at how you can share a component you have developed with the rest of your development team. The Visual Component Manager facilitates this by providing a way to *publish* your component. Publishing allows you to thoroughly describe your component and then add it to the Repository. You publish a component using the *Publishing Wizard*.

The first two steps (not counting the intro screen) of the publishing process might be the most important steps of all. These steps, shown in Figures 14-12 and 14-13, allow you to set the properties of your component. These properties provide a way to categorize and describe your component, and they are also used when you are finding a component.

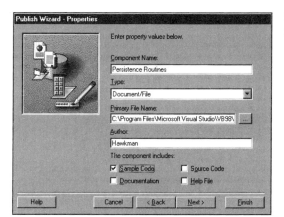

Figure 14-12: Publishing a component—
setting properties, first step

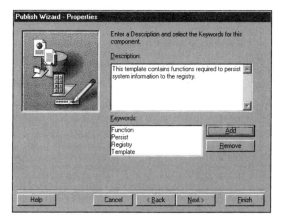

Figure 14-13: Publishing a component—
setting properties, second step

The properties of a component are described in Table 14-6. Many of these
properties are set by a user in the Publishing Wizard. The other properties are
automatically maintained by the Visual Component Manager.

Table 14-6
Some Component Properties

Property	Description
Component Name	The name of the component
Type	The category of the component
Primary Filename	The name of the actual file that is being referenced
Author	The name of the person who developed the component
Component Includes	A set of options to further describe the component
Description	A brief description of the component
Keywords	A set of searchable keywords that pertain to this component
Date Published	The date the component was added to the Repository using the Publishing Wizard

Note   Many of these properties can be modified even after a component is published. To modify a property, right-click on the object in the VCM Explorer pane and choose one of the menu items, such as Change Description or Edit Properties.

Once you have set the properties, you can then specify additional files that are related to your component that you wish to publish. Next, you tell the wizard which of the files you are about to publish require an entry in the system's registry on the computer where you will be installing the wizard. The VCM will use this information when a component is added to a project that is on a system where the registration may be required. In these cases, the VCM will add the required entry into the system registration database when the component is used. You are now ready to publish your component. This component is now available to anyone using the same VCM repository.

Finding a component

One of the most important aspects of a centralized reusable component library is the ability to locate a particular component. If this is a tedious process or one that does not yield the desired results, you probably will not use the Repository at all. What we mean by this is that if it takes more time to find a component than to build one, or if repository searches are not fruitful, then it is not worth the time investment to use the Repository. Therefore, one of the goals of the Repository is to provide a simple and effective search mechanism for component retrieval. Figure 14-14 shows the search mechanism in the Visual Component Manager.

Figure 14-14: Finding a component

Using a component

It is easy to use a component located within the VCM. There are three basic steps:
(1) Start the VCM, (2) Locate the component, and (3) Add it to your project. To find
a component, use the tree control to navigate your repository or use the Find
facility as described earlier. If you select a component in the top-right pane, its
properties show up in the bottom-right pane. You can also view the properties of a
component by right-clicking on an object and selecting Properties. A tabbed dialog
allows you to view all the properties for the selected object. Having located the
desired component, right-click on it and select Add to my Project (Figure 14-15).
The component and any related files will be automatically added to your project.

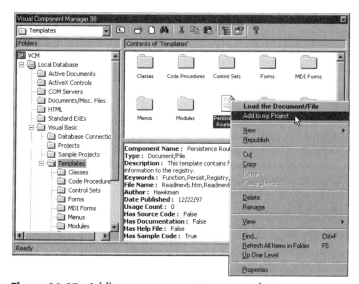

Figure 14-15: Adding a component to your project

A Word About Reusability

Nobody will argue that reusability is a desirable and strategic initiative. Reusability promises quicker application-development times, better quality through use of proven components, and increased maintainability with an overall reduction of the code base. But for many companies, reusability *is a myth*. Why is this? It obviously can't be due to technology — our current technologies have given us the greatest reuse opportunities ever. Integrated version-control systems. ActiveX controls. OLE servers. A plethora of engineering and modeling tools. If all these technologies exist, then why is it so hard for companies to realize these tools' potential? It is probably true that most companies have achieved some level of reusability by using a small set of homegrown objects — but the "big kahuna" (as they say) still remains on the horizon.

The reason that reusability is so hard to achieve is not due to the technology; it is due to people and organizations. Reusability requires systems, discipline, and communication. Systems include such things as physical repositories that create and maintain libraries of components and frameworks. A library of this type — the Microsoft Visual Component Manager — is included with Visual Basic. Systems, however, also include the policies and procedures necessary to use these libraries on a daily basis. The use of these systems requires discipline. Too often it seems easier or just more fun to create something from scratch. Locating an available component takes time. Finally, such reusability requires a method of communicating the availability of reusable components throughout the internal development community.

If these people and organizational problems can be tackled, reusability is available for you right now — the rest is just a matter of well-thought-out components and frameworks.

Summary

It is important to plan your application, a process referred to as *software architecture*.

✦ The amount of planning should directly correlate to the complexity of your application.

✦ There are many approaches to constructing a new application. You could build one from scratch, or (preferably) build upon an existing software base — a *framework*.

✦ A framework can be a set of generic component templates a sophisticated organization of items maintained in a repository.

✦ In any case, the more thorough and clever the architecture of your products — and the more you can reuse existing components — the more productive you will be.

✦   ✦   ✦

Externalizing Resources

◆   ◆   ◆   ◆

In This Chapter

Introduction to resources

Creating resource files

Using resources in Visual Basic programs

◆   ◆   ◆   ◆

Many Visual Basic programmers we have spoken to don't know much about externalizing program resources — moving all the strings (menus, captions, messages, and so on) and pictures from within a program to external files. On the other hand, every C++ programmer knows about resources — this knowledge is required in order to produce just about any program. Historically, Visual Basic has shielded developers from needing to manage resources directly — it does that job for you. There are, however, many reasons why every VB developer, yourself included, should become knowledgeable about externalizing resources. The need for this technique is obvious when you are developing an application that must support more than one language. You also gain the benefits of sharing common resources more efficiently and improved ways to quality-test your application. In this chapter we will start with some of the basic ways to externalize resources using Visual Basic and end with some more advanced topics that utilize both Visual Basic and Visual C++.

Introduction to Resources

The term *resource* refers to those elements of the program that do not directly relate to code or the program logic. For example, the pictures, captions, menus, and even sounds that your program uses can be considered resources. Resources primarily relate to the parts of your program that interact with the user. These are the parts of the program that potentially need to change, depending on your audience.

Collections of resources can be compiled into a *resource file* by a *resource compiler*. This file is then used by the application to retrieve resources. Typically, this file has the .RES extension, for instance, `MyApp.res`. This file can be added to a Visual

Basic project to access all the resources within. Later in this chapter we will show you how to edit resources and ultimately compile them into a resource file.

If you're planning to market your application worldwide, you will definitely need to externalize your resources. Even if you have no current plans for worldwide marketing, it may make sense to plan for this possibility up front. It can be very difficult and painstaking to retrofit an application to another language if such a process has not been planned for from the start. Several design issues must also be considered, and they will be discussed later in this chapter.

There are, however, other reasons to externalize your resources besides internationalization of your application. It may be easier to manage resources if they are all grouped together in a common place. For instance, suppose you wanted to make sure that all the messages your application generates have a consistent style or tone. It would be a difficult process to find all these messages manually throughout your application and edit them for consistency. In addition, there would be a greater chance of not catching all your messages in this fashion. If, however, all these messages were grouped in a single, sequential resource file, editing them all would be easy. You would also have the added benefit of seeing them all together to help develop your style. Another advantage to externalization has to do with modification of your resources. If your style were to change, having all these messages in one place would make them easier to modify.

Let's take a look at another compelling reason for externalization. What if you found an error in some message or some other string after you have shipped thousands of copies of your prize-winning application? Without externalization, you would have to fix the strings in the design stage, then recompile and redistribute the corrected application. Even when using Visual Basic's inherent ability to use resource files, you would have a similar problem. You would still have to fix the resource file, recompile it into your application, and redistribute your application. Later in this chapter, however, we are going to show you the power-user way of making such a fix by side-stepping Visual Basic's inherent abilities and making your resources into a callable DLL.

A final reason to externalize resources, other than localization, is for efficiency. After you have gained mastery over Visual Basic language fundamentals, efficiency becomes a big motivator to try new techniques. When coding, it should be a standard practice for you to create reusable functions that handle logic used in more than one place. Wouldn't it make sense to reuse graphics in a similar way? Every picture that you reuse *directly* removes the size of that picture from the size of the compiled executable file.

It is possible to reuse pictures in ways other than through externalization. One technique is to set the picture property of one control to the picture property of another control. The problem with this technique is that it does not support good code encapsulation due to the fact that the "master" pictures must be made global to the whole project. Another technique is to use the PictureClip control to create an array of graphics and then to extract a particular graphic by using a row and column offset. The problem with this technique is the same as the master picture technique — *plus* the fact that the PictureClip does not support icons. If you require pictures to have transparent backgrounds, you will need icons. Another advantage of externalizing picture resources is that these resources are then easier to reuse *among* projects, not just within a project. You will find that over time you will build a symbol library that can be easily added to each new project.

Locale

If you are marketing your application internationally, you will need to provide it in different *locales*. A locale is a user's environment — the language, culture, and conventions for a particular geographic region. A locale is a unique combination of *language* and *country*. Two examples of locales are English/U.S. and French/Canada.

When you define a locale, the combination of language and country helps to distinguish important cultural differences that must be considered. For example, French is spoken in France, Canada, and Belgium as well as many other countries. Although these countries share a common language, their cultures vary dramatically.

Localization

Localization is the process of adapting an application to a particular locale. This involves much more than a mere translation of words — it is important that the meaning be communicated to a user. In addition to the translation of words (or meanings), a translation of application symbols may be required. It is possible that the icons or other graphical symbols that have a meaning to one locale have a very different, even offensive, meaning to a different locale. For this reason, it may be necessary to provide specific symbols to a locale or, preferably, to design a set of symbols that will work with all locales.

String resources

String resources are all the text that appears in the user interface. This includes menus, captions, any messages that might be displayed using the `MsgBox` or `InputBox` functions, and any other text that might be displayed to a user. These resources can be moved from the Visual Basic development environment to an external *string table*. This string table is a sequential list of strings individually identified by a resource identifier. Visual Basic has a built-in function, `LoadResString`, used to retrieve string resources from a resource file.

Binary resources

Binary resources include pictures and any other binary data. Picture resources are all the graphical symbols that appear in the user interface. This includes bitmaps, cursors, icons, and, possibly, graphics in other formats. These resources are maintained as separate files that are brought together by the resource compiler.

Visual Basic has a built-in function, LoadResPicture, used to retrieve picture resources.

It is also possible to store other resources of unspecified types as binary data. For example, you may want to include a .WAV sound file as a resource to be used by your application. As with pictures, these resources are separate files that are brought together by the resource compiler. Visual Basic has a built-in function, LoadResData, used to retrieve binary resources.

Design considerations

The externalization of resources is much like many other design processes the segregation of an application. The process involves a separation of an *application component* and *resource component* into individual pieces. These pieces, when combined, create a *localized product*.

Figure 15-1 shows that by merely changing the resource data and recombining it with the application code, you will be able to create various localized versions of your product. Although this is basically true, some design considerations must be made while developing the application. These primarily have to do with allocating adequate dialog real estate to handle varying lengths of localized strings as they appear in the interface.

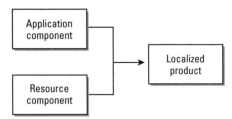

Figure 15-1: Code and data create an application.

Figure 15-2 shows a typical dialog for adding a new user to a database. This dialog has just enough real estate allocated to accommodate the label captions in English. Figure 15-3 shows the same dialog that has been designed to be localized into other languages. As you can see, space has been added to the captions to accommodate the different lengths of localized captions. Table 15-1 provides some specific guidelines to spacing, but as a rule, you should allocate about 50% more space to each caption than you would normally need in English.

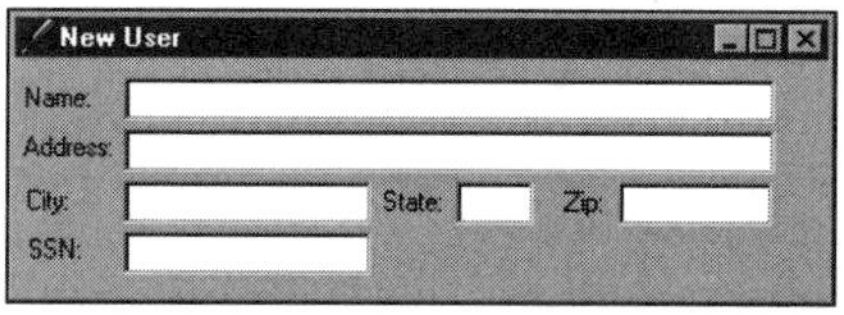

Figure 15-2: A typical New User dialog box

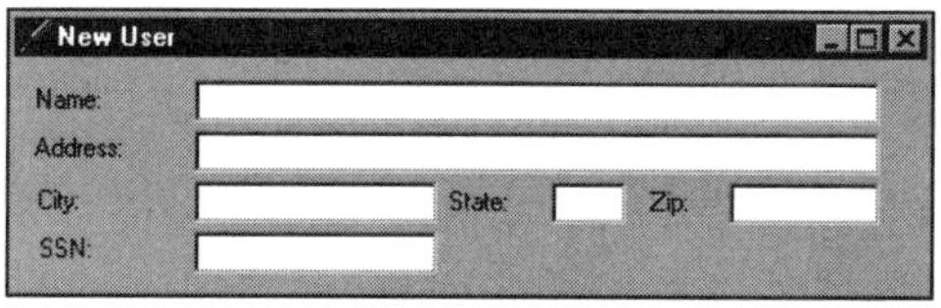

Figure 15-3: The New User dialog box, ready to localize

Table 15-1
Additional Spacing for Localized Strings

Characters in English	Additional Spacing for Localized Strings
1 – 4	100%
5 – 10	80%
11 – 20	60%
21 – 30	40%
31 – 50	20%
Over 50	10%

This requirement for you to allocate more space leads to some interesting and potentially beneficial design decisions. We have all seen dialogs jam-packed with various controls, making them hard to work with. The fact that you *must* allocate additional real estate leads to decisions to break apart such complex forms into subforms. This will have the effect of simplifying some of your dialogs, and may actually improve your user interface (UI).

Graphical symbols such as icons and bitmaps are often used to portray particular functionality without using text. These are a few considerations for using symbols that need to be localized:

✦ Avoid using symbols that portray a functionality that is not an international standard. For example, users from some locales may not recognize a mailbox symbol. There are many books that deal entirely with internationalization that may be helpful in this regard.

✦ Avoid using symbols that contain text. Try to portray the functionality of the symbol with graphics only.

✦ Avoid using symbols that are culturally sensitive. You may need a locale expert to help you determine what the various sensitivities are.

Performance considerations

Oftentimes we hear the argument that loading resources from a file is slower than not loading them, and that this is a good enough reason not to externalize resources. Logic would tell us this is true — it *must* be slower to perform this load operation. In the old days, when computers were much slower (possibly as little as two years ago), loading of resources might have had an impact on load time. Today, this initial load impact is negligible.

There may actually be a performance *advantage* to using externalized resources. Normally, when a form is loaded, all the pictures and strings that the form utilizes are also loaded. This means all interface strings, all message strings, and all pictures will be loaded — all of which affects memory usage and load time. It is possible that many of these strings might not be accessed, as would be the case with error messages. Likewise, some pictures may be hidden so that visible pictures can change as the session dictates. If all these strings and pictures were externalized, only the ones that were actually used would be loaded, and thus the memory impact and the initial load time would be less.

Creating Resource Files

In order to use resources within your program, you must first create a resource file. This involves editing the individual resources and then compiling them into a .RES file. Visual Basic includes an image editor and a resource compiler on the program CD. These tools *are not* installed by default, but must be manually installed by the user. In Visual Basic 6.0, they can be found in the following directories:

\Common\Tools\Vb\Imagedit — Contains the image editor used to edit bitmaps, icons, and cursors.

\Common\Tools\Vb\Resource — Contains the resource compiler used to compile individual resources into a resource file.

To generate the RES file, the resource compiler uses a resource definition file . This file, which has an .RC extension, contains a number of resource definition statements used to identify the various resources. Although some of these statements are mentioned in this chapter, a complete listing can be found in the resource compiler help file RC.HLP. String resources, as noted by the STRINGTABLE statement, are actually contained within the definition file. Binary resources, which are contained in separate files, are referenced in the definition by the name of their file.

If you want to use the inherent Visual Basic tools, you will have to manually create this RC file with any standard text editor. There are, however, alternatives. We recommend using the resource creating capabilities of Microsoft Visual C++

(VC). VC will automatically create the RC file and will compile it within the development environment. If you have no other need for VC, then this is an expensive proposition — but if you already are using VC within your development team, then this would be the preferable alternative. Beyond Microsoft Visual C++, many other C++ compilers will also have this capability. Since this book is primarily dealing with Visual Basic's inherent capabilities, we will be concentrating on creating resource files with VB-available tools.

The Imagedit tool

We're going to talk a little bit about the image-editor tool that comes with Visual Basic, but for full documentation refer to the tool itself and its associated help file. This editor, whose filename is `Imagedit.exe`, allows you to edit cursors, icons, and bitmaps. If you do not have a more powerful editor of this type, then Imagedit will have to suffice. In this case, we recommend using the Microsoft Paint application that comes with Windows to edit bitmaps, and use Imagedit to edit icons and cursors. Paint is a more appropriate bitmap editor for the larger bitmap files.

To make Imagedit available to your Windows desktop, copy all the files in the \Common\Tools\Vb\Imagedit directory on the Visual Basic CD to a directory of your choice. There is no need to perform any installation or register this tool — just copy it to your hard drive.

To create a new icon, do the following:

1. Start the Imagedit program.

2. Select File ↪ New.

3. Select Icon as the resource type.

4. Select the Target Device of this icon. Your choices are 2-color or 16-color, and 16 x 16 (small icon) or 32 x 32 (large icon) size. Select a full-color large icon, which is the 16-color 32 x 32 choice.

5. Draw your icon, save it, and exit the program.

It is important to note that icons can contain *both* small and large icon images in the same file. To add a small icon to your current icon, select Edit ↪ New Image and then select the 16-color small icon.

Although icon files can contain both large and small images, some unsatisfactory results have been reported when such files are used with the ImageList control. Remember, this is the control that contains images which can then be utilized by many of the Microsoft Windows Common Controls, such as the Toolbar, ListView, and TreeView. It appears that these controls will use the 32 x 32 icon and scale it down to 16 x 16, even when a 16 x 16 image is available within the file (this is still the case with Visual Basic 6.0). For this reason, you should create separate large and small icon files and place them into separate ImageLists when using them in conjunction with the controls listed here.

The resource definition file

The *resource definition file* is a script used by the resource compiler to create a resource file. This file — or, more accurately, this script — is a text file with the .RC extension. The script lists all the resources within your application and describes some types of resources in great detail. For binary resources that exist in separate files (such as icons or cursors), the script will name the resource and the file that contains it. For some other resources (such as strings), the entire definition of the resource will exist within the script.

A script file can contain the following types of information:

✦ **Preprocessing directives** instruct RC to perform actions on the script before compiling it. Directives can also assign values to names. We will not be discussing most of these directives in this chapter — for details, refer to the compiler documentation.

✦ **Statements** name and describe resources.

Resource IDs

Each resource is identified by a unique integer within the script. This integer is referred to as the *resource ID* and is used when retrieving a resource from the RES file. The Visual Basic functions refer to this ID as the resource *index*. For example, the function used to retrieve strings is LoadResString(index), where index is an integer variable serving as the resource ID. Oftentimes it is useful to substitute a constant name for the ID when referring to a resource. This can be done by defining a constant/ID pair and then using the constant instead of the actual ID when declaring the resource. This is done using the #define directive:

```
#define btnOK                          3001
#define btnCancel                      3002
```

All these constant/ID definitions can be placed in a separate header file, having the .H extension. In fact, if you create your resources using other tools such as Visual C++, this is exactly where these definitions are placed. A header file is a useful way to organize such definitions together in a single place. If you do use such a header file, use the #include directive to tell the script about it:

```
//name of the resource file
#include "resource.h"
```

Notice the double slash // in the above statement. This is used to add comments to your resource script or header file.

Organizing your resources is key to successfully managing them. This organization begins in your resource script and carries through to your Visual Basic code. It's accomplished by grouping like resources into a number of categories. Categories can be devised for whatever makes sense to you. For each category, you can establish a starting number for the category; then each item under it can be offset from the starting point, or *baseid* (pronounced "base-eye-dee"). The following segment shows some of the resource definitions using this nomenclature:

```
#define baseidButton                 3000
#define btnOK                        3001
#define btnCancel                    3002
#define baseidCompany                4000
#define comName                      4001
#define comPhone                     4002
```

In addition to providing a starting point, each baseid also has a unique prefix assigned to it. In the above example, all buttons that can be found under `baseidButton` have a `btn` prefix and so on. These same definitions carry through to a Visual Basic module that declares the resource constants:

```
'<Button> ——————————————————
Public Const baseidButton As Integer = 3000
Public Const resbtnOK     As Integer = (baseidButton + 1)
Public Const resbtnCancel As Integer = (baseidButton + 2)
'</Button> ——————————————————-

'<Company> —————————————————
Public Const baseidCompany As Integer = 4000
Public Const rescomName   As Integer = (baseidCompany + 1)
Public Const rescomPhone  As Integer = (baseidCompany + 2)
'</Company> —————————————————
```

This module will be discussed in more detail in the section "Using Resources in Visual Basic Programs" later in this chapter.

The resource compiler

The resource compiler RC.EXE is a DOS command-line compiler used to compile individual resources into a .RES file. It uses a resource definition (script) file to bring together the various resources into a single file. Also, a number of optional switches may be specified while compiling this .RES file. These switches are not needed for most simple resource files you will be using with your Visual Basic program.

The following sections show you how to define bitmaps, icons, cursors, and strings within the resource script. For additional documentation on these and other resources, refer to the help files associated with RC.EXE. For each resource type listed below there is a resource-definition statement, which is a *keyword* recognized by the resource compiler. The general syntax for each statement is as follows:

Syntax

```
resourceID STATEMENT [load-mem] "filename"
```

Part	Description
resourceID	An integer, or a constant that has been specified using the #define directive.
STATEMENT	The resource compiler keyword.
load-mem	Loading and memory attributes. The only attribute used by Win32 (the 32-bit Windows API library) is the DISCARDABLE attribute. This attribute specifies that the resource can be discarded if it is no longer needed.
filename	Specifies the name of the file that contains the resource. The name must be a valid filename; it must be a full path if the file is not in the current working directory. The path can be either a quoted or nonquoted string.

Bitmaps

The BITMAP resource definition statement is used to specify a bitmap resource to be included in the RES file:

Syntax

```
resourceID BITMAP [load-mem] "filename"
```

Examples

```
bmpFinish      BITMAP  DISCARDABLE    "FINISH.BMP"
1024           BITMAP  DISCARDABLE    "TRASH.BMP"
```

Icons

The ICON resource definition statement is used to specify an icon resource to be included in the RES file:

Syntax

```
resourceID ICON [load-mem] "filename"
```

Examples

```
icoFolderClosed  ICON    DISCARDABLE    "Folder Closed.ico"
2096             ICON    DISCARDABLE    "FolderOpen.ico"
```

Cursors

The CURSOR resource definition statement is used to specify a cursor resource to be included in the RES file:

Syntax

```
resourceID CURSOR [load-mem] "filename"
```

Examples

```
curFolderClosed     CURSOR      "Hand.cur"
4127                CURSOR      "c:\MyApp\Point.cur"
```

Strings

The `STRINGTABLE` resource definition statement is used to specify that a string table will immediately follow within the script file. Each string resource is a null-terminated string, enclosed in double quotation marks. The string must be no longer than 255 characters and must occupy a single line in the source file. To add a carriage return to the string, use the character sequence `\n`. For example, `Error Number:\nError Code:` would define a string that would be displayed as follows:

```
Error Number:
Error Code:
```

You can have as many different `STRINGTABLE`s in the script file as needed. Grouping strings in separate tables allows all related strings to be read in at one time and discarded together.

Syntax

```
STRINGTABLE [load-mem]
[optional-statements]
BEGIN
    resourceID "string"
    . . .
END
```

Example

```
STRINGTABLE DISCARDABLE
BEGIN
    IDS_HELLO,    "Hello"
    IDS_GOODBYE   "Goodbye"
END
```

Using the RC compiler

The resource compiler RC.EXE is found in the Resource directory on the Visual Basic CD-ROM. Install it by copying the files into a directory of your choice. To start the RC resource compiler, exit Windows to a DOS prompt and use the RC command. The following line shows RC command-line syntax:

Syntax

```
RC [options] script-file
```

Examples

To compile a file and show status messages:

```
RC /v resfilename.rc
```

To display a list of all the RC command-line options, type the following:

```
RC /?
```

Once the compiler has successfully compiled the resource file, the compiled file can be found in the directory that contained the original source. The filename, by default, will be the name of the RC file with a .RES extension. This file is now ready to load into a Visual Basic project.

Using Resources in Visual Basic Programs

Any valid resource file can be loaded into a Visual Basic project, but you can only have one such file per project. To load the file, select Project ➪ Add file and pick the resource file you wish to add. This resource file is now a part of your project and will, in fact, be linked into the EXE by Visual Basic. Although the file shows up in your Project Explorer under the Related Documents folder, it cannot be opened from within the development environment. However, all the resources contained within this file are now available to your project at runtime.

Note   There can be only one resource file per project.

Once the RES file has been added to your project, you can access these resources using the following built-in Visual Basic functions.

LoadResString

Loads a string resource as referenced by the resource ID or index. Returns a string. In the following example, a string with the resource ID of 1027 is being loaded into the Text property of a TextBox:

Syntax

```
LoadResString(index)
```

Example

```
Text1.Text = LoadResString(1027)
```

LoadResPicture

Loads a picture resource as identified by the resource index. To make use of this function, set a picture property of a PictureBox or Image control to the returned value.

Syntax

```
LoadResPicture(index, format)
```

Supported formats

Constant	Value	Resource type
vbResBitmap	0	Bitmap resource
vbResIcon	1	Icon resource
vbResCursor	2	Cursor resource

Example

Set Picture1.Picture = LoadResPicture(2145, vbResBitmap)

LoadResData

Loads a binary resource as identified by the resource index. Returns a byte array.

Syntax

```
LoadResData(index, format)
```

Supported formats

Value	Resource type
1	Cursor resource
2	Bitmap resource
3	Icon resource
4	Menu resource
5	Dialog box

6	String resource
7	Font directory resource
8	Font resource
9	Accelerator table
10	User-defined resource
12	Group cursor
14	Group icon

Example

The following example loads the custom resource SOUND_BYTE and plays it using an API call. Refer to the resource compiler help file RC.HLP for information on creating custom binary resources.

```
'— the API declaration to play sounds
Declare Function sndPlaySound Lib "WINMM.DLL" Alias _
"sndPlaySoundA" (ByVal lpszSoundName As Any, _
ByVal uFlags As Long) As Long

Sub BeginPlaySound(ResId As Integer)
    Dim SoundBuf As String

    '— return string is converted to Unicode
    SoundBuf = StrConv( _
  LoadResData(ResId, "SOUND_BYTE"), vbUnicode)

Call sndPlaySound(SoundBuf, SND_ASYNC Or _
    SND_NODEFAULT Or SND_MEMORY)

    '— needed to play sound asynchronously
    DoEvents
End Sub
```

Note   The terms *resource ID* and *index* are identical. Visual Basic refers to the resource identifier as *index,* whereas the resource compiler refers to this same identifier as *resource ID.*

Designing with string resources

Technically, the examples shown earlier provide everything you need to load and use external string and picture resources. The use of binary resources requires a more detailed understanding than we can adequately discuss in this book. Although you now know enough to basically use resources, we are now going to introduce some techniques to organize your work and test your resources.

String resources should replace the use of *all* strings in your project that have interaction with a user. This means that the form and label captions, menus, messages, and even URLs must potentially be externalized. As you will still need to create the string captions and menus at design time, it is important to differentiate the design-time strings from runtime strings. A design-time string is one entered into a form or menu within the Visual Basic IDE. A runtime string is one assigned to a text, caption, or similar property programmatically during the execution of a program. For this reason, we have come up with the technique of preceding all design-time strings with an asterisk (*). At design time, you can clearly read every caption — this is important for your everyday development. At runtime, you will be replacing all the captions with resource strings that do not include the asterisk. In this way, you can quickly look at your form and determine whether all the design-time strings have been replaced or not. Figure 15-4 shows a form in the design stage where strings that appear within label controls are marked with asterisks, as a signal to replace them later.

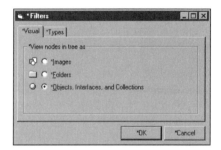

Figure 15-4: Design-time strings that are marked

It is very easy to test all the visible string resources in your application in this way. Any string resources that have been inadvertently omitted will show up easily. Once resources have been properly externalized, the same form can be made to appear as shown in Figure 15-5.

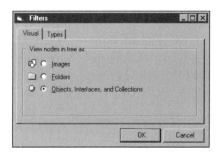

Figure 15-5: The runtime form with resource strings loaded

Organizing your resources

The resource ID itself is an integer. Although you use this raw integer when referencing a resource in the RES file, if you create a set of constants it will be easier to understand what resource you are referencing. In addition, if the value of a constant needs to change, you only have to change it in one place. Instead of just creating some sequential set of constants for the IDs, you should categorize resources into various groups. This categorization begins with the resource script and carries through to your Visual Basic program.

Categorization of resources can be done in a number of different ways; try different techniques until you settle on one that is meaningful for you. To begin your organization, assign each category a baseid, which is the starting number for that category. Also, assign a common prefix to each category. Next, assign all the resources belonging to that category a sequential offset from that ID. Make sure you leave enough space between baseids to provide for future expansion within the category.

All resource constants are placed in a separate code module so that they are easy to locate and maintain. At the top of this resource module is a resource map that is used to identify the categories of resources that you will be using. This map helps to coordinate your resource categories within Visual Basic and your resource script. Portions of such a map appear here in Listings 15-1 and 15-2. In the next section, we will show you how this map can also be used to facilitate testing of your resources.

Listing 15-1: **The Resource Map Defines Resource Categories**

```
'<ResourceMap>
'                   Res              BaseID
'Category           Type    Prefix*  Name            Value
'_____ ___ ____ _____
'<Bitmap>          Bitmap  (bmp)    baseidBitmap     2000
'<Button>          String  (btn)    baseidButton     3000
'<Company>         String  (com)    baseidCompany    4000
'<Cursor>          Cursor  (cur)    baseidCursor     5000
'<Dialog>          String  (dlg)    baseidDialog     6000
'<Icon>            Icon    (ico)    baseidIcon       7000
'<Menu>            String  (mnu)    baseidMenu       8000
'<String>          String  (str)    baseidString     9000
'<Toolbar>         String  (tbr)    baseidToolbar    10000
'<Message>         String  (msg)    baseidMessage    13000
'<Object>          String  (obj)    baseidObject     14000
'<Application>     String  (app)    baseidApp        29000
'<Error>           String  (err)    baseidError      30000
'
' * all prefixes are preceded by a 'res' to indicate
'    a resource; for example: 'resappName'
'</ResourceMap>
```

Listing 15-2: **Each Resource Category Defined
in Separate Section**

```
'<Application> ———————————
Public Const baseidApp            As Long = 29000
Public Const resappName           As Long = (baseidApp + 1)
Public Const resappPrefix         As Long = (baseidApp + 2)
Public Const resappVersion        As Long = (baseidApp + 3)
Public Const resappCopyright      As Long = (baseidApp + 4)
Public Const resappRoot           As Long = (baseidApp + 5)
Public Const resappMyComputer     As Long = (baseidApp + 6)
Public Const resappDesktop        As Long = (baseidApp + 7)
Public Const resappContentsOf     As Long = (baseidApp + 8)
Public Const resappObjects        As Long = (baseidApp + 9)
'</Application> ———————————
```

The resource script can include a reference to a resource header file (for example #include "resource.h") that defines a set of constants and resource IDs. This header file contains the same set of categories used to group resources together as is found in the Visual Basic resource module. An example of a resource header file appears in Listing 15-3.

Listing 15-3: **Resource Header File Containing
Same Categories and IDs**

```
#define baseidApplication        29000
#define appName                  29001
#define appPrefix                29002
#define appVersion               29003
#define appCopyright             29004
#define appRoot                  29005
#define appMyComputer            29006
#define appDesktop               29007
#define appContentsOf            29008
#define appObjects               29009
```

The resource constants as used in the header file have only the category prefix followed by a descriptive name. When this constant is defined within Visual Basic, another prefix, res, is added to denote that the constant is a resource-related constant.

Testing external resources

Testing of external resources presents some unique problems. You must find a way to ensure that every resource ID referenced in your program can be found in the resource file. If you reference an ID that does not exist, you will generate a runtime error. This presents a unique problem that we painfully experienced when we first started using resource files. To understand this problem, take a look at Listing 15-4.

Listing 15-4: Attempting to Handle Bad Resource ID References

```
Public Function AddNode(NewNode As INode) As String
    Dim NodeKey As String
    On Error GoTo BadNode

    '— create the key
    NodeKey = "Node." & Nodes.Count + 1
    Call Nodes.Add(NewNode, NodeKey)
    AddNode = NodeKey
  Exit Function

BadNode:
    '— show error message
    Call MsgBox(LoadResString(reserrAddNode),_
              vbOKOnly + vbInformation)
    AddNode = ""
End Function
```

As you can see, a message box is displayed when an error has occurred. An error message is then loaded out of the resource file and displayed as the message. If the ID of the string (reserrAddNode = 1024) is not a valid resource ID, an error will be generated. Unfortunately, the only reason that this resource string is being displayed in the first place is because an error has *already* been generated — and this bad ID would then cause a fatal error. This anomaly could probably be handled in several ways — such as moving the display of error messages to a separate function, which then checks for bad resource ID errors. However, this kind of error trapping can lead to a vicious circle that needs to be avoided.

Fear not — the authors of this book, having experience with this problem, have developed a way to test the availability of resources. A fully functional test application is included on the CD-ROM that accompanies this book. The resource test application ResTest.vbp is used to test that all the resources referenced within a Visual Basic application can actually be found in the RES file used by the app. It does this by going through each resource that is declared and attempting to load it. Figure 15-6 shows ResTest at work.

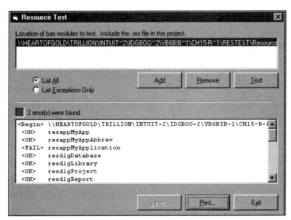

Figure 15-6: Resource test application

The ResTest application requires a code module that contains all the resource declarations preceded by a resource map. This singular map will define *all* the resources that will be used within the entire project. The resource map begins with the HTML-style tag <ResourceMap> and ends with the closing tag </ResourceMap>. The map contains a number of tags that define the resource category and attributes regarding each category. Each resource category "record" is of fixed-length and conforms to the format listed in Table 15-2.

Table 15-2			
Resource Map Record			
Field	**Start**	**Length**	**Description**
Tag	2	18	Resource category
Type	20	7	Resource type
Prefix	28	11	Prefix unique to the category
Name	40	23	Name of the baseid
Value	64	7	Value of the baseid

Here is how you use ResTest:

1. Create a resource file using the category groupings described in this chapter.

2. Create a resource module in Visual Basic with the same category groupings and a resource map.

3. Add the RES file to the ResTest project by choosing the file from the Add File dialog: Project ➪ Add File.

Note Note that you can only have one resource file per project. You may have to remove any existing resource files before adding the new one you want to test. Currently, the project is only designed to work with the resource file ExtRes.res included with the project. Other resource files should work, but they must be constructed as per the instructions in this chapter.

4. Run the project.

5. In the *Location of bas modules. ListBox* found on the main form, add the resource code module that contains your resource map.

6. Press Test to have ResTest examine your resources.

ResTest builds an internal structure that correlates to each resource category in the map. It then locates all the resource constants for each category and attempts to load the resources they reference. ResTest builds a complete log of its activity, or just provides a log of any exceptions it finds.

Note Note that this test application will only work when you use the ExtRes.res file and Resource.bas files supplied with this project. You may have to modify the source to have it work with your own files. The project simply provides a starting framework that you can use to test your resource files.

This program has proven to be successful in locating resource errors in a production application that was shipped by one of the authors. With a little bit of work, it can be adapted to fit your particular needs. In any case, it is very important that you provide thorough testing of your resources, just as you would test any other component of your application.

Servicing multiple locales

Basically, two approaches provide ways for your externalized resources to service multiple locals:

> **All locales in a single resource file:** Place a number of complete sets of resources in the same file in groups. Each group is offset from another group by a fixed number.

> **Each locale in a separate resource file:** Each file represents a certain locale.

Placing all your resources in a single file gives you the benefit of having a single place to store and modify all resources. The disadvantage of this technique is twofold: (1) Your application size will increase because you will have duplicate strings to support the various locales; and (2) A change required to a particular locale will require a change to all localized versions of the application. An example of this would be if you had four localized versions of your program: English, French, Spanish, and German. If you only had to change a French term, you would still have to recompile a resource file that was used by all the versions. Despite these disadvantages, the single-file approach is surely the easiest way to localize strings and has the advantage of being able to produce a single executable that will "play" in multiple locales.

To create an offset-based system, you merely create a bank of strings for each locale, each laid out in an identical fashion, but each starting at a different point or offset. You could still categorize your resources, but then you would have to have language offsets within your category offsets, which would result in less overall resources that could be assigned to any category. Once the resource file is laid out to this specification, a locale offset is read in by the application and applied to every use of a resource. This language offset can be obtained from a command-line prompt, or some registry setting, or from any similar technique.

For example, let's say that English starts at resource ID 1000, Spanish starts at 2000, and French starts at 3000. In this example, the English sentence, "Hello, there," would be assigned the resource ID 1001, the Spanish equivalent of that sentence 2001, and the French equivalent 3001. Listing 15-5 completes this example.

Listing 15-5: **Example of Using a Language Offset**

```
'—- offsets:
' 1000 = English
' 2000 = Spanish
' 3000 = French
Public LangOffset As Integer

Sub Main()
'— get the offset
LangOffset = GetSetting("MyApp", "Resource", _
    "LangOffset")

  '— using the resource
  HelloText.Text = GetResString(1 + LangOffset)
End Sub
```

A second way to service different locales is to create separate RES files for each locale. This has the advantage of allowing changes to any locale as needed, but has a distinct disadvantage. Because of the way that Visual Basic includes resource files in the project, you will have to compile a different executable for each locale. Because of the significant advantages of this technique, and to overcome its serious drawback, the next section is going to show you how to create separate resource files that can be used by a single executable. The only way to do this is to turn to the Windows API for help.

Using the Windows API to Access Resources

So far we have concentrated on accessing resources using inherent Visual Basic functions. In many cases, this will be sufficient; however, there are times when it will be advantageous to access resources directly using Windows API functions. Some of the information in this section requires a general knowledge of C++. For more information on Windows API programming in Visual Basic, see Part VI.

This section will provide some working examples of how you can create a DLL that contains your resources and how this DLL can be accessed from within Visual Basic. We will be using Microsoft Visual C++ to create this DLL, but you should be able to create it with other tools as well.

To begin this exercise, you create a C++ project that contains all your resources. You will only need to compile a single source file with the following code as a DLL:

```
void DLLMain();

void DLLMain()
{
};
```

Now, from within Visual Basic, we are going to load this resource library, access the resources as needed, and then unload the library before we completely exit the program. Listing 15-7 presents the necessary declarations for the API functions.

Listing 15-7: **Declarations for Windows API Functions**

```
Public Declare Function LoadLibrary Lib "kernel32" _
  Alias "LoadLibraryA" (ByVal lpLibFileName As String) _
  As Long
Public Declare Function LoadString Lib "user32" _
  Alias "LoadStringA" (ByVal hInstance As Long, _
  ByVal wID As Long, ByVal lpBuffer As String, _
  ByVal nBufferMax As Long) As Long
Public Declare Function LoadIconByNum Lib "user32" _
  Alias "LoadIconA" (ByVal hInstance As Long, _
  ByVal lpIconName As Long) As Long
Public Declare Function DrawIcon Lib "user32" _
  (ByVal hdc As Long, ByVal X As Long, _
  ByVal Y As Long, ByVal hIcon As Long) As Long
Public Declare Function FreeLibrary Lib "kernel32" _
  (ByVal hLibModule As Long) As Long
```

The handle to the DLL is placed in a modular variable. A *handle* is a number used to access a Windows resource:

```
Private hResDLL As Long   '— handle to the res dll
```

Load the resource DLL when appropriate:

```
hResDLL = LoadLibrary(App.Path & "\MyRes.dll")
```

If the resource you need to retrieve is a string, the code in Listing 15-8 can accomplish that task.

Listing 15-8: **Retrieving a String Resource**

```
Public Function GetDLLString(ResID As Long) As String
    Dim ReturnCode  As Long
    Dim ReturnStr   As String * 255

  ReturnCode = LoadString(hResDLL, ResID, _
        ReturnStr, 255)
    GetDLLString = Mid(ReturnStr, 1, _
        InStr(1, ReturnStr, Chr(0)) - 1)

End Function
```

If the resource you need to retrieve is an icon, use the code in Listing 15-9.

Listing 15-9: **Retrieving an Icon Resource**

```
Public Sub GetDLLPicture(ResID As Long, _
    PicCtrl As VB.Control)

    Dim ReturnCode  As Long
    Dim hIcon       As Long

    hIcon = LoadIconByNum(hResDLL, ResID)
    ReturnCode = DrawIcon(PicCtrl.hdc, 0, 0, hIcon)

End Sub
```

When you finish retrieving resources, use the following line of code to unload the DLL before you end the application:

```
Call FreeLibrary(hResDLL)
```

Once all the code just given is in place, to change locales just create a new C++ project for each locale and translate the string tables within each project. Compile a different DLL for each local and include the appropriate DLL with your distribution and installation. Once you have mastered this technique, you will be able to perfect it to your particular needs.

Summary

In this chapter, we have described what resources are, how to create them, and how to manage them. We have taken you beyond Visual Basic's inherent capabilities and introduced you to some advanced techniques of creating resource DLLs.

✦ There are many compelling reasons to externalize your resources.

✦ If you are planning to distribute your Visual Basic application in more than one language, then the practice of externalizing and localizing your resources is an obvious choice.

✦ Yes, externalizing resources does take more work, and yes, it also requires a new programming discipline. But this chapter has shown you many of the benefits you can realize by using resources — these rewards may be enough to make this effort worth your while.

✦   ✦   ✦

Persisting State

A *state* can be thought of as a snapshot of a system at a
given time. Any system comprises multiple states. For
the most part, a user controls the movement from state to
state by the actions he or she takes while using the system.
The capability of a system to remember the state of a system
when the application is exited and then return the system to
that same state when the system is restarted is known as *state
persistence*.

Persistence of state is all about providing the user with that
additional comfort level and making the user feel that he or
she is in control of the system. Many systems are not well
behaved in that they don't "listen" to what a user is telling
them to do, or just arbitrarily change their state even though
they have not been directed to do so. For example, there is a
particular mail system we use at work (see if you can figure
out which one on the basis this description). This system
never returns to the place it is left in — it always returns to
some initial state. If mail-related subfolders are opened and
the system is exited and reentered, the system always returns
to the inbox. This behavior screams that the system is in
control, not the user. Another nasty habit this system has is
to minimize itself when an attachment document that requires
the launching of an application is opened — users should be
able to minimize a window when they want to (thank you
very much). This is an example of persisting state during
the operation of the system. Apparently, the designers of the
system think they know a user's work habits better than the
user does. A system should work around a user's habits —
and that means persisting the state the system is left in.

We are all conscious of some aspects of how a system persists
(or does not persist) states, like the example described above.
This nasty mail program is just downright smarter than any
user and is not going to relinquish control even if the user did
pay good money for it. Other aspects of state persistence are
much more subtle — such as the positions of forms, or widths
of columns in a grid. The combination of these conscious
actions by the system, along with the more unconscious but
comforting behaviors, makes a highly usable system. This

chapter, then, is about which system behaviors are candidates to persist — and the technical techniques required to accomplish this persistence.

Learning About State

A computer program can be thought of as a state machine, or to be more precise, a *finite state machine*. That is, a system consists of a finite number of states and it can only be in one state at any given time. Figure 16-1 shows the system DataMan in a given state.

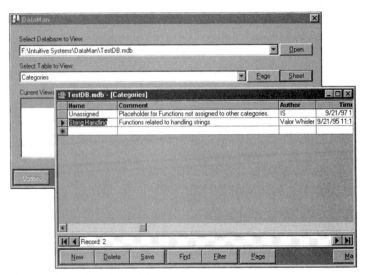

Figure 16-1: A system state

What can we tell about the state of this system?

- ✦ There are two forms visible.
- ✦ The bottom form has a database and table selected in the combo boxes.
- ✦ The top form has a view of the selected table within a grid control.

What is not obvious by looking at the above figure is the work that has been done behind the scenes by the state engine built into this product. Figure 16-2 helps illustrate this work.

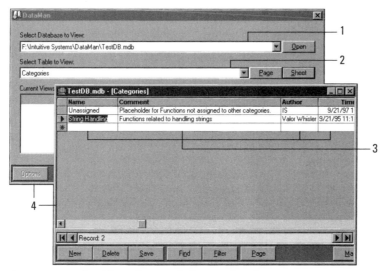

Figure 16-2: The things that are being persisted

Item 1 in Figure 16-2 shows a combo box that has a list of all of the databases that have been opened by this system in the past. The last database used is selected in this combo box when the system is initialized.

Item 2 illustrates a combo box that has a list of all of the tables that are found within the selected database. *For each database*, the last table used is persisted and selected when the system is initialized.

Item 3 shows the widths of the column in the grid *for each table that is viewed*. The widths are persisted so the grid can be returned to its previous state.

Item 4 shows the size and screen position of each form persisted so they can be returned to the state they were left in.

Tracking System Information

We think all developers are familiar with state persistence in its simplest form — saving system options. Many programs offer some type of Options dialog that facilitates the review and modification of these options. These options are used to modify the behavior of a system on the basis of a user's likes or needs. Options of this type are stored during each system session and retrieved for use by a new session.

In this section, we provide a working example of how such options can be tracked in a very encapsulated fashion. We also show you how to track many of the visual attributes of your system.

Persisting system options

Just about any system of consequence offers some type of options, generally offered in an Options dialog. This dialog displays the currently selected options and allows a user to change them. The dialog shown in Figure 16-3, which is included on the accompanying CD, is a template for an encapsulated Options dialog.

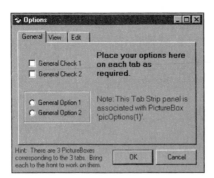

Figure 16-3: The Options dialog box

There are many ways to persist the dialog options and many ways to use those options within a program. This information can be stored in global (public, in a code module) properties, in a user-defined type, or in a class module. They can also be stored in and "owned" by the Options dialog itself. We like this method the best because the form used to set those options is also the form responsible for maintaining them within the program. To complete this encapsulation of options, the form is also responsible to persist them and to retrieve them from their persistent store.

It is important at this time to take a look at the life of a form and how that relates to its memory footprint. Before we do so, let's take a quick historical look back. In versions 4 and earlier of Visual Basic, a form had only two states: *loaded* and *unloaded*. A loaded form had (and still has) a high impact on memory — and the more controls on a form, the more memory is eaten up. For this reason, it was very important to unload forms that were not being used, so the memory they were using could be released. You may also want to completely remove a form from memory by setting it to Nothing — this removes all traces of the form from memory, not just the visual footprint. In addition to having only two states, forms in early versions did not have public properties or public procedures.

Many of the earlier adapters of object-oriented programming (OOP) wanted to encapsulate functionality within a form. We fired events by setting the Text property of invisible TextBoxes on the form to a particular value and then executing logic within the click event of that control. Different types of events could be fired by using a Select Case statement that would use the text value. Likewise, values "owned" by the form could be read by reading text values in invisible TextBoxes.

Although this technique gave us encapsulation, it was very much a workaround, having limited capabilities. However, the biggest problem when using such a technique was the memory impact. It turns out that *a form is implicitly loaded when any of the properties of the form or any control on the form is accessed, even if the form is not visible*. As you can see, this technique gave us a sort of cruder encapsulation, but was not very efficient.

When the capability to have public properties and procedures in forms came along, these problems went away. In addition to public properties and procedures, two new form events were added: Initialize and Terminate. Figure 16-4 shows the life of a form object and describes what occurs in each of the life-related events.

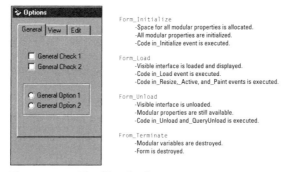

Figure 16-4: The life of a form

Careful coding is required so a form's memory footprint is properly managed. As mentioned, the visual components of a form generally have the highest memory impact. However, a form object can be initialized and not loaded. In this initialized state, the public properties and procedures are available, yet the memory impact is minimal. Here are some rules to follow:

1. Retrieve the values of public properties from your persistence store in the Initialize event. These values are then accessible to your program. DO NOT get or set any control properties. If you do, you cause the form to be loaded. The first function that accesses a public property automatically causes the Initialize event to fire.

2. Set the initial properties of the visible controls on your form in the Load event. Use the public properties that have been retrieved in step 1 to set the CheckBoxes, OptionButtons, and other controls on your form.

3. Make sure you set the public properties to any new values the user may have set when you dismiss the form, such as when a user presses an OK button.

4. Persist the properties in the QueryUnload or Terminate events. We prefer using the QueryUnload event for this task, although the Unload event can also be used.

Figure 16-5 shows the memory that is used by a form in its various states. It is not accurate in percentages of uses, but does give you an idea of the relative amounts of memory used. By understanding the life of a form and its memory implications, we can design an Options form that encapsulates our options yet efficiently handles memory.

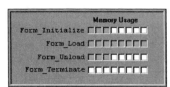

Figure 16-5: A form's memory utilization

Now, let's take a look at some code associated with the Options form. The code in Listing 16-1 begins with declaring modular properties in the general section of the form. The values of these properties are retrieved from the system Registry in the `Initialize` event. Remember, the `Initialize` event is fired when the properties are accessed by any code that refers to them. In this way, the properties are always correctly set prior to the property values being returned by the form. When the form is loaded, the property settings are used to configure the visual controls on the form. Finally, the property settings are stored back into the system Registry when the form is unloaded.

Listing 16-1: **Code for the Options Form**

```
General properties of the form:
'<Public>————————————————————————
'— whether a user pressed the OK, or Cancel buttons
Public PressedOK           As Boolean

'— public properties that correspond to form options
Public GeneralCheck1       As Integer
Public GeneralCheck2       As Integer
Public GeneralOption       As Integer
'</Public>———————————————————————

'<Private>———————————————————————
'— used to temporarily store info during edit session
Private tmpGeneralOption    As Integer

'— the last tab that was selected
Private LastTab            As Integer

'— used for Registry functions
Private AppName            As String
'</Private>————————————————————————
```

Retrieving property values from the Registry:

```
Private Sub Form_Initialize()

    AppName = "MyApp"  '— set to name of your app

    '— initialize public properties

    '— Syntax: GetSetting(appname, section, key[, default])
    GeneralCheck1 = Val(GetSetting(AppName, "Options", _
        "chkGeneral1", "1"))
    GeneralCheck2 = Val(GetSetting(AppName, "Options", _
        "chkGeneral2", "1"))
    GeneralOption = Val(GetSetting(AppName, "Options", _
        "optGeneral", "1"))

End Sub
```

Accessing an option from within code:

```
'— causes the form to initialize which retrieves the
'— value of the property from the Registry
PropertyValue = frmOption.GeneralOption
```

Showing the property values in the form:

```
Private Sub Form_Load()

    '— show values in controls
    chkGeneral1.Value = GeneralCheck1
    chkGeneral2.Value = GeneralCheck2
    optGeneral(GeneralOption) = True

End Sub
```

Persisting the property values to the Registry:

```
Private Sub Form_Terminate()

    '— save options to the Registry

    '— Syntax: SaveSetting appname, section, key, setting
    Call SaveSetting(AppName, "Options", "chkGeneral1", _
        CStr(GeneralCheck1))
    Call SaveSetting(AppName, "Options", "chkGeneral2", _
        CStr(GeneralCheck2))
    Call SaveSetting(AppName, "Options", "optGeneral", _
        CStr(GeneralOption))
End Sub
```

Window state

Figure 16-2 illustrated a system that has two windows visible. Each window is of a certain size and position on the screen. Wouldn't it be nice to have a set of functions that could easily "remember" these positions and sizes and restore them the next time that form is displayed. This is very easy to do with the code shown in Listing 16-20.

Chapter 14 discusses the use of *frameworks* and *templates*. If you make these window-persistence routines part of your application framework, they're included automatically in all new projects.

To persist window state, add the two functions shown in Listing 16-2 to your project, and then add the calls to these functions in each form.

Note   The `GetWindowState` and `SetWindowState` functions use the App object's `ProductName` property. In order for them to work properly, you must have that property set in the "Version Information" area of the project Properties dialog. This information is found on the Make tab.

Listing 16-2: **Adding Functions to Persist Window State**

```
Getting the window state in the form:
Private Sub Form_Load()

    Call GetWindowState(Me, "FormName", True)

End Sub

The GetWindowState() code:
Public Sub GetWindowState(ThisWindow As Form, _
KeyName As String, Optional SizeWindow As Variant)
    Dim i        As Integer
    Dim CharPos  As Integer
    Dim Height   As Integer
    Dim LLeft    As Integer
    Dim Top      As Integer
    Dim Width    As Integer
    Dim State    As Integer
    Dim Setting  As String

    On Error GoTo err_GetWindowState

    If (App.ProductName = "") Then
        MsgBox "You must enter a 'Product Name' using"  & _
        "the EXE Options dialog box before you continue." _
        ,vbOKOnly + vbInformation
        Exit Sub
    End If
```

```
'— get the window info from the Registry
'— Syntax: GetSetting(appname, section, key[, default])
Setting = GetSetting(App.ProductName, "WindowState", _
    KeyName)
If (Setting = "") Then
    Call CenterForm(ThisWindow)
    Exit Sub
End If

'— parse the window info
Do
    CharPos = InStr(Setting, ".")
    If CharPos = 0 Then
        Height = Val(Setting)
        Exit Do
    End If
    Select Case i
        Case 0: State = Left(Setting, CharPos - 1)
        Case 1: LLeft = Left(Setting, CharPos - 1)
        Case 2: Top = Left(Setting, CharPos - 1)
        Case 3: Width = Left(Setting, CharPos - 1)
    End Select
    Setting = Mid(Setting, CharPos + 1)
    i = i + 1
Loop

'— perform the move
Select Case State
    Case vbNormal
        On Error Resume Next
        If (Not IsMissing(SizeWindow)) Then
            If CBool(SizeWindow) Then
                ThisWindow.Move LLeft, Top, Width, Height
            Else
                ThisWindow.Move LLeft, Top
            End If
        Else
            ThisWindow.Move LLeft, Top
        End If
        On Error GoTo 0
    Case vbMinimized: ThisWindow.WindowState = State
    Case vbMaximized: ThisWindow.WindowState = State
End Select

Exit Sub

err_GetWindowState:
    Call CenterForm(ThisWindow)

End Sub
```

(continued)

Listing 16-2 *(continued)*

The CenterForm() companion function:

```
Public Sub CenterForm(ThisForm As Form)
    '— move is fastest
    With ThisForm
        .Move (Screen.Width / 2) - (.Width / 2), (Screen.Height
        / 2) - (.Height / 2)
    End With
End Sub
```

Saving the window state in the form:

```
Private Sub Form_QueryUnload(Cancel As Integer, UnloadMode _
    As Integer)

    Call SetWindowState(Me, "FormName")

End Sub
```

The SetWindowState() code:

```
Public Sub SetWindowState(ThisWindow As Form, KeyName As _
    String)
    Dim Setting As String

    If (App.ProductName = "") Then
        MsgBox "You must enter a 'Product Name' using the _
            EXE Options dialog box before you continue.", _
            vbOKOnly + vbInformation
        Exit Sub
    End If

    Setting = ThisWindow.WindowState & "." & ThisWindow.Left _
        & "." & ThisWindow.Top & "." & ThisWindow.Width & _
        "." & ThisWindow.Height
    '— Synatx: SaveSetting appname, section, key, setting
    Call SaveSetting(App.ProductName, "WindowState", _
        KeyName, Setting)

End Sub
```

These code segments are used to save the size and position of a form to the system Registry and then to retrieve these values and return a form to its previous size and position. This technique is used to provide yet another level of usability — an application that implements this code will have forms that "remember" where you left them.

Persisting Explorer-style settings

Let's take a look at another example of how information can be persisted to enhance the user experience. In this example, we work with an Explorer-style interface: the Microsoft Repository Browser. This type of interface is very popular for navigating any type of dataset — any time that you can offer a familiar metaphor, you are ahead of the game.

The Explorer has several pieces of information that are persisted, but we are going to just describe how the splitter bar and ListView column-width settings are persisted. Let's face it — it would be a real pain in the neck if you had to always set the Explorer to the view you like every time you use it. Yet when this type of functionality is added to your application, it tends to go unnoticed — persistence is one of those things that gives a user a better feeling about your application. Figure 16-6 shows additional items that can be saved and restored to enhance usability. These include the placement of a splitter and the widths of columns that have been set by a user.

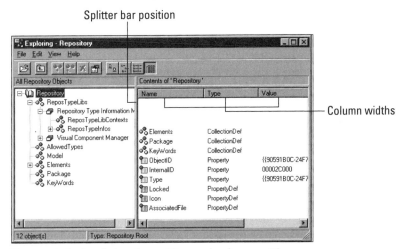

Figure 16-6: Persisting the splitter and column settings

The settings are physically stored in the Registry, like the settings listed previously in this chapter. The settings are restored in the _Load event and saved in the _QueryUnload event. The code in Listing 16-3 will persist the settings. The splitter bar and column-width functions have been created separately to increase their potential to be reused.

Listing 16-3: **Code for Persisting the Splitter
and Column Width Settings**

```
Calls to restore the states:
Private Sub Form_Load()
    '— restore browser state
    Call GetWindowState(Me, "Browser", True)
    Call GetSplitterBarState(Me, "Browser")
    Call GetColumnHeaderState(lvwItemsPane, "Browser")
End Sub
```

Note　It is important to size the window using GetWindowState prior to retrieving the splitter bar's state.

Getting the splitter position and column widths:

```
Public Sub GetSplitterBarState(ThisForm As Form, ThisSection _
    As String)
    Dim Setting As String

    '— get the splitter info
    Setting = GetSetting(App.ProductName, ThisSection, _
        "SplitterPos")

    '— call function to move splitter to previous position
    If (Setting <> "") Then
        Call ThisForm.SplitPanes(CInt(Setting))
    End If

End Sub
```

Note　The SplitPanes function moves the splitter bar to a position and also sizes the TreeView and ListView controls.

Getting the column header settings:

```
Public Sub GetColumnHeaderState(ThisListView As _
    VB.ListView, ThisSection As String)
    Dim InstHeader      As ColumnHeader
    Dim Header          As Integer
    Dim Setting         As String
```

```
    Dim Section         As String

    On Error Resume Next     '— account for bad settings

        Header = 1
        For Each InstHeader In ThisListView.ColumnHeaders
            Section = "ListHeader " & Header
            Setting = GetSetting(App.ProductName, _
                ThisSection, Section)
            If (Setting <> "") Then
                ThisListView.ColumnHeaders(Header).Width = _
                    CInt(Setting)
            End If
            Header = Header + 1
        Next

    On Error GoTo 0

End Sub
```

Calls to save the states:

```
Private Sub Form_QueryUnload(Cancel As Integer, UnloadMode _
    As Integer)

    '— explicitly destroy all objects
    Set LastNode = Nothing
    Set SelectedNode = Nothing
    Set ThisItem = Nothing
    Set ThisNode = Nothing
    Set WorkingNode = Nothing

    Set ContextMenu = Nothing
    Set RepNameSpace = Nothing

    '— save browser state
    Call SetWindowState(Me, MyName)
    Call SetSplitterBarState(Me, MyName, CStr(Splitter.Left))
    Call SetColumnHeaderState(lvwItemsPane, MyName)

End Sub
```

Setting the splitter position:

```
Public Sub SetSplitterBarState(ThisForm As Form, _
    ThisSection As String, Setting As String)

    Call SaveSetting(App.ProductName, ThisSection, _
        "SplitterPos", Setting)

End Sub

Setting column widths:
Public Sub SetColumnHeaderState(ThisListView As VB.ListView, _
    ThisSection As String)
    Dim InstHeader       As ColumnHeader
    Dim Header           As Integer
    Dim Setting          As String
    Dim Section          As String

    Header = 1
    For Each InstHeader In ThisListView.ColumnHeaders
        Section = "ListHeader " & Header
        Setting = CStr(InstHeader.Width)
        Call SaveSetting(App.ProductName, ThisSection, Section, _
            Setting)
        Header = Header + 1
    Next

End Sub
```

When you combine the persistence of the splitter and the column settings with the persistence of window state and the user options, you have a very nice and well-behaved system. Interestingly enough, none of this has anything to do with the functionality of the system — but you've got to do it to take your application to the next level of usability.

Examining State's Physical Storage

There are many ways to physically store state within a system, including INI files, the system Registry, a database, or within a proprietary file structure. Each of these techniques has its pros and cons, and the choice of one technique over another should be carefully considered. Table 16-1 helps to outline the different attributes of each storage technique.

Table 16-1
Comparing Ways to Persist Information

Attribute	INI Files	System Registry	Database	Proprietary File
VB intrinsic language calls for read/write		yes		
Windows API calls to read/write	yes	yes		
Easy to edit	yes	yes		
Easy to locate settings	yes			
Easy to view structure of information	yes	yes	yes[1]	
Easy to replicate settings to new system	yes		yes	yes
Inherent security mechanisms			yes[2]	yes[3]
Settings are sharable between users			yes	
Fast read/write of settings	yes	yes	(see note)[4]	(see note)[4]
Use of data types is restricted	yes	yes	(see note)[5]	(see note)[5]
Easiest to create generic, reusable functions		yes[6]		
Supports global and local settings for multiuser systems	yes[7]		yes[7]	yes[7]

[1] The structure of information in INI files and the system Registry can be easily viewed using existing tools. The structure of the information in a database may also be easy to comprehend, but may not be as easy to access as with the other techniques.

[2] The inherent database security mechanisms can be used.

[3] A proprietary file can be made highly secure. The structure need not be published, and the settings can be encrypted.

[4] Database access will be inherently slower than either INI or Registry access. The proprietary technique requires the development of special functions to read and write the data; thus it, too, will be slower.

[5] The INI files and Registry support only strings and numeric data types. The database or proprietary techniques can be extended to support any data type.

[6] Since no special functions are required and there is no concern for the physical location of files (as with all other techniques), and there is intrinsic support for the Registry, this technique is probably the easiest to use to create generic functions.

[7] It may be advantageous to the design of a multiuser system to support a set of global system settings that are common to the whole system, as well as local settings that are specific to a user.

In addition to the four state-persisting techniques described above, there are several other techniques available that are not covered in this chapter. For example, it might be possible to store state information in some type of structured storage file or in some type of binary object. In the purest sense, any storage mechanism that allows for information to be saved to it and retrieved from it can be used to store state.

The system Registry

Whereas we used to store all our configuration settings in INI files, we are now moving to storing them in the system Registry. We're not going to talk much about the Registry itself, as it is fairly ubiquitous to our development lives. We are going to discuss the functions provided by Visual Basic to read and write Registry, data as well as show you how to create your own Registry-handling functions.

Using VB's intrinsic functions

Visual Basic provides four Registry-related functions. These are intrinsic to the core language and therefore are available to all projects without requiring the addition of any references:

* `GetSetting`—Gets the value of a setting from the system Registry.

* `GetAllSettings`—Gets all of the settings for a section; places them in a variant array.

* `SaveSetting`—Saves a value to a key in the Registry.

* `DeleteSetting`—Deletes either a key, or an entire section from the Registry.

Examples of the `GetAllSettings` and `DeleteSettings` functions are provided in Listing 16-4. Refer to the coding examples for the `GetSetting` and `SaveSetting` functions in Listing 16-3 earlier in this chapter.

Listing 16-4: **DeleteSettings and GetAllSettings functions**

```
The DeleteSetting() function used to delete a key:
Call DeleteSetting("MyApp", "Options", " optGeneral")


The DeleteSetting() function used to delete a section:
Call DeleteSetting("MyApp", "Options")


The GetAllSettings() function:
Private Sub PrintSettings()
    Dim SectionSettings As Variant
    Dim i              As Integer
    Const regKeyName   As Integer = 0
    Const regKeyValue  As Integer = 1
```

```
      SectionSettings = GetAllSettings("MyApp", "Options")

      For i = LBound(SectionSettings, regKeyValue) To _
          UBound(SectionSettings, regKeyValue)
          Debug.Print SectionSettings(i, regKeyName) & vbTab & _
              SectionSettings(i, regKeyValue)
      Next

  End Sub
```

Listing 16-4 references the values set in the Options dialog described in this chapter. If you run this function, the immediate window shows the following results:

```
chkGeneral1 1
chkGeneral2 1
optGeneral  0
```

The Visual Basic Registry functions provide an easy way to incorporate handling of Registry values within your application. They are, however, limited in what they allow you to do. You cannot specify a particular location within the Registry to store your information. All the information is stored under the following path:

My Computer\HKEY_CURRENT_USER\Software\VB and VBA Program Settings

Figure 16-7 shows a snapshot of the Registry and how the settings from the options dialog would be stored.

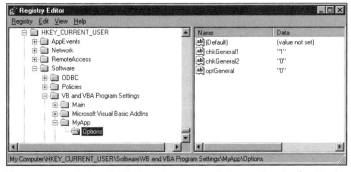

Figure 16-7: Where VB's functions store information in the Registry

The nice part about using VB's intrinsic functions is that they are pretty painless to implement. The bad part is that you don't have a lot of control over where the values are written, and thus have limited abilities to organize your data. The next section explains how you can create your own Registry-handling functions and have maximum flexibility.

Writing your own Registry functions

There are times when it would be nice to have more control over how your Registry settings are being stored. For example, you may want to organize all of the applications you develop for your company under your company name. Or, you may want to write information to a completely different Registry key. To do so, you will have to use the Windows API calls related to the Registry.

Figure 16-8 shows how information can be organized using the API calls. Compare this to Figure 16-7, which shows how Visual Basic stores information. As you can see, you have a lot more flexibility using the APIs. The trade-off is that the APIs will be a little harder to use than the intrinsic functions — you be the judge if the added flexibility is worth the price.

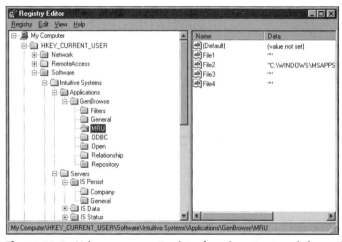

Figure 16-8: Using your own Registry functions to store information

Most of the frequently used Registry function declarations are given in Listing 16-5. The complete set of declarations can be found in the file Win32API.text that ships with Visual Basic.

Listing 16-5: **Declarations for Frequently Used Registry Functions**

```
'<Declaration>
Public Declare Function RegCloseKey Lib "advapi32.dll" _
    (ByVal hKey As Long) As Long
Public Declare Function RegCreateKeyEx Lib "advapi32.dll" _
```

```
      Alias "RegCreateKeyExA" (ByVal hKey As Long, ByVal _
      lpSubKey As String, ByVal Reserved As Long, ByVal _
      lpClass As String, ByVal dwOptions As Long, ByVal _
      samDesired As Long, ByVal lpSecurityAttributes As Long, _
      phkResult As Long, lpdwDisposition As Long) As Long
Public Declare Function RegOpenKey Lib "advapi32" Alias _
      "RegOpenKeyA" (ByVal hKey As Long, ByVal lpSubKey As _
      String, phkResult As Long) As Long
Public Declare Function RegOpenKeyEx Lib "advapi32.dll" _
      Alias "RegOpenKeyExA" (ByVal hKey As Long, ByVal _
      lpSubKey As String, ByVal ulOptions As Long, ByVal _
      samDesired As Long, phkResult As Long) As Long
Public Declare Function RegQueryValueEx Lib "advapi32" _
      Alias "RegQueryValueExA" (ByVal hKey As Long, ByVal _
      lpValueName As String, ByVal lpReserved As Long, lpType _
      As Long, lpData As Any, lpcbData As Long) As Long
Public Declare Function RegQueryValueExString Lib _
      "advapi32.dll" Alias "RegQueryValueExA" (ByVal hKey As _
      Long, ByVal lpValueName As String, ByVal lpReserved As _
      Long, lpType As Long, ByVal lpData As String, lpcbData _
      As Long) As Long
Public Declare Function RegQueryValueExLong Lib _
      "advapi32.dll" Alias "RegQueryValueExA" (ByVal hKey As _
      Long, ByVal lpValueName As String, ByVal lpReserved As _
      Long, lpType As Long, lpData As Long, lpcbData As Long) _
      As Long
Public Declare Function RegQueryValueExNULL Lib _
      "advapi32.dll" Alias "RegQueryValueExA" (ByVal hKey As _
      Long, ByVal lpValueName As String, ByVal lpReserved As _
      Long, lpType As Long, ByVal lpData As Long, lpcbData As _
      Long) As Long
Public Declare Function RegSetValueExString Lib _
      "advapi32.dll" Alias "RegSetValueExA" (ByVal hKey As _
      Long, ByVal lpValueName As String, ByVal Reserved As _
      Long, ByVal dwType As Long, ByVal lpValue As String, _
      ByVal cbData As Long) As Long
Public Declare Function RegSetValueExLong Lib "advapi32.dll" _
      Alias "RegSetValueExA" (ByVal hKey As Long, ByVal _
      lpValueName As String, ByVal Reserved As Long, ByVal _
      dwType As Long, lpValue As Long, ByVal cbData As Long) _
      As Long
'</Declaration>————————————--
```

Now, let's put some of these declarations to use. The functions shown in Listing 16-6 use the Windows API to save and retrieve settings to the system Registry.

Listing 16-6: **Windows API Registry Settings Functions**

```
A function to get a Registry setting:
Public Function GetRegSetting(RegKeyName As String, Item As _
    String, ValueName As String, Optional Default As _
    String = "") As Variant
    Dim lRetVal     As Long      '— result of the API _
        functions
    Dim hKey        As Long      '— handle of opened key
    Dim vValue      As Variant   '— setting of queried value
    Dim Setting     As String

lRetVal = RegOpenKeyEx(HKEY_CURRENT_USER, RegKeyName & Item, _
    0, KEY_ALL_ACCESS, hKey)

    '— if no key exists, exit
    If (hKey = 0) Then
        GetRegSetting = Default
        Exit Function
    End If

    lRetVal = QueryValueEx(hKey, ValueName, vValue)

    '— deal with various types of return values
    If IsEmpty(vValue) Then
        GetRegSetting = Default
    ElseIf IsNull(vValue) Then
        GetRegSetting = Default
    ElseIf (CStr(vValue) = "") Then
        GetRegSetting = Default
    Else
        Setting = CStr(vValue)
        '— remove null, if present
        If (Right(Setting, 1) = Chr(0)) Then
            Setting = Left(Setting, Len(Setting) - 1)
        End If

        GetRegSetting = Setting
    End If

    Call RegCloseKey(hKey)

End Function
```

Calling GetRegSetting:

```
Setting = GetRegSetting("Software\Intuitive _
    Systems\ISPersist" , "WindowState", "Main")
```

Saving to the Registry:
```
Public Function SetRegSetting(RegKeyName As String, Item As _
    String, ValueName As String, Value As Variant) As Boolean
    Dim lRetVal     As Long        '— result of the _
        SetValueEx function
    Dim hKey        As Long        '— handle of open key
    Dim FullKey     As String      '— the section plus the key

'— open the specified key
    lRetVal = RegOpenKeyEx(HKEY_CURRENT_USER, RegKeyName & _
        Item, 0, KEY_ALL_ACCESS, hKey)

    '— may have to create the new key
    If (hKey = 0) Then
        If CreateNewKey(HKEY_CURRENT_USER, RegKeyName & Item) _
Then
            '— if the key was created, try one more time
            lRetVal = RegOpenKeyEx(HKEY_CURRENT_USER, _
                RegKeyName & Item, 0, KEY_ALL_ACCESS, hKey)
            If (hKey = 0) Then
                SetRegSetting = False
                Exit Function
            End If
        Else
            SetRegSetting = False
            Exit Function
        End If
    End If

    lRetVal = SetValueEx(hKey, ValueName, REG_SZ, Value)
    Call RegCloseKey(hKey)

End Function
```

Creating a new key:

```
Public Function CreateNewKey(RegKey As Long, sNewKeyName As _
    String) As Boolean
    Dim hNewKey As Long        '— handle to the new key
    Dim lRetVal As Long        '— result of the _
        RegCreateKeyEx function

    lRetVal = RegCreateKeyEx(RegKey, sNewKeyName, 0&, _
        vbNullString, REG_OPTION_NON_VOLATILE, KEY_ALL_ACCESS, _
        0&, hNewKey, lRetVal)
    Call RegCloseKey(hNewKey)

    CreateNewKey = True

End Function


Calling SetRegSetting():
Setting = SetRegSetting("Software\Intutive Systems\ISPersist" _
    , "WindowState", "Main", Setting)
```

It would be fairly easy to take the GetRegSetting and SetRegSetting Registry functions, combine them with all of the supporting functions and declarations, and make them into a template (see Chapter 14). This template could then be added to all projects right from the start. Over time, you could tailor the functions provided here and add other persistence-related functions. You should soon get to the point where persisting system state is a routine and painless part of your development practices.

Summary

In this chapter, we have explained that an application exhibits a number of "states" — a state corresponding to a particular configuration that a system is in. A user works with a system by moving it from one state to another — this movement is controlled by the user's interactions with menus, buttons, and other system elements, and the underlying program logic.

✦ Often, it is possible to capture some elements of a system's state and save them so a system can be returned to that same state when an application is restarted.

✦ This state can be saved to the Windows system Registry by one of two techniques — using native functions provided by Visual Basic, using Windows API functions.

✦ Although the native Visual Basic functions are easier to use, they have less flexibility when storing this information.

✦ Many state-storing and retrieval functions can be wrapped into procedures that can easily be added to any application; thus any system can provide that added comfort level to a user.

✦   ✦   ✦

Integrating the Internet into Visual Basic

♦   ♦   ♦   ♦

In This Chapter

Using the WebBrowser control

Adding Web browsing capabilities to your application

Sending electronic mail through MAPI

♦   ♦   ♦   ♦

Visual Basic applications, while they may live on a user's PC, aren't limited to using just that PC. For instance, wouldn't it be nice to automatically jump to a customer's Web page with the click of a button? What about sending e-mail instead of printed correspondence? You've already got information about your customers; why not gather a few more pieces of data like e-mail and Web site addresses, and expand your application to be even more useful?

This chapter will show you how to use some common features of the Internet within your program. There are many other ways to use the resources of the Internet, but this chapter should give you some introduction to the capabilities available to Visual Basic. You'll also see how to take advantage of MAPI (Windows Messaging API) to make sending e-mail a piece of cake. Instead of having to write directly to the Windows Sockets layer, you can simply manipulate a series of prebuilt objects to get your messages out to the world.

Note   The Web-based examples in this chapter use Microsoft's Internet Explorer 4.0 exclusively. If you don't have IE installed already, you can install it from the CD-ROM included with this book. You can also download the latest version from Microsoft's Web site: hyperlink http://www.microsoft.com/ie.

Using the WebBrowser Control

Visual Basic makes it easy to integrate Web browsing into your application by way of the WebBrowser control. This control provides access to whatever version of Internet Explorer is on your (or your user's) machine. With the release of Internet Explorer 4.0, Microsoft has relaxed the licensing restrictions, and now you can install just the DLLs needed to perform Web browsing. This prevents your having to install Internet Explorer on every machine in your organization, which can be especially helpful if you're working in a shop that is partial to other browsers.

To see how the WebBrowser control works, do the following:

1. Create a new Standard EXE project in Visual Basic.

2. Select Project ➪ Components.

3. From the dialog shown in Figure 17-1, select Microsoft Internet Controls and click the OK button. The filename you're loading is not actually an OCX; it's a DLL named SHDOCVW.DLL, which should be located in your Windows\System directory.

Figure 17-1: The WebBrowser control is part of Microsoft Internet Controls.

The WebBrowser control is the small globe on the Toolbox, shown in Figure 17-2.

— WebBrowser control

Figure 17-2: The WebBrowser
control in the Toolbox..

The other new control is part of the SHDOCVW.DLL library, and is not usable in a
meaningful way within your Visual Basic project. If you add it to your form, you'll
just get a box with an X through it and no properties you can set.

The WebBrowser control, on the other hand, has quite a different look to it and
has a wide variety of properties you can set. To see the list of properties, add a
WebBrowser control to the form Visual Basic created for you already. As shown in
Figure 17-3, the control really doesn't have much to look at in design mode. The real
power is under the hood, in the control's vast array of properties and objects that
are only accessible through code.

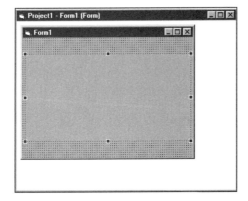

Figure 17-3: The WebBrowser control is
pretty dull to look at in design mode.

Even though the Web Browser control has properties that would appear to control
whether a toolbar is shown, these properties don't work in Visual Basic as they
should. Setting the Toolbar property makes absolutely no difference in how the
window looks when you run your program. The following properties have a similar
lack of function: AddressBar, CausesValidation, FullScreen, MenuBar,
Offline, Silent, StatusBar, and TheaterMode.

An interesting property of the WebBrowser control is that, by default, it can accept drag-and-drop shortcut targets. This means you can drag an Internet shortcut from Windows Explorer (or your desktop) onto the WebBrowser control. If the RegisterAsDropTarget property is set to True, the WebBrowser control will automatically navigate to that URL.

Just because some of the WebBrowser control's properties don't work automatically, however, doesn't mean you can't use the functions that would normally be on the toolbar, for instance. The WebBrowser provides methods to do everything normally available in your Internet Explorer interface. The next section shows you how to use these methods to add a browser to your own application.

Adding a Browser to Your Application

Now that you're a bit more familiar with the WebBrowser control, you can integrate it with your application. The sample application in this segment uses a simple Data form with an extra button to start a Web browser. You also have a few extra features on the Web browser to make it more than just a single-page viewer.

You can start your browser using the form you built in the last section. Give the control a name, such as ctlWeb, so you can more easily identify it. The form should be named also, such as frmWebBrowser. These names will be used in the sample code in this section.

The first thing you need to do is to add one line of code to the Form_Load procedure, shown in Listing 17-1.

Listing 17-1:

```
Sub Form_Load()
    ctlWeb.Navigate "about:blank"
End Sub
```

This one little line can save you hours of headaches. Internet Explorer, if you start it without this line, will simply appear to hang, never actually showing up on the form and never responding to your commands. By telling the control to navigate to this special URL, it loads a blank page and stops.

With that little "gotcha" out of the way, you can start adding functionality. First, you'll want to add some navigation controls to your form. Because we're not trying to replicate a full browser, you don't have to add every control. However, we like the feature of having a button to launch a full browser window. You'll also be providing the user a Forward and a Back button, as well as a place to type URLs. The form will also have some convenience features, such as resizing, and loading

Web pages by default so the user doesn't have to type **http://** every time. The finished browser is shown in Figure 17-4.

Figure 17-4: The completed Web browser form

The graphics used were included with Visual Basic. You can use any of these graphics you want in your own application without having to pay royalties or give credit for them.

The controls and the important properties you need to set are shown in Table 17-1. The controls are listed left to right, top to bottom as shown in Figure 17-4.

Table 17-1 frmWebBrowser Control Properties		
Control	**Property**	**Value**
cmdBack	Picture	(any valid picture)
	Style	1 - Graphical
	ToolTipText	Previous Page
cmdForward	Picture	(Any valid picture)

(continued)

Table 17-1 *(continued)*		
	Style	1 - Graphical
	ToolTipText	NextPage
cmdStartIE	Picture	(Any valid picture)
	Style	1 - Graphical
	ToolTipText	Full Browser
txtURL	Text	about:blank

No additional properties need to be set for the WebBrowser control.

The code required to make this form work is shown in Listing 17-2. It includes a few helpful techniques that will be explained after the listing.

Listing 17-2: **frmWebBrowser Code**

```
Option Explicit
Const MARGIN = 60

Private Sub cmdBack_Click()
    On Error Resume Next
    ctlWeb.GoBack
End Sub

Private Sub cmdForward_Click()
    On Error Resume Next
    ctlWeb.GoForward
End Sub

Private Sub cmdStartIE_Click()
    Dim objIE As Object
    Set objIE = _
        CreateObject("InternetExplorer.Application")
    objIE.Visible = True
    objIE.Navigate2 CStr(txtURL.Text), Null, Null, Null, Null

End Sub

Private Sub Form_Load()
    ctlWeb.Navigate "about:blank"
End Sub

Private Sub Form_Resize()
    On Error Resume Next
    txtURL.Width = Me.ScaleWidth - txtURL.Left - MARGIN
    ctlWeb.Width = Me.ScaleWidth - (2 * MARGIN)
```

```
    ctlWeb.Height = Me.ScaleHeight - ctlWeb.Top - MARGIN
End Sub

Private Sub txtURL_GotFocus()
    txtURL.SelStart = 0
    txtURL.SelLength = Len(txtURL)
End Sub

Private Sub txtURL_KeyPress(KeyAscii As Integer)
    If KeyAscii = 13 Then
        KeyAscii = 0        ' Gets rid of beep
        If InStr(txtURL, "://") = 0 Then
            txtURL = "http://" & txtURL
        End If
        ctlWeb.Navigate txtURL
    End If

End Sub
```

Here are the important parts of this code:

cmdForward_Click, cmdBack_Click — These event procedures simply use
the built-in GoForward and GoBack methods of the WebBrowser control. Error
handling exists to make sure the user doesn't try to go back to a page that
doesn't exist.

cmdStartIE — This event handler creates a new instance of Internet Explorer
and feeds it the URL to load. Note that you have to make the object visible, or
nothing will appear to happen.

Form_Resize — This event handler resizes the WebBrowser control and the
URL text box so they fill the form.

txtURL_GotFocus — This little snippet of code causes the URL to be
highlighted when you click your mouse in the box or tab into the field. This
enables you to start typing over the URLimmediately without having to
highlight the text.

txtURL_KeyPress — This event procedure listens for the Enter key and
causes the navigation to start immediately afterward. It also will prepend
http:// if no protocol (ftp://, mailto://, and so on) is listed.

Quite a few more methods and properties are available for the WebBrowser control,
but these are the basics. An easy enhancement would be to create a public method
on the form that accepts a URL to show. Simply call the Navigate() method on the
ctlWeb control (after first going to about:blank) and show the form. An example
of this code is shown in Listing 17-3.

Listing 17-3: **Public Navigate Method**

```
Public Sub Navigate(sURL As String)
    If Instr(sURL, "://") = 0 Then
        txtURL = "http://" & sURL
    Else
        txtURL = sURL
    End If
    ctlWeb.Navigate txtURL
    Show
End Sub
```

The code to create the correct URL (that is, adding the `http://` prefix) could be placed in a function procedure for simplicity. In addition, this form can be used as an MDI Child form if you're building an MDI-based application.

Sending E-Mail with MAPI

MAPI is the Messaging API designed by Microsoft. It is included as part of the Windows operating system. It specifies a method by which messages can be sent with a variety of providers, such as fax and Internet e-mail. Because each provider and user is using the Messaging API, you can interchange providers without having to rewrite your application.

This section will show you how to send e-mail using MAPI. The next section in this chapter will show you how to access the other information stored in Outlook, but here we will deal exclusively with e-mail.

The first object you'll be creating is a `Session` object, which defines a connection with a particular MAPI provider. For instance, you'll need a `Session` object to use a mailbox. To get started, use the following lines of code to create a MAPI Session:

```
Dim objSession As Object
Set objSession = CreateObject("Mapi.Session")
```

You need to refer to this `Session` object in most of the code, but you can use the `With` statement to shorten your code and avoid having to retype the entire object hierarchy in each line of code.

Once the `Session` object is created, you need to use it to log on to a MAPI provider. In this case, you'll be logging into your mailbox. The code is as follows:

```
objSession.Logon ProfileName:="Joe Smith"
```

The `ProfileName` parameter should contain the name of the profile you wish to use. This might be "Default Exchange Settings" or a name as in this example. You have to provide this argument because the `Session` object has to use a profile to connect to a server.

Other than the `Session` object, all other objects are defined in the Active Messaging 1.1 Object Library, which you can add using the Project ⇨ References menu item. Adding the library will provide the AutoComplete features you're used to when dealing with complex objects like these.

At this point, your VB application will be logged into a MAPI Session. Because you're planning to send a message, the next thing you need to do is to create a new message. This is done with the following lines of code:

```
Dim objMsg As MAPI.Message
Set objMsg = objSession.Outbox.Messages.Add
```

The variable `objMsg` is now an empty message object, just waiting for you to fill it with data. The first thing you should do is to give the message some recipients. You can have three different types of recipients:

Standard — Names that show in the To: header line.

Carbon copy (CC) — Names that show in the CC: header line. This line is typically used when you are sending someone a message and want to let them know about other people who are getting a copy of the same message simultaneously.

Blind carbon copy (BCC) — Any addresses added as BCC recipients will be hidden from the person who received the original message. This is helpful if you want to send a message to someone and copy it to someone else without the original recipient's knowing it.

Adding a recipient is very easy to do. The code is as follows:

```
Dim objRecipient As MAPI.Recipient
Set objRecipient = objMsg.Recipients.Add
objRecipient.Name = "joe.smith@northcomp.com"
objRecipient.Type = mapiTo
```

This adds joe.smith@northcomp.com as a standard recipient to this message. You can add as many recipients to this message as you wish.

If you want to add a CC'd recipient to this message, use the following code:

```
Set objRecipient = objMsg.Recipients.Add
objRecipient.Name = "Mary Jones"
objRecipient.Type = mapiCC
```

Mary Jones will be CC'd with a copy of this message. You can use any valid e-mail address in the Name property, including both Internet and non-Internet (local) e-mail addresses.

The last type of recipient is a BCC. This uses similar code:

```
Set objRecipient = objMsg.Recipients.Add
objRecipient.Name = "Jeff Martin"
objRecipient.Type = mapiBCC
```

Jeff Martin will get a blind carbon copy of this message.

Now that you have all the recipients added, you still have to *resolve the addresses*, which is a process that verifies whether the addresses are in the local (LAN) or remote (Internet) domain, and adds additional information to each address if it is outside of the local domain. To resolve addresses, use the following code:

```
Dim i As Integer
For i = 1 To objMsg.Recipients.Count
    objMsg.Recipients(i).Resolve showdialog:=False
Next I
```

This will process all the recipients, regardless of type, to whom the message is directed. If you are writing a program that sends mail and the mail doesn't seem to get sent, make sure you are resolving the recipients. In Outlook, this process happens during the time and that you enter an address and the name is underlined in the message. Once the address is underlined, Outlook has determined that it is a good address. Outlook can't check, however, to see whether an Internet e-mail address is correct. All it can do is check for a properly formatted address.

With the addressees added correctly, you can create the actual message you want to send. This is done using the properties of the Message object you created (objMsg), as shown in the following code:

```
objMsg.Subject = "Test Message"
objMsg.Text = "This is a test message."
objMsg.Importance = mapiHigh
```

The Subject property is obviously the subject of the message, which will show in the lists of nearly every mail program automatically. The Text property contains the text of the message. This can contain any type of text, including blank lines and even HTML.

The Priority property can take three values:

mapiHigh — High priority, which shows a red flag in Outlook

mapiNormal — Normal priority

mapiLow — Low priority, often shown with a down-arrow symbol

If you use the Object Browser, you may see some additional constants: ActMsgHigh, ActMsgNormal, and ActMsgLow. These constants have exactly the same values as those prefixed with mapi, so you can use the constants that you want. The mapi prefix is shorter than ActMsg, so we use mapi instead.

The last thing to do is to send the message, using this line of code:

```
objMsg.Send ShowDialog:=False
```

As you might guess, using the ShowDialog parameter indicates whether the message you created should be shown in a dialog before it is sent. Since most e-mail you create through code should be sent immediately, there is no reason to show the Confirmation dialog.

That's all there is to sending a basic message through MAPI. However, many messages you'll want to send through code would benefit from being able to attach files to the message. For instance, if you have a watchdog program of some sort, wouldn't it be helpful to send an extract of a log file whenever something happens? That way the recipient(s) of the message can determine if anything needs to be done.

Attachments are easy to add with the MAPI object library you've been using. The code shown in Listing 17-4 attaches a text file to the existing message object (objMsg).

Listing 17-4: **Adding Attachments to Messages**

```
Dim objAttachment As MAPI.Attachment
Set objAttachment = objMsg.Attachments.Add
With objAttachment
    .Name = "Customers.txt"
    .Type = mapiFileData
    .Position = 2880
    .ReadFromFile filename:="C:\Examples\Customers.txt"
End With
```

After creating a new Attachment object, it is populated with the name to show in the message, the type of data, and the position within the message. Because this message is actually including a copy of the file in the message, the ReadFromFile() method is used to read the file being attached.

In cases where you just want to send a shortcut or link to your data file, you use a different type of data and specify a Source parameter, as in code shown in Listing 17-5.

Listing 17-5: **Adding File Links to Messages**

```
Dim objAttachment As MAPI.Attachment
Set objAttachment = objMsg.Attachments.Add
With objAttachment
    .Name = "Customers.txt"
    .Type = mapiFileLink
    .Position = 2880
    .Source = "C:\Examples\Customers.txt"
End With
```

This takes care of programs like Outlook that show an icon for each attachment. Some programs, like Qualcomm's Eudora, simply decode the message immediately and append a text string indicating where the attachment was placed.

The `Type` property of an `Attachment` class object may be set to any of the following types of data:

> `mapiEmbeddedMessage` — The message contains another message object.

> `mapiFileData` — An actual file is included with the message.

> `mapiFileLink` — A shortcut or link to a file is included with a message. This enables the user (in programs that support it) to double-click a shortcut in a message to open the file being referenced.

> `mapiOLE` — The message includes an OLE object.

That's the bulk of what you need to know about using MAPI with Visual Basic. If you don't want to get into the coding you saw here, Visual Basic still includes several controls (MAPISession, MAPIMessages) that are designed to simplify some of the code for you. To add these controls to your project, click Project ➪ Components and select them from the dialog shown in Figure 17-5.

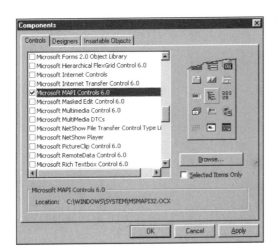

Figure 17-5: The Microsoft MAPI Controls

The MAPISession control handles things such as logon/logoff, supplying a login interface when needed, and so on. The MAPIMessages control handles the bulk of the messaging work, including accessing message stores, sending and retrieving e-mail, and other related functions. Windows Messaging has come quite far since these controls were released. Unfortunately, these controls have not kept pace with the current state of Windows Messaging, so using them will constrain you to an older version of the technology. For best results, use the technologies discussed in this section to do your messaging in Visual Basic.

Summary

No longer are your applications constrained to the information that you have on your own computer or your local network. Empower your users to get more information from an original source: the Internet. Why spend time typing in stock quotes every day when you can pull them from a half-dozen sites for free? By using the free sources of information on the Internet, you can save your users and yourself time and energy.

Adding e-mail capabilities to your programs makes it easy for users to collaborate and share data, even if there is no network available for shared drives. Users can send e-mail back and forth to anyone who wants it. With the common formats currently available for e-mail, anyone can get and send e-mail as part of their normal Internet services.

✦   ✦   ✦

Creating IIS Applications

Although many of the new features in this version of Visual Basic are enhancements or upgrades of existing features, the features you'll learn about in this chapter are entirely new. This chapter introduces the WebClass feature of Visual Basic 6.0. If you're building applications for Microsoft's Internet Information Server (IIS)or Personal/Peer Web Server, you can now avoid the problems inherent in building VBScript code. Unlike VBScript code, your compiled application will run faster, and your code will be more reliable because you're writing real Visual Basic code in the VB environment. You'll also be able to *debug* your Web-based application — a capability unheard of until now. No more plunking down lots of Print statements everywhere that you'll only have to remove later, just to give yourself messages as to why the page isn't working in the first place. You can fully test your Web page before it even touches your Web server.

One of the best things about IIS applications is that they are browser independent. If you are dealing with more than one type of browser, you can either write HTML that will work on any browser, or detect the browser's type and use its particular capabilities. Either way, the end users only see what you want them to see. You don't have to worry about someone stealing your source code, since (1) the code is never sent across the Internet, and (2) the code is compiled into a library and resides entirely on your server.

Note   In order to deploy WebClass applications, you need either Personal Web Server installed on your Windows 95 machine or you need access to Internet Information Server running on a Windows NT machine. The applications will work on both platforms the same way.

WebClass Basics:
The "Hello World" WebClass

To introduce you to WebClass applications, we'll build a simple program. This program will be known as the "Hello, World!" WebClass. The WebClass is called this because one of the first things most programmers do when using a new tool or feature is write a simple program to generate some sort of output, like a printed line or a message box. This example will show you how to generate some simple output to your Web browser. You'll create a new WebClass project, add a little bit of code, debug and test it, and then deploy it to your Web server.

To get started, you'll be creating a new application. Start Visual Basic, select New from the File menu, and select IIS Application from the dialog box, shown in Figure 18-1.

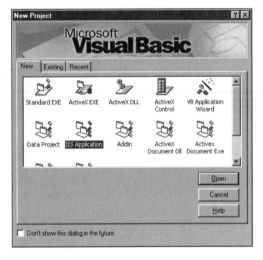

Figure 18-1: IIS Application is a new entry in the New Project dialog box in Visual Basic.

Once Visual Basic is done creating the new project, you might expect to see a class module in your project. That's not the case. A WebClass isn't quite the same as a regular class module. It has many of the same events and properties of a class, but it is designed to do much more. For this reason, you'll be saving a *designer file* (.DSR) as part of your project for each WebClass you build. Designer files are used by some of the more complex VB tools to store all the relevant data to a particular type of module, like a WebClass. When you created your new IIS application, Visual Basic automatically added a designer file to your project and named it WebClass1, as shown in Figure 18-2.

Figure 18-2: WebClass1 is added by default to your new IIS Application project.

The designer file saves quite a bit more information than what is normally saved in a class file. In addition, even though you can instantiate this class within Visual Basic, you can't export it to a regular class module — and thus can't use it in any versions of Visual Basic before the current one. In general, don't plan on using a WebClass where you would normally use a standard class module. It works, but it's really not designed for that purpose.

To continue, double-click on the WebClass1 item in the Project Explorer window. You'll see the WebClass designer, as shown in Figure 18-3.

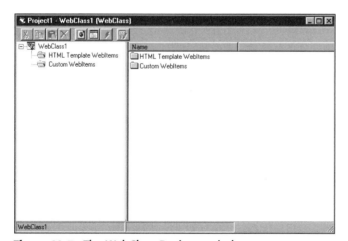

Figure 18-3: The WebClass Designer window

Figure 18-4 shows the Properties window, which is displaying the WebClass's most relevant properties. If you wish, you can rename the WebClass to HelloWorld or another valid name (no spaces allowed). The other property values should remain as is — you'll learn about them later in the chapter.

Figure 18-4: The Properties window shows the properties for this WebClass.

Most of the work involved in building a WebClass involves the WebClass designer. This window shows you two categories of items: HTML templates and custom WebItems.

HTML templates

An *HTML template* is an HTML document used by a WebClass. This document consists of plaintext and is edited in either Notepad or your default HTML editor. This template uses special tags that allow it to manipulate the HTML without your having to write all the HTML through code. The HTML template is not compiled into the WebClass, so you can make changes without having to rebuild the WebClass itself.

Custom WebItems

A *custom WebItem* is simply a name that you define as part of the WebClass module. A WebItem can have custom events, giving you essentially a two-level hierarchy. Compared to standard VB, a WebItem could be a standard code or class module, while an event is like a procedure that is part of the module or class. Custom WebItems are the heart of your code when you start building IIS applications.

Besides what you see in the Designer window, you can also look at the underlying code by selecting View ➪ Code. When you create a new WebClass, the code that is added is shown in Listing 18-1.

Listing 18-1: **WebClass Default Code**

```
Private Sub WebClass_Start()
    Dim sQuote As String
    sQuote = Chr$(34)
    'Write a reply to the user
    With Response
        .Write "<HTML>"
        .Write "<body>"
        .Write "<h1><font face=" & sQuote & "Arial" _
```

```
                 & sQuote _
                 & ">WebClass1's Starting Page</font></h1>"
            .Write "<p>This response was created " _
                 & "in the Start event of WebClass1.</p>"
            .Write "</body>"
            .Write "</html>"
        End With
    End Sub
```

This code, which can obviously be altered, is shown if you use the WebClass by itself without creating any WebItems. To see this in action, select Run ➪ Start. The dialog box shown in Figure 18-5 appears.

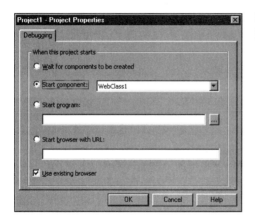

Figure 18-5: This dialog box appears when you run your WebClass for the first time.

In this case, VB assumes that we want to run WebClass1, and shows its output in the browser that exists on your system. The HTML code works with any Web browser, including non-Microsoft models.

In the Project Properties dialog box, click OK to continue. At this point, Visual Basic creates a temporary virtual directory for testing these applications. Figure 18-6 shows the dialog box that appears. The directory you have defined as your temporary Windows directory (typically C:\Windows\Temp) becomes a shared directory known as Temp. This shared directory is used by Personal Web Server, running on your Windows 95 or NT machine. This allows VB to load the page in your browser. If you've already saved your files and project, VB creates a shared name for the folder in which your project resides. For this reason, you should create a new directory for each IIS application you build — doing so makes it easier to manage the shared directories that are created.

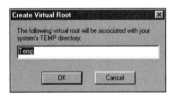

Figure 18-6: VB creates a virtual directory for testing the WebClass.

The results of all this are shown in Figure 18-7. The code in the `WebClass_Start()` event procedure has been executed, and has produced some HTML output.

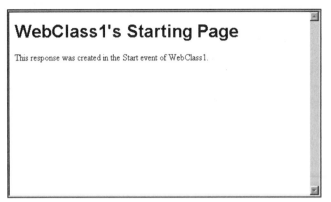

WebClass1's Starting Page

This response was created in the Start event of WebClass1.

Figure 18-7: The output of your WebClass running successfully

The HTML code is not magical by any means, and is listed in Listing 18-2 for reference.

Listing 18-2: HTML from WebClass

```
<HTML><body><h1><font face="Arial">WebClass1's Starting
    Page</font></h1><p>This response was created in the Start
    event of WebClass1.</p></body></html>
```

Why is it all on one line, you might ask? It's because the WebClass didn't add any line breaks to the HTML that is put in the page. Even though your code is generating HTML that the browser can read in any format or layout, it is good to add line breaks so that *you* can tell whether the HTML is correct. Having one long line of HTML tends to hamper readability. To break up the HTML, use the `vbCr` constant within the WebClass procedure. The revised code for the `WebClass_Start` event procedure is shown in Listing 18-3.

Listing 18-3: WebClass_Start Code with Line Breaks

```
Private Sub WebClass_Start()
    Dim sQuote As String
    sQuote = Chr$(34)
    'Write a reply to the user
    With Response
        .Write "<HTML>" & vbCr
        .Write "<body>" & vbCr
        .Write "<h1><font face=" _
            & sQuote & "Arial" & sQuote _
            & ">WebClass1's Starting Page</font></h1>" _
            & vbCr
        .Write "<p>This response was created " _
            & "in the Start event of WebClass1.</p>" & vbCr
        .Write "</body>" & vbCr
        .Write "</html>" & vbCr
    End With
End Sub
```

The resulting HTML is much easier to read with the line breaks in place, as shown in Listing 18-4.

Listing 18-4: HTML with Line Breaks

```
<HTML>
<body>
<h1><font face="Arial">WebClass1's Starting Page</font></h1>
<p>This response was created in the Start event of
WebClass1.</p>
</body>
</html>
```

Notice that the URL in the address line of your browser is referencing a file ending in .ASP. This extension stands for Active Server Page and is Microsoft's main method of generating dynamic Web pages using Personal Web Server or Internet Information Server. Active Server Page code is evaluated before it is sent down to the user's browser and is thus much faster than alternatives such as client-side scripting. And you are probably wondering where it came from. If you haven't stopped your VB program yet, use Explorer to look in your temporary directory and you'll see the ASP page. However, when you stop your program, it disappears. If you're quick, you can open up the ASP page to see what it contains. The contents are shown in Listing 18-5.

> ### Listing 18-5: **The Contents of Project1_WebClass1.ASP**
>
> ```
> <%
> Server.ScriptTimeout=600
> Response.Buffer=True
> Response.Expires=0
>
> Set WebClass = Server.CreateObject("Project1.WebClass1")
> WebClass.[_Process] True
> %>
> ```

Visual Basic is automatically creating this Active Server Page for you. All it is doing is creating an instance of your WebClass1 and executing it. When you compile and deploy your application, VB builds a copy of this file for you and puts it with your compiled library. Both the ASP and the library need to be placed on your Web server. You can't run the library by itself — it has to be started in exactly the manner shown in the ASP. You probably should avoid editing the ASP as well, since VB simply overwrites your changes later. The ASP is simply a wrapper around your class; any HTML you want to build yourself should be made part of your WebClass through a standard code module.

The last thing you would need to do if you were really deploying this WebClass is compile it. You do this by selecting File ➪ Make Project1.dll. VB compiles your code and creates a DLL and the corresponding ASP for you automatically. You can then use a tool called the Packaging and Deployment Wizard (covered later) to create a cabinet file (.CAB) that can be deployed to your Web server. You can also simply copy the library and the other required files to your server and register them manually. The wizard finds the files you need to deploy and can combine them into a single file for download.

That covers the basics of how WebClasses are built. Later in the chapter, you'll learn how to really exploit some of the cool features of WebClasses. You'll also learn how to combine these features with HTML templates, which allows for rapid updates to the output format without having to change a line of code in your WebClass.

Creating and Using an HTML Template

As you can see from the previous example that built HTML through many lines of code, dealing with HTML is a bit of a pain in VB. Not only do you have to add your own line breaks, you also have to deal with double-quote characters around addresses and values in HTML; you can't take advantage of the WYSIWYG HTML editors on the market, such as Microsoft Visual InterDev and Microsoft FrontPage. For this reason, you're likely to appreciate the features of VB's HTML templates.

This section of the chapter shows you how to build a template and use it with your WebClass.

The first thing you'll need to do is create a simple HTML document. You can do this in Notepad or your favorite HTML editor. Because you need to write raw HTML, WYSIWYG editors like FrontPage are probably not a good choice. They tend to add a lot of extra tags everywhere that you really don't need, and may simply confuse you when you have to code with the page. As an example, use a text editor to write the following HTML text:

```
<HTML>
<HEAD>
<TITLE><WC@Title>Title</WC@Title></TITLE>
</HEAD>
<BODY bgColor=<WC@BGCOLOR>BGColor</WC@BGCOLOR>>
<H1><WC@TITLE>Title</WC@TITLE></H1>
This is a test of the HTML Template feature
in combination with WebClasses. Both the background color and
the Title have been substituted through code.
</BODY>
</HTML>
```

The extra, non-HTML tags beginning with WC@ are *substitution tags* used by the WebClass. You'll see how these work shortly, so for now just type the text as is. You should also notice that you can put these tags within other HTML tags, such as where the background color for the document would go. Because these special tags are never parsed by the user's browser, you won't have to worry about errors occurring when these tags are in the page. Save this file in a directory different from where your IIS project is located.

Once you have the HTML template built and saved, you can add it to your IIS application. To do this, perform the following steps:

1. If you're not already in a new IIS application (the one from the previous section is fine to use), create a new project.

2. Open the Designer window and right-click on HTML Template WebItems. From the menu that appears, select Add HTML Template.

3. From the dialog box shown in Figure 18-8, select your HTML file and click Open to let VB load it.

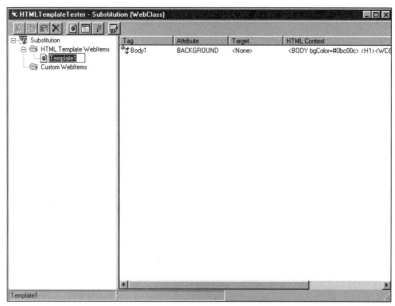

Figure 18-8: Add your HTML template to your project with this dialog box.

At this point, VB has added your template and is prompting you for a name. The code that follows uses `tmpSubstitution` as a name, but use your own judgment. You can see some of the HTML shown under the column heading "HTML Context."

You might also notice that the HTML doesn't quite look the way it did when you last saved your work. VB made a copy of your HTML file and placed it into the directory of your project. If you select the template in the Web Designer, right-click, and select the Edit HTML Template option, you'll see a few changes to it, as shown in Figure 18-9.

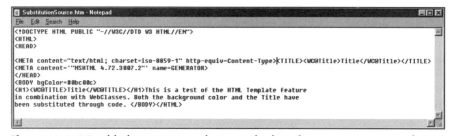

Figure 18-9: VB added some tags and removed others from your HTML template.

As you can see, some extra `<META>` tags were added to your document. In addition, the formatting has been altered and the `<BGCOLOR>` substitution tags have been removed and replaced with what is a very nasty shade of green.

All these changes probably mean you'll have to reedit your template file. Once you've added the template to your WebClass project, you have to edit the copy located in the project directory and not the original file. VB uses its copy as the source instead of the original file. There are various reasons for this, but mainly it's to simplify things when you deploy your application. VB doesn't have to worry about whether the file you used is still available; it makes its own copy. When you save your changes, VB detects it and asks if you want to refresh the copy in the project. Always let it do the refresh, or you'll have some ugly problems later.

Now that you've got the template into the project, you can start using it. The first thing you need to do is remove the code in the WebClass_Start event procedure. You'll replace it with the following code:

```
Private Sub WebClass_Start()
    tmpSubstitution.WriteTemplate
End Sub
```

This tells VB to use the tmpSubstitution template and send it to the user. Your project can have any number of HTML templates; typically, you'll have one for each resulting HTML page you plan to send to the user. You may also have different templates based on variable browser capabilities.

Once the WriteTemplate() method has been called, the first thing your HTML template does is execute the following code for each substitution tag that it finds in the HTML source code. The code to make this happen is shown here:

```
Private Sub tmpSubstitution_ProcessTag _
    (ByVal TagName As String, _
    TagContents As String, _
    SendTags As Boolean)

    TagName = Mid$(TagName, _
        Len(tmpSubstitution.TagPrefix) + 1)
    Select Case UCase$(TagName)
    Case "TITLE"
        TagContents = "The Test Worked!"
    Case "BGCOLOR"
        TagContents = "#FF0000"
    End Select
    SendTags = False
End Sub
```

The first thing this procedure does is remove the WC@ prefix from the substitution tag, which is represented by the TagName parameter. For instance, one of the values you can find in TagName may originally look like WC@Title. Removing the prefix from the tag and uppercasing it with the UCase$ function allows it to be matched more easily in the Select Case clause. We highly recommend matching uppercased tags against uppercase letters only; because HTML is case insensitive, and you don't want to have errors because someone decided to use lowercase or mixed-case letters in their tag names. Using the UCase$ function can solve these problems very quickly.

Once the `Private Sub tmpSubstitution_ProcessTag` procedure has determined what tag is being read, the new contents for the tag are assigned to variable `TagContents`, which is an output parameter. The assigned contents are placed between the substitution tags. The final line sets the `SendTags` parameter to `False`. This parameter indicates whether to print the substitution tags along with the existing contents of the HTML template. Such an arrangement enables you to do multiple levels of substitutions. For instance, when the first tag is read, the substitution routine could replace it with another set of substitution tags. These tags are reprocessed by the same routine just as if they were in there from the beginning. Because this type of recursion can be very confusing to read, we recommend against using this technique unless there is no other alternative. In most cases, you can get everything done with just a single level of substitutions.

The end result of this work: Your browser now shows the HTML template with the correct values substituted, as shown in Figure 18-10.

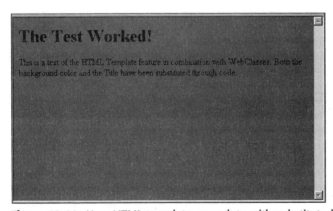

Figure 18-10: Your HTML template, complete with substituted values

The background color of the form is red (#FF0000), and the title of the document has been set correctly and is showing up in both your browser's title bar and on the document.

Although this substitution scheme may appear to only work with simple strings, you can set the `TagContents` property equal to any amount of text you wish, or to an expression, or to the result of a function procedure. You can add regular class modules and code modules to your application, also; the Project menu is automatically changed to show you what you can add. For instance, you could allow a collection, such as one you built in a previous chapter to manage customers, to generate an HTML table for its member objects. That HTML could be generated either by the collection or the objects themselves. The entire block of HTML could be returned and stored in a substitution tag. You'll see how to do this type of coding later in the chapter.

With the basics of HTML templates down, you're ready to move on to custom WebItems and events.

Using Custom WebItems and Events

Although the WebClass has some default events in which you can have various types of processing, those few events are too generic to respond to specific actions, such as a user clicking on a customer on a page with 100 different customers. If you didn't have another method, you'd have to have all your code in a single event, which would of course work fine. However, WebClasses provide a better approach. You can add your own custom WebItems to a WebClass. As was mentioned in the introduction to this chapter, you can think of a WebItem as a set of functions or a class. Within each WebItem, you can have a number of custom events, which are the actual methods that can be performed by the WebClass. WebItems and custom events belonging to a WebClass module may be triggered from the same ASP, simply through varying arguments supplied to the page. You can then use these arguments internally to produce URLs in the HTML output that the user can click, or you can call the URLs from other HTML pages you may have on your site. You'll see the syntax for this later in the section.

For now, you'll see how to add custom WebItems and custom events to perform processing on the HTML template you just built. You'll be using a combination of custom WebItems and events to provide additional functionality to the user. In the process, you should start seeing how to use these features to make your own Web-based applications more modular and reliable.

The first thing you'll need to do is to add three custom WebItems to your WebClass. To do this, perform the following steps:

1. Open the designer window.

2. Right-click on Custom WebItems and select Add Custom WebItem from the popup menu.

3. VB will add a new WebItem to the tree and prompt you to rename it. Add three WebItems with these names: `ShowInRed`, `ShowInYellow`, `ShowInBlue`.

At this point, your designer window should look like the one in Figure 18-11.

Figure 18-11: Your WebClass now has three custom WebItems.

The next thing to do is add some code behind the scenes. As mentioned, the WebClass can have variables just like any other class. In the Declarations section of the WebClass, add the following variable declaration:

```
Dim sColor As String
```

Listing 18-6 shows the code you need for the three custom WebItems.

Listing 18-6: **Custom WebItem Code**

```
Private Sub ShowInBlue_Respond()
    sColor = "#0000FF"
    tmpSubstitution.WriteTemplate
End Sub

Private Sub ShowInRed_Respond()
    sColor = "#FF0000"
    tmpSubstitution.WriteTemplate
End Sub

Private Sub ShowInYellow_Respond()
    sColor = "#FFFF00"
    tmpSubstitution.WriteTemplate
End Sub
```

These are all essentially event handlers for the custom WebItems. The next thing you have to do is change the `WebClass_Start` event procedure. Because we need to give the user a few choices, `WebClass_Start` will have to generate some HTML dynamically. You'll see shortly why this is done. Add the code in Listing 18-7 to your WebClass.

Listing 18-7: **WebClass_Start Code**

```
Private Sub WebClass_Start()
    sColor = "#FFFFFF"
    With Response
      .Write "<HTML><HEAD><TITLE>"
      .Write "Pick Your Color"
      .Write "</TITLE></HEAD>" & vbCr
      .Write "<BODY BGCOLOR=#FFFFFF>" & vbCr
      .Write "Pick the color you'd like to see:<P>" & vbCr
      .Write "<A HREF=""" _
          & URLFor(ShowInRed) _
          & """>Red</A><BR>" & vbCr
      .Write "<A HREF=""" _
          & URLFor(ShowInYellow) _
          & """>Yellow</A><BR>" & vbCr
      .Write "<A HREF=""" _
          & URLFor(ShowInBlue) _
          & """>Blue</A><BR>" & vbCr
      .Write "</HTML>"

    End With

End Sub
```

The important feature of this code is the `URLFor` function. This method generates the proper URL to access this WebClass's Custom WebItems. The first time it is used, it generates the URL to access the `ShowInRed` custom WebItem. The advantage of using `URLFor` is that it generates the internal ID number used by the Web server to access the method. This number is used to retrieve the location of the method within the WebClass object. This makes referencing a method faster, because the WebClass doesn't have to look up a name reference. If you're generating code, always use the `URLFor` method for WebItems that are in your WebClass.

The last piece of code you need is a slightly modified version of the `tmpSubstitution_ProcessTag` procedure. The changes are highlighted in Listing 18-8.

Listing 18-8: **ProcessTag Code**

```
Private Sub tmpSubstitution_ProcessTag _
    (ByVal TagName As String, _
    TagContents As String, _
    SendTags As Boolean)

    TagName = Mid$(TagName, _
        Len(tmpSubstitution.TagPrefix) + 1)
    Select Case UCase$(TagName)
    Case "TITLE"
        TagContents = "The Test Worked!"
    Case "BGCOLOR"
        TagContents = sColor
    End Select
    SendTags = False
End Sub
```

Instead of always using a particular color, this procedure will now use the color stored in the sColor variable. The correct color was assigned earlier by the custom WebItem triggered by the user.

Save your work and then run your project. The first page you see, shown in Figure 18-12, shows the HTML generated in the WebClass_Start event.

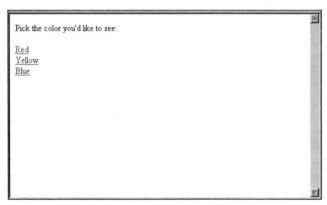

Figure 18-12: The first page is generated from the WebClass_Start event procedure.

If you look at the source, you will see the code shown in Listing 18-9.

Listing 18-9: **HTML Generated by WebClass_Start Event Procedure**

```
<HTML><HEAD><TITLE>Pick Your Color</TITLE></HEAD>
<BODY BGCOLOR=#FFFFFF>
Pick the color you'd like to see:<P>
<A HREF="HTMLTemplateTester_Substitution.ASP?WCIID=1281">
Red</A><BR>
<A HREF="HTMLTemplateTester_Substitution.ASP?WCIID=1282">
Yellow</A><BR>
<A HREF="HTMLTemplateTester_Substitution.ASP?WCIID=1280">
Blue</A><BR>
</HTML>
```

If you haven't saved your project yet, HTMLTemplateTester may be shown as Project1 or whatever your project is currently named.

The WCIID reference following the question mark, and the number following it and the equal sign, are known in ASP lingo as a *parameter*. This is one method by which one page can talk to another page. The number refers to the custom WebItem you built. The rest of the URL is the same as before: the project name followed by the WebClass name.

If you click on one of these items, you will see the same HTML template as before, except you'll now see a different background color for each. Although this may seem like a trivial example, the basic idea really expands the scope of how you can use WebClasses and HTML templates.

With the creation of custom WebItems under your belt, creating custom events is just as easy. The main difference is that instead of using the default Respond() event handler, you'll have a different event handler for each event you build, all under a particular WebItem. The example you'll build simply converts the previous example to use a single WebItem and three events instead of using three different WebItems. All the modified code will be marked so you can see the differences between the two techniques.

First of all, you need to open your designer window and do the following: Add a custom WebItem named ChangeColor. Then right-click on ChangeColor in the list and select Add Custom Event from the popup menu. Add three custom events named Red, Yellow, and Blue. Your Designer window should look like the one in Figure 18-13 when you're done.

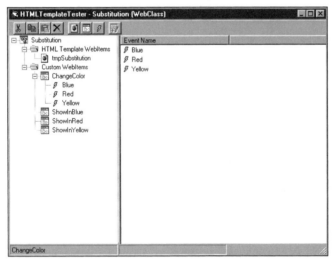

Figure 18-13: Your WebClass now has a new custom
WebItems with three custom events.

You now have to add new event handlers to deal with the new events you just built. That code is shown in Listing 18-10.

Listing 18-10: **Custom Event Handlers for WebClass**

```
Private Sub ChangeColor_Blue()
    sColor = "#0000FF"
    tmpSubstitution.WriteTemplate
End Sub

Private Sub ChangeColor_Red()
    sColor = "#FF0000"
    tmpSubstitution.WriteTemplate
End Sub

Private Sub ChangeColor_Yellow()
    sColor = "#FFFF00"
    tmpSubstitution.WriteTemplate
End Sub
```

As you can see, these procedures use the same instructions as the ones for the WebItems built earlier, though the procedures' names are different to take account of the new events.

The last change you need to make is in the WebClass_Start event handler. The changes are to the three calls to URLFor, as marked in Listing 18-11.

Listing 18-11: **WebClass_Start Event Handler**

```
Private Sub WebClass_Start()
    sColor = "#FFFFFF"
    With Response
      .Write "<HTML><HEAD><TITLE>"
      .Write "Pick Your Color"
      .Write "</TITLE></HEAD>" & vbCr
      .Write "<BODY BGCOLOR=#FFFFFF>" & vbCr
      .Write "Pick the color you'd like to see:<P>" & vbCr
      .Write "<A HREF=""" _
          & URLFor(ChangeColor, "Red") _
          & """>Red</A><BR>" & vbCr
      .Write "<A HREF=""" _
          & URLFor(ChangeColor, "Yellow") _
          & """>Yellow</A><BR>" & vbCr
      .Write "<A HREF=""" _
          & URLFor(ChangeColor, "Blue") _
          & """>Blue</A><BR>" & vbCr
      .Write "</HTML>"

    End With

End Sub
```

Although the name of the WebItem (ChangeColor, in this case) is actually an object defined to Visual Basic, the name of the event has to be passed as a string in quotes. It is not defined to Visual Basic and thus has to be "protected" from Visual Basic's syntax checker. When you run your program, the string will be passed to the URLFor function, which understands how to interpret it. The end result of this code is very similar to the previous version, except in the starting page. The new HTML for the starting page is shown in Listing 18-12.

Listing 18-12: **WebClass_Start HTML Using Custom Events**

```
<HTML><HEAD><TITLE>Pick Your Color</TITLE></HEAD>
<BODY BGCOLOR=#FFFFFF>
Pick the color you'd like to see:<P>
<A HREF="HTMLTemplateTester_Substitution.ASP?WCIID=
1280&WCE=Red">Red</A><BR>
<A HREF="HTMLTemplateTester_Substitution.ASP?WCIID=
1280&WCE=Yellow">Yellow</A><BR>
<A HREF="HTMLTemplateTester_Substitution.ASP?WCIID=
1280&WCE=Blue">Blue</A><BR>
</HTML>
```

Appended to the end of each URL is the name of the event to be called, prefixed with WCE (WebClass Event). This particular part of the URL is always passed as text, even in this version.

If you prefer to write this HTML page manually, you can still call the three WebItems, but in a different way. Instead of using the WCIID parameter that VB utilizes, you write the WCI parameter followed by the WebItem's name, as in this example:

```
<A HREF="HTMLTemplateTester_Substitution.ASP?WCI=
ChangeColor&WCE=Red">Red</A><BR>
```

This syntax enables you to create plain HTML pages that can start WebClass applications. When you use this syntax, make sure you have a default response in case parameters are omitted from the name of the ASP. This may happen if plain HTML pages are referring to ASPs that require certain information to run properly. Typically, you want a URL entered by hand to be as simple as possible. In most cases, you'll call the main Respond() event in a class first, after which all other URLs will be generated by the WebClass itself. You'll see more of this later in the chapter.

Using ADO with WebClasses

Now you're ready to start using databases with your templates. This will show you more of the real power behind this new technology. If you've done ASPs by hand previously (as we have), you may not be doing a lot of them by hand any longer. We know that *we* won't be.

The main point of the Active Server Pages technology was primarily to make it easier to publish dynamic pages. These pages were typically based on database tables and queries. WebClasses are no different, and even make it easier yet to build these types of applications. In this section, you'll build an HTML template with substitution tags. These tags will be replaced by data from a database that you access by way of ADO. You'll also be building something called a UserEvent to make it easier to show more detailed information on records in a table of data.

The database you'll be using is (no surprise here) the Northwind Traders database. You'll be building a list of the customers in the database and giving the user the ability to click on a customer to see more information about the customer's company. The functionality here is very similar to what you built using VB forms, except that the output is directed through the Web to any browser supporting a minimal set of HTML.

We'll start by creating a new IIS application. Be sure to put it in its own directory, since VB will need to create a share for it. Once the project is created, you'll probably want to rename both the project and the WebClass. In the example included, the project is named ADOWebClass and the WebClass is named NWind.

The next thing you need to do is to build an HTML template that will be used for the customer list. The only things you need to put in this page are general tags, such as TITLE and BODY. All the customer entries will be generated dynamically with the WebClass. The HTML template should look something like the one in Listing 18-13.

Listing 18-13: **CustomerList HTML Template**

```
<HTML>
<HEAD>

<TITLE>Northwind Traders - Customer List</TITLE>
<STYLE>
<!-
H1 {
        font-family: Arial;
        font-weight: bold;
        font-size: 16px;
        color: #800000;
}

H3 {
        font-family: Arial;
        font-size: 12px;
        color: #800000;
}
H4 {
        font-family: Arial;
        font-size: 10px;
        color: #000000;
}
->
</STYLE>

</HEAD>
<BODY bgColor=#ffffcc>
<H1>Northwind Traders Customer List<BR>
<H3>As Of <WC@CURRENTDATE></WC@CURRENTDATE> </H3></H1>
<HR>
<WC@CUSTOMERDATA></WC@CUSTOMERDATA>

</BODY></HTML>
```

If you're not familiar with embedded style sheets (ESS), this HTML document has one. The ESS feature works in the latest versions of both Netscape and Internet Explorer; it enables you to define fonts, colors, and other text formatting features in one place in the document instead of every time you use the text. These fonts will be used to generate the data for the page. By leaving the font properties here instead of in the WebClass, you can change the format of the data without having to change the WebClass itself.

Once you've saved this template in another directory, add it to your IIS application and name it tmpCustomerList. Next, add a custom WebItem to show the customer list, since your WebClass will probably have a wide variety of other features that will be shown first on a menu or other interface. Name the WebItem ShowCustomer. The default event for this will trigger an event that handles showing the list of customers. Create a custom event called ListAll as part of the ShowCustomer WebItem.

With the WebItems and custom events defined, you can start writing some code. We'll start with the WebClass_Start event handler. As mentioned earlier, you'd probably want to have a menu from which to show the customer list, but these instructions will serve as test code so that the list of customers will come up automatically when the WebClass is started:

```
Private Sub WebClass_Start()
    Set NextItem = ListCustomer
End Sub
```

The ListCustomer_Respond event handler is next, and is very simple:

```
Private Sub ListCustomer_Respond()
    tmpCustomerList.WriteTemplate
End Sub
```

This triggers the CustomerList template to load and be processed. Because we have substitution tags to deal with, the tmpCustomerList_ProcessTags event handler is next. The code for it is shown in Listing 18-14.

Listing 18-14: **ProcessTags Event Handler**

```
Private Sub tmpCustomerList_ProcessTag _
    (ByVal TagName As String, _
    TagContents As String, _
    SendTags As Boolean)

    Dim sTag As String

    sTag = UCase$(Mid$(TagName, _
        Len(tmpCustomerList.TagPrefix) + 1))
    Select Case sTag
        Case "CURRENTDATE"
            TagContents = Format$(Date, "mmmm d, yyyy")
        Case "CUSTOMERDATA"
            TagContents = fnGenerateCustomerList
    End Select
```

```
        SendTags = False

End Sub
```

The function procedure fnGenerateCustomerList, called toward the end of
Listing 18-14, actually reads the database and creates a table with the customers in
it. This procedure is listed in Listing 18-15. Remember to use the path to your
Northwind Traders database in the ADO connection.

Listing 18-15: **The fnGenerateCustomerList Function**

```vb
Private Function fnGenerateCustomerList() As String
    Dim dcnNWind As ADODB.Connection
    Dim rsCust As ADODB.Recordset
    Dim sOutput As String

    Set dcnNWind = New ADODB.Connection
    dcnNWind.CursorLocation = adUseClient
    dcnNWind.Open "PROVIDER=Microsoft.Jet.OLEDB.3.51;" _
        & "Data Source=C:\Visual Studio\VB98\NWind.MDB;"

    Set rsCust = New ADODB.Recordset
    rsCust.Open "SELECT * FROM Customers " _
        & "ORDER BY CompanyName", _
        dcnNWind, adOpenForwardOnly, adLockReadOnly

    If rsCust.RecordCount = 0 Then
        sOutput = _
            "<H1>No records are in the database.</H1>"
    Else
        sOutput = "<TABLE CELLPADDING=3 BORDER=1>" & vbCr _
            & "<TR><TH><H4>Customer Name</TH>" & vbCr _
            & "<TH><H4>City</TH>" & vbCr _
            & "<TH><H4>State/Region</TH>" & vbCr _
            & "<TH><H4>Country</TH>" & vbCr _
            & "</TR>" & vbCr

        Do While Not rsCust.EOF
            sOutput = sOutput & "<TR>" & vbCr _
                & "<TD><H4>" _
                & rsCust("CompanyName") & "</TD>" & vbCr _
                & "<TD><H4>" _
                & rsCust("City") & "</TD>" & vbCr _
                & "<TD><H4>" _
                & rsCust("Region") & "</TD>" & vbCr _
                & "<TD><H4>" _
                & rsCust("Country") & "</TD>" & vbCr _
```

(continued)

Listing 18-15 *(continued)*

```
            & "</TR>" & vbCr
        rsCust.MoveNext
    Loop
    sOutput = sOutput & "</TABLE>" & vbCr
    sOutput = sOutput & "<HR><H3><I>" _
        & rsCust.RecordCount _
        & " customers listed.</I></H3>" & vbCr

  End If
  fnGenerateCustomerList = sOutput

  '
  ' Clean up objects
  '
  rsCust.Close
  Set rsCust = Nothing
  dcnNWind.Close
  Set dcnNWind = Nothing
End Function
```

After making a connection to the Northwind Traders database, a recordset is created of all the customers, sorted by company name. The TABLE header tags are generated next, including column headers. All the HTML is appended to the sOutput string variable, since it all needs to be returned to the ProcessTags event procedure at the end. For each record retrieved, a new table row is added. When it is generated, the HTML looks like this for a single row:

```
<TR>
<TD><H4>Alfreds Futterkiste</TD>
<TD><H4>Berlin</TD>
<TD><H4></TD>
<TD><H4>Germany</TD>
</TR>
```

Leaving the <H4> tags unclosed will actually save some vertical space since adding an </H4> tag will add extra white space after the text. The CELLPADDING parameter of the <TABLE> tag, generated by fnGenerateCustomerList, has already taken care of this. A summary line is printed listing the number of records and then, finally, the database objects are closed and eliminated by Visual Basic.

At this point, you can run your project and look at the results. Both browsers will give you output similar to that shown in Figure 18-14.

Figure 18-14: The completed Northwind Traders customer list

Now that you've learned the basics of combining ADO with WebClasses, you can move on to some more advanced techniques for building useful applications.

Advanced Techniques

In this section, you'll learn how to create a dynamic event associated with a WebClass. These events enable you to respond with a varying result, based on the event that is triggered. To see how this works, you're going to be modifying the example from the previous section, and to enable users to click on a company name see more information about the company. In addition, you'll learn a few tricks to help simplify your code when dealing with WebClasses.

The first thing you need to do is build a new HTML template. This template will be used to show a customer's information. An example HTML template is shown in Listing 18-16.

Listing 18-16: **ViewCustomer HTML Template**

```
<HTML>
<HEAD>
<TITLE>Northwind Traders - View Customer</TITLE>
<STYLE>
<!-
H1 {
     font-family: Arial Black;
     font-size: 16px;
     color: #800000;
}
H3 {
```

(continued)

Listing 18-16 *(continued)*

```
        font-family: Arial;
        font-size: 12px;
        color: #800000;
}

H4 {
        font-family: Arial;
        font-size: 10px;
        color: #000000;
}
-->
</STYLE>

</HEAD>
<BODY bgColor=#ffffcc>
<H1><WC@FIELDCOMPANYNAME></WC@FIELDCOMPANYNAME></H1>
<HR>

<TABLE border=1 cellPadding=3>
<TBODY>
<TR>
<TD>
<H3>Customer ID:</H3>
</TD>
<TD>
<H3><WC@FIELDCUSTOMERID></WC@FIELDCUSTOMERID></H3>
</TD></TR>

<TR>
<TD>
<H3>Contact Name:</H3></TD>
<TD>
<H3><WC@FIELDCONTACTNAME></WC@FIELDCONTACTNAME></H3>
</TD></TR>

<TR>
<TD>
<H3>Contact Title:</H3></TD>
<TD>
<H3><WC@FIELDCONTACTTITLE></WC@FIELDCONTACTTITLE></H3>
</TD></TR>

<TR>
<TD>
<H3>Address:</H3>
</TD>
<TD>
<H3><WC@FIELDADDRESS></WC@FIELDADDRESS></H3>
</TD></TR>
```

```
<TR>
<TD>
<H3>City:</H3></TD>
<TD>
<H3><WC@FIELDCITY></WC@FIELDCITY></H3>
</TD></TR>

<TR>
<TD>
<H3>Region:</H3>
</TD>
<TD>
<H3><WC@FIELDREGION></WC@FIELDREGION></H3>
</TD></TR>

<TR>
<TD>
<H3>Postal Code:</H3>
</TD>
<TD>
<H3><WC@FIELDPOSTALCODE></WC@FIELDPOSTALCODE></H3>
</TD></TR>

<TR>
<TD>
<H3>Country:</H3>
</TD>
<TD>
<H3><WC@FIELDCOUNTRY></WC@FIELDCOUNTRY></H3>
</TD></TR>

<TR>
<TD>
<H3>Phone:</H3>
</TD>
<TD>
<H3><WC@FIELDPHONE></WC@FIELDPHONE></H3>
</TD></TR>

<TR>
<TD>
<H3>Fax:</H3>
</TD>
<TD>
<H3><WC@FIELDFAX></WC@FIELDFAX></H3>
</TD></TR>
</TBODY>
</TABLE>
</BODY>
</HTML>
```

In this particular template, all the tags to be filled with data from the database are prefixed with the word FIELD. You'll see the reason for this shortly. For now, add the template to your WebClass and name it tmpViewCustomer or another appropriate name of your choosing.

Next, add the following declarations to the general Declarations section of the WebClass:

```
Dim dcnNWind As ADODB.Connection
Dim rsCust As ADODB.Recordset
```

These declarations enable event handlers to communicate and to save some database activity that would be required otherwise. The next changes are to the fnGenerateCustomerList procedure, highlighted in Listing 18-17.

Listing 18-17: **Changes in the fnGenerateCustomerList Procedure**

```
Private Function fnGenerateCustomerList() As String
    Dim sOutput As String

    Set dcnNWind = New ADODB.Connection
    dcnNWind.CursorLocation = adUseClient
    dcnNWind.Open "PROVIDER=Microsoft.Jet.OLEDB.3.51;" _
        & "Data Source=C:\Visual Studio\VB98\NWind.MDB;"

    Set rsCust = New ADODB.Recordset
    rsCust.Open "SELECT * FROM Customers " _
        & "ORDER BY CompanyName", _
        dcnNWind, adOpenForwardOnly, adLockReadOnly

    If rsCust.RecordCount = 0 Then
        sOutput = _
            "<H1>No records are in the database.</H1>"
    Else
        sOutput = "<TABLE CELLPADDING=3 BORDER=1>" & vbCr _
            & "<TR><TH><H4>Customer Name</TH>" & vbCr _
            & "<TH><H4>City</TH>" & vbCr _
            & "<TH><H4>State/Region</TH>" & vbCr _
            & "<TH><H4>Country</TH>" & vbCr _
            & "</TR>" & vbCr

        Do While Not rsCust.EOF
            sOutput = sOutput & "<TR>" & vbCr _
                & "<TD><H4><A HREF="""" _
                & URLFor(ViewCustomer, _
                    CStr(rsCust("CustomerID"))) _
                & """>" & rsCust("CompanyName") _
                & "</A></TD>" & vbCr _
                & "<TD><H4>" & rsCust("City") _
```

```
                 & "</TD>" & vbCr _
                 & "<TD><H4>" & rsCust("Region") _
                 & "</TD>" & vbCr _
                 & "<TD><H4>" & rsCust("Country") _
                 & "</TD>" & vbCr _
                 & "</TR>" & vbCr
         rsCust.MoveNext
      Loop
      sOutput = sOutput & "</TABLE>" & vbCr
      sOutput = sOutput & "<HR><H3><I>" _
          & rsCust.RecordCount _
          & " customers listed.</I></H3>" & vbCr

   End If
   fnGenerateCustomerList = sOutput

   '
   ' Clean up objects
   '
   rsCust.Close
   Set rsCust = Nothing
   dcnNWind.Close
   Set dcnNWind = Nothing
End Function
```

The first change is the removal of the declarations for dcnNWind and rsCust, since
they are now defined at the WebClass level. The other change is that now, instead of
just printing the company name, the name is wrapped with a URL by the URLFor
function. Omitting all the host and directory information, the URL looks like this
when it is complete:

```
ADOWebClass_NWind.ASP?WCIID=1282&WCE=ALFKI
```

The customer ID has been appended to the URL by way of the URLFor method and
is called a user-defined event. Obviously, we're not going to create a separate event
for each possible customer ID. What we're going to do instead is have the
ViewCustomer WebItem respond to the UserEvent event handler and show
the customer's information when it is requested. This task is very easy, and is
significantly simpler than the same task using ordinary Active Server Pages without
VB. In the ASP environment, you would have to break up the URL yourself (using
the Request object) and then fill the page yourself. In addition, you wouldn't get
the benefit of being able to change the template for the page without changing the
code, because the HTML and VBScript code are linked in ASP programming.

The next piece of code you need is shown in Listing 18-18. When a user clicks on a
customer name, this code will be triggered because we are providing an unknown
event name (the customer ID). The customer ID will be placed in the EventName
parameter to the ViewCustomer_UserEvent subroutine. It is then used in the SQL
query to retrieve the correct piece of data.

Listing 18-18: ViewCustomer_UserEvent Event Handler

```
Private Sub ViewCustomer_UserEvent(ByVal EventName As String)
    Set dcnNWind = New ADODB.Connection
    dcnNWind.CursorLocation = adUseClient
    dcnNWind.Open "PROVIDER=Microsoft.Jet.OLEDB.3.51;" _
        & "Data Source=C:\Visual Studio\VB98\NWind.MDB;"

    Set rsCust = New ADODB.Recordset
    rsCust.Open "SELECT * FROM Customers " _
        & "WHERE CustomerID = '" & EventName & "'", _
        dcnNWind, adOpenForwardOnly, adLockReadOnly

    tmpViewCustomer.WriteTemplate
End Sub
```

The main purpose of this code is to find the customer record and place it in the module-level recordset. This action is done here because we don't want the ProcessTags event handler to create a new recordset for every single tag that it processes.

The next code is the ProcessTags event handler for the tmpViewCustomer template, and is shown in Listing 18-19.

Listing 18-19: The tmpViewCustomer_ProcessTags Event Handler

```
Private Sub tmpViewCustomer_ProcessTag _
    (ByVal TagName As String, _
    TagContents As String, _
    SendTags As Boolean)

    '
    ' At this point, we only care about tags
    ' that have the word "Field" in them.
    ' You may wish to expand this over time
    ' to handle other tags.
    '
    Dim iLoc As Integer
    iLoc = InStr(TagName, "FIELD")
    If iLoc > 0 Then
        TagContents = rsCust(Mid$(TagName, iLoc + 5)) & ""
    End If
    SendTags = False
End Sub
```

This handler looks for all tags beginning with the word FIELD and substitutes data from the field in the database whose name appears to the right of FIELD in the HTML template — giving you the capability of changing the database and the template without changing the code in the WebClass. Simply reference the field in the template, and this handler will find the corresponding database field.

The last change is to the WebClass_Terminate event procedure. This cleans up the open recordsets and connections that may have been left open by the UserEvent handler. This code is shown in Listing 18-20.

Listing 18-20: **The WebClass_Terminate Event Handler**

```
Private Sub WebClass_Terminate()
    On Error Resume Next

    rsCust.Close
    Set rsCust = Nothing
    dcnNWind.Close
    Set dcnNWind = Nothing

End Sub
```

Because the WebClass has ceased execution anyway, the Resume Next error handler will skip any errors in which the recordset or connection is not open.

With these changes in place, you can run your WebClass. The customer list will now have a link for each customer that shows the customer data when you click on it, as shown in Figure 18-15.

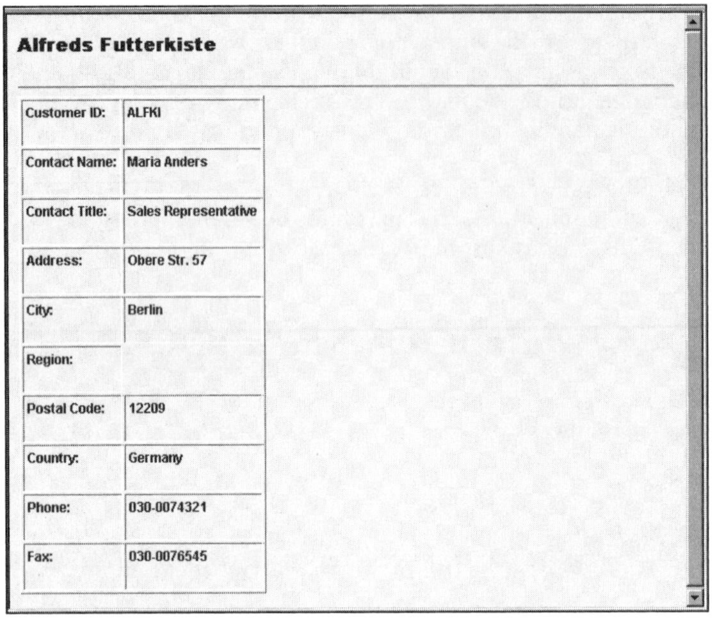

Figure 18-15: The completed Northwind Traders customer viewer

At this point, you have a model for many Web database publishing projects that you've probably been planning, or may have done using Active Server Pages. You can now make your code quicker and more reliable by using a WebClass to consolidate all your code and be able to build it all in Visual Basic.

Summary

As you can see from the material and examples in this chapter, WebClasses are one of the most exciting parts of this release of Visual Basic. For everyone who dreads having to write and debug Web applications built using ASPs and VBScript, this will save you many headaches and a lot of time.

✦ Performance and reliability have increased in VB6, making it worth your while to learn this new technology.

✦ Not only can you build simple pages, you can also build dynamic pages using the user-defined events you learned about.

✦ VB also provides you with the entire ASP object model to further expand your developer's palette.

✦ WebClasses are a great combination of the Visual Basic environment with the new Web programming model.

✦   ✦   ✦

ActiveX Development

ActiveX Server Planning Strategies

◆ ◆ ◆ ◆

In This Chapter

Encapsulating
functionality in
DLLs and ActiveX
components

Considering
in-process and
out-of-process servers

Analyzing what your
server should do

◆ ◆ ◆ ◆

I t's certainly hard to keep up with the name changes that
Microsoft is always coming up with. Architecturally, we
have client/server, three-tiered, and now *n*-tiered systems.
Object-wise we have always had DLLs, and of course VBXs,
and now OCXs. You have most certainly heard of OLE, but
what's this about ActiveX? In addition, what's the difference
between objects and classes and interfaces and . . . well, all
those other components?

In this chapter, we explain the differences and similarities
among all these concepts, because they are all relevant to our
discussion about ActiveX server planning strategies. It turns
out that all these "things" we just mentioned have to do with
breaking down a problem into smaller parts.

We'll also talk a lot about constructing an architecture that
exploits this world of objects. This requires a different kind of
problem solving and design methodology than would be
applied to building a monolithic application. There are many
design decisions along the way, including planning for reuse,
scalability, portability, and the like.

Encapsulating Functionality

You have all heard the buzzwords by now: Object-Oriented
Design (OOD), Object-Oriented Programming (OOP),
reusability, portability, objects, servers, services, and so on.
If you understand these concepts completely then you should
skip this section. On the other hand, if you need to get a good
idea of what these concepts are, then read on.

All these concepts share a common theme—taking a problem and reducing it into smaller pieces. Alternatively, if you prefer the bottom-up perspective, all these concepts help you create a set of building blocks with which to construct an application. Within this chapter, we're going to call this notion of creating small functional pieces *encapsulation*. Of course, the term carries a lot of varied meaning, but we are considering it only in its abstract sense of *providing a way to isolate functionality*.

Windows DLLs

The acronym DLL stands for Dynamic Link Library. This is a library of functions that are available to an application at run-time. The term *dynamic* denotes that the functions are loaded as needed from a separate file and not linked directly into the executable. The functions contained within a DLL are each independent of one another. The persons developing the DLL try to assemble similar functions into libraries.

Within Visual Basic, the functions must be independently declared within a code module. When declared, a function can be called, or executed, as needed—just like a native VB function.

Within a DLL, there is typically no notion of state, no notion of properties, and no notion of events. A DLL function would be equivalent to an ActiveX method. As you can see, a DLL is most useful to assemble functions that are designed to operate independently into a package—thus encapsulating their functionality. However, a DLL is not useful if you need a component to participate in the logic or execution of your program.

Figure 19.1 shows the relationship of a DLL to an application. As you can see, an application calls a DLL function, supplying the necessary and proper parameters. The DLL then processes these parameters and returns a value. Note that a void function, which is equivalent to a Visual Basic Sub, does not return a value. The DLL in turn may do external processing due to the function call. An example of this would be when a Windows drawing function is called. That's really all there is to the application-DLL relationship; thus the limited usefulness of DLLs in your system's architecture.

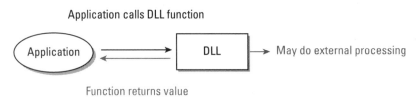

Figure 19-1: The relationship of a DLL to an application

ActiveX components

Before we get into the discussion of ActiveX, let's make one thing perfectly clear: ActiveX is OLE (Object Linking and Embedding). The core technology used by ActiveX components is OLE. The term *ActiveX* is Microsoft's way of extending OLE technologies to the Internet and branding it with a new, catchy name.

Figure 19-2 shows the possible types of ActiveX components. It also shows the construction of an ActiveX component, highlighting the fact that a component is primarily based on OLE technologies. There are three types of components: *controls*, *servers*, and *documents*. Servers and documents each come in two flavors: EXEs and DLLs.

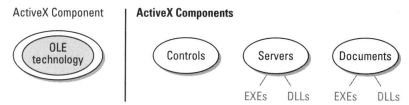

Figure 19-2: ActiveX components

An ActiveX control is a component that is designed to be used by an ActiveX control-consuming application such as Visual Basic or Visual C++. The ActiveX control supercedes an OCX control, which superseded a VBX control. We're not going to go into a lot of discussion about ActiveX controls and documents, since Chapters 25–28 do go into such detail; and this and the next two chapters are really concerned with servers.

An ActiveX document is a special type of server that can be used in an Web page. It's kind of a cross between an ActiveX control and an ActiveX server. It's like a control because it is always used within a consuming application, in this case Microsoft Internet Explorer (IE). It's also like a server because you can build a set of ActiveX documents within the same project that operate together. In our opinion ActiveX documents currently have limited usage and may, in fact, be slightly ahead of their time. The main problem is that these components are relatively large and can be painfully slow to use over the Internet. Although increases in network bandwidth may solve that problem, there may be more suitable solutions to building Internet applications, such as Active Server Pages (ASP), Dynamic HTML (DHTML), and similar programming techniques.

Finally, on to ActiveX servers. An ActiveX server is very much like a standalone application with some specialized interfaces required by OLE. Such a server gives you the ability to encapsulate functionality in a much different way than a DLL.

An ActiveX server is available to any ActiveX client, such as a Visual Basic application. When we talked about DLLs, we discussed the fact that the DLL supplied functions. We might also take a little stretch here and say that a DLL *serves* up functions. An ActiveX server, on the other hand, not only serves up methods (equivalent to functions) but also provides properties, events, as well as subordinate objects. Another big distinction between a server and a DLL is in how the client application uses the server. In a DLL, there is only one type of interaction—a function call. The Windows system and Visual Basic take care of loading and unloading the DLL, as needed. The client, on the other hand, must create a server in order to use it. This act of creating the server is known as *instantiation*. When a server is instantiated, the client can get to all the properties, events, methods, and objects that are made visible by the server (Figure 19-3).

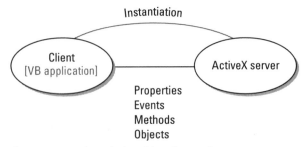

Figure 19-3: The relationship of an ActiveX server to an application

Because a server is really a fully functional application, it can be used in collaboration with your main application to create your system solution. In the next sections, we talk about how an application can be broken out into separate servers and what strategy and methodology to employ when doing so. However, before we get into this process of dissection, we talk about process spaces, which should help you understand the differences between ActiveX server DLLs and ActiveX server EXEs.

Are You In or Out?

By now you've probably heard about in-process (*in-proc*) and out-of-process (*out-of-proc*) servers, but what do these terms really mean? To answer that question and to understand the ramifications of building such servers, we need to take a look at Windows *process spaces*.

The Windows operating system is a multitasking OS. It performs multitasking by assigning *process spaces* to applications that are currently executing on the system. A process space is a reserved area of memory that is only available to a particular application. The application loads and executes entirely within this space.

Windows does not allow various loaded applications or processes to interfere with each other's memory directly. Windows does, of course, allow processes to intercommunicate, but only in an orderly fashion.

Figure 19-4 shows a client process and a server process communicating via a third process — a system message-passing facility. In the figure, a line divides these two classes of processes, representing the relationship between a client and out-of-process ActiveX server. Figure 19-4 shows how the operating system facilitates communications between an out-of-process DLL and an application.

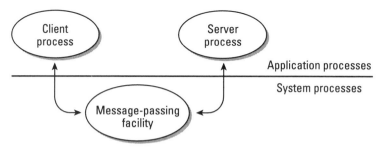

Figure 19-4: Out-of-process servers

All communications between a client and out-of-process server must be made via an external mechanism — in this case, a system-provided message-passing facility. The use of this facility adds a lot of overhead to communications. In addition, this is not necessarily just a flow-through type of message passing, but rather an internal messaging protocol. Take, for example, modem communications. First, there is a handshake, then a piece of a message, then some error checking and correction. Although this is not the same mechanism used by Windows, the analogy helps to understand the amount of overhead associated with out-of-process communications. An in-process server, on the other hand, can directly communicate with the client and vice versa. Figure 19-5 shows how a client and an in-process server communicate. Notice that all communications occur within the process space of the application — thus eliminating the overhead associated with interprocess communications.

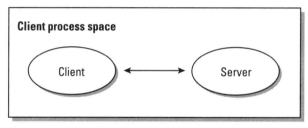

Figure 19-5: In-process servers

So if in-process is so much more efficient for communications, why not just make all your servers in-process? As with most of your design decisions, there are trade-offs. Let's take a look at a couple of scenarios that would benefit from in-proc and out-of-proc servers.

The forms server

This scenario describes a *forms server*. This server is responsible to generate forms that are used within the client application. Let's say that these forms are fairly complex, bursting with controls and graphics, and that they are generated according to the particular need of the client. For example, one could envision a tabbed dialog that might have more or fewer tabs depending on the session-state that the client is in. This session-state is the state that the system is in based on the cumulative interactions a user has had with the system. For example, a system that provides database connectivity can be in either a connected or an unconnected state. If the system was unconnected, a tab defining database-connection properties may not need to be displayed. In addition, before this dialog is displayed it would have to be populated with current values from the client.

This usage scenario probably points to the use of an in-proc server, for two reasons. First, the forms are complex and are generated as needed. This can be computationally intensive. Second, the generation of forms is dependent on the session-state of the client. It may be useful to store some of this state in the server. An out-of-process server would potentially be shared, though, and thus this technique could not be used in view of possible conflicting property settings from various clients.

The credit-card validation server

This scenario describes a credit-card validation server. This server is used to validate credit-card information that is supplied by the client. The server maintains a fixed number of communication channels to a validation bureau. A client requests a validation and the server uses the next available channel to perform the validation. There are large numbers of clients that need credit-card validation.

This usage scenario definitely points to the use of an out-of-proc server for the following reason: The scenario describes a fixed number of channels that are available to the validation bureau. These channels really need to be a pooled resource.

As you can see, the selection of an in-proc versus out-of-proc server depends heavily on the expected usage of the server. When you make this decision, take a look at not only the client-server interactions, but also the server-to-other-processes interactions. Other factors are also involved — for example, the way you expect to deploy your server and what expected future uses the server may have. Tables 19-1 and 19-2 help to highlight some trade-offs between these types of servers.

Table 19-1
Characteristics of In-Process Servers

Item	Comment
Speed	The communications to the client can be much faster than an out-of-proc server.
Maintaining client state	It is possible for the client to set state information in the server without concern for contention with other clients. Such information can be maintained in server properties, if desired. This technique may alleviate the necessity to pass in state with each method call.
Scalability	An in-process server runs on the same machine as its client, so it cannot be moved to machines that are faster or have more available system resources.
Resource impact	Each client creates a new instance of the server and thus has a greater overall resource impact on the system.

Table 19-2
Characteristics of Out-of-Process Servers

Item	Comment
Speed	The communication to the client is slower than an in-process server.
Maintaining client state	A client should not try to maintain state in the server, but must pass in state information to methods as needed. If a client tries to use properties to maintain state, other clients may interfere with those property settings.
Shared Resources	A server may have resources that it can share with multiple clients.
Scalability	It is easier to scale an out-of-proc server as the demands grow.
Distributed computing	It is easier to move out-of-process servers to remote locations as the demands dictate.
Resource impact	The server is shared amongst many clients and thus has a lesser overall resource impact on the system.

These tables help to clarify when to create and use an in-proc server, or an out-of-proc server. You should choose your architecture wisely from the start, if possible. It is possible to convert an in-process to an out-of-process server, but there are some definite differences to the internal architectures of the servers. The main physical differences have to do with the `Instancing` property of your class modules (this is an actual property of a class module that appears in the Visual

Basic IDE), yet there are many other design decisions that you will make along the way that may make change difficult in the future. For example, since a single client can depend on a single in-process server to service its requests, a developer might choose to store client data in the server. Because of this one-to-one relationship, they could always be assured that the data would be accurate to that particular client. In an out-of-process server, however, each client could not be guaranteed that its particular data would not be changed. This is one example of a design decision that would be very hard to modify as you moved an in-process to an out-of-process server.

Any system that you design can utilize multiple servers. There is no reason you have to stick to one server type or the other. So why not utilize both types of server as the architecture dictates. Figure 19-6 shows a system that utilizes both the in-process forms server and out-of-process credit-card validation server we described earlier.

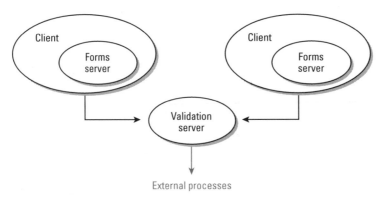

Figure 19-6: A hybrid system using both server types

Analyzing What Your Server Should Do

Now that you have seen the differences between the types of servers you can create with Visual Basic, we need to look at exactly what your server will do. There are a lot of important design decisions that must be made to build a server. A server does some tasks that would otherwise be done within your application. To determine what the server will do, we must design it as an *object*. To begin that process, analyze and consider the following five key concepts as you designyour server

✦ *Usage scenarios* — By gaining an understanding of how the servers will be used, you will be able have the servers provide the appropriate services and interfaces.

✦ *Services-based modeling* — Your server will provide services; these are embodied in the properties, events, and methods exposed by your server.

✦ *Understanding relationships* — Your server will potentially have relationships, including dependencies to other servers, to its client, and even to other resources. It is important for you to understand these relationships in order to properly design the server.

✦ *Defining interfaces* — The exposed properties, events, and methods provided by your server are its interfaces. When you understand your server's usage role and dependencies, you should be able to define a set of appropriate interfaces.

✦ *Reuse considerations* — Are you about to develop a server that has reuse potential? If so, you may want to add additional interfaces to better enable that reuse. This reuse consideration may additionally lead to some design decisions on how the server is constructed. (For more information on how Visual Basic encourages reuse, see Chapter 15.)

Usage scenarios

A *usage scenario* is a narrative that describes how the system will be used from a user's perspective. It does not concern itself with any architectural or technical problems; it only describes a real-life or desired set of user-system interactions. There are many ways to develop scenarios — in fact, entire methodologies exist.

In general, a scenario is developed by first stating the business problem and then describing the steps necessary to solve it. When you develop a scenario, it is particularly useful to interview the potential users of the system. These are the *domain experts* who can quickly identify what the system *must* have and what they would *like* the system to have. A scenario that describes an order-entry system might be similar to the one outlined in the following paragraph:

> A telephone agent sees an alert on the screen that a customer is on-line waiting to place an order. The customer's background data is already displayed on the screen; the system has used its Caller ID capability to look up the customer and retrieve the appropriate data. The agent can accurately access the level of inventory on any item and ensure that any stock item will be reserved for the customer when an order is taken. The agent can process the order with a minimum amount of information from the customer and using as few keystrokes as possible.

It is often useful to develop different scenarios that equate to specific system usage roles. For example, a system might have an administrator, a manager, and a user role. Each type of user interacts with the system in a different way. In addition to the different roles, each role might have several usage scenarios. The more accurately you can describe each scenario, the more accurately the system can satisfy the requirements extracted from the scenarios.

When the scenarios are developed, they need to be analyzed. The narrative itself will give clues as to the system's objects, *services*, and *interfaces*. Remember that a scenario is merely a methodology to help you rough out the system's architecture. The details will come out as you explore each item more thoroughly, as we will do below.

Services-based modeling

This approach separates the various components of a system's architecture into discrete services. A service is an encapsulation of a related set of functions. Although it is possible to encapsulate such functionality within an application using classes, we're only going to consider encapsulation of services into ActiveX servers.

You have probably heard of a three-tiered architecture. This architecture defines user services, business services, and data services. Services do not necessarily correspond to physical components and do not in any way define locations of components; they merely are a way of breaking up a system into conceptual layers. There really is no magic number of tiers, and in fact, much of the literature lately is no longer discussing three-tiered systems, but *n-tiered* systems. This is probably a more appropriate way of looking at services-based architectures. The total number of tiers will vary depending on the requirements of the system and the breakdown of the services.

Try to think of service objects as they relate to real-world objects. For example, in the scenario given earlier we might identify a display object, inventory object, order object, and customer object (Figure 19-7). These objects relate to some of the nouns used in the narrative. The verbs relate to the services these objects provide via properties, events, and methods. After you have identified the basic objects and services, you should then further consider what your objects should do. For example, we can all think of many things that an inventory object should do that were not mentioned in the narrative. Therefore, it is necessary to expand the services your object provides by extending your design into what you know about the modeled object's behavior in the real world.

Figure 19-7: Objects described in the scenario

If we analyze the customer object, we see several services we would like it to provide. Figure 19-8 shows that this object provides the following services:

✦ *Contact Information Service* — Customer name, phone, fax, and e-mail.

✦ *Address Information Service* — Customer address(es).

✦ *Account Information Service* — Account numbers and credit history.

✦ *Transaction History Service* — A list, or collection, of all the customer's transactions.

✦ *Call History Service* — A list, or collection, of all the customer's calls.

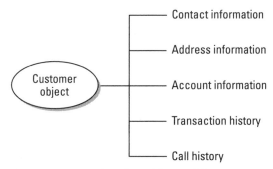

Figure 19-8: Services found in an object

When you think about how the object works and the services it provides, don't think of just a place where you can go and get data. Think of an object that encapsulates the data but provides you with a way to "ask" for the data. This thought process really helps you get away from having to consider where the data is, or in what format. All you have to be concerned with is that when you ask the customer object for some contact information, you can get it — perhaps in the form of a contact object. Try to think of how you want to work with the object (use its services), and don't even consider how the object performs a service. Figure 19-9 shows show you might model this interaction.

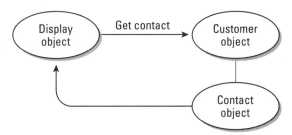

Figure 19-9: Getting contact information

The code to get the contact information might look like the following segment. This segment assumes that the Customer object has already been instantiated. It uses the ContactInfo method to retrieve a contact object. It knows the "footprint" of the contact object and so can query it to get specific contact information. In the next chapter, we will get into the specifics of how these objects are created, instantiated, and used.

```
Private Sub GetContact(CustomerID As Long)
    Dim ThisContact As Object

    Set ThisContact = Customer.ContactInfo(CustomerID)

End Sub
```

Understanding relationships

Objects have relationships to other objects. There are many different types of relationships. Sometimes an object is the parent, or a child, of another object; sometimes an object is a collection of other objects; and sometimes an object is dependent on another object. If you want to really get a flavor for the many different types of relationships, open the Microsoft Repository using the Repository Browser (RepBrows.exe). Browse some of the items and then view the relationship by opening the Relationship dialog. By doing this you will start to get an idea of the hundreds of possible relationship types.

Figure 19-10 shows the relationships between a customer and his or her transactions. The Customer object has a Transactions collection. The collection represents all the transactions for a particular customer — the transaction history. The collection contains several individual Transaction objects. Each Transaction object contains all the information about a particular transaction.

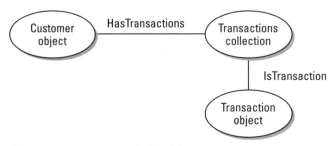

Figure 19-10: Contact relationships

It is important to understand the relationships among objects in order to properly design an object's interfaces. Often you can create dependencies among objects by defining their relationships.

For example, it is clear that the Transactions collection and Transaction object shown in Figure 19-10 are dependent on a particular Customer object. The Customer object is not so directly dependent on the Transactions to exist, but must be able to get to them to satisfy methods it has related to getting the Transaction history. It might be useful to view relationships in a type of hierarchy to get a different view of dependencies. Figure 19-11 shows a partial hierarchy for Visual Basic's add-in model. The add-in model is discussed in Chapter 24.

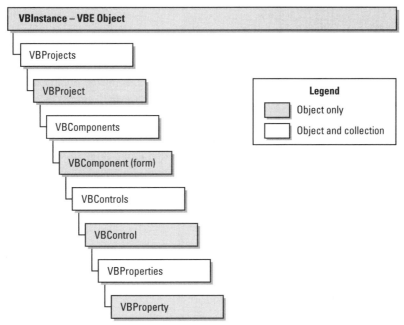

Figure 19-11: An object hierarchy

Defining interfaces

When the individual objects and their relationships have been identified, you can start designing the interfaces of the objects. The interfaces are the properties, events, and methods a particular object provides — these should correlate to the services provided by the object.

Figure 19-8 presented some of the services provided by the Customer object. These services correspond to interfaces that the object provides. There is not necessarily a one-to-one relationship between services and interfaces — there may be several interfaces for a particular service.

There are many ways to implement a service within an object. One approach might be to set some properties and then call a method. The method would then use the property settings to process the method call. Another approach would be to pass in a complete set of arguments with each method call. Although this is less efficient, there is less chance of contention for property settings by multiple clients. Remember that the type of server you have chosen (in-proc or out-of-proc) greatly affects how you design your interfaces.

Reuse considerations

Anytime an object is designed, you should stop and consider its reuse potential. Obviously, some objects have much greater reuse potential than other objects. For example, the customer object described earlier could provide many different types of services, whereas the transaction object is much more specific and thus potentially less reusable. It is generally true that *greater reuse = more generic*. More generic generally means that the design of an object will take more time, have more interfaces, and be more bloated.

You might consider a couple of different levels of designing your object for reuse. The first level would be an actual full implementation of a set of interfaces to make your object more generic, and thus more reusable. The second level would be a consideration for future reuse by designing existing interfaces to accommodate varying use.

Methodologies and modeling tools

The are many methodologies and many modeling tools that can assist you in the design of your servers. You should explore the various methodologies to come up with one that is suitable for you and your team. Even if you choose a simple and unstructured methodology, it is important to come up with a consistent approach to your designs. As far as the use of modeling tools go, it is probably true that simple designs to not require such tools, whereas complex designs will greatly benefit from tool usage.

Many discussions of such methodologies can be found in the Visual Basic documentation, as well as within other Microsoft literature. Microsoft has an entire development discipline devoted to systems development. As far as tools go, Rational's Visual Modeler is included with some of the editions of Visual Basic. This tool is capable of performing sophisticated system modeling. Another emerging technology to explore is the Microsoft Repository. The Repository provides a way to describe different types of systems in a common fashion. Various vendors provide tools on top of the Repository for their own particular needs, but all share the underlying data structures. This ability for custom tools to share a single data representation is an important step towards creating a single reusability library.

Summary

✦ There are two basic types of servers: in-process and out-of-process. An in-process server runs much faster but may be less efficient, because it cannot be shared among applications. An out-of-process server can be shared by multiple applications and is easy to distribute to remote file servers, but may prove too slow for calculation-intensive uses.

✦ As you construct your server, it is important to correctly dissect a large problem into small pieces. Each piece must then be examined to determine if it should be externalized to a server, or not. There are always design trade-offs to be considered — it is generally harder, less efficient, and more time consuming to build a more generic server, but it may also be more reusable. There are also usage trade-offs to consider — how far should you go when you consider product improvement and prepare your architectures for future generations?

We hope you now have a better understanding of what an ActiveX server is and when you should build one. In the next chapters, we use an example to show you exactly how to build a server.

✦   ✦   ✦

Building an ActiveX Server

In the previous chapter, we discussed some strategic reasons why you should build an ActiveX server and some techniques and methodologies you can employ to build it.

In this chapter, we will show you in detail how to build an ActiveX server. We will actually be building a server and a test application. Much of the code and conceptual framework of the server will be provided within this chapter. The entire server and test applications are provided on the CD-ROM that accompanies this book, in the Status Server directory.

We will continue this discussion in the next chapter by talking about how you can use ActiveX servers throughout your system's architecture.

Examining the Project

It's often useful to have a way to display information related to the execution of your application, or other session-related messages. A simple way to do this would be to use message boxes or the Debug window to display such information. These techniques, obviously, have very limited use. They only can display one message at a time, typically are not suitable to ship with the product, and thus are relegated to being used during the development/debug cycle only.

The *StatusServer* we build in this chapter is a fully functional ActiveX server that provides a way to display application messages. It provides a window with a RichTextBox so the messages can be displayed in color, as well as some Save and Print buttons. Figure 20-1 shows the StatusServer with several formatted status messages.

Figure 20-1: The StatusServer

The StatusServer is created as an in-proc server (ActiveX DLL). It is designed to be generic so that it can easily be used by any application. A server test application, *TestStatus*, has also been created to facilitate testing of the server. Finally, a Visual Basic project group, SSGroup.vbg, has been created that loads both the StatusServer and the TestStatus projects, as shown in Figure 20-2.

Figure 20-2: The StatusServer and TestStatus projects

Features of the server

The server comes with a fairly complete set of features. The Status window itself can be positioned and sized. A persistence mechanism persists the window state (size and position) between sessions. Formatted status items can be written to the window. The contents of the window can also be printed or saved. The features are explained in more detail in Table 20-1.

Table 20-1 Server Features	
Feature	**Description**
Window Persistence	The left, top, height, and width settings of the Status window are written to the Registry when the server is destroyed. The window is then returned to its previous size and position the next time that it is displayed.
Add Status Line to Display	Status text is displayed, line by line, in a RichTextBox. The text color and bold attributes can be individually set for each status line. In addition, an HTML-style tag can be added to each line. The color of this tag can be set independent of the status text.
Set Form Caption	The caption of the status form can be set.
Print Contents of Status Window	The status text can be printed.
Save Contents of Status Window	The status text can be saved as an RTF or TXT file.
Show or Hide Buttons	The Print and Save buttons can be made visible or invisible.
Maintain a Status Items Collection	In addition to being displayed, each status line is added to a collection as a status item. This collection is maintained within the server and can be retrieved by any client. This provides a way for the client to manipulate status items in ways not inherently provided by the server.
Clear Status Text	Clears the status text and the status items collection.

Architectural overview

An ActiveX DLL must have at least one public class module that exposes properties, events, or methods. This class module provides a way for client applications to use the server. The StatusServer exposes a class named Application. This .class provides all the properties and methods that encapsulate the server's functionality. These properties and methods are actually the interfaces that a client sees when using the server.

Note   In the next chapter, we talk more about naming of servers and classes. We also discuss standardizing server interfaces across all your servers.

Figure 20-3 provides a high-level overview of the StatusServer. To use the server, a client would create an instance of the server's application object (class). The class would then provide ways to manipulate the Status window, even though the client has no direct access to this window. A StatusItems collection is maintained by the window itself. This collection contains a number of StatusItem objects. The application object can return the StatusItems collection from the Status window to the client.

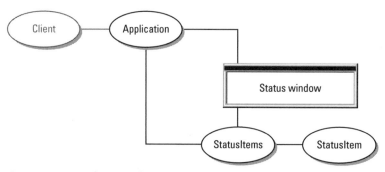

Figure 20-3: Architectural overview of StatusServer

Note   Think of a Visual Basic form as a class that provides a visual interface. This train of thought allows for the StatusItems collection to be maintained by the form.

Building the Server

This section goes into detail regarding the construction of the server. Each project component will be analyzed, as well as most procedures. Some interesting code segments are included in this book, but refer to the code on the accompanying CD-ROM in order to get the complete picture.

The following forms, code modules, and class modules are found in the status server project StatusServer.vbp. This project is the actual ActiveX DLL server. There is also a test project, TestStatus.vbp, that is used to test the server. This project exercises most of the methods found within the server. The test project is described in the following section. Visual Basic has the ability to load more than one project into a workspace and save this workspace as a *project group*. The project group, SSGroup.vbg, contains both the server and test projects. This project group allows you to debug the test application and server simultaneously. You can also jump directly into server code when in Debug mode.

Forms

The StatusServer project has two forms: frmAbout and frmStatus. The form frmAbout is a typical About box. You can modify this About box for your particular needs. The main Status form, frmStatus, is the form the server uses to display status text. The Status form, as shown in Figure 20-4, has four controls:

txtStatus — This RichTextBox displays the status text.

cmdPrint — Contains the procedures to print the contents of the RichTextBox.

cmdSave — Contains the procedures to save the contents of the RichTextBox as a TXT or RTF file.

ComDialog — This Common dialog control is used by the printing and saving procedures.

Figure 20-4: The main Status form: frmStatus

Although a client of the status server cannot actually get to the Status form directly, many of the form's public methods are mirrored in the *application* class module. In this way, a client can successfully manipulate the Status form. The server is designed in this way to isolate, or encapsulate, the form. This technique makes it easy to replace the entire form with any other visual representation of status, as usage might dictate.

Let's now look at some important methods and properties of this form. In the form's general section, you will find a function declaration for the Windows API SendMessage function. This function is used to suppress or enable the drawing of a window. Each time a status line is added to the form, the drawing is first turned off and then turned back on using this function. This prevents the display of character selection within the RichTextBox, because characters must be selected in order to apply formatting to them.

```
'<Constant>————————————
'— drawing messages and parameters used in SendMessage
Const WM_SETREDRAW    As Long = &HB
Const REDRAWOFF       As Long = 0
Const REDRAWON        As Long = 1
'</Constant>———————————

'<Declare>————————————
Private Declare Function SendMessage Lib "user32" _
    Alias "SendMessageA" (ByVal hWnd As Long, _
    ByVal wMsg As Long, ByVal wParam As Long, _
    ByVal lParam As Any) As Long
'</Declare>———————————
```

Status lines are added to the server using a method in a line-by-line fashion. Each line that is added to the display is also added to a collection known as the `StatusItems` collection. This collection can be useful if you need to find out what was added to the window without having to look at the contents of the RichTextBox itself. The `StatusItems` collection is a collection of all the status lines in the window:

```
'<Public>————————————————————————--
Public StatusItems      As Collection
'</Public>————————————————————————
```

The `StatusItems` collection is declared in the General section of the form. It is important to note that when the form is created by Visual Basic, this declaration causes memory to be allocated for a collection-type object but it does not actually create a collection. The actual collection is not created, or *instantiated*, until the object is set using the `New` keyword. Instantiating of form-level objects can be done in the `_Initialize` event:

```
Private Sub Form_Initialize()

    Set StatusItems = New Collection

End Sub
```

Although the Visual Basic documentation suggests that such objects will automatically be destroyed by Visual Basic, we like to be on the safe side and explicitly destroy all the objects we create. We like to place such code in the `Terminate` event:

```
Private Sub Form_Terminate()

    Set StatusItems = Nothing

End Sub
```

Exploring usability features

There are two sets of usability features built into the Status form. These are the ability of the form to persist its size and position, and the ability for the RichTextBox to stretch to the size of the form. The persistence mechanism is performed by two functions found in the code module Persist — the actual functions will be discussed in the following section. The previous window state is retrieved when the window is loaded, and the current window state is stored when the form is unloaded:

```
Private Sub Form_Load()

    '— restore the last window settings
    Call GetWindowState(Me, "StatusWindow", True)

End Sub
```

```
Private Sub Form_QueryUnload(Cancel As Integer, _
    UnloadMode As Integer)

    '— store the window settings
    Call SetWindowState(Me, "StatusWindow")

End Sub
```

The second feature, which resizes the RichTextBox, is found in the _Resize event of the form. The size of the RichTextBox depends on whether the Print and Save buttons are currently visible or not. The resize code is error-wrapped in case negative values are generated due to minimizing of the form or similar reasons. Notice also that the move method is used rather than individually setting the left, top, width, and height properties. The move method is not only more compact, but also faster than this other technique.

```
Private Sub Form_Resize()

    On Error Resume Next
    If cmdSave.Visible Then
        txtStatus.Move 0, txtStatus.Top, _
            Me.ScaleWidth - 1235, (Me.ScaleHeight - 75)
        cmdSave.Left = Me.ScaleWidth - 1175
        cmdPrint.Left = Me.ScaleWidth - 1175
    Else
        txtStatus.Move 0, txtStatus.Top, _
            Me.ScaleWidth, (Me.ScaleHeight - 75)
    End If
    On Error GoTo 0

End Sub
```

Adding status lines to the RichTextBox

The main method provided by the status form is AddStatusLine. This method adds a status line to the RichTextBox and adds a Status object to the StatusItems collection. A lot of the code in this procedure has to do with the formatting of the new status line. We will examine some code in this discussion, but refer to the actual source to identify all this format-related code. Table 20-2 shows the parameters that can be passed into this method. Here is the syntax:

```
AddStatusLine(Status, StausColor, StatusBold, Tag, TagColor)
```

Table 20-2	
AddStatusLine Parameters	
Parameter	*Description*
Status	Required. Status text to display.
StatusColor	Optional. The color of the status text. Default is vbBlack.
StatusBold	Optional. Set the status to bold. Default is False.
Tag	Optional. An HTML-style tag to surround the status text . Default is no tag.
TagColor	Optional. The color of the status tag. Default is vbBlack.

Now let's look at some code in the procedure. This procedure extensively uses a With block when referring to the RichTextBox control. The use of With provides a way for the compiler to grab a reference to the control and then iterate through its methods and properties more efficiently. All the methods and properties beginning with a dot (".") belong to the RichTextBox named txtStatus.

The first thing to do is turn off the system's painting of the RichTextBox by sending this control a message to turn off Redraw. We then add the tag, followed by the status, and so on. When you work with the RichTextBox, you work with text selections, not the entire text contents (as you would if you were working with a normal text box). A text selection is defined as the text contained between a starting and an ending point. The starting point is defined using the SelStart property, and the ending point is defined by specifying the selection length SelLength that is forward from the starting point. After a selection is made, you can apply several formatting properties such as SelBold, SelColor, and so on. Refer to the RichTextBox help for a complete description of these properties. By the way, if we had not turned off the drawing of the RichTextBox, we would see all these selections being made in the control. Listing 20-1 shows the beginning block of code for the AddStatusLine method.

Listing 20-1: **Beginning of AddStatusLine**

```
With txtStatus
        Call SendMessage(.hWnd, WM_SETREDRAW, _
            REDRAWOFF, 0&)

        '— cache to select status text
        FirstChar = Len(.Text)

        '— create the start of the tag, if supplied
        IsTag = (Tag <> "")
        If IsTag Then
            Temp = "<" & Tag & ">"
```

```
            FullText = Temp & Status
            LastChar = FirstChar
            .SelStart = LastChar
            .SelText = Temp
            .SelStart = LastChar
            .SelLength = Len(Temp)
            .SelColor = TagColor
    End If

    '— add the status text
    LastChar = Len(.Text)
    .SelStart = LastChar
    .SelText = Status
    .SelStart = LastChar
    .SelLength = Len(Status)
    '— assign color
    .SelColor = StatusColor
```

The next step is to skip down in this procedure to where the status line is added
to the StatusItems collection (see Listing 20-2, and then add the status line as a
Status object, which is actually an instance of the class module named Status.
The first thing to do is to create a new instance of the Status object. We will name
this instance ThisStatus. After the instance is created, we will again use the
efficient With block when setting the objects properties. After all the properties
are set, the object is added to the collection using the collection's Add method.

Listing 20-2: **Adding the Status Line to the Collection**

```
    '— add the status to the collection
    Dim ThisStatus As New Status

    With ThisStatus
        .RawText = Status
        .StatusText = DisplayText
        .StatusBold = StatusBold
        .StatusColor = StatusColor
        If (Tag = "") Then
            .Tag = ""
        Else
            .Tag = "<" & Tag & ">"
        End If
        .TagColor = TagColor
    End With

    StatusItems.Add ThisStatus
```

Interestingly enough, a timestamp is automatically added to this status item when it is added to the collection. The addition of the timestamp is not obvious when you look at the above code—there is no reference to such a timestamp. To find the timestamp, take a step back and think about encapsulation and object-oriented design. One of the goals is to have an object responsible for as much of its own data as possible. With this in mind, it is easy to understand why the setting of the timestamp property is done when the instance of the `Status` object is created. The line `Dim ThisStatus As New Status` creates a new instance of the object and fires the `_Intialize` event of that object. A timestamp is automatically created when the Status object is instantiated:

```
Private Sub Class_Initialize()

    '— time is captured when the instance is created
    CurTimeStamp = Now

End Sub
```

Although the previous example shows a simple application of object-oriented design, the concept that is introduced is very important. In a more complex example, we could have retrieved information from a database, or started up another server, instead of just setting a property. The important idea is that the `Status` object itself took care of things that a new instance needed rather than depending on external influences for the setting of such properties.

Code modules

There is only one code module in the status server, named `Persist`. This module contains code to save and retrieve the window size and position to and from the Windows system Registry. This functionality is placed in a separate module so that it can easily be used in other projects.

Let's take a good look at the procedure used to retrieve a window's size and position from the Registry and apply it to a form (Listing 20-3). The idea here is that all the information about a window is placed in a delimited string that is created in the `SetWindowState` function.

Listing 20-3: Saving a Window's State to the Registry

```
'_____
'<Purpose> sets the window state for persistence
'_____
Public Sub SetWindowState(ThisForm As Form, _
    ThisSection As String)
    Dim Setting As String

    On Error Resume Next
    If (ThisForm.WindowState = vbMinimized) Then Exit Sub
```

```
        Setting = ThisForm.WindowState & "." _
            & ThisForm.Left & "." & ThisForm.Top _
            & "." & ThisForm.Width & "." & ThisForm.Height
        Call SaveSetting("StatusServer", _
            ThisSection, "WindowState", Setting)
        On Error GoTo 0

End Sub
```

As you can see from the above code, the window state (minimized, normal, maximized) is saved, followed by a period ("."), followed by the left property, and so on. This function is called when the form is unloaded. The GetWindowState function (Listing 20-4) then retrieves this string from the same key and parses the information back out again so that it can be used. It is possible that the key string retrieved information contains bad settings, so some key code segments in this procedure are error-wrapped.

Listing 20-4: **Getting a Window's State from the Registry**

```
'_____
'<Purpose> gets the window state for persistence
'_____
Public Sub GetWindowState(ThisForm As Form, _
    ThisSection As String, _
    Optional SizeWindow As Boolean = False)
    Dim Setting     As String
    Dim i           As Integer
    Dim CharPos     As Integer
    '— window state
    Dim WinState    As Integer
    '— size and position attributes
    Dim RegLeft     As Integer
    Dim RegTop      As Integer
    Dim RegWidth    As Integer
    Dim RegHeight   As Integer

    '— get and parse the window info
    Setting = GetSetting("StatusServer", _
        ThisSection, "WindowState")

    If (Setting = "") Then
        Call CenterForm(ThisForm)
        Exit Sub
    End If

    On Error GoTo BadSetting
    Do
```

(continued)

Listing 20-4 *(continued)*

```
            CharPos = InStr(Setting, ".")
            If CharPos = 0 Then
                RegHeight = Val(Setting)
                Exit Do
            End If
            Select Case i
                Case 0
                    WinState = Left(Setting, CharPos - 1)
                    If (WinState = vbMinimized) Then
                        Call CenterForm(ThisForm)
                        Exit Sub
                    End If
                Case 1: RegLeft = Left(Setting, CharPos - 1)
                Case 2: RegTop = Left(Setting, CharPos - 1)
                Case 3: RegWidth = Left(Setting, CharPos - 1)
            End Select
            Setting = Mid(Setting, CharPos + 1)
            i = i + 1
        Loop
        On Error GoTo 0

        On Error Resume Next  '— account for bad settings in _
                                Registry
        '— perform the move
        Select Case WinState
            Case vbNormal
                If SizeWindow Then
                    ThisForm.Move RegLeft, RegTop, _
                        RegWidth, RegHeight
                Else
                    ThisForm.Move RegLeft, RegTop
                End If
            Case vbMaximized: ThisForm.WindowState = WinState
            Case Else:        ThisForm.WindowState = vbNormal
        End Select
        On Error GoTo 0

        Exit Sub

    BadSetting:
        Call CenterForm(ThisForm)

    End Sub
```

We use Visual Basic's intrinsic function GetSetting in this procedure, and SaveSetting in the corresponding procedure that saves the window state. These functions always place information in the same area within the Registry tree. If you would like to store your information elsewhere in the Registry, you will have to write a little more code to deal with the system Registry API functions more directly. Examples of how this is done can be found in Chapter 16.

Class modules

There are two class modules in the project: Application and Status. The Status class represents a status line that has been added to the server using the AddStatusLine method. This merely contains a number of property sets and gets with no additional methods. The most interesting class, and the one that provides all the client methods, is the Application class.

We can start with a look at a few methods found within this class. First, we will look at what is probably the most important method — the one used to add a status line to the display and also to the collection — the AddStatusLine method:

```
'_____
'<Purpose> main routine to show text in the status window
'_____
Public Sub AddStatusLine(Status As String, _
    Optional StatusColor As Long, _
    Optional StatusBold As Boolean, _
    Optional Tag As String, Optional TagColor As Long)

    Call frmStatus.AddStatusLine(Status, _
        StatusColor, StatusBold, Tag, TagColor)
End Sub
```

This method is merely a *pass-through* method provided by the application class. It just accepts parameters and passes them to the method in the Status form with the same name. Note the fact that the parameter names and method names in the application class and form do not have to be the same names — this is merely done for convenience. We could have just as easily called a method with a completely different name and with completely different parameter names. We could have also broken up this single application method call into two or three internal method calls. The point is that what we do inside this method is of no importance to the client. Their only concern is that when they call the method, a status line is displayed within the status form and a status item is added to the collection.

The only other procedure to discuss at this time is used to retrieve the StatusItems collection. Although we will be discussing some other methods in the section explaining how we test this server, you should take the time to review the code on your own time. The retrieval of the StatusItems collection by a client is through a property procedure.

```
Public Property Get StatusItems() As Object
    Set StatusItems = frmStatus.StatusItems
End Property
```

Wow, that was easy! The procedure is set up to return an object; all we do is set that object to the `StatusItems` object, which is a public property of the Status form. Again, the fact that the name of this property procedure coincides with the name of the collection in the form is by design, but is not required.

Procedure attributes

Each procedure you create within a Visual Basic project has various attributes. To view a procedure's attributes, open up a Code window containing the desired procedures and select Tools ⇨ Procedure Attributes. One of the attributes, `Description`, allows you to set text describing any procedure. This text can then be viewed in the Visual Basic Object Browser. Figure 20-5 shows how text set in the Attributes dialog corresponds to the description displayed in the browser.

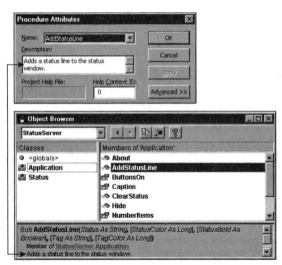

Figure 20-5: Setting procedure attributes

It is a good idea to go through all your procedures and set this description text. As far as the use of the server is concerned, you will need to set descriptions for only procedures that are exposed by the server. If you don't set this text, it will not affect how your server works — it's just one of those "finishing touches" for a professional-looking server.

Testing the Server

An ActiveX server is not designed to be self-sufficient — that is, it does not operate as an application. A server provides a service to its client, and it is the client that must drive this service. Thus, in order to test an ActiveX server, you must develop a client that will exercise all the server's interfaces.

Visual Basic allows you to have both an ActiveX server and a test client in the same workspace, by creating a project group.

The source that comes on the CD-ROM has a project group named SSGroup.vbg. This group can be found in the Test Server directory on the CD. When you open the SSGroup, both the server project file (StatusServer.vbp) and the test project file (TestStatus.vbp) open as well.

Debugging practices

Before we discuss what is in the test project, let's look at how you can debug the server while you are running the test project. When you open the project group, notice how the TestStatus project is bolded in the Project Explorer. The bolding indicates that TestStatus is the startup project, which means it is the project that will be run when you hit F5 (Run ➪ Start). The server project named StatusServer is, in fact, not even started by the Visual Basic development environment — it is the test application that starts the server. By the way, you can assign a different startup project by highlighting the desired server in the Project Explorer, right-clicking on it, and setting it as the startup project.

Now, let's set a couple of breakpoints (Listing 20-5) and see how the two projects work together in the workspace. Open up the form `frmTest` found in the test project. Find the `Form_Initialize` event and set a breakpoint on the line that says `Set StatusServer =...` . Now run the project. The execution of the test project should stop at your breakpoint. Step into the procedure by hitting F8. Note that the context of your debugging session switched from the test project into the server project. You should be on the `Class_Initialize` event of the server. As you can see, you are in the initialization code of a new instance of the server that is being created.

Listing 20-5: **Setting a Breakpoint in the Test Project**

```
Private Sub Form_Initialize()

    TextColor = optTextColor(0).ForeColor
    TagColor = optTagColor(1).ForeColor

    Set StatusServer = New StatusServer.Application

    IsAlive = (Not (StatusServer Is Nothing))

    Call ShowIsAlive

End Sub
```

Now let's look at debugging from a different angle. First, remove the breakpoint that you set in the test project. Open the form frmStatus found in the server project. Find the procedure named AddStatusLine and scroll down toward the bottom of the procedure. Put a breakpoint on the line that says End With (Listing 20-6).

Listing 20-6: **Setting a Breakpoint in the Server Project**

```
Call SendMessage(.hWnd, WM_SETREDRAW, REDRAWON, 0&)    .Refresh
    End With

    '— add the status to the collection
    Dim ThisStatus As New Status

    With ThisStatus
        .RawText = Status
        .StatusText = DisplayText
        .StatusBold = StatusBold
        .StatusColor = StatusColor
        If (Tag = "") Then
            .Tag = ""
        Else
            .Tag = "<" & Tag & ">"
        End If
        .TagColor = TagColor
    End With

    StatusItems.Add ThisStatus

    Set ThisStatus = Nothing

End Sub
```

Again, run the application by pressing F5. When the test form comes up, click the Add to Status button. You will now stop at the breakpoint that you set in the server. If you single-step out of this procedure, you will eventually step back into the button click event in the test project. As you can see, it is easy to set breakpoints in either project, as your debugging needs dictate.

Instantiating the server

In order to use the server within your test application, you must create an instance of it. The technique we like to use is to declare an object variable of the server's type and then create the actual instance of the server. However, before Visual Basic will allow you to create a variable of the server's type, you must first create a reference to that type. This is done with the References dialog (Project ➪ References), as is shown in Figure 20-6. At times, you may have to reset this reference if your test project loses the connection to the original reference. This can happen if you register some other instance of your server's DLL with the system.

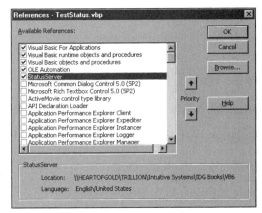

Figure 20-6: The References dialog

The following code declares an object variable of the appropriate type for the Server object:

```
'— the server itself
Private StatusServer          As StatusServer.Application
```

By the way, you also could have declared the StatusServer to be of the generic `Object` type—this would be what is known as *late binding*. It is always more efficient to use *early binding*, which is declaring an object of a specific type. Declaring the object in the general section only causes Visual Basic to allocate a memory and handling mechanism that will accommodate the object. It does not actually create the object in this area until you use the `New` keyword. This keyword is used in the `_Initialize` event of the test application. As you have already seen in the debugging session above, the use of this word actually creates and starts an instance of the server.

Exercising the server

The purpose of a test application is to exercise the interfaces found on the server. In addition, since this application was written for this book, we are spending a little more time illustrating some capabilities of the server. Figure 20-7 shows the main screen of the test project with the various sections of the screen noted as to their usage.

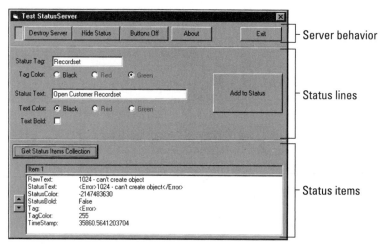

Figure 20-7: The Test StatusServer

The Test form is divided into three areas: a *server behavior* area, a *status line* area, and a *status items* area. The behavior area exercises the creation and destruction of the server and its visible properties. The status line area shows how you can create, format, and add status lines to the server. Finally, the status items area shows how you can retrieve and display the status items collection created by the server. You should review and step through the code in the top two areas; this chapter focuses on the status items area.

When we discussed the StatusServer in the section, it was noted that the server maintains a collection of status items. Every time a new status line is added to the server using the AddStatusLine method, the server also adds a Status object to the StatusItems collection. This collection can then be retrieved by using the StatusItems property get procedure located in the Application class. To retrieve this collection, we first declare a collection object in the general section of the Test form.

```
'— the status items collection from the server
Private StatusItems        As Collection
```

Next, we set this collection to the collection in the server. We do this by first destroying the old collection, if any. This is done by setting the object to nothing. We then create a new collection and finally set this new collection to the server's collection. Notice that the set statement actually calls the property get procedure on the server (Listing 20-7).

Listing 20-7: **Retrieving the Collection (Code Segment)**

```
'_____
'<Purpose> gets the status items collection from
' the server
'_____
Private Sub cmdGetItems_Click()

    '— reset the status items collection
    Set StatusItems = Nothing
    Set StatusItems = New Collection

    '— get the items
    Set StatusItems = StatusServer.StatusItems

    '— set the new state
    If (Not (StatusItems Is Nothing)) Then
        If (StatusItems.Count > 0) Then
     vsrItems.Max = StatusItems.Count
            Call ShowItem
        End If
    End If

End Sub
```

After we have the collection, we can then iterate through all the items within the collection. The test server does this with the vertical scroll bar vsrItems. We set the max property of this scroll bar equal to the number of items in the collection in the previous procedure. The number of items in a collection is found in the collection's Count property. An item is actually displayed in the ListBox on the test form in the ShowItem procedure (Listing 20-8).

Listing 20-8: **Showing an Item (Code Segment)**

```
'_____
'<Purpose> shows a status item in the ListBox
'_____
Private Sub ShowItem()
    '— an object of type "Status" found in the server
    Dim ThisItem As StatusServer.Status

    Set ThisItem = StatusItems(vsrItems.Value)

    lstStatusItem.Clear

    With ThisItem
      lstStatusItem.AddItem "RawText: " & .RawText
      lstStatusItem.AddItem "StatusText: " & .StatusText
      lstStatusItem.AddItem "StatusColor: " & .StatusColor
      lstStatusItem.AddItem "StatusBold: " & .StatusBold
      lstStatusItem.AddItem "Tag: " & .Tag
      lstStatusItem.AddItem "TagColor: " & .TagColor
      lstStatusItem.AddItem "TimeStamp: " & .TimeStamp
    End With

    lblItemNum = " Item " & vsrItems.Value

    Set ThisItem = Nothing

End Sub
```

We get to a particular item in the collection by first creating a suitable object in our procedure and setting that object to one of the collection items. Because Status is a public class in the server, we can create an object of type StatusServer.Status. This is an instance of the same type of object that was added to the collection by the server. By taking the value of the scroll bar, we are accessing an item in the collection by its index. We can then iterate through all the properties of that object and display them.

This is a good time to digress into an interesting discussion on working with foreign objects in the development environment. In this case, we know that the collection contains objects of type Status. Since we know the type of object, we know what properties it exposes and we can readily use them. However, oftentimes you will be working with objects that you don't know a lot about. It is possible to get some information about an object by looking at it in Visual Basic's Watch window. You can always get to an object by referring to it by its index in the collection, and all collections begin with index #1. Therefore, to interrogate an unknown object, do the following:

1. Create a variable of type `Object`.

2. Set it to the first item in the collection.

3. Put a breakpoint on the line directly following the one where the object is being set:

```
Dim ThisItem As Object

Set ThisItem = StatusItems(vsrItems.Value)
1stStatusItem.Clear
```

4. Highlight the object by double-clicking on it, and then bring up the Context menu in the editor.

5. Select Add Watch and then click OK.

The object now shows up in the Watch window, as shown in Figure 20-8. If you open the object, you can view all its properties. This technique can be extremely useful in debugging foreign objects.

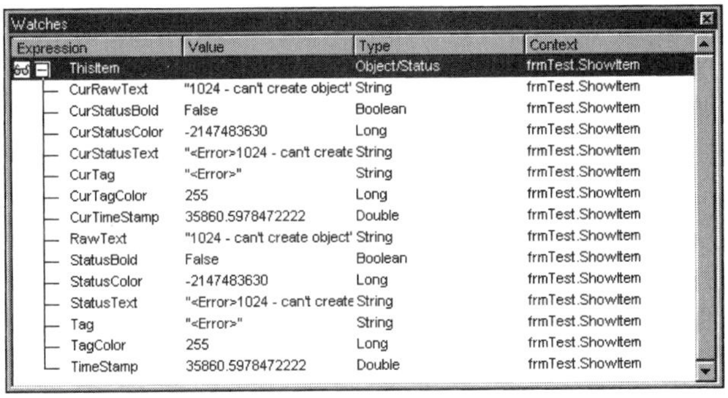

Figure 20-8: Interrogating an object

Summary

This chapter discusses, by example, how to build an ActiveX server. Specifically, we have built a status server — one capable of displaying formatted status messages.

✦ During our discussion, we discussed the logic behind the code, as well as the reason a particular procedure was built a certain way or was placed in a particular component.

✦ In addition, we discussed how to build an application that is used to test the server during its development.

✦ The server and test applications are in a single workspace, made possible by Visual Basic's capability to create a project group.

Having read this chapter, you should be able not only to understand the status server but also to build your own server using this new knowledge. In the next chapter, we discuss how to use ActiveX servers in your system's architecture.

✦   ✦   ✦

Building Systems with ActiveX Servers

The previous two chapters have set the stage; you should have an understanding of what an ActiveX server is and how you should approach designing one. And by following the example, you've actually built one. This chapter discusses how you can utilize ActiveX server technology to create systems based on so-called three-tiered, or *n*-tiered, architectures. To illustrate how such a system can be created, we discuss an order entry system as an example.

We'll be talking a lot about how you define the requirements and services that your system provides, and how you then encapsulate these services into separate ActiveX objects. It is very important in this requirements-definition stage to define the appropriate boundaries for each of your servers. After the requirements and services have been defined, the physical servers can be constructed. At this stage, it's important to understand how the system will be deployed. In addition, although the servers are physically separate objects, it is important to create a standard set of interfaces and behaviors across the whole system.

Comprehending Architectural Tiers

As software has evolved, it has developed from *monolithic*, to *client/server*, to *three-tiered*, and now to *n-tiered* architectures. A monolithic application has everything all rolled into one — there may be some physical segregation of functionality into DLLs, but the program is primarily a single entity. A client/server application has a distinct segregation of client and server, and database, activities. Typically, the server processes much of the business logic, such as rules and transactions that are embedded within the database as stored procedures. Although this approach can be advantageous with large, high-performance systems, the program becomes very dependent on the database itself. It becomes difficult to move such a system to a different DBMS if the need arises. For example, if you designed a small client/server application using Microsoft Access and then wanted to move it to Microsoft SQL Server, you might have difficulty moving some of the logic embedded in the DBMS. In addition, the development and programming model for stored procedures is very different in client/server from that of Visual Basic. Therefore, you have to sustain two areas of development expertise simultaneously to implement such a system.

A final problem with client/server architecture is that if you are building a commercial software product, you may have difficulties installing your database logic into a customer's existing DBMS. Three-tiered architecture solves these problems by taking this business logic and separating it out into another layer. By relegating the DBMS to pure data storage and retrieval tasks, it is much easier to change out a DBMS as the need arises. Remember, three-tiered architecture does not necessarily mean that there are three physical components to the system. Three tiers means that there are three distinct kinds of services within the system, and that each service may comprise a number of physical objects, including ActiveX servers.

This takes us to *n*-tiered architectures. An application built around an *n*-tiered system has any number of services, the actual number of which are implemented being variable with the changing requirements of the application. This is a much more meaningful and natural approach to designing an application. There really is no reason to restrict yourself to a certain number of tiers, nor is there any reason to try and arbitrarily make your functionality conform to a particular tier. An *n*-tiered system allows you to create the number of services that are appropriate for your particular application.

Throughout this chapter, we talk about an order entry system for a fictional company that utilizes an *n*-tiered architecture. The shell of this order entry system is included on the CD-ROM that is provided with this book.

Scalability

The word *scalability* means a system can grow or shrink to meet an increase (or decrease) in user demand. Such a system is not necessarily designed to add new functionality easily — that characteristic is the *robustness* of the system. Scalability has more to do with the load on a system and how the system is designed to accommodate an increasing load.

Figure 21-1 shows a small networked application on the left that comprises four
services and a DBMS. An example of this might be a typical desktop contact-
management system. The system application on the right extends this small
system into a medium-scale system. Notice that the medium system employs the
same services as the small system, but some of the services have been moved to
different machines. One of the beauties of implementing services using ActiveX is
that they can easily be moved to different machines using remote automation. We
like to say "you get a lot for free" by designing with ActiveX. What this statement
means is that there is a huge amount of functionality provided by this platform —
some of which may not be used until a later time, but it is there when you need it.
Another interesting thing to note — also an important aspect of scalability — is
that the user interface service is shown to have two separate server instances,
both using the same middle tier. This makes the middle tier a pooled resource.
ActiveX also makes it possible to pool resources as your workload grows.

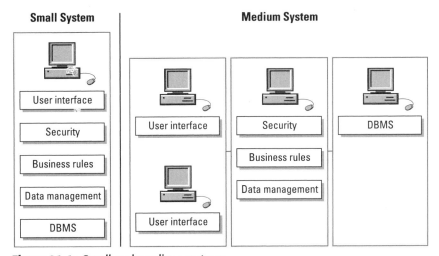

Figure 21-1: Small and medium systems

Figure 21-2 shows the exact same services that have now been deployed to
accommodate a much larger workload. Notice how the data management service
has been moved to a different physical layer and is a pooled resource. Additionally,
the DBMS is now a pooled resource. Finally, several larger computers have been
added into the system. As illustrated by these figures, the services provided by the
large-scale network application have not changed, but their physical deployment
has drastically changed in conversion from the small to the large system. Of course,
this is a simplified example of how an application designed with ActiveX servers
can be scaled. You should expect to have to do some tuning as you scale your
system; with any luck, the amount of tuning will be minimal.

Large System

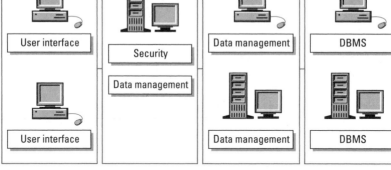

Figure 21-2: Large systems

Resource usage

A finite amount of processing resources are available in any given application, system, network, or enterprise. As we scale a system and move servers to different computers, we are spreading around the resources the application uses; all do not belong to any one computer. There are good reasons to scale a system — for instance, to take advantage of certain security mechanisms or network bandwidth availability. However, one of the most attractive reasons is to take advantage of a certain system's processing capacity — that is, some computer systems physically have more processing power than others.

In addition to the "raw horsepower" advantages that are achieved by moving a service to a more powerful machine, there are advantages within a particular machine's operating environment. As each ActiveX server runs in its own thread, the multitasking capabilities of Windows allow an *n*-tiered system that is deployed on a single computer to outperform a similar monolithic application. This would especially be true if processor-intensive tasks were separated out into individual servers.

Reusability

Reusability certainly seems an elusive goal. It is very easy to understand and talk about but, in practice, is hard to achieve. Having said this, it should not stop us from looking at ways of making our ActiveX servers more reusable. One of the interesting phenomena of reusability is that as the scope of the reused object increases, its potential for reuse decreases. It stands to reason, then, that the greatest reuse opportunity exists with small or primitive servers.

Aggregation

The term *aggregation* refers to the process whereby a number of smaller servers are grouped, or *wrapped*, into a larger server. This technique allows you to build simple, primitive servers for reuse and then group their capabilities into an aggregate object. The problem with this is that the aggregate object is not likely to perform as well as it would if the functionality provided by the simple servers were inherent to the aggregate object. Even if the primitives were built as in-process servers, which reduces the overhead, there still would be more overhead than if the functions were built into the aggregate server.

For this reason, you must really pick and choose which functions you want to encapsulate in these generic, primitive servers. You must weigh the reusability potential of the server versus the performance impact.

Interface reusability

An interface is the smallest visible, functional part of a component. Conceivably, if you could package an interface as a reusable unit, you could build a new object that consisted of a group of interfaces. If you are interested in this kind of a concept, you should read some in-depth materials on the Microsoft Repository and study some of the object construction tools, such as the Microsoft Visual Modeler. This way of thinking of a system is really a metalevel above the architectural discussions in this chapter. Oftentimes, by exploring some of these more sophisticated concepts, it is easy to understand the ones we are actually going to be employing.

Development efforts

Designing an *n*-tier application using ActiveX servers gives the development process a tremendous boost. Since each server is a separate physical entity, the development effort can be split into teams that are each responsible for a particular server. You can assign developers with particular expertise to servers that need that type of expertise. For example, developers that prefer database work can be assigned to database-related servers, and developers that are skilled with user interfaces can be assigned to client-side servers.

The teams have to come together to agree on how the servers interact; these server interactions will be the *interfaces* provided by the servers. The interfaces are exposed as *properties*, *events*, and *methods*. After the interfaces have been designed, the teams can split up and concentrate on implementing the interfaces and all the supporting code that is internal to the server. Each server is tested independently —this is known as *unit testing*. Finally, the servers are brought together and their interactions are tested—this is known as *integration testing*.

Maintainability

A system comprising a group of ActiveX servers is usually easier to maintain than a similar monolithic system. The reason we say "usually" is that, as with most development decisions, there are always trade-offs.

The maintainability advantage derives from each server's being developed independently, so each server is maintained independently. Changes to the networked application generally do not affect all the servers. Therefore, once all the servers are developed, debugged, and tested, you have only to develop, debug, and test the individual servers where changes have occurred. Similar changes to a monolithic system would require a complete development, debug, and test cycle for the entire application. The problem is that *dependencies* exist between the servers in your system. Such dependencies can be directional; in Figure 21-3, the user interface server is dependent on the security server, but the reverse is not true. Conceivably, a change to a server could create a change in the interface supporting another server. Therefore, even when changes only affect a portion of the servers within a given system, it would be prudent to do integration testing once the changes are made.

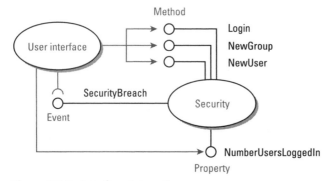

Figure 21-3: Interface interactions

Even with the trade-off we just described, a system containing ActiveX servers is usually much more maintainable than an equivalent monolithic system. Of course, there are interface dependencies between servers, but similar dependencies exist within a monolithic application — these are internal dependencies among the functional modules that make up this type of application. The beauty of ActiveX server architecture is that if you ensure that changes internal to your servers do not affect your interfaces, those changes do not afflict the body of your system.

Defining the System

In this chapter, we're going to construct a number of ActiveX servers belonging to a sample order-entry system. We'll assume this fictitious system is capable of checking items in inventory and entering orders against inventory. We're not going to actually build the entire system, but we describe how this system could be constructed using ActiveX servers. Here is the process that we outline in this chapter:

Requirements definition — The requirements of the system are defined. At this stage, we need not be concerned with the final architecture of the system.

Services definition — Using the requirements as a platform to build onto, we group similar requirements into services. This is the *logical design* of the system.

Other considerations — At this point, we consider such matters as server reuse potential and deployment strategies.

Server construction — After the services and servers have been well defined, it is time to actually implement the servers. This effort concentrates on the interfaces between the servers, as well as other implementation considerations.

Requirements definition

The requirements-definition process is necessary so you and your CD-developers can get down on paper what you expect the system to do. Depending on your development methodology, there may be several different types or levels of requirements definitions. We are going to talk about three levels of requirements definition: marketing requirements, functional requirements, and technical requirements.

Requirement definition begins with the marketing requirements. This involves such things as describing features of the product, identifying a target customer, identifying competitors, and answering many other questions related to what it takes to produce such a product. For a commercial product, these requirements translate to the features of the product that you expect to be selling to a potential customer. Even on an in-house project, there may be some "selling" of the product, especially if you work for a large, distributed company. Typically, at this stage, you should merely describe the raw functionality without spending time trying to describe any particular implementation of those features. This is true because your initial audience will be managers and executives who need to grasp the overall concept before anything can proceed.

There is an interesting and useful technique that can be used to generate a high-level set of marketing requirements. This involves developing a two- to four-page marketing "slick," like the one you later hand out to potential customers. The slick will, of course, highlight the key features of your system and describe the benefits of each feature. The process of forcing yourself to reduce the system's features down to those that fit on such a marketing slick helps you to understand what the important features really are.

From the marketing requirements, you derive a set of functional requirements. Typically, a single marketing requirement expands into several functional requirements. For example, a marketing requirement might be, "Provides a real-time check of product availability." The corresponding functional requirements might be as follows:

✦ Provide a user interface (UI) that displays the availability of a product.

✦ Provide a way for the UI to retrieve information from the database about a product.

✦ Provide a way for the database to notify the UI when a change is made in the product count.

Although the functional requirements do not provide a complete description of how anything is implemented, certain implementation elements are starting to show up. In the above example, we are definitely seeing a user interface and some database interaction.

As you can see in Table 21-1, each level of the requirements-definition process has increasing granularity. The final level — technical requirements — expands on the functional requirements and describes the technical impact of each requirement. At this point, there should be a clear definition of what the system has to do and a fairly clear idea of how the system does it.

Table 21-1
Levels of the Requirements-Definition Process

Marketing Requirement	Functional Requirements	Technical Requirements
Provide a real-time check of product availability	Provide a UI to display product availability	Implement a form that provides a way to display a product
	Provide a way to retrieve the latest availability for a particular product	Provide a way to switch between a brief list of products and a detailed view of a particular product
	Provide a way to inform the UI if the product count changes	Provide a Find dialog to locate and retrieve a product
		Provide an event that can be fired if the product count changes; provide a mechanism for the UI to hook into this event

The amount of time and level of detail devoted to the requirements process usually is directly related to the scope of the project. In a small project, it may not be important to distinguish between marketing, functional, and technical requirements. It may be entirely appropriate to combine these into a small document that can be completed in a day or two by one person. On the other hand, the requirements definition for a large project may be a formal process that requires a number of teams from various disciplines.

Services definition

In the requirements-definition process, there isn't a great concern for the overall architecture of the system; we are more concerned with defining what the system will do. In the services-definition process, we start to develop the architecture of the system. Although we are describing requirements definition and services definition as separate processes, in practice they overlap a great deal. As the granularity of the requirements is uncovered, the services that are provided will emerge.

A service is a logical or conceptual way of organizing a set of related features. An application can then be viewed as a set of services — this is the *services model* of your application. There are many advantages to looking at your application as a set of services. A service is an abstracted high-level view of the features of your system. This abstraction provides a more natural way of looking at a software system from a real-world perspective.

To illustrate this point, let's consider an example. You may describe the functions of a system in how it allows a user to add or remove money from a bank account. This system might also provide several other features, but our view of the application is constrained by the features it is providing. If, on the other hand, we said that we were going to provide a *banking service*, we are immediately flooded with ideas about what this service will do. This is because we all have experiences and opinions about a banking service, but we may not have similar perspectives as to the details that lie within the service.

By thinking of our application as a system of discrete services, we can look at a system from a new perspective. It is this type of perspective that effectively maps into an object-oriented design, which has many inherent advantages. These advantages include object (service) reuse, encapsulation of functionality, and distributed architectures.

Another advantage to the services approach is how it helps to describe the system to other people. It is easier to communicate to nontechnical people the services that a system provides versus trying to describe to them the technical details.

The services model is a conceptual way of looking at a system; it does not necessarily conform to the physical implementation of the system. This means a service might be a collection of objects that are deployed across several machines, or a service might be a single object contained on one machine. A service might also be a combination of ActiveX servers, database procedures, and Web servers. Of course, when you actually begin to implement your application services, you will need to consider a number of system constraints.

Another good way to help define your system services is to develop *usage scenarios*. A usage scenario is a narrative that describes a typical user session with your application. A possible usage scenario might be as follows: The telephone order center receives a call from a customer. They want to check price and availability on a product they have just read about. The system operator enters a description of the product and receives a list of products matching that description. After isolating the desired product, the availability is quoted. After the customer decides to purchase the product, the operator enters an order and secures the stock. The system must provide a lot of information about the services that can be found within such a narrative. For example, we may derive a display service, a lookup service, and an order service from this narrative.

Deployment considerations

There are a number of other items to consider as you make your design decisions. It is always important to "step back" or "climb out of your box" so that you don't miss some potentially important aspects of your design. Here is a list of other considerations to keep in mind when designing deployment of your system:

✦ **Reuse potential** — As each component is designed, consider its reuse potential — that is, the potential for a component to be used within another product. When doing so, take a look at what additional time and effort would be required to make a particular component reusable.

✦ **Object dependencies** — It is important to understand dependencies among objects within your system, as well as dependencies that exist between your objects and external systems or data sources. Try to minimize the total number of interactions, and thus dependencies, that are required. If two objects have a large number of interactions with each other, yet have a small number of interactions with other objects, it might be advantageous to combine these objects and reduce their dependencies.

✦ **Deployment** — There are a number of factors related to how the objects within your system will be deployed. There is network bandwidth — both public and private. There is the availability of the systems that will contain your objects. In addition, you can expect to use only a limited amount of resources in any given system — these include such things as the disk and memory footprints required to run your application.

✦ **Strategic directions** — It is usually good to have some type of understanding as to the future and strategic direction of your system. It may be possible to make changes to your current design that can greatly affect the future use of your system. Design considerations of this type should be cautiously pursued, since requirements of future systems can be expected to change.

Server construction

By now, we have looked at the application in a number of different ways. We have considered marketing requirements, technical requirements, services, and possible usage scenarios. We should have a well-rounded and balanced perspective of the application. Building on the definition of services, we define the actual ActiveX servers that implement the services. This is the *physical design* of the system. The design of the servers must take into account not only what each server can do, but also the relationships between the servers.

Many different types of relationships may exist between ActiveX servers. Oftentimes, these servers are dependent on one another, as in the case of one server's requiring a service the other has. For example, a service that captures the status of an application might require another service that has the capability to store the data it creates. ActiveX servers are organized in a hierarchical fashion, such that parent/child relationships exist between server objects. The child object cannot be instantiated, or created directly; it is only available through the parent object. To illustrate this, let's look at the set of database objects shown in Figure 21-4.

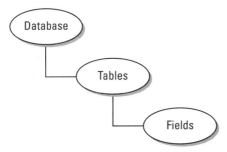

Figure 21-4: Objects with a hierarchical relationship

A database object contains a number of table objects, which in turn contain a number of field objects. This type of hierarchical organization makes sense — obviously, a field must ultimately be contained within a database. In order to access a field object, you must first have a valid database and table object. The following code segment is accessing the first field in the *fields collection* of a table object:

```
Dim ThisField As Field
Set ThisField = ThisDatabase.ThisTable.Fields(1)
```

Building the order entry system

On the CD-ROM accompanying this book, there are several sample projects and a project group. The projects are located in the Order System, Client, and Servers directories. The project group, found in the Order System directory, is named OESystem.vbg. When you open this group, all the related projects are opened into one workspace. You also need Nwind.mdb, the database that comes with Visual Basic, in order to correctly use these sample projects. It might be helpful to have this group open as you follow along with the rest of this discussion.

Note   The ActiveX servers in this sample have all been designated as ActiveX DLLs. This has been done merely for convenience so that they can be referenced within the project workspace. When a server is referenced in the workspace in this way, you can step into the server code as you are debugging.

Figure 21-5 shows the four projects belonging to the order entry system: a *client*, a *security server*, a *business rules server*, and a *data engine server*. The client contains most of the user interface. The security server provides a login dialog and login services to the client. If the security server accepts the login, it creates a valid business-rules object for the client. The security server does not actually perform the validation itself — it does so indirectly through a business rules object. The business rules object, in turn, passes the login request to a database engine object. Figure 21-6 helps to illustrate the relationships and interactions between the servers in this system.

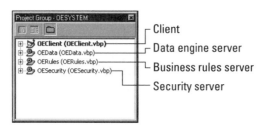

Figure 21-5: The order entry system workspace

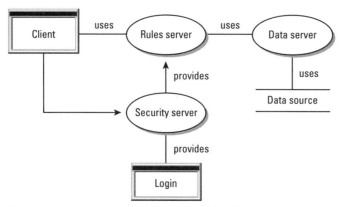

Figure 21-6: Interactions and relationships between objects

Logging In to the system

Let's take a more detailed look at the server interactions, starting with the client logging into a database. The login is initiated by clicking the Login button. The procedure that is fired creates a security server object and then calls the

SystemLogin method. If the login method returns True, indicating a valid login, the client then retrieves a business rules object from the security server. Listing 21-1 shows the event procedure that is triggered by the user's clicking on the Login button on the introductory form.

Listing 21-1: **A Client Logging In to the System**

```
Private Sub cmdLogin_Click()
    Dim SecurityServer As Object

    Set SecurityServer = New OESecurity.Application
    If (SecurityServer Is Nothing) Then
        MsgBox "Unable to create the login server.", _
            vbOKOnly + vbCritical, "OES Client"
    Else
        If (SecurityServer.SystemLogin()) Then
            MsgBox "Login successful.", _
                vbOKOnly + vbInformation, "OES Client"


            '_____

            'If the login was successful, retrieve the
            'rules server — this server will provide all
            'data interactions to the client
            '_____

            Set TheseRules = SecurityServer.BusinessRules
            Set SecurityServer = Nothing
            cmdRetrieve.Enabled = True
        Else
            MsgBox "Unable to login to the database.", _
                vbOKOnly + vbInformation, "OES Client"
            cmdRetrieve.Enabled = False
        End If
    End If

End Sub
```

The role of the security server is to prevent unauthorized access to a database. In order to do so, it passes the login information to a server that has the capability to attempt the login. In the order entry system, it is the data engine that ultimately provides all database access. The security server could have created an instance of the data engine directly and tested the login. However, since the client is only going to be able to access a business rules server through the security server, the security server passes the login information through a business rules server to the data engine server. It is the business rules server that needs the relationship to the data engine; future client interactions will be filtered through the rules into the database. After a connection is established, the security server drops out of the picture. Listing 21-2 shows the general procedure that validates the login, which is called by Private Sub cmdLogin_Click in Listing 21-1.

Note In an actual system, you may want the security server to perform additional services other than just the login service.

Listing 21-2: The SystemLogin Starts in the Application Class

```
Public Function SystemLogin(_
    Optional DBName As String = "", _
    Optional User As String = "", _
    Optional Pass As String = "", _
    Optional ShowDialog As Boolean = True) As Boolean

    Dim ValidLogin  As Boolean

    '_____
    ' Performs a login, with or without a
    ' dialog.  If login is valid, makes
    ' available a Data Engine object
    '_____
    With frmLogin
        '— pre-populate form properties
        .DBName = DBName
        .UserName = User
        .Password = Pass
        If ShowDialog Then
            .Show vbModal
            ValidLogin = .LoginPassed
        Else
            '— just perform validation,
            '— if user/pass were provided
            ValidLogin = .TryLogin()
        End If
    End With

    SystemLogin = ValidLogin

End Function
```

The preceding procedure is contained within the Application class of the security server. All the servers, by convention, have an Application class that provides an entry point into the server. Although the security server can provide a login dialog, it is not necessary to use this dialog to log in to a database. If the ShowDialog argument is False, a login is attempted using the TryLogin method, using the database, user, and password parameters supplied as arguments. The TryLogin method in Listing 21-3 is also called if the login dialog is displayed, this time using the parameters set in the dialog.

Listing 21-3: The TryLogin Method

```
Public Function TryLogin() As Boolean

    Set CurRules = New OERules.Application
    TryLogin = CurRules.OpenRules(DBName, _
        UserName, Password)

End Function
```

The `TryLogin` method creates a new business rules object and calls a method that ultimately tries to open a database. The `OpenRules` method creates a new database engine object and passes the login information to it; the database engine finally tries to connect to the physical database. The result of the login attempt is either True (login was successful), or False (login failed). This result is passed up from the database engine to the business rules, to the security server, and finally to the client. This may seem like a lot of work, or a convoluted way of doing things, but let's look at the state of the system after a successful login:

✦ **Client object** has a connection to a valid business rules object. The client always uses this object to access data. This relationship provides a way for the business rules object to apply its rules to data proceeding to or from the client. In addition, the client does not have to be concerned with any of the inner workings of the database.

✦ **Security object** has provided a login dialog and a pass-through of the login information. If the login was valid, a business rules object was made available to the client. The security object populates the rules object with the username that logged in and assigns a *privilege level* that is used in future transactions.

✦ **Business rules object**, originally instantiated by the security object, was initialized to a state that would be ready for the client. The rules object also created a database engine object, which it maintains as private so that it can process database requests. The rules object is eventually handed off to the client by the security object; the client uses the rules object for all data interactions.

✦ **Data engine object** is created by the rules object and performs all database interactions. The rules object performs business validations and filtering before making any calls to the data engine. The data engine is the only object that has a direct connection to a database, and is responsible for all direct data management and manipulation.

Requesting data

Figure 21-7 models a request for data placed by the client and forwarded through all the server objects in the chain of this application. A client makes a data request to the rules server it acquired during the login process. The rules server may accept or reject this request, depending on a set of internal criteria it applies to the request. The criteria takes into account who the user making the request is, or what their system access privilege level is, or it may even take into account some state that the overall system is in. For example, if the system is unavailable or extremely busy, the rules server may deny the request. The rules server may also modify the request before it passes the request to the data engine.

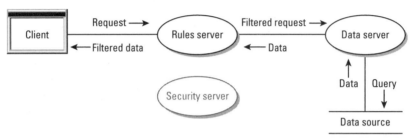

Figure 21-7: A client's data request

Data retrieval starts with a request to the rules server by the client. In the demo included on the CD-ROM, this is done by the user pressing the Retrieve button. Listing 21-4 shows the event procedure executed when this user event occurs.

Listing 21-4: **The Client Request for Data**

```
Private Sub cmdRetrieve_Click()
    Dim i          As Integer
    Dim ReturnVal  As Integer
    Dim ClientMsg  As String

    '— clear the list
    lvwData.ListItems.Clear
    lvwData.ColumnHeaders.Clear

    '— normally, the client would not supply their
    '— privilege level
    '— this is maintained by the rules server
    ReturnVal = TheseRules.GetData(TableNumber, _
        AssignedLevel, ClientMsg)

    If (ReturnVal = 0) Then '— failed
        MsgBox ClientMsg, _
            vbOKOnly + vbInformation, "Retrieve Data"
        Exit Sub
    Else '— not call the rules to show the data
        Call TheseRules.ShowData(lvwData, AssignedLevel)
    End If

End Sub
```

The client first calls a method named GetData. In the demo, the client passes its privilege level as a parameter to the rules server; but in a real system, this server would probably maintain that value on behalf of its client. The client also supplies a little information — in this case, the table number. If the method call is successful, the client calls a second method named ShowData. The client passes a ListView control, represented by lvwData, to this method.

Listing 21-5 shows the GetData method called by the Private Sub cmdRetrieve_Click event procedure.

Listing 21-5: **The GetData Method**

```
'— modular property
Private CurRecordset        As DAO.Recordset

Public Function GetData(TableNumber As Integer, _
    AssignedLevel As Integer, _
    ClientMsg As String) As Integer

    Dim SQLStatement    As String

    If (AssignedLevel = 3) Then
        ClientMsg = "Insufficient privileges" _
            & "to retrieve data."
        GetData = 0 '— failed
        Exit Function
    End If

    Select Case TableNumber
        Case 0: SQLStatement = "Select * From Categories"
        Case 1: SQLStatement = "Select * From Customers"
        Case 2: SQLStatement = "Select * From Employees"
        Case 3: SQLStatement = "Select * From Orders"
    End Select

    Set CurRecordset = _
    DataEngine.CreateRecordset(SQLStatement)

    If (CurRecordset Is Nothing) Then
        GetData = 0 '— failure
    Else
        GetData = 1 '— success
    End If

End Function
```

In the GetData method, we are showing how the business rules server could be used to filter data requests. In this demo, the privilege level (assigned by the UI) must be at least as a user; guests are not allowed to retrieve data. The rules server then issues an SQL statement to the data engine and gets back a recordset. This method returns a 0 if the method failed, or a 1 if the method succeeded.

If the client's data request was successful, the client then calls a method to display the data. The client issues this request to the rules server and passes the reference for a ListView control to be populated. In the demo, we have added another rule: Only an admin can see the first field in the recordset. This was done to further illustrate how the rules server can be used to filter information. We are assuming that the first field contains some kind of system ID, and that this ID is only pertinent to system administrators.

Notice how the client is completely isolated from any data chores — the rules server maintains the recordset and uses it to populate the control for the client. Because of this isolation, the data could be easily moved from a recordset to any other data source by the rules server; the client really doesn't know or care where the data actually is.

Finally, Listing 21-6 shows the method responsible for populating the ListView object with results.

Listing 21-6: **Populating the Client's ListView**

```
Public Function ShowData(ThisListView As Object, _
    PrivilegeLevel As Integer) As Boolean

    Dim i           As Integer
    Dim NumColumn   As Integer
    Dim StartCol    As Integer
    Dim WorkingItem As Object

    If (CurRecordset Is Nothing) Then
        ShowData = False
        Exit Function
    End If

    '— create the column headers
    For i = 0 To CurRecordset.Fields.Count - 1
        If (i = 0) Then
            '— only admin can see the first field
            If (PrivilegeLevel = 0) Then
                ThisListView.ColumnHeaders.Add
                ThisListView.ColumnHeaders(1).Text = _
                    CurRecordset.Fields(i).Name
                NumColumn = 1
            End If
        Else
            ThisListView.ColumnHeaders.Add
```

```
                ThisListView.ColumnHeaders(NumColumn _
                    + 1).Text = CurRecordset.Fields(i).Name
                NumColumn = NumColumn + 1
            End If
        Next

        CurRecordset.MoveFirst
        Do While (Not CurRecordset.EOF)
            '— create a new list item
            Set WorkingItem = ThisListView.ListItems.Add

            If (PrivilegeLevel = 0) Then
                WorkingItem.Text = _
                    CurRecordset.Fields(0).Value & ""
                NumColumn = 1
            Else
                WorkingItem.Text = _
                    CurRecordset.Fields(1).Value & ""
                NumColumn = 2
            End If

            For i = 1 To ThisListView.ColumnHeaders.Count - 1
                WorkingItem.SubItems(i) = _
                    CurRecordset.Fields(NumColumn).Value & ""
                NumColumn = NumColumn + 1
            Next

            CurRecordset.MoveNext
        Loop

    End Function
```

This demo is meant to show you how several servers can be used to create a system. Each server provides a particular set of services and has a particular role within the system. The client is isolated from any direct database manipulations; it can now concentrate on user-related tasks. The other servers work together to ultimately deliver data to the client. Both the security server and the data engine server are potential candidates for reuse; their roles are fairly generic versus the client and rules servers. In addition, any of the servers could be physically distributed to other machines in an effort to increase performance, or for any other strategic reason.

Summary

After the introduction, we discussed how you would actually create a system that utilizes ActiveX servers. Our examination proceeded all the way from the definitions phases to the actual implementation phase.

✦ Defining the system includes the processes of requirements definition, services definition, and servers definition.

✦ Effective server construction grows directly from a careful definition process.

✦ Conceptual examples and practical techniques have been discussed in balance with each other.

✦   ✦   ✦

Add-Ins and Extensibility

Visual Basic provides a development framework that can be extended and enhanced through the use of add-ins. Add-ins allow you to manipulate your design-time objects, such as forms, controls, and even code. This manipulation is accomplished through an object library that provides a set of properties and methods. This library is collectively known as the *extensibility model* and is implemented through a system known as the IDTExtensibility interface.

Add-ins allow you to automate everything from the mundane, such as tedious tasks, to the very sophisticated, such as preparing entire forms with associated code. Add-ins can also be employed to do such things as code auditing and code generation.

In this chapter, we provide you with an understanding of what an add-in is and how to create one. We then attempt to plant some seeds as to how this capability can be used to take you to the next generation of development.

Examining Add-Ins

Visual Basic began life as a rapid application-development tool — a way to create Windows programs without having to know a lot about the Windows internals. Based on how this product initially appeared, many of us expected Visual Basic to evolve into some sort of fifth-generation development tool. Such a tool would have automatic form and code generation, and perhaps some next-generation programming metaphors such as graphical logic assembly. However, instead of taking this route, Visual Basic has slowly evolved with an ever-increasing set of features and functionality. This larger feature set has compounded the complexity of the Visual

Basic programming environment while at the same time allowing us to solve more sophisticated problems with each revision. With constant pressures to improve and expand the core product, Microsoft has left the tasks of creating such fifth-generation features to the Visual Basic user-and tools-development community, by providing a way to extend the development environment — through add-ins.

An *add-in* is a tool that interacts with the development environment. In order to understand the relationship between Visual Basic and an add-in, it may be useful to consider how VB uses components such as OCXs. An OCX (OLE custom control) is a software component that is designed to perform a particular set of tasks. It usually provides a visual interface and also has methods, properties, and events. A Visual Basic programmer uses the OCX by setting the properties, calling the methods, and responding to the events. Similarly to Visual Basic's use of the OCX, an add-in uses, or "drives" if you will, Visual Basic. The add-in sets VB properties, calls its methods, and responds to its events. The difference is that Visual Basic uses an OCX to provide a set of functionality within an application program being delivered to a customer, whereas an add-in uses VB to automate and extend the development environment, making it easier to program. Figure 22-1 shows the relationships between Visual Basic, an OCX component, and an add-in.

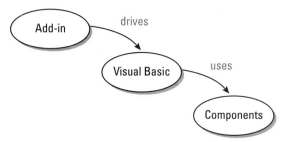

Figure 22-1: Visual Basic, add-ins, and components

The ability for an add-in to drive Visual Basic is provided through a set of objects, collectively known as the *extensibility model*, or *add-in object model*. As with other object models you are familiar with, the objects within this model are organized into a hierarchy starting with a root object known as the Visual Basic Extensibility object, or *VBE*. Figure 22-2 shows a simplified object diagram of the top-level objects and collections contained within the VBE. It pays special attention to the VBProjects collections, as this is where much of the work is done related to your project and interface elements.

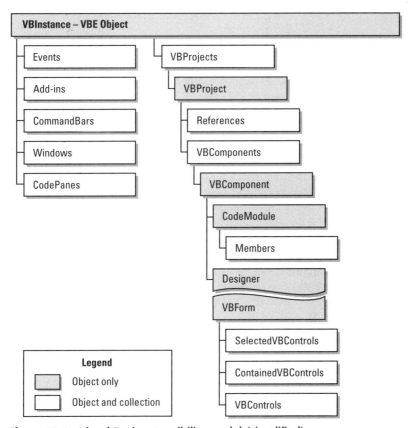

Figure 22-2: Visual Basic extensibility model (simplified)

The following items summarize the top-level objects and collections shown in this object model. They are explained in complete detail later in this chapter.

✦ The VBInstance object represents an instance of the Visual Basic development environment. It contains the VBE object that is used to derive all the other objects and collections within the extensibility model.

✦ The Events object contains a number of properties that are used to return *event source objects*. These event source objects fire events that notify you of changes in the Visual Basic development environment. The properties of the Events object return objects of the same type as the property name. For example, the CommandBarEvents property returns the CommandBarEvents object.

✦ The properties found in the events object are `CommandBarEvents`, `VBComponentsEvents`, `FileControlEvents`, `VBControlsEvents`, `ReferencesEvents`, `VBProjectsEvents`, and `SelectedVBControlsEvents`.

✦ The `Add-Ins` collection returns a collection of every add-in that is registered with Visual Basic. An add-in registers with Visual Basic by adding an entry into the `vbaddin.ini` file located in the Windows directory. Once registered, the add-in shows up in the Add-In Manager dialog, accessed from Add-Ins ➪ Add-In Manager.

✦ The `CommandBars` collection contains all the command bars in a project, including command bars that support shortcut menus. A command bar unifies menus and toolbars into a single programmatic object. An add-in can use this collection to add custom command bars and controls specific to the add-in, or to add custom controls to built-in command bars that are native to the Visual Basic development environment.

✦ The `Windows` collection contains all the windows contained with a project. This includes all open or permanent windows. Each window is represented by a `Window` object. Windows, such as Code windows, are added to the collection when they are opened and removed when they are closed. Other windows, such as the Project window, are considered permanent windows and are always present in this collection. The properties and methods of a `Window` object can be used to manipulate the appearance of the windows in a Visual Basic project.

✦ The `CodePanes` collection is used to access all the open code panes in your project. At first this may seem confusing, as you may think this is what the `Windows` collection does. However, the `Windows` collection includes *all* windows, such as Visual Basic's Project and Properties windows — not just windows containing code (code panes). Use the `CodeModule` property of a `CodePane` object to get to the actual code contained within the pane.

✦ The `VBProjects` collection contains all the projects that are available within your development environment. Remember, you can have more than one project open within a Visual Basic instance, starting with version 5.0. A `VBProject` object contains all the components that you are intimately familiar with, such as forms, code modules, and controls. If you have followed the extensibility model since its beginnings in Visual Basic 4.0, you will recognize the `VBProject` object; this was the only hierarchy available in the original extensibility model.

Add-ins can be created with Visual Basic. In fact, the wizards that ship with Visual Basic are add-ins created in Visual Basic. The purpose of these wizards is to automate various programming tasks. To get a quick look at what an add-in can do, load the VB Wizard Manager add-in that comes with Visual Basic. This add-in assists in the development of new add-ins that utilize a wizard-style interface.

An add-in may be designed to automate a set of tasks, similar to a macro, or it may be designed to provide integration between Visual Basic and another tool, as is the case with the Visual Component Manager. The following sections highlight some of the possible uses for add-ins.

Task automations

A *task automaton* is an add-in that is used to automate a repetitive or tedious task. Let's take a look at a simple example of how such an automaton might work. There are several control structures within Visual Basic that open and close with a certain set of keywords. Some examples of these structures are as follows:

```
Select Case testexpression
Case expressionlist-n
[statements-n] ...
Case Else
    [elsestatements]
End Select
```

and

```
If condition Then
[statements]
[ElseIf condition-n Then
[elseifstatements]] ...
[Else
[elsestatements]]
End If
```

It would be possible to build an add-in that laid down a control structure template so that you would not have to type in each part of the required structure manually. In addition to laying out the structure template, the add-in might also provide a standard comment header and even a comment containing information regarding the author of the code segment. Figure 22-3 shows a dialog that facilitates the creation of a code segment. This dialog allows you to select a few parameters for creation of the segment.

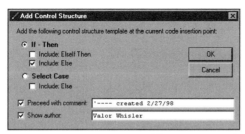

Figure 22-3: Automating addition of control structures

Framework generators

A *framework* is a starting place for an application. It might also be thought of as a project template or project shell. It consists of a collection of forms, class modules, code modules, components, and references that are added to a new project. Any of these objects can be added to a Visual Basic project using methods provided in the extensibility model. In fact, many of the templates you see in the New Project dialog utilize add-ins to create your project framework. In addition, the Microsoft Visual Component Manager uses the add-in capabilities to interact with Visual Basic. Although it is possible to build your own special-purpose framework generator using an add-in, we recommend using Visual Basic's built-in template capabilities or the Visual Component Manager for this task.

If you want to know more about frameworks, they are covered in great detail in Chapter 14 of this book.

Forms generators

A *forms generator* add-in would use some type of script, or form definition, to generate a form and add it to the active project. The forms that are added via the Add Form dialog (Project ⇨ Add Form) are *not* generated via an add-in, but rather with a form template (see Chapter 3). On the other hand, the Data Form Wizard *is* an example of a form generated through the extensibility model. This tool uses a wizard-style interface to provide a way to select a database, table, fields, form layout, and other options used to generate this form. The wizard then interacts with the VBE objects to generate a form, add controls to that form, set properties on those controls, and finally add code behind the controls and form.

You can use this same set of capabilities to generate any type of form that suits your need. It is conceivable that you would provide a set of wizards that could generate several different types of forms. These forms could all conform to some corporate interface and coding standard styles. By autogenerating these forms, you would not only save time but also be assured more consistent results. And this generator does not need to create only a single form; it could be used to generate sets of forms that are designed to work together.

Style wizards

A *style* is a set of properties for a particular control, or form. For example, the fact that a CommandButton has a particular height, width, and font might be considered a style. An add-in can be created to set a group of property values all at once for a single control, for all the controls that are selected on a form, or for all the controls on a form. Of great importance to most developers is a consistent style within an application, and often throughout an entire product line. A style wizard can be created to facilitate the setting of properties to assure this consistent style.

What's even more interesting than merely setting styles is the ability to capture the existing properties for any control and save them in some sort of style library. Each style could be assigned a name so that it would be easy to identify for reuse. Such a library could be created by a design committee and then made available for every developer on the team. Figure 22-4 shows how the properties found on a form (the Properties dialog is shown) can be saved into an external library. These property settings can then be applied to any new object having the same properties.

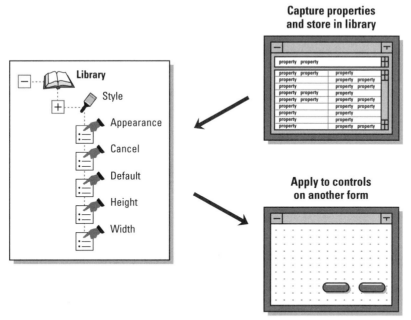

Figure 22-4: Capturing and applying styles

Application bridges

An add-in can act as a *bridge*, or *conduit*, between Visual Basic and another application. The previous add-in examples are of tools that are used to automate the development environment. These tools have generally been small, single-purpose wizards designed specifically for use with Visual Basic. But what if you had a fully functional standalone application that would also like to interact with Visual Basic?

In this case, you want to create a set of functions within the application to enable this communication. These functions act as the conduit to perform this interaction. The bridge can be provided by code that is contained within the other application, or it might be placed in a separate object. Figure 22-5 shows a fully functional application communicating to Visual Basic using an application bridge. This bridge knows how to communicate with the application on one side using any suitable mechanism, and with Visual Basic on the other side using the add-in mechanism.

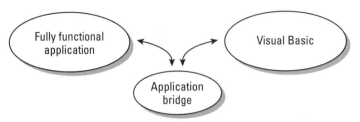

Figure 22-5: An application bridge add-in

An example of this type of relationship can be found between Visual Basic and the Visual Component Manager. The VCM is a fully functional application that not only interacts with Visual Basic but also with other Microsoft Visual Tools.

Code generators

A *code generator* supplies some avenue to select, or build, a set of logic and then produce corresponding program code. In a simple sense, a dialog or wizard allows you to pick from a fixed set of logic choices and then generate the code. This could be useful if you were selecting from lists of available functions that you wanted to include in your program.

A more advanced code generator might allow you to build program logic through a graphical interface. You would connect logic blocks together by dragging lines between such blocks to indicate program flow. The generator would then build an entire set of code to support the logic defined in this interface. This is not as far-fetched as it might initially sound. Everything is currently in place to support such an effort — Visual Basic could be used to build the interface, and the Visual Basic extensibility model would provide a way to generate the code.

Expert assistants

The last "breed" of add-ins we talk about might be the most interesting. What if you could capture the expertise of one or more individuals and make this expertise available to your programming sessions? This add-in might be known as an *expert assistant*. The expert assistant would provide a number of services to its users:

✦ *Pattern Finder* — Suggests syntax or organizational changes in code.

✦ *Naming Janitor* — Looks for adherence to standard naming conventions, both variable prefixes and use of abbreviations.

✦ *Type Checker* — Makes sure that all variables have their data type explicitly declared, and also that all function calls pass in the correct data types and have appropriate data-type variables declared for function returns.

✦ *Scope Detective* — Makes sure that all variables are declared with appropriate scope in mind. For example, a variable that is declared at a modular level but only used in a single procedure should, in fact, be declared in that procedure.

As you can see in these add-in examples and suggestions, there are many uses for add-ins in your development process. We have discussed everything from a simple add-in that automates repetitive tasks to an expert assistant that helps to analyze your project. The interesting point about all these add-ins is that each and every one can be implemented *today* with the add-in technology that is available. The following sections tell you how to create an add-in, and cover the extensibility model in more detail.

Building Your Own Add-In

This section tells you how to create your first add-in — and it couldn't be easier! To create your first add-in, just select the Addin template from the new project dialog (File ➪ New Project). Visual Basic adds the following two components:

- ✦ frmAddIn (Form) — This form is a shell that provides the developer with the beginnings of the add-in's interface. It doesn't really do a lot, but it does have two public properties that show you how to tie a form in with the other components of the add-in.

- ✦ Connect (Class Module) — This is a designer that contains the operational code for the add-in's interactions with Visual Basic. It also contains a custom designer interface that is used to set many of your add-ins' properties.

Using a capability that first appears in Visual Basic version 5.0, a developer merely has to implement the IDTExtensibility add-in interface to access the extensibility model. Once this interface is implemented, four methods are available in the class module implementing the interface. These methods are all that is needed to connect, disconnect, and manage the connection between Visual Basic and your add-in.

Note   See the Implements keyword in Visual Basic for more information on implementing another object's interface.

Note   There have been only minor changes to the extensibility model between versions 5.0 and 6.0.

One of the methods available through the implemented interface is the OnConnection method. This event is fired when the Visual Basic session instantiates your add-in. One of the arguments in this event, VBInst, is an object that represents the instance of Visual Basic that instantiated your add-in and is, in fact, the VBE root object. It is from this object that all other objects and collections within the extensibility model are derived (see Figure 22-2). The VBE object(s) allow you to query, manipulate, and receive events related to the extensibility of your current Visual Basic session.

In the following sections, we are going take this add-in template and modify it so that we can perform a particular task.

Giving your add-in an identity

In order for an add-in to work with Visual Basic, there are four things that have to happen:

1. Register with Visual Basic — This is accomplished by adding an entry to the VBAddin.ini file. This file is located in the Windows directory and contains a list of all the Visual Basic add-ins. Each add-in must somehow make an entry into this file with the following format:

   `ApplicationName.ClassName=0/1`

   The `ApplicationName` is the compiled name of your application. The `ClassName` is the name of the class that implements the `IDTExtensibility` interface and contains all the required `IDTExtensibility` methods. The value is either 0, indicating that the add-in is not loaded when Visual Basic starts, or 1, indicating that it is loaded at start time.

2. Implement the `IDTExtensibility` interface — An add-in must provide a class module that implements this interface, and the instancing of class must be public and creatable (`MultiUse` is recommended).

3. Register in the System Registry — An add-in must have an entry in the system Registry in order to work. Visual Basic looks for the Registry entry that is defined in `VBAddin.ini` in order to be able to launch your add-in. *Visual Basic automatically creates the required entry in the Registry when your add-in is either run in Debug mode or compiled.*

4. Provide an interface — If you have done all these items properly, Visual Basic can launch your add-in, but without an interface it cannot be useful. You must provide some type of interface to enable your add-in to do work.

You can use the `ApplicationName` and `ClassName` to provide an identity for your add-in. Although from time to time we have seen recommendations on naming standards, our conclusion is that there really are none. It's best for you to come up with a convention and use it. Because of the fact that an add-in is actually an *ActiveX server* with the special extensibility interface, try to devise a naming convention that will work for all your ActiveX servers (Chapters 21 – 23 talk a lot more about ActiveX servers).

Table 22-1 shows some possible naming styles; Figure 22-6 shows a name being assigned.

	Table 22-1	
	Add-In Naming Conventions	
ApplicationName	*ClassName*	*Comment*
ISData	`Application`	The application name uses the initials of the company name, followed by a word that describes the add-in. The class name is always `Application`, by convention.
ActiveXDocumentWizard	`Connect`	The application name describes the add-in; in this case a document wizard. The class name is always `Connect`, by convention.
Repository	`VBAddIn`	The application name denotes that this add-in is part of the Microsoft Repository collection of tools. The class name denotes the type of tool.
IS_VBE_017	`CodeManager`	The application name uses a naming system that corresponds to an internal company convention. The class name describes the use of this particular add-in.

As you can see, the names can technically be any valid name that you choose. The point is that you should do some thinking about a convention that you would like to employ up front — changing this after the fact is much more work.

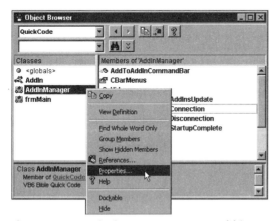

Figure 22-6: Assigning a name to your add-in

The name of the add-in that appears in the Add-In Manager dialog is set in yet another place. This is a text string that is defined in the Object Browser. To set this string, bring up the browser by pressing F2. Next, select the class that implements the `IDTExtensibility` interface and provides the startup and shutdown methods. (This naming process is shown in Figure 22-6.)

Tip

If you only want to see the objects associated with your active project, you can select the name of that project from the ComboBox at the top-left of this dialog. Once you have the correct class object selected, right-click on it and select Properties from the context menu.

Figure 22-7 shows the Member Options dialog. The Description property is the name that will appear in Visual Basic's Add-In Manager dialog in the Available Add-Ins column.

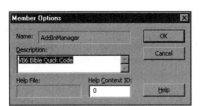

Figure 22-7: Your add-in name as it appears in the Add-In Manager

Debugging your add-in

If you want to follow along with some of the examples discussed in this and the following sections, you should copy the QuickCode project, from within the directory of the same name, off the CD-ROM that is supplied with this book. QuickCode is an add-in that adds some control structure templates to the active code module. It has a class named AddInManager that implements the extensibility interface.

To debug an add-in, you must run two instances of Visual Basic. The first instance is the instance that contains the add-in, and the second instance is a project that is used to test and debug the add-in. You should start by only having the add-in instance loaded. Set any breakpoints you desire and run the project. Once the add-in project is running, start the second instance of Visual Basic. Now select your add-in from the Add-In Manager dialog and begin your testing and debugging. Remember, you must have your add-in registered with Visual Basic to effectively do this.

When you are debugging, you can set any breakpoints you like in either instance of Visual Basic. If your add-in instance is minimized, Visual Basic will not only stop at your breakpoint but will return that instance to normal and with focus. The correct way to stop debugging is to stop the instance that is using your add-in and completely shut down that instance. Once this testing instance is unloaded, return to your add-in instance and stop it.

Creating your add-in interface

It is possible to create custom menus and toolbar buttons for your add-in that become part of the Visual Basic menu and toolbars. Even though menus, toolbars, and toolbar buttons have different physical and visual characteristics, they are internally treated by Visual Basic as the same kinds of objects. Visual Basic considers all these interface elements as command bars or, technically, as `CommandBar` objects. All these objects can be found in the `CommandBars` collection. A `CommandBar` object, in turn, has a collection of `Controls` contained within it. Figure 22-8 helps to illustrate these collections and objects.

VBE . CommandBars ("File")   VBE . CommandBars ("Add-Ins")

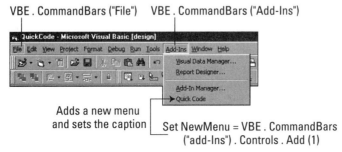

Adds a new menu
and sets the caption   Set NewMenu = VBE . CommandBars
                         ("add-Ins") . Controls . Add (1)

Figure 22-8: CommandBars and CommandBar controls

Note

Interestingly enough, the `CommandBars` collection is actually part of the Microsoft Office object library — this library is added by Visual Basic if you do not have Office installed. This is an example of how Microsoft reuses software by sharing libraries between applications.

We're going to discuss how to hook a menu into Visual Basic and then bring up a dialog that controls your add-in. First, we're going to create a variable that is public to the `AddInManager` class in the QuickCode project, to cache the `VBInst` coming in from the `OnConnection` event. We will need this to traverse the extensibility model. We are also going to create a private variable to store the menu object we will be creating. The final modular variable we will need handles the events created by our menu — this is done with our `MenuEvents` object, shown in Listing 22-1.

Listing 22-1: **Creating Some Modular Variables to Store Objects and Handle Events**

```
'<Public>—————————————————
Public VBInstance    As VBIDE.VBE
'<Public>—————————————————

'<Private>————————————————
Private CBarMenus    As Office.CommandBarControl
'</Private>———————————————

'<Events>—————————————————
'— command bar event handler
Public WithEvents MenuEvents As CommandBarEvents
'</Events>————————————————
```

Listing 22-2 shows how the `VBInst` argument that is passed into the `OnConnection` event is cached. Listing 22-3 shows how the function that will add our Add-Ins menu to Visual Basic is called. We will then handle any of the events that are generated via our menu.

Listing 22-2: **The OnConnection Event**

```
Private Sub IDTExtensibility_OnConnection(ByVal VBInst _
    As Object, ByVal ConnectMode As vbext_ConnectMode, _
    ByVal AddInInst As VBIDE.AddIn, Custom() As Variant)

    '— cache the vb instance
    Set VBInstance = VBInst

    Set CBarMenus = AddMyMenu("Quick Code")

    '— sink the event
    Set Me.MenuHandler = _
        VBInst.Events.CommandBarEvents(CBarMenus)

End Sub
```

Listing 22-3: **Adding Our Menu to Visual Basic**

```
Function AddMyMenu(MenuCaption As String) _
    As Office.CommandBarControl
    Dim MyMenu      As Office.CommandBarControl
    Dim AddInMenu   As Object

    '— see if we can find the Add-Ins menu
    Set AddInMenu = VBInstance.CommandBars("Add-Ins")
    If (AddInMenu Is Nothing) Then
        '— not available so we exit
        Exit Function
    End If

    '— add our menu and set the caption
    Set MyMenu = AddInMenu.Controls.Add(1)
    MyMenu.Caption = MenuCaption

    '— return our menu so we can handle its events
    Set AddMyMenu = MyMenu

End Function
```

This next snippet of code shows the handling of our Menus events:

```
Private Sub MenuEvents_Click(ByVal CommandBarControl _
    As Object, Handled As Boolean, _
    CancelDefault As Boolean)
    frmMain.Show
End Sub
```

The preceding listings show you how to add a custom menu to Visual Basic and handle the Click event that is generated when a user selects the menu. These segments have been simplified for print — refer to the included project for the complete routines.

Accessing Visual Basic code

This section provides a discussion of how an add-in can access and manipulate Visual Basic code. To do this, we will primarily use three kinds of extensibility objects: CodePanes, CodeModules, and Members. The CodePane object represents a visible Code window. A given component can have several CodePane objects. The CodeModule object represents the code within a component. A component can only have one CodeModule object. A member of a code module is an identifier that has module-level scope and can be considered a property, method, or event of that code module. Using these objects, it is possible to view and manipulate every line of code in a Visual Basic project. Figure 22-9 shows the hierarchy of the code-related objects.

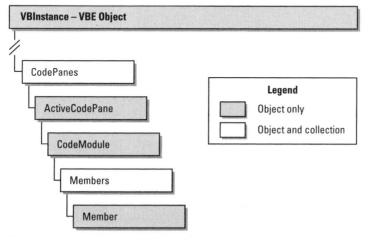

Figure 22-9: CodePanes, CodeModules, and Members

A special code pane, the ActiveCodePane, represents the Code window that has the focus in a project. Listing 22-4 shows how to get a handle to the ActiveCodePane and its CodeModule objects when the expert agent form is activated. It sets the CodeModule to a modular level variable: ThisCodeModule. This variable is now available for code manipulation.

Listing 22-4: **Getting the ActiveCodePane and CodeModule**

```
'<Private>—————————————————
Private ThisCodePane     As VBIDE.CodePane
Private ThisCodeModule   As VBIDE.CodeModule
'</Private>——————————————————

Private Sub Form_Activate()
    Dim ThisCodePane As VBIDE.CodePane

    On Error GoTo InvalidCodePane

    '— destroy previous CodeModule object
    Set ThisCodeModule = Nothing

    '— get the active pane and its module
    Set ThisCodePane = VBInstance.ActiveCodePane
    Set ThisCodeModule = ThisCodePane.CodeModule

    cmdOK.Enabled = True

    Exit Sub

InvalidCodePane:
    cmdOK.Enabled = False
    Call MsgBox("Activate a code module before _
        activating this form.", vbOKOnly + vbInformation)

End Sub
```

The CodeModule object contains a Members collection that represents the actual code and contains a number of Member objects. There are seven types of member objects, as shown in Table 22-2.

Table 22-2
Type of Member Objects of a CodeModule

Type	Description
vbext_mt_Method	Represents a method (procedure, or proc)
vbext_mt_Property	Represents a property procedure
vbext_mt_Variable	Represents a modular-level variable
vbext_mt_Event	Represents an event
vbext_mt_Enum	Represents an enumerated value
vbext_mt_Const	Represents a modular-level constant
vbext_mt_EventSink	Represents an event sink

The Member object contains several properties — some of which define the starting location and number of lines of code belonging to the particular Member. This information is then supplied to the Lines method of a CodeModule object to retrieve the actual code. Listing 22-5 shows how to retrieve all the procedures, or members, within a code module and place them in a ListView control. In order to use this function properly, make sure your ListView control (lvwMembers) has the following four columns: Name, Type, Location, and Number of Lines.

Listing 22-5: **Retrieve All the Members of a Code Module**

```
Private Sub GetMembers()
    Dim TheseMembers    As VBIDE.Members
    Dim InstMember      As VBIDE.Member
    Dim WorkingItem     As ListItem
    Dim NumberLines     As Long
    Dim ThisType        As String

    '— clear the lists
    lvwMembers.ListItems.Clear

    '— get the Members collection
    Set TheseMembers = ThisCodeModule.Members

    On Error Resume Next
    '— list each member
    For Each InstMember In TheseMembers

    Select Case InstMember.Type
```

(continued)

Listing 22-5 *(continued)*

```
            Case vbext_mt_Event
                NumberLines = 1
                ThisType = "Event"
            Case vbext_mt_Property
                '_____

                ' this example only retrieves the
                ' "_Get" property procedure there may
                ' also be "_Set" and "_Let" procedures
                '_____

                NumberLines = _
                    ThisCodeModule.ProcCountLines _
                    (InstMember.Name, vbext_pk_Get)
                ThisType = "Property"
            Case vbext_mt_Const
                NumberLines = 1
                ThisType = "Constant"
            Case vbext_mt_Variable
                NumberLines = 1
                ThisType = "Variable"
            Case vbext_mt_Method
                NumberLines = _
                    ThisCodeModule.ProcCountLines _
                    (InstMember.Name, vbext_pk_Proc)
                ThisType = "Method"
        End Select

        '— add the member information to the list
        Set WorkingItem = _
            lvwMembers.ListItems.Add _
            (, , InstMember.Name, , InstMember.Type)
        WorkingItem.SubItems(1) = ThisType
        WorkingItem.SubItems(2) = InstMember.CodeLocation
        WorkingItem.SubItems(3) = NumberLines

    Next

Cleanup:
    Set InstMember = Nothing
    Set TheseMembers = Nothing
    Set WorkingItem = Nothing

    Exit Sub

InvalidObject:
    MsgBox "Unable to get a required object." & vbCrLf _
        & Err.Description, vbOKOnly + vbInformation
    GoTo Cleanup

End Sub
```

Listing 22-6 retrieves lines of code using the `ThisCodeModule` object and a starting point, and the number of lines to retrieve (the previous function showed you how to get the starting point and number of lines).

Listing 22-6: **Retrieve Code from Visual Basic into the Add-In**

```
Private Function RetrieveCode(StartLine As Long, _
    NumLines As Long) As String

    RetrieveCode = ThisCodeModule.Lines(StartLine, NumLines)

End Function
```

Earlier, we talked about expert assistants that would look through your code and make suggestions. Now that you know how to get to the code, the next step to build an intelligent code-parser and pattern-recognition engine combined with a knowledge base.

Adding code to Visual Basic

Okay, we've shown you a way for an add-in to access all the code within Visual Basic. Now, let's take a look at how your add-in can add code to a code module. Listing 22-7 adds an `If-Then-Else` statement at the top of a code module.

Listing 22-7: Code for Adding an If-Then-Else Statement

```
Private Sub cmdOK_Click()
    Dim ThisStr     As String
    Dim StartLine   As Long
    Dim StartCol    As Long
    Dim EndLine     As Long
    Dim EndCol      As Long


    '— get the current cursor position
    Call ThisCodePane.GetSelection _
       (StartLine, StartCol, EndLine, EndCol)

    ThisStr = "If expression Then" & vbCrLf & vbCrLf
    ThisStr = ThisStr & "ElseIf expression Then" _
       & vbCrLf & vbCrLf

    ThisStr = ThisStr & "Else" & vbCrLf & vbCrLf
    ThisStr = ThisStr & "End If"
    Call ThisCodeModule.InsertLines(StartLine, ThisStr)

End Sub
```

There are other methods that can be used to add code to a `CodeModule` object.
These are as follows:

✦ `AddFromFile`—Inserts the contents of a file starting on the line preceding the
first procedure in the code module. If the module doesn't contain procedures,
`AddFromFile` places the contents of the file at the end of the module.

✦ `AddFromString`—Inserts the text starting on the line preceding the
first procedure in the module. If the module doesn't contain procedures,
`AddFromString` places the text at the end of the module.

✦ `ReplaceLine`—Replaces an existing line of code with a specified line of code.

More on the Extensibility Model

So far we have explained how to create your first add-in and use it to add code to a
`CodeModule`. Now, let's use our new capability to add a form to a project, add
controls to that form, and finally set some of the properties of those controls.
Figure 22-10 shows the collections and objects associated with these activities.

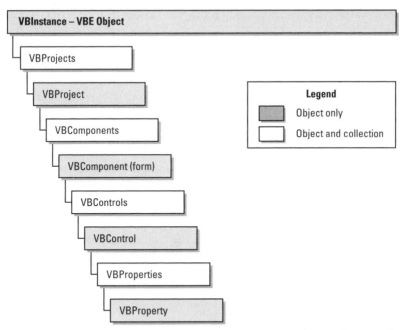

Figure 22-10: Extensibility objects and collections related to VB forms and controls

To add a new form to a project, you will actually be adding a form to the VBComponents collection contained within a VBProject. All the forms, class modules, and code modules, as well at other design objects, are considered to be *components* in the extensibility model. We will use the Add method of the VBComponents collection to add our form. The Add method returns a VBComponent object that we will cache in a modular variable, as shown in Listing 22-8.

Listing 22-8: **Adding a Form**

```
'<Private>────────────────────
Private NewForm    As VBIDE.VBComponent
'</Private>────────────────────

Private Sub cmdAddForm_Click()
    Set NewForm = VBInstance. _
        ActiveVBProject.VBComponents.Add(vbext_ct_VBForm)
End Sub
```

Some other component types are as follows:

`vbext_ct_StdModule` — The component is a code module.

`vbext_ct_ClassModule` — The component is a class module.

`vbext_ct_VBMDIForm` — The component is an MDI form.

In this example, as in previous examples, the variable `VBInstance` was set to be the instance of the Visual Basic session that was passed into our add-in in the `OnConnection` event.

Now let's add two controls to this new form. To manipulate design attributes, we must use the `Designer` object. We will also use the `VBControls` collection, which is a collection of all the controls on a particular form. As in the form we added, we're going to save the new controls in modular variables so that we can use these variables to set properties of the new controls. This process is shown in Listing 22-9.

Listing 22-9: **Adding the Controls**

```
'<Private>——————————————
Private NewOK          As VBIDE.VBControl
Private NewCancel      As VBIDE.VBControl
'</Private>——————————————

Private Sub cmdAddControl_Click()
    Dim TheseControls As VBIDE.VBControls

    Set TheseControls = NewForm.Designer.VBControls

    Set NewOK = TheseControls.Add("VB.CommandButton")
    Set NewCancel = TheseControls.Add("VB.CommandButton")

End Sub
```

Notice how we are using the `NewForm` object that was returned and the `Add` method of the `VBComponents` collection. Finally, to complete our example, we will set some properties of these new controls, as shown in Listing 22-10.

Listing 22-10: **Setting Properties of Controls**

```
Private Sub cmdSetProps_Click()

    With NewOK
        .Properties("Top") = 200
        .Properties("Left") = 5000
        .Properties("Height") = 375
        .Properties("Width") = 1125
        .Properties("Caption") = "OK"
        .Properties("Default") = True
    End With

    With NewCancel
        .Properties("Top") = _
            NewOK.Properties("Top") _
            + NewOK.Properties("Height") + 45
        .Properties("Left") = NewOK.Properties("Left")
        .Properties("Height") = 375
        .Properties("Width") = 1125
        .Properties("Caption") = "Cancel"
        .Properties("Cancel") = True
    End With

End Sub
```

The entire extensibility model is too diverse and complex a subject for just one chapter, but we have shown you how to manipulate code, add forms, add controls, and set object properties. We hope you have come up with ideas of your own on how to exploit these capabilities.

Summary

There are many obvious uses for add-ins, yet the capability also offers opportunities to create some really neat tools, such as expert assistants. Such an add-in is able to capture the experiences of one or more experts and make it available to every developer on your team. Dream on!

✦   ✦   ✦

ActiveX Components

One of the most exciting and powerful features of Visual Basic is its capability to create reusable *components*. The significant benefits of using component-based architecture are as follows:

> ◆ Components let you encapsulate program functionality into easily transportable units.

> ◆ Components' functionality may be shared by all your applications that require it.

> ◆ You can update the application by simply updating the components that it uses.

Visual Basic-Authored Components

The power of components is not new. Windows started using independent, shared, reusable code modules with the dynamic link library (DLL). A testament to its success is that 10 years later the modules are still in use. Over time, this concept has evolved from simple shared blocks of reusable code into dynamic, active participants in applications — components.

Visual Basic utilizes two main classes of components: OLE servers and ActiveX UserControls (OCXs). The major difference between these two classes lies in how they interact with an application.

OLE servers

OLE servers are blocks of shared code that are executable programs in their own right. You create an OLE server and compile it into a separate executable program with an .EXE or .DLL extension. OLE servers with a .DLL extension are called *in-process servers*; those with an .EXE extension are *out-of-process servers*.

"Out-of-process" means that the component is a separate program or process from the application that addresses it, and does not share address space with that application. As discussed in Chapters 21 – 24, this out-of-process mechanism results in lower performance but has advantages, too. For an out-of-process server, an intermediary is required to communicate back and forth between the application process in one address space and the component process in another address space. That intermediary technology is object linking and embedding — hence the name, OLE server. "In-process" means that the component shares address space with the application using it; no intermediary is required for the component to communicate with the application or with other in-process components, resulting in higher performance.

These types of components are unidirectional with regard to Visual Basic program flow. That is to say, your VB application accesses the properties and methods of the OLE server component, and the OLE server returns information to your application. An OLE server cannot make contact with your application of its own accord; your application is the originator of all activity with the OLE server. Figure 23-1 shows the communication flow between an OLE server and a VB application.

Properties and Methods of OLE Server

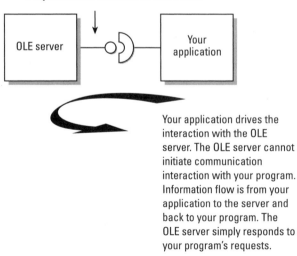

Your application drives the interaction with the OLE server. The OLE server cannot initiate communication interaction with your program. Information flow is from your application to the server and back to your program. The OLE server simply responds to your program's requests.

Figure 23-1: The direction of information flow between an OLE server and an application

UserControl components

UserControls are truly advanced. Visual Basic UserControls are ActiveX controls with the file extension .OCX. Note that Visual Basic-authored UserControls are ActiveX controls, but not all ActiveX controls are written using Visual Basic. Further, just because a file possesses the .OCX extension, that does not make it an ActiveX control. ActiveX is a specification developed by Microsoft that defines a software interface between an application and a component.

ActiveX components are in-process; however, they have the capacity for bi-directional interaction. Unlike OLE servers, UserControls can generate standard VB events in your applications. This allows your UserControls to communicate with your VB application, even if the application did not initiate the request. This is a key benefit to ActiveX UserControls because they allow for components to perform work and then notify the application if an error occurs or the work completes. Figure 23-2 shows the communication flow between a UserControl and a VB application.

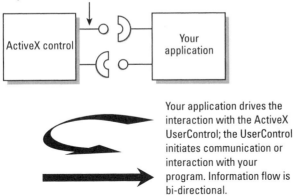

Figure 23-2: The direction of information flow between an ActiveX UserControl and a VB application

ActiveX is a Microsoft component technology supported by dozens and dozens of applications, including Internet Explorer, Netscape Navigator, Access, Word, Excel, PowerPoint, Visio, and AutoCAD. Further, you can create ActiveX components using Visual C++, Borland C++ or C++ Builder, Borland Delphi, or Visual Basic.

The *host container* is that part of an application that actually connects to, queries, and manages the ActiveX component and its interfaces. If you develop carefully, your Visual Basic UserControls will run in a variety of host containers. We created an ActiveX UserControl and then displayed it in several ActiveX hosts. Take a look at how Microsoft Excel displays available ActiveX components (Figure 23-3) versus

Microsoft Access (Figure 23-4) and Microsoft Visual Basic (Figure 23-5). In each case, you'll find our Modern GuardX Protection Control, which is exactly the same component made available to all three containers.

Figure 23-3: How ActiveX components are accessed in the Microsoft Excel ActiveX host

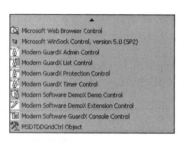

Figure 23-4: How ActiveX components are accessed in the Microsoft Access ActiveX host

Figure 23-5: How ActiveX components are accessed in the Microsoft Visual Basic IDE

Even though many applications support ActiveX, most have slightly different host container implementations. Although the interprocess communications interfaces that define ActiveX are standardized, the mechanisms used to interact with the ActiveX object via programming source code are completely nonstandard. This is even true with regard to Microsoft.

Extender Object

Potential problems derive from the fact that an ActiveX control is hosted by another program. The program that hosts the ActiveX control may or may not make available certain additional properties via what's referred to as the Extender Object.

The Extender Object is a late bound interface through which you can access properties of the control that are maintained and controlled by the container of the control rather than by the control itself. Some examples of extender properties include the Name, Tag, and Left properties. If your controls will need to access and change extender properties, then you will be using the Extender Object.

The problem mentioned above arises because the ActiveX specification suggests that certain extender properties be available, but not all containers implement them. Further, many extender properties are unique to a given ActiveX host. You can create a control to access extender properties unique to a specific ActiveX host container, but this makes the control only fully usable in that specific ActiveX host. The ActiveX specification suggests that the Extender Object provide the following properties:

- ✦ Cancel — Returns True (-1) if the control is the default Cancel button for the container.
- ✦ Default — Returns True (-1) if the control is the default button for the container.
- ✦ Name — Returns the user-defined name of the control. Same value as the UserControl.DisplayName() property, but available in the InitProperties() event.
- ✦ Parent — An object that represents the container of the control. For example, in Visual Basic, a form, picture box, or frame control.
- ✦ Visible — Specifies whether the control is visible or not.

Note that all ActiveX hosts might not provide the above standard properties, and that specific ActiveX hosts may provide additional extender properties as well. For example, Visual Basic provides the following specific extender properties:

- ✦ Container — Returns an object that represents the container of the control.
- ✦ DragIcon — Specifies the icon to use when the control is dragged.
- ✦ DragMode — Specifies that the control will automatically drag, or that the user of the control must call the Drag() method.
- ✦ Enabled — Specifies that the control is enabled.
- ✦ Height — Specifies the height of the control in the container's scale units.
- ✦ HelpContextID — Specifies the help file context ID number to use when the F1 key is pressed and the control has the focus.

✦ `Index` — Specifies a position in a control array.

✦ `Left` — Specifies the left edge of the control with respect to the left edge of the container.

✦ `TabIndex` — Specifies the position of the control in the tab order of the container.

✦ `TabStop` — Specifies that the control will be in a tab list.

✦ `Tag` — Contains a user-defined value.

✦ `ToolTipText` — Contains text to display when the cursor hovers over the control for more than one second.

✦ `Top` — Specifies the top edge of the control with respect to the top edge of the container.

✦ `WhatsThisHelpID` — Specifies the help file context ID number to use when "What's This" help is used on the control.

✦ `Width` — Specifies the width of the control.

ActiveX hosts may also provide methods, objects, and events via the Extender Object. Visual Basic provides the following methods and events:

✦ `Drag()` — Begins, ends, or cancels a drag operation of the control.

✦ `DragDrop()` — An event raised when another control is dropped on this control.

✦ `DragOver()` — An event raised when another control is dragged over this control.

✦ `GotFocus()` — An event raised when the control gets focus.

✦ `LostFocus()` — An event raised when the control loses focus.

✦ `Move()` — Moves the control.

✦ `SetFocus()` — Sets focus to the control.

✦ `ShowWhatsThis()` — Displays the help file topic defined by `WhatsThisHelpID`.

✦ `ZOrder` — Moves the control to the front or back of the z-order.

If you choose to use the Extender Object, you must take great care — otherwise, your control will be limited to a specific ActiveX host. If you want your control to only work with one ActiveX host, this is fine. For example, if your control is used only in other Visual Basic applications you create, you may safely take advantage of the Extender Object and the additional features it provides. However, if you want to create commercial control that you plan to sell to as many developers (and for as many ActiveX hosts) as possible, then you will probably not want to use the Extender Object at all.

When using the Extender Object, note that it is not available to you in the UserControls `Initialize` event. However, it is available to you in the UserControls `InitProperties` and `ReadProperties` events. Always implement error handling, in case the Extender property you access is not available in the current ActiveX host of your control. Visual Basic will generate error number 438, "Object doesn't support this property or method" if you attempt to access an extender property or method that the current ActiveX host does not provide. If an error occurs, you should degrade as gracefully as possible. For example:

```
Private Sub UserControl_InitProperties()
    ' set this controls Caption property
    ' the default Name of this control.
    ' turn on error handling
    On Error Resume Next
    ' try to access extender objects name property
    Caption = Extender.Name
    ' if an error occurs, fall back on a hard coded
    ' name.
    If Err.Number = 438 Then
        Caption = "my control"
    End If
End Sub
```

The above code attempts to assign the `Caption` property of a control to the Extender Object's `Name` property. If the ActiveX hosts provides a `Name` property, no error is generated. However, if the Extender Object does not provide a `Name` property, Visual Basic will generate error 438. If error 438 occurs, the code above then assigns the `Caption` property with a hard-coded default value.

In summary, if you know your ActiveX host will always be the same, you can take advantage of Visual Basic UserControl Extender Object properties. If you want your control to be portable to as many ActiveX hosts as possible, avoid using the Extender Object.

Creating ActiveX UserControls

To begin creating an ActiveX UserControl, choose ActiveX Control from the Visual Basic New Project dialog. Visual Basic creates a new project with UserControl as a special type of form.

Think of this UserControl design window as a form. You can drop controls onto it, just as you do on a form. You can print to a UserControl, just like a form. However, unlike a form, the UserControl will compile into an ActiveX control. You can then use your ActiveX control in any host that supports it, including Visual Basic.

Basic UserControl settings

When you create a new control, there are a number of decisions you need to make. These decisions affect how your control operates and how it interacts with the users. In this case, there are two users to take into account rather than just one: the ultimate end-user of the application that utilizes your control, and the developer/user who employs your control in an application being built within their own Visual Basic environment.

UserControls are quite flexible and offer a wide range of capabilities. You can create UserControls that don't have a visual user interface, or you can create UserControls with dialogs that require substantial user interaction — the choice is yours.

No matter your end goal, there are a number of basic requirements that all UserControls have in common. Although there are dozens of UserControl properties, you really only need to focus on a few basic ones initially. Every control will be faced with the following basic requirements:

  ✦ Your control will require a name.

  ✦ You will need to decide if your control will have a toolbar icon.

  ✦ You will need to decide if your control will be visible or invisible to the developer/user, as well as to the end user.

  ✦ You will need to determine the default size and properties of your control.

UserControl name

Every UserControl requires a unique `Name` property. In fact, when you create a new UserControl, Visual Basic automatically assigns a new `Name` property to it — usually `UserControl`*x*, where *x* is the next available whole number, starting with 1.

> **Note** Choose your UserControl's name carefully; it must be unique. If another control has the same name as your control, Visual Basic will not load it.

The name of the control is quite important. Not only is it shown to the developer who uses your control, it is also used to represent your control in the developer's source code. When the developer/user of your control attempts to manipulate its methods and properties, its `Name` property is used to distinguish the specific control being addressed. The value of this property is referred to as the control's *display name*. The developer may rename this instance of the control to whatever he or she chooses, but this only changes the display name for a particular instance, not for the control itself. You can access the `UserControl.DisplayName` property to read the value, or you can also get to this value via the `UserControl.Extender.Name` property.

The display name contrasts with the control's *class name*, which you define for the UserControl at design time as you create your UserControl. You set the name of your control via the Visual Basic Property Browser. The following steps show how you access the UserControl and set its basic properties:

1. From the Project Explorer window shown in Figure 23-6, right-click on your new UserControl, and from the popup shown in Figure 23-7, choose View Object.

Figure 23-6: The Visual Basic Project Explorer

Figure 23-7: Viewing the new UserControl object

2. The new UserControl window, which looks like a form, should look similar to the one in Figure 23-8. Click on the gray "pegboard" area of the UserControl window, and press F4.

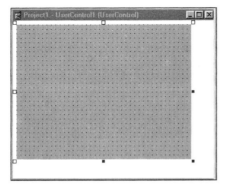

Figure 23-8: The new UserControl

3. In the Properties window shown in Figure 23-9, enter the name for your control under the listing for the Name property. You'll find it at the very top, under (Name), *not* under *N* in the alphabetized list.

Figure 23-9: The UserControl shown in the Property Browser

Figure 23-9 shows the properties for a UserControl whose `Name` property is set to `myControl`. Of course, you can give it any name you want. Every time a user drops an instance of your control into a host form, it will be labeled with a default name of `myControl` next to a whole number. The first instance of the control in a single container would be `myControl1`. If you were to drop another instance of your control into the same container, it would be titled `myControl2`, and so on. Of course, the user of your control can change the name at design time — but only the display name.

The name you enter during the control's design time remains constant, and is referred to as the *class name*. Users of your control can make use of its class name (as opposed to its display name) by using the Visual Basic `TypeOf` keyword. `TypeOf` works only in conjunction with a Visual Basic `If` block. `TypeOf`, `If`, and the `Is` keyword combine to form a code construct that lets you examine an object to determine its class name. The syntax for using `TypeOf` is as follows:

```
If TypeOf txtText1 Is TextBox Then
    ' do something cool
    txtText1.Text = Date$
End If
```

In the above code, `txtText1` is a Visual Basic control — intrinsic, like a `TextBox`, a UserControl, or another ActiveX control. The `TypeOf` statement then evaluates the control (in this case, `txtText1`) to see if its class is `TextBox`. If the object represented by `txtText1` is of class `TextBox`, then the `If` block executes as `True`; otherwise, the `If` block executes as `False`. You can replace `txtText1` with any control, and `TextBox` with any class name. Even if the user changes the display name of your control, the internal class name remains constant.

UserControl Toolbar icon

All Visual Basic UserControls, with or without a visible user interface at runtime, possess a visible user interface for you, the developer, at design time. During design time, you can interact with the control as you develop it. To be able to identify controls at design time, all controls contain a Toolbar icon. The Toolbar icon is displayed in the Toolbox of the ActiveX host IDE (Visual Basic or VBA, for example). This icon defaults to the internal icon that Visual Basic uses for all UserControls, but you can change it to any image you desire.

The steps are simple: Create a bitmap 16 pixels high by 15 pixels wide and assign it to the ToolboxBitmap property in the Property Browser. The steps for doing this are easy:

1. Select your UserControl from the Visual Basic Project window.

2. Choose to View Object or simply double-click on the name of your UserControl in the Project window.

3. When the UserControl design sheet appears, press F4 to pull up the Visual Basic Property Browser.

4. Scroll down the Property Browser entries until you come to the property titled ToolboxBitmap.

5. Assign a bitmap to the ToolboxBitmap property and press Enter.

Then, when your control is loaded into the Visual Basic IDE, your custom image will appear in the toolbar. Note that this image will also be the image used by users of your control when they add your control to their Toolbox, and when they drop an instance of your control on a form in their project.

Note   The toolbar will automatically size a bitmap to fit, but for best results, use the defined measurements of 16 × 15 pixels.

The toolbar image is important; a well-designed icon will help the developer/user of your control understand what it does. This is often hard to accomplish in the small space given for a toolbar bitmap, but you should still strive to develop a system for drawing your toolbar bitmaps. If the project has more than one control, try to create a visual relationship among them using your bitmaps. The developer/user should be able to see that the controls belong together.

UserControl visibility

UserControls may be visible or invisible to the end user. Typically, controls that interact with the user of the software employing the control are visible. Controls that interact solely with the developer of the software are invisible. For example, if you are creating a formatted input control, you would want it to be visible so that the user can enter data into it. However, if the purpose of the control is to manage an INI file for the developer, then that control would be invisible. There is no sense in showing the end user an icon or control with which he or she cannot interact.

You determine the visibility of controls by setting the InvisibleAtRuntime() property of the Property Browser. Setting InvisibleAtRuntime() to True makes the control invisible to end users of the software; False makes it visible.

Note   You cannot change the InvisibleAtRuntime() property at runtime; it is a design-time-only property.

UserControl default property values

There are numerous other default properties of your UserControl component. You can designate the mouse pointer's shape and size, as well as the background colors and font settings. Although Visual Basic handles all the COM and OLE system interactions in the background, you are left to actually write the code that will implement your control's functionality.

Custom default properties are useful for implementing unique functionality into your controls. One of Visual Basic's most popular aspects is that it provides useful default values for many items. For example, when you drop a CommandButton control on a form, VB automatically names it Command*x* (where *x* is the next number in an incrementing numeric sequence). This makes it obvious what the object is (a Command button) and speeds development (you don't have to rename it to be useful unless you want to). Contrast this with other languages like Visual FoxPro and Access — dropping a new control into a FoxPro or Access form names the control Actxtctl*x* (where *x* is the next number in an incrementing numeric sequence). You are almost forced to stop work and define a name for the new control, because the default name is almost useless.

You can implement your own property defaults quite easily, as shown in the next section of this chapter. When you implement your control's default values, strive to create useful and laborsaving default values. Choose data for the default that is most likely to be what the user wants. For example, if you are creating a default value for a Caption() property, use the Extender.Name() property so that the Caption() property will mimic the action of the standard Visual Basic Label control.

Your initial Visual Basic UserControl has only some basic default properties (from the Visual Basic Extender Object), among them the size and position properties of Left, Top, Height, and Width, plus the crucial Enabled and Visible properties.

Constituent controls

One of the most exciting aspects of Visual Basic-authored UserControls is that you can embed other controls into your own UserControls. You then use these other controls, called *constituent controls*, as you would on a normal Visual Basic form. This allows you to leverage the functionality of controls that are already built.

Note Take note of license and legal issues relative to including other controls in your UserControls. Microsoft grants you the right to embed the intrinsic Visual Basic controls such as TextBox, Image, and Label into your UserControls. But others, such as the Tab Control and Grid Control have different license requirements.

A Visual Basic UserControl at design time may contain other controls in the same manner that a form does. You simply highlight your UserControl, then drag and drop other controls onto your UserControl. You then use these other controls as you would any control on a Visual Basic form.

Using constituent controls lets you create custom functionality. For example, you can mimic the very cool Access LabelBox — a text box with a label that stays attached. This is really handy for creating database entry screens that invariably require a text box with a descriptive label. If you create a UserControl that is composed of a standard Visual Basic TextBox and Label controls, you can then move, size, and place them as a single unit. This saves a lot of time when developing, because moving the UserControl moves both constituent controls at the same time. Because the constituent controls are contained in the UserControl, their size and positional relationship remain constant unless you change them via properties and methods of your UserControl.

Custom UserControl interfaces

You can add custom functionality to your controls quite easily. Writing code for a UserControl is exactly the same as writing code for any other Visual Basic component, such as a form, module, or class. You create variables, define constants, and declare procedures. Your procedures implement whatever functionality your control requires. You respond to events generated by the control during the lifetime of your UserControl or any constituent controls.

In most cases, the code you write for a form, module, or class is completely portable to UserControls. However, UserControls contain additional capabilities not found in forms, classes, or modules. UserControls also do not contain all the events of forms. UserControls are extended with special objects, events, properties, and methods found exclusively in the UserControl. You will need to use the special extensions found in UserControls to create the custom properties, methods, and events UserControls require. You can add properties, methods and events to your controls that allow the developer/user to interact with the control. These interfaces allow the developer/user and end users of your controls to access, store, and retrieve the value (in the form of functionality) your control provides.

Controls that you create using Visual Basic can support three basic types of customization. You can add custom

✦ Properties

✦ Methods

✦ Events

Custom properties may be read or written; custom methods are implemented by way of both `Function` and `Sub` procedures. A `Sub` procedure does not return a value, whereas a `Function` procedure does return a value.

Custom events will occur only in the `UserControl` class, which represents a host that employs your control's functionality. In the `UserControl` module, you simply generate the event with the `Raise` statement. The developer/user of your control may write code to handle the event within his or her own application. Certain events already occur within the `UserControl` class. So, do not confuse custom events you add to your control with these intrinsic events, which are designed as signals for the developer/user during the runtime of your control.

Custom properties

ActiveX UserControls have properties just like a form. In fact, you access the properties of the UserControl by clicking in the UserControl Design window and pressing F4, just like a form. However, you can also add custom properties, methods, and events to your UserControls that the developer/user of your control can access. For example, your application might require formatted text input, with special handling of nonstandard input. You might decide to create a control that automatically formats input depending on how a property has been set. The control then could fire an event if the data input was incorrect.

You can create a custom property using the Property Wizard or by writing code yourself. All the wizard does is autogenerate the rough code for you. For this example, we will create the code ourselves.

Properties are typically exposed interfaces to the code of the control. For example, your control might have a `Caption` property that stores a text string to be displayed. Let's create a new UserControl and give it a custom property titled `Caption`.

The first step is to create the UserControl itself. From the Visual Basic File menu, select New and choose User Control from the list.

The new UserControl has no custom methods, properties, or events. To give the UserControl a custom property, make one of your UserControl's Code windows the active window, switch to the code view of your UserControl, and then from the Tools menu select Add Procedure. VB will bring up the Add Procedure dialog shown in Figure 23-10.

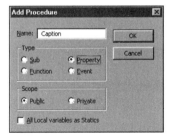

Figure 23-10: The Add Procedure dialog

To follow along with our example and create a custom property for UserControl, in the Add Procedure dialog, in the text box marked Name, type **Caption**. Then choose Property in the Type frame, and Public in the Scope frame. When done, click on OK and VB will create the framework for your new custom property automatically, in the form of two procedure declarations as shown in Figure 23-11.

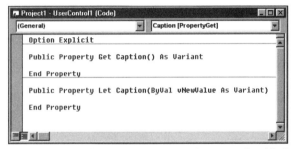

Figure 23-11: The custom property framework added by Visual Basic

The Add Procedure Dialog

The Add Procedure dialog allows you to create custom methods (Sub and/or Function procedures), custom properties, and events. In the Scope frame, you designate whether your procedure is to be made *private* or *public*. Public method and property procedures are accessible to developers/users, whereas Private procedures are only accessible to other procedures within the same UserControl module. Use Private when the procedure is only to be used by the control itself, and not accessed from an outside application. All user-accessible procedures — in other words, all your control's custom properties and methods — must be declared Public.

Visual Basic handles the interface to your users and the world outside of your UserControl, but you have to do all the work inside your control. When you use the Add Procedure dialog to generate procedure frameworks for the Property Get and Property Let procedures, those frameworks are capable of nothing, since there is no code in them. All these code frameworks do is expose the control to the developer/user. As the UserControl module stands now, if the developer attempts to read the Caption property, Visual Basic returns an empty variant. If the developer attempts to write to the Caption property, the data passed to the Property Let procedure is lost, since there is no code written yet to store or act on the data.

Let's add some code to the Property Get procedure to return a value. Before we can do this, we need to add a private variable to hold the data that the Property Get procedure will return. Add a variable to the Declarations section of the UserControl, like this:

```
Option Explicit

' property variables
Dim m_Caption As String
```

The m_Caption variable will be used to store the text string that the Caption property represents. Now we can update the Property Get procedure by assigning the m_Caption variable's contents to the procedure return value:

```
Public Property Get Caption() As Variant
    Caption = m_Caption
End Property
```

Now, when the user reads the Caption() property, the value stored in m_Caption is returned through the Caption property. We are halfway to a complete property! Next, add the code to allow the user to store information into the property as well. This is simply assigning a value to m_Caption:

```
Public Property Let Caption(ByVal vNewValue As Variant)
    m_Caption = vNewValue
End Property
```

Now, if the user writes to the property, the value carried in the vNewValue argument will be assigned to m_Caption, and stored. In this example, vNewValue is set by being the recipient of the argument on the right side of the equal sign in a property assignment equation, like this:

```
        MyControl.Caption = "Now is the time"
```

After the above code fragment is executed, vNewValue will contain "Now is the time," which in turn is stored in m_Caption. The Caption custom property may now be read or written. It stores a user-defined string, and returns that string when the user requests it.

Default property values

At this point, a feature you probably would like to see is *persistent data*, which is data that remains constant from instance to instance. For example, suppose the user starts a program that uses your control, and sets its Caption property to "Now is the time." Normally, when the user ends the program, the control "forgets" the value of m_Caption. What you may prefer is for the UserControl to store a default value for m_Caption, but also to allow the user of your control to be able to replace that default value with a persistent value. Visual Basic accomplishes this by way of an internal object called the property bag. The property bag stores user-defined data in the UserControl's host container. For example, in the case of a Visual Basic form, the data is stored on disk in the form's FRM file if the data is of ASCII format, like a string; or the form's FRX file if the data is of binary format, like a picture.

The default property value is a value you, the developer, decide on. For our Caption() property, let's make the default value be the name of the control. We start by declaring a constant to hold the name of the control, in the general Declarations section of the project:

```
Const m_Def_Caption = "MyControl 1.0"
```

After you have defined a default value for a property, you need to assign the default value to the property. You need to assign the default value just once, when the control is created. Thereafter, the users can change the value to whatever they want. A UserControl has several events that are not visible to the user of the completed control. Rather, these events occur to communicate information to you, the developer, about the status of the control. One event that the UserControl fires only occurs when the control is created, the first time it is dropped on a form. That event is titled InitProperties.

In the InitProperties event, you add code to assign the default value to the variable that maintains the value of the property; in the example of our Caption property, that variable is titled m_Caption.

```
Private Sub UserControl_InitProperties()
    ' assign default one time only
    m_Caption = m_Def_Caption
End Sub
```

The InitProperties event fires the first time the developer places a control on a form. Use the Private Sub UserControl_InitProperties event procedure to set up the default values of your properties. Here, we set up m_Caption (which is returned from the Caption property) to have a default value of m_Def_Caption. Now, each time the developer creates an instance of our control, the Caption property is preset with the value contained in the m_Def_Caption constant.

The new control now has a default value for Caption, but user-defined values assigned to Caption are lost when the program using the control ends. However, using the PropertyBag, we can also store user-defined values for custom properties. Only user-defined values entered during design time are saved, but this is exactly the behavior we want.

The user of your control may be another developer, who may choose to have the Caption property default to a different value. Visual Basic provides two additional events that allow you to create persistent user-defined values for your properties: ReadProperties and WriteProperties.

Default properties

The properties of our new control may be read or written to, but the control does not yet possess a value. Controls may have a property defined that is the default for the control. This property may be read or set by using the control's name without indicating a specific property. For example, for Visual Basic TextBox controls, the Text property is the default. In this case, the following two lines are equivalent:

```
Text1.Text = "My Control"
Text1 = "My Control"
```

You, the developer, can define any custom property to be the default for the control. To define a default property, use the following steps:

1. Create a property with both Get and Let (or Set) methods.

2. Switch to the Code view of your UserControl and position the cursor into the code for either of the property's methods.

3. Choose the Tools menu, then the Procedure Attributes submenu to display the Procedure Attributes dialog.

4. On the Procedure Attributes dialog, choose the Advanced button to expand the dialog to show advanced property options.

5. Under the Procedure ID drop-down, choose the entry marked (Default).

6. Choose OK to accept and close the dialog.

After these steps, the property will act as the default for the control. Note that you can only define one property as the default property. From this point on, that property will operate as the default value for the control.

Saving values with the WriteProperties event

Visual Basic fires the UserControl's WriteProperties event when the value or setting of one of the properties you created for the UserControl is changed by the developer/user. Given the state of our code right now, you might ask yourself how

Visual Basic knows that a user-defined property has changed. The answer is, you need to tell VB the property has changed! For this purpose, an intrinsic method titled `PropertyChanged` is provided. You use `PropertyChanged` to tell Visual Basic a property value has changed, as in the following example:

```
Public Property Let Caption(ByVal vNewValue As Variant)
    m_Caption = vNewValue
    PropertyChanged "Caption"
End Property
```

Here, `PropertyChanged` tells Visual Basic that the `Caption` property has a new value. If this control is currently in design mode (that is, being used by a developer or designer in the Visual Basic IDE), then Visual Basic will fire another event when the project or form is saved. That event is the `WriteProperties` event. In the `WriteProperties` event procedure, you write the code to save the changed value into the host container — in our example, a form:

```
Private Sub UserControl_WriteProperties(PropBag As PropertyBag)
    Call PropBag.WriteProperty("Caption", m_Caption,
m_Def_Caption)
End Sub
```

Note how you again refer to the property by a string representation of its actual exposed name, `"Caption"`. The second argument to the `WriteProperty` method is the value to write into the property, in this case `m_Caption` (which contains the value "Now is the time"). The last argument is a default value to write into the property in case the user-defined property data is not available. It is good practice to use the default value for the property as the third argument to `WriteProperty`.

Note   Remember that the name of the member property must be passed by the `WriteProperty` method as a string. Do not change the name of the text string when you internationalize your control. The text of the name must match the name of the declaration for that property.

Now, when the user sets the `Caption` property, that setting is stored in `m_Caption`. In the `Property Let` procedure, you tell Visual Basic that the property has changed value, and VB then fires the `WriteProperties` event if the control is in design mode. The `WriteProperties` event procedure stores the value of the property into the `PropertyBag` object, which represents the host's data storage.

Reading values with the ReadProperties event

After the user-defined data is stored in the `PropertyBag`, you will also want to be able to read it. Visual Basic calls the `ReadProperties` event any time the `PropertyBag` is read. This occurs when the control initializes at runtime, and

during design time when you edit a property using the Property Browser. The
ReadProperties event procedure is where you set up values for the control; again,
Visual Basic handles the hard work, while you have to write the actual code to
assign values:

```
Private Sub UserControl_ReadProperties(PropBag As PropertyBag)
    m_Caption = PropBag.ReadProperty("Caption", m_Def_Caption)
End Sub
```

The first argument to the ReadProperty method is the name of the property to
read — in this case, "Caption". The second argument is a default value in case
there is nothing stored in the PropertyBag object for this property. This is true if
the developer/user has never changed the default value of this property.

> **Note**　You can hard-code default values; however, declaring a default constant allows for
> more maintainable code.

The code is now complete. Your custom property can be read and written to. And if
the user of the control is a developer in design-time mode of the IDE, any changes
made to the property using the Property Browser are persistent — that is, they are
stored and may be retrieved at a later date.

Custom events

One of the most powerful features of ActiveX UserControls is their bi-directional
communications capability. Your control can signal its host by firing a custom
event. You define custom events in your source code, in the Declarations section.
Then, anywhere in the body of your control, you can tell Visual Basic to fire the
event in the user's host.

The first step is to define the custom event. To continue our example, in the
Declarations section of the UserControl module, add the new event as shown here:

```
Option Explicit
' events
Event CaptionChanged()
```

> **Note**　Custom events do not occur in the UserControl; rather, they occur in the host that is
> currently running the UserControl.

Using the Event keyword tells Visual Basic that the following name will be an event.
In this case, the name of the event is CaptionChanged. Unlike custom properties,
custom events are never enclosed in quotes. You are required to close the event
declaration with a set of parentheses.

You may optionally pass arguments to your event as well. In this case, you declare the event arguments just like a custom property. You can permit the user to modify the argument data you pass when calling the event. This allows for the user of your control to communicate back to your control. For example, you might define an argument to allow the user to indicate what action to take on an error — perhaps a value of 1 means try again, 2 means give up, and so on. If you want to allow the user to modify the argument, then you must not declare the event using ByVal. If you declare the event using ByVal, no changes made to the argument will be returned to your code. Again, note that no quotes are used in the declaration:

```
Option Explicit
' events
Event CaptionChanged(Msg As String)
```

In this case, the event will accept a single argument Text, declared as a string. The developer/user of your control will see the custom event in the event drop-down when he or she uses your compiled control. The following code shows how this user will see the custom event CaptionChanged() within his or her own source code:

```
Option Explicit
Private Sub UserControl1_CaptionChanged(Msg As String)
        ' user writes code in here
End Sub
```

After you have declared the custom event, you need to *raise* it in the user's code. This is done using the Visual Basic RaiseEvent method. RaiseEvent causes the custom event to be recognized by your control's host. You call RaiseEvent with the event name and any optional arguments:

```
RaiseEvent CaptionChanged(vNewValue)
```

Notice that the custom event name is not in quotes, and also that the arguments are enclosed within parentheses.

Note   You can also pass arguments to the event procedure. If the user makes changes to the argument passed, you can read the changes in the argument. To prevent the user from changing the value you pass to the event procedure, declare the event using the ByVal **keyword.**

You can raise custom events from anywhere in the body of your control; for our example, we will raise the event from within the Property Let procedure for the Caption property. This means that when the user of your control sets the Caption property, the control's CaptionChanged event will also fire, and it will pass the value of the string the user set in the Text argument of the CaptionChanged event.

```
Public Property Let Caption(ByVal vNewValue As Variant)
    m_Caption = vNewValue
    PropertyChanged "Caption"
    RaiseEvent CaptionChanged(vNewValue)
End Property
```

Appropriate Uses for User Controls

Just because you *can* do something, doesn't mean that you *should* do something. This is true more than ever with ActiveX. An ActiveX control can quickly become quite complex. If you are not careful, the work required to create the control may outweigh the benefits. Valid uses for UserControls should include those places where you desire a component that can raise events in its host, or to encapsulate some code or dialogs into a reusable format that may be updated outside of the actual host application.

UserControls should be focused toward creating reusable components of a larger application. UserControls work best for providing custom functionality not available elsewhere. Other uses of UserControls are for their unique capability to generate events in user code. In some cases, this capability alone is enough to justify using a UserControl — for example, an object that can signal the container when a function is complete, replicating a Windows callback function.

Combining constituent controls into a UserControl provides very powerful customization capabilities. However, don't spend more time on the UserControl than it would take to simply use the constituent controls themselves.

If you require no more than an object with properties and methods and to raise events, consider using a class instead. UserControls consume more resources than a class due to their relatively complex interface to an application. Classes get compiled into your application and cannot be updated outside of the application — if you desire properties, methods, and events without persistent data storage, a class is the way to go.

If you require properties, methods, and events with persistent data storage, or require the component to be updatable outside of the application, then UserControls are the way to go. Just remember that the time and energy required to design, test, and build a component are about the same as for any normal Visual Basic-authored piece of software. When you decide to create your own UserControls, do not underestimate the testing and debugging requirements — you will need to test each and every property, method, and event to ensure proper functioning. Also, you will need to implement sophisticated error-handling because any error in the control can be fatal, rendering your application useless.

Summary

UserControls are a powerful feature of Visual Basic. You can create encapsulated functionality with custom properties, methods, and events that provide custom solutions to common programming problems.

✦ Because the actual physical ActiveX UserControl resides in a separate file from the application, you can update the UserControl without updating the entire application. This is one of the most compelling reasons to consider using UserControls in your applications.

✦ A UserControl has an Extender Object that makes available additional properties, methods, and possible events for your control. However, not all ActiveX hosts implement all extender properties — in fact, many do not. Therefore, use Extender Object properties with great care or you can render your control nonfunctional in ActiveX hosts that do not support the Extender Object properties your control relies on. For controls that require maximum ActiveX host support, we recommend that you avoid the Extender Object.

✦ You can create custom solutions that include other constituent controls which greatly reduce your workload — this is often one of the main reasons for creating your own UserControls.

✦ Writing a custom property requires multiple lines of code, with several declarations under multiple UserControl events. The process is straightforward; without patience and practice, however, it's easy to overlook a step and face maddening problems. We recommend you use the UserControl Wizard, which allows you to implement custom properties, methods, and events quickly and easily.

✦   ✦   ✦

ActiveX UserControl Secrets

✦ ✦ ✦ ✦

In This Chapter

Property sheets

Hiding properties
and methods

Keeping public
properties out of the
Object Browser

Default methods

Enum and custom
properties

✦ ✦ ✦ ✦

Enough idiosyncrasies exist in the creation of Visual Basic ActiveX UserControls to make you think someone set out to make it difficult to access all the features Visual Basic provides. This is, of course, not true.

However, it is a symptom of the growing complexity that has affected Visual Basic since Version 1.0. With each new release come new features. It becomes more and more difficult for Microsoft to fit those features into the old interface and maintain the look and feel of Visual Basic. Microsoft engineers do their best to squeeze new features, such as ActiveX, into the existing shell — but sometimes things get lost.

Some useful features for finishing off a professional-quality control are either quite poorly documented or not documented at all, anywhere. You need access to these ActiveX UserControl secrets if you want the following:

- ✦ Default properties
- ✦ Default methods
- ✦ Default events
- ✦ Property sheets
- ✦ To hide properties or methods from the user
- ✦ To keep public properties out of the Property Browser
- ✦ To implement Enum data types in your control properties
- ✦ To manage the name that appears for your controls in various hosts

You can customize many aspects of the UserControls you create. This isn't required in many cases. If you want to sell your UserControl or create a complete UserControl with all the bells and whistles of commercial ActiveX controls, however, then you will need to delve a little deeper into the Visual Basic implementation of ActiveX UserControls.

Customization of UserControls

The key to customization of UserControls is the Visual Basic Object Browser. The Object Browser enables you to do the following:

✦ Add custom help to any custom property, method, or event

✦ Add custom help to the control itself

✦ Provide a description of each custom property, method, and event

✦ Provide a description for the control itself

✦ Create default properties and events

✦ Connect property pages to custom methods and properties

✦ Define the Visual Basic Property Browser section in which the custom properties or methods will appear

✦ Hide any custom method or property

✦ Prevent any custom method or property from appearing in the property browser

✦ Bind any property to a database field

Object Browser

Figure 24-1 shows the Visual Basic Object Browser. You invoke the Object Browser from within your UserControl Code window. Simply view your UserControl code, click anywhere in the body of the code, and press F2 to call up the Object Browser.

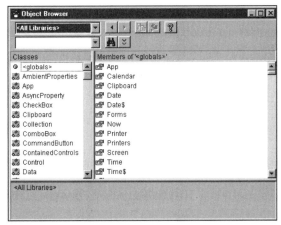

Figure 24-1: The Visual Basic Object Browser

In Figure 24-1, we are ready to select an object to browse. The Object Browser shows all the ActiveX interfaces (controls, property pages, constants, and so on) that this object exposes.

The Object Browser is composed of four sections:

The top of the dialog contains searching and filtering capabilities to enable you to locate a particular object — and any property of that object — quickly.

The left pane, titled Classes, contains all the properties, methods, and events the currently selected object exposes.

The right pane, titled Members, contains all the properties, methods, and events that the class contains.

The bottom section shows extra information about the currently selected object or member.

To select our UserControl, choose the UserControl's project name from the drop-down list, as shown in Figure 24-2.

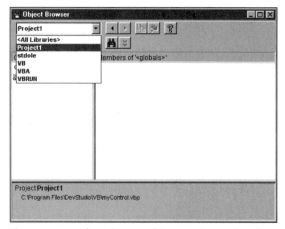

Figure 24-2: Choosing an object to view using the Visual Basic Object Browser

After selecting our project from the list of available objects to browse, notice our UserControl named `UserControl1`, now in the Classes pane (Figure 24-3). After you click on `UserControl1`, you will be able to see all the methods, properties, constants, enums, and events contained within that object.

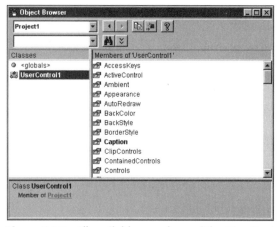

Figure 24-3: All available members of the UserControl1 object

Notice the `UserControl` class contains many properties. It also contains a single custom property: `Caption`, added to the UserControl project in the last chapter. Custom properties, methods, and events are indicated in boldface in the Object Browser. The Object Browser enables you to peruse an object, seeing its exposed methods, properties, constants, and events. The Object Browser also serves as a method for accessing the definition of a custom property, method, or event. The Object Browser also provides access to the procedure attributes of your UserControls properties, methods, and events. The procedure attributes are accessible via the Tools menu's Procedure Attributes submenu — the Object Browser simply provides a shortcut.

The panes of the Object Browser enable you to choose objects and their properties and methods. When you select an object or one of its properties and methods, you can then customize them. By choosing the class from the left-hand pane of the Property Browser, we can then see the customization options.

To set custom options for the `UserControl` object, right-click `UserControl` in the Classes pane of the Object Browser, and then choose Properties from the Context menu, as shown in Figure 24-4.

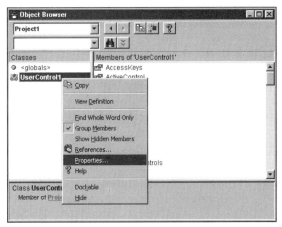

Figure 24-4: The Context menu for the UserControl1 object of the Object Browser Classes list

Member Properties dialog

Choosing Properties from the Context menu pulls up the Members dialog. Here, you can enter a help context ID number to link your control to a help file. You may also enter a description of your control (Figure 24-5).

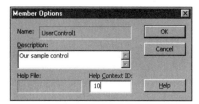

Figure 24-5: Entering a description for our UserControl

The description entered into the Member Options dialog is displayed in the lower pane of the Object Browser, as shown in Figure 24-6. The description enables users of your controls to identify your control and its purpose.

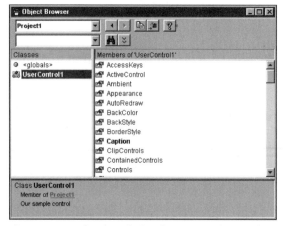

Figure 24-6: The description for our UserControl displayed in the Object Browser

The Help Context ID field enables you to connect your control to a help file. You enter the help context ID number of the page of help you want to display whenever the user selects your control and presses F1. This help is also used as default help for the control's design time. Whenever the developer/user highlights a method or property and presses F1, or whenever the user chooses Help from a property page, this help page is shown.

Procedure Attributes dialog

You can further customize each individual method and property of your UserControl to provide custom help. Choose the member to be customized from the Members pane of the Object Browser, then right-click and choose Properties from the Context menu, as shown in Figure 24-7.

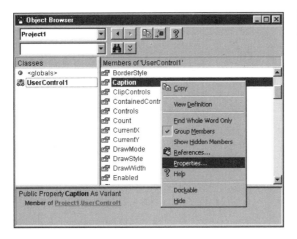

Figure 24-7: Pulling up the Procedure Attributes dialog for the custom Caption property

This pulls up the Procedure Attributes dialog, where you can enter a help context number to link this property, method, or event to a help file. The default view of the Procedure Attributes dialog shows the procedure name (which you cannot change here), an optional description, and a help context ID.

Much like the Member Properties dialog, the Procedure Attributes dialog lets you define a description that explains the function or purpose of your custom property, to be shown in the lower pane of the Object Browser. Also, like the Member Properties dialog, you can connect your member (method, property, or event) to a help page by setting the help context ID number in the Help Context ID field.

The Procedure Attributes dialog appears quite similar to the Member Properties dialog for classes. However, as Figure 24-8 shows, there is an important addition: the Advanced button, which allows the setting of more custom options than the Member Properties dialog does for classes.

Figure 24-8: The Procedure Attributes dialog has an Advanced button

Clicking the Advanced button displays quite an array of secret options for your UserControl. As you can see in Figure 24-9, the majority of the Procedure Attributes dialog is well hidden — perhaps hidden too well, as evidenced by the fact that it is so poorly documented. Be that as it may, this dialog is your key to creating highly functional UserControls.

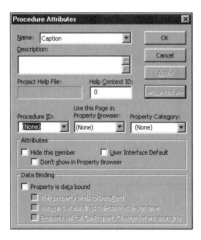

Figure 24-9: More custom options for UserControl properties, methods, and events

Procedure ID field

Unlike the Member Properties dialog for classes, the Procedure Attributes dialog allows the setting of default methods and other custom features. First is the Procedure ID field, shown in the middle of Figure 24-9. This field enables you to associate a standard ActiveX *member ID* with the chosen member. An ActiveX member ID is used to exclusively identify a property, method, or event with a type known to OLE.

Many ActiveX hosts support known member IDs. For example, Visual Basic understands a standard member called Font. You can add a property titled Font, and then connect it to the standard member Font in the Procedure ID list. Then, when the developer/user chooses your Font property from the Property Browser, Visual Basic will automatically display the Windows common Choose Font dialog, giving the user complete access to Windows's font system with a few lines of code:

```
Public Property Get Font() As Font
    Set Font = UserControl.Font
End Property

Public Property Set Font(ByVal New_Font As Font)
    Set UserControl.Font = New_Font
    PropertyChanged "Font"
End Property
```

The preceding code is all it takes to have Visual Basic display the standard Font dialog for your control. It assumes you are also saving font changes using the ReadProperties and WriteProperties event procedures explained in the last chapter.

Use This Page In Property Browser field

The Use This Page In Property Browser field of the Procedure Attributes dialog enables you to attribute any custom property pages you have defined for this control to the chosen member. This way, when the user chooses that member (property) from the Visual Basic Property Browser, Visual Basic will display the property page directly.

Property Category field

The Property Category field enables you to position your custom members in the Visual Basic Property Browser. The Property Browser has several optional areas defined under the Categorized tab, shown in Figure 24-10. This tab enables you to locate and identify properties quickly, based on their functional area.

Figure 24-10: The Categorized tab of the Visual Basic Property Browser

You can define any custom member of your UserControl to be displayed under any of the available sections by choosing that section from the Property Category field of the Procedure Attributes dialog. Note that the property will only appear in the Property Browser after you compile your UserControl project.

To follow along with our example, use the Procedure Attributes dialog to set the Caption property's category to Misc. This will place it into the Misc section of the categorized display, as demonstrated in Figure 24-11. When the developer/user of your UserControl highlights the control and presses F4 in the IDE, the Property Browser will appear and browse your UserControl's properties.

Figure 24-11: Our custom Caption property, listed under the Misc section

Also note how the `Caption` property has a default value of `My Control 1.0`. To read about defining and setting default values for properties, see Chapter 25.

Hide This Member option

The Hide This Member option causes the selected member to be excluded from the Property Browser by default. This is useful if your control requires a public member but you do not want the member to be visible to users. Setting this item hides the item in the Property Browser but does not disable or make the item unavailable for use. A common example of this is a property designed to be used by another control — perhaps a hidden gateway to some instance information that a developer would have little use for. You can't really make the member invisible forever because, as Figure 24-12 demonstrates, simply choosing the View Hidden Members option from the Object Browser will show any members that have been hidden using this technique.

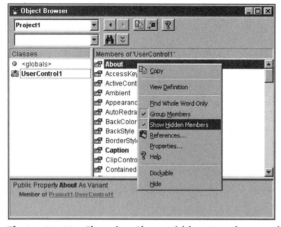

Figure 24-12: Choosing Show Hidden Members makes your hidden custom properties visible to the Browser.

If you cannot make your custom properties truly hidden, then you might wonder why you would ever want to use this feature. The answer is *ease of use*. You should always strive to make the control as easy to use as possible. Hiding irrelevant information from the user helps reduce the clutter, making your control easier to learn and use.

Don't Show In Property Browser option

A related clutter-control tool is the Don't Show In Property Browser option. This option is useful for removing properties from the Property Browser at *design time*, as opposed to runtime. As a general rule, any property you make persistent (using `ReadProperties` and `WriteProperties`, as discussed in Chapter 25) should be available to the Property Browser. Any properties you do not make persistent should not be in the Property Browser. Remember that users are accustomed to making changes in the Property Browser and having them persist.

User Interface Default option

Every Visual Basic UserControl supports default methods and properties. The default property is the property you can reference without explicitly using the property name. A well-known example of a default property is the common Visual Basic TextBox control, which has a property titled `Text`. This property is used to read or write a textual string of information to or from the control. This is also referred to as the *value* of the control. In reality, this is a standard member ID of zero (0). Users access the `Text` property with code similar to the following:

```
Private Sub Form_Load()
    Text1.Text = "Hank was here"
End Sub
```

This transfers the string "Hank was here" into the `Text` property of the control. Because `Text` just happens to be the default property for the TextBox control, you could instead access it as follows:

```
Private Sub Form_Load()
    Text1 = "Hank was here"
End Sub
```

Note how the string "Hank was here" is transferred into the `Text` property of the control without specifically naming the `Text` property. To read the default `Text` property, you assign the TextBox control (which defaults to the `Text` property) to a variable:

```
Public Sub Foo()
    Dim sText As String
    sText = Text1
End Sub
```

Again, note how the TextBox is directly assigned to a variable without explicitly naming the `Text` property.

You may wonder why you would use a default property. Well, the answer is *performance and compatibility*. The default property is "hard-wired" into the ActiveX control. This means the control can return information about the default property faster than it could by searching property name by property name. The end result: Using a default property is faster than stating the property by name. Also, since Microsoft has built default properties into its own ActiveX controls, developers/users of your UserControls will expect the same high level of functionality.

Any ActiveX control may posses only one default property, so choose yours wisely. To be of benefit to the developer/user of your control, the default property you choose should be the one the developer/user will access most often.

You can define any of your properties to be the default, using the Visual Basic Object Browser. For instance, to make the `Caption` property the default, right-click the `Caption` member and choose Properties from the Context menu. This will pull up the Procedure Attributes dialog. Then, enable the User Interface Default option on the Procedure Attributes dialog. From this point, the `Caption` property may be set using the control's own name or the explicit property name, as shown in the following:

```
Private Sub Form_Load()
    ' Either of these work ok
    UserControl1 = "Hank was here"
    UserControl1.Caption = "Hank was here"
End Sub

Public Sub Foo()
    Dim sText As String
    ' Either of these work ok
    sText = UserControl1
    sText = UserControl1.Caption
End Sub
```

In the preceding code, the default property of the control is accessed by referring to the control's display name without referencing a specific property.

Data binding

Database applications are quite common in Visual Basic. Not surprisingly, given Microsoft's commitment to data access, you can connect a property to a field in a database. To assign a database field to a property, use the Procedure Attributes dialog. Expand the dialog by choosing the Advanced button. Then select the Property is Data Bound check box and the This Property Binds to Data Field check box. From that point on, your property will operate like a standard bound control — meaning that in the Property Browser you will be able to select database control and field name for this control.

Custom Properties and Behaviors

You can use several "tricks" to implement custom actions in your UserControls. You have used controls in the past with properties that are read-only during runtime. Using some standard programming techniques and built-in Visual Basic capabilities, it's easy to give your controls some custom behavior.

Two distinct modes of operation exist for your controls: runtime and design time. *Runtime* is when the control is executing; *design time* is when you are developing your control. When a user of your control is developing an application using your control, they, too, are in design time — however, they cannot edit your control's source code. For the purposes of this discussion, design time refers specifically to your development of the control. Depending on the mode Visual Basic is in (runtime or design time), you can create custom properties that are read-only, write-only, or not available.

You may frequently want to make some aspect of your UserControl available to the developer/user but not to the end user of your controls. There is no command or option to make properties read-only (or write-protected, depending on your viewpoint). However, several methods are available for your use.

Read-only properties

A *read-only property* is one that can only be read — it cannot be written to. An example of a read-only property is one that returns free disk space. You cannot force a disk to have more space, so there is no reason for the property to have a write capability.

Note   Properties that are not relevant to the end user should be read-only during runtime.

A more practical example would be some sort of formatting control — for example, font size or window color. The developer/user of your control will probably want to change these options while developing his or her application. The end user will simply use the application as the developer/user has designed it.

There are three types of read-only status:

- ✦ Read-only during design time
- ✦ Read-only during runtime
- ✦ Read-only all the time

Before we go into the ways of creating a read-only property, here's an example of a control that enables read/write capabilities:

```
Public Property Get RTProp0() As Variant
    RTProp0 = m_RTProp0
End Property
```

```
Public Property Let RTProp0(ByVal New_RTProp0 As Variant)
    m_RTProp0 = New_RTProp0
    PropertyChanged "RTProp0"
End Property
```

The preceding code is a standard property with read and write capabilities. Remember, this code allows the RTProp0 property to be read or written to at any time, runtime or design time. To make properties read-only, you need to write code that detects the Visual Basic mode and then allows or disallows user access.

Read-only during runtime

To make a control property read-only during runtime, you first detect the run mode of Visual Basic using the Ambient object. This object has many properties, but the one we care about right now is the UserMode property.

Ambient.UserMode returns True when the control is in use by an end user. While the control is running from the Visual Basic IDE, this is an indicator the control is in run mode. If the control is part of a compiled application that is not running from the IDE, and the control itself has already been compiled, UserMode will also return True. When the control is in use by a developer/user, Ambient.UserMode returns False. In the Visual Basic IDE, you are developing or coding your control in design mode.

Let's make this a little clearer: A developer/user of your control sets methods and properties using the Visual Basic Property Browser. These property settings are stored in the control; however, the control is not considered to be running. It is not in run mode until the application that uses the control is placed in run mode. Up to this point, the control is considered to be in design time — not from your perspective as the developer of the control, but rather from the perspective of the developer/user of your control.

Note

Remember, for a read-only property, you restrict access to the *write* aspects of the property.

Ambient.UserMode can tell you how the control is being used. For example:

```
If Ambient.UserMode Then
     ' we are in run mode
Else
     ' we are in design mode
End If
```

Using Ambient.UserMode is the key to creating custom read- or write-only properties. Consider the following code:

```
Public Property Let RTProp3(ByVal New_RTProp3 As Variant)
    If Ambient.UserMode Then Err.Raise 382
```

```
        m_RTProp3 = New_RTProp3
        PropertyChanged "RTProp3"
End Property
```

If the preceding code executes during run mode (Ambient.UserMode = True), it does allow the property to be set, and instead returns error 382, "Set not supported at runtime." If, on the other hand, Ambient.UserMode resolves to False, indicating design mode, the property is set and no error is raised, allowing the Property procedure to store the value.

Read-only during design time

Runtime is when the control is executing its code in the context of a running program or application. *Design time* is when the control is being written and edited by you, the developer. A custom ActiveX control may have code that runs at design time, because it has functionality that may only be pertinent to the developer/user of your control. Consider the following code:

```
Public Property Let DTPRop2(ByVal New_DTPRop2 As Variant)
    If Ambient.UserMode = False Then Err.Raise 387
    m_DTPRop2 = New_DTPRop2
    PropertyChanged "DTPRop2"
End Property
```

If this code executes during design mode (not run mode), do not allow the property to be set; instead, return error 387, "Set not permitted." If, on the other hand, Ambient.UserMode resolves to True, indicating run mode, the property is set and the error is not raised, allowing the property to store the value.

Read-only all the time

For some properties, it would make sense for you to disallow any writing all the time. Two methods achieve this. The first option is to create a Visual Basic Function (method) that returns a value:

```
Public Function DiskSpace() As Long
    DiskSpace = GetFreeDiskSpace * 1024
End Function
```

The preceding function returns the amount of disk space. There is only one problem: Because this is a method and not a property, it cannot appear in the Property Browser. Only properties appear in the Property Browser.

A further wrinkle on the rules for getting a value displayed in the Property Browser is that only properties with both Property Let and Property Get can appear in the Browser. So, to get our imaginary disk-space property value into the Property Browser, we need both halves of the property. But because this is a read-only property, we will need to implement code like the following sample so that the `Property Let` procedure raises an error whenever it is called:

```
Public Property Get DTProp1() As Variant
    DTProp1 = m_DTProp1
End Property

Public Property Let DTProp1(ByVal New_DTProp1 As Variant)
    Err.Raise 383
End Property
```

The `Property Let` raises error 383, "Set not supported (read-only property)" — exactly what we want. Don't let this sleight of hand using `Err.Raise` distract you. It's perfectly legal and appropriate to raise errors for conditions; that's why the `Err` object has a `Raise` method.

Write-only properties

A *write-only property* is one that may only be written to — it may not be read. Common examples include password properties — they may be set, but for security reasons they may not be read. The logic and implementation is quite similar to that presented for read-only properties.

> **Note** Remember, to create a write-only property, you restrict access to the *read* aspects of the code.

There are two situations for creating write-only properties — one for design time and one for runtime. For runtime write-only access, the `Property Get` procedure for the property checks `Ambient.UserMode` for `True` and then raises error 393, "Get not supported at runtime." The following code shows how to implement a write-only property for runtime:

```
Public Property Get RTProp2() As Variant
    If Ambient.UserMode Then Err.Raise 393
    RTProp2 = m_RTProp2
End Property
```

The preceding code simply does not allow the read to occur if the control is in run mode.

The following code raises an error and does not allow the property to be read if the control is in design mode. The message text for error 382 is "Set not supported at runtime."

```
Public Property Get DTPRop2() As Variant
    If Ambient.UserMode = False Then Err.Raise 382
    DTProp2 = m_DTProp2
End Property
```

The `Ambient` and `Err` objects, along with an understanding of run mode and design mode, together enable you to implement read- or write-only properties for both design time and runtime.

Fine-Tuning Your ActiveX UserControls

When creating your ActiveX UserControls, you will be compiling them many, many times. By default, each time you compile your UserControl, Visual Basic generates new GUIDs and type library information. This information (GUID and TypeLib) are used by ActiveX hosts to understand your control's interface. These items are required, and (unlike developing using C++) Visual Basic takes care of them for you automatically.

Visual Basic also registers your control's GUID in the Registry when you compile the control, saving you from having to use RegSvr32.EXE to manually register or unregister your controls. This is a nice feature of Visual Basic. However, by default, Visual Basic does this for you *each time* you compile. For example, if you compile once, the GUID and TypeLib are created and stored in the Registry. The next time you compile, a new GUID and a new TypeLib are created and then stored in the Registry — the old GUID and TypeLib are left "dangling" in the Registry. This means the old information is no longer connected to any executable objects (your controls), but it still takes up space. This is a real problem that can degrade system performance as your Registry swells with invalid GUID and TypeLib entries.

Take heart. You bought this book, so we are going to tell you how to get out of this fix. The answer lies in the Visual Basic Project Properties dialog, buried and undocumented in the Component tab.

The Project Properties dialog contains five tabs, each of which enables you to fine-tune your control. To view the Project Properties dialog, follow these steps:

1. While in the Code viewing mode of your project, choose the Project menu.

2. Near the bottom of the Project menu will be a submenu entry with your project's name and the word Properties...; for example, if your project is titled Project1, the submenu would be Project1 Properties.... Choose this entry to display the Project Properties dialog.

With the Project Properties dialog visible, click on the Component tab so the dialog appears as shown in Figure 24-13.

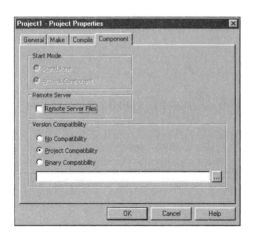

Figure 24-13: The Visual Basic Project Properties dialog, Component tab

The options in the Start Mode frame pertain to the project's type and control how the program starts up. Any project that is an OLE server (for example, ActiveX DLL, ActiveX EXE, Active Document, and so on) can start up as a program or as a server, depending upon the Start Mode setting.

The Remote Server Files check box indicates whether you want Visual Basic to create the extra runtime files required for remote program execution. When this option is checked, Visual Basic creates a file with a .VBR extension and a filename the same as that of the project. The VBR file contains information that is added to the Windows Registry in order an ActiveX Server on a remote computer.

Version Compatibility is both important and misunderstood. The three options in this frame (No Compatibility, Project Compatibility, and Binary Compatibility) control how your program is compiled with regard to its GUID, version, and type library. No Compatibility is a poor choice, because by default Visual Basic creates a new GUID and TypeLib every time you compile, quickly filling the Registry with dangling entries. You should develop your controls with the Project Compatibility option set, so VB knows to use the existing GUID and type library rather than create new ones. This also allows any existing Registry entries to be reused, resulting in much less clutter in the Registry. This also means projects that use your control needn't be completely rebuilt, since the GUID has not changed. Therefore, any application that uses the control will still contain valid pointers to it.

The last option, Binary Compatibility, is used when you are ready to ship your control. Set Binary Compatibility, and in the text box enter the component (OCX, DLL, or EXE) with which you want to maintain interface compatibility. Setting this option will compare a saved copy of your project (OCX, DLL, EXE, and so on) to verify that no exposed properties, methods, or events have changed in the new version. If there are any changes to the existing exposed properties, methods, or events, Visual Basic will notify you with a dialog indicating what has changed. You then have the option of canceling the compile to remove the changes, or compiling and creating a new version — one incompatible with the new file. Note that you should copy the compiled project OCX, DLL, or EXE with which you want to maintain compatibility into another file, and store it in a safe place. This way, you always have it. You can add new methods and properties while maintaining binary compatibility, but you cannot delete or modify the existing properties or methods in any way.

Custom Enumerations

After you build a control or two, you will find yourself paying closer attention to other controls and how they operate. You may have already noticed that some controls display a drop-down list of choices in the Visual Basic Property Browser. Typically, these lists have a numeric value to the left and a textual string to the right, as shown in Figure 24-14. The content of such a list is called an *enumeration*.

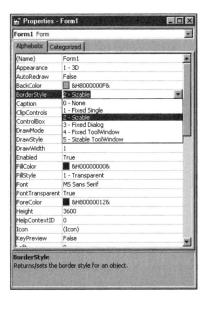

Figure 24-14: The Visual Basic Property Browser showing an enumerated property

As you can see, the enumeration presents a list of valid options to the developer/user of the control. Using an enumeration makes for foolproof property settings, because the user is not left to his or her own devices in order to properly enter one of several valid entries. Instead, the Visual Basic UserControl does the job for you (and the developer/user) by presenting a list.

Adding your own custom enumeration properties is quite easy, but rather poorly documented. To implement an enumeration property, you first must create an `Enum` structure. This structure stores lists of constants and associates them with a textual string, as shown in the following code fragment:

```
Enum Fruits
    Apples
    Oranges
    Bananas
    Grapes
    Melons
End Enum
```

The `Enum` enumerates a set of constants, beginning with the first constant in the list. Visual Basic starts counting at zero, so the value of `Fruits.Apples` is 0, the value of `Fruits.Oranges` is 1, and so on to `Fruits.Melons`, which equals 4.

Note, however, that you can arbitrarily assign values to any member of an `Enum`. Subsequent members of the `Enum` will take incremental values. If you assigned `Fruits.Apples = 100` as follows, then `Fruits.Oranges` would be 101, and so on to `Fruits.Melons`, which would = 104:

```
Enum Fruits
    Apples = 100
    Oranges
    Bananas
    Grapes
    Melons
End Enum
```

You can also restart numbering at any point in the `Enum`, as long as the values assigned do not conflict with any existing values:

```
Enum Fruits
    Apples = 100
    Oranges
    Bananas = 200
    Grapes
    Melons
End Enum
```

In the preceding example, `Fruits.Apples` is 100 and `Fruits.Oranges` = 101; however, `Fruits.Bananas` would restart the numbering with 200.

To implement the `Enum` property, you create a standard property with both `Property Get` and `Property Let` procedures. The trick here is to declare the data type of the property to be of type `Fruits`. This is legitimate because Visual Basic considers an `Enum` to be a data type. Therefore, our sample project has a `Fruits` data type.

The code to implement the property is presented here as Listing 24-1. Note how the data type of the Property Get and the argument to the Property Let are defined as Fruits, referencing the Fruits enumeration.

Listing 24-1: A Sample Program That Creates a Custom Fruit Property

```
Option Explicit

Enum Fruits
    Apples = 100
    Oranges
    Bananas
    Grapes = 99
    Melons = 1
End Enum

'Default Property Values:
Const m_def_Dessert = Fruits.Apples

'Property Variables:
Dim m_Dessert As Fruits

Public Property Get Dessert() As Fruits
    Dessert = m_Dessert
End Property

Public Property Let Dessert(ByVal New_Dessert As Fruits)
    m_Dessert = New_Dessert
    PropertyChanged "Dessert"
End Property

' Initialize Properties for User Control
Private Sub UserControl_InitProperties()
    m_Dessert = m_def_Dessert
End Sub

' Load property values from storage
Private Sub UserControl_ReadProperties(PropBag As _
    PropertyBag)

    m_Dessert = PropBag.ReadProperty("Dessert", _
        m_def_Dessert)
End Sub

' Write property values to storage
Private Sub UserControl_WriteProperties(PropBag _@srAs
PropertyBag)
```

(continued)

Listing 24-1 *(continued)*

```
        Call PropBag.WriteProperty("Dessert", _
            m_Dessert, m_def_Dessert)
    End Sub
```

Listing 24-1 creates an Enum titled Fruits. It creates a variable, titled m_Dessert, to maintain the value of a property titled Dessert, and a constant to contain the default value of the property m_def_Dessert. Figure 24-15 shows the Dessert property selected with the Fruits enumeration listed. The code establishes a default value for m_def_Dessert of Fruits.Apples—which, unless the user changes it, will be the value returned when the Dessert property is read. The UserControl_InitProperties procedure assigned the default value constant (m_def_Dessert) to the state maintenance variable (m_Dessert). The Property Let and Property Get procedures read or set the m_Dessert variable. The code also implements persistence of data by using the UserControl_WriteProperties and UserControl_ReadProperties events to read and write to and from the PropertyBag object.

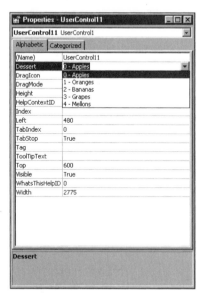

Figure 24-15: The Visual Basic Property Browser showing the Dessert property, which uses the Fruits enumeration

You can use this methodology to create custom enumeration properties for your controls. You can also customize the numeric values associated with the Enum members. It is normally a good idea to use zero-based enumerations for ease of understanding by the users of your control. However, there are many instances when you will want to have your own numeric enumeration scheme. One example might be custom error constants, for which you want to assign your own values for use with Err.Raise.

Note   At runtime, the enumeration list cannot be modified. Visual Basic enables you to modify enumeration lists only at design time.

As you can see in Figure 24-16, Visual Basic displays the numeric values we assigned. Notice that Oranges and Bananas follow enumeration from Apples. That is because, in the program in Listing 24-1, Apples is defined as 100 and Oranges and Bananas are defaulted to sequential enumeration because there are no explicit values assigned.

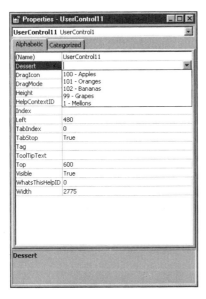

Figure 24-16: The Property Browser showing an enumeration property that uses nonsequential numbers

Of course, for custom enumeration properties you also need to be able to read, write, store, and retrieve property values. You use the same techniques for enumeration properties as for properties defined as standard data types.

Summary

Many methods are available for customizing your ActiveX UserControls. Some of these require knowing the hidden functionality of certain Visual Basic dialog options, while others require your use of code techniques. In either case, the result is a fine-tuned, highly functional and professional-looking ActiveX UserControl.

The Object Browser is a powerful aid to the Visual Basic development environment — the Object Browser enables you to view all the properties, methods, and events of all the objects in your project. For objects you created, you can use the Object Browser to take you to definitions, as well as being a shortcut to the Procedure Attributes dialog in which you can edit the attributes of your custom properties, methods, and events.

Several means prevent access to properties you do not want users to get at easily. You can make them read-only or write-only, and you can also hide them from the Property Browser.

Though this chapter shows you how to achieve fine control of your controls manually, many of the options presented here are also available through the various wizards that Visual Basic employs. Feel free to either use the wizards or code it yourself.

✦　　✦　　✦

ActiveX Control Portability

Portability is the term used to describe the capability of a software component, in this case, to operate with modification in a number of hosts. A classic example is a Windows DLL (Dynamic Link Library). The code is compiled and distributed with an application but as a separate disk file, allowing updates to application functionality without requiring that the entire application be replaced.

A truly portable ActiveX component retains all functionality from host to host. If not written with portability in mind, ActiveX components can suffer from reduced functionality when certain methods and properties do not operate in all hosts.

This chapter will describe the reasons ActiveX portability is important, why you should consider developing for more than one host, and some of the issues that you will face when you develop.

Why Care About Portability?

Although portability will probably not make you rich and famous, it can reduce the amount of work you have to do — and that is typically a good thing!

ActiveX technology has enabled you for the first time to develop a product for one market and, with careful development effort, sell that product into new markets. With Visual Basic's capability to create ActiveX components, you can create a component for the Visual Basic market and also sell it to the Microsoft Access market. This is an important benefit, if not the key benefit, of ActiveX technology. Understanding the market forces that are driving these changes helps to clarify why you should write portable code.

Requirements for Portability

The number of potential ActiveX hosts is enormous: over 160 at the time of this writing and growing daily. It is impossible for you to create a complex control that operates with full functionality within every single possible ActiveX host. However, with planning and discipline, you can create ActiveX components that operate with full functionality in many hosts.

Regardless of the marketing hype, ActiveX is not yet a complete standard. The implementation of ActiveX varies from vendor to vendor. You can even see this variety from Microsoft itself — the inventor and chief promulgator of ActiveX. Figure 25-1 shows the Components dialog, which is where you add an ActiveX control to your Visual Basic IDE.

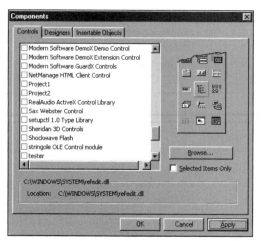

Figure 25-1: The Visual Basic Components dialog

Note, in Figure 25-1, the available controls are listed. What might not be readily apparent is that this dialog shows one entry for each ActiveX OCX file. A single ActiveX file can contain more than one control. For example, the entry labeled Modern Software GuardX Controls is a single disk file titled GDXP100.OCX that contains six ActiveX controls, each with its own label. However, looking at the Visual Basic Component dialog, you would not know that.

Figure 25-2 shows the Additional Controls dialog of Visual Basic for Applications (VBA), the procedural language for Microsoft Office.

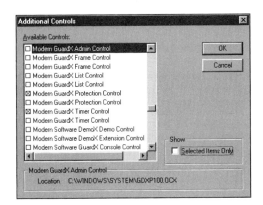

Figure 25-2: VBA's Additional Controls dialog

At first glance, the VBA Additional Controls dialog seems similar to the Visual Basic Component dialog. However, look at the ActiveX control entries, especially Modern GuardX Admin through Modern GuardX Timer. These are the individual ActiveX controls contained within the single file GDXP100.OCX.

This issue of portability becomes more convoluted as you move to other Microsoft products. Figure 25-3 shows Microsoft Excel, which supports ActiveX components directly hosted into spreadsheets. Notice the drop-down list indicating the available controls. It is completely different from VBA or Visual Basic. In Excel, you are provided with a list of the individual component names. If an ActiveX control file on disk contains more than one ActiveX component, which is common, the name of each individual control inside the file is shown. For example, the disk file GDXP100.OCX is a single disk file — however, it contains five separate ActiveX controls. When browsing this component from Excel, you see five distinct controls. When browsing this component from Visual Basic, you see a single component name.

This little example just serves to illustrate my point: ActiveX is not a uniform environment, even from the same vendor. Take heart; don't get depressed. With discipline, you can create portable ActiveX components. It's simply a matter of careful development.

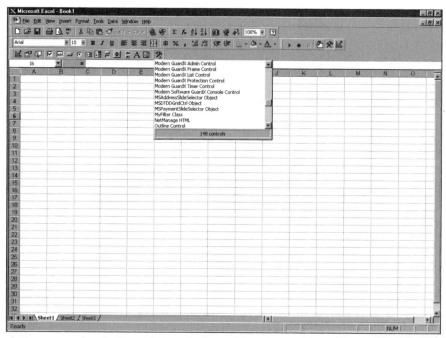

Figure 25-3: The Excel Controls drop-down list

Achieving ActiveX Portability

Given the enormous market support for ActiveX component technology, it is clear that one component standard will be ActiveX. It almost sounds too good to be true — write once and run anywhere. Can you really create a component in any development language and have it run in virtually any application? The answer is yes, but there are a number of bumps in the road.

Portability requires more than just being able to browse a standard user interface. You need to be confident of a control's standard behavior as well. Unfortunately, this seems to be the area of weakness with ActiveX.

Visual Basic frame ActiveX components

One commonly used control is the frame. A frame contains other controls. An example of the frame is the standard Windows grouping frame so common on user interfaces that use options buttons. When you create a frame control in Visual Basic, the frame control makes use of features unique to Visual Basic. This results in your ActiveX component's working properly in Visual Basic only. Your Visual Basic-authored frame control will work fine in Visual Basic — but Access won't even display it as a valid control. Excel will let you browse the control, but it won't let you add other controls to it. In short, if your ActiveX host is known to be Visual Basic, you can create frame controls; but if you want a portable solution, Visual Basic is not the appropriate means to create a frame control.

Earlier, Figure 25-3 showed the drop-down list for choosing ActiveX controls from Excel. Note in that figure the control labeled Modern GuardX Frame Control. Now look at Figure 25-4, which shows how Access displays controls that can be used there for database forms.

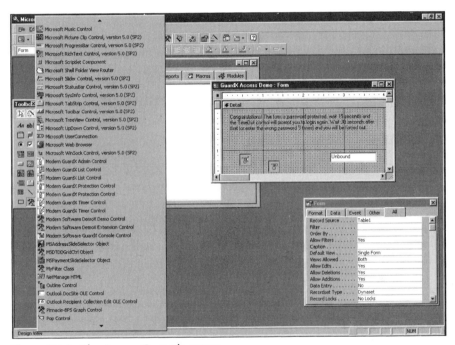

Figure 25-4: The Access Controls menu

Note that there is no entry for the Modern GuardX Frame control. Because the Visual Basic-authored frame control is specific to Visual Basic, Access cannot use the control. Thus, Access decides for you that you cannot use nor even browse the frame control.

Now this is not a bad thing, unless of course you really want your frame control to run under some host other than Visual Basic. In that case, you will need to write the control in C++, not Visual Basic.

Images and controls

Controls often require an image of some sort. If you are developing in Visual Basic, it's easy to add an image to a control. Simply add a PictureBox (or Image control) to your new control. Then set the `Picture` property to an image. Simple, fast, and easy — except images done this way won't display in all ActiveX hosts.

Displaying an image is one of the most basic Windows programming functions, so it should be easy. However, it took me several maddening days to come to the only solution that draws the control image properly in all my test hosts. My solution was to fall back on traditional C programming and attempt to draw the image the old-fashioned way — hand-coding the image painting. I put my image into a resource file that would compile into the control. In the control's `Paint` event function, which maps to the `WM_PAINT` message, I loaded the image and painted it to the control.

In C, I would use `LoadResource` and `BitBlt` to do this job, but I wanted an all-Visual Basic solution. So, at the top of the control's `Paint` event procedure, I created an object reference using the standard OLE Picture object template, followed by a simple single-precision variable I would need later for screen measurements:

```
Private Sub UserControl_Paint()
    Dim x As Picture
    Dim p As Single
```

Next, I used Visual Basic's `LoadResPicture` method to load and store the image into my empty picture object, with this instruction:

```
Set x = LoadResPicture(IDB_Cipher, vbResBitmap)
```

Then, the `PaintPicture` method was used to draw the image on the control. To make sure the image was positioned properly, I used the `Screen` object, which reads GDI driver information into its properties for you to account for various screen resolutions. Here's the method instruction I came up with:

```
UserControl.PaintPicture x, (Width - (15 * _
    Screen.TwipsPerPixelX)) / 2, (Height - (16 * _
    Screen.TwipsPerPixelY)) / 2
```

Finally, to border my image, I used the `Line` method of the control, as follows:

```
    p = Screen.TwipsPerPixelX
    UserControl.Line (p, p)-(UserControl.Width - (p * 2), p)
    UserControl.Line (p, p)-(p, UserControl.Height - (p * 2))
    UserControl.Line (UserControl.Width - p, 0)-
        _(UserControl.Width - p, UserControl.Height)
    UserControl.Line (p, UserControl.Height - p)-
        _(UserControl.Width - p, UserControl.Height - p)
End Sub
```

At long last, I had it. My control now painted properly in all the ActiveX hosts I chose as test cases. After three days of trial and error, I had both a solution and an important lesson about portability: *It's often the simple things that are the hardest to resolve, so plan accordingly.*

Host conflicts

The next problem I encountered was more serious than an image that wouldn't display. Most host containers wrap the controls they load with the host's own properties and methods, which, of course, vary from host to host. On the surface, this seems not to be a problem — until you realize that, for example, the host container might have a method or property defined to be the same name as a method or property of your control — in which case you have real trouble.

Case in point: Excel wraps your controls with its own properties, one of which is named `Enabled`. If your control has a property titled `Enabled`, the Excel property "overrides" your control's property, effectively removing your `Enabled` property. Not good.

In this case no workaround exists, other than to accept that if you want your control to be portable, it simply cannot have a property named `Enabled`. Or `Locked`, or `Shadow`, or `Placement`, or any other property name "reserved" for use by Excel or any other host you might want to support.

The bad news is, no list of ActiveX reserved property names exists. The good news is that once you are aware of the limitations, you can code around them.

And so I learned my next important lesson: *Do not assume that, because a host supports ActiveX, it will support your controls.* To write portable ActiveX controls, you need to completely research and understand each host you want to support.

Visual Basic 4.0

Visual Basic-authored ActiveX controls can be used under 32 bit Visual Basic 4.0 — with a few extra precautions.

First, make sure all your properties are declared with `ByVal`, or they will not appear in the Visual Basic 4.0 Property Browser. The following code shows a property declaration for a fictional `Audit` property.

```
Option Explicit
Dim m_Audit As Boolean
```

```
Public Property Get Audit() As Boolean
    Audit = m_Audit
End Property

Public Property Let Audit(New_Audit As Boolean)
    m_Audit = New_Audit
    PropertyChanged "Audit"
End Property
```

This property works fine under Visual Basic 4.0; note how in Figure 25-5, the Audit property appears in VB 6.0's Property Browser. Also note that VB6 has detected that the property is of type Boolean and created a True/False drop-down for it.

Figure 25-5: The Visual Basic 6.0 Property Browser showing the Boolean property, Audit

Now look at Figure 25-6, which shows Visual Basic 4.0-32 using your control. Notice how Audit does not appear in the Property Browser. For Visual Basic 4.0-32 portability, always declare property arguments as ByVal, as in the following amended instruction:

```
Public Property Let Audit(ByVal New_Audit As Boolean)
```

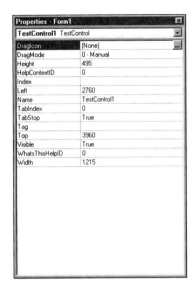

Figure 25-6: The Visual Basic 4.0 Property Browser in which Audit does not show

State of ActiveX Technology

Components have been around a long time. Yet, to read the headlines you would think component-based development is a new thing. Many companies are changing their entire product focus to support components. Microsoft now even licenses VBA — which supports ActiveX controls — to anyone who wants it; and many, many diverse companies have chosen to adopt and support ActiveX.

So the question is, why? What's happening now to cause such interest and acceptance of components and ActiveX? The answer is that component-based development has now reached critical mass.

To describe critical mass in this context, I recall IBM and the original personal computer, the IBM PC. IBM invented the PC/AT bus and then standardized the entire industry around it. Hundreds of vendors around the world created thousands of products to support the PC/AT bus. They put their energy into the PC/AT bus because it was a safe bet that their products would work in virtually any hardware configuration that used the PC/AT bus.

When IBM attempted to change the market with the PS/2 bus, they made a terrible mistake. In an attempt to "control" the marketplace, they created a "new" standard without properly considering the marketplace. What IBM missed was that the PC/AT bus had critical mass — the industry no longer needed IBM or its support. The PC/AT bus was by now the *de facto* standard. Any company that wanted to sell into the lucrative PC marketplace now had to choose whether to support the industry standard and widely implemented PC/AT bus, or the new, closed, and proprietary PS/2 bus. That's not a very tough business question to answer, and the entire industry went right on around IBM. IBM lost big because the AT bus had critical mass.

Today, ActiveX has attained critical mass. For a product to reach critical mass, four elements must exist:

✦ Enabling technology

✦ Applications

✦ Market acceptance/demand

✦ Standardization

Enabling technology

Before anything can attain critical mass, an infrastructure must support the technology. Support systems for the technology and a body of people with expertise in the technology must exist. The technology itself is not the product. Rather, it is the accumulation of support systems, expertise, and technology that come together to enable the creation or implementation of a larger result.

In the case of ActiveX technology, the expertise and support systems are already in place. Today we have tools to develop components quickly and easily. Visual Basic lets you build ActiveX components about as easily as it ever could be. However, Borland Delphi creates components, and C/C++ can make them, too—and the list goes on and on. Clearly the technology of components is here to stay, for good reason.

A fundamental requirement of component creation is the ability to design, debug, and tune components. Although Microsoft pioneered operating system and language infrastructures for components, the debugging, designing, and tuning technologies are driven by non-Microsoft sources.

This third-party buy-in to a technology is key to its attaining critical mass. Companies such as NuMega Labs, Rational, and others allow developers and managers to tackle real-world projects, knowing they can complete them successfully. No organization will adopt a new technology without a complete understanding of the implications of that technology.

As a company researches the paradigm shift that Visual Basic represents, the company also looks for tools and support systems for that technology. Without the proper support systems, the company can't be sure that it can complete the project. The infrastructure for ActiveX technology has the support systems in place to enable component development and adoption.

Applications

Applications are the bread and butter of the software world. Even though Microsoft gets a lot of attention for Visual Basic and Windows, $8 billion of the company's recent $10 billion yearly revenue came from Microsoft Office—word processor, spreadsheet, and so forth. The application is the heart of software. So how do components fit into the application strategy? For components, the application is the host, where they are actually used.

The biggest thing to hit components is ActiveX. ActiveX components work with Visual Basic, Visual C++, Visual J++, Word, Excel, PowerPoint, Access, PowerBuilder, Internet Explorer — yes, even Netscape — and hundreds of other titles. Applications now exist in sufficient quantity to drive a component market.

Market acceptance

Market acceptance is required to push third-party organizations to adopt and enhance a technology. Market acceptance occurs once developers learn how to leverage technology so as to make users demand it.

Key to the success of Windows 3.0 were Common Dialogs and the goal of standardizing usage to reduce learning curve and training costs. It worked. Few programs now deviate from "File/Open." Users expect it, they understand it, and they demand it. How many programs have you written that do not try to mimic or adopt standard interface elements?

This is classic critical mass: Users who learn and thus actually use software result in market acceptance and demand. Which in turn forces developers like us to adopt and implement that technology.

The market demands the benefits delivered by component solutions.

Standardization

You cannot reach critical mass without mass production, which requires a standard. Using the previous example of the original IBM PC, standardization was the definition of the bus structure. With a standard, defined bus architecture, any hardware manufacturer could make a plug-in board for the PC—all they had to do was follow the standard. The swell of applications, tools, and features to follow has been mind boggling.

There are several defined standards for component-based software. These include CORBA, JavaBeans, and ActiveX. For Visual Basic applications, the component standard is ActiveX. Any objective analysis shows this to be true. Visual C++, Delphi, Visual Basic, PowerBuilder, AutoCAD, and dozens more applications all support ActiveX. Like it or not, a component standard has arrived and, more importantly, has been accepted by the marketplace.

Summary

In the end, it turns out you really can write an ActiveX component that works properly, with full functionality across multiple platforms. However, it is not an easy task with obvious choices. Nor is there much guidance or assistance along the way. It also turns out that the language in which you choose to write your control does make a difference.

You can safely create many controls in Visual Basic that are fully functional in many different ActiveX hosts. However, certain Visual Basic-authored controls, such as frame controls, are specific to Visual Basic and are therefore not fully usable in other hosts.

With diligence, testing, and a few good debugging tools, however, you too can create portable ActiveX components. Just take into account these following simple rules:

✦ Determine the capabilities of your ActiveX development environment in advance. Choice of development language does make a difference. You might not be able to do what you want — as evidenced by the frame-control escapade.

✦ In advance of development, determine the clients you expect to support (Excel, Access, Visual Basic, Visual C++, etc.). Rigorously examine them before you start coding. Examine their default properties and methods, to make sure your properties and methods won't conflict. Test your code with as many test containers as you can. Test early and test often.

✦ Make sure you have solid testing tools to see what's going on under the surface. Without NuMega FailSafe (for internal procedure tracing) and NuMega SmartCheck (for Windows messages and OLE event spying), I don't think I could have got my controls working at all, and I certainly wouldn't know why they didn't work.

✦ Write down your experience and document it for the rest of your team. There are no user guides for writing portable components. It's all trial and error, so your documented experience may be what gives you and your company the edge over your rivals.

✦　　✦　　✦

Using ActiveX Documents

O ne of the biggest problems facing large organizations today is the delivery of software to the desktop. It seems that no sooner is an application deployed than, for whatever reason, an update — or, to use Microsoft-speak, a hyperlink `"mailto:\"service pack\"-"` is required.

Such an update may be required to fix a bug or to respond to diverse and changing user requirements. No matter what the reason, the issue of managing such frequent updates is huge. The fundamental question is how to synchronize your entire enterprise with the same version of your software. If your enterprise comprises multiple locations with many users, the very thought of an upgrade can give you shivers of fear. Yet, we do it every day; it's part of life in corporate IS/IT shops.

Some expensive and hard-to-maintain custom solutions are available for this purpose, and a new and simple solution also exists — ActiveX Document.

What Is ActiveX Document?

Today, when people mention components, you probably think about ActiveX (OCX controls) or Java (applets). ActiveX is actually a family of component technologies, that includes the well-known ActiveX Control (OCX) and the lesser-known ActiveX Document.

ActiveX documents are very similar to Visual Basic forms. They may contain other controls, just like a form; however, unlike a form, they may be hosted by an Internet browser using HTML commands to load. These special "forms" are called `UserDocument` objects. When compiled, every

`UserDocument` object will create a special disk file with a .VBD extension, which may be displayed using a browser.

ActiveX documents provide a unique solution to problems common in today's modern software. If you find yourself in a service pack nightmare with many updates to your software, you should consider the powerful benefits that ActiveX documents may provide for your organization.

Potential benefits

ActiveX documents are Visual Basic 6.0 components that essentially wrap application dialogs into an ActiveX component that runs in your browser. Think of an ActiveX document as a turbocharged HTML page. There are some real benefits to using ActiveX documents:

✦ ActiveX documents can be stored on a central server, creating a single repository for your application.

✦ ActiveX documents are most commonly hosted in HTML pages, which are displayed under Internet Explorer 3.0 or higher, with Internet Explorer 4.0 preferred. You can then mix and match traditional HTML pages with ActiveX documents for custom Internet or intranet Web-based solutions.

✦ When using ActiveX documents, you update your entire user base by simply updating the server where the ActiveX documents are stored. Then, as the users connect to your ActiveX documents, they get the newest version of the program.

ActiveX documents are easy to create using Visual Basic. There is even a conversion wizard to help you port existing applications to ActiveX Document. To view the conversion wizard, follow these steps:

1. From the Add-Ins menu, choose the Add-In Manager option.

2. From the Add-In Manager dialog, select the VB 6 ActiveX Doc Migration Wizard.

3. Still on the Add-In Manager dialog, set the Loaded/Unloaded check box.

4. Choose the OK button to close the Add-In Manager dialog.

5. Now, in the Add-Ins menu you will see the ActiveX Document Migration Wizard option. Choosing this option starts the Wizard, which will prompt you through the conversion process.

For you to understand the ActiveX Document better, the analogy to remember is of an HTML page. ActiveX documents are hosted in the user's browser. The browser provides standard Internet and/or intranet features such as image support, navigation via hyperlinks, and file download capabilities. One of the intrinsic features of an Internet browser is that it can navigate using the HTTP protocol — a simple and uniform syntax for reaching a variety of network resources locally or remotely. Using a browser, you can access computers on the network anywhere in the world.

When a user navigates to an ActiveX document, the HTML commands can download the ActiveX document just like an HTML page is downloaded to your browser when you visit a site on the Internet. In the same way, the ActiveX document is also stored locally on the user's machine. When the user navigates to your ActiveX document, the browser compares the local (downloaded) copy to the copy on the server. If the ActiveX document does not exist locally or the local copy is of a lesser version, the browser then automatically downloads the new copy and — here's the kicker — updates any earlier existing version on the user's computer. Automatic upgrades to enterprise applications are now as simple as using ActiveX Document.

ActiveX documents also support a hyperlink object that lets you provide complete Web URL navigation or manipulation of the history list. An ActiveX document can also merge its own menu commands into the menu of the browser, extending or modifying the browser interface to its own specifications. ActiveX Document also possesses the `PropertyBag` object, just as ActiveX controls do.

A `PropertyBag` is an object with properties and methods that allow you to store and retrieve arbitrary data values. Typically these data values are used to store and retrieve your components' properties and methods. `PropertyBags` are much more robust than using HTML cookies.

Microsoft chose the word *document* in ActiveX Document to draw a parallel between ActiveX components and the well-known Word document (as in "Microsoft Word document"). In a somewhat convoluted way, the analogy works. Users are accustomed to working in documents, like HTML pages. ActiveX documents provide a way to create dynamic programmatic HTML pages — thus the name ActiveX Document, according to Microsoft.

Potential drawbacks

By this point you're probably thinking this sounds too good to be true; there must be a catch. While there are no catches, you should be aware of a few details when you set out to build your next killer app based on ActiveX documents.

ActiveX documents are the user interface components to Visual Basic applications. They are forms (dialogs). They may contain source code, and even classes and other controls, but they are not standalone applications. You can only run them in a proper container, such as Internet Explorer — which leads to an important issue: portability.

An ActiveX document can only run in an ActiveX container; however, as there is no standardization between ActiveX hosts (even from Microsoft), there are numerous pitfalls. You should target one container — for example, Internet Explorer — and make sure your project works in that container or host.

Any variables you declare within an ActiveX document cannot be made persistent — that is to say, existing beyond the lifetime of the document itself. For example, you declare a variable in an ActiveX document, and modify it while the ActiveX document is activated in the browser. When the user navigates to another page, the modifications are lost — unless you implement a series of global variables and references.

You may need to create an ActiveX DLL that incorporates your data — and pass references to the individual pages as they come in and out of scope. Another approach is to implement public properties or methods for your ActiveX document and set them as needed.

Lastly, while you can include many third-party controls on your ActiveX document, you cannot use the OLE Container control or embedded objects such as an Excel spreadsheet. You may, however, include other ActiveX controls, including Visual Basic-authored ActiveX controls.

Also, your ActiveX document cannot contain certain keywords, such as End. The conversion wizard automatically flags your code and notifies you of the changes you must make.

Creating an ActiveX Document

ActiveX documents make use of the UserDocument object. As you might gather from looking at it in the Visual Basic workspace, a UserDocument object is similar to a Visual Basic form. Yet there are several important exceptions:

✦ You cannot include OLE objects such as Word or Excel documents, or the OLE container control.

✦ UserDocument objects have many but not all of the standard events that a form has. Among the standard form events that are missing in UserDocument objects are Activate, Deactivate, LinkClose, LinkError, LinkExecute, LinkOpen, Load, QueryUnload, and Unload. If you are translating from a standard form to a UserDocument, you may need to move code from the form's events to the corresponding UserDocument events. However, in some cases you will need to rethink your logic, because there is no corresponding event.

✦ On the other hand, UserDocument objects also possess events that the form does not. Some events unique to UserDocument objects include AsyncReadComplete (occurs when the browser completes a download); Hide (occurs when the Visible property changes to False.); Scroll (occurs when the user clicks the browser's scroll bar); and Show (occurs when the Visible property changes to True).

Tip You will have pretty good success if you use the ActiveX Document Migration Wizard to port your standard Visual Basic 5 or Visual Basic 6 projects to ActiveX Document. However, the Migration Wizard does not move code from events not supported by the UserDocument — you will have to move this code manually.

Step-by-Step ActiveX documents

Outside of the issues noted previously, creating a new ActiveX document project is pretty easy. The steps are quite similar to developing a standard interface using forms:

1. Lay out the features of your ActiveX Document interface.

2. Design the communications interface of your ActiveX document — the properties, methods, and events required.

3. Create a new ActiveX document and add any required classes, modules, forms, and so on.

4. Design your document using standard Visual Basic tools such as text boxes, labels, and so on. Add third-party controls, too.

5. Compile your document to create the .VBD file, or run the project and use an instance of Internet Explorer to test your code.

6. Test your ActiveX document with all your targeted applications. Do not forget or omit this last step!

Visual Basic creates two types of ActiveX documents — EXE and DLL. The major difference between EXE and DLL is how they run in the host. DLL ActiveX documents are called *in-process servers,* and those with an .EXE extension are *out-of-process servers*. Out-of-process means the component is a separate program or process and does not share address space with the applications that use it. This makes it necessary for an intermediary (OLE) to communicate back and forth between the application process in one address space and the component process in another address space. In-process means that the component shares address space with the application using it, so no intermediary is required to communicate between processes.

After you determine which sort of ActiveX document to create, choose it from the Visual Basic File ➪ New menu dialog. By default, the new project contains a single, empty, ActiveX UserDocument object.

When you have the UserDocument as you wish, it's time to try it out. Unlike a traditional project, you cannot run the ActiveX document in the IDE — you need a host. For this testing, we will use Microsoft Internet Explorer 4.01, included on the companion CD-ROM.

Remember, the project is a DLL (or OLE Server) and at least one of the interface forms are now UserDocuments. For an example, we created a small directory application that connects to a database using the Visual Basic Data control. Our little directory application can look up names of colleagues and return information about them, including their company Web site. Using the Hyperlink object of the UserDocument, the directory application can also connect to their Web site. This little applet not only uses a database, it also uses the PropertyBag object of the UserDocument to save and retrieve the last URL that was visited.

You could cobble this together with a series of CGI or other scripts, but it took us about 10 minutes total to do this in Visual Basic — and that is the real reason to think about ActiveX documents.

We started this applet as a standard Visual Basic executable program. Figure 26-1 shows the form and its contents before we converted it to an ActiveX document using the ActiveX Migration Wizard.

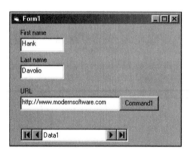

Figure 26-1: A standard Visual Basic program before conversion to an ActiveX document

The ActiveX Migration Wizard (see Figure 26-2) is a real help when you're Web-a-cizing existing applications. The ActiveX Migration Wizard is also easy to use. Here's how you perform the conversion process using the Migration Wizard:

1. Load your existing non-ActiveX Document/Visual Basic 5 or Visual Basic 6 project.

2. If the ActiveX Document Migration Wizard option is not visible in the Add-Ins menu, choose the Add-In Manager option from the Add-Ins menu and start the VB 6 ActiveX Document Migration Wizard.

3. Choose the ActiveX Document Migration Wizard option from the Add-Ins menu.

4. Note that the wizard's first panel explicitly states its job is simply to convert forms to UserDocument objects. This is a key concept you must grasp. Click Next to continue.

5. The next step, shown in Figure 26-3, is for you to choose which forms you want to convert. The list shows all of the forms in the active VB project. Note that your ActiveX document can also contain conversions of standard forms.

Remember, though, that your ActiveX Document project must have at least one `UserDocument`. Typically, the `UserDocument` calls and loads the forms as needed. You may also have multiple `UserDocument` objects that load one another. Having chosen the forms to be converted, click Next to continue.

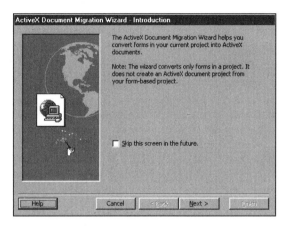

Figure 26-2: The ActiveX Migration Wizard Introduction screen

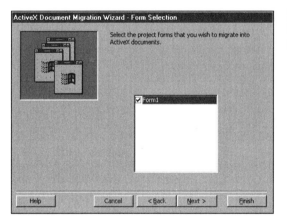

Figure 26-3: The ActiveX Migration Wizard Form Selection screen

6. Next, select Conversion options (Figure 26-4). Although the ActiveX Migration Wizard will not create an ActiveX Document project for you, it can convert the project type of your current project to ActiveX Document. After the conversion, you will need to move any now-invalid code manually. For example, code that was previously in `Form_Load` might need to be moved to the `UserDocument_InitiProperties` event. You may also have to work around a few issues — such as the fact that forms have a `Caption` property, but a `UserDocument` does not. Click Next to continue.

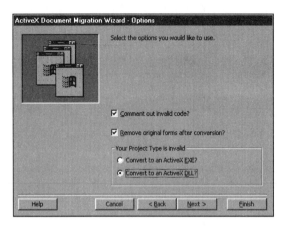

Figure 26-4: The Migration Wizard's Options screen

7. Your new `UserDocument` is almost ready to debug or test. Click Finish to exit the wizard (Figure 26-5).

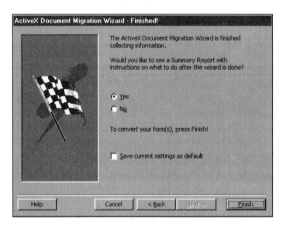

Figure 26-5: The final panel of theActiveX Migration Wizard

The Migration Wizard will probably make some changes to your code, as shown in Listing 26-1. The wizard inserts incompatible code into ActiveX Document as comments, but it marks the offending code so you can find it and work around it if you must.

The following code is the result of the ActiveX Migration Wizard's having converted our original form, and then our having added a custom property to make the current URL location persistent. The wizard displays a message if comments were added (option selected in step 5), and it displays the summary report (if "yes" was selected in step 7). Note how the Migration Wizard has commented out certain aspects of the code. The wizard replaces invalid code and syntax with comments, as shown in Listing 26-1. The complete code for the ActiveX Document applet in this chapter is shown in this listing.

Listing 26-1: **Complete Code for the ActiveX Document Applet**

```
Option Explicit

'Default Property Values:
Const m_def_website = "http://www.modernsoftware.com"

'Property Variables:
Dim m_website As String

Public Property Get website() As String
    website = m_website
End Property

Public Property Let website(ByVal New_website As String)
    m_website = New_website
    PropertyChanged "website"
End Property

'Initialize Properties for User Control
Private Sub UserDocument_InitProperties()
    m_website = m_def_website
End Sub

'Load property values from storage
Private Sub UserDocument_ReadProperties(PropBag As PropertyBag)
    m_website = PropBag.ReadProperty("website", m_def_website)
End Sub

'Write property values to storage
Private Sub UserDocument_WriteProperties(PropBag As _
    PropertyBag)
    Call PropBag.WriteProperty("website", m_website, _
        m_def_website)
End Sub

Private Sub Command1_Click()
    ' Use Hyperlink NavigateTo
    ' to go to the URL in txtURL.
    On Error Resume Next
    Hyperlink.NavigateTo txtURL.Text
    If Err.Number = 0 Then
        'save this URL
        website = txtURL.Text
    End If
End Sub
```

(continued)

Listing 26-1 *(continued)*

```
Private Sub UserDocument_Initialize()
    ' called before InitProperties, setup default values
    m_website = m_def_website
End Sub

Private Sub mnuExit_Click()
'[AXDW] The following line was commented out by the _
    ActiveX Document Migration Wizard.
'    End
End Sub

Private Sub Form_Load()

'[AXDW] The following line was commented out by the _
    ActiveX Document Migration Wizard.
'    Caption = "Company directory"
    Label1 = "First name"
    Label2 = "Last name"
    Label3 = "URL"
Command1.Caption = "GO"
End Sub
```

The preceding code implements a database control that connects to a database of names and URLs. The code stores the last-used URL for a contact in a persistent data member, and choosing the GO button uses the ActiveX Documents Hyperlink method to navigate the browser to that URL. This is a powerful integration feature of your ActiveX documents — you can use Visual Basic code and controls to create an interface to filter or navigate to standard HTML pages and Web locations.

Basically, the wizard gets rid of invalid statements. For example, the standalone directory had a caption in the title bar; when hosted in the browser, the title bar will read whatever the HTML page title tells it to — and no VB property can override that. The wizard also gets rid of any End statements, because now this code is simply a dialog and no longer a standalone application. To end the application now, the user moves to another page. Figure 26-6 shows the project running under Internet Explorer 4.01.

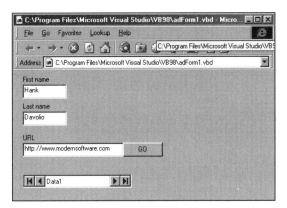

Figure 26-6: The ActiveX document now running in Internet Explorer

Figure 26-6 shows our directory running as a Web page; pretty cool, huh? ActiveX documents let you quickly develop Visual Basic applications that tightly integrate with your intranet or Internet. ActiveX documents also offer the wonderful ability to make sure each and every user in the entire enterprise is using the exact version of your software. You can make and update the entire enterprise by simply making changes to the ActiveX document and posting it on your server.

Hosting ActiveX Documents

Once your ActiveX document is created, you will need to get somewhat proficient with HTML and things Web related. ActiveX documents are hosted in Internet browsers and make use of HTML commands to "boot" the ActiveX document from an HTML page.

After creating an ActiveX document in Visual Basic, you compile it. You have choices when it comes to compiling and creating your ActiveX documents — you can create an in-process or out-of-process document. As with Visual Basic-authored OLE Servers (or ActiveX servers), you can create an ActiveX Document EXE or an ActiveX Document DLL. The difference between them is how they interact with their host. An ActiveX Document EXE runs out-of-process; an ActiveX Document DLL runs in-process. (See the discussion in Chapter 19.) ActiveX Document DLLs are faster because they share space with their host. ActiveX Document EXEs are slower, but they may be shared by other programs. The choice you make depends on the usage model of your ActiveX document. Generally speaking, an in-process ActiveX document shares address and memory space with its host, resulting in faster operation. You use in-process servers when you want to make sure no other application can share data with your component. An in-process server cannot be used by external programs. An out-of-process document, however, may be used by multiple applications. There is slightly more overhead in calling an out of process server's methods and properties, but the same server may support many client programs.

Essentially, your ActiveX Document is a program (EXE or DLL) that has one or more of its dialogs created using the Visual Basic `UserDocument` instead of a form. You can mix and match `UserDocument` objects and `Form` objects in your ActiveX document — however, only the `UserDocument` objects are hosted by the browser. `UserDocument` objects can display forms, but forms cannot display `UserDocument` objects.

When you compile your ActiveX document, Visual Basic creates a file with the extension .VBD for each `UserDocument` object in the ActiveX Document project. These VBD files are the definition files that the browser uses to locate, load, and activate your ActiveX documents. A single ActiveX Document project could consist of the main EXE or DLL and a series of VBD files, and perhaps some forms, too.

The browser loads the VBD file, which in turn describes the ActiveX Document EXE (or DLL) to load. Typically, you would use HMTL and/or VBScript to load and reference the ActiveX document. The trick is to make a plain HTML page that loads the ActiveX document — this is because the ActiveX document replaces the HTML page in Internet Explorer. You use the HTML <OBJECT> tag to load the ActiveX document. You also use HTML to provide a means for the browser to download, register, and navigate to the ActiveX document.

Debugging ActiveX Documents

To view an ActiveX document, you need to load the VBD file Visual Basic creates into a container such as Internet Explorer (included on the companion CD-ROM). Visual Basic automatically creates a new VBD file for every ActiveX document in your project whenever the project is run or compiled.

You can create your own ActiveX document or use the AD_DEMO.VBP project (included on the companion CD-ROM). To view the ActiveX document AD_DEMO.VBP, follow these steps:

1. Run the project by pressing F5. Once the project is running, if you change to the directory where the project is located, you will find a file named ADFORM1.VBD — this is the VBD file that contains the information Internet Explorer needs to load and access your ActiveX document.

2. Visual Basic will automatically start Internet Explorer for you and display the `UserDocument`.

Debugging ActiveX documents is similar to debugging other ActiveX components, and you can use all the tools Visual Basic has to offer. While you are debugging your project, you can switch from Internet Explorer back to Visual Basic.

Note When you debug this way, Internet Explorer is now the client of Visual Basic and your ActiveX document. If you end or close Visual Basic during the session before closing Internet Explorer, an error will occur in Internet Explorer. Always end Internet Explorer before ending your program in Visual Basic.

This interactive development lets you see and test the logic of your program in real time. For changes to the interface, however, you will need to end Internet Explorer, then end your program in Visual Basic. When your changes are complete, you repeat the cycle.

Running ActiveX Documents

As mentioned earlier, Visual Basic forms are different from UserDocuments — UserDocuments have different events and methods. Key events in the life of a UserDocument are as follows:

✦ UserDocument_Initialize

✦ UserDocument_InitProperties

✦ UserDocument_Show

✦ UserDocument_Hide

✦ UserDocument_Terminate

The Initialize event precedes the InitProperties event, so do your setup and default variable assignments in the Initialize event. Initialize occurs prior to the invocation of any form-level (document-level) variables. InitProperties occurs when the document requests its default property settings. ReadProperties takes place whenever the PropertyBag class variable is polled. WriteProperties occurs whenever the contents of the PropertyBag class variable are changed, generally by way of a PropertyChanged statement. Pay attention to this behavior — it impacts your startup. Remember, if you want a procedure to run on startup, put a call to it into the Initialize event. If you want a procedure to run only the first time a user views your ActiveX document, place it in the InitProperties event. However, note that container properties are unavailable at the time Initialize occurs, because the ActiveX document has not yet connected to the host.

When the ActiveX UserDocument is shown, the Show event occurs. This event occurs each time the document is navigated to, and is analogous to the Form_Load event of a form. The Terminate event occurs when the ActiveX document moves out of the cache of Internet Explorer. Use the Terminate event to clean up before your ActiveX document terminates.

Deploying ActiveX documents

Users can navigate between HTML pages and your ActiveX documents. ActiveX documents that are not on users' computers are automatically downloaded when the user navigates to them — just like HTML. Further, ActiveX documents can automatically upgrade existing copies on a user's computer if fresher versions are on the server.

You devise links to ActiveX documents within an HTML page using a combination of HMTL and VBScript. It is not practical to think users will load and view your pages using the method presented above for debugging ActiveX documents. So, you need to use HTML to control the browser functions. You can then use VBScript to instruct Internet Explorer to load your ActiveX document through its VBD file.

The following HTML page embeds VBScript into the page, which in turn loads the VBD file. This code programmatically performs the same function as using the Internet Explorer File ➪ Open dialog to load the VBD file. Listing 26-2 shows how to programmatically load the VBD file.

Listing 26-2: **HTML Code for Loading an ActiveX Document**

```
<html>
<head>
<title>New Page 1</title>
</head>
<body>
<script LANGUAGE="VBScript">

Sub Window_OnLoad
    Document.Open
    Document.Write "<FRAMESET>"
    Document.Write "<FRAME SRC=""c:\program _
        files\devstudio\vb\adform1.vbd"">"
    Document.Write "</FRAMESET>"
    Document.Close
End Sub

</script>
</body>
</html>
```

Internet download packaging

Visual Basic-authored components that can be used in Internet Explorer can be packaged for automatic download and installation. This is a key feature for making practical use of ActiveX Documents. Using the tools provided by HTML, VBScript, and Visual Basic, you can package your ActiveX document for intranet or Internet download.

When the user accesses your Web page, your package is activated — downloaded (in the form of a compressed CAB file) along with the HTML Web page. Then, the package is verified for safety (optionally checking any digital certificates embedded into it via code signing). Internet Explorer also registers your ActiveX components in the registry, and finally loads and runs your ActiveX document. The browser does a lot for your automatically — you, however, have to package your application so that that browser can do its job for you.

The Visual Basic Package and Deployment Wizard is used to perform this packaging of your ActiveX Components. The Package and Deployment Wizard collects all the files your application requires and compresses them into a CAB file, then creates a sample HTML page that contains the information required to load your component. A CAB file consists of one or more compressed files.

The Package and Deployment Wizard creates a CAB file that contains the following information and files from your project:

- ✦ The ActiveX DLL or ActiveX EXE that hosts your ActiveX documents
- ✦ Visual Basic support files and other controls (if any) required by your project
- ✦ Information about whether or not the component is safe for scripting and initialization
- ✦ Registry information to install and activate your components

One nice feature is all the runtime components like MSVBVM60.DLL and data access components are available directly from the Microsoft Web site — meaning you don't have to include them in your own package.

The Package and Deployment Wizard also asks you to decide whether your components are safe for scripting and initialization. The rules for these statements are fuzzy — it's really up to you to decide just what *safe* means to you. When you say your components are safe, you guarantee your components never do bad things — nebulous at best. The end result is that selection *safe* for scripting and *safe* for initialization result in extra registry entries under the ActiveX Document Class ID storage that tell Internet Explorer to skip the annoying "Warning, this page contains controls that are not safe" message.

The Wizard is long-winded, with many screens, but the effort is well worth the time it takes you to enter the data! To create an Internet download package, here is what you do:

1. Start the Package and Deployment Wizard. You can run the Wizard from the Visual Basic IDE for the current project or as a stand-alone program. The icon to start the Package and Deployment Wizard is located in the program group where the Visual Basic icon is located. Once you choose the wizard, you'll soon see the wizard's main panel, as shown in Figure 26-7.

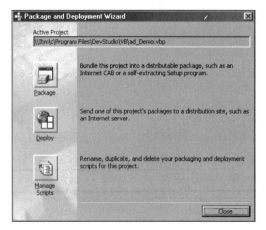

Figure 26-7: The first panel of the Package and Deployment Wizard

2. Enter your project's project (.VBP) filename or choose the Browse button to navigate to your project.

3. Choose the Package button to display the Package Type dialog, where you can choose how to package your software. The options are Standard Setup (uses setup.exe program), Internet Package (creates a downloadable Internet package with .CAB extension), or Dependency file (creates a file listing the runtime components you project uses). For this example, choose Internet Package, which will create an installation package suitable for use on your intranet or via the Internet. Choose Next to continue.

4. In the combo box marked Select Project, choose your ActiveX Document project.

5. Click the Package button. Soon, you'll see the panel shown in Figure 26-8.

6. In the list marked Package type, choose Internet Package to start the Internet Package Wizard. Click Next to continue. You'll see the Build Folder screen (Figure 26-9).

7. In the combo box marked Build Folder, choose the location where the wizard is to place your packaged files. Click Next to continue to the Files screen (Figure 26-10).

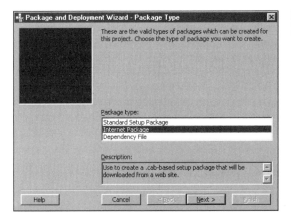

Figure 26-8: The wizard's Package Type screen

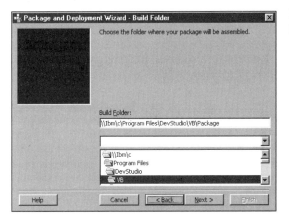

Figure 26-9: The wizard's Build Folder screen

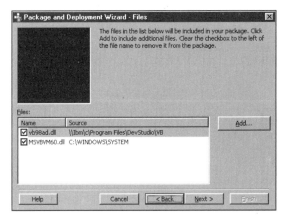

Figure 26-10: The wizard's Files screen

8. In the Files list, choose which files to include. At this step, all files need to be selected, including those that can be downloaded. Note that the wizard detects most of the files your application requires. Click Next to continue to the Components screen (Figure 26-11).

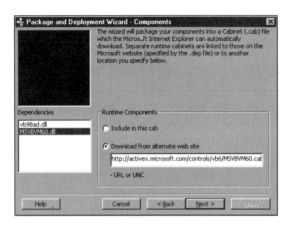

Figure 26-11: The wizard's Components screen

9. In the Runtime Components frame, choose whether the user is to download the system runtime files that are listed in the Dependencies list at left, from Microsoft's Web site. If the user is to download these files, they need not be included in your final package; otherwise, if you choose Include in this cab, the user's browser will download this package from your own deployment site. If any of the listed components are already on the user's machine, his or her browser will not attempt to download them again. Click on Next to continue to the Safety screen (Figure 26-12).

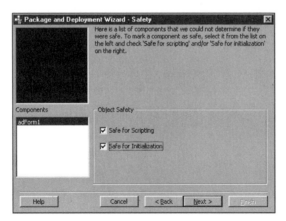

Figure 26-12: The Safety panel

10. In the frame marked Object Safety, check whether you've decided if your component is safe for scripting and for initialization. Safe for Initialization indicates that during initialization of the component, the component does not create, change, or delete any files or change system settings. Safe for Scripting indicates that the component, when used by scripts, does not create, change, or delete any files or change system settings.

Note the possible legal implications of using these options, as shown, by pressing the Help button. Consult your company management before using these options with Internet Web sites. Click Next to continue to the Install Locations screen (Figure 26-13).

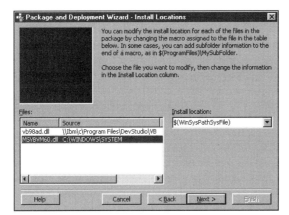

Figure 26-13: The wizard's Install Locations screen

11. In the combo box marked Install location, choose where the files will be installed. Macros are used to indicate where to install files. The macros take a value in parentheses and return a path. For example, $(ProgramFiles) returns the directory into which applications are usually installed (for Windows 98 and 95 or Windows NT 4.0, this is usually c:\Program Files). Press Help to view a complete listing of macros and values. Click Next to continue to Shared Files (Figure 26-14).

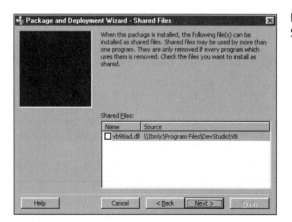

Figure 26-14: The wizard's Shared Files screen

12. The next step shows a list of files that, after installation, the Registry may treat as shared files. Click Next to continue to the last screen (Figure 26-15).

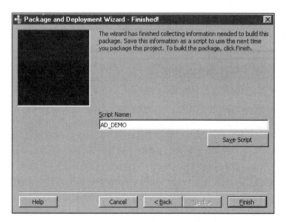

Figure 26-15: The final panel of the Package and Deployment Wizard

13. Continue through the Package and Deployment Wizard and then choose Finish to create the Internet download package.

The Package and Deployment Wizard creates a number of files and places them into the directory you specify. Use an HTML editor to view the files the Package and Deployment Wizard creates for you.

Code signing

Several advanced operations are available to you if you choose to use ActiveX Documents. These advanced features let you control versioning, licensing, validation, and compression of the components used. One of these key technologies accommodates *code signing* and *digital signatures*.

ActiveX documents and ActiveX controls have full access to the system and all its resources, allowing powerful solutions for Internet and intranet Web sites — and an opening for malicious behavior. Not surprisingly, security has arisen as a topic of discussion. In order to make component use safer, and make users feel more secure, the industry has embarked on a security campaign. One result of this campaign is digital code signing.

Signing adds extra information to an object (program, control, and so on) so that a browser can determine the trustworthiness of the component. Signing embeds information about the control in such a way that any changes to the signed object will be detected by the browser.

Authenticode

Microsoft's solution to the security issue is Authenticode, which comprises the code signing and authentication techniques Microsoft provides. There are two related security issues — ensuring authenticity and ensuring integrity. Ensuring authenticity refers to a way to determine if the software comes from the vendor that claims to have created it. Ensuring integrity refers to a way to determine if the software has been modified since it was signed. Though Authenticode does not guarantee that signed code is safe, it does provide a means to inform users about the publisher of the software and to determine if the program has been modified since it was signed.

The operating system component of Authenticode is the Microsoft Cryptography Application Programming Interface (CryptoAPI). The browser components of Authenticode use the CryptoAPI with the extra information in the signed component to present the user security dialogs.

To sign your ActiveX documents, you will need to get a copy of the ActiveX SDK — free from Microsoft — currently available at

```
http://www.microsoft.com/workshop/prog/
```

Authenticode alone is not enough for code signing if you also require *trust*. Trust comes from an independent third party, called a *certification authority*. The trusted authority is the grantor of a key component of the code-signing scheme — your credentials. The certification authority is a third party that verifies your information and grants you a digital key. One such certification authority is a company called VeriSign (`http://www.verisign.com`).

Credentials

Ensuring authenticity and ensuring integrity are accomplished by having a trusted body (the certification authority) grant you *credentials*. The credentials are called a *software publisher certificate*. The software publisher certificate is issued by the certification authority after it verifies your identity. Your certificate includes your public cryptographic key, which you will use to sign your code.

The software publisher certificate contains coded information that provides a verifiable hierarchy security. This hierarchy is how the trust is communicated. The software publisher certificate also contains a digital signature that identifies you (the developer or firm developing the software) and your public key. VeriSign offers two classes of digital IDs to meet the needs of two types of software publishers. VeriSign describes their digital IDs as follows:

> A Class 2 digital ID is designed for individual software publishers — in other words, people who publish software independently of an organization or company. This class of digital ID provides assurance regarding an individual's identity.

> A Class 3 digital ID is designed for commercial software publishers. These are companies and other organizations that publish software. This class of digital ID provides greater assurance about the identity of a publishing organization and is designed to represent the level of assurance provided today by retail channels for software.

What this means is, if you want to sell software, get a Class 3 digital ID; otherwise, get a Class 2 digital ID.

Signing your code

Once you have a certificate and the ActiveX SDK, you are almost ready to sign your code. Before you can sign code, you need to make sure the proper operating system and cryptography options are installed. The test program for the correct CryptoAPI is API.EXE, which is installed as a part of the ActiveX SDK. To make sure your computer is configured, you simply run API.EXE from the DOS prompt as follows:

```
C:\ACTXSDK\API.EXE *
```

This displays messages as it tests out your system. If your version of Windows supports the CryptoAPI, you may begin to use the SIGNCODE.EXE program installed from the ActiveX SDK to sign your code.

Signing your code adds overhead, usually around 1,000 bytes. This small overhead is usually not significant. There is also a small amount of delay induced when loading the signed control. This is do to the processing of the digital certificate wrapper placed around your control by SIGNCODE.EXE — the impact is minimal on most systems.

The steps for production code signing are as follows:

1. Get Internet Explorer 4.01 or 3.02.
2. Download the free ActiveX SDK from
   `http://www.microsoft.com/workshop/prog/`.
3. Purchase digital credentials from VeriSign, GTE, or another CA (certification authority).
4. When you receive your credentials, the browser will create your SPC (software publisher certificate).
5. Create your ActiveX document.
6. Use SIGNCODE.EXE with your credentials and key to sign your code.
7. Use CHKTRUST.EXE to test your signed code. It should indicate the code is safe and display the information you used to sign your code.

Component compression

If you require Registry updates, component licensing, code signing, or CAB file creation, you need to get the Microsoft ActiveX Development SDK, available from `www.microsoft.com`. The Enterprise Edition of Visual Basic includes elementary capabilities for these features; but for custom work, get the SDK — it's worth it.

The CAB file extraction, licensing, and registry update functionality all reside with the browser and are controlled using HTML tags and values to make the browser do your bidding. The ActiveX SDK has all the tools you need, and Visual Basic Enterprise Edition also has beginner-level tools for getting your ActiveX documents posted and working on the Web or your intranet. The code signing requires a digital certificate from a certificate authority. The most common certificate authority is Verisign.

Advanced Operations with Active Documents

ActiveX documents offer some pretty amazing and easy-to-use features that can enable you to customize the look and feel of not only your Web pages, but also the browser itself. Some key features include menu hosting and custom properties.

Menu hosting

Using the Visual Basic Menu Editor, you can add menus to your ActiveX documents. Your ActiveX documents cannot have their own menus when displayed in Internet Explorer; however, the menu you create can be merged into Internet Explorer. This means you have to take into account menu negotiation for menus you add to your ActiveX documents.

Figure 26-16 shows the menus of the sample directory application used in this chapter. Notice the Lookup menu and its Find Them submenu item.

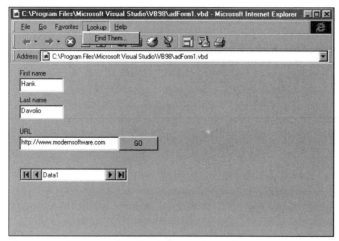

Figure 26-16: Menu hosting in Internet Explorer

Note

While in the Visual Basic IDE, you cannot see the menu on your UserDocument. However, by using the Ctrl+E menu shortcut while the UserDocument has focus, you can use the standard Visual Basic Menu Editor.

You needn't do anything special other than add the menu to the UserDocument.

Custom properties

Using the UserDocument PropertyBag object, you can save data values for custom properties. Visual Basic gives us two additional events that enable you to create persistent user-defined values for your properties: ReadProperties and WriteProperties.

Saving values with WriteProperties()

Visual Basic fires the UserDocument object's WriteProperties event when any user-defined properties change. All you need to do is tell Visual Basic that property has changed, and then Visual Basic will fire the WriteProperties event. For this purpose an intrinsic method titled PropertyChanged is provided. You use the PropertyChanged statement to tell Visual Basic a property value is changed, as in the following example:

```
Public Property Let Caption(ByVal vNewValue As Variant)
    m_Caption = vNewValue
    PropertyChanged "Caption"
End Property
```

In the `Property Let` procedure for the `Caption` property, we use `PropertyChanged`. This tells Visual Basic that the `Caption` property has a new value. Then, Visual Basic will trigger the `WriteProperties` event. In `WriteProperties`, you write code to save the incoming value into the host container.

```
Private Sub UserDocument_WriteProperties(PropBag As _
    PropertyBag)
    Call PropBag.WriteProperty("Caption", m_Caption, _
        m_Def_Caption)
End Sub
```

Note how you again refer to the property by a string representation of its actual exposed name, `Caption`. The second argument to `WriteProperty` is the value to write into the property, in this case `m_Caption` (which contains the value "Now is the time"). The last argument is a default value to write into the property in case the user-defined property is not available.

Note

> Remember, the name of the member property must be passed as a string. Do not change the name of the text string when you internationalize your `UserDocument`. The text string of the name must match the name of the declaration for that property.

A good practice is to follow the guidelines presented here and use the default value for the property for the third argument. Now, when the `Caption` property is set, it is stored in `m_Caption`. In the `Property Let` procedure, you tell Visual Basic the property has changed value, and Visual Basic then calls the `WriteProperties` event. In the `WriteProperties` event procedure, you then write code to store the value of the property into the `PropertyBag` (that is, the host's data storage).

Reading values with ReadProperties

Once the data is stored in the `PropertyBag` (the host's data storage), you will also want to be able to read it. Visual Basic calls the `ReadProperties` event to load the values from the `PropertyBag`. For `UserDocuments`, `ReadProperties` won't occur until the second time the user navigates to your ActiveX document, so plan accordingly. The `ReadProperties` event is where you set up values for the `UserDocument` — again, Visual Basic handles the hard work, while you have to write the actual code to assign values.

```
Private Sub UserControl_ReadProperties(PropBag As PropertyBag)
    m_Caption = PropBag.ReadProperty("Caption", m_Def_Caption)
End Sub
```

The first argument to `ReadProperty` is the name of the property to read — in this case, `Caption`. The second argument is a default value in case there is nothing stored in the `PropertyBag` for this property. This is true if the user of your control has never changed the default value of this property.

The code is now complete. Your custom property is ready for read/write operations. Any changes made to the property using are now persistent — that is, they are stored and may be retrieved at any later date. Any changes the user makes to the document are reflected in the state of that document when the user goes away and comes back to it. The complete code to implement a single, persistent custom property is shown below in Listing 26-3.

Listing 26-3: Code Required to Implement Persistent Properties in ActiveX UserDocument

```
Option Explicit

' default values
Const m_Def_Caption = "MyActiveX Document 1.0"
' property variables
Dim m_Caption As String

Public Property Get Caption() As Variant
    Caption = m_Caption
End Property

Public Property Let Caption(ByVal vNewValue As Variant)
    m_Caption = vNewValue
    PropertyChanged "Caption"
End Property

Private Sub UserDocument_InitProperties()
    m_Caption = m_Def_Caption
End Sub

Private Sub UserDocument_ReadProperties(PropBag As _
    PropertyBag)
    m_Caption = PropBag.ReadProperty("Caption", m_Def_Caption)
End Sub

Private Sub UserDocument_WriteProperties(PropBag As _
    PropertyBag)
    Call PropBag.WriteProperty("Caption", m_Caption, _
        m_Def_Caption)
End Sub
```

Targeting hosts

ActiveX documents require a host or container. Three containers that are common targets of ActiveX Documents are as follows:

✦ Microsoft Internet Explorer

✦ Microsoft Office Binder

✦ Visual Basic Development Environment Tool Window

Each of these containers has certain issues associated with it based on its implementation of ActiveX interfaces. How your ActiveX document operates depends on its host, so these issues are important to you. You should test all features of your ActiveX document with your host of choice to make sure it operates as you expect.

Summary

✦ ActiveX documents are similar to Visual Basic forms. They can contain other controls, just like a form; however, unlike a form, they can be hosted by an Internet browser. ActiveX documents run in HTML pages hosted under Internet Explorer—enabling you to mix and match traditional HTML pages with ActiveX documents. This browser hosting provides a powerful solution for integrating Internet and intranet resources into Visual Basic programs.

✦ ActiveX documents may also be stored on the server, creating a single repository for your application. This allows easy updating of all users of the application, because ActiveX documents' VBD files contain the information the browser requires to automatically update the local copy—ensuring that all users always have the most recent versions.

✦ ActiveX documents are easy to create using Visual Basic. There is even a conversion wizard to help you port existing applications to ActiveX Document. The conversion wizard will make changes to your code, so be prepared. However, the changes the wizard makes are all commented and noted in the code, so you can easily find and resolve them.

✦ Using the Package and Deployment Wizard makes creating your setup a breeze. You can code your signing before using the wizard, resulting in a robust and secure installation process.

✦ ActiveX documents support three host container types (Microsoft Internet, Explorer, Microsoft Office Binder, and the Visual Basic Development Environment Tool Window), but each of these containers has certain associated issues based on its implementation of ActiveX Documents. Therefore, you need to test your ActiveX documents carefully with the host you plan to use.

✦   ✦   ✦

Windows API Programming

Using the Windows Application Programming Interface

Before Visual Basic, all programmers who wanted to write Windows programs had to use the Windows API. Programs had to use the Windows API to access the internal data structures, information, and system functions of Windows. With the advent of Visual Basic, use of Windows API is optional. In many cases, you can "work around" a particular limitation. However, when you cannot, the Windows API is often the only way to accomplish some tasks.

The Windows API was not, and is not, designed to be used from Visual Basic. This sad fact often makes using the Windows API seem more difficult than you might expect. The Windows API is based on C, not Visual Basic. Windows API calls (APIs for short) follow a set of rules foreign to most Visual Basic developers. Many APIs implement callbacks, others demand that you create string buffers before you use them, and yet others append annoying null strings (Chr$(0)) to the end of strings they return to you.

All these things are normal for C/C++ programmers and are a part of everyday programming in those languages. We Visual Basic developers need to expand our horizons and realize that to use this powerful, free source of information and utility, we must learn the ways of the API.

It is well worth the trouble of learning, too. Using the functionality exposed by the Windows operating system, there is very little that you cannot accomplish. It is very important to realize that there are many Windows API calls. Grouped by function, Windows API calls allow access to many custom Windows services such as encryption, compression, and networking. However, Visual Basic itself also has many methods and properties. The key to successfully incorporating usage of Windows API calls into your programs is to learn what services the Windows API provides.

Understanding Windows API Calls

Windows API calls are contained in DLLs external to your program. You declare the API call and the DLL that contains it; this is done in the Declarations section of a module, class, form, property page, user control, and so on. The functions exposed by Windows via the Windows API are external to your program. The Windows API is contained within Windows system files such as kernel32.exe, gdi32.exe, user32.exe, and others. These files are parts of Windows, and in fact Windows itself uses the same functions you will. Most Windows API calls are fast, well written, and optimized for performance. That is not to say that using the Windows API is always going to make your code faster; in some cases, it will not. What it does say is that this functionality is largely stable and quite functional.

Windows API calls encapsulate many system functions in a standard and uniform manner. The Windows API provides access to system resources such as configuration information, the keyboard, the mouse, the screen, and the file system, to name a few.

Over the years, the Windows API has grown to handle more and more tasks. Microsoft has, thankfully, left many API calls the same. In some cases, Microsoft has extended the original API calls with newer versions. Often, you can choose from several Windows API calls to perform a given task. To use the Windows API, you need to declare the API, the name of the DLL it's located in, and all the arguments it takes. For a function, you must also define the data type it returns. The process of declaring the API includes defining all aspects of its usage with regard to arguments and data types. Remember that the Windows API is not a part of your program, or of Visual Basic. The only information Visual Basic can use to implement your API calls is what you tell VB when you declare the API. Additionally, many Windows API calls take *structures* as arguments. In Visual Basic, you call a "structure" a user-defined type, or UDT. More data types exist in Windows and other languages than Visual Basic supports. At times, you may need to translate from Windows data types to Visual Basic types. During the declaration process, you will also need to include and define those structures the API requires.

If all this sounds like more work, you're right. It is more work, but the rewards outweigh the costs. And to make it easier, Visual Basic comes with an add-in that has almost all the Windows API declarations properly defined. The API add-in lets you choose declarations, constants, and structures and paste them directly into your programs.

Visual Basic does so much of the hard work for us that many Visual Basic developers are not prepared for using the Windows API. Using the Windows API is programming the old-fashioned way — you do all the work yourself, and any error can unceremoniously dump your program. A Windows API call often returns a Boolean value that indicates success or failure — unlike a Visual Basic call, which generates a runtime error that returns a unique numeric value representing precisely which error occurred. Most Windows API calls, if you use them incorrectly, simply don't perform the task you expect. In the worst cases, using an API call incorrectly can corrupt your program and cause it to fail.

Windows API calls are sticklers for detail. You must properly declare and define each argument, constant, and function member you expect to use. Failure to do so often results in a very sour experience, because the Windows API expects that you know what you are doing. Passing a string variable when the API expects an integer can crash not only your program but also Windows. However, with proper planning, you can safely incorporate advanced features directly into your programs.

Learning When to Use Windows API Calls

Windows contains dozens of API categories. A complete list is beyond the scope of this book. However, experience shows that almost all Visual Basic developers require several specific, well-defined categories during the development of most reasonably complex applications. Table 27-1 lists Windows API functions commonly required by Visual Basic developers.

Table 27-1
Common Functionality Provided by Windows API

Category	Description
Keyboard	Determining keyboard type, number of function keys, keyboard language, and key mappings; checking the state of any keyboard key; setting key states; synthesizing keystrokes; controlling key repeat and delay rates
Mouse	Determining presence or absence of a mouse; ascertaining type of mouse, number of mouse buttons; determining whether buttons are pressed or released; swapping and determining whether buttons are swapped (left- vs. right-handed mouse); locating mouse cursor; synthesizing mouse movement; tracking location of mouse
File System	Checking for existence of file(s); determining type of drive (that is, network, location, CD-ROM, read-only, and so on); modifying file attributes; determining disk space used and free; checking file system attributes; converting to/from long and short filenames

(continued)

Table 27-1	
Category	**Description**
Video Display (Screen)	Determining color depth; checking resolution; calculating true window position; retrieving, moving, and sizing information under various resolutions; optimizing screen/graphical operations
System Information	Determining operating system version; getting operating system name (Windows 95, Windows NT, and so on); checking number of processors; retrieving memory installed; setting or getting advanced properties of Windows and controls

Although Table 27-1 is not all-inclusive, it represents a fair amount of additional functionality that is commonly needed by Visual Basic developers. In general, if what you want to accomplish is in Table 27-1, the Windows API is where you need to be looking.

For example, suppose you want to determine the number of function keys on a keyboard. The Windows API has a function that returns this information quickly and accurately — GetKeyboardType:

```
Private Declare Function GetKeyboardType Lib "user32" _
(ByVal nTypeFlag As Long) As Long
```

When you call GetKeyBoardType and pass it an argument of 2, it returns the number of function keys.

Technically, you can use Windows API calls whenever you want to. Of course, just because you can do something does not always mean you should. The same is true for Windows API calls. Windows contains many API calls that duplicate what Visual Basic already does—for example, the DeleteFile API:

```
Declare Function DeleteFile Lib "kernel32" Alias _
    "DeleteFileA" (ByVal lpFileName As String) As Long
```

DeleteFile performs the same task as the Visual Basic Kill method. Although they perform the same basic function, DeleteFile does not generate a trappable error if the file to delete is not found; the Kill method does. DeleteFile returns a code indicating whether it succeeds or fails. Therefore, using DeleteFile with a structured Visual Basic application that includes planned error-handling requires extra code to check whether the file was truly deleted or not and then raise the appropriate error. If not implemented properly, this extra code may result in hard-to-find bugs.

On the other hand, the Visual Basic `Kill` method works with intrinsic Visual Basic error-handling systems like `On Error`, `On Error Resume`, `On Error Resume Next`, and the `Error` object. Whenever you're presented with a choice of using an internal method or property or a Windows API call, choose the internal method unless there is a very good reason for not doing so. Some sound reasons for choosing Windows API calls are listed here:

✦ **Because you can:** If you are learning Windows API programming, then by all means use every Windows API you can. Except for use as a learning or training experience, however, this reason will most likely be counterproductive. Never use APIs in production or commercial programs unless it's required by the needs of that application.

✦ **Enhanced performance:** In some cases, but not all, a Windows API call may be faster than the Visual Basic counterpart. You will need to test carefully to verify any alleged performance enhancement. Except for a very few well-documented cases, this reason is dubious at best.

✦ **Because Visual Basic cannot do something:** This is by far the best reason to use the Windows API—to augment and extend Visual Basic.

Windows API Usage Secrets

To successfully integrate Windows API function calls into your programs, you will need to know not only how to properly declare, set up, and call Windows API, but also how to handle error conditions and integrate them into your existing program logic. You should implement a fairly rigid error-handling process to test the success or failure of each Windows API you call. This is required, because Windows API calls often fail silently. Therefore, if you do not test return results and code appropriately to handle failures, you will induce subtle and often hard-to-find bugs in your code. For example, if an API fails and you then attempt to use a string that was supposed to be returned by the API with a Visual Basic keyword, that Visual Basic keyword might fail because the string is empty. APIs that do not fail subtly will fail spectacularly—corrupting your program and sometimes even crashing Windows itself.

Successfully Integrating Windows API Calls

You should use a well-defined process for integrating Windows API calls into your Visual Basic program. Follow these steps:

1. **Plan your mission.** Identify the task or tasks you want to accomplish, and define the results expected.

2. **Collect API functions.** Often, you will need several Windows API calls to accomplish a single task. Windows API calls are not named or grouped in the way you might think. For example, the API that determines the name of a user logged on to Windows is grouped under system information — not where you might think it would be located. A good reference, such as the Win32 Software Development Kit (SDK), MSDN, or other API reference work, is required.

3. **Test the API function calls.** A good plan often starts with coding the functionality of the Windows API portion of your code outside of the program that will use it. In most cases, writing a class wrapper for the APIs is the best solution, since you can develop and test the API solution using the class. See the example given in Listing 27-4 for an example of encapsulating Windows API function calls into a class. You can then reuse later, in other projects, the class and the Windows API functionality it encapsulates.

4. **Validate the solution.** Once the Windows API calls are collected into a class and tested together, make sure that class does what you thought it would. Many times, Windows API calls have unexpected side effects, or they generate results that require extra work on your part. Great examples of this are the need to declare strings and pad them with spaces before calling the API, and needing to strip trailing null (`Chr$(0)`) characters from returned strings.

5. **Write and test validation code.** Once all the mechanics are in place, write and test the code you will need in order to use the implemented class. For example, if your class does not implement a failure using Err.Raise, you will need to test for and handle the failure result in your code in the main body of your program.

One trick to remember: Due to the manner in which Visual Basic implements declared functions external to itself, including Windows API calls, you cannot use the `GetLastError` API function. `GetLastError` is used from C/C++ to return the error code of a failing API call — it sounds like something you really want to use. Unfortunately, Visual Basic can execute dozens of additional Windows API calls itself while calling your declared function. This means that the result of `GetLastError` will never be valid for the Windows API calls you declare and use.

Performance Implications of Using Windows API Calls

A common fallacy is that Windows API calls are always more efficient and faster than Visual Basic's built-in methods and properties. The story goes something like this: "Visual Basic wraps all its function in paranoid validation and error-handling code, making them slow, slow, slow." While it is true that certain Windows API calls are much faster than their Visual Basic counterparts, in general the opposite is true. Once you understand how Visual Basic implements an API call, you will understand why this is so.

Visual Basic implements declared API calls to external DLLs via the most flexible method possible. When the API function is called by your code, Visual Basic uses the `LoadLibrary` API function to first load an image of the module containing the declared function. Next, Visual Basic uses `GetProcAddress` to locate the start of the declared function's executable code. `GetProcAddress` is a Windows API that locates the executable starting address in memory of a function declared in a Windows DLL. Visual Basic then sets up the Windows error-tracking system using the `SetErrorMode` API function. When the staging is complete, Visual Basic indicates a critical thread section and calls the declared function. After the function executes, Visual Basic releases the critical thread semaphore and stores any failure codes in the Error object's `LastDLLError` member. After cleaning up, Visual Basic copies any argument values from the API function into the variables you declared, unloads the module, releases memory, and returns control to your program.

This process is lengthy but flexible. All declared functions external to Visual Basic are late bound this way. *Late binding* refers to the process of locating the code to execute in another program or DLL after the calling program is already compiled. The benefit of this late binding method is that your program can run even if the required or referenced DLL is not present — Visual Basic simply generates an error. The downside of this process is that it takes quite a bit of time for all the overhead involved. On the other hand, the Visual Basic run time is fairly optimized. An assembly language dump of the Visual Basic runtime library DLLs shows some pretty slim internal functions — without all the overhead. This is why, except for a few well-documented exceptions, you are better off from a performance perspective in sticking to Visual Basic methods.

When higher performance counts

Some Windows API calls outperform built-in Visual Basic methods. However, before embarking on a performance-enhancement journey, you should understand that there is lots of optimization you can do to Visual Basic's own methods. Often, these optimizations will dramatically improve performance while still allowing you to use built-in Visual Basic methods and properties. A great example of this is a control's Left and Top properties.

You often move controls about on a form using their Left and Top properties. For example:

```
txtText1.Left = 500
txtText1.Top = 500
```

A simple test run with 5,000 iterations took about 1.1s on a 133MHz Pentium machine. A quick optimization of this code results in a dramatic improvement:

```
txtText1.Move 500, 500
```

This optimization using Move instead of Left and Top ran in about .7s — a whopping 36 percent performance improvement.

The Windows API call MoveWindow (shown below), the counterpart to the Move method, ran in about 1.7s — 242 percent slower than using the Move method.

```
Declare Function MoveWindow Lib "user32" Alias "MoveWindow" _
    (ByVal hwnd As Long, ByVal x As Long, ByVal y As Long, _
     ByVal nWidth As Long, ByVal nHeight As Long, ByVal _
     bRepaint As Long) As Long
```

If you have gone through the motions of understanding how to optimize Visual Basic itself, then in many cases you have the most optimized program. Seldom if ever will an API call actually be faster than the Visual Basic counterpart. One exception to this rule-of-thumb is graphical operations. Visual Basic performs a tremendous amount of work whenever it accesses graphical components of the screen — to validate device contexts, window handles, and so on.

The net result is that for operations like reading pixels from the screen or writing pixels to the screen, the Windows API equivalent is more efficient. Instead of validating all the operands and parameters as Visual Basic does, the Windows API counts on your having made all the checks yourself. Therefore, the Windows API call has less direct overhead and can operate more efficiently. This is especially true for operations in loops in your programs.

For example, consider a loop to read a series of pixels from the screen. (Note that for ease of understanding, the following code is not optimized by using constants for colors.)

```
Dim i As Long
Dim j As Long
For i = 0 to 31
```

```
    For j = 0 To 31
        If Form1.Point(i, j) = QBColor(7) Then
            Form1.PSet(i, j), QBColor(0))
        End IF
    Next j
Next i
```

This code loops through an icon, changing all gray pixels to black. Each time Visual Basic reads a pixel using `Point`, it must validate all the Windows handles and device contexts, as well as set up internal error handlers in case an instruction attempts to read a pixel outside of the bounds defined by the device context.

The same happens when the pixel is being set to black. This is because Visual Basic doesn't know that this method is being addressed repetitively from a loop. As far as Visual Basic knows, each time you use the `Point` method, you could be using it for a different object. Therefore, for safety, Visual Basic always verifies all the arguments of every Visual Basic property and method every time the property or method is called. This results in a significant slowdown over the run of the loop as tremendous duplication of work is done over and over again.

When using the associated Windows API calls `SetPixel` and `GetPixel`, you pass the handle and device context one time — the APIs expect them to be correct, and they probably will remain unchanged for the duration of this loop.

The API equivalent of Visual Basic's `Point` and `PSet` methods are `SetPixel` and `GetPixel`. These APIs operate using a variable containing a data structure called a device context. A device context is a long integer into a table that Windows maintains. The device context is used by Windows to indicate which window to operate on. In Visual Basic, you use the object name, such as `Form1`, with graphical methods such as `Point`. However, when using the Windows API, you cannot use the object name (such as `Form1`) directly; you must deduce and use the object's device context, or `hDC`. Fortunately, Visual Basic exposes the device context of most of its graphical objects via a property titled `hDC`. The following code shows how to use the `hDC` of a form with API function calls:

```
Declare Function SetPixel Lib "gdi32" Alias "SetPixel" _
    (ByVal hdc As Long, ByVal x As Long, ByVal y As Long, _
    ByVal crColor As Long) As Long
Declare Function GetPixel Lib "gdi32" Alias "GetPixel" _
    (ByVal hdc As Long, ByVal x As Long, ByVal y As Long) _
    As Long

Dim i As Long
Dim j As Long
Dim hDC As Long

hDC = Form1.hDC
```

```
For i = 0 to 31
   For j = 0 To 31
      If GetPixel(hDC, i, j) = QBColor(7) Then
         SetPixel(hDC, i, j, QBColor(0))
      End IF
   Next j
Next i
```

The code using this method executes several times faster than when using Visual Basic's `Point()` method.

In summary, you can more often than not get the best results from optimizing Visual Basic's internal methods. There are, however, exceptions where using the API will be faster overall: for instance, in the case of loops of instructions that are executed many, many times.

Understanding Windows API Arguments and Result Codes

Windows itself is built on the C programming language. The data structures of C (and C++) allow parsing of data into fundamental data elements called words, bytes, and bits. Throughout the Windows API, you will need to be able to locate and evaluate the values of these data units. Unfortunately, Visual Basic has no function to do this for us. Visual Basic looks at data as whole units. You can, however, reliably parse out the information you need.

Before we jump into explaining how to extract information from data structures, we need to talk a little bit about binary data. At the lowest level, all data is stored as a grouping of bits. The word *bit* is a contraction of the term *binary digit*. All data is stored as groupings of bits. A bit represents a logical one (1) or zero (0), an on or off state, or the presence or absence of a value. In fact, the numbering system called *binary* uses only two digits: 1 and 0.

Using binary, or *base 2* arithmetic, you can then represent any number. Just like the decimal system, you can represent numbers as powers of the base. Visual Basic gives us the exponential operator: ^. For example, 2 is the result of the expression 2^1, or "two to the first power." Likewise, 4 is the result of 2^2, and so on. Given 8 bits, you can represent any number from 0 to 255 (Figure 27-1). Each bit position represents a continuing power of 2; thus, $2^0 = 1$, $2^1 = 2$, $2^2 = 4$, and so on. Setting bits lets us represent numeric values. For example, the number 5 may be represented by setting bits 0 and 2: 00000101.

2^7	2^6	2^5	2^4	2^3	2^2	2^1	2^0	(powers of 2)
7	6	5	4	3	2	1	0	(bit positions)
128	64	32	16	8	4	2	1	(values in each position)

Figure 27-1: How 8 bits can represent the numbers 0 to 255

At this point, you have the basic structure upon which all software is built. The next important concept is that of grouping. Groups of bits are collected together, stored, and operated upon as a data structure or unit of data. Table 27-2 lists the data types used by Windows and their corresponding Visual Basic data type.

Table 27-2
Translations of VB and Windows Basic Data Structures

Visual Basic	Windows
Long integer (32 bits)	Double word
Integer (16 bits)	Word
Byte (8 bits)	Byte

On the Intel processor family, 8 bits make a byte; 16 bits, or 2 bytes, in turn, create a word; 32 bits, or two words, create a double word; as shown in Table 27-3. (In some computer operating systems and communications protocols, 4 bits, half a byte, is referred to as a *nybble*. Nybbles are not a part of the vernacular of Windows, however.)

Table 27-3
How Groups of Bits Create Windows Data Structures

Data Type	Bytes	Bits
Double word	4	0 to 31
Word	2	0 to 15
Byte	1	0 to 7

Bit order indicates which bit (bit 0 or bit 7) represents the most value. This is referred to as the "most significant bit." The "least significant bit" is the bit position that represents the least value. On Intel-based machines, data is stored from least significant bit to most significant bit order, called *little-endian*. Other processor families — for example, the Motorola 68k series processor used predominantly in Apple computers — store data in *big-endian* order: most significant bit to least significant bit.

When you need to examine the most significant bit of the integral return value of a Windows API call, you really need to check the state of bit 15. To examine the state of individual bits, you use Visual Basic's built-in Boolean algebraic functions: And, Or, XOr, and Not.

When using Windows API calls, you often need to set individual bits of flags and arguments. Many times, you need to examine just certain parts of the return value — for example, GetAsyncKeyState, which indicates the state of a given keyboard key. The result of the GetAsyncKeyState API is a 16-bit integer for all versions of Windows. If the most significant bit of the result of GetAsyncKeyState is set (a logical 1), then the key is currently down; if it is not set (a logical 0) then the key is not down. If the least significant bit is set, then the key was pressed at least once since the last call. You can determine which bits are set by examining the numeric value of the return code; for example, in a 16-bit integer, the most significant bit would be bit 15 (the 16th bit). The value of 2^{15} is 32,768; therefore, if the result of GetAsyncKeyState is 32,768 or higher, then the most significant bit is set.

The logic of Windows

Once data is arranged into groups (double words, words, and bytes), you can operate on the individual bits these data structures contain. The concept is called *logic*.

Logic refers to the operation you want to perform on the data. These operations refer to the True or False condition of bits. Unlike Visual Basic, in which True equates to -1; in Boolean logic, true is 1, or the opposite of zero. Common logical operators include AND, OR, NOT and XOR. Others include EXP and MOD. These operators work on the bits in a data structure.

The way that they work is best represented by what's referred to as a *truth table*. The truth table for a logical operator indicates what that operator will do in the presence of logical 1s and 0s.

The And operator

The And operator is used to logically compare two bits. And results in a logical 1 when both of the two bits are 1. Table 27-4 shows the truth table for And.

Table 27-4 **Truth Table for the *And* Operator**	
Comparison Bits	*Result*
1 × 1	1
1 × 0	0
0 × 1	0
0 × 0	0

The truth table indicates that the result of comparing two bits through And is always a logical 0 unless both bits are logical 1. You use And to pluck out the value of any given bit or group of bits. For example, to determine the state of any bit, you use And to see if that bit is set or not. A set bit is one whose value is 1. Imagine you wanted to check the fourth bit of some number (remember that the fourth bit position is 2^3, and represents the number 8):

```
If SomeNum And 8 Then Beep
```

If SomeNum were 8, then the example would beep. If SomeNum were 9, it would also beep — because 9 contains an 8 and a 1. Therefore the fourth bit position has to be set as well as the first bit position — (2^3) + (2^0) = 8 + 1 = 9. Keep in mind that we are examining the pattern of bits, not a numerical operation. For example, if SomeNum were 16, there would be no beep because 16 = (2^4), meaning bit 5 was set, and clearing bit 3 (the 8's place).

A complete function that uses And to check the state of any bit of a Long Integer follows. It returns True (–1) if the bit passed is set, or False (0) if the bit is not set. (Note that this function is zero-based; that is, it will examine bits 0 to 15.)

```
'returns True (-1) if bit passed in iBit is set
'or False (0) otherwise. On entry iBit is an
'value from 0 to 15 indicating which bit to
'examine
Function GetBit(lArray As Long, iBit As Integer)
    GetBit = (lArray \ (2 ^ iBit)) > 0
End Function
```

The Or operator

The Or operator is used to logically compare two bits. The result of Or is a logical 1 when any one of the two bits are 1. Table 27-5 shows the truth table for the Or operator.

Table 27-5 Truth Table for the *Or* Operator	
Comparison Bits	**Result**
1 × 1	1
1 × 0	1
0 × 1	1
0 × 0	0

The truth table for Or indicates that the result of comparing two bits through Or is always a logical 1 unless both bits are logical 0. You use Or to set the state of any given bit. For example, to set the state of bit 4 you would use code like the following (note that this logic is zero-based—that is, bits are indicated as 0 to 15, counting from right to left):

```
X = X Or 2^4
```

Using Or this way lets you set bits quickly. You will typically want to set flags with this technique when you are storing information into a flag variable. For example, to conserve memory, you might pack multiple program options into a variable. Then you could use Or to see if a flag is set.

The XOr operator

The XOr operator is used to logically compare two bits. XOr results in a logical 1 when one and only one of the two bits is 1. Table 27-6 shows the truth table for the XOr operator.

Table 27-6 Truth Table for the *XOr* Operator	
Comparison Bits	**Result**
1 × 1	0
1 × 0	1
0 × 1	1
0 × 0	0

The most common use of XOr is in the logic of ciphering. Due to the unique action of XOr, if you XOr two numbers twice, you wind up with the same number. This is very handy for a low-security scrambling of data. For example, take the number 16 and XOr it with a key value of 10. The result is 26 (16 XOr 10 = 26). Now, XOr 26 with 10 and you will get 16, the original value. Knowing this, you can create a function that operates on the ASCII value of characters. The following simple example shows how this is done:

```
Private Sub Form_Load()
    Dim secrets As String
    Dim key As String
    Dim i, j
    Show
    key = "password"
    secrets = "VB Rules"
    For i = 1 To Len(secrets)
        Mid$(secrets, i, 1) = Chr$(Asc(Mid$(secrets, i, 1)) Xor
        Asc(Mid$(key, i, 1)))
    Next
    Print secrets ' prints "&#S!___"
    For i = 1 To Len(secrets)
        Mid$(secrets, i, 1) = Chr$(Asc(Mid$(secrets, i, 1)) Xor
        Asc(Mid$(key, i, 1)))
    Next
    Print secrets ' print "VB Rules"
End Sub
```

The Not operator

The Not operator simply flips the state of a bit from logical 1 to logical 0 or vice versa. Table 27-7 shows the truth table for the Not operator.

Table 27-7
Truth Table for the *Not* Operator

Bit	Result
1	0
0	1

When used together, And, Or, Not, and XOr provide all the power you need to manipulate data at the bit level.

Parsing arguments

Once data is arranged into groups (double words, words, and bytes), you can then operate on the bits using the logical operators. In addition to And, Or, Not, and so on, you will also use simple division to literally chop double words into words, and words into bytes.

Remember that groupings of bits represent numbers. Visual Basic data types of long and integer are also numbers. Therefore, simple mathematics can help us by removing the piece of the number we no longer want. For example, it is very common in the Windows API to need what's called the "high word," "low word," "low byte," or "high byte." This is referring to which of the bytes you care about.

As shown in Figure 27-2, a double word (a Visual Basic Long Integer) contains 32 bits, which you can consider to be 2 words or 4 bytes. The low word refers to bits 0 to 15 of the double word; the high word refers to bits 16 to 31. The low byte refers to bits 0 to 7 of the low-order word of the double word; the high bytes refer to bits 8 to 15 of the low-order word.

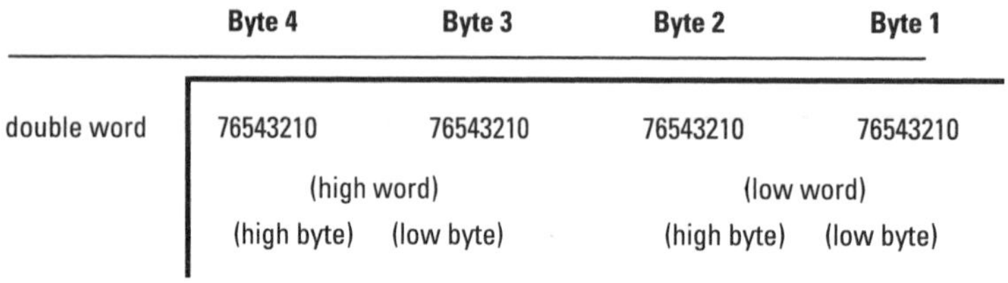

	Byte 4	Byte 3	Byte 2	Byte 1
double word	76543210	76543210	76543210	76543210
	(high word)		(low word)	
	(high byte)	(low byte)	(high byte)	(low byte)

Figure 27-2: This image shows high and low bytes and words.

For example, the first bit of the high byte of the low-order word is, in fact, bit number 8. Using this somewhat bizarre nomenclature, you can easily identify any piece of the data structure. In fact, this is just how Windows API wants us to think, too!

You can now extract information using basic mathematics. Each byte can represent any of 256 (2^8) values in the range 0 to 255. Each word can represent any of 65,536 (2^{16}) values in the range 0 to 65,535. Each double word can represent any of 4,294,967,296 (2^{32}) values in the range 0 to 4,294,967,295.

Using this information, you mathematically extract portions of numbers using logical operators. To extract the high byte from a word (16-bit integer), you would divide the word by 255 to chop off the remainder, with the result being the value left over after removing the maximum value of the low word. When working with words, interpret the low-byte value as the number of 1s, and the high-byte value as the number of 256s; for example, the number 513 is $(2 \times 256) + 1$. This allows us to use division to determine the number of 256s in an integer as follows:

```
'return HIGH byte (bits 8 to 15) from a integer
Dim hb As Byte
Dim someword As Integer
someword = 513
hb = someword \ 255      'chop out high byte
```

We use the integer division operator (\ ) above to preclude any fractional portions. You divide by 255, since that is the maximum value of an 8-bit byte. This tells you the number of 256s the word contains. In the case of the above example, it is 2, and thank goodness that's what the variable hb contains. Now, to extract the value of the low-order byte from the above value of 513, you need to use the logical And operator, which tells us the value left over after clearing out anything above the value of 255:

```
'return LOW byte (bits 0 to 7) from an integer
Dim lb As Byte
Dim someword As Integer
someword = 513
lb = someword And 255      'chop out low byte
```

This time, lb contains the value 1, indicating the 513 contains two 256s and one 1. One thing you need to take into account is that Visual Basic integers may be from -32,768 to 32,767 in value—not 0 to 65,535 as in Windows API calls. Microsoft did this in order to give Visual Basic support for negative numbers. You need to modify the above formula just a bit to handle the possibility that the Integer return value from the API could be more than 32,767. Here's how:

```
Public Function HighByte(wByte As Integer) As Byte
   'return the HIGH byte (bits 8 to 15) from a byte
   Dim hb&, HByte&
   hb& = wByte \ 255
   If hb& < 0 Then hb& = 65535 + HByte&
   HighByte& = hb&
End Function

Public Function LowByte(wByte As Integer) As Byte
   'return the LOW byte (bits 0-7) from a given word
   Dim LB&
   LB& = wByte And 255
   If LB& < 0 Then LB& = 65535 + LB&
   LowByte& = LB&                        'assign function
End Function
```

What you do is add 65,535 to the value if it is less than 0, thus compensating for any number greater than 16,387. This same logic applies for high and low words as well, except of course to replace 255 and 65,535 with 65,535 and 4,294,967,295, respectively.

In many cases, you will need to extract portions of the return value of a Windows API call—now you know how. This parsing of arguments seems a little bit abstract, but in return you gain capabilities far outside those of Visual Basic.

Determining the Operating System and Version of Windows

The last critical factor in successfully using the Windows API is realizing that the APIs for Windows NT are different from Windows 98's. Further, Windows NT 4.0 has its own APIs and is not the same as Windows NT 3.51.

It is often critically important to be able to dynamically determine the version of Windows you are running under. Examples are trying to determine if long filenames are supported or not, and trying to access Windows 95 OEM 2-specific features. These are just a few of many situations where it is imperative to know which operating system you are running under.

It is important to note that "the version of Windows" also means which of the five different operating systems called Windows you are talking about. There are currently five major 32-bit versions of Windows in the world: Windows 95, Windows 95 OEM 2, Windows NT 3.51 and 4.0, and Windows 98.

Tip   Don't forget to check Windows 98 for operating-system-specific features.

Table 27-8 lists the Windows API functions that this chapter will use to determine the operating system and version. It lists the Windows API name, function, and how you use it for the purpose of determining versions.

Table 27-8
Windows APIs Used in This Chapter

API	Function	Description
GetVersion	Returns the version of DOS and Windows	Used to determine version information
GetVersionEx	Returns version and operating system information	Used to determine the version of Windows before accessing OS or version-specific APIs

Note   You can see these and many more Windows APIs by using the API Viewer Add-In that comes with Visual Basic, or by obtaining the Windows Software Development Kit documentation from Microsoft.

Table 27-9 lists the named constants used in this chapter. These constants control the actions of the Visual Basic keyword or Windows API with which they are used. Table 27-9 lists the constant name, where it is defined, and its ordinal (numeric) value.

Table 27-9
Constants Used in This Chapter

Constant	Where Defined	Value (Decimal)
VER_PLATFORM_WIN32_NT	Windows API	2
VER_PLATFORM_WIN32_WINDOWS	Windows API	1
VER_PLATFORM_WIN32s	Windows API	0

Using Windows API calls and some sleight of hand, any Visual Basic program can determine the version of Windows it's running under. You will determine at least two major components of any operating system: the major and minor version numbers of the operating system.

For example, for Windows NT 3.51, the major version number is 3 and the minor version number is 5. For 32-bit operating systems, even more information is available — for example, for NT 4 and Windows 95, you can gather the build number of the operating system and platform supported by the operating system.

The keys to our success are the GetVersion and GetVersionEx Windows API calls. These two calls deliver important information you need to determine the true version numbers.

GetVersion

The Windows API GetVersion seems like a reasonable place to start when trying to determine the version of the operating system you're working under.

```
Declare Function GetVersion Lib "kernel32" Alias _
    "GetVersion" () As Long
```

GetVersion is available to all applications running under all Windows versions. Table 27-10 shows GetVersion API results for various operating systems.

Table 27-10
GetVersion Results

Windows 95	Windows 95 OEM 2	Windows NT 3.51	Windows NT 4.0
3.95	3.95	3.10	3.10

GetVersion tells us a lot; however, GetVersion does not give us correct information under 32-bit windows. Before there was Windows NT, there was 16-bit Windows. GetVersion returned the version number of Windows, but with Windows NT came a problem — there were now multiple versions of Windows.

For a 32-bit application running under 32-bit Windows, GetVersion returns version 4 for Windows 95 and for Windows NT version 4! Since you cannot trust GetVersion for 32-bit Windows, you need to use GetVersionEx.

GetVersionEx

Consider the following lines of code:

```
Declare Function GetVersionEx Lib "kernel32" Alias _
    "GetVersionExA" (ByVal lpVersionInformation As _
    OSVERSIONINFO) As Long
```

GetVersionEx is only available under 32-bit Windows. GetVersionEx fills out a user-defined type with major and minor versions, build number, platform information, and an additional custom or OEM-defined operating system field.

Table 27-11 shows GetVersionEx results.

Table 27-11 GetVersionEx Results			
Windows 95	**Windows 95 OEM 2**	**Windows NT 3.51**	**Windows NT 4.0**
4.00	4.00	3.51	4.00

As you can see from the tables, even though you can figure out the version of Windows pretty quickly, you still need to determine which operating system your program is running under.

Identifying Windows 95

You use the GetVersionEx API to determine the operating system. GetVersionEx uses a user-defined type — OSVERSIONINFO. The members of this type accurately indicate the 32-bit operating system (Windows 95, Windows NT, Win32s) as well as the correct version of the operating system.

Note

For 32-bit Windows applications, GetVersionEx reliably indicates operating system and version.

Listing 27-1 shows a simple function (for 32-bit applications) that uses GetVersionEx to determine whether the operating system is Windows 95.

Listing 27-1: A Function to Determine Whether the Operating System Is Windows 95

```
' this function returns True (-1) if
' the operating system is Windows 95
' otherwise it returns False (0)
Function Win95() As Boolean
    Dim typOS As OSVERSIONINFO
    typOS.dwOSVersionInfoSize = Len(typOS)
    GetVersionEx typOS
    Win95 = typOS.dwPlatformId = _
        VER_PLATFORM_WIN32_WINDOWS
End Function
```

Identifying Windows NT

Detecting Windows NT from 32-bit Windows is easy — just use GetVersionEx. If the dwPlatformId member of the OSVERSIONINFO user-defined type argument is VER_PLATFORM_WIN32_NT, this is Windows NT. Listing 27-2 shows a simple function that uses GetVersionEx to determine if the operating system is Windows NT.

Listing 27-2: A Function to Determine Whether the Operating System Is Windows NT

```
' this function returns True (-1) if
' the operating system is Windows NT
' otherwise it returns False (0)
Function WinNT() As Boolean
    Dim typOS As OSVERSIONINFO
    typOS.dwOSVersionInfoSize = Len(typOS)
    GetVersionEx typOS
    WinNT = typOS.dwPlatformId = _
        VER_PLATFORM_WIN32_NT
End Function
```

Once you have determined the operating system, you will need to determine the version. For Windows 95, this is not so important; for Windows NT, this is a major requirement. To figure out which version of NT your program is under, you need to check the dwMajorVersion member of OSVERSIONINFO for 4. NT version 4 returns the value 4; NT version 3 returns 3.

A 32-bit application can easily detect NT as the operating system and the version, by using GetVersionEx as follows:

```
GetVersionEx typOS
WinNT4 = typOS.dwMajorVersion = 4
```

Listing 27-3 shows a simple function that uses GetVersionEx to determine if the operating system is Windows NT, and then to see if the version is Windows NT 3 or Windows NT 4.

Listing 27-3: **A Function to Detect Windows NT and the Version**

```
' this function returns True (-1) if
' the operating system is Windows NT
' and the version of Windows NT is
' 4
Public Function WinNT4() As Boolean
    Dim typOS As OSVERSIONINFO
    typOS.dwOSVersionInfoSize = Len(typOS)
    GetVersionEx typOS
    If typOS.dwPlatformId = VER_PLATFORM_WIN32_NT Then
    ' this is Windows NT, get version
    WinNT4 = typOS.dwMajorVersion = 4
End If
End Function
```

32-bit extensions

You can use the GetVersionEx function to return build and service pack numbers, also, using the GetVersionEx information available from 32-bit Windows. OSVERSIONINFO is a user-defined type that GetVersionEx fills out with operating system and version information. So far, you have used the dwPlatformId, dwMajorVersion, and dwMinorVersion members.

You can get even more information from the dwBuildNumber and szCSDVersion members. The dwBuildNumber member contains the build number of the operating system. The build number may be important to know, because certain versions of software may only run reliably under certain builds or later. A great example of this is Visual Basic 5.0, which refuses to install if your Windows NT build is not compatible. SzCSDVersion provides "arbitrary information about the operating system." This can include service pack information or other information. For example, for Windows NT, SzCSDVersion carries a note, such as "service pack 2."

Putting it all together

Listing 27-4 is the entire version and operating system code. It determines the operating system and version of Windows from any Visual Basic program. Throughout the following chapters, the operating system and version will reference this code.

On the CD-ROM

The code in Listing 27-4 is on the CD-ROM as VERSION.CLS.

Listing 27-4: Module to Encapsulate Keyboard into Object for Use in Any Program

```
DefInt A-Z
Const VER_PLATFORM_WIN32_NT = 2
Const VER_PLATFORM_WIN32_WINDOWS = 1
Const VER_PLATFORM_WIN32s = 0
Type OSVERSIONINFO
    dwOSVersionInfoSize As Long
    dwMajorVersion As Long
    dwMinorVersion As Long
    dwBuildNumber As Long
    dwPlatformId As Long
    szCSDVersion As String * 128
End Type
Dim typOS As OSVERSIONINFO
Declare Function GetVersionEx Lib "kernel32" Alias _
    "GetVersionExA" (lpVersionInformation As OSVERSIONINFO) _
    As Long Declare Function GetVersion Lib "kernel32" () _
    As Long
Function Win95() As Boolean
    typOS.dwOSVersionInfoSize = Len(typOS)
    GetVersionEx typOS
    Win95 = typOS.dwPlatformId = VER_PLATFORM_WIN32_WINDOWS
End Function
Function WinNT() As Boolean
    typOS.dwOSVersionInfoSize = Len(typOS)
    GetVersionEx typOS
    WinNT = typOS.dwPlatformId = VER_PLATFORM_WIN32_NT
End Function
Public Function WinName() As String
    If WinNT3 Then
        WinName = "Windows NT 3.x"
    ElseIf WinNT4 Then
        WinName = "Windows NT 4.x"
```

(continued)

Listing 27-4 *(continued)*

```
        ElseIf Win95 Then
            WinName = "Windows 95"
        Else
            WinName = "Windows"
        End If
End Function
Public Function WinNT3() As Boolean
    typOS.dwOSVersionInfoSize = Len(typOS)
    GetVersionEx typOS
    If typOS.dwPlatformId = VER_PLATFORM_WIN32_NT Then
        'NT
        WinNT3 = typOS.dwMajorVersion = 3
    End If
End Function
Public Function WinNT4() As Boolean
    typOS.dwOSVersionInfoSize = Len(typOS)
    GetVersionEx typOS
    If typOS.dwPlatformId = VER_PLATFORM_WIN32_NT Then
        'NT
        WinNT4 = typOS.dwMajorVersion = 4
    End If
End Function
```

Summary

The Windows API is a rich set of extended functionality that often solves complex programming codes and lets you work around a particular limitation of Visual Basic.

✦ The Windows API is often the only way to accomplish some tasks under Windows — regardless of language.

✦ In order to use the Windows API for maximum results, you need to remember that Windows API function calls are not always faster than intrinsic Visual Basic methods. Your best results will come from using the Windows API when Visual Basic cannot perform a given task.

✦ When you choose to use the Windows API, remember that API function calls operate outside of Visual Basic's error-handling and protection schemes — making you responsible for correct usage and implementation. However, with a little thought, planning, and common sense (and the code presented in this chapter), you can reliably and safely integrate Windows API calls into your own programs.

✦ Using simple math and the Visual Basic And, Or, and XOr operators, you can parse API results into bits, bytes, and words. Using the formulas and functions presented, you will be able to extract the information you require from the result codes and arguments that the Windows API provides.

✦ Remember to make sure the Windows API function calls you choose are supported on all the platforms your programs may run on. A Windows NT-only API will mean that your program cannot run on Windows 95 and vice versa.

✦ Furthermore, as Windows has advanced, certain API function calls are only found in certain service packs and versions. Double-check to make sure the API function calls you plan to use are available—use the routines for detecting operating system and version, presented in this chapter, to ensure your API function calls have what they need to run.

✦ Finally, don't worry! Using the Windows API is only slightly more complex than using Visual Basic. The trick to using the API successfully is taking care of the details as summarized here.

✦   ✦   ✦

Expanding Keyboard Control Using the Windows API

◆   ◆   ◆   ◆

In This Chapter

Understanding the keyboard

Determining keyboard states

Getting and setting individual key state

Determining the number of function keys

Custom keyboard layouts

◆   ◆   ◆   ◆

O ne of the most fundamental input devices for any program is the keyboard. Virtually all programs will need to receive input from the user via keystrokes. You can easily determine the user's keystrokes by the manner in which Visual Basic implements event-driven programming. As the user presses and releases keys or groups of keys on the keyboard, Visual Basic generates events for objects that support them.

For example, if a text box has focus and the user presses a key, Visual Basic updates the text in the window of the text box and fires the `TextBox_Changed` event. You can then respond to the events if you want to, but since Visual Basic has taken care of all the chores required to accomplish this feat, you can often just let the text box gather the user input. Then, when the user changes focus to another control, you can simply check the contents of the text box. This is the sort of input operation Visual Basic does well.

Visual Basic actually encapsulates quite a lot of functionality automatically. To implement this keyboard input, Windows creates and sends a series of messages to the TextBox control. Windows interacts with the hardware to interpret user actions and create messages that get posted to your application's message queue. Windows sends messages to the control procedure for the control—in this case, our text box. These messages include WM_KEYDOWN, WM_SYSKEYDOWN, WM_KEYUP, and WM_SYSKEYUP. Visual Basic then translates these messages and raises the familiar KeyPress, KeyDown, and KeyUp events.

To monitor keystrokes from Visual Basic, you can simply set the KeyPreview property of a form to True, then monitor the KeyDown, KeyUp, and KeyPress events of that form. As the user hits keys, you get a chance to preview them. You can detect most keyboard characters—alphabetic, numeric, or extended. You can even detect if the user is holding down a Shift key while pressing another key.

However, using Visual Basic alone, you cannot determine the state of a keyboard key *asynchronously*—asynchronously means when you want to, not when a user hits a key. For example, you may need to know if the Caps Lock key is on right now, or you may want to force Num Lock off. You may also need to know if a given key has been pressed, or is being held down by the user. The built-in Visual Basic events cannot tell us this sort of real-time, asynchronous information; and Visual Basic has no built-in method of letting us get or set the state of keyboard keys.

Luckily, however, there are Windows API calls that can tell you all you need to know about the keyboard and its state. With a little work to understand how these API functions work, you can tackle virtually any keyboard task. In fact, not only can you query the keyboard to determine the current state of any key, you can also set any key to any state! Using these Windows API calls, you can easily check the state of Num Lock or determine which Caps Lock is on. You can also detect if the user has pressed and is continuing to hold a key down. Further, you can determine the physical keyboard implementation, the number of function keys it has, and the language Windows has mapped onto the physical keys. For Windows NT, other pertinent keyboard information includes which Shift, Alt, or Control key is down.

Note   Only the Windows NT operating systems provide indication of which Shift, Alt, or Control key (Left or Right) is pressed.

Table 28-1 lists the Windows API functions that this chapter will use to implement keyboard control.

Table 28-1
Windows API Functions Used in This Chapter

Function	Return Data	Description
keybd_event	None	Used to simulate presses of Caps Lock, Num Lock, Scroll Lock, or any other key
GetKeyboardState	Current state of all the keys	Used to determine current state of one or more keys
GetAsyncKeyState	Current state of an individual key	Used to determine the state of a single key
GetKeyboardLayoutName	Name of the currently loaded keyboard driver software	Used to determine how the user's keyboard is configured
GetKeyState	The toggled state of a key	Used to determine past user activity on the keyboard; for example, "Has the Alt key been pressed?"
GetKeyboardType	A value that indicates the physical type of keyboard connected to the computer	Used to determine the type of keyboard
SystemParamsLong	Various system state information	Used to determine/set software operating system-controlled options for the keyboard
SystemParamsInt	Various system state information	Used to determine/set software operating system-controlled options for the keyboard

Note   You can see these and many more Windows API functions by using the API Viewer Add-In that comes with Visual Basic.

Table 28-2 lists the named constants used in this chapter. These constants control the actions of the Visual Basic keyword or Windows API function with which they are used. The table lists the constant name, where it is defined, and its ordinal (numeric) value. Constants preceded with a lowercase vb prefix are intrinsic to Visual Basic.

Table 28-2 Constants Used in This Chapter	
Constant	**Value (Decimal)**
KEYEVENTF_EXTENDEDKEY	1
KEYEVENTF_KEYUP	2
SPI_GETKEYBOARDDELAY	22
SPI_GETKEYBOARDSPEED	10
VK_CAPITAL	14
VK_NUMLOCK	90
VK_SCROLL	91
VK_LSHIFT	160
VK_RSHIFT	161
VK_LCONTROL	162
VK_RCONTROL	163
VK_LMENU	164
VK_RMENU	165
VK_SNAPSHOT	44
vbKeyMenu	4
vbKeyShift	18

Understanding the Keyboard

Understanding how keyboards actually operate helps you understand how to assemble, plan, and use the Windows API calls.

Keyboard components

The keyboard is really a fairly complex system of hardware and software. The main components are the physical keyboard itself, the driver software, and the Windows API underneath that controls it all.

Keyboard types

A keyboard is the physical device used to input character-based information to a program. There are many types of keyboards in use, including the following:

✦ IBM® PC/XT® or compatible (83-key) keyboard

✦ Olivetti® ICO (102-key) keyboard

✦ IBM® PC/AT® (84-key) or similar keyboard

✦ IBM® enhanced (101- or 102-key) keyboard

✦ Nokia® 1050 and similar keyboards

✦ Nokia® 9140 and similar keyboards

✦ Dvorak keyboards

✦ Microsoft® Natural keyboards

Each of these keyboards is physically different from the others. Some have 16 function keys, some have 12, and others have only 10. The arrangement and placement of keys differs in most cases. However it is implemented, the physical keyboard takes input from the user, through software drivers, and converts the keypresses into standard characters.

Windows keyboard drivers

When the user presses a key on a keyboard, Windows's keyboard driver software translates the keypress into a series of keyboard messages. These keyboard messages indicate what the user is typing as keys are pressed and released. Visual Basic translates these messages into KeyUp, KeyDown, KeyAscii, and related events. You can easily respond to these events by writing code for the associated event procedure.

The actual physical keys on a keyboard are represented by *scan codes*. These are device-dependent, manufacturer-defined values representing each key on a keyboard. Every keyboard generates one scan code when a key is pressed and a different scan code when the key is released. Not all keyboards have the same scan code mapping, as depicted in Figure 28-1.

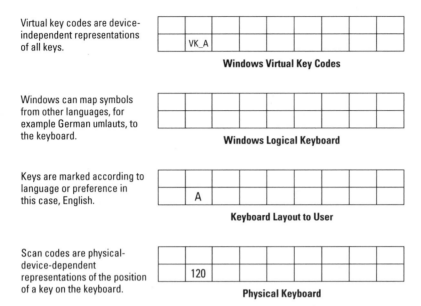

Virtual key codes are device-independent representations of all keys.

Windows Virtual Key Codes

Windows can map symbols from other languages, for example German umlauts, to the keyboard.

Windows Logical Keyboard

Keys are marked according to language or preference in this case, English.

Keyboard Layout to User

Scan codes are physical-device-dependent representations of the position of a key on the keyboard.

Physical Keyboard

Figure 28-1: Four views of a keyboard available to a Windows program

This potentially show-stopping nonstandardization of keyboards does have a solution: *virtualization*. Windows virtualizes many services. Virtualization is the process whereby hardware is managed by a low-level software program called a device driver. The device driver interprets the manufacturer-specific hardware and presents a common API to the programmer. This is why Windows needs specific mouse, video, and CD-ROM drivers, and why virtualization is also required for keyboards.

Tip   Never use Windows API calls to monitor/change scan codes directly, since all keyboards are not the same.

Device independence is achieved when Windows maps the actual scan code of a key on a keyboard to software virtual keys. Figure 28-2 depicts the relationship between elements in a computer system that handle keyboard input.

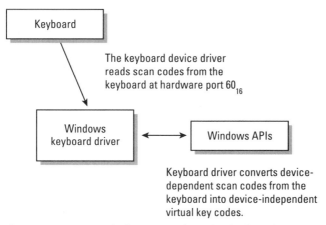

Figure 28-2: How Windows virtualizes the keyboard

Virtual keys are defined constants that logically represent any key on any keyboard (assuming, of course, that all keyboards have that particular key). So, while the scan code for the Shift key on a Microsoft Natural keyboard (which itself is emulating an IBM® enhanced 101- or 102-key keyboard) might be 42, the virtual key code for any keyboard's Shift key is defined as follows:

```
Const VK_SHIFT = 16          'either Shift key
```

Now, when the user hits the Shift key on any keyboard, no matter what its scan code, Windows generates VK_SHIFT, which is always the value 16. Device independence has been achieved! Virtualization is one of the key benefits that Windows provides.

Windows also maps the character sets of a variety of languages onto keyboards. Windows supports English, Chinese, Hebrew, German, and dozens of other languages. You can change your language preference easily in Windows; just use the Control Panel to select another keyboard layout or language. After a language has been mapped to the physical keyboard, the keyboard becomes a *logical keyboard*.

Windows has quite a number of keyboard API functions. Some allow direct query of the keyboard; others work on a copy of the state of the keyboard, called a *virtual keyboard buffer*. A virtual keyboard buffer is in reality a block of memory wherein the individual keys of the keyboard are represented. Using the virtual keyboard buffer allows you to set several keys to some state and then update the keyboard all at once by writing the virtual keyboard buffer to the keyboard.

Another issue you need to be aware of is that 16-bit Windows shares services between all applications. A single logical keyboard is used by all applications. Any single application can change the keyboard used by all other applications. With the arrival of 32-bit Windows, this was considered to be "bad behavior" and applications were virtualized, or "sandboxed." This means no single application can (easily!) change the state of shared services, and you will need all the tricks in the book to coerce Windows NT into doing what you want.

Determining keyboard state

Before you can change the keyboard, you need to be able to query the keyboard to determine its physical and logical limitations. There are two main information-retrieval API functions that are relevant to Visual Basic programmers working with the keyboard: GetKeyboardLayoutName and GetKeyboardType.

GetKeyboardLayoutName

The GetKeyboardLayoutName function returns a value representing the current keyboard language layout — for example, English, Chinese, Hebrew, and so on. Its declaration is

```
Declare Function GetKeyboardLayoutName Lib "user32" Alias _
"GetKeyboardLayoutNameA" (ByVal pwszKLID As String) As Long
```

The GetKeyBoardLayoutName API uses a string argument that must be 9 characters long when you call GetKeyBoardLayoutName. The best way to ensure this is so is to declare a public constant and then use the constant when creating the argument for GetKeyBoardLayoutName:

```
Public Const KL_NAMELENGTH = 9
```

Note

For Windows NT, GetKeyboardLayoutName returns the name of the keyboard in use by the system. For Windows 95, GetKeyboardLayoutName returns the name of the keyboard in use by the application calling the function.

The function's return value is a code representing the language in a hexadecimal-derived string format. The following code fragment demonstrates this:

```
Dim sLayOutName As String
Dim iSize As Long

' create a string to receive the keyboard
' layout name
SLayOutName = Space$(KL_NAMELENGTH)
' get the name
```

```
GetKeyboardLayoutName sLayOutName$
' find the null character
iSize = Instr$(sLayOutName$, Chr$(0))
' now parse out the name, sans null
sLayOutName = Left$(SlayOutName, iSize - 1)
```

This example returns 00000409 for a U.S. English system. A complete listing of codes is available in the Windows SDK.

The preceding code works by first declaring a string variable, SLayOutName, and setting to a string of spaces as controlled by the KL_NAMELENGTH constant. GetKeyboardLayoutName is then used to fill SLayOutName with the name of the keyboard layout. GetKeyboardLayoutName terminates its return string with a null character, represented in Visual Basic by the Visual Basic syntax Chr$(0). When the null is located, indicating the end of the returned string, the sLayOutName is trimmed to length of the string without the null.

GetKeyboardType

The GetKeyboardType function returns information about the physical keyboard. It takes as its argument an index indicating which information to return. GetKeyboardType can determine the number of function keys on a keyboard and the physical type of keyboard installed. The API function's declaration is:

```
Declare Function GetKeyboardType Lib "user32" Alias _
"GetKeyboardType" (ByVal nTypeFlag As Long) As Long
```

To determine the number of function keys on a keyboard, use GetKeyboardType with an index of 2, as in this example:

```
'number of function keys
FKeyCount = GetKeyboardType(2)
```

Note   With GetKeyboardType(2), a return value of 7 indicates that there is no way to determine the number of function keys.

You can query the status of any key, but if that key does not exist on the keyboard, Windows returns 0, indicating that the key is not pressed. Clearly, what is required is a method for determining if the keyboard physically contains the key in question. This information is critical, especially for those developers wanting to access extended function keys of F13 or higher — which most keyboards don't offer.

To determine the keyboard type, use GetKeyboardType with an index of 0. Listing 28-1 shows how to use GetKeyboardType to return the physical keyboard name. The Select Case block determines this name.

> ### Listing 28-1: **A Function to Return the Name of the Keyboard Installed**
>
> ```
> ' returns a string with the name
> ' of the physical keyboard attached
> Function kbName() As String
> ' index 0 is type of keyboard
> Select Case GetKeyboardType(0)
> Case 1
>     kbName = "IBM® PC/XT® or compatible  (83-key) keyboard"
> Case 2
>     kbName = "Olivetti® 'ICO' (102-key) keyboard"
> Case 3
>     kbName = "IBM® PC/AT® (84-key) or similar keyboard"
> Case 4
>     kbName = "IBM® enhanced (101- or 102-key) keyboard"
> Case 5
>     kbName = "Nokia® 1050 and similar keyboards"
> Case 6
>     kbName = "Nokia® 9140 and similar keyboards"
> Case 7
>     kbName = "Japanese Keyboard"
> Case Else
>     kbName = "unknown"
> End Select
> End Function
> ```

Tip   Never assume the presence of a given extended key or function key — it might not be there. Always check for the presence of the key before attempting to access it directly.

If you intend to refer to keys only found on a certain keyboard — for example, an IBM® enhanced (101- or 102-key) keyboard — then you need to make sure those keys are present. With GetKeyboardType, you can quickly determine if the keys you need are physically present.

Getting and Setting Individual Key States

Most of us want to control Caps Lock, Num Lock, or Scroll Lock at one time or another. You either want to check their status or make sure they are in a particular state before you accept data input. You may also want to know if the user is holding down an *extender key* (such as Shift, Control, or Alt). You may also want to know if a key has been pressed at least once before, or is currently being held down. Before you can take control over these keys, you need to learn how to check key status.

Getting the state of a key

There are two methods for checking the status of a key: You can ask Windows for the state of an individual key, or you can read a copy of the entire keyboard into an array and check it there.

There are two primary Windows API functions available to check the status of a key. They are GetKeyState and GetAsyncKeyState. Although both of these are Windows API calls that read and return key-state information directly, there is a subtle difference in how they operate. GetKeyState returns the toggled state of a key (whether a key was pressed and then released prior to the function call). GetAsyncKeyState checks to see if the specified key is "up" or "down" at the time the function is called.

Virtual key codes

Both GetKeyState and GetAsyncKeyState return information about a key on the keyboard. They take as an argument a *virtual key code*. Virtual key codes are standard constants that identify the actual physical keyboard scan code of the key you care about. You will use these constants to identify the key you want information about. Visual Basic has you declare these codes as global constants. The common virtual key codes are presented here:

```
Const VK_SHIFT = 16      'either Shift key
Const VK_CONTROL = 17    'either Control key
Const VK_ALT = 18        'either Alt key
```

GetKeyState

There are three special keys on the keyboard: Caps Lock, Num Lock, and Scroll Lock. These keys — which Microsoft calls *toggle keys* — modify the overall action of the keyboard. Caps Lock causes the keyboard driver to convert lowercase to uppercase, and Num Lock causes the numeric keypad to switch from navigation to numeric entry.

GetKeyState returns the toggled state of any of these keys, as well as any key on the keyboard. Its declaration is

```
Declare Function GetKeyState Lib "user32" Alias "GetKeyState" _
(ByVal nVirtKey As Long) As Integer
```

All keys can toggle. Toggling simply means whether or not the key has been pressed and released. If the result of GetKeyState is 1 (least significant bit set), then the key is on; otherwise it is off. Figure 28-3 depicts the differences among these three key states.

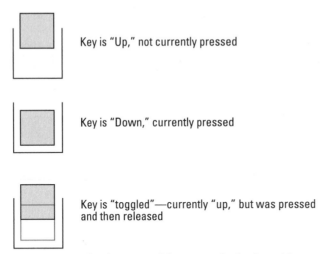

Key is "Up," not currently pressed

Key is "Down," currently pressed

Key is "toggled"—currently "up," but was pressed
and then released

Figure 28-3: The three possible states of a keyboard key

In most cases, you will only care about the toggled state for the Caps Lock, Num
Lock, and Scroll Lock keys. These toggle keys have virtual key codes just like any
key, as shown in these constant declarations:

```
Const VK_CAPITAL = 20
Const VK_NUMLOCK = 144
Const VK_SCROLL = 145
```

Although these keys have virtual key codes, GetAsyncKeyState may not correctly
recognize their key states. For instance, GetAsyncKeyState treats Caps Lock like
all other keys, returning its up or down state. However, you may actually want to
see the logical "on" or "off" state of this key (represented by the light on your
keyboard), as opposed to its physical up or down state.

GetKeyState returns the *toggled* state of an extender key, especially for those keys
whose purpose is to change the computer's response to a keypress. For example, if
the Caps Lock key is pressed once, then GetKeyState returns 1 (least significant
bit set). GetKeyState continues to return 1 until the next time the Caps Lock key is
pressed, at which time it is toggled back to 0.

Note   GetKeyState **returns the toggled state of a key;** GetAsyncKeyState **returns the**
current state of a key.

GetKeyState is passed the virtual key code of the toggle key of interest. This code
would return CapsLock as True (-1) or False (0), depending on the key's state:

```
CapsLock = GetKeyState(VK_CAPITAL) = 1
```

Listing 28-2 presents a simple set of functions showing how to use GetKeyState to return the Caps Lock and Num Lock state.

Listing 28-2: **Functions to Determine the State of Caps Lock and Num Lock keys**

```
' returns True (-1) if the CapsLock key
' is On, otherwise False (0)
Function CapsLock() As Boolean
    CapsLock = GetKeyState(VK_CAPITAL) = 1
End Function
' returns True (-1) if the NumLock key
' is On, otherwise False (0)
Function NumLock() As Boolean
    NumLock = GetKeyState(VK_NUMLOCK) = 1
End Function
```

Remember: If the result of GetKeyState is 1 (least significant bit set), then the key is logically on; otherwise it is logically off.

GetAsyncKeyState

For real-time keyboard queries, use GetAsyncKeyState. From the point of view of this function, the keys on the keyboard are considered up or down. A key that is up is not pressed; a key that is down is considered pressed. Toggle keys are down when they are engaged. For example, if the Caps Lock key is engaged, meaning that all input is shifted to uppercase, then it is considered down.

GetAsyncKeyState checks to see if the specified key is up or down at the time the function is called. Its declaration is

```
Declare Function GetAsyncKeyState Lib "user32" Alias _
"GetAsyncKeyState" (ByVal vKey As Long) As Integer
```

GetAsyncKeyState can also reveal whether the key has been pressed at least once since the last call to GetAsyncKeyState — handy if you are polling the keyboard for some special key.

To use GetAsyncKeyState you need to know the virtual key code for the key in question. In Visual Basic, virtual key codes are prefaced with vbKey*xxx*, where *xxx* represents the key. For example, vbKeyShift is the key code for the Shift key, whose value is 16.

GetAsyncKeyState returns both the current and previous state of the key. This means it can indicate if a key was pressed, even if it is not currently down. The result of GetAsyncKeyState is a 16-bit integer for all versions of Windows. To check to see if a key has been pressed since the last call, check the least significant bit of the result of GetAsyncKeyState. If the key has been pressed since the last call to GetAsyncKeyState, then the least significant bit of the result will be set, resulting in a value of 1, indicating that the key was pressed at least once since the last GetAsyncKeyState call. If the most significant bit of this integer is set, then the key is currently down.

GetAsyncKeyState returns 0 if a window in another thread or process currently has the keyboard focus. So, to see if the Shift key is currently down, use this equation:

```
ShiftKeyDown = (GetAsyncKeyState(VK_SHIFT) < 0)
```

If a key is down, the return value of GetAsyncKeyState normally has its most significant bit set, resulting in a value of -32,767. It is possible to query the keyboard and get a result of -32,768, indicating that the key is down but that the toggle flag is not yet set. This can happen if GetAsyncKeyState is executed prior to Windows setting the toggle flag — rare, but it has happened to us. So, we check for less than zero (< 0 in the example) to handle the case where the key may be down and the toggle flag is not yet set. Checking for < 0 covers all possibilities at once.

Armed with this knowledge, you can build a nice little Function procedure that states whether any key is currently pressed. Listing 28-3 shows how to use GetAsyncKeyState to return the state of any key. Note that this tells only whether the user is holding the key down, not whether the key is toggled.

Listing 28-3: **A Function to Return Toggled State of Any Keyboard Key**

```
' returns True (-1) is the key passed in
' vKeyCode is "down" right now, otherwise
' returns False (0)
Function KeyIsDown(vKeyCode) As Boolean
    KeyIsDown = (GetAsyncKeyState(vKeyCode) < 0 )
End Function
```

Tip   Always check the state of a toggle key *before* setting it. If a key is already down, do not attempt to force it down; in reality, you will force it up.

You can call this Function procedure in loop clauses that have Visual Basic do something while the user holds a key down. For example, while the user holds down the S key, you could increase the volume of an imaginary CD player control, like this:

```
While KeyIsDown(vbKeyS)
    CDPlayer1.Volume = CDPlayer1.Volume + 1
Wend
```

To reduce our imaginary volume, make the user press Shift+S:

```
While KeyIsDown(vbKeyS) And KeyIsDown(vbKeyShift)
    CDPlayer1.Volume = CDPlayer1.Volume - 1
Wend
```

GetAsyncKeyState also works on mouse buttons. You can quickly determine which mouse button (if any) the user is holding down. Often we need to "do something as long as the user holds the mouse down" — for example, incrementing a counter as long as the mouse is down. The following code shows how to update a text box by incrementing its value while the mouse is held down:

```
While GetAsyncKeyState(VK_LMOUSEBUTTON) < 0
    'user has mouse held down
    Text1.Text = Val(Text1.Text) + 1
    Text1.Refresh
Wend
```

The preceding code adds 1 to the value of the text box. The Refresh method is used to force an update to the text box, since in this tight loop the text box would not normally get a change to refresh.

This next example returns True (-1) if the Shift key has been pressed since the last call to GetAsyncKeyState, or False (0) otherwise:

```
ShiftKeyWasPressed = (GetAsyncKeyState(VK_SHIFT) And 1) = 1
```

If you know that your operating system is Windows NT, you can get extra information from GetAsyncKeyState. The following virtual key code constants are used to determine which specific Shift, Control, or Alt key is down. These are only available under Windows NT:

```
Const VK_LSHIFT = 160
Const VK_RSHIFT = 161
Const VK_LCONTROL = 162
Const VK_RCONTROL = 163
Const VK_LMENU = 164
Const VK_RMENU = 165
```

These constants will cause GetAsyncKeyState to return 0 if you use them under any operating system other than Windows NT.

Note

Right and Left virtual key codes are only available under Windows NT. You need to determine the operating system (Windows 95 or Windows NT) before relying on these constants.

These virtual key codes are recognized only by the Windows NT implementations of GetAsyncKeyState and GetKeyState. Determine if you are running under Windows NT, and if so, use the VK_R*xxx* or VK_L*xxx* constants to check for the left or right versions of the given key.

Getting the state of the keyboard: GetKeyboardState

GetKeyState and GetAsyncKeyState return the state of individual keys. If you want to process multiple keys, the GetKeyboardState Windows API function is a more efficient option. You can use this function to read the state of every key on the entire keyboard into an array. Its declaration is

```
Declare Function GetKeyboardState Lib "user32" Alias
"GetKeyboardState" (pbKeyState As Byte) As Long
```

An example of using GetKeyboardState to read the keyboard into a buffer follows. This example gets a copy of the virtual keyboard buffer and then accesses the Shift key:

```
Dim bBuffer(0 to 255) As Byte
GetKeyBoardState bBuffer
ShiftKeyState = bBuffer(VK_SHIFTKEY)
```

Note The virtual keyboard buffer is shared between all 16-bit applications. Each 32-bit application, however, has its own buffer and key state.

To read the state of a key such as Caps Lock, use the Visual Basic And operator to determine the key's on or off state. Listing 28-4 shows how to read the keyboard into an array and then use And to determine the on or off state of any key.

Listing 28-4: A Function to Determine the State of Any Keyboard Key

```
' reads entire keyboard into an array
' then returns True (-1) if the
' Caps Lock key is On or False (0)
' if Caps Lock in Off
Public Property Get CapsLock() As Boolean
    Dim bKeyState(0 To 255) As Byte
    GetKeyboardState bKeyState(0)
    CapsLock = bKeyState(VK_CAPITAL) And 1
End Property
```

GetKeyboardState is most useful when you want to load a copy of the keyboard and poll the state of multiple keys all at once. GetKeyboardState does not provide real-time access to the keys. So, when you want to query a single key state for its status, use GetKeyState or GetAsyncKeyState. When you are preparing for multiple key edits, use GetKeyboardState.

Tip

If you read the entire keyboard state and store it, be aware that the user might change keyboard keys and their states — for example, by pressing the Caps Lock key. Always read, edit, and write/update the keyboard with as little delay as possible, and never store the keyboard state for use "later on."

Setting the state of a key

Now that you have conquered the task of asking the keyboard for information, it's time to teach the keyboard how to do what you want it to do. Under 32-bit Windows, any one application is not supposed to change a service (such as keyboard state) that is shared by other applications — it's not considered proper application etiquette. However, when you need to change the keyboard, there is a method for 32-bit Windows that works nicely.

There are two methods available for updating the keyboard. One is useful for setting individual keys, the other for setting multiple keys at once. The first method simulates keystrokes; the second method directly manipulates the keyboard.

Simulating keystrokes

Visual Basic has a function called SendKeys that may be used to route simulated keystrokes to the form or application. SendKeys cannot, however, change the state of the keyboard. Fortunately, this change can be accomplished with a lesser-known and more powerful Windows API equivalent to SendKeys: the keybd_event API function. Its declaration is

```
Declare Sub keybd_event Lib "user32" Alias "keybd_event" _
    (ByVal bVk As Byte, ByVal bScan As Byte, ByVal dwFlags _
    As Long, ByVal dwExtraInfo As Long)
```

Much like SendKeys, keybd_event synthesizes, or "fakes," a keystroke just as if the user had pushed the key. Using keybd_event is not quite as easy as using SendKeys, but it is not that hard, either.

Note

With the release of Windows NT 4.0 Service Pack 3, the SendInput API function has been introduced to replace the keybd_event API function; however, the keybd_event still exists and still operates as indicated. SendInput offers the capability to synthesize mouse or keyboard input, as opposed to keybd_event, which can only synthesize keyboard events.

The following code generates a press of the Caps Lock key under Windows 95 or Windows NT:

```
' fake a press on Caps Lock
keybd_event VK_CAPITAL, 0, 1, 0
```

The keybd_event function takes as its arguments the virtual key code to toggle, followed by that key's scan code, then a flag to indicate if the key is to be pressed or released, and, finally, by a long integer containing optional information to pass to the API. The last argument is not used when using the API from Visual Basic and may safely be left zero (0). Remember that a keyboard scan code is a hardware-specific code that identifies an actual key on the keyboard, as opposed to the logical and device-independent virtual key code. You may opt to leave the scan code set to 0, or you could use the MapVirtualKey API function to figure it out dynamically. MapVirtualKey translates virtual key codes into scan codes.

To make keybd_event work correctly, you need to call it once to press the key and once more to release the key. For our purposes, the following code does the trick and simulates a keypress of the virtual key code of choice:

```
'press CapsLock
keybd_event VK_CAPITAL, 0, 1, 0
'release CapsLock
keybd_event VK_CAPITAL, 0, 3, 0
```

The call to release is quite important; otherwise, the keyboard will stay in a position simulating a user holding that particular key down! Although this may be desired for some occasions, most of the time you simply want to simulate a normal press/release cycle of a key.

Let's now create a function to wrap keybd_event and toggle the Caps Lock key. For clarity, we are showing this as a property in Listing 28-5.

Listing 28-5: **A Property to Set the Caps Lock Key to On or Off**

```
' sets the state of the Caps Lock
' to bState.
Property Let CapsLock (bState As Boolean)
   ' if the current state of Caps Lock
   ' is not already what we want
   If GetKeyState(VK_CAPITAL) <> Abs(bState) Then
      ' "press" Caps Lock key
      keybd_event VK_CAPITAL, 0, 1, 0
      ' release Caps Lock key
      keybd_event VK_CAPITAL, 0, 3, 0
   End If
End Property
```

The `CapsLock` Property toggles the Caps Lock key if the current state is not `bState`. In essence, this code says, "If the current toggled state of the Caps Lock key is not the same as the desired state (as indicated by `bState`), press and release the Caps Lock key."

The `Abs` function is used in Listing 28-5 to account for the fact that `GetAsyncKey State` returns 1 for `True`, and in Visual Basic -1 means `True`. So `Abs` converts a negative one (-1) to positive one (1) and leaves 0 alone.

The following is the `Property Get` partner for the above `Property Let` procedure. The `Property Get CapsLock` procedure just returns the current state of the Caps Lock key.

```
' returns True (-1) if Caps Lock is
' On, otherwise returns False (0)
Property Get CapsLock() As Boolean
    CapsLock = GetKeyState(VK_CAPITAL)
End Property
```

At this point, you have a working model for setting or getting any toggle key on the keyboard. To create a Num Lock property, replace `VK_CAPITAL` with `VK_NUMLOCK`.

Triggering a screen capture to the Clipboard

One of the things most developers want to be able to do is to simulate a press of the Print Scrn key to capture a screenshot and place it in the Clipboard. Using `keybd_event`, you can easily do this.

To simulate a press of the Print Scrn key, call `keybd_event` with the `bVk` parameter set to `VK_SNAPSHOT`, and the `bScan` parameter set to 0 for a snapshot of the full screen, as follows:

```
keybd_event VK_SNAPSHOT, 0, 0, 0 'full screen
```

Or you can set `bScan` to 1 for a snapshot of the active window, as follows:

```
keybd_event VK_SNAPSHOT, 0, 1, 0 'active window
```

Setting the state of the keyboard

The `keybd_event` API function simulates a keystroke. To set or get multiple keys at once, or to set the keyboard state directly, you will need to take a different approach. For direct keyboard manipulation, you will need to access the Windows *virtual keyboard buffer*.

The virtual keyboard buffer represents 256 keys on a keyboard. Think of the virtual keyboard buffer as an array with 256 elements. The offset into the virtual keyboard buffer array for any given key is equivalent to the virtual key code for that key. The process of polling the keyboard buffer is to read the keyboard state into an array, then check the array element that represents the particular key of interest.

Manipulating the keyboard

To change the state of the keyboard, you will first use `GetKeyboardState` to fetch a copy of the virtual keyboard buffer. Then you will modify the buffer state and use `SetKeyBoardState` to update the keyboard with your modifications.

GetKeyboardState

Use the `GetKeyboardState` API function to read the state of the entire keyboard all at once. Its declaration is

```
Declare Function GetKeyboardState Lib "user32" Alias _
"GetKeyboardState" (pbKeyState As Byte) As Long
```

You use an array of the Visual Basic `Byte` data type (a byte array) to store the keyboard state. First, you declare a string of 256 bytes:

```
vKeyBuffer = String$(256, 0)
```

Next you call `GetKeyboardState` and pass the string, which simulates an array. Windows then copies the current keyboard state into your buffer when you execute this instruction:

```
GetKeyBoardState vKeyBuffer
```

To check whether the Caps Lock key is down, you introduce the old constants to your new API function. If the byte state is 1 (least significant bit set), the key is on. For example, in the following code, the value of the buffer entry for Caps Lock would be `True` or `False` depending on its state:

```
If Mid$(vKeyBuffer, VK_CAPITAL + 1, 1) = Chr$(0) Then
    Mid$(vKeyBuffer, VK_CAPITAL + 1, 1) = Chr$(1)
Else
    Mid$(vKeyBuffer, VK_CAPITAL + 1, 1) = Chr$(0)
End If
```

This code flips the bit state of the `VK_CAPITAL` key in `vKeyBuffer`. If it was 0, it becomes 1; if it's 1, it becomes 0. Note that the virtual key code is used as the offset into the string. The Visual Basic `Mid$` method allows you to access a single character in a string. If you consider the keyboard buffer string as an array, then `Mid$` lets you access any given position in the string just as though it were an array. The virtual key code constants align numerically with the position in the keyboard buffer string; however, the virtual keyboard buffer is zero based, so you need to add 1 to the virtual key code to arrive at the proper key position. This technique works very nicely, with a minimum of coding.

The keys on the keyboard, represented by the virtual keyboard buffer, are considered to be up or down. A key that is up is not pressed; a key that is down is pressed. Toggle keys are down when they are engaged. For example, if the Caps Lock key is engaged — meaning that all input is shifted to uppercase — it is considered down. If an entry in the buffer is 1, then it means that key is down; if it is 0, the key is up.

SetKeyboardState

Lastly, you need to update the keyboard with our changes. The SetKeyboardState API function updates the keyboard with the contents of the buffer you pass to it. Its declaration is:

```
Declare Function SetKeyboardState Lib "user32" Alias _
"SetKeyboardState" (lppbKeyState As Byte) As Long
```

SetKeyboardState **effectively sets the keys you modified to the state you want.** SetKeyboardState **must be used with** GetKeyboardState. **The process is to read the keyboard using** GetKeyboardState:

```
' make an string to hold keyboard state
vKeyBuffer = String$(256, 0)
' read keyboard state into vKeyBuffer
GetKeyBoardState vKeyBuffer
```

After the keyboard state has been read into the vKeyBuffer string, you can manipulate it. For example, to set the Num Lock key to on, you would modify the Num Lock key position using the virtual key code for the Num Lock key:

```
Mid$(vKeyBuffer, VK_NUMLOCK + 1, 1) = Chr$(1)
```

Normally, if you are using this technique, you have more than one key to set. When you are done setting the keyboard state, you use SetKeyboardState. SetKeyboardState **writes the contents of the** vKeyBuffer **string to the keyboard driver, updating the keyboard key states:**

```
SetKeyboardState vKeyBuffer
```

Accessing key repeat and delay rates

You now have the skills to reliably determine and configure your keyboards. The last area to talk about is key repeat and delay rates. Keyboards have both repeat-delay and repeat-speed settings. *Repeat-delay* is the time interval between holding a key down and when it starts to be repeated. *Repeat-speed* is the time interval between repetitions of the key while it is held down. You can control both of these settings with the SystemParametersInfo API function.

SystemParametersInfo

The `SystemParametersInfo` API function lets you set or get many system preferences, including repeat-delay and repeat-speed. Because this API function takes different arguments, depending on the index you are setting or getting, using `SystemParametersInfo` is not very straightforward.

When using the Windows API from C/C++, you can dynamically change the types of data presented to the API using pointers. Visual Basic does not directly support pointers, so each argument to an API declaration must be declared of a specific data type. Visual Basic does, however, allow you to *alias* the API — change its name and its argument data types. In effect, using the Visual Basic `Alias` keyword tells Visual Basic to create a declaration to the API with your unique arguments and name.

To use the Visual Basic `Alias` keyword, you first will need to create a pair of declarations, each defining a different value for the parameter `lpvParam`:

```
Declare Function SystemParamsLong Lib "user32" Alias _
    "SystemParametersInfoA" (ByVal uAction As Long, ByVal _
    uParam As Long, lpvParam As Long, ByVal fuWinIni As _
    Long) As Long
Declare Function SystemParamsInt Lib "user32" Alias _
    "SystemParametersInfoA" (ByVal uAction As Long, ByVal _
    uParam As Long, lpvParam As Integer, ByVal fuWinIni As _
    Long) As Long
```

After these are defined, the constants for the repeat function follow:

```
Const SPI_SETKEYBOARDDELAY = 23
Const SPI_SETKEYBOARDSPEED = 11
Const SPI_GETKEYBOARDSPEED = 10
Const SPI_GETKEYBOARDDELAY = 22
```

Note   Typically, the user has already established a keyboard usage configuration. You should not change keyboard speed, delay, or repeat rate unless the user verifies it.

After the constants and the APIs are declared, call `SystemParamsInt` or `SystemParamsLong` as needed. To get the current repeat-delay and repeat-speed settings, execute the following:

```
Dim iRepeatDelay As Integer
Dim lRepeatSpeed As Long

SystemParamsInt SPI_GETKEYBOARDDELAY, 0, iRepeatDelay, 0
SystemParamsLong SPI_GETKEYBOARDDELAY, 0, lRepeatSpeed, 0
```

To set the repeat-delay and repeat-speed settings, execute the following:

```
SystemParamsInt SPI_SETKEYBOARDDELAY, 0, iRepeatDelay, 0
SystemParamsInt SPI_SETKEYBOARDSPEED, 0, lRepeatSpeed, 0
```

Note The entire keyboard control code is available on the CD-ROM as KEYS.CLS. The file contains a class module that encapsulates the keyboard into an extensible object, and is ready for use in any program.

Summary

Windows supports many types of keyboards, and some of these keyboards have special keys not found on other keyboards. Using the keyboard APIs, you can determine the type of keyboard and then query to see if the keyboard supports a particular key.

✦ You should never assume a certain function key is present — instead, query the keyboard driver using the Windows API before accessing that key.

✦ The Windows API lets you query the keyboard directly, enhancing Visual Basic's capability to provide events. When using the keyboard APIs, you can determine keyboard state when your program requires key state information.

✦ When you are simply querying a certain key state, you should not use the keyboard APIs that use a virtual keyboard buffer.

✦ Reserve use of the virtual keyboard buffer for those times when you need to update several keys at once.

✦ Remember that the user can change the state of the keyboard at any time, and that your use of the virtual keyboard buffer should be kept as quick as possible.

✦ Using the Windows API calls and techniques presented in this chapter, you can take control of your keyboard.

✦   ✦   ✦

Expanding Mouse Control Using Windows API

Windows provides a rich set of information and control capabilities for the mouse. Using Windows API calls, you can quickly determine the state of the mouse or its current location. You can even move the mouse programmatically or lock the mouse to a given control or form. There are even Windows API functions that do what you can do with Visual Basic — for example, changing mouse pointers.

The mouse is a magnificent mechanism for speedy navigation of large amounts of data. In Visual Basic, you can quickly set the mouse pointer icon using the `MousePointer` property. You can trap user input, and determine whether the user clicks on screen objects with the mouse, via the `MouseMove`, `MouseDown`, `MouseMove`, and `MouseUp` events. Unfortunately, however, Visual Basic stops right there with regard to giving programmers access to the mouse.

If you want to determine whether a mouse is present, see how many buttons the mouse has, check the state of a mouse button, move the mouse to a given point, or accomplish many other common mouse tasks, you will need to use the Windows API. Table 29-1 lists the Windows API functions that this chapter will use to effect mouse control. The table lists each Windows API function name, along with a description of how you use it for the purpose of mouse control.

Note

Windows refers to the mouse pointer at times as the cursor. Several Windows API calls use *cursor* where you might expect them to use *mouse pointer*. Don't worry about the name; when you see *cursor*, we are correctly referring to what you normally call the *mouse pointer*.

We will at times also use the common description of *mouse pointer* for enhanced clarity. To avoid confusion with another Windows term, pointer, which means a location in memory, we will use the entire phrase *mouse pointer*.

Table 29-1 Windows API Functions Used in This Chapter	
API Function	**Description**
GetSystemMetrics	Returns information about the system. Used to determine mouse button count and mouse existence.
SwapMouseButton	Swaps left and right mouse button.
SetCursorPos	Positions the mouse cursor on the screen.
GetCursorPos	Returns position of cursor on the screen. Use this function to determine location of the mouse before moving it. Also useful to determine the window or control a mouse is over.
ShowCursor	Shows or hides the cursor.
ScreenToClient	Converts absolute screen coordinates into relative window coordinates.
ClientToScreen	Converts relative window coordinates into absolute screen coordinates.
GetAsyncKeyState	Returns the state of a mouse key.
GetWindowRect	Returns the dimensions of a window or control. Used when determining where and how to clip the cursor.
ClipCursor	Restricts the cursor to a defined control or window.
GetDoubleClickTime	Returns the duration, in milliseconds, in which a double-click must occur.
SetDoubleClickTime	Sets the duration, in milliseconds, in which a double-click must occur.
GetDesktopWindow(	Returns the handle to the entire screen. Used to restore a clipped cursor.
WindowFromPoint	Returns the handle of a window, given a screen coordinate. Used to determine the window (or control) a mouse is currently over.

Note You can see these and many more Windows APIs by using the API Viewer Add-In that comes with Visual Basic.

Table 29-2 lists the named constants used in this chapter. These constants control the actions of the Visual Basic keyword or Windows API function with which they are used. The table lists the constant name and its ordinal (numeric) value.

Table 29-2 Constants Used in This Chapter	
Constant	*Value (Decimal)*
VK_LMOUSEBUTTON	1
VK_RMOUSEBUTTON	2
VK_MMOUSEBUTTON	4
SM_MOUSEPRESENT	19
SM_SWAPBUTTON	23
SM_CMOUSEBUTTONS	43

Understanding the Mouse

The mouse is a frequently used input device; however, it can also do much more for you. Aside from simply letting the user choose menu options or size windows, the mouse can also be used to collect information. For example, there are Windows API calls that return the window handle (hWnd) of the window the mouse is currently over. This is handy for creating popup or context-sensitive help as the user glides the mouse over your interface elements.

Mouse components

The mouse is really a fairly complex system of hardware and software, including the physical mouse itself, the driver software, the graphical elements displayed on the screen, and the Windows API underneath that controls it all.

Mouse hardware

Mouse is now a relative term describing an input device alternative to the keyboard, which reflects user movement as a screen location or action. A mouse today may be the traditional two-button mouse, a three-button mouse, a trackball, or even a small finger tab like the IBM TrackPoint. However it is implemented, the physical mouse takes input from the user and, through software drivers, converts the movement into a screen location or action.

Windows mouse drivers

When the user positions (drags) the mouse, Windows mouse driver software translates the movement into a series of mouse messages. These mouse messages indicate what the user is doing (scrolling) and whether any keys are pressed (or released). Visual Basic translates these messages into `MouseMove`, `MouseOver`, `MouseUp`, and `MouseDown` events. You can easily respond to these events by writing code under the event of choice.

Mouse cursor

The mouse *cursor* is the official designation of what most of us call the mouse *pointer*. It's easy to get confused using the lingo of Windows. Most of us think a cursor is the insertion indicator in a text or word processor. In fact, the insertion point is represented by the *caret*. In Windows API lingo, however, the mouse pointer is referred to as the cursor. The text insertion indicator is referred to as the caret.

Windows provides visual feedback to the user by moving an onscreen icon called the *cursor* in coordination with the user's physical mouse movement. As the user moves the mouse, Windows moves the mouse pointer. As the cursor glides over windows, controls, and screen areas, Windows or your application can change the cursor.

You can also change the appearance of the cursor whenever you want by using the Visual Basic `MousePointer` property. For example, when your program starts a lengthy operation, you can set the `MousePointer` property to `vbHourGlass`, which causes the cursor to show the Windows Waiting icon. When the operation is complete, you can set the `MousePointer` property to `vbDefault`, which turns the cursor back into the default image.

Cursor hot spot

The *hot spot* is the point in the cursor that indicates the exact x,y position on the screen that the mouse action applies to. For example, as you slowly glide the mouse pointer over a window border, at one point along the edge of the border the cursor changes appearance. That point is the hot spot.

Windows mouse driver software tracks this point as the position of the cursor. The rest of the cursor is there for appearance only. As far as Windows is concerned, the hot spot is the cursor.

Determining the mouse state

The first step to making the mouse do what you want it to do is learning how to access the mouse information and status data. The most basic question you need to ask is whether the mouse is even installed. Believe it or not, Windows fully supports mouse emulation! The Windows SDK states that the mouse may be important, but it isn't required to operate Windows. This means you cannot assume there is a mouse present. If there is no mouse present, Windows shows the cursor only when the user chooses certain system commands — for example, sizing or moving a window.

There are many mouse-related Windows API calls, not all of which make sense for use by the Visual Basic developer. However, the most common functions — for determining whether a mouse is present, detecting the number of buttons the mouse has, checking the state of a mouse button, and moving the mouse to a given point — are quite commonly required and fairly easy to implement.

There are two primary Windows API functions available to check the status of the mouse. They are GetSystemMetrics() and GetAsyncKeyState().

Detecting mouse presence

Basic system information about the mouse can be retrieved using GetSystemMetrics, whose declaration is

```
Declare Function GetSystemMetrics Lib "user32" Alias _
    "GetSystemMetrics" (ByVal nIndex As Long) As Long
```

GetSystemMetrics returns a wide variety of system information and configuration data. To use GetSystemMetrics, assign its result to a variable. Before calling, set the index to the constant that indicates what to return. In this case, the constant is SM_MOUSEPRESENT. The following code shows how to determine whether a mouse is installed:

```
Public Function MouseThere() As Boolean
    MouseThere = GetSystemMetrics(SM_MOUSEPRESENT) = 1
End Function
```

MouseThere will contain True if there is a mouse installed or False if there is no mouse installed. MouseThere calls GetSystemMetrics with the SM_MOUSEPRESENT constant, which instructs GetSystemMetrics to indicate whether a mouse is installed. If a mouse is installed, GetSystemMetrics returns a value of one (1); any other value indicates an error occurred.

In order for the function to return a Visual Basic Boolean value of True (—1) or False (0), the code sets MouseThere to the following result: GetSystemMetrics(SM_MOUSEPRESENT) = 1. If GetSystemMetrics(SM_MOUSEPRESENT) = 1, MouseThere returns True (—1); otherwise, it returns False (0).

Determining the number of mouse buttons

After figuring out whether the mouse is there, the next step is to determine the number of buttons on the mouse. Windows fully supports two- and three-button mice. If the middle button is present, you can use it for your own purposes in your programs.

To check the number of buttons on the mouse, you call GetSystemMetrics again, this time with the constant SM_CMOUSEBUTTONS, as follows:

```
Public Function ButtonCount As Integer
    ButtonCount = GetSystemMetrics(SM_CMOUSEBUTTONS)
End Function
```

With this index, GetSystemMetrics returns the number of buttons on the mouse, or zero (0) if there is no mouse installed. ButtonCount now holds the number of buttons.

ButtonCount() calls GetSystemMetrics with the SM_CMOUSEBUTTONS constant, which instructs GetSystemMetrics to indicate the number of buttons on the mouse. A value of 2 is returned for most mice, but three buttons are available for some mice.

Detecting left- or right-handed mouse

One of the other things users can do is to swap the mouse buttons. (My setup is Windows for a left-handed mouse.) Because you are going to be accessing mouse buttons by their logical positions of left or right, you need a method to determine whether they have been swapped.

Once again, you can use the Windows API GetSystemMetrics, this time with index SM_SWAPBUTTON to determine whether mouse buttons are swapped, as follows:

```
Public Function ButtonsSwapped() As Boolean
    ButtonsSwapped = GetSystemMetrics(SM_SWAPBUTTON) = 1
End Function
```

Now ButtonsSwapped returns True if the user has swapped the mouse buttons using the Control Panel, or if some other program has swapped them.

If you want to swap mouse buttons, use the SwapMouseButton Windows API function. This swaps the left and right mouse buttons, reversing or restoring the original settings. If you call SwapMouseButton with its argument set to True, the left mouse button will generate right-button messages, and the right mouse button will generate left-button messages. If you call SwapMouseButton with its argument set to False, the mouse buttons are restored to their original state.

The example property in Listing 29-1 wraps the previous Windows API functions into a simple set of procedures. The Property Let procedure sets or resets the mouse buttons, while the Property Get procedure returns whether the buttons are swapped at all.

Listing 29-1: **Complete Mouse Button Swapping Property**

```
Private Declare Function SwapMouseButton Lib "user32" _
    (ByVal bSwap As Long) As Long

' API constant
Private Const SM_SWAPBUTTON = 23

' swap mouse buttons.
' on entry bState = False (0) means to restore (unswap)
' buttons; while bState = True (-1) means to swap
' them
Public Property Let ButtonsSwap(bState As Boolean)
    SwapMouseButton bState
End Property

' determine if mouse buttons are swapped,
' returns True (-1) is buttons are swapped,
' otherwise returns False
Public Property Get ButtonsSwap() As Boolean
 ButtonsSwap = GetSystemMetrics(SM_SWAPBUTTON) <> 0
End Sub
```

The previous code implements a complete mouse button swapping property. The ButtonSwap property Let uses the SwapMouseButton API to set the swap state to True or False depending on the value of the bState argument passed. If bState is True (-1), the buttons are swapped; if bState is False (0), the buttons are unswapped.

The ButtonSwap property Get uses the GetSystemMetrics API with the SM_SWAPBUTTON constant to return a True (-1) or False (0) value for the current swap state of the mouse. If the mouse buttons are swapped, ButtonSwap returns True (-1); otherwise, ButtonSwap returns False (0).

The code compares the result of GetSystemMetrics API with the SM_SWAPBUTTON constant and checks to determine whether it's equal to zero. This is because with the SM_SWAPBUTTON constant, GetSystemMetrics returns a nonzero number if the buttons are swapped.

Mouse button state

Although Visual Basic is great at telling us when the user does something, you will often want to do or know more than what Visual Basic allows. For example, if you want to "do something as long as the user holds the mouse button down," you need to write some fairly complex Visual Basic code to monitor several events and set global shared flags accordingly. A much easier method is to access this information directly from Windows using mouse-oriented Windows API functions.

When checking mouse button states, you use the same logic as when working with keyboard Windows API functions. This is because mouse buttons are represented to Windows as extensions of the keyboard; in fact, Windows keyboard API functions consider the mouse just another set of keys.

You can easily determine whether a mouse button is up or down using the same methods as those used for standard keyboard keys, as discussed in Chapter 28. The mouse buttons are considered to be up or down. A mouse button that is up is not pressed. A mouse button that is down is considered pressed. Because mouse buttons are considered keys, there are virtual key codes for them as well.

Windows virtual key code constants for the mouse are as follows:

```
Const VK_LMOUSEBUTTON = 1    'left mouse button
Const VK_RMOUSEBUTTON = 2    'right mouse button
Const VK_MMOUSEBUTTON = 4    'middle button - yes, it's true!
```

The GetAsyncKeyState() Windows API function returns keyboard information and mouse key information. Its declaration is

```
Declare Function GetAsyncKeyState Lib "user32" Alias
"GetAsyncKeyState" (ByVal vKey As Long) As Integer
```

You can quickly determine which mouse key, if any, the user is holding down. To check the state of a mouse key, you call GetAsyncKeyState with the virtual key code constant of choice. GetAsyncKeyState returns both the current and previous state of mouse keys. This means it can indicate whether a mouse key was pressed, even if it is not currently down.

The result of GetAsyncKeyState is a 16-bit integer for all versions of Windows. If the most significant bit is set, the key is currently down. If the least significant bit is set, the key was pressed at least once since the last call. For 32-bit Windows, GetAsyncKeyState returns zero (0) if a window in another thread or process currently has the keyboard focus. So, to see whether the left mouse button is currently down, execute the following instruction:

```
LeftMouseDown = GetAsyncKeyState(VK_LMOUSEBUTTON) < 0
```

You could put the previous code in a loop to execute while the user holds the left mouse button down. This is handy for operations that you need to execute as long as the user holds a mouse button down — for example, drawing or dragging operations. The following code shows how this is done:

```
Private Sub Form_MouseDown(Button As Integer, _
    Shift As Integer, X As Single, Y As Single)

    While GetAsyncKeyState(VK_LMOUSEBUTTON) < 0
        'user has mouse held down
        'do whatever it is that you need to do in here
    Wend

End Sub
```

To check to see whether a mouse key has been pressed since the last call to GetAsyncKeyState, use the following instruction:

```
LeftMouseWasPressed = (GetAsyncKeyState(VK_LMOUSEBUTTON) = 1)
```

Listing 29-2 shows code that takes into account the swap state of the mouse, and then modifies itself accordingly to return correct information.

Note

GetAsyncKeyState operates on the physical mouse buttons, and may appear to work inverted if SwapMouseButton has been used to swap buttons.

Listing 29-2: **Complete Mouse Button State Function**

```
' this function returns True (-1) if the left mouse
' button is down, other wise returns False (0).
Public Function LeftMouseDown() As Boolean
    If GetSystemMetrics(SM_SWAPBUTTON) = 1 Then
        'buttons are swapped, so use R mouse key constant
        LeftMouseDown = GetAsyncKeyState_
                        (VK_RMOUSEBUTTON) < 0
    Else
        'buttons are not swapped, so use L mouse key constant
        LeftMouseDown = GetAsyncKeyState_
                        (VK_LMOUSEBUTTON) < 0
    End if
End Function
' this function returns True (-1) if the right mouse
' button is down, other wise returns False (0).
Public Function RightMouseDown() As Boolean
    If GetSystemMetrics(SM_SWAPBUTTON) = 1 Then
        'buttons are swapped, so use L mouse key constant
        RightMouseDown = GetAsyncKeyState_
                        (VK_LMOUSEBUTTON) < 0
    Else
        'buttons are not swapped, so use R mouse key constant
        RightMouseDown = GetAsyncKeyState_
                        (VK_RMOUSEBUTTON) < 0
    End if
End Function
```

The code in Listing 29-2 requires a bit of explanation. Both the `LeftMouseDown` and `RightMouseDown` properties first use the `GetSystemMetrics` API with the `SM_SWAPBUTTON` constant to check whether the mouse buttons are currently swapped. If the buttons are swapped, `GetSystemMetrics` will return a value of 1, which is used in a Visual Basic `If/End If` block to branch between the two states.

If the mouse buttons are not currently swapped, the code uses the `GetAsyncKeyState` API with the appropriate left (`VK_LMOUSEBUTTON`) or right (`VK_RMOUSEBUTTON`) mouse button constant. However, if the mouse buttons are swapped, then the code reverses the mouse buttons, switching `VK_LMOUSEBUTTON` and `VK_RMOUSEBUTTON`. This has the effect of querying the opposite mouse button — which is what we need to do because the left and right mouse buttons are currently swapped.

Setting mouse state

There are times when you will want to hide and then redisplay the cursor. There is a single Windows API that handles this task for us and can hide or show the mouse pointer: `ShowCursor`. Its declaration is

```
Declare Function ShowCursor (ByVal bShow As Long) As Long
```

`ShowCursor` is not a simple on or off mechanism. Instead, `ShowCursor` either increments or decrements the internal visibility counter of the mouse. `ShowCursor` toggles the cursor visibility flag up or down and maintains a counter that keeps track of the state of the cursor. The following instruction increments this counter:

```
ShowCursor True
```

and this decrements the counter:

```
ShowCursor False
```

Windows makes the cursor visible only if the counter is greater than or equal to zero (0). This means that `ShowCursor True` does not always show the cursor! To help you set the cursor visibility to what you want, `ShowCursor` returns the cursor's previous state when you set its new state. This way, you can set the new state, read the previous state, and then put the old state back. So, to get the current state of the mouse cursor visibility, the following property is used within a class module dedicated to mouse pointer functionality:

```
Public Property Get Visible() As Boolean
    Visible = ShowCursor(True) 'increment state
    ShowCursor False           'decrement state
End Property
```

Note   The mouse pointer is a shared resource. If you hide it, it is hidden from all applications — not just yours!

To set the visibility of the cursor, more complex code is needed. Here, the logic is to walk back through the existing cursor states until you arrive at the visibility state that corresponds to what you want. Listing 29-3 shows code that takes into account the current visible state and then modifies itself accordingly to return correct information.

Listing 29-3: **Complete Mouse Pointer State Function**

```
' this property shows or hide the mouse pointer
' based on the value of bNewValue. If bNewValue
' is True (-1), then mouse pointer is shown. If
' bNewValue is False (0) then the mouse pointer
' is hidden.
Public Property Let Visible(ByVal bNewValue As Boolean)
    Dim oldmode As Integer
    If bNewValue Then
        oldmode = -1 'to make sure the loop executes
        While (oldmode < 1)
            oldmode = ShowCursor(True)'toggle up
        Wend
    Else
        oldmode = 1'to make sure the loop executes
        While (oldmode >= 0)
            oldmode = ShowCursor(False)'toggle down
        Wend
    End If
End Property
```

The code in Listing 29-3 is fairly complex and requires a bit of explanation. Before we explain the code, remember that the mouse pointer state is a counter, not a toggle. As applications show or hide the mouse pointer, the counter is incremented and decremented, respectively. Therefore, it is possible to use ShowCursor True and still have the mouse pointer be invisible. To handle this possibility, the previous code steps through the counter value attempting to show or hide the mouse pointer. When ShowCursor finally reaches the proper state and returns the requested state, the loop exits.

Getting and setting mouse position

Now that you know that there is a mouse, how many buttons it has, which button is down or has been pressed, and can turn the cursor on or off, you need to figure out where the cursor is. Windows refers to the visible mouse pointer as the *cursor*. There is one and only one cursor in Windows, and it is shared by all applications — even under 32-bit Windows.

Many Visual Basic objects generate events as the mouse moves over them. For example, Visual Basic fires the MouseMove event when the mouse moves over a form. Sometimes, however, the mouse is over an object that does not give MouseMove events, or the mouse could be over the window of another process altogether.

There are lots of times when you need to know where the mouse pointer is. The Windows API functions that handle these tasks are GetCursorPos and ScreenToClient.

Getting mouse position

The Windows API function that indicates where the mouse is located is called GetCursorPos. Its declaration is

```
Declare Function GetCursorPos Lib "user32" (lpPoint As _
    POINTAPI) As Long
```

GetCursorPos takes as its argument a user-defined type that it fills in with the current (x,y) coordinates of the mouse, relative to the upper-left corner of the visible display screen. These coordinates are paired together within a Type clause that appears in the general Declarations section of your VB application, along with the API function declaration. The proper clause is as follows:

```
Private Type POINTAPI
    x As Long
    y As Long
End Type
```

To use GetCursorPos, make a copy of the type and then call GetCursorPos, as in the following example:

```
Dim typPt As POINTAPI
GetCursorPos typPt
```

Variable typPt now contains the (x,y) coordinates of the mouse pointer. You can wrap this Windows API function in a reusable property that returns the (x,y) position of the mouse using the familiar Visual Basic CurrentX and CurrentY syntax, as follows:

```
Public Property Get CurrentX() As Long
    Dim typPt As POINTAPI
    GetCursorPos typPt
    CurrentX = typPt.x
End Property

Public Property Get CurrentY() As Long
    Dim typPt As POINTAPI_TYPE
    GetCursorPos typPt
    CurrentY = typPt.Y
End Property
```

The location of the mouse is returned in the form of *screen coordinates*. What this means is that the mouse position is given in relation to the upper-left corner of the screen. To convert from screen coordinates to coordinates that you can use with forms and other controls, you will need the ScreenToClient Windows API function. Its declaration is

```
Declare Function ScreenToClient Lib "user32" Alias _
    "ScreenToClient" (ByVal hwnd As Long, lpPoint As _
    POINTAPI) As Long
```

ScreenToClient converts the (x,y) screen coordinates in the Type clause that GetCursorPos fills, to (x,y) values that are relative to the upper-left corner of a given window.

To convert the raw cursor position into a relative cursor position for a given window, call GetCursorPos and then pass the window handle and the point type to ScreenToClient. For example, to get the position of the mouse pointer while it is over Form1, use the following instructions:

```
Dim typPt As POINTAPI
GetCursorPos typPt
ScreenToClient Form1.hWnd, typPt
```

The result is that typPt.X and typPt.Y are now (x,y) coordinates relative to the upper-left corner of Form1. Using these Windows API functions together, you can update the properties by adding an hWnd property to the class or module, then inside the function use ScreenToClient to translate the absolute screen coordinates into relative window coordinates.

Listing 29-4 shows code that returns the x and y location of the mouse pointer using the familiar CurrentX and CurrentY implementation.

Listing 29-4: **Complete Mouse Position Retrieval Properties**

```
' returns the Y (vertical) location of
' the mouse according to the Form where this code
' is called from.
Public Property Get CurrentY() As Long
    Dim typPt As POINTAPI
    GetCursorPos typPt
    ScreenToClient Me.hWnd, typPt
    CurrentY = typPt.Y
End Property
' returns the X (horizontal) location of
' the mouse according to the Form where this code
' is called from.
```

(continued)

Listing 29-4 *(continued)*

```
Public Property Get CurrentX() As Long
    Dim typPt As POINTAPI
    GetCursorPos typPt
    ScreenToClient Me.hWnd, typPt
    CurrentX = typPt.X
End Property
```

Now you can tell where the mouse is at all times, even when your application does not control the mouse.

The preceding code assumes that this property is hosted in a form. The Visual Basic Me keyword is then used to return the hWnd property of the form hosting the code. If you use this code in a module or class, Me.hWnd will not be available because modules and classes do not have an hWnd property. If you plan to use this code in modules or classes, replace Me.hWnd with a public variable and make sure to set the variable to the hWnd of the form you wish to use as the coordinates source.

Setting mouse position

When you are ready to take control of the mouse, you will need additional API functions to move the mouse to a given spot on the screen. The API functions that handle these tasks are SetCursorPos and ClientToScreen.

The SetCursorPos function positions the cursor at a specified (x,y) point on the screen. In other words, SetCursorPos can move the mouse for you. The API function's declaration is

```
Declare Function SetCursorPos Lib "user32" (ByVal x As Long, _
    ByVal y As Long) As Long
```

To use SetCursorPos, fill in a point type with the desired (x,y) coordinates, then call SetCursorPos. For example, to move the mouse to coordinates 100 pixels in and 100 pixels down from the upper-left corner of the screen, use the following routine:

```
Dim typPt As POINTAPI
typPt.X= 100
typPt.Y = 100
SetCursorPos typPt.X, typPt.Y
```

To use `SetCursorPos` with your own forms, you need the counterpart to `ScreenToClient` — which is aptly named `ClientToScreen`! Its declaration is

```
Declare Function ClientToScreen Lib "user32" Alias
"ClientToScreen" (ByVal hwnd As Long, lpPoint As POINTAPI) _
    As Long
```

`ClientToScreen` fixes up coordinates relative to a window so that they refer to an origin that is in the upper-left corner of `Form1`. To fix up our last example, you would just add a call to `ClientToScreen`, as follows:

```
Dim typPt As POINTAPI_TYPE
typPt.X= 100
typPt.Y = 100
ClientToScreen Form1.hWnd, typPt
SetCursorPos typPt.X, typPt.Y
```

The preceding code now moves to a point 100 pixels in and 100 pixels down from the upper-left corner of `Form1`. The following property procedure provides the `Let` functionality to complement the previous `CurrentX Get` property procedure:

```
' set X (horizontal) position of mouse pointer
Public Property Let CurrentX(X As Long)
    Dim typPt As POINTAPI
    GetCursorPos typPt
    typPt.X= X
    ClientToScreen Form1.hWnd, typPt
    SetCursorPos typPt.X, typPt.Y
End Property
```

The following property procedure provides the `Let` functionality to complement the previous `CurrentY Get` property procedure:

```
' set Y (vertical) position of mouse pointer
Public Property Let CurrentY(Y As Long)
    Dim typPt As POINTAPI
    GetCursorPos typPt
    typPt.Y= Y
    ClientToScreen Form1.hWnd, typPt
    SetCursorPos typPt.X, typPt.Y
End Property
```

The foregoing code examples implementing the `Let` functionality again use `Form1.hWnd` as the windows handle of the window to map coordinates. This, of course, assumes you have a form titled `Form1`. If you plan to use this code in a module or class, or with other forms, create a public variable to represent the `hWnd` property of the form you want to use. Replace the `Form1.hWnd` with the name of the variable. Then, set the public variable to that form before calling this code. The code in Listing 29-5 shows how to implement this technique — it shows code that sets or gets the position of the mouse, encapsulated into a reusable class property.

Listing 29-5: Complete Mouse Position Properties

```
' variable to hold hWnd of form to use this with
Public Hwnd As Long

' returns the Y (vertical) location of
' the mouse according to the Form where this code
' is called from.
Public Property Get CurrentY() As Long
    Dim typPt As POINTAPI
    GetCursorPos typPt
    ScreenToClient Hwnd, typPt
    CurrentY = typPt.Y
End Property
' set Y (vertical) position of mouse pointer
Public Property Let CurrentY(Y As Long)
    Dim typPt As POINTAPI
    GetCursorPos typPt
    typPt.Y = Y
    ClientToScreen Hwnd, typPt
    SetCursorPos typPt.X, typPt.Y
End Property
' returns the X (horizontal) location of
' the mouse according to the Form where this code
' is called from.
Public Property Get CurrentX() As Long
    Dim typPt As POINTAPI
    GetCursorPos typPt
    ScreenToClient Hwnd, typPt
    CurrentX = typPt.X
End Property
' set X (horizontal) position of mouse pointer
Public Property Let CurrentX(X As Long)
    Dim typPt As POINTAPI
    GetCursorPos typPt
    typPt.X= X
    ClientToScreen Hwnd, typPt
    SetCursorPos typPt.X, typPt.Y
End Property
```

You now have an encapsulated method for determining or positioning the mouse on the display screen (desktop), any window (even Windows in other applications), or your own application. Assuming you name this class cMouse, usage of this class module from within a form titled Form1 would be as follows:

```
' declare instance of mouse class
Dim myMouse As New cMouse

' assign mouse class window handle to form
cMouse.hWnd = Form1.hWnd
```

```
' now use mouse class properties
cMouse.CurrentX = 100
cMouse.CurrentY = 100

' more code here to do whatever your
' code does

' clean up after using cMouse
Set cMouse = Nothing
```

This example shows how to declare an instance of the cMouse class and then set the cMouse class's hWnd property to that of the form where you are using the cMouse class properties. As always, when you're done with an instance of a class, use the Visual Basic Set keyword to remove its resources.

Mouse Secrets

The Windows mouse system can also offer you some valuable extra information — if you know the "secret" Windows API functions to use. For example, there are system-related API functions that can tell you which window the mouse is currently over — even if that window is not in your application! The API functions that give you this extra power are as follows:

✦ WindowFromPoint

✦ ClipCursor

✦ GetWindowRect

✦ GetDoubleClickTime

✦ SetDoubleClickTime

Identifying windows

The WindowFromPoint API function takes a set of raw coordinates and then looks up which window owns that point. It returns the window handle (hWnd) of that window. This function's declaration is

```
Declare Function WindowFromPoint Lib "user32" Alias _
    "WindowFromPoint" (ByVal xPoint As Long, ByVal yPoint _
    As Long) As Long
```

In the following example, the current cursor coordinates are retrieved by GetCursorPos, and then the window that owns those coordinates is returned by WindowFromPoint:

```
Public Function IsOver() As Long
    Dim typPt As POINTAPI
    GetCusorPos typPt
    IsOver = WindowFromPoint(typPt.Y, typPt.x)
End Function
```

IsOver receives the window handle (hWnd) that the mouse pointer currently resides over. This is especially handy for controls that don't offer MouseMove events. For example, as the mouse flies over the controls of your form, you might offer popup help.

Clipping the mouse pointer

Windows also lets you limit the mouse to certain areas of the screen. The Windows API function for this is ClipCursor, whose declaration is

```
Declare Function ClipCursor Lib "user32" (lpRect As Any) _
    As Long
```

ClipCursor limits the mouse to an area of the screen — normally, this is a control or a window. For example, you might want to force the user to choose an option or press a button. You can lock the mouse to that control, making sure the user cannot exit that part until he or she clicks the button.

Note   It is not normally considered acceptable user-interface design to clip the mouse pointer, but sometimes situations require special solutions.

ClipCursor requires as its argument a user-defined type that represents a rectangle. The GetWindowRect Windows API function returns the dimensions of the given window referenced in the hWnd property passed to it. This function's declaration is

```
Declare Function GetWindowRect Lib "user32" Alias _
    "GetWindowRect" (ByVal hwnd As Long, lpRect As _
    RECT_TYPES) As Long
```

GetWindowRect uses a user-defined type named RECT_TYPE. This type's members are filled in with the left, top, right, and bottom coordinates of a rectangular section of the screen:

```
Private Type RECT_TYPE
    Left As Long
    Top As Long
    Right As Long
    Bottom As Long
End Type
```

So, let `GetWindowRect` figure out the dimensions and coordinates (in screen coordinates relative to upper-left corner of the screen) for you. The following example shows how to limit the mouse pointer to a given control. Listing 29-6 centers the mouse in the middle of the control passed to it.

Listing 29-6: **Restricts or "Clips" the Mouse Pointer to the Area of a Control**

```
Sub ClipToControl(ctl As Control)
    Dim hwnd As Long
    Dim typ_RECT As RECT_TYPE
    hwnd = ctl.hWnd
    GetWindowRect hwnd, typ_RECT
    SetCursorPos typ_RECT.Left + ((typ_RECT.Right - _
    typ_RECT.Left) / 2), _
    typ_RECT.Top + ((typ_RECT.Bottom - typ_RECT.Top) / 2)
    ClipCursor typ_RECT
End Sub
```

If you consider using the preceding code, you will eventually need the partner to `ClipCursor`, which is `GetClipCursor`. This API function returns the screen coordinates of the rectangle that contains the mouse. Its declaration is

```
Declare Function GetClipCursor Lib "user32" _
    (lprc As RECT_TYPE) As Long
```

To rescind a clipped mouse region, you need to set the mouse pointer to the entire screen. There is no "ReleaseClipCursor" function. Instead, use Listing 29-6, but pass to `ClipCursor` the hWnd of the desktop. This effectively clips the mouse to the entire desktop. The `GetDesktopWindow` Windows API function returns the window handle (hWnd) of the desktop. Its declaration is

```
Declare Function GetDesktopWindow Lib "user32" Alias
"GetDesktopWindow" () As Long
```

Putting it all together, you can now unclip the cursor. Listing 29-7 restores the mouse pointer to the entire screen.

Listing 29-7: Restoring or Unclipping Mouse Movement

```
Public Sub ClipToDesktop()
    Dim typ_RECT As RECT_TYPE
    GetWindowRect GetDesktopWindow(), typ_RECT
    ClipCursor typ_RECT
End Sub
```

Mouse timing

An operation commonly performed by users of Windows is the double click. Double clicks are typically used to indicate selection of items. Users can change the double click interval — the maximum number of milliseconds permitted between the first and second click — at any time.

In some applications you will want to maintain a given double click interval; for example, unattended kiosk applications and games commonly need to control the double click interval. For these situations, you can override the user-defined double click settings and institute your own.

The `GetDoubleClickTime` API function retrieves the current double click interval for the mouse. Its declaration is

```
Declare Function GetDoubleClickTime Lib "user32" () As Long
```

Note   Typically, the user has already established a mouse configuration. You should not change the double click interval unless the user verifies it.

Windows enables you to set the mouse double-click interval using the `SetDoubleClickTime` API function, whose declaration is

```
Declare Function SetDoubleClickTime Lib "user32" (ByVal _
    wCount As Long) As Long
```

A sample property that encapsulates these two Windows APIs follows:

```
Public Property Get DoubleClickTime() As Long
    ' assign API function
    DoubleClickTime = GetDoubleClickTime
End Property
Public Property Let DoubleClickTime(ByVal vNewValue As Long)
    ' assign API
    SetDoubleClickTime vNewValue
End Property
```

Putting It All Together

Listing 29-8 presents a class module that encapsulates the mouse pointer API functions into an extensible object ready for use in any VB program. This class module — which also is available in its entirety on the CD-ROM — includes a complete working demo program written in Visual Basic that implements all the mouse APIs and code used in this chapter. The class module then abstracts the mouse into an extensible object.

On the CD-ROM

This code is located on the accompanying CD-ROM in the file MOUSE.CLS.

Listing 29-8: **Complete Listing of MOUSE.CLS**

```
Option Explicit
DefInt A-Z
Private Const VK_LMOUSEBUTTON = 1
Private Const VK_RMOUSEBUTTON = 2
Private Const VK_MMOUSEBUTTON = 4
Private Const SM_MOUSEPRESENT = 19
Private Const SM_SWAPBUTTON = 23
Private Const SM_CMOUSEBUTTONS = 43
Private Type POINTAPI_TYPE
    x As Long
    y As Long
End Type
Private Type RECT_TYPE
    Left As Long
    Top As Long
    Right As Long
    Bottom As Long
End Type
Declare Function GetSystemMetrics Lib "user32" Alias
"GetSystemMetrics" (ByVal nIndex As Long) As Long
Private Declare Function SwapMouseButton Lib "user32" (ByVal _+
    bSwap As Long) As Long
Private Declare Function SetCursorPos Lib _
    "user32" (ByVal x As Long, ByVal y As Long) As Long
Private Declare Function GetCursorPos Lib _
    "user32" (lppoint As POINTAPI_TYPE) As Long
Private Declare Function ShowCursor Lib _
    "user32" (ByVal bShow As Long) As Long
Private Declare Function GetAsyncKeyState Lib "user32" _
    (ByVal vKey As Long) As Integer
Private Declare Function GetWindowRect Lib "user32" _
    (ByVal hwnd As Long, lpRect As RECT_TYPE) As Long
Private Declare Function ClipCursor Lib _
    "user32" (lpRect As RECT_TYPE) As Long
Private Declare Function GetDesktopWindow Lib "user32" _
    () As Long
```

(continued)

Listing 29-8 *(continued)*

```
Private Declare Function WindowFromPoint Lib "user32" _
    (ByVal xPoint As Long, ByVal yPoint As Long) As Long
Public Sub ButtonsSwap()
    SwapMouseButton True
End Sub
Public Property Get CurrentX() As Long
    Dim pt As POINTAPI_TYPE
    GetCursorPos pt
    CurrentX = pt.x
End Property
Public Property Let CurrentX(x As Long)
    Dim pt As POINTAPI_TYPE
    GetCursorPos pt
    pt.X= x
    SetCursorPos pt.x, pt.Y
End Property
Public Property Let CurrentY(y As Long)
    Dim pt As POINTAPI_TYPE
    GetCursorPos pt
    pt.Y = y
    SetCursorPos pt.x, pt.Y
End Property
Public Property Get CurrentY() As Long
    Dim pt As POINTAPI_TYPE
    GetCursorPos pt
    CurrentY = pt.Y
End Property
Public Property Get Visible() As Boolean
    Dim oldmode As Integer
    oldmode = ShowCursor(True)
    ShowCursor False
    Visible = oldmode
End Property
Public Property Let Visible(ByVal bNewValue As Boolean)
    Dim oldmode As Integer
    If bNewValue Then
        oldmode = -1
        While (oldmode < 1)
            oldmode = ShowCursor(True)
        Wend
    Else
        oldmode = 1
        While (oldmode >= 0)
            oldmode = ShowCursor(False)
        Wend
    End If
End Property
Public Function IsPresent() As Boolean
    IsPresent = GetSystemMetrics(SM_MOUSEPRESENT) = 1
End Function
Public Sub ButtonsUnswap()
```

```
        SwapMouseButton False
End Sub
Public Function ButtonsSwapped() As Boolean
    ButtonsSwapped = GetSystemMetrics_
                     (SM_SWAPBUTTON) <> 0
End Function
Public Function ButtonDownLeft() As Boolean
    GetAsyncKeyState vbKeyLButton
    ButtonDownLeft = Not (GetAsyncKeyState(vbKeyLButton) _
        And &HFFFF) = 0
End Function
Public Function ButtonDownMiddle() As Boolean
    GetAsyncKeyState vbKeyMButton
    ButtonDownMiddle = Not (GetAsyncKeyState(vbKeyMButton) _
        And &HFFFF) = 0
End Function
Public Function ButtonDownRight() As Boolean
    GetAsyncKeyState vbKeyRButton
    ButtonDownRight = Not (GetAsyncKeyState(vbKeyRButton) _
        And &HFFFF) = 0
End Function
Public Sub Move(x As Long, y As Long)
    SetCursorPos x, y
End Sub
Public Sub ClipToControl(ByVal ctl As Object)
    On Error GoTo myError
    Dim hwnd As Long
    Dim typ_RECT As RECT_TYPE
    hwnd = ctl.hwnd
    GetWindowRect hwnd, typ_RECT
    SetCursorPos typ_RECT.Left + _
        ((typ_RECT.Right - typ_RECT.Left) / 2), _
        typ_RECT.Top + ((typ_RECT.Bottom - typ_RECT.Top) / 2)
    ClipCursor typ_RECT
myExit:
    Exit Sub
myError:
    On Error Resume Next
End Sub
Public Sub ClipToDesktop()
    Dim typ_RECT As RECT_TYPE
    GetWindowRect GetDesktopWindow(), typ_RECT
    ClipCusor typ_RECT
End Sub
Public Sub ClipToRectangle(Left As Long, Top As Long, Width _
    As Long, Height As Long)
    Dim typ_RECT As RECT_TYPE
    typ_RECT.Left = Left
    typ_RECT.Top = Top
    typ_RECT.Right = Left + Width
    typ_RECT.Bottom = Top + Height
```

(continued)

Listing 29-8 *(continued)*

```
        SetCursorPos typ_RECT.Left + ((typ_RECT.Right - _
            typ_RECT.Left) / 2), typ_RECT.Top + ((typ_RECT.Bottom _
            - typ_RECT.Top) / 2)
        ClipCursor typ_RECT
End Sub
Public Function ButtonCount() As Long
    ButtonCount = GetSystemMetrics(SM_CMOUSEBUTTONS)
End Function
Public Sub Reset()
    Screen.MousePointer = vbDefault
End Sub
Public Function IsOver() As Long
    Dim lppoint As POINTAPI_TYPE
    GetCursorPos lppoint
    IsOver = WindowFromPoint(lppoint.Y, lppoint.x)
End Function
```

Summary

Using the Windows API, you can accomplish many tasks that Visual Basic alone cannot perform. One confusing aspect of using the Windows mouse-related APIs is that Windows refers to the mouse pointer as the cursor. However, once you understand this nomenclature, using the mouse APIs is straightforward.

✦ Windows supports several types of mouse input devices — some of which are not "mice" at all! Fortunately, Windows virtualizes the mouse and presents you with a series of information and control APIs that let you determine the type of mouse device installed and then manipulate the "mouse" using standard methods.

✦ The mouse is one of the most used elements of a Windows computer. Therefore, the user has great control over its position, appearance, and how it operates.

✦ The Windows API enables you to override the user and take control of the mouse away. This power should be used judiciously; otherwise, users of your software may not find your software usable.

✦ For those situations where your application or environment requires direct control of the mouse, the code presented in this chapter allows you to perform virtually any action a user could.

✦   ✦   ✦

File, Disk, and Directory Control Using the Windows API

Reading data from disk files and writing data to files are fundamental program functions. Visual Basic provides very flexible and powerful methods for creating and opening files, as well as reading and writing data.

Any application of significant breadth soon requires advanced functions for manipulation of information stored on disk, as well as manipulation of the media itself. For example, a drive attached to a system might be a floppy drive, a hard drive, or a CD-ROM drive, but Visual Basic itself has no built-in function to determine a drive's type. An example of this is when one or more CD-ROM drives are installed on a system. A CD-ROM is read-only, and an attempt to write to it will generate a runtime error. Other examples include detecting if a drive is out of space or not, whether or not long filenames are allowed, and if directories or files are read-only. Using the Windows API, you can quickly determine not only the drive type but also other essential information about the drive including free space and support for long filenames.

Windows supports several types of file systems, and each type includes features unique to it. For example, not all file systems that support Windows support long filenames. Regardless of the specific features of the file system, however, all file systems have means to store data and methods for retrieving information about the data and the media upon which the data is stored.

Windows File Systems

A file system is a method of storing and retrieving data. File systems also store information about the data stored — such as creation date, filenames, and space allocated. As mentioned previously, specific features of the file system may vary. Not all drives support all capabilities — for example, you cannot write to a CD-ROM drive. However, all drives store information using the same basic techniques.

In general, information is allocated into *clusters* of bytes. The exact number of bytes in a cluster varies depending on the drive type and how it was partitioned and formatted. Clusters are composed of disk regions called *sectors*. All data stored on a drive is grouped into sectors, which in turn are grouped into clusters. A table listing the starting cluster for any file is also maintained by the file system. This table is called the file allocation table, or FAT. Used together, the sectors, clusters, and the FAT allow a drive's file system to allocate and preserve space for the data stored on a drive.

The region of a disk managed by a single file allocation system is referred to as a *volume*. Note that a drive may have one or more volumes on it, and a drive's volumes may have different file allocation systems.

Common file system types

Other information, such as whether the file is read-only or when it was created or written to, is also stored by the file system. Where that data is stored varies from file system to file system. Depending on computer and network configuration, your programs might access one of four very different file systems:

✦ Windows NT® New Technology File System (NTFS)

✦ High Performance File System (HPFS)

✦ File allocation table (FAT)

✦ Virtual file allocation table (VFAT, or "protected-mode FAT")

If you are writing network applications, or applications that access or may access network drives, you could connect to more than one type of file system. Thankfully, Windows manages the differences between physical data storage for you automatically. Even so, you may encounter drives that offer unique features — for example, long filename support.

For example, on a peer-to-peer network, there might be Windows NT workstations and Windows for Workgroups (WFW) workstations. The NT workstation might offer long filename support; however, the WFW workstations cannot, because WFW does not support long filenames. In these sorts of situations, where advanced features may not be available, Windows "gracefully degrades" — that is, it falls back to the least common denominator of the system. Specifically, for example, Windows 95 and Windows NT support long filenames and can also maintain a file *alias*, or short filename, as well. You may then refer to a long filename by its short filename alias. There are Windows APIs that let you locate a short filename if you provide the long filename, and vice versa.

NTFS

Windows NT® New Technology File System (NTFS) provides a faster access methodology than many other file systems. NTFS also supports compression for individual files and directories, as well as security and Unicode filenames. NTFS is designed to automatically (most of the time) detect and recover from system crashes, which on other file systems requires a recovering utility. NTFS filenames may be up to 255 characters in length. A compatibility feature of NTFS is that it also provides for short filename aliases to long filenames.

FAT

The file allocation table (FAT) file system is the MS-DOS® file system. One of the main advantages to FAT is that it is supported by MS-DOS, Windows, and OS/2. FAT is also the only file system supported for floppy disks. FAT systems do not support long filenames, nor do they distinguish between uppercase and lowercase characters in filenames. FAT system support the classic 8.3 naming convention — up to 8 characters followed by a period and then up to 3 more characters.

VFAT (protected-mode FAT)

VFAT, or Virtual FAT, is the Windows 95 default. It is compatible with MS-DOS FAT file systems and uses a similar logic in storing data. Protected-mode FAT also adds support for long filenames up to 255 characters. When a file or directory is created under protected-mode FAT, the file system automatically creates an alias, which is a filename compatible with MS-DOS, using the familiar 8.3 filename notation.

File system information

Regardless of the type of file system, certain characteristics are always available for query, including file attributes and file and directory names.

File attributes

All file and directory names on the volume contain *attributes* that describe the data stored. Attributes are really bits that are set in the allocation table entry for a file or directory to indicate special or additional information. Common file and directory attributes stored by file allocation systems include the following:

✦ **Archive** — A flag to mark an entry for backup. Typically, files with this bit not set are backed up; when you modify a file, this bit may be set, indicating that it should be backed up.

✦ **Missing name of attribute.** This entry in the volume is a directory. Directories are really just files with this bit set.

> ✦ **Hidden**—This entry is hidden and does not appear in listings, as when using the DOS `Dir` command or Windows Explorer.
>
> ✦ **Readonly**—This entry is read-only. Program are allowed to read the file data, but cannot modify it.
>
> ✦ **System**—This entry is a part of the operating system. These files are typically also hidden and sometimes read-only.

Note that a file may have one or all of the above attributes set at the same time, or it might have none of them set.

File and directory names

All entries in a volume have some type of name associated with them. The name represents a user- or system-defined label to be used as a reference for the chain of data clusters. A common example is the directory where Windows system DLLs are typically installed—Windows\System.

Long/short filenames

Robust programs are developed to gracefully degrade—that is, fall back to a "plan b" if "plan a" doesn't work. Not all volumes support long filenames, and this is often the cause of severe program problems. If your program assumes long filenames are present simply because you developed your application using Visual Basic on a version of Windows that supports long filenames, you may be in for a rude awakening. During the installation phase of Windows, the installer can determine whether to enable long filename support. See the "Files" section later in the chapter for methods of determining support for long filenames.

Windows-supported drive types

Windows can access low-level information stored on a disk drive that denotes its logical structure. Using this structural information and some simple math, you can determine the amount of free and used disk space, the quantity of physical drives installed, the drive's volume mappings, the drive's name, its serial number, and whether it supports long filenames.

It is also important for robust applications to make sure the drive you are writing to allows write access—attempting to write to a read-only drive, such as a CD-ROM or write-protected floppy, can crash your program. Table 30-1 lists the Windows API functions that this section will use to gather drive information.

Table 30-1
Windows API Functions for Determining Drive Metrics

Function	Return Data	Description
GetDiskFreeSpace	Returns logical disk structure information	Used to calculate the amount of free, used, and total disk space.
GetLogicalDrives	Returns bitwise value indicating installed disk drives	Used to determine physical quantity of drives installed and if a particular drive is installed.
GetLogicalDriveStrings	Returns a string with volume letter mappings	Used to determine a drive's volume mappings or drive letter, for example, C: or F:.
GetVolumeInformation	Returns information about a volume	Used to identify a volume.
SetVolumeLabel	Sets the name of a volume on a drive.	Drives may have names as well as letters, and you can use this API to change the name of a drive.

Note   You can see these and many more Windows APIs by using the API Viewer Add-In that comes with Visual Basic.

Table 30-2 lists the named constants used in this section. These constants are necessary in order for you to effectively phrase the Visual Basic instructions and Windows API calls that gather drive information. The table lists the constant name, the class of drive with which the name is associated, and the constant's ordinal (numeric) value.

Table 30-2
Constants Windows Uses to Represent Drive Types

Constant	Drive Class	Value (Decimal)
DRIVE_CDROM	CD-ROM	5
DRIVE_FIXED	Fixed	3
DRIVE_RAMDISK	RAM Drive	6
DRIVE_REMOTE	Remote	4
DRIVE_REMOVABLE	Removable	2

Note   You should not assume that a removable drive is a floppy drive. Many "hard drives" from SyQuest and others are also removable.

Windows supports five classes of drives, which are listed in Table 30-2. Although Visual Basic has no built-in method to assess the class of any particular drive, the Windows API can detect the class to which any given drive belongs. This is important because you cannot assume that drive letter C, or any other letter for that matter, will always be the same kind of drive. The drive types supported by Windows are as follows:

- ✦ CD-ROM drive
- ✦ Fixed drive
- ✦ RAM drive
- ✦ Remote drive
- ✦ Removable drive

Note   All CD drives are considered read-only storage media by Windows's native APIs. Using special device drivers, CD-R and CD-RW drives may be writable; however, they cannot be written to using standard Visual Basic or Windows methods. You should not attempt to write directly to a CD drive.

Determining the number of drives

A PC may have up to 26 drives, numbered from 0 to 25 and carrying a character name of A to Z. Using the Windows API, you often refer to a drive by its number instead of its letter — for example, drive 0 would be drive A and so on. Developers coming to Visual Basic from C or C++ are especially so inclined. However, these are dangerous assumptions to make.

Rather than assuming anything at all about the PC your software will run on, a better plan is to dynamically determine the number and type of drives at runtime. The Windows API function GetLogicalDrives returns a bit mask indicating which drives are physically installed. This in turn lets you determine the actual number of drives (including any RAM drives) installed on the PC. This function's Declare statement appears in the Declarations section of your VB project, as follows:

```
Private Declare Function GetLogicalDrives Lib "kernel32" () As
Long
```

GetLogicalDrives returns a long integer, within which each of the individual bits represents a drive. Bit 0 (the least significant bit) represents drive A, bit 1 is drive B, bit 2 is drive C, and so on for up to 25 drives. If a bit is "set" (not zero), then the drive represented by that bit is present; otherwise, that drive is not present. A simple function procedure, DriveCount, shown in Listing 30-1, returns an integer value indicating the number of drives on a PC.

Listing 30-1: **A Function That Determines the Number of Drives in the System**

```
Public Function DriveCount() As Integer
    Dim BitMask As Long
    Dim j, i
    BitMask = GetLogicalDrives()
    For i = 0 To 24
        If BitMask And 2 ^ i Then
            j = j + 1
        End If
    Next
    DriveCount = j
End Function
```

DriveCount works by getting the result of the GetLogicalDrives API into a long integer, named BitMask. Then, each bit from 0 to 25 (26 drive slots) is examined to see if it is set or cleared. If set, the drive indicated by that bit position is present; if clear, it is not present. If the bit is set, indicating that the drive is present, the variable j is incremented. When all bits are examined, the function returns the value of j as the result of the function.

Another use for GetLogicalDrives is to quickly determine if a drive is present. Remember that drive A is represented by bit 0, drive B is bit 1, drive C is bit 2, and so on. Listing 30-2 shows a simple function that performs this task.

Listing 30-2: **A Function That Quickly Determines If a Drive Is Available**

```
Public Function Exists(nDrive As Integer) As Boolean
    Exists = (GetLogicalDrives And 2 ^ nDrive) <> 0
End Function
```

You could extend this little function by passing it a string, like A or C, and then using the ASCII value of the string and converting it to a zero-based drive identifier instead of passing it a zero-based drive identifier.

Detecting drive type

The type of drive represented by a drive letter may be determined by using the
GetDriveType Windows API function. GetDriveType takes a drive string as its
argument and returns a value ranging from DRIVE_REMOVABLE to DRIVE_RAMDISK
(integer 2–6). Any other value is an error code, indicating the API call failed. The
declaration for this API function follows, along with some constants you can use to
better interpret its return value:

```
Private Declare Function GetDriveType Lib "kernel32" Alias _
    "GetDriveTypeA" (ByVal nDrive As String) As Long
Private Const DRIVE_CDROM = 5
Private Const DRIVE_FIXED = 3
Private Const DRIVE_RAMDISK = 6
Private Const DRIVE_REMOTE = 4
Private Const DRIVE_REMOVABLE = 2
```

Listing 30-3 shows a simple function procedure that returns the name of the
drive class.

Listing 30-3: **A Function That Returns a Drive Type String**

```
Public Function TypeIs(Optional sDrive As String) As String
    Select Case GetDriveType(Left$(sDrive, 1) + ":\")
    Case 0   'The drive type cannot be determined.
        TypeIs = "unknown"
    Case 1   'The root directory does not exist.
        TypeIs = "unknown"
    Case DRIVE_REMOVABLE 'The disk can be removed from the _
        drive.
        TypeIs = "removable"
    Case DRIVE_FIXED 'The disk cannot be removed from the _
        drive.
        TypeIs = "fixed"
    Case DRIVE_REMOTE    'The drive is a remote (network) _
        drive.
        TypeIs = "remote"
    Case DRIVE_CDROM 'The drive is a CD-ROM drive.
        TypeIs = "CD-ROM"
    Case DRIVE_RAMDISK   'The drive is a RAM disk.
        TypeIs = "RAM-disk"
    Case Else 'not a valid disk drive
        TypeIs = "error!"
    End Select
End Function
```

`TypeIs` works by comparing the result of the `GetDriveType` API to the various values it can return and assigning a string value if a match is made. Note: Call `GetDriveType` using the drive letter complete with colon and optional slash — for example, C:\.

You should only pass valid drive strings to the API; by this we mean do not pass anything except the characters A to Z, a colon, and an optional slash. You can use another API function to determine the drive names of all currently mapped drives. That API function is `GetLogicalDriveStrings`, whose declaration is

```
Private Declare Function GetLogicalDriveStrings Lib "kernel32" _
    Alias "GetLogicalDriveStringsA" (ByVal nBufferLength As
Long, _
    ByVal lpBuffer As String) As Long
```

`GetLogicalDriveStrings` returns a string containing a list of drive letters (with colon and slash, for example a:\ c:\ d:\) separated with null (`Chr$(0)`) characters. The last drive letter is followed by two nulls. Using the result of `GetLogicalDriveStrings`, you can create a function to return an array of valid drives; then use the array of drives as arguments to `GetDriveType`. Listing 30-4 shows how to call `GetLogicalDriveStrings`.

Listing 30-4: A Function That Returns an Array With All Available Mapped Drive Letters

```
Public Function LoadDrivenames(An_Array() As String) As Long

    Dim j, i
    Dim lpBuffer As String
    ReDim An_Array(128) As String

    lpBuffer = Space$(1024)
    GetLogicalDriveStrings Len(lpBuffer), lpBuffer
    j = InStr(lpBuffer, Chr$(0))
    Do While j > 0
        An_Array(i) = Left$(lpBuffer, j - 1)
        i = i + 1
        lpBuffer = Mid$(lpBuffer, j + 1)
        j = InStr(lpBuffer, Chr$(0))
    Loop
    ReDim Preserve An_Array(i - 2)

End Function
```

This code gets the drive string from GetLogicalDrives, then parses the drive string into a string array. (Note that An_Array is passed by reference so that we can modify its contents and return the drive data in it. Passing ByRef is the default for Visual Basic, but you could also explicitly pass An_Array as ByrefAn_Array if you wanted to.) When you know the actual drives available on a system, you can then use GetDriveType safely to return the drive type for each or any one. It is then easy to implement a series of functions to indicate the drive type.

Listing 30-5 shows a set of simple functions to validate drive type. Each of these assumes you have validated the drive argument using GetLogicalDrives.

Listing 30-5: **Functions That Return True or False on the Basis of Drive Type**

```
Public Function IsRemote(sDrive As String) As Boolean
    IsRemote = GetDriveType(sDrive) = DRIVE_REMOTE
End Function

Public Function IsRemovable(sDrive As String) As Boolean
    IsRemoveable = GetDriveType(sDrive) = DRIVE_REMOVABLE
End Function

Public Function IsFixed(sDrive As String) As Boolean
    IsFixed = GetDriveType(sDrive) = DRIVE_FIXED
End Function

Public Function IsCDROM(sDrive As String) As Boolean
    IsCDROM = GetDriveType(sDrive) = DRIVE_CDROM
End Function

Public Function IsRAMDisk(sDrive As String) As Boolean
    IsRAMDisk = GetDriveType(sDrive) = DRIVE_RAMDISK
End Function
```

These functions let you quickly determine whether a drive is of a certain type.

Free and used space

The next thing you are going to want to do is determine the amount of free (or used) space on the volume. After taking all the time to make sure the drive is there, and writable, it would be a waste to have your program fail because the volume is out of free space!

Windows exports the GetDiskFreeSpace function to return information about the physical structure of the volume. This information varies depending on drive type. Some information common to all drives includes how data is gathered into clusters and sectors — and this is what GetDiskFreeSpace returns. You need to use a little math to calculate the used, free, and total volume space, but it's not that hard if you know the algorithm. The declaration for GetDiskFreeSpace is

```
Private Declare Function GetDiskFreeSpace Lib "kernel32" Alias
"GetDiskFreeSpaceA" _(ByVal lpRootPathName As String,
lpSectorsPerCluster As Long, lpBytesPerSector As Long,
_lpNumberOfFreeClusters As Long, lpTotalNumberOfClusters As
Long) As Long
```

Remember that bytes are stored in sectors, which are in turn grouped into clusters. To calculate the total size of a volume, use this formula:

```
Size = TotalNumberOfClusters * SectorsPerCluster * _
    BytesPerSector
```

Listing 30-6 shows a function to implement this formula using the Windows API.

Listing 30-6: **A Function That Determines the Total Space on a Drive**

```
Public Function Size(sDrive As String) As Long
    Dim lpSectorsPerCluster&
    Dim lpBytesPerSector&
    Dim lpNumberOfFreeClusters&
    Dim TotalNumberOfClusters&
    If GetDiskFreeSpace(Left$(sDrive, 1) + ":\", _
        lpSectorsPerCluster, lpBytesPerSector, _
        lpNumberOfFreeClusters, TotalNumberOfClusters) _
        Then Size = TotalNumberOfClusters * _
        lpSectorsPerCluster * lpBytesPerSector
    End If
End Function
```

Size works by using the GetDiskFreeSpace API to return the total number of clusters, sectors, and bytes per sector. It then calculates the total amount of disk space using the following formula:

```
Size = TotalNumberOfClusters * SectorsPerCluster * _
    BytesPerSector
```

You can modify Size to calculate the free space within a volume by modifying the formula to use the `NumberOfFreeClusters` variable instead of the `TotalNumberOfClusters` argument that `GetDiskFreeSpace` returns:

```
FreeSpace = NumberOfFreeClusters * SectorsPerCluster * _
    BytesPerSector
```

Listing 30-7 shows a function to implement this formula using the Windows API.

Listing 30-7: A Function that Determines the Free Space on a Drive

```
Public Function FreeSpace(sDrive As String) As Long
    Dim lpSectorsPerCluster&
    Dim lpBytesPerSector&
    Dim lpNumberOfFreeClusters&
    Dim TotalNumberOfClusters&
    If GetDiskFreeSpace(Left$(sDrive, 1) + ":\", _
        lpSectorsPerCluster, lpBytesPerSector, _
        lpNumberOfFreeClusters, TotalNumberOfClusters) _
        Then FreeSpace = lpNumberOfFreeClusters * _
        lpSectorsPerCluster * lpBytesPerSector
    End If
End Function
```

Finally, to calculate the space used on a volume, subtract `FreeSpace` from `Size` as follows:

```
UsedSpace = Size - FreeSpace
```

Listing 30-8 shows a function to implement this formula using the Windows API.

Listing 30-8: A Function That Determines the Amount of Space Used on a Drive

```
Public Function UsedSpace(sDrive As String) As Long
    UsedSpace = Size(sDrive) - FreeSpace(sDrive)
End Function
```

GetDiskFreeSpace doesn't really return the amount of free space in bytes on a volume — but using a little bit of math in conjunction with an understanding of how drives store data lets you get the same result anyway. GetDiskFreeSpace is a classic example of using the Windows API — a single API call returning low-level information that you use to determine the information you really want.

Volume information

The volume contains information about itself as well as the data it contains. To access this volume information, you use the GetVolumeInformation API function, whose declaration is

```
Private Declare Function GetVolumeInformation Lib "kernel32" _
    Alias "GetVolumeInformationA"_ (ByVal lpRootPathName As _
    String, ByVal lpVolumeNameBuffer As String, _
    ByVal nVolumeNameSize As Long, lpVolumeSerialNumber As _
    Long, lpMaximumComponentLength As Long, lpFileSystemFlags _
    As Long, ByVal lpFileSystemNameBuffer As String, ByVal _
    nFileSystemNameSize As Long) As Long
```

The information returned by GetVolumeInformation includes the following:

✦ Whether or not the volume supports long filenames

✦ The name of the volume

✦ The volume's serial number

✦ The name of the file system (such as FAT or NTFS)

✦ Information about how the file system stores data on the volume

Using GetVolumeInformation is easy; simply call the API function with the drive name of the drive to query — like C: — then read the arguments returned by the API.

When you perform a directory listing (MS-DOS' DIR command) on a drive, you will see the line "Volume serial number: XXXX-XXXX." Each drive has a unique number to represent it, and the Xs in the example are replaced with hexadecimal values. A real serial number might be 4168-0CCE. To determine the serial number of the drive, use a function like that in Listing 30-9.

Listing 30-9: **A Function That Returns the Drive Serial Number**

```
Public Function Serial(sDrive As String) As String

    Dim tmp$
    Dim j
    Dim lpVolumeNameBuffer As String
    Dim lpVolumeSerialNumber As Long
    Dim lpMaximumComponentLength As Long
    Dim lpFileSystemFlags As Long
    Dim lpFileSystemNameBuffer As String
    Dim nFileSystemNameSize As Long
    sDrive = Left$(sDrive, 1) + ":\"
    lpVolumeNameBuffer = Space$(128)
    GetVolumeInformation sDrive, lpVolumeNameBuffer, _
        Len(lpVolumeNameBuffer), lpVolumeSerialNumber, _
        lpMaximumComponentLength, lpFileSystemFlags, _
        lpFileSystemNameBuffer, nFileSystemNameSize

    j = InStr(lpVolumeNameBuffer, Chr$(0))
    If j > 0 Then
        tmp$ = Hex$(lpVolumeSerialNumber)
        Serial = Left$(tmp, 4) + "-" + Mid$(tmp, 5)
    End If

End Function
```

The only tricky part about using this API function is to realize that the data is not returned in a ready-to-use fashion. The volume serial number is returned as a single long integer, not a pair of four-digit hexadecimal numbers. If you want your serial number function to return a value that looks like what you see when you use the MS-DOS DIR command, you have to convert it. The preceding code handles the conversion and returns a string value identical to what you see when you invoke the DIR command.

Other information is extracted the same way; for example, returning the volume name. Listing 30-10 shows a Property Get that returns the drive's name. The volume name is not read-only — you may also write or change the name as you desire. Therefore, Listing 30-11 shows the Property Let counterpart to the Property Get shown in Listing 30-10.

Listing 30-10: **A Function That Returns a Drive's Name**

```
Public Property Get Name(Optional ByVal sDrive As String) _
    As String

    Dim j
    Dim lpVolumeNameBuffer As String
    Dim lpVolumeSerialNumber As Long
    Dim lpMaximumComponentLength As Long
    Dim lpFileSystemFlags As Long
    Dim lpFileSystemNameBuffer As String
    Dim nFileSystemNameSize As Long

    If Len(sDrive) = 0 Then sDrive = CurDir

    sDrive = Left$(sDrive, 1) + ":\"
    lpVolumeNameBuffer = Space$(128)
    GetVolumeInformation sDrive, lpVolumeNameBuffer, _
        Len(lpVolumeNameBuffer), lpVolumeSerialNumber, _
        lpMaximumComponentLength, lpFileSystemFlags, _
        lpFileSystemNameBuffer, nFileSystemNameSize

    j = InStr(lpVolumeNameBuffer, Chr$(0))
    If j > 0 Then Name = Left$(lpVolumeNameBuffer, j - 1)

End Property
```

You can also set the volume label using the SetVolumeLabel API function, declared here:

```
Private Declare Function SetVolumeLabel Lib "kernel32" Alias _
    "SetVolumeLabelA" (ByVal lpRootPathName As String, ByVal _
    lpVolumeName As String) As Long
```

Listing 30-11 shows the Property Let procedure that sets the drive's name.

Listing 30-11: **A Function That Sets a Drive's Name**

```
Public Property Let Name(ByVal sDrive As String, ByVal sName _
    As String)
    sDrive = Left$(sDrive, 1) + ":\"
    SetVolumeLabel sDrive, sName
End Property
```

Using the information GetVolumeInformation provides, you can create some very
powerful low-level functions. A common use for these sorts of functions is copy
protection—limiting a program to running on a single drive, for example.

Putting it all together

Listing 30-12 presents the entire code to a file information and control class module.
The class will encapsulate file API functions into an extensible object ready for use
in any program.

This code is on the CD-ROM as FILES.CLS.

**Listing 30-12: A class module that provides
disk metrics to a VB project**

```
Option Explicit

DefInt A-Z
Private Declare Function GetDiskFreeSpace Lib "kernel32" _
    Alias "GetDiskFreeSpaceA" (ByVal lpRootPathName As String, _
    lpSectorsPerCluster As Long, lpBytesPerSector As Long, _
    lpNumberOfFreeClusters As Long, lpTotalNumberOfClusters As _
    Long) As Long
Private Declare Function GetLogicalDrives Lib "kernel32" () _
    As Long
Private Declare Function GetDriveType Lib "kernel32" Alias _
    "GetDriveTypeA" (ByVal nDrive As String) As Long
Private Const DRIVE_CDROM = 5
Private Const DRIVE_FIXED = 3
Private Const DRIVE_RAMDISK = 6
Private Const DRIVE_REMOTE = 4
Private Const DRIVE_REMOVABLE = 2

'Name
Private Declare Function GetVolumeInformation Lib "kernel32" _
    Alias "GetVolumeInformationA" (ByVal lpRootPathName As _
    String, ByVal lpVolumeNameBuffer As String, ByVal _
    nVolumeNameSize As Long, lpVolumeSerialNumber As Long, _
    lpMaximumComponentLength As Long, lpFileSystemFlags As _
    Long, ByVal lpFileSystemNameBuffer As String, ByVal _
    nFileSystemNameSize As Long) As Long
Private Declare Function GetLogicalDriveStrings Lib _
    "kernel32" Alias "GetLogicalDriveStringsA" (ByVal _
    nBufferLength As Long, ByVal lpBuffer As String) As Long
Private Declare Function SetVolumeLabel Lib "kernel32" Alias _
    "SetVolumeLabelA" (ByVal lpRootPathName As String, ByVal _
    lpVolumeName As String) As Long
```

```
Public Function FreeSpace(Optional sDrive As String) As Long

    Dim lpSectorsPerCluster&
    Dim lpBytesPerSector&
    Dim lpNumberOfFreeClusters&
    Dim lpTtoalNumberOfClusters&
    Dim j

    If Len(sDrive) = 0 Then sDrive = Left$(CurDir$, 1)

    If GetDiskFreeSpace(Left$(sDrive, 1) + ":\", _
        lpSectorsPerCluster, lpBytesPerSector, _
        lpNumberOfFreeClusters, lpTtoalNumberOfClusters)
    Then
        FreeSpace = lpNumberOfFreeClusters * _
        lpSectorsPerCluster * lpBytesPerSector

    Else
        Error 5
    End If

End Function
Public Function Size(Optional sDrive As String) As Long

    Dim lpSectorsPerCluster&
    Dim lpBytesPerSector&
    Dim lpNumberOfFreeClusters&
    Dim lpTtoalNumberOfClusters&
    Dim j

    If Len(sDrive) = 0 Then sDrive = Left$(CurDir$, 1)

    If GetDiskFreeSpace(Left$(sDrive, 1) + ":\", _
        lpSectorsPerCluster, lpBytesPerSector, _
        lpNumberOfFreeClusters, lpTtoalNumberOfClusters)
    Then
        Size = lpTotalNumberOfClusters * lpSectorsPerCluster _
            * lpBytesPerSector

    Else

        Error 5

    End If

End Function


Public Function Count() As Integer
```

(continued)

Listing 30-12 *(continued)*

```
        Dim BitMask As Long
        Dim j, i

        BitMask = GetLogicalDrives()

        For i = 0 To 26

            If BitMask And 2 ^ i Then
                j = j + 1
            End If

        Next

        Count = j

    End Function

    Public Function TypeIs(Optional sDrive As String) As String

        If sDrive = "" Then sDrive = CurDir$

        Select Case GetDriveType(Left$(sDrive, 1) + ":\")
        Case 0    'The drive type cannot be determined.
            TypeIs = "unknown"
        Case 1    'The root directory does not exist.
            TypeIs = "unknown"
        Case DRIVE_REMOVABLE 'The drive can be removed from the_
            drive.
            TypeIs = "removable"
        Case DRIVE_FIXED 'The disk cannot be removed from the drive.
            TypeIs = "fixed"
        Case DRIVE_REMOTE    'The drive is a remote (network) drive.
            TypeIs = "remote"
        Case DRIVE_CDROM 'The drive is a CD-ROM drive.
            TypeIs = "CD-ROM"
        Case DRIVE_RAMDISK    'The drive is a RAM disk.
            TypeIs = "RAM-disk"
        End Select

    End Function

    Public Function TypeOfIs(Optional sDrive As String) As Long

        If sDrive = "" Then sDrive = CurDir$

        TypeOfIs = GetDriveType(Left$(sDrive, 1) + ":\")

    End Function
```

```
Public Function Serial(Optional sDrive As String) As String

    Dim tmp$
    Dim j
    Dim lpVolumeNameBuffer As String
    Dim lpVolumeSerialNumber As Long
    Dim lpMaximumComponentLength As Long
    Dim lpFileSystemFlags As Long
    Dim lpFileSystemNameBuffer As String
    Dim nFileSystemNameSize As Long

    If Len(sDrive) = 0 Then sDrive = CurDir

    sDrive = Left$(sDrive, 1) + ":\"
    lpVolumeNameBuffer = Space$(128)
    GetVolumeInformation sDrive, lpVolumeNameBuffer, _
        Len(lpVolumeNameBuffer), lpVolumeSerialNumber, _
        lpMaximumComponentLength, lpFileSystemFlags, _
        lpFileSystemNameBuffer, nFileSystemNameSize

    j = InStr(lpVolumeNameBuffer, Chr$(0))
    If j > 0 Then

        tmp$ = Hex$(lpVolumeSerialNumber)
        Serial = Left$(tmp, 4) + "-" + Mid$(tmp, 5)

    End If

End Function

Public Property Get Name(Optional ByVal sDrive As String) _
    As String

    Dim j
    Dim lpVolumeNameBuffer As String
    Dim lpVolumeSerialNumber As Long
    Dim lpMaximumComponentLength As Long
    Dim lpFileSystemFlags As Long
    Dim lpFileSystemNameBuffer As String
    Dim nFileSystemNameSize As Long

    If Len(sDrive) = 0 Then sDrive = CurDir

    sDrive = Left$(sDrive, 1) + ":\"
    lpVolumeNameBuffer = Space$(128)
    GetVolumeInformation sDrive, lpVolumeNameBuffer, _
        Len(lpVolumeNameBuffer), lpVolumeSerialNumber, _
        lpMaximumComponentLength, lpFileSystemFlags, _
        lpFileSystemNameBuffer, nFileSystemNameSize
```

(continued)

Listing 30-12 *(continued)*

```
            j = InStr(lpVolumeNameBuffer, Chr$(0))
            If j > 0 Then Name = Left$(lpVolumeNameBuffer, j - 1)

End Property

Public Property Let Name(ByVal sDrive As String, ByVal sName _
    As String)

            sDrive = Left$(sDrive, 1) + ":\"
            SetVolumeLabel sDrive, sName

End Property

Public Function LongFilenames(Optional sDrive As String) As _
    Boolean

            Dim j
            Dim lpVolumeNameBuffer As String
            Dim lpVolumeSerialNumber As Long
            Dim lpMaximumComponentLength As Long
            Dim lpFileSystemFlags As Long
            Dim lpFileSystemNameBuffer As String
            Dim nFileSystemNameSize As Long

            If Len(sDrive) = 0 Then sDrive = CurDir

            sDrive = Left$(sDrive, 1) + ":\"
            lpVolumeNameBuffer = Space$(128)
            GetVolumeInformation sDrive, lpVolumeNameBuffer, _
                Len(lpVolumeNameBuffer), lpVolumeSerialNumber, _
                lpMaximumComponentLength, lpFileSystemFlags,_
                lpFileSystemNameBuffer, nFileSystemNameSize

            j = InStr(lpVolumeNameBuffer, Chr$(0))
            If j > 0 Then LongFilenames = lpMaximumComponentLength > 12

End Function
Public Function FileSystem(Optional sDrive As String) _
    As String

            Dim j
            Dim lpVolumeNameBuffer As String
            Dim lpVolumeSerialNumber As Long
            Dim lpMaximumComponentLength As Long
            Dim lpFileSystemFlags As Long
            Dim lpFileSystemNameBuffer As String
            Dim nFileSystemNameSize As Long

            If Len(sDrive) = 0 Then sDrive = CurDir$
            sDrive = Left$(sDrive, 1) + ":\"
            lpVolumeNameBuffer = Space$(128)
```

```
        lpFileSystemNameBuffer = Space$(32)
        GetVolumeInformation sDrive, lpVolumeNameBuffer, _
            Len(lpVolumeNameBuffer), lpVolumeSerialNumber, _
            lpMaximumComponentLength, lpFileSystemFlags, _
            lpFileSystemNameBuffer, Len(lpFileSystemNameBuffer)

        j = InStr(lpFileSystemNameBuffer, Chr$(0))
        If j > 0 Then FileSystem = Left$(lpFileSystemNameBuffer, _
            j - 1)

End Function

Public Function IsRemote(Optional sDrive As String) As Boolean

    If sDrive = "" Then sDrive = CurDir$ 'default to current _
        drive
    sDrive = Left$(sDrive, 1) + ":\"

    IsRemote = GetDriveType(sDrive) = DRIVE_REMOTE

End Function
Public Function IsRemoveable(Optional sDrive As String) As _
    Boolean

    If sDrive = "" Then sDrive = CurDir$
    sDrive = Left$(sDrive, 1) + ":\"

    IsRemoveable = GetDriveType(sDrive) = DRIVE_REMOVABLE

End Function

Public Function IsFixed(Optional sDrive As String) As Boolean

    If sDrive = "" Then sDrive = CurDir$
    sDrive = Left$(sDrive, 1) + ":\"

    IsFixed = GetDriveType(sDrive) = DRIVE_FIXED

End Function

Public Function IsCDROM(Optional sDrive As String) As Boolean

    If Len(sDrive) = 0 Then sDrive = CurDir$
    sDrive = Left$(sDrive, 1) + ":\"

    IsCDROM = GetDriveType(sDrive) = DRIVE_CDROM

End Function

Public Function IsRAMDisk(Optional sDrive As String) As Boolean
```

(continued)

Listing 30-12 *(continued)*

```
        If sDrive = "" Then sDrive = CurDir$
        sDrive = Left$(sDrive, 1) + ":\"

        IsRAMDisk = GetDriveType(sDrive) = DRIVE_RAMDISK

End Function

Public Function LoadDrivenames(An_Array() As String) As Long

    On Error GoTo myError

    Dim j, i
    Dim lpBuffer As String

    ReDim An_Array(128) As String

    lpBuffer = Space$(1024)
    GetLogicalDriveStrings Len(lpBuffer), lpBuffer
    j = InStr(lpBuffer, Chr$(0))
    Do While j > 0
        An_Array(i) = Left$(lpBuffer, j - 1)
        i = i + 1
        lpBuffer = Mid$(lpBuffer, j + 1)
        j = InStr(lpBuffer, Chr$(0))
    Loop
    ReDim Preserve An_Array(i - 2)

myExit:
    Exit Function

myError:
    Error 5

End Function

Public Function Used(Optional sDrive As String) As Long

    If Len(sDrive) = 0 Then sDrive = Left$(CurDir$, 1)

    Used = Size(sDrive) - FreeSpace(sDrive)

End Function
```

Directories

Table 30-3 lists the Windows API functions that this section will use to gather directory information.

<table>
<tr><td colspan="3" align="center">Table 30-3
Windows API Functions for Accessing Directory Information</td></tr>
<tr><td>*Function*</td><td>*Return Data*</td><td>*Description*</td></tr>
<tr><td>GetTempPath()</td><td>Returns path of a directory useful storing temporary files</td><td>Used to determine for temporary drive and directory.</td></tr>
<tr><td>GetFileAttributes()</td><td>Returns information about a file or directory</td><td>Used to determine advanced information about a directory.</td></tr>
</table>

Locating Windows directories

Windows has three special directories that are used to store three special types of files. These directories may be of any name. They are as follows:

✦ Windows System directory

✦ Windows directory

✦ Temp directory

Each directory is used by the operating system — and your programs. You might not know it, but these special directories are available to you and are, in fact, designed so that you can have known repositories for these certain special file types.

Windows System directory

The System directory contains files that are used by all Windows applications and by Windows itself. These files include Windows libraries (OCXs, DLLs, and so on), drivers, and font files.

Note that you (and your applications) are should not place files in the System directory. This is because some versions of Windows may have the System directory write-protected. This is also true of networked Windows, where Windows itself is stored on a server.

Although the issue of a write-protected directory is a potential problem, in many cases your setup programs will install controls, fonts, and libraries into the System directory anyway. Even the Setup Wizard that comes with Visual Basic will break this rule and place your files into the System directory. However, technically, instead of putting files into the System directory, you are supposed to put them into the Windows directory. Now you can plan for the potential problem of a write-protected System directory — however rare that may be.

The `GetSystemDirectory` API retrieves the path of the Windows System directory. This directory is typically titled System on Windows 95 or System32 for Windows NT, but it can have any name — thus the need to query Windows for this information. Here is the function's declaration:

```
Private Declare Function GetSystemDirectory Lib "kernel32"_
    Alias "GetSystemDirectoryA" (ByVal lpBuffer As String, _
    ByVal nSize As Long) As Long
```

The following function titled `SystemDir` calls `GetSystemDirectory` and returns a string containing the complete path; for example, `C:\Windows\System` or `C:\Winnt\System32`. You should always use this function (or a similar one) to access the System directory. Never assume that the System directory has a certain name.

The `SystemDir` function declares a string variable to contain the System directory name, `tmp`. The variable is then set to a prefilled string of spaces. This is a crucial step, because `GetSystemDirectory` requires a padded string of at least 260 bytes, which is the maximum size of a Windows path name. To make this easier, we declare a constant called `MAX_PATH`, and set it equal to 260.

`GetSystemDirectory` takes as its arguments the variable to contain the string, padded to `MAX_PATH` spaces, and another argument that indicates the length of the string, which is `MAX_PATH`. `GetSystemDirectory` returns the length of the actual path name character string as its result. Listing 30-13 shows the code for a function that finds the System directory.

Listing 30-13: **A Function to Locate the System Directory**

```
' this const goes in the declaration section of the
' module
Private Const MAX_PATH = 260

Public Function SystemDir() As String

    Dim tmp As String

    tmp = Space$(MAX_PATH)

    SystemDir = Left$(tmp, GetSystemDirectory(tmp, MAX_PATH))

End Function
```

You should not create files in the Windows System directory. This is because the System directory is not always available for writing. Certain implementations and installations of Windows do not give applications write access. If you need to create a file, use the Windows directory instead.

Windows directory

The Windows directory contains files that are used by Windows applications. These types of files include initialization (INI) files, help files, and license files.

The Windows directory is where you are supposed to store your private applications files. Even if the user is running a shared version of Windows, the Windows directory will be write-enabled. This may seem counterintuitive, and you may want to store your files in the System directory.

However, Windows always searches the System directory and then the Windows directory when you (or your program) attempt to load a library (DLL, OCX), help file, or other file. So, placing your files in the Windows directory will not "hide" them from your application, and you do not need to make any changes to the path statement in the AUTOEXEC.BAT file of the user's computer.

The GetWindowsDirectory function retrieves the path of the Windows directory. This directory is typically titled Windows on Windows 95 or Winnt for Windows NT, but it can have any name — thus the need to query Windows for this information:

```
Private Declare Function GetWindowsDirectory Lib "kernel32"_
    Alias "GetWindowsDirectoryA"(ByVal lpBuffer As String, _
    ByVal nSize As Long) As Long
```

The function titled Home, shown in Listing 30-14, calls GetWindowsDirectory and returns a string containing the complete path; for example, C:\Windows or C:\Winnt. You should always use this function (or a similar one) to access the system directory. Never assume that the Windows directory has a certain name.

The Home function declares a string variable to contain the Windows directory name, lpBuffer. The variable is then set to a prefilled string of spaces. This is a crucial step, because GetWindowsDirectory requires a padded string of at least 260 bytes, which is the maximum size of a Windows path name. To make this easier, declare a constant called MAX_PATH and set it equal to 260.

GetWindowsDirectory takes as its arguments the variable to contain the string, padded to MAX_PATH spaces; and another argument that indicates the length of the string, which is MAX_PATH. GetWindowsDirectory returns the length of the actual path-name character string as its result.

> ### Listing 30-14: **A Function to Locate the Name of the Windows Directory**
>
> ```
> ' this const goes in the declaration section of the
> ' module
> Private Const MAX_PATH = 260
>
>
> Public Function Home() As String
>
>     Dim lpBuffer As String
>
>     lpBuffer = Space$(MAX_PATH)
>
>     Home = Left$(lpBuffer, GetWindowsDirectory( _
>         lpBuffer, MAX_PATH))
>
> End Function
> ```

Temporary directory

Windows also provides a place to store temporary files — files that your program creates and will not need the next time Windows boots. The `GetTempPath` API retrieves the path of the directory specifically designated to hold temporary files.

Never put files into a temporary directory that your program will need at the time either your program or Windows starts! Users (present company included) clean out the various temporary directories at will. Here is the function's declaration:

```
Private Declare Function GetTempPath Lib "kernel32" Alias_
    "GetTempPathA" (ByVal nBufferLength As Long, _
    ByVal lpBuffer As String) As Long
```

The `GetTempPath()` API returns the temporary file path using the following logic:

If the AUTOEXEC.BAT file (or initialization for Windows NT) has set an environment variable titled TMP, that path is returned — for example, an AUTOEXEC.BAT entry of

```
SET TMP = C:\WINDOWS\TEMP
```

If TMP is not found in the environment, then `GetTempPath` checks for an environment variable titled TEMP — for example, an AUTOEXEC.BAT entry of

```
SET TEMP = C:\WINDOWS\TEMP
```

If no entry for TMP or TEMP is found, GetTempPath returns the currently active directory, as set by using Windows or the Visual Basic ChDir or ChDrive commands.

The function titled TmpDir, shown in Listing 30-15, calls GetTempPath and returns a string containing the complete path — for example, C:\TEMP or C:\WINDOWS\TEMP. You should always use this function (or a similar one) to access the temporary directory. Never assume that the temporary directory has a certain name.

The TmpDir function declares a string variable to contain the temporary directory name, lpBuffer. The variable is then set to a prefilled string of spaces. This is a crucial step, because GetTempPath requires a padded string of at least 260 bytes, which is the maximum size of a Windows path name. To make this easier, declare a constant called MAX_PATH and set it equal to 260.

GetTempPath takes as its arguments the variable to contain the string, padded to MAX_PATH spaces; and another argument that indicates the length of the string, which is MAX_PATH. GetWindowsDirectory returns the length of the actual path-name character string as its result.

Listing 30-15: A Function to Locate the Name of the Temporary Directory

```
' this const goes in the declaration section of the
' module
Private Const MAX_PATH = 260

Public Function TmpDir() As String

    Dim lpBuffer As String

    lpBuffer = Space$(MAX_PATH)

    TmpDir = Left$(lpBuffer, GetTempPath(MAX_PATH, lpBuffer))


End Function
```

Note Never put any files that you need in a temporary directory. The temporary directory is for storing work files and nonpersistent data for this instance of your application only. If your program needs this data the next time it runs, then the data does not belong in the temporary directory.

Files

Virtually every program requires interaction with data files on disk. You may want to check for a file's existence, move a file to a new location, or determine a short filename. In any case, Visual Basic has built-in functions that you, with enough experience, could use to accomplish any of these tasks. So why use the Windows API? Speed, efficiency, and accuracy. For example, consider the Visual Basic Dir$ (or Dir) function. It claims to return a filename matching a pattern — except that passing even an empty string will return a filename, too! This sort of unreliable or unexpected operation is typical of trying to "shoehorn" Visual Basic into doing something it was not designed to do. By way of example, consider the Dir$ command. Dir$ is designed to return a filename — not check for a file's existence. You can write enough code to coerce Dir$ into checking for a file, but why not use a function designed for just that purpose?

Additionally, Visual Basic just cannot do some things — for example, determining the long filename from a filename, or vice versa. Windows API calls can take care of these sorts of tasks as well. This section provides Windows API solutions to common file-manipulation requirements.

Table 30-4 lists the Windows API functions that this section will use to gather file information. It lists the Windows API name, function, and why it is used.

Table 30-4
Windows API Functions for Accessing File Storage Information

Function	Return Data	Description
FindFirstFile()	Starts a disk search to find a disk entry	Used to determine short or long filename.
FindClose()	Closes a disk search	Used to determine short or long filename.
GetShortPathName()	Returns the "short" filename (MS-DOS 8.3 style) of a file	Used to create "portable" filenames.

Function	Return Data	Description
GetTempFileName	Returns a temporary filename	Used to get a unique filename for temporary operations.
MoveFileEx	Moves a file	Used to move files, even across drives.
OpenFile	Opens a file	Used to prepare a file for writing or reading; also used to check for file existence.

Table 30-5 lists the named constants used in this section. These constants control the actions of the Visual Basic keyword or Windows API they are used with. The table lists the constant name and its associated ordinal (numeric) value.

Table 30-5
Constants Used in This Section

Constant	Value (Decimal)
MOVEFILE_COPY_ALLOWED	2
MOVEFILE_REPLACE_EXISTING	1
OF_EXIST	16,384
OF_READWRITE	2
OFS_MAXPATHNAME	128

Listing 30-16 contains the user-defined types used in this section. These types are used with Windows APIs to return or communicate information. They should appear in the Declarations section of any VB project that utilizes the API functions discussed here.

Listing 30-16: **Types Used in This Section**

```
Private Type FileTime
    dwLowDateTime As Long
    dwHighDateTime As Long
End Type
Private Type OFSTRUCT
    cBytes As Byte
    fFixedDisk As Byte
```

(continued)

> **Listing 30-16** *(continued)*
>
> ```
>         nErrCode As Integer
>         Reserved1 As Integer
>         Reserved2 As Integer
>         szPathName(OFS_MAXPATHNAME) As Byte
>     End Type
>
>     Private Type SystemTime
>         Year As Integer
>         Month As Integer
>         DayOfWeek As Integer
>         day As Integer
>         Hour As Integer
>         Minute As Integer
>         Second As Integer
>         Milliseconds As Integer
>     End Type
>
>     Private Type WIN32_FIND_DATA
>             dwFileAttributes As Long
>             ftCreationTime As FileTime
>             ftLastAccessTime As FileTime
>             ftLastWriteTime As FileTime
>             nFileSizeHigh As Long
>             nFileSizeLow As Long
>             dwReserved0 As Long
>             dwReserved1 As Long
>             cFileName As String * OFS_MAXPATHNAME
>             cAlternate As String * 14
>     End Type
> ```

Determining existence

One of the most common requirements in programming is to determine if a file is present. Checking for a file before attempting to open it for reading or writing can prevent crashes. Checking for the existence of a file can also control logic for creating any files not found. In either case, a reliable method of checking for files is an important requirement. As discussed previously, the Visual Basic Dir$ (or Dir) function can be used to implement a file-checking routine — however, it takes a fair bit of code to handle all the conditions. For example, if the string representing the filename passed to Dir$ is empty, the Dir$ function will return an error, so you need to add code to check for a valid string. Also, if the string has invalid characters in it, Dir$ won't work right.

Clearly, you could use Dir$, but using the OpenFile API function with the OF_EXIST constant is much more reliable and efficient — after all, it was designed to detect the presence or absence of a file! The function's declaration is

```
Private Declare Function OpenFile Lib "kernel32" (ByVal _
    lpFileName As String, lpReOpenBuff As OFSTRUCT, ByVal _
    wStyle As Long) As Long
```

OpenFile takes a constant to indicate what the API should do. OpenFile
can open a file, create a file, or even delete a file — all depending on the mode.
The particular mode for checking for a file's existence is OF_EXIST (integer value
16,384). When OF_EXIST is used with OpenFile, it causes a user-defined type
to be filled with information. The user-defined type is OFSTRUCT. The szPathName
member is defined to be of size OFS_MATHPATHNAME, which is 128. You can declare a
constant OFS_MAXPATHNAME = 128 and place this definition before the type
declaration:

```
Const OFS_MAXPATHNAME = 128

Private Type OFSTRUCT
    cBytes As Byte
    fFixedDisk As Byte
    nErrCode As Integer
    Reserved1 As Integer
    Reserved2 As Integer
    szPathName(OFS_MAXPATHNAME) As Byte
End Type
Private typOfStruct As OFSTRUCT
```

Part of the information in the definition is used to determine if the file is there or
not, as shown next. Listing 30-17 shows a simple function that quickly determines if
a file exists or not.

Listing 30-17: **AFunction That Quickly Determines if a File Exists**

```
Public Function Exists(ByVal sFilename As String) As Boolean

    Dim typOfStruct as OFSTRUCT
    On Error Resume Next
    If Len(sFilename) > 0 Then
        apiOpenFile sFilename, typOfStruct, OF_EXIST
        Exists = typOfStruct.nErrCode <> 2
    End If

End Function
```

Write this function once; use it forever. It always works, taking into account all
the problems mentioned by trying to use Dir$. After using OpenFile, if the
typOfStruct.nErrCode is not 2, it means the file is present; any other value
means the file is missing.

Long and short filenames

One of the most requested features of Microsoft for Windows 95 and Windows NT was long filename support — something other operating systems have had for years. The implementation of long filenames has been a boon for users, making it easy to remember file contents by replacing cryptic 8.3 names with description strings up to 255 characters long. Unfortunately for developers, supporting long filenames has been tough. This is because all the classic parsing routines that work on filenames no longer apply. A long file can contain more than one period (dot) and may also contain spaces. Further, as discussed earlier, not all operating systems' file systems support long filenames.

Good programming practice dictates that you program for the least common denominator, and degrade gracefully. When it comes to long filenames, this means your users can do whatever they want, but *you* should never use long filenames. A surefire method of handling long filenames is to convert them to short filenames.

Getting the short filename

Determining the short filename or alias of a long filename is easy — just use the GetShortPathName API function. To convert a short filename into a long filename is not quite so easy, but with a little coding it's not too tough to do. The function is declared as follows:

```
Private Declare Function GetShortPathName Lib "kernel32" _
    Alias "GetShortPathNameA" (ByVal lpszLongPath As String, _
    ByVal lpszShortPath As String, ByVal cchBuffer As Long) _
    As Long
```

Windows file systems maintain a list of aliases for compatibility with MS-DOS and older Windows programs. GetShortPathName returns the short name or alias of a file. For example, the filename c:\program files\hanks text.txt is converted into c:\PROGRA~1\HANKST~1.TXT and stored as the alias for the filename hanks text.txt. Windows aliases replace trailing text over the 8.3 boundary with the tilde (~) character, and a number denoting the position in the repetition sequence of this six-character sequence within this directory. If there were another file named hanks textfile.txt, and it was created after hanks text.txt, its alias would be c:\PROGRA~1\HANKST~2.TXT.

Listing 30-18 shows you how to use GetShortPathName to return the alias of any long filename. Note that you should use the complete path (for example, c:\windows\foo.txt) when using this method. If no path is supplied, the API defaults to the current directory.

> **Listing 30-18: A Function Procedure That Returns a Short Filename Given a Long Filename**
>
> ```
> Public Function ShortName(sFilename As String) As String
>
>     Dim lpszShortPath As String
>     Dim j
>
>     lpszShortPath = Space$(OFS_MAXPATHNAME)
>
>     GetShortPathName sFilename, lpszShortPath, Len(lpszShortPath)
>
>     j = InStr(lpszShortPath, Chr$(0))
>     If j > 0 Then ShortName = Left$(lpszShortPath, j - 1)
>
> End Function
> ```

Getting the long filename

Determining the long filename given the short filename is not as simple. This is because Windows APIs provide us the information we need at a low level, but there is no high-level API along the lines of GetShortPathName. Instead, we need to make use of a feature of another API function, FindFirstFile, which is declared here:

```
Private Declare Function FindFirstFile Lib "kernel32" Alias _
    "FindFirstFileA" (ByVal lpFileName As String, _
    lpFindFileData As WIN32_FIND_DATA) As Long
```

FindFirstFile locates and loads information about a filename into a user-defined type. One of the fields of the type that FindFirstFile populates carries the short filename; another carries the long filename. Unfortunately, FindFirstFile does not work on complete filenames that include the files' paths. In such a circumstance, you will need to parse the long filename into pieces and then use FindFirstFile on each piece. Listing 30-19 shows an implementation of this technique.

Listing 30-19: A Function That Returns a Long Filename Given a Short Filename

```
Public Function LongName(sFilename As String) As String

    Dim typFind As WIN32_FIND_DATA
    Dim work As String
    Dim newwork As String
    Dim i
    Dim hFile As Long

    hFile = FindFirstFile(sFilename, typFind)
    If hFile > 0 Then
        'filename part
        work = Left$(typFind.cFileName, InStr( _
            typFind.cFileName, Chr$(0)) - 1)
    Else
        Exit Function
    End If
    FindClose hFile

    ' now do path
    For i = Len(sFilename) To 4 Step -1
        If Mid$(sFilename, i, 1) = "\" Then
            hFile = FindFirstFile(Left$(sFilename, i - 1),_
            typFind)
            If hFile > 0 Then
                newwork = Left$(typFind.cFileName, _
                InStr(typFind.cFileName, Chr$(0)) - 1) _
                + "\" + newwork
            Else
                Exit Function
            End If
            FindClose hFile
        End If
    Next

    ' add path to filename and prepend drive
    LongName = Left$(sFilename, 3) + newwork + work

End Function
```

The function in Listing 30-19 processes the short filename, determines its long filename, and then appends the pieces into a result string. It does this in three steps. First, FindFirstFile is used to locate the file entry for the filename passed as sFileName. FindFirstFile fills in the typFind user-defined type — the typFind.cFileName member contains the long filename with a trailing null (Chr$) character appended to it. The path name, however, is still in alias or short form. In the second part, the short path is stripped from the short filename sFileName, and

each delimited (separated with slashes) part of the path is then read using
`FindFirstFile`, which in turn returns the long path equivalent of the short path.
The results are concatenated to create a completely qualified path name; the result
is the long filename equivalent of the short filename passed in `sFileName`.

Putting it all together

Listing 30-20 presents the entire code for a file information and control class
module that encapsulates file APIs into an extensible object ready for use in any
program.

This code is on the CD-ROM as VB98FILE.CLS.

Listing 30-20: **A Class Module That Gathers File Information**

```
Option Explicit

DefInt A-Z

Private Const OFS_MAXPATHNAME =128


Private Type OFSTRUCT
    cBytes As Byte
    fFixedDisk As Byte
    nErrCode As Integer
    Reserved1 As Integer
    Reserved2 As Integer
    szPathName(OFS_MAXPATHNAME) As Byte
End Type
Private typOfStruct As OFSTRUCT

'GetTempName
Private Declare Function GetTempFileName Lib "kernel32" _
    Alias "GetTempFileNameA" (ByVal lpszPath As String, _
    ByVal lpPrefixString As String, ByVal wUnique As Long, _
    ByVal lpTempFileName As String) As Long
Private Declare Function apiOpenFile Lib "kernel32" Alias _
    "OpenFile" (ByVal lpFileName As String, lpReOpenBuff As _
    OFSTRUCT, ByVal wStyle As Long) As Long
'Copy and Move
Private Declare Function MoveFileEx Lib "kernel32" Alias _
    "MoveFileExA" (ByVal lpExistingFileName As String, ByVal _
    lpNewFileName As String, ByVal dwFlags As Long) As Long
'Find
```

(continued)

Listing 30-20 *(continued)*

```
Private Declare Function SearchPath Lib "kernel32" Alias _
    "SearchPathA" (ByVal lpPath As String, ByVal lpFileName _
    As String, ByVal lpExtension As String, ByVal _
    nBufferLength As Long, ByVal lpBuffer As String, ByVal _
    lpFilePart As String) As Long
'Qualify
Private Declare Function GetFullPathName Lib "kernel32" _
    Alias "GetFullPathNameA" (ByVal lpFileName As String, _
    ByVal nBufferLength As Long, ByVal lpBuffer As String, _
    ByVal lpFilePart As String) As Long
'ShortName
Private Declare Function GetShortPathName Lib "kernel32" _
    Alias "GetShortPathNameA" (ByVal lpszLongPath As String, _
    ByVal lpszShortPath As String, ByVal cchBuffer As Long) _
    As Long
' time stuff
Private Declare Function lopen Lib "kernel32" Alias "_lopen" _
    (ByVal lpPathName As String, ByVal iReadWrite As Long) _
    As Long
Private Declare Function lclose Lib "kernel32" Alias "_lclose" _
    (ByVal hFile As Long) As Long
' constants
Private Const OF_READWRITE = &H2
Private Const OF_EXIST = &H4000
Private Const MOVEFILE_COPY_ALLOWED = &H2
Private Const MOVEFILE_REPLACE_EXISTING = &H1
Public Function Exists(ByVal sFilename As String) As Boolean

    On Error Resume Next
    If Len(sFilename) > 0 Then
        apiOpenFile sFilename, typOfStruct, OF_EXIST
        Exists = typOfStruct.nErrCode <> 2
    End If

End Function

Function Move(sFilename1 As String, sFilename2 As String) As_
    Boolean

    On Error Resume Next

    If MoveFileEx(sFilename1, sFilename2, _
        MOVEFILE_COPY_ALLOWED Or _
        MOVEFILE_REPLACE_EXISTING) < 0 Then Error 5

End Function

Function GetTemp(Optional sDrive As String) As String

    On Error Resume Next
```

```
        Dim lpTempFileName As String
        Dim j As Long
        Dim psDrive As String

        If Len(sDrive) Then
            psDrive = Left$(sDrive, 1) + ":\"
        Else
            psDrive = CurDir$
        End If

        lpTempFileName = Space$(OFS_MAXPATHNAME)
        j = GetTempFileName(psDrive, "hm", 0, lpTempFileName)

        If Len(lpTempFileName) > 1 Then
            j = InStr(lpTempFileName, Chr$(0))
            Kill Left$(lpTempFileName, j - 1)
            GetTemp = Left$(lpTempFileName, j - 1)
        End If

    End Function
```

The `Find` function locates a file by checking for it in several well-known locations. `Find` checks the following directories for a file, in the order presented:

1. The application directory

2. The current default directory, as set by Windows or the Visual Basic `Chdir` or `ChDrive` methods

3. The Windows System directory

4. The Windows NT 16-bit System directory and the 32-bit System directory

5. The Windows directory

6. Directories in the PATH environment variable

```
Public Function Find(sFilename As String, Optional sPath _
    As String) As String

    Dim lpBuffer As String
    Dim j
    Dim lpFound As String

    lpBuffer = Space$(OFS_MAXPATHNAME)
    j = SearchPath(sPath, sFilename, vbNullString, _
        Len(lpBuffer), lpBuffer, lpFound)

    If j > 0 Then Find = Left$(lpBuffer, j)

End Function
```

Qualify will attempt to append a complete path, given just a filename:

```
Public Sub Qualify(sFilename As String)

    Dim j
    Dim lpBuffer As String
    Dim lpFilePart As String

    lpBuffer = Space$(OFS_MAXPATHNAME)
    lpFilePart = Space$(OFS_MAXPATHNAME)
    j = GetFullPathName(sFilename, Len(lpBuffer), lpBuffer, _
        lpFilePart)

    If j > 0 Then sFilename = Left$(lpBuffer, j)

End Sub

Public Function ShortName(sFilename As String) As String

    Dim lpszShortPath As String
    Dim j

    lpszShortPath = Space$(OFS_MAXPATHNAME)

    GetShortPathName sFilename, lpszShortPath, _
        Len(lpszShortPath)

    j = InStr(lpszShortPath, Chr$(0))
    If j > 0 Then ShortName = Left$(lpszShortPath, j - 1)

End Function
```

Years ago there was a UNIX utility called Touch. Touch would take every file that matched a mask and mark it with the current date and time stamp. This allowed you to be able to see changed files, as well as to mark files prior to distribution. If you spend any time working with lots of files, you will probably find a need for your own Touch function to mark all files matching the mask with the current date and time. Here it is:

```
Public Sub Touch(ByVal sMask As String)

    Dim myName As String

'get first entry
    myName = Dir$(sMask)

    'start the loop
```

```
      Do While myName <> ""
          FileTimeSet myName, Year(Date$), Month(Date$), _
              day(Date$), Hour(Now), Minute(Now)
          myName = Dir$     'get next entry
      Loop

  End Sub
```

Summary

Windows supports many types of drives: fixed, removable, RAM, local, and remote. No matter what kind of drive it is, it has a number and a name—which may be accessed using the Windows API. Drives are numbered from 0 to 25, and will have a drive letter of A to Z. Using the Windows API, you can quickly determine both the type of drive and whether or not a given drive is installed or not.

✦ File systems store information using bytes, sectors, and clusters. Various schemes are used to store data, but they all rely on bytes, sectors, and clusters. Using the Windows API to access a volume's information, you can then calculate the total size of the volume, the amount of free space, and used space in bytes.

✦ Three special types of directories are available to you under Windows—the System directory, the Windows directory, and the temp directory. Windows APIs return the names of these directories, since they might not always be named "System," "Windows," or "temp." Remember never to store any program files in the System directory, and don't place any files you want to maintain in the temp directory.

✦ Using the OpenFile Windows API, you can quickly and reliably determine if a file exists, saving you from tedious and possible unreliable dependence upon Visual Basic keywords that were not really designed for determining file existence.

✦ File systems offer varying functionality. Long filenames are found on VFAT and NTFS volumes. Using the Windows API, you can determine the long filename given a short filename, and vice versa.

✦   ✦   ✦

Retrieving System Information Using Windows API

At one time or another, most developers want to know how much memory is installed on a PC. Or what kind of processor is installed. As software evolution moves forward, it becomes more important than ever to understand the platform your software is to run on.

A great example of this is multiprocessor systems; or battery information from laptops; or basic performance capabilities. For example, if the system is fairly slow, you might want to present a wait dialog or splash screen during a long process; for a fast machine, you might not need to do so.

Windows can also start in a number of different modes — Normal, Safe, and Safe Without Network Support. Again, knowing the startup mode enables you to handle these conditions gracefully.

Most applications require access to data that may be stored remotely and accessed via network connections. It becomes important, then, to be able to determine whether a network is available to your programs before you attempt to access network resources.

If all this seems a little paranoid to you, then you just haven't yet been developing long enough to run into "the wall" that these seemingly tedious details can throw into your path. Trust me — taking care of the details is what effective application development is all about. If you assume the worst and plan for it, then you (and more importantly the users of your software) are pleasantly unaware of all the little things going wrong. In short, to be a good developer, you need a healthy amount of paranoia.

Windows provides significant system status information through the Windows API. In this chapter, you learn the APIs to use to retrieve system configuration and status information.

Retrieving System Information

System information refers to the current configuration of the operating system and the PC host platform running the operating system. System information includes

✦ Memory

✦ Total memory installed and available

✦ Windows start mode

✦ Detecting network support

Note   To determine the operating system, version, and type, see Chapter 27, which includes complete code and instructions on how to determine this operating system information.

Memory

All developers need to worry about memory. As our applications and their runtimes grow ever larger, the memory available becomes critical. Insufficient memory can reduce any program to a crawl, resulting in a very unsatisfactory user experience. Windows has powerful APIs that provide all the memory information you need. Windows APIs can provide

✦ Total physical memory installed

✦ Available physical memory

✦ Total paging file space

✦ Available paging file space

The Windows API that gives us this wealth of memory information is GlobalMemoryStatus. GlobalMemoryStatus fills a user-defined type (MEMORYSTATUS) with raw memory information; using this raw information, you can then calculate the desired result.

The MEMORYSTATUS user-defined type is placed in the Declarations section of a Visual Basic code module. If you want to use the memory APIs in more than one module (code, class, form, user control, and so on), then place it into a code module and declare it as Public instead of Private. When declared private (as shown here) it is only available to the module in which it is declared.

```
Private Type MEMORYSTATUS
    dwLength As Long
    dwMemoryLoad As Long
    dwTotalPhys As Long
    dwAvailPhys As Long
    dwTotalPageFile As Long
    dwAvailPageFile As Long
    dwTotalVirtual As Long
    dwAvailVirtual As Long
End Type
Private Declare Sub GlobalMemoryStatus Lib "kernel32" _
    lpBuffer As MEMORYSTATUS)
```

Members of the MEMORYSTATUS Type

After a call to GlobalMemoryStatus, the members of the MEMORYSTATUS Type structure contain the memory information. Several members provide information about virtual memory—a memory management technique beyond the scope of Visual Basic, often used for device driver developers. Only relevant members for Visual Basic memory retrieval are outlined in the following list.

dwMemoryLoad—Returns a value from 0 to 100 that represents an approximation of how much memory is currently in use. A value of 0 means no memory is in use; 100 means all memory is in use. Use this value as a relative gauge of how "loaded down" the PC is when you call it. You might decide that if the PC has a load of more than 75 (that is, less than 25% remaining), then your software won't start. This member is similar to the 16-bit Windows concept of system resources.

dwTotalPhys—Returns a value that represents how many total bytes of physical memory are installed. Use this value to determine the amount of memory the PC has. For example, you might decide your software cannot run on a machine with 8MB of memory.

dwAvailPhys—Returns a value that represents how many total bytes of physical memory are currently available. Unlike dwMemoryLoad, this member is useful to determine the actual amount of memory in bytes.

dwTotalPageFile—Returns a value that represents how many bytes may be stored in the paging file at the time you call GlobalMemoryStatus. It is important to remember that this member's value is not the actual size of the paging, but rather how much space in the paging file is available for storing data.

dwAvailPageFile—Returns a value that represents how many total bytes are available in the paging file. Note that this member's value is not how many bytes are available for storage at the time you call GlobalMemoryStatus, but rather the entire size of the paging file.

Determining memory installed and available

Retrieving memory information using `GlobalMemoryStatus` is straightforward, as the following code shows. The process is to create a copy of the user-defined type `MEMORYSTATUS`, then call `GlobalMemoryStatus`. `GlobalMemoryStatus` in turn fills in the members of the user-defined type. Then, you simply query the members of the user-defined type to retrieve the information of interest. This example returns the total number of bytes the PC has.

Listing 31-1 shows a simple function that uses `GlobalMemoryStatus` to determine the total amount of memory installed.

Listing 31-1: A Function That Determines the Total Amount of Memory Installed

```
Public Function MemoryTotal() As Long
    Dim memsts As MEMORYSTATUS
    GlobalMemoryStatus memsts
    MemoryTotal = memsts.dwTotalPhys
End Function
```

The total information is useful, but more often you may want to know how much memory is available to your program. Listing 31-2 shows how easy it is to determine this information using `GlobalMemoryStatus`.

Listing 31-2: A Function to Determine Total Available Memory

```
Public Function MemoryAvailable() As Long
    Dim memsts As MEMORYSTATUS
    GlobalMemoryStatus memsts
    MemoryAvailable = memsts.dwAvailPhys
End Function
```

Using `GlobalMemoryStatus` is easy; in no time, you can add detailed memory usage and status information to your project's About boxes and system information displays. You can also make sure there is sufficient memory for your application to operate.

Determining Windows start mode

Consider the following lines of code:

```
Declare Function GetSystemMetrics Lib "user32" Alias _
    "GetSystemMetrics" (ByVal nIndex As Long) As Long
```

GetSystemMetrics is one of the most useful Windows API functions for Visual Basic developers. It returns a wealth of information about the user interface, as well as diverse peripheral information such as network installations and mouse configurations. It also returns a value that indicates how the user's Windows session started.

Windows can boot in a number of configurations. Normal mode is when Windows starts without any problems or limiting factors. Exactly how Windows starts is a function of the PC platform and the state of the operating system (Windows). For example, if Windows experiences a registry problem during startup, it may start in Safe mode.

During this Safe mode startup period, users can decide whether they want to attempt to load configuration files and drivers for peripherals such as the network. During the period of operation with problems detected, Windows operates in what is called "fail-safe" or "safe" boot mode.

Knowing how Windows starts can make your software more reliable. There are three possible modes:

✦ Normal boot

✦ Safe boot

✦ Safe boot with network

There are a number of defined constants that you can use with GetSystemMetrics. The constant you pass as an argument to GetSystemMetrics tells that function what information to return. There are dozens and dozens of these constants, including constants for determining the start mode of Windows. The constant to use to determine the Windows start mode is SM_CLEANBOOT. SM_CLEANBOOT is defined as follows:

```
Const SM_CLEANBOOT = 67
```

Listing 31-3 shows a simple function titled StartMode that polls GetSystemMetrics using the SM_CLEANBOOT constant. The result of the StartMode function is an integer value from 0 to 2 that indicates the start mode of the current Windows session.

Listing 31-3: A Function That Determines Windows Start Mode

```
Public Function StartMode() As Integer
    StartMode = GetSystemMetrics(SM_CLEANBOOT)
End Function
```

A return value of zero (0) indicates a normal boot, which means no restrictions are in effect and the system should have a drivers and devices available.

When Windows boots, you can press F5 to select a method of loading Windows. This is often done to boot DOS instead of Windows. However, when Windows experiences a problem during its boot up, or when it determines that the last attempt to start Windows failed due to a problem, Windows presents this screen and defaults to booting up in Safe mode. When in Safe mode, Windows loads a subset of drivers—the bare minimum required to load. This is called a *safe boot*— meaning that no "dangerous" or "failing" drivers are loaded.

GetSystemMetrics provides two return values that indicate whether the current Windows session is in Safe mode or not.

A return value of one (1) indicates that a safe boot was performed. This means a severe system problem (often registry related) has prevented Windows from booting properly. The user configuration files have been skipped, all nonsystem device drives are not loaded, and there is no network support.

A return value of two (2) indicates a safe boot with network support. This is the same as a safe boot, but Windows was able to load the network drivers and make network support available.

Detecting network support

Most applications written in Visual Basic seamlessly support networks—this is because Microsoft enables you to reference remote servers and network resources using UNC conventions—for example, \\server\files\hank.txt instead of g:\files\hank.txt. This sort of "drive independence" enables users to map drive letters to whatever they want; your program remains properly pointed and connected to appropriate resources.

However, you can't just assume the network is omnipresent; and even when one *is* present, Windows can fail to load drivers for it. Some networks can fail rather ungracefully if a server is not found while booting. In short, enough potential issues can arise to warrant checking for whether a network is installed before attempting to access remote files.

The Windows API function that can tell us whether a network is available is
GetSystemMetrics. To determine whether network support is present, you use
GetSystemMetrics with a special constant. The constant to use to determine
whether a network is available is SM_NETWORK. SM_NETWORK is defined as follows:

```
Const SM_NETWORK = 63
```

The following function titled Network is all it takes to determine whether a
Windows supported network is available for your use.

Listing 31-4 shows a simple function that uses GetSystemMetrics to determine
whether a network is available.

> **Listing 31-4: A Function to Determine Whether
> a Network Is Available**

```
Public Function Network() As Boolean
    Network = GetSystemMetrics(SM_NETWORK) And &H1
End Function
```

Locating Windows directories

Windows has three special directories that are used to store three special types of
files. These special directories may be of any name. They are called

✦ Windows System directory

✦ Windows directory and

✦ Temp directory

Each directory is used by the operating system — and your programs. You might not
know it, but these special directories are available to you and are in fact designed so
that you can have known repositories for these certain special file types.

Windows System directory

The *System directory* contains files used by all Windows applications and by
Windows itself. These files include Windows libraries (OCXs, DLLs, and so on),
drivers, and font files.

Note that you (and your applications) should not place files in the System
directory. The reason is that some versions of Windows may have the system
directory write-protected — which is also true of networked Windows, where
Windows itself is stored on a server.

Although the issue of a write-protected directory is a potential problem, in many cases your setup programs may install controls, fonts, and libraries into the System directory anyway. Even the Setup Wizard that comes with Visual Basic may break the don't-use-the-System-directory rule and place your files there. Technically, however, it's better practice to put your files into the Windows directory instead of the System directory. Now you know, and can plan for the potential problem of a write-protected System directory — however rare.

The `GetSystemDirectory` API retrieves the path of the Windows System directory. This directory is typically titled "System" on Windows 95 or "System32" for Windows NT, but it can have any name, thus the need to query Windows for this information.

```
Private Declare Function GetSystemDirectory Lib "kernel32"_
Alias "GetSystemDirectoryA" (ByVal lpBuffer As String, _ByVal
nSize As Long) As Long
```

The following function titled `SystemDir` calls `GetSystemDirectory` and returns a string containing the complete path. For example, `C:\Windows\System32` or `C:\Winnt\System32`. You should always use this function (or a similar one) to access the System directory. Never assume that the System directory has a certain name.

The `SystemDir` function shown in Listing 31-5 declares a string variable to contain the System directory name, `tmp`. The variable is then set to a prefilled string of spaces. This is a crucial step because `GetSystemDirectory` requires a "padded string" of at least 260 bytes, which is the maximum size of a Windows path name. To make this easier, I declare a constant called `MAX_PATH`, and set it equal 260.

`GetSystemDirectory` takes as its arguments the variable to contain the string, padded to `MAX_PATH` spaces, and another argument that indicates the length of the string, which is `MAX_PATH`. `GetSystemDirectory` returns the length of the actual path name character string as its result.

Listing 31-5: **A Function to Locate the System Directory**

```
' this const goes in the declaration section of the
' module
Private Const MAX_PATH = 260


Public Function SystemDir() As String

    Dim tmp As String
```

```
        tmp = Space$(MAX_PATH)

        SystemDir = Left$(tmp, GetSystemDirectory(tmp, MAX_PATH))

    End Function
```

Windows directory

The Windows directory contains files used by Windows applications. These types of files include initialization (INI) files, Help files, and license files.

The Windows directory is where you should store your private applications files. Even if the user is running a shared version of Windows, the Windows directory is write-enabled. This situation may seem counterintuitive; you may want to store your files in the System directory.

However, Windows always searches the System directory and then the Windows directory when you (or your program) attempt to load a library (DLL, OCX), help file, or other file. So placing your files in the Windows directory won't "hide" them from your application, and you don't need to make any changes to the path statement in the Autoexec.bat file of the user's computer.

The GetWindowsDirectory function retrieves the path of the Windows directory. This directory is typically titled "Windows" on Windows 95 or "Winnt" for Windows NT, but it can have any name, thus the need to query Windows for this information.

```
    Private Declare Function GetWindowsDirectory Lib "kernel32"_
        Alias "GetWindowsDirectoryA"(ByVal lpBuffer As String, _
        ByVal nSize As Long) As Long
```

The following function titled Home calls GetWindowsDirectory and returns a string containing the complete path — for example, C:\Windows or C:\Winnt. You should always use this function (or a similar one) to access the System directory. Never assume that the Windows directory has a certain name.

The Home function shown in Listing 31-6 declares a string variable to contain the Windows directory name, lpBuffer. The variable is then set to a prefilled string of spaces. This is a crucial step; GetWindowsDirectory requires a "padded string" of at least 260 bytes, the maximum size of a Windows path name. To make this whole process easier, declare a constant called MAX_PATH, and set it equal to 260.

GetWindowsDirectory takes as its arguments the variable to contain the string, padded to MAX_PATH spaces, and another argument that indicates the length of the string, which is MAX_PATH. GetWindowsDirectory returns the length of the actual path name character string as its result.

Listing 31-6: A Function to Locate the Name of the Windows Directory

```
' this const goes in the declaration section of the
' module
Private Const MAX_PATH = 260


Public Function Home() As String

    Dim lpBuffer As String

    lpBuffer = Space$(MAX_PATH)

    Home = Left$(lpBuffer, GetWindowsDirectory(lpBuffer, _
        MAX_PATH))

End Function
```

Temporary directory

Windows also provides a place to store temporary files — files that your program creates and won't need to the next time Windows boots. The GetTempPath API retrieves the path of the directory specifically designated to hold temporary files.

Never put into a temporary directory files that your program needs when your program — or Windows — starts! Users (present company included) clean out the various temporary directories at will. Consider the following code:

```
Private Declare Function GetTempPath Lib "kernel32" Alias_
    "GetTempPathA" (ByVal nBufferLength As Long, _
    ByVal lpBuffer As String) As Long
```

The GetTempPath API returns the temporary file path using the following logic:

If the AUTOEXEC.BAT file (or initialization file for Windows NT) has set an environment variable titled TMP, that path is returned. For example, in an AUTOEXEC.BAT entry of

```
SET TMP = C:\WINDOWS\TEMP
```

if TMP is not found in the environment, then GetTempPath checks for an environment variable titled "TEMP". For example, in an AUTOEXEC.BAT entry of

```
SET TEMP = C:\WINDOWS\TEMP
```

if no entry for TMP or TEMP is found, `GetTempPath` returns the currently active directory, as set by using Windows or the Visual Basic `ChDir` or `ChDrive` commands.

The following function titled `TmpDir()` calls `GetTempPath` and returns a string containing the complete path — for example, `C:\TEMP` or `C:\WINDOWS\TEMP`. You should always use this function (or a similar one) to access the temporary directory. Never assume that the temporary directory has a certain name.

The `TmpDir` function shown in Listing 31-7 declares a string variable to contain the temporary directory name, `lpBuffer`. The variable is then set to a prefilled string of spaces. This is a crucial step; `GetTempPath` requires a "padded string" of at least 260 bytes, the maximum size of a Windows path name. To make this process easier, declare a constant called `MAX_PATH`, and set it to equal 260.

`GetTempPath` takes as its arguments the variable to contain the string, padded to `MAX_PATH` spaces, and another argument that indicates the length of the string, which is `MAX_PATH`. `GetWindowsDirectory` returns the length of the actual path name character string as its result.

Listing 31-7: A Function to Locate the Name of the Temporary Directory

```
' this const goes in the declaration section of the
' module
Private Const MAX_PATH = 260

Public Function TmpDir() As String

    Dim lpBuffer As String

    lpBuffer = Space$(MAX_PATH)

    TmpDir = Left$(lpBuffer, GetTempPath(MAX_PATH, lpBuffer))

End Function
```

A system-information class — putting it all together

Listing 31-8 is an entire system-information class, encapsulating all the code in this section — plus some additional system information and control capabilities — into an extensible object ready for use in any program. The additional routines allow you to determine the computer name.

The code in Listing 31-8 is on the CD-ROM as VB98SYSIN.CLS.

Listing 31-8: Encapsulating Common Windows System Information as an Extensible Object

```
Option Explicit
DefInt A-Z
Const MAX_PATH = 260
Const myDescription = "Host platform information and control
library"
Declare Function GetSystemMetrics Lib "user32" Alias
"GetSystemMetrics" (ByVal nIndex As Long) As Long
Private Declare Function GetComputerName Lib "kernel32" _
    Alias "GetComputerNameA" (ByVal lpBuffer As String, _
    nSize As Long) As Long

Private Declare Function GetEnvironmentVariable Lib _
    "kernel32" Alias "GetEnvironmentVariableA" (ByVal _
    lpName As String, ByVal lpBuffer As String, ByVal _
    nSize As Long) As Long
Private Declare Function SetEnvironmentVariable Lib _
    "kernel32" Alias "SetEnvironmentVariableA" (ByVal _
    lpName As String, ByVal lpValue As String) As Long

Private Declare Function GetVersion Lib "kernel32" () As Long
Private Declare Function GetSystemDirectory Lib "kernel32" _
    Alias "GetSystemDirectoryA" (ByVal lpBuffer As String, _
    ByVal nSize As Long) As Long
Private Declare Function GetWindowsDirectory Lib "kernel32" _
    Alias "GetWindowsDirectoryA" (ByVal lpBuffer As String, _
    ByVal nSize As Long) As Long

'OS info
Private Type OSVERSIONINFO
    dwOSVersionInfoSize As Long
    dwMajorVersion As Long
    dwMinorVersion As Long
    dwBuildNumber As Long
    dwPlatformId As Long
    szCSDVersion As String * 128
End Type
Private Declare Function GetVersionEx Lib "kernel32" Alias _
    "GetVersionExA" (LpVersionInformation As OSVERSIONINFO) _
    As Long

'memory info
Private Type MEMORYSTATUS
    dwLength As Long
```

```
        dwMemoryLoad As Long
        dwTotalPhys As Long
        dwAvailPhys As Long
        dwTotalPageFile As Long
        dwAvailPageFile As Long
        dwTotalVirtual As Long
        dwAvailVirtual As Long
End Type
Private Declare Sub GlobalMemoryStatus Lib "kernel32" _
    (lpBuffer As MEMORYSTATUS)

Private Declare Function ExitWindowsEx Lib "user32" (ByVal _
    uFlags As Long, ByVal dwReserved As Long) As Long
Private Const EWX_FORCE = 4
Private Const EWX_REBOOT = 2
Private Const EWX_LOGOFF = 0
Private Const EWX_SHUTDOWN = 1
'start mode
Private Const SM_CLEANBOOT = 67
Private Declare Function IsWindowVisible Lib "user32" Alias _
    "IsVisible" (ByVal hwnd As Long) As Long
Private Declare Function SetWindowPos Lib "user32" (ByVal _
    hwnd As Long, ByVal hWndInsertAfter As Long, ByVal x As _
    Long, ByVal y As Long, ByVal CX As Long, ByVal cy As _
    Long, ByVal wFlags As Long) As Long
Private Declare Function FindWindow Lib "user32" Alias _
    "FindWindowA" (ByVal lpClassName As String, ByVal _
    lpWindowName As String) As Long
Private Const SWP_HIDEWINDOW = &H80
Private Const SWP_SHOWWINDOW = &H40

Public Function TmpDir() As String

    Dim lpBuffer As String

    lpBuffer = Space$(MAX_PATH)

    TmpDir = Left$(lpBuffer, GetTempPath(MAX_PATH, lpBuffer))


End Function


Public Function ComputerName() As String

    Dim lpBuffer  As String
    Dim j
    lpBuffer = Space$(255)

    GetComputerName lpBuffer, Len(lpBuffer)
    j = InStr(lpBuffer, Chr$(0))
```

(continued)

Listing 31-8 *(continued)*

```
    If j > 0 Then ComputerName = Left$(lpBuffer, j - 1)

End Function

Function IsNT() As Boolean

    Dim verinfo As OSVERSIONINFO
    verinfo.dwOSVersionInfoSize = Len(verinfo)
    GetVersionEx verinfo
    IsNT = verinfo.dwPlatformId = 2

End Function

Public Function IsNT3() As Boolean

    Dim verinfo As OSVERSIONINFO
    verinfo.dwOSVersionInfoSize = Len(verinfo)
    GetVersionEx verinfo
    If verinfo.dwPlatformId = 2 Then IsNT3 = _
        verinfo.dwMajorVersion = 3

End Function

Public Function IsNT4() As Boolean

    Dim verinfo As OSVERSIONINFO
    verinfo.dwOSVersionInfoSize = Len(verinfo)
    GetVersionEx verinfo
    If verinfo.dwPlatformId = 2 Then IsNT4 = _
        verinfo.dwMajorVersion = 4

End Function

Public Function IsNT5() As Boolean

    Dim verinfo As OSVERSIONINFO
    verinfo.dwOSVersionInfoSize = Len(verinfo)
    GetVersionEx verinfo
    If verinfo.dwPlatformId = 2 Then IsNT5 = _
        verinfo.dwMajorVersion = 5

End Function

Public Function SystemDir() As String

    Dim tmp As String
    tmp = Space$(MAX_PATH)

    SystemDir = Left$(tmp, GetSystemDirectory(tmp, _
        MAX_PATH)) + "\"
```

```
End Function

Public Function Home() As String

    Dim lpBuffer As String

    lpBuffer = Space$( MAX_PATH)
    Home = Left$(lpBuffer, GetWindowsDirectory(lpBuffer, _
        MAX_PATH)) + "\"

End Function

Public Function Is95() As Boolean

    Dim verinfo As OSVERSIONINFO
    verinfo.dwOSVersionInfoSize = Len(verinfo)
    GetVersionEx verinfo
    Is95 = verinfo.dwPlatformId = 1

End Function

Public Function WindowsName() As String

    Dim verinfo As OSVERSIONINFO

    verinfo.dwOSVersionInfoSize = Len(verinfo)
    GetVersionEx verinfo

    Select Case verinfo.dwPlatformId
    Case 1 'Win95
        WindowsName = "Windows95"
    Case 2 'NT
        WindowsName = "Windows NT " & verinfo.dwMajorVersion _
            & "." & verinfo.dwMinorVersion
    End Select

End Function

Public Property Let TaskBarVisible(ByVal bNewValue As Boolean)

    If bNewValue Then
        SetWindowPos FindWindow("Shell_traywnd", ""), 0, 0, _
            0, 0, 0, SWP_SHOWWINDOW
    Else
        SetWindowPos FindWindow("Shell_traywnd", ""), 0, 0, _
            0, 0, 0, SWP_HIDEWINDOW
    End If

End Property
```

(continued)

Listing 31-8 *(continued)*

```vb
Public Property Get TaskBarVisible() As Boolean

    TaskBarVisible = _
        IsWindowVisible(FindWindow("Shell_traywnd", ""))

End Property

Public Function MemoryTotal() As Long

    Dim memsts As MEMORYSTATUS

    GlobalMemoryStatus memsts
    MemoryTotal = memsts.dwTotalPhys

End Function

Public Function MemoryAvailable() As Long

    Dim memsts As MEMORYSTATUS

    GlobalMemoryStatus memsts
    MemoryAvailable = memsts.dwAvailPhys

End Function

Public Sub ShutDown()

    Dim dwReserved As Long
    ExitWindowsEx EWX_FORCE Or EWX_LOGOFF Or EWX_SHUTDOWN, _
        dwReserved

End Sub

Public Sub Reboot()

    Dim dwReserved As Long
    ExitWindowsEx EWX_FORCE Or EWX_REBOOT, dwReserved

End Sub

Public Function StartMode() As Integer

    StartMode = GetSystemMetrics(SM_CLEANBOOT)

End Function

Public Function GetVariable(sVariable As String) As String
```

```
    On Error GoTo myError

    Dim result As Long
    Dim tmp As String

    tmp = Space$(1024)

    result = GetEnvironmentVariable(sVariable + Chr$(0), _
        tmp, Len(tmp))

    If result = 0 Then
        Error 5
    Else
        GetVariable = Left$(tmp, result)
    End If

myExit:

    Exit Function

myError:

    Resume myExit

End Function

Public Sub SetVariable(sVariable As String, sValue As String)

    Dim result
    result = SetEnvironmentVariable(sVariable, sValue)

End Sub

Public Sub KillVariable(sVariable As String)

    Dim sValue As String

    SetEnvironmentVariable sVariable, sValue

End Sub

Public Function Name() As String

    Dim lpBuffer  As String
    Dim j
    lpBuffer = Space$(255)

    GetComputerName lpBuffer, Len(lpBuffer)
    j = InStr(lpBuffer, Chr$(0))
```

(continued)

Listing 31-8 *(continued)*

```
    If j > 0 Then Name = Left$(lpBuffer, j - 1)

End Function

Public Function Network() As Boolean
    Network = GetSystemMetrics(SM_NETWORK) And &H1

End Function
```

As you can see, using the code given in Listing 31-8 enables your program to provide quite a bit of valuable system information.

System-level information that your program requires can include the Network, Name, and MemoryAvailable functions. You may also need program-level information for your own use — for instance, the location of any directories that use the TmpDir, Home and SystemDir functions.

System control functions — for example, the ShutDown and ReBoot functions — give you actual control of the system. Other functions also provide useful capabilities; for example, you can use the GetVariable, SetVariable and KillVariable functions to read and manipulate environment variables.

Windows status functions — for example, TaskBarVisible, WindowsName, or other version functions such as Win95 and WinNT3 — return information about the system itself.

Viewing Hardware Information

Windows 95 and Windows NT run on a number of diverse platforms with very different CPUs. Windows runs on anything from an Intel 80386, 80486, or Pentium to a DEC Alpha. There are even widely available "clone" chips from AMD, IBM, and others. These CPUs all offer widely differing performance characteristics. For example, consider "the" Intel Pentium — actually a range of chips with varied capabilities. In my office I have one 75MHz Pentium, two 90MHz Pentiums, and a 233MHz Pentium with MMX capabilities — quite a spread of performance and technology.

Given the complexity and sheer size of today's runtime libraries and support systems, even a simple little Visual Basic DLL can require multiple megabytes of memory and a significantly speedy processor to operate.

The hardware information offered in this section relates to the PC itself — specifically, the processor or CPU. Windows enables you to determine the CPU type, the number of CPUs, and the relative performance capabilities of the CPU.

✦ CPU type

✦ CPU count

✦ CPU performance

CPU type

Depending on your applications, you might need to know and even require a certain type of processor. The Windows API function that can tell you this information is GetSystemInfo.

```
Private Declare Sub GetSystemInfo Lib "kernel32" _
    (lpSystemInfo As SYSTEM_INFO)
```

GetSystemInfo() returns a user-defined type whose members are populated with a tremendous amount of information. In classic Windows API fashion, the exact value of the member's data varies on the basis of operating system and Windows version.

The SYSTEM_INFO user-defined type is placed in the Declarations section of a Visual Basic code module. If you want to use the memory APIs in more than one module (code, class, form, user control, and so on), then first place it into a code module, and then declare it as Public instead of Private. When declared Private (as shown in the following code) it is only available to the module in which it is declared:

```
Private Type SYSTEM_INFO
    dwOemID As Long
    dwPageSize As Long
    lpMinimumApplicationAddress As Long
    lpMaximumApplicationAddress As Long
    dwActiveProcessorMask As Long
    dwNumberOfProcessors As Long
    dwProcessorType As Long
    dwAllocationGranularity As Long
    dwReserved As Long
End Type
```

You can also use a set of constants with GetSystemInfo and SYSTEM_INFO to help you identify the information contained in the members' elements after a call to GetSystemInfo(). For determining CPU type, these constants are defined as shown in the following list:

```
Const PROCESSOR_INTEL_386 = 386
Const PROCESSOR_INTEL_486 = 486
Const PROCESSOR_INTEL_PENTIUM = 586
Const PROCESSOR_MIPS_R4000 = 4000
Const PROCESSOR_ALPHA_21064 = 21064
```

Note To determine the operating system, version and type, see Chapter 27, which includes complete code and instructions on how to determine this operating system information.

Listing 31-9 shows how to extract some base-level information from this API.

Listing 31-9: **A Function to Determine CPU Type**

```
Public Function CPUName() As String
    Dim lpSystemInfo As SYSTEM_INFO
    GetSystemInfo lpSystemInfo
    Select Case lpSystemInfo.dwProcessorType
    Case PROCESSOR_INTEL_386
        CPUName = "386"
    Case PROCESSOR_INTEL_486
        CPUName = "486"
    Case PROCESSOR_INTEL_PENTIUM
        CPUName = "Pentium"
    Case PROCESSOR_MIPS_R4000
        CPUName = "MIPS"
    Case PROCESSOR_ALPHA_21064
        CPUName = "Alpha"
    End Select
End Function
```

In this example, we determine the name of the CPU. You might use this to prevent your software from running on a 386 machine or to slow down animation on a Pentium class machine.

CPU count

Even though Visual Basic itself does not implement multiprocessing, knowing whether more than one processor is available may help you make decisions about how your software loads and runs. GetSystemInfo returns in one of its members a mask indicating the number of processors in the system. Listing 31-10 shows a simple function to return the number of processors a machine has installed:

Listing 31-10: **A Function to Determine CPU Count.**

```
Public Function CPUCount() As Integer
    Dim lpSystemInfo As SYSTEM_INFO
    GetSystemInfo lpSystemInfo
    CPUCount = lpSystemInfo.dwNumberOfProcessors
End Function
```

CPU performance

Aside from the CPU name information provided, Windows gives you a binary value indicating whether the CPU is "slow." This is a subjective decision Windows makes using an internal formula. At best, this enables you make a somewhat informed decision about how your software should load and run.

To determine this information, use the GetSystemMetrics API and the SM_SLOWMACHINE constants.

```
Declare Function GetSystemMetrics Lib "user32" Alias_
    "GetSystemMetrics" (ByVal nIndex As Long) As Long

Private Const SM_SLOWMACHINE = 73
```

Listing 31-11 shows how to access this information in a simple function that returns True if the CPU is "slow," or False otherwise.

Listing 31-11: **A Function to Determine Relative CPU Performance**

```
Public Function IsSlow() As Boolean
    IsSlow = GetSystemMetrics(SM_SLOWMACHINE)
End Function
```

CPU system-information class – putting it all together

Listing 31-12 contains the entire code for the CPU system-information class. As before (in Listing 31-8), this class module encapsulates the information into an extensible object, ready for use in any program.

The code for Listing 31-12 is on the CD-ROM as VB98CPU.CLS.

Listing 31-12: **Encapsulating the CPU Information API as an Extensible Object**

```
Option Explicit
DefInt A-Z
Const myDescription = "PC information and control library"
Declare Function GetSystemMetrics Lib "user32" Alias _
    "GetSystemMetrics" (ByVal nIndex As Long) As Long

Private Declare Function GetComputerName Lib "kernel32" _
    Alias "GetComputerNameA" (ByVal lpBuffer As String, _
    nSize As Long) As Long
'CPU type etc
Private Declare Sub GetSystemInfo Lib "kernel32" _
    (lpSystemInfo As SYSTEM_INFO)
Private Type SYSTEM_INFO
    dwOemID As Long
    dwPageSize As Long
    lpMinimumApplicationAddress As Long
    lpMaximumApplicationAddress As Long
    dwActiveProcessorMask As Long
    dwNumberOfProcessors As Long
    dwProcessorType As Long
    dwAllocationGranularity As Long
    dwReserved As Long
End Type
Private Const PROCESSOR_INTEL_386 = 386
Private Const PROCESSOR_INTEL_486 = 486
Private Const PROCESSOR_INTEL_PENTIUM = 586
Private Const PROCESSOR_MIPS_R4000 = 4000
Private Const PROCESSOR_ALPHA_21064 = 21064

Private Const SM_NETWORK = 63
Private Const SM_SLOWMACHINE = 73

Public Function CPUCount() As Integer
    Dim lpSystemInfo As SYSTEM_INFO
    GetSystemInfo lpSystemInfo
    CPUCount = lpSystemInfo.dwNumberOfProcessors
End Function

Public Function CPUName() As String

    Dim lpSystemInfo As SYSTEM_INFO
```

```
        GetSystemInfo lpSystemInfo

        Select Case lpSystemInfo.dwProcessorType
        Case PROCESSOR_INTEL_386
            CPUName = "386"
        Case PROCESSOR_INTEL_486
            CPUName = "486"
        Case PROCESSOR_INTEL_PENTIUM
            CPUName = "Pentium"
        Case PROCESSOR_MIPS_R4000
            CPUName = "MIPS"
        Case PROCESSOR_ALPHA_21064
            CPUName = "Alpha"
        End Select

    End Function

    Public Function IsSlow() As Boolean

        IsSlow = GetSystemMetrics(SM_SLOWMACHINE)

    End Function
```

Summary

Using the Windows API calls and techniques presented in this chapter, you can create more robust software by ensuring that the platform contains the processing power and system resources your application requires.

✦ You can create powerful system-level information displays showing the status and configuration of Windows and the resources that Windows has available.

✦ Using the program-level information you gather, you can ensure that your applications use the proper directories to store special files, and avoid problems caused by write-protected directories.

✦ The system control functions give you control of the system, enabling you to manipulate environment variables, reboot Windows, or exit to DOS.

✦ The code on the CD-ROM includes all APIs and code used in this chapter.

✦   ✦   ✦

Retrieving Display Information Using the Windows API

◆ ◆ ◆ ◆

In This Chapter

Setting display
configurations

Controling system
colors

Managing your
windows

◆ ◆ ◆ ◆

Virtually all programs output information to the display. Displays come in all sizes and styles. Some support color; some do not. Some offer more resolution than others. Windows attempts to level the playing field through a process of *virtualization*, which is the creation of a consistent high-level interface that abstracts and standardizes all the device-dependent issues.

For the display, Windows implements a standard measuring system as well as a series of information points that describe the capabilities of the display. This information is crucial, since your program may attempt to use graphics images with more colors than the display permits. In this case, you would load another, lower-resolution image instead.

Another common requirement is for an application to be able to manipulate windows on the screen. You will often want to make a window "topmost"—floating on top of all other windows, never becoming obscured. Other times, you will want to determine whether a window is minimized or maximized. Of course, the Visual Basic WindowState property tells you this for your own windows, but what about other windows? Once again, you will need the Windows API to get this sort of information.

Display Capabilities

Windows lets you query the display to determine a standard set of information from which you can deduce the configuration and capabilities of the display. Information you can retrieve includes the following:

✦ Number of color planes

✦ Number of bits per pixel

✦ Number of colors a display supports

Acquiring and releasing device contexts

In order to use the Windows API functions that refer to the display, you need to understand the concept of a *device context*. A Windows device context is a data structure that defines graphical objects. The device context contains all the attributes that make a graphical image. The colors of a bitmap, the text drawn in a textbox — all are in reality manipulation of Windows device contexts. A device context is referred to in Windows shorthand as an *hDC* ("handle to a device context").

All Windows API functions with device contexts require a handle — a long integer that points to the data structure Windows maintains for each graphical object. You can get the handle and create a device context for any graphical object using the GetDC API function. GetDC creates an entry in the list Windows maintains and returns a handle to it, an hDC.

The following code shows how to get the hDC of the entire Windows desktop. This is useful for situations when you require a device context and don't have one available in your program. First, you need a declaration for an API function that gives you the hWnd of the desktop; this is because GetDC returns the hDC of a Window, as referenced by the hWnd. GetDeskTopWindow returns the hWnd of the desktop:

```
Declare Function GetDesktopWindow Lib "user32" Alias _
    "GetDesktopWindow" () As Long
```

Then, you will need the declaration for the GetDC API. Its declaration (for the general Declarations section of your VB application) is

```
Declare Function GetDC Lib "user32" Alias "GetDC" (ByVal _
    hwnd As Long) As Long
```

Finally, in the body of your procedure, use variable hDC (either declared Long or left as a variant) within an assignment expression, as follows:

```
hDC = GetDC(GetDesktopWindow())
```

Once you have the hDC, you can begin using the API functions that return information about the display. Just one note here: Whenever you use GetDC, you are required to use ReleaseDC to release the handle to the DC you secured with GetDC. Continual failure to do so can cause Windows to run out of resources — something you don't want to happen. Of course, you'll need a declaration for the ReleaseDC function, which appears here:

```
Declare Function ReleaseDC Lib "user32" Alias "ReleaseDC" ↵
    (ByVal hwnd As Long, ByVal hdc As Long) As Long
```

The following instruction shows how to release a DC once you are done with it.

```
ReleaseDC GetDesktopWindow(), hDC
```

Used together (and used properly as shown here) it is perfectly safe and effective to access and use Windows device contexts. The value that GetDC returns varies, depending on your version of Windows and the state of Windows when the call is made. Don't worry about the actual value returned; just keep it in a variable and remember to use ReleaseDC when done using the device context.

 Note   Always release any device contexts you get or create, when you've done with them.

Number of color planes

Color planes represent the separate red, green, blue, or intensity components for an image contained in a bitmap. When the number of color planes is combined with the number of bits per pixel, you can determine the number of colors an image is composed of. In this sample, we also use the GetDesktopWindow API function, which returns the window handle (hWnd) of the Windows desktop. The hWnd is the value used to represent individual windows, but you can also use it as an index for looking up its associated device context.

To determine how many bit planes are in use requires that you use a permutation of the now-familiar GetDeviceCaps API function. Here is the declaration for GetDeviceCaps

```
Private Declare Function GetDeviceCaps Lib "gdi32" (ByVal hDC _
    As Long, ByVal nIndex As Long) As Long
```

Listing 32-1 shows how to use GetDeviceCaps() to determine the number of color planes.

**Listing 32-1: How to Use GetDeviceCaps() to
Return the Color Plane Count**

```
' Windows API constant, place in declarations
' section.
Private Const PLANES = 14

Dim myDC As Long
Dim myGetDeviceCaps As Long
myDC = GetDC(GetDesktopWindow())
myGetDeviceCaps = GetDeviceCaps(myDC, PLANES)
ReleaseDC GetDesktopWindow(),myDC
```

The above listing declares a variable titled myDC. Then, the GetDC API is used to return the device context (hDC) of the desktop and store it in the variable myDC. At this point, a device context has been created, and myDC contains a value that may be used with other Windows APIs that require an hDC.

The variable myGetDeviceCaps is then used to receive the result of the GetDeviceCaps API. GetDeviceCaps can return a variety of useful pieces of information. In this case, we use GetDeviceCaps with the PLANES constant, which instructs GetDeviceCaps to return the number of color planes in use. The number of color planes is then stored in the myGetDeviceCaps variable for later use.

Finally, because we used GetDC to create and return a handle (hDC), we must use ReleaseDC to free the resources we used with GetDC. ReleaseDC() takes as its arguments the hWnd of the window as well as the hDC of the window to release, so we use the GetDeskTopWindow API again to provide ReleaseDC with the hWnd of the desktop.

This is a lot of explanation for what would seem to be a simple matter of querying a system variable. However, this is how the Windows API operates, and you have to explicitly declare, define, and call each API in order to achieve the results you want.

Number of bits per pixel

The number of bits per pixel indicates the color depth of an image. Windows supports 1, 4, 8, 16, 24, or 32 bits per pixel. When working directly with bitmaps using Windows API calls, this information is crucial. Even if you're not creating and manipulating bitmaps directly, this value is used with the color planes to indicate the number of colors an image supports (a calculation you'll witness for yourself shortly). Listing 32-2 shows how to use GetDeviceCaps to determine the number of bits per pixel.

Listing 32-2: How to Use GetDeviceCaps() to Return the Number of Bits per Pixel

```
' Windows API constant, place in declarations
' section.
Private Const BITSPIXEL = 12

Dim myDC As Long
Dim myGetDeviceCaps As Long
myDC = GetDC(GetDesktopWindow())
myGetDeviceCaps = GetDeviceCaps(hDC, BITSPIXEL)
ReleaseDC GetDesktopWindow(), hDC
```

The preceding listing declares a variable titled myDC. Then, the GetDC API is used to return the device context (hDC) of the desktop and store it in the variable myDC, just as in the previous example. At this point, a device context has been created, and myDC contains a value that may be used with other Windows APIs that require an hDC, specifically GetDeviceCaps.

The variable myGetDeviceCaps is then used to receive the result of the GetDeviceCaps API. GetDeviceCaps() can return a variety of useful pieces of information. In this case, we use GetDeviceCaps with the BITSPIXEL constant, which instructs GetDeviceCaps to return the number of bits used to represent each pixel displayed. The bits-per-pixel value is then stored in the myGetDeviceCaps variable for later use.

Finally, just like the previous example, because we used GetDC to create and return a handle (hDC), we must use ReleaseDC() to free the resources we used using GetDC.

Number of colors a display supports

Color planes and bits per pixel come together to represent the total number of colors that a device context supports. Listing 32-3 shows how to use GetDeviceCaps to determine the colors a device context supports.

Listing 32-3: How to Use GetDeviceCaps to Return the Colors a Device Context Supports

```
' Windows API constants, place in declarations
' section.
Private Const PLANES = 14
Private Const BITSPIXEL = 12

Public Function Colors() As Long
    Dim myBits As Long, myPlanes As Long
    Dim myDC As Long
    myDC = GetDC(GetDesktopWindow())
    myPlanes = GetDeviceCaps(hDC, PLANES)
    myBits = GetDeviceCaps(hDC, BITSPIXEL)
    Colors = myPlanes * myBits
    ReleaseDC GetDesktopWindow(), hDC
End Function
```

The above `Colors` function returns a value indicating the colors supported by the desktop, which you can assume to be the number of colors configured for Windows when this call is made.

The code declares three variables: `myBits`, `myPlans`, and `myDC`. The first step is to get the `hDC` of the desktop using the `GetDC` API with `GetDeskTopWindow` as its argument. Remember that `GetDeskTopWindow()` returns the `hWnd` of the desktop. Also, remember that `GetDC` returns the `hDC` of the window represented by the `hWnd` passed as its argument.

Once the `hDC` of the desktop is obtained, it is stored in the `myDC` variable. Then, `GetDeviceCaps` is queried for the number of color planes and bits per pixel supported. The color plane count is stored in `myPlanes`, and the bits-per-pixel count is stored in `myBits`.

To determine colors supported, the code then multiplies bits per pixel (`myBits`) by the number of color planes (`myPlanes`). The result of the multiplication is stored as the return value of the function.

Finally, the code releases the `hDC` using the `ReleaseDC` API.

Display Configuration

Any user of Windows can change color depth to any supported value at any time. This makes it hard for developers to maintain a consistency of appearance within their applications. Many developers use the standard "green, gray, white, and blue" Windows default interface colors. This works OK, right up until the user decides he or she wants something other than the default system colors — at which point your application sticks out and looks plain ugly.

Windows does, however, provide you with the ability to determine and then use system colors in your applications. This is very important if you want an application to fit in and match the standard colors of the other windows on a user's desktop. Using Windows APIs, you can determine and set the following:

✦ System colors

✦ Width and height of the screen (with and without the system tray)

✦ Dimensions of title bars and other windows elements

Determining system colors

Following the color scheme Windows uses is important. Thankfully, you have complete access to every color used anywhere in Windows. Windows implements standard colors for the pieces of each window displayed. For example, the window title bar has a unique color for its background and its text. The same holds true for menus and menu bars. Each individual piece of a window has a standard color reference, and you can read each of them using the `GetSysColor` API function, whose declaration is as follows:

```
Private Declare Function GetSysColor Lib "user32" (ByVal _
    nIndex As Long) As Long
```

`GetSysColor` takes as its argument an index value, which indicates the window element for which you want the function to return the color. The function returns the color as a long integer — ready to use with standard Visual Basic `ForeColor` and/or `BackColor` properties. Table 32-1 lists the index values for use with `GetSysColor`.

Table 32-1
Index Values for GetSysColor

Constant	Value (Decimal)
COLOR_SCROLLBAR	0
COLOR_BACKGROUND	1
COLOR_ACTIVECAPTION	2
COLOR_INACTIVECAPTION	3
COLOR_MENU	4
COLOR_WINDOW	5
COLOR_WINDOWFRAME	6
COLOR_MENUTEXT	7
COLOR_WINDOWTEXT	8
COLOR_CAPTIONTEXT	9
COLOR_ACTIVEBORDER	10
COLOR_INACTIVEBORDER	11
COLOR_APPWORKSPACE	12
COLOR_HIGHLIGHT	13
COLOR_HIGHLIGHTTEXT	14
COLOR_BTNFACE	15
COLOR_BTNSHADOW	16
COLOR_GRAYTEXT	17
COLOR_BTNTEXT	18
COLOR_INACTIVECAPTIONTEXT	19
COLOR_BTNHIGHLIGHT	20

Using GetSysColor at the start of your application lets your program mimic the current Windows color scheme.

Note Note that you can choose to use Visual Basic "system colors" for your applications as well; this lets your application reflect any changes the user makes to the system colors.

For example, to fill a picture box with the current background color of a command button, you would use GetSysColor with the COLOR_BTNFACE index within an instruction like this:

```
Picture1.BackColor = GetSysColor(COLOR_BTNFACE)
```

Determining width and height of screen

Visual Basic gives you the Screen object, which has methods and properties for working directly with the display. However, the Screen object has no ability to determine the available size of the screen, including the taskbar. The Windows API functions `GetSystemMetrics` and `SystemParametersInfo` provide you with just this functionality. First, we'll look at `SystemParametersInfo`, whose declaration is as follows:

```
Declare Function SystemParametersInfo Lib "user32" Alias _
    "SystemParametersInfoA" (ByVal uAction As Long, ByVal _
    uParam As Long, ByVal lpvParam As Any, ByVal fuWinIni _
    As Long) As Long
```

`SystemParametersInfo` is a very interesting API function. In classic API form, it likes to use pointers. Pointers refer to a numeric value that indicates the position in memory where some specific data begins. In this case, parameter `lpvParam` must be a `RECT` structure. `RECT` is a defined Windows data structure. In Visual Basic, you create structures using the `Type` keyword. Following is the Visual Basic equivalent of the Windows `RECT` structure:

```
' declare the type
Private Type RECT
    Left As Long
    Top As Long
    Right As Long
    Bottom As Long
End Type

' now create a variable of type RECT
Private myRect as RECT
```

The `myRect` variable now has properties of `Left`, `Top`, `Right`, and `Bottom` — which we will use to define a rectangular section of the screen.

To change the `SystemParametersInfo` API declaration to accept a `RECT` instead of a `Long`, we could use some undocumented Visual Basic keywords (`ObjPtr`, `StrPtr`, and so on) and "hack it," but we prefer the much safer and more portable method of *aliasing* the API function.

To alias an API, you take advantage of Visual Basic's ability to give any API function any name you want. You also declare the function's arguments with the data type that this call to `SystemParametersInfo` requires. In this case, we will recast `SystemParametersInfo` to take a `RECT` structure instead of a long. Then, when you call the new alias function, it will fill in the `RECT` structure for you. In the following code fragment, a constant is declared for later use, a `Type` clause defines the rectangle that will represent the screen area, and the alias function is declared:

```
' re-cast with alias to take a rect
Private Const SPI_GETWORKAREA = 48
```

```
Private Type RECT
    Left As Long
    Top As Long
    Right As Long
    Bottom As Long
End Type

Declare Function apiWorkArea Lib "user32" Alias _
    "SystemParametersInfoA" (ByVal uAction As Long, ByVal _
    uParam As Long, lpvParam As RECT, ByVal fuWinIni As Long) _
    As Long
```

Now the apiWorkArea function will return a RECT structure with the dimensions of the usable screen area; that is, the screen without the taskbar. Listing 32-4 encapsulates your new SystemParametersInfo API and returns the usable height and width of the screen.

Listing 32-4: A Function to Return the Usable Screen Height and Width

```
Public Sub WorkArea(sWidth As Long, sHeight As Long)
    Dim myRect As RECT
    Dim uParam As Long
    Dim fuWinIni As Long
    apiWorkArea SPI_GETWORKAREA, uParam, myRect, fuWinIni
    sWidth = myRect.Right - myRect.Left
    sHeight = myRect.Bottom - myRect.Top
End Sub
```

The above WorkArea procedure takes two arguments by reference: sWidth and sHeight. The procedure creates a user-defined type titled myRect and declares two variables to be used with the renamed SystemParametersInfo() API.

The apiWorkArea takes the SPI_GETWORKAREA constant and then fills in the members of the myRect type with the right, left, top, and bottom of a rectangle, representing the usable screen area. uParam and fuWinIni are not used in this example because they don't return any useful information when used with the SPI_GETWORKAREA constant.

Finally, sWidth is calculated by subtracting the left of the rectangle from the right, and sHeight is calculated by subtracting the top from the bottom.

Determining dimensions of Windows elements

Often, complex programs will require you to manipulate windows like panes — sizing, moving, and stretching them to fit your application window. You can use a third-party control or you can "roll your own." If you plan to create your own sizing routines, you will need to know the dimensions of a window border, the height of the title bar, and similar measurements. Windows provides the GetSystemMetrics API function for just this purpose. Its declaration is as follows:

```
Declare Function GetSystemMetrics Lib "user32" (ByVal nIndex _
    As Long) As Long
```

GetSystemMetrics takes an index as its argument. For example, the index you need to examine the title bar height is SM_CYCAPTION, decimal value 4. Table 32-2 shows several common constants for use with GetSystemMetrics.

Table 32-2 Index Values for GetSystemMetrics		
Constant	**Query Purpose**	**Value (Decimal)**
SM_CXBORDER	Height in pixels of a window border	5
SM_CYBORDER	Width in pixels of a window border	6
SM_CYCAPTION	Height in pixels of a normal window caption	4

Listing 32-5 encapsulates GetSystemMetrics into a sample Function procedure that returns the height of any window's title bar.

Listing 32-5: **A Function to Return the Height of Any Windows Title Bar**

```
Public Function TitleBarHeight() As Long
    TitleBarHeight = GetSystemMetrics(SM_CYCAPTION)
End Function
```

The above code simply calls GetSystemMetrics with the SM_CYCAPTION constant and returns the result as the function's value. The result is the height, in pixels, of the caption of a normal Windows window.

Putting it all together

Listing 32-6 is the entire code for a display-oriented class module. It encapsulates the display API functions into an extensible object, ready for use in any program.

On the CD-ROM

This code is on the CD-ROM as VB98DISP.CLS.

Listing 32-6: **Display Information Class Module**

```
Option Explicit

DefInt A-Z
Private Type RECT
        Left As Long
        Top As Long
        Right As Long
        Bottom As Long
End Type

Private Declare Function GetSysColor Lib "user32" (ByVal _
    nIndex As Long) As Long
Private Declare Function SystemParametersInfo Lib "user32" _
    Alias "SystemParametersInfoA" (ByVal uAction As Long, _
    ByVal uParam As Long, ByVal lpvParam As Any, ByVal _
    fuWinIni As Long) As Long
' re-cast with alias to take a rect
Private Declare Function apiWorkArea Lib "user32" Alias _
    "SystemParametersInfoA" (ByVal uAction As Long, ByVal _
    uParam As Long, lpvParam As RECT, ByVal fuWinIni As Long) _
    As Long

Private Const SPI_GETWORKAREA = 48

Private Declare Function GetDeviceCaps Lib "gdi32" (ByVal hDC _
    As Long, ByVal nIndex As Long) As Long
Private Declare Function GetSystemMetrics Lib "user32" (ByVal _
    nIndex As Long) As Long
Private Const DRIVERVERSION = 0
Private Const TECHNOLOGY = 2
Private Const HORZRES = 8
Private Const VERTRES = 10
Private Const VERTSIZE = 6
Private Const LOGPIXELSX = 88
Private Const LOGPIXELSY = 90
Private Const BITSPIXEL = 12
Private Const PLANES = 14
Private Const NUMBRUSHES = 16
Private Const NUMCOLORS = 24
Private Const NUMFONTS = 22
Private Const NUMPENS = 18
Private Const ASPECTX = 40
Private Const ASPECTY = 42

Private Declare Function GetDC Lib "user32" (ByVal hwnd As _
    Long) As Long
Private Declare Function GetDesktopWindow Lib "user32" () _
    As Long
Private Declare Function ReleaseDC Lib "user32" (ByVal hwnd _
    As Long, ByVal hDC As Long) As Long
```

```vb
Private myScreenMode As Integer
Private Const SM_CYCAPTION = 4

Public Function Height() As Long
    Select Case myScreenMode
    Case 1 'twip
        Height = Screen.Height
    Case 2 'pixel
        Height = Screen.Height / Screen.TwipsPerPixelX
    End Select
End Function

Public Function Width() As Long
    Select Case myScreenMode
    Case 1 'twip
        Width = Screen.Width
    Case 2 'pixel
        Width = Screen.Width / Screen.TwipsPerPixelY
    End Select
End Function

Public Property Get Mode() As Integer
    Mode = myScreenMode
End Property

Public Property Let Mode(ByVal vNewValue As Integer)
    Select Case vNewValue
    Case Is > 0
        myScreenMode = vNewValue
    Case Else
    End Select
End Property

Public Function Colors() As Long
    Dim myColors As Long
    myColors = p_myGetDeviceCaps(NUMCOLORS)
    If myColors = -1 Then
        Dim myBits As Long, myPlans As Long
        myPlans = p_myGetDeviceCaps(PLANES)
        myBits = p_myGetDeviceCaps(BITSPIXEL)
        Colors = myPlans * myBits
    End If
End Function

Private Function p_myGetDeviceCaps(nIndex As Integer) As Long
    Dim hDC As Long

    hDC = GetDC(GetDesktopWindow())
    p_myGetDeviceCaps = GetDeviceCaps(hDC, nIndex)
    ReleaseDC GetDesktopWindow(), hDC
End Function

Public Function Pixel2TwipH(nPixels As Integer) As Long
```

(continued)

Listing 32-6 *(continued)*

```
    Pixel2TwipH = nPixels * Screen.TwipsPerPixelX
End Function

Public Function Pixel2TwipV(nPixels As Integer) As Long
    Pixel2TwipV = nPixels * Screen.TwipsPerPixelY
End Function

Public Function Twip2PixelH(nTwips As Long) As Long
    Twip2PixelH = nTwips \ Screen.TwipsPerPixelX
End Function

Public Function Twip2PixelV(nTwips As Long) As Long
    Twip2PixelV = nTwips \ Screen.TwipsPerPixelY
End Function

Public Function TitleBarHeight() As Long
    TitleBarHeight = GetSystemMetrics(SM_CYCAPTION)
End Function

Public Sub WorkArea(sWidth As Long, sHeight As Long)
    Dim myRect As RECT
    Dim uParam As Long
    Dim fuWinIni As Long
    apiWorkArea SPI_GETWORKAREA, uParam, myRect, fuWinIni
    sWidth = myRect.Right - myRect.Left
    sHeight = myRect.Bottom - myRect.Top
End Sub
```

Listing 32-6 includes some interesting functions not covered elsewhere in this chapter. The functions `Pixel2TwipH`, `Pixel2TwipV`, `Twip2PixelH`, and `Twip2PixelV` are provided to help you convert from pixels to twips. The default unit of measurement for Visual Basic is the twip. There are 1,440 twips per inch. The twip was designed to give Visual Basic a screen resolution-independent means of placing objects, windows, and information on the screen.

The reason you need to convert to and from twips and pixels is because the Windows API uses pixels. Visual Basic helps out quite a bit by providing the Screen object, and specifically the `Screen.TwipsPerPixelY` and `Screen.TwipsPerPixelX` members. These members return the number of twips that a single horizontal or vertical pixel contains.

This information is very useful when moving or positioning items on the screen and you want to move or size them a fixed amount. For example, if you want a command button to be exactly 5 pixels high, the following code is what you use:

```
Command1.Height = 5 * Screen.TwipsPerPixelX
```

Managing windows

At one time or another, we all want to create a "topmost" window — one that cannot be obscured by other windows. These sorts of windows are often used for tips, help, or wizard interfaces, when you need to be able to show the entire contents of a window even while that window does not have focus and the user is working in another window.

When working with forms and windows in complex Visual Basic programs, you also often work with the window handle, as represented by the form's hWnd property (Form1.hWnd), instead of the complete window name (Form1). This is also how you use Windows APIs, too.

When working with Windows API calls, many standard Visual Basic methods and properties no longer work because they require an object name to work against — for example, Form1.Left to return the left position of a form, or Form1.Command1.Name to return the display name of a command button. When all you have is an hWnd, you cannot use the standard Visual Basic object properties such as Name or Left, and so on.

However, using the Windows API, you can easily replicate all (or at least as many as you need) of the methods and properties built into Visual Basic. Common window-management tasks easily accomplished using the Windows API include the following:

✦ Getting the parent of any window

✦ Determining whether a window handle is a valid window

✦ Determining whether a window is enabled

✦ Setting the enabled state of any window

✦ Determining whether a window is visible

✦ Setting the visible state of any window

✦ Determining whether a window is maximized

✦ Determining whether a window is minimized

✦ Determining whether a window is a child of another window

✦ Moving any window to the top of the z-order

✦ Making a window topmost or not topmost

Changing z-order

The z-order of any window can be changed using BringWindowToTop, whose declaration is

```
Private Declare Function BringWindowToTop Lib "user32" (ByVal _
    hwnd As Long) As Long
```

BringWindowToTop puts the window indicated via its hWnd argument at the top of the z-order. Listing 32-7 shows a simple function that moves any window on top of other windows.

Listing 32-7: A Function That Moves a Window to the Top of the Z-Order

```
Public Sub BringToTop(hwnd As Long)
    BringWindowToTop hwnd
End Sub
```

Making a window topmost

You can control all overlapped windows using the SetWindowPos API function. SetWindowPos takes a lot of arguments, but it makes sense if you read the argument names. To use SetWindowPos, pass the window handle of the window you want moved in the hWnd argument and pass the window handle of the window to position it after in the hWndInsertAfter argument. You can safely leave hWndInsertAfter set to 0; or set it to an empty long integer variable if you just want to move the window to the top.

SetWindowPos also has another more common use: to make a window topmost. The instructions below include all the constants you need for SetWindowPos, plus its API function declaration:

```
Private Const SWP_NOMOVE = 2
Private Const SWP_NOSIZE = 1
Private Const Flags = SWP_NOMOVE Or SWP_NOSIZE
Private Const HWND_TOPMOST = -1
Private Const HWND_NOTOPMOST = -2
Private Declare Function SetWindowPos Lib "user32" (ByVal _
    hwnd As Long, ByVal hWndInsertAfter As Long, ByVal x As _
    Long, ByVal y As Long, ByVal CX As Long, ByVal cy As _
    Long, ByVal wFlags As Long) As Long
```

A topmost window is one that remains completely visible even if another window has the focus. Creating a topmost window is a snap, as shown in Listing 32-8.

```
Public Sub TopMost(ByVal vNewValue As Long)
    SetWindowPos vNewValue, HWND_TOPMOST, 0, 0, 0, 0, Flags
End Sub
```

In this example, vNewValue is the window handle (hWnd) of the window to make
topmost. To make the window normal (not topmost) again, use the logic shown in
Listing 32-9.

```
Public Sub NotTopMost(ByVal vNewValue As Long)
    SetWindowPos vNewValue, HWND_NOTOPMOST, 0, 0, 0, 0, Flags
End Sub
```

Determining window state

Using a series of thoughtful Windows API calls, you can also determine the state
of any window from any process (even programs outside your own!). These API
functions' declarations are as follows:

```
Private Declare Function IsWindowValid Lib "user32" Alias _
    "IsWindow" (ByVal hwnd As Long) As Long
Private Declare Function IsWindowEnabled Lib "user32" Alias _
    "IsEnabled" (ByVal hwnd As Long) As Long
Private Declare Function IsWindowVisible Lib "user32" Alias _
    "IsVisible" (ByVal hwnd As Long) As Long
Private Declare Function IsWindowZoomed Lib "user32" Alias _
    "IsZoomed" (ByVal hwnd As Long) As Long
Private Declare Function IsWindowIconic Lib "user32" Alias _
    "IsIconic" (ByVal hwnd As Long) As Long
Private Declare Function IsWindowChild Lib "user32" Alias _
    "IsChild" (ByVal hWndParent As Long, ByVal hwnd As Long) _
    As Long
```

You can use these API functions directly, without wrappers, or you can add them to
your class module as public methods, as shown in Listing 32-10.

Listing 32-10: **Functions that Return Window State Information**

```
Public Function IsWindow(lChild As Long) As Boolean
    IsWindow = IsWindowValid(lChild)
End Function

Public Function IsVisible(lWindow As Long) As Boolean
    IsVisible = IsWindowVisible(lWindow)
End Function

Public Function IsIconic(lWindow As Long) As Boolean
    IsIconic = IsWindowIconic(lWindow)
End Function

Public Property Get IsZoomed(lWindow As Long) As Boolean
    IsZoomed = IsWindowZoomed(lWindow)
End Property
```

The functions in Listing 32-10 provide commonly required status information for windows when all you have is the hWnd of the window. IsWindow returns True (-1) if the argument passed is a valid window handle (hWnd), and False (0) otherwise. IsVisible returns True (-1) if the argument passed is a valid window handle (hWnd) and the window is visible, and False (0) otherwise. IsIconic returns True (-1) if the argument passed is a valid window handle (hWnd) and the window is minimized, and False (0) otherwise.

Putting it all together

Listing 32-11 presents a class module that encapsulates the windows-management API functions used in this chapter into an extensible object ready for use in any program.

On the CD-ROM

This code is on the CD-ROM as VB98DISP.CLS.

Listing 32-11: **Complete Listing of VB98DISP.CLS**

```
Option Explicit
DefInt A-Z

Private Declare Function BringWindowToTop Lib "user32" (ByVal _
    hwnd As Long) As Long
Private Declare Function SetWindowPos Lib "user32" (ByVal _
    hwnd As Long, ByVal hWndInsertAfter As Long, ByVal x As _
    Long, ByVal y As Long, ByVal CX As Long, ByVal cy As _
    Long, ByVal wFlags As Long) As Long
```

```vb
Private Const SWP_NOMOVE = 2
Private Const SWP_NOSIZE = 1
Private Const Flags = SWP_NOMOVE Or SWP_NOSIZE
Private Const HWND_TOPMOST = -1
Private Const HWND_NOTOPMOST = -2

Private Declare Function GetParent Lib "user32" (ByVal hwnd _
    As Long) As Long
Private Declare Function IsWindowValid Lib "user32" Alias _
    "IsWindow" (ByVal hwnd As Long) As Long
Private Declare Function IsWindowEnabled Lib "user32" Alias _
    "IsEnabled" (ByVal hwnd As Long) As Long
Private Declare Function IsWindowVisible Lib "user32" Alias _
    "IsVisible" (ByVal hwnd As Long) As Long
Private Declare Function IsWindowZoomed Lib "user32" Alias _
    "IsZoomed" (ByVal hwnd As Long) As Long
Private Declare Function IsWindowIconic Lib "user32" Alias _
    "IsIconic" (ByVal hwnd As Long) As Long
Private Declare Function IsWindowChild Lib "user32" Alias _
    "IsChild" (ByVal hWndParent As Long, ByVal hwnd As Long) _
    As Long
    Private Declare Function EnableWindow Lib "user32" _
    (ByVal hwnd As Long, ByVal fEnable As Long) As Long

Public Sub BringToTop(hwnd As Long)
    BringWindowToTop hwnd
End Sub

Public Sub TopMost(ByVal vNewValue As Long)
    SetWindowPos vNewValue, HWND_TOPMOST, 0, 0, 0, 0, Flags
End Sub

Public Sub NotTopMost(ByVal vNewValue As Long)
    SetWindowPos vNewValue, HWND_NOTOPMOST, 0, 0, 0, 0, Flags
End Sub

Public Function Parent(lChild As Long) As Long
    Parent = GetParent(lChild)
End Function

Public Function IsWindow(lChild As Long) As Boolean
    IsWindow = IsWindowValid(lChild)
End Function

Public Function IsVisible(lWindow As Long) As Boolean
    IsVisible = IsWindowVisible(lWindow)
End Function

Public Property Let Enabled(lWindow As Long, bState As Boolean)
    EnableWindow lWindow, CLng(Abs(bState))
End Property
```

(continued)

Listing 32-11 *(continued)*

```
Public Property Get Enabled(lWindow As Long) As Boolean
    Enabled = IsWindowEnabled(lWindow)
End Property

Public Function IsIconic(lWindow As Long) As Boolean
    IsIconic = IsWindowIconic(lWindow)
End Function

Public Property Get IsZoomed(lWindow As Long) As Boolean
    IsZoomed = IsWindowZoomed(lWindow)
End Property
```

Listing 32-11 contains some code not previously discussed in this chapter, including the Parent and NotTopMost procedures.

The Parent function uses the GetParent Windows API to return the owner window handle of a given window. GetParent is useful for manipulating the owner or parent of a window; for example, a form containing a command button control — if you have the hWnd of the command button control, you can use GetParent to return the hWnd of the form.

NotTopMost is a variation of the TopMost code shown earlier. In NotTopMost, we are removing a topmost window from the topmost position; that is, returning it to normal z-order placement. NotTopMost uses the SetWindowPos API with the HWND_NOTOPMOST constant.

Summary

Windows supports many display types and many resolutions. Using Windows API calls, you can determine the color depth as well as working height and width of the currently configured display.

- ✦ The Windows API you will use virtually every time you manipulate a window or image is the device context, or hDC. You acquire an hDC using the GetDC API. When acquiring an hDC using GetDC, you must remember to explicitly free the resources allocated by GetDC, with ReleaseDC.

- ✦ To make sure your program uses standard windows colors, you can use the GetSysColor API to determine the current color scheme for any windows object.

✦ When working with windows via their hWnds, use Windows API calls to return status information about the handle — IsWindowValid and the others presented in this chapter will let you determine status for most common requirements.

✦ Using the Windows API calls and techniques presented in this chapter, you can determine the video display support your application requires, and ensure that it is present. Additionally, you can manage and control windows of your own and other applications.

✦　　✦　　✦

Reliable Programming

Debugging and Error Handling

T he very word brings a painful look to most developers'
faces. The very thought connotes drudgery. *Debugging* is
an odd term that hails from the very beginning of the
computer revolution.

I am old enough to remember hearing my mother, who was a
systems analyst in the 1960s, talking about "debugging." She
implemented programs, prior to the wide-scale use of computer
languages, by physically implementing the logic using wires and
plugs. In those early days, to debug a program meant to
physically remove the carcasses of insects that had died inside
the wiring of the program. The debris created an electrical
short circuit, which in turn caused the program to fail.

Today, we use the term *debugging* to represent the activities
developers must undertake to make a program function as
designed. Developers often fear debugging as tedious and
treacherous ground. Nothing can cause a cold sweat like
hearing that your application, deployed to hundreds of users,
has a bug in it.

The purpose of this chapter is to arm you with the tools,
tips, tricks, and techniques required to face any debugging
challenge — *any* challenge. You can debug any program if you
have the correct tools and training, and in this chapter you will
get them.

Many developers face debugging in a reactionary mode; when
a bug is reported, they sweat, and then try to figure it out. You
can find many problems in this reactionary mode. However,
truly robust programs require as much forethought and plan
future maintenance and debugging as is devoted to the user
interface. Unfortunately, most organizations spend very little
time, if any, contemplating the future support implications of
their programs. Those organizations that do, know how
important a planned error-recovery system is. They
implement code reviews; they test at milestones for memory
leaks and problems with third-party components.

Organizations that do not plan for future support and maintenance are doomed to develop poor products and fear ringing telephones.

Levels of Debugging

Typically, debugging occurs on several levels. This chapter identifies at least three separate levels of debugging that occur in virtually every software program of any size, termed *level 1*, *level 2*, and *level 3 debugging*.

Level 1 debugging

The first level of debugging is the implementation of a debugging procedure and the requisite tuning to make it operate as expected.

For example, when you set out to write a function, you have in mind only the expected output of that procedure — in other words, you know what the procedure is supposed to accomplish, but you have not yet determined the optimal method of coding its functionality. As you develop the procedure, perhaps you realize it might require additional input. You then code these as arguments, providing data to the procedure and returning modified data from the procedure

Most of the time, the code you write will change as you write it — you may have an idea about how to implement a procedure, but as you try to code it, you realize another method might work better, so you change your code on-the-fly. Finally, your function performs the basic operation you intend; however, you need to test and fine-tune it to make sure the procedure as a whole performs as expected. This includes making sure that it works under many circumstances — especially when passed invalid data.

This fine-tuning and tweaking is what I call *level 1 debugging*. Most of us do it all the time, without thinking or consciously knowing that we are indeed "debugging." Rather, we think we are simply "coding" — making the program work.

The excitement of developing — the ability to create something from nothing — is why most people are developers in the first place. Little did you know that part of the excitement of developing code is debugging! You may think I am taking this a bit too far, but it's true — we all debug code whenever we write code.

The example shows how debugging evolves as you write code. For the sake of clarity, I am using a simple example. As this chapter evolves, our simple function will expand in complexity to incorporate many of the most useful techniques you will need to debug any program of any size.

The following function, `FileSize`, is a public member of a larger imaginary file-handling class, called `cFile`. The `Size` member returns the number of records in an imaginary database that uses a random file with a record size of 512. The first record is used to store field names, so `Size` determines the number of records and then subtracts 1 to arrive at the actual file size. The file handle comes from another member.

```
Public Function Size(lFilehandle As Long) As
    ' return number of records in a random file
    ' less header, assuming 512 bytes records
    Size = (LOF(lFilehandle) \ 512) - 512
End Function
```

The `Size` member seems straightforward. Your function works wonderfully during your test cases, so you call it a day, check it into source code control so that other members of your work group can access your completed code, and move on to the next part of the job.

The painful debugging occurs after the code is written, however. I call this *level 2 debugging*, and it is often perceived as less fun.

Level 2 debugging

Using the `Size` example from the preceding discussion of level 1 debugging, let's say another developer reports that your `Size` function crashes with Error 52, `Bad file name or number`. The bug is assigned to you, and you have to find and fix it. This is what I call *level 2 debugging*.

Second-level debugging is the activity required to make a functional unit of code interact according to plan with other units of code, typically before shipping or deploying your completed project. Ordinarily, you find yourself in this mode of development when your procedure does not operate properly in a test case.

In this example, you have written a procedure to return the number of records in a database. The file handle is passed to your function from another code block. Your procedure works fine until something causes the file handle passed to your procedure to be invalid. The invalid handle then causes the Visual Basic runtime error 52, and because you have not added error handling to `Size`, this error is fatal, crashing the program. Not pretty.

Level 3 debugging

Level 3 debugging is the diagnosis and repair of problems occurring in deployed applications. These bugs are often the most difficult to locate because they occur on a remote machine. They may be the result of variable or unanticipated circumstances, such as the following:

✦ User actions (keystrokes, menu choices, options settings)

✦ Program configuration (option settings, states, call stack)

✦ System configuration (operating system versions, system DLL versions, disk space, memory, drivers, and so forth)

Visual Basic Errors

Visual Basic is a great language, but it is terribly unforgiving. Any little thing that goes wrong causes Visual Basic to generate a runtime error, which, if not managed with error-handling code, will terminate your program. Microsoft made Visual Basic this way so that developers could at least know a problem occurred.

Figures 33-1 and 33-2 show how Visual Basic displays errors during runtime and design time; Figure 33-3 shows the code that generated those errors. In the case of runtime, all unhandled Visual Basic errors are fatal — terminating the program. In the Integrated Development Environment (IDE), Visual Basic enables you to end the program or drop into the debugger for isolation and repair.

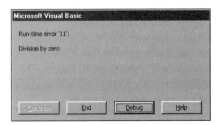

Figure 33-1: A Visual Basic error in the IDE for division by zero

Figure 33-2: A Visual Basic error in a compiled program for division by zero

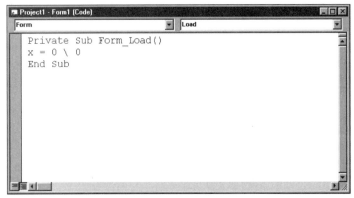

Figure 33-3: Visual Basic code that generated the errors shown in Figures 33-1 and 33-2

If you are not familiar with other languages, let me tell you how C works. A program error may or may not generate a fault in C, depending upon the severity of the error. For example, consider an array of integers. Visual Basic and C both provide for arrays of integers. In Visual Basic the array is declared using the `Dim` statement:

```
Dim myArray(1 to 10) As Integer
```

This code creates an array with 10 elements. If you attempt to access element 0 (or anything less than 1) or element 11 (or anything greater than 10), then Visual Basic generates the trappable Error 9, `Invalid array element`. This can easily occur if your array offsets are calculated in your program. You might think that Visual Basic is harsh for causing a runtime error that, if not handled, is fatal to your application — until you consider the C example.

In C, you can happily go on accessing memory locations that are *out of bounds* — that is, memory not reserved for use in the array. C generates no errors and indicates nothing to you about that fact that you have read memory from outside of the array.

In effect, it's possible to access the C equivalent of `myArray(12)` — 4 bytes away from the end of your actual array data. Worse still, it's possible with C to write to the C equivalent of `myArray(12)`, potentially overwriting valid program or data code from some other part of the application. Reading and writing memory this way results in corrupt data. Your program is not working correctly — you might even have corrupted the data of some other function, or the program may crash later on because of the now-corrupted memory.

Visual Basic implements a more restrictive approach to prevent you from hurting yourself or other programs. Visual Basic checks each and every argument before a procedure uses that argument. In the case of your array, this means checking the reference index against the bounds of the array. If you attempt to access an element outside the defined size of the array before using it, Visual Basic will generate a runtime error.

Where Bugs Occur

You will run into bugs during the entire development cycle:

✦ Design time

✦ Compile time

✦ Runtime

Design-time bugs

Errors that occur while you are in the IDE and before you compile your program are called *design-time bugs*. These are the common ones. Typically, design-time bugs are caused by misuse of some component. For example, the following code fragment shows a function that works great as long as you pass it a TextBox control; it fails if you pass any other type of control:

```
Sub SetText(ctrl As Text box, txt As String)
        ctrl.Text = LCase$(Trim$(txt)) + " : " + Date$
End Sub
```

This is not the type of error a user could cause after the product is released; you, the developer, are responsible for detecting and resolving these sorts of errors. Only by means of complete testing can you locate and eliminate this type of bug.

The next code fragment converts a string to an integer. A developer would probably always enter strings that result in numbers — however, a user may enter a formatted value or any arbitrary string. For example, if the user entered the string $1,234.00, Visual Basic would generate an error.

```
Function Str2Int(sTxt As String) as Integer
        Str2Int = Val(sTxt)
End Function
```

You, the developer, must test to locate such logical errors. Unfortunately, most developers are "too close" to their work. Generally, they make what constitutes a legal entry for each and every input field in the program. Then, during testing, they enter only good values — resulting in test cases that "work." On the other hand, the users of software may not necessarily know what is valid in all cases and may type anything into a field.

As a rule, you should always enter random data into input fields — data you know to be incorrect, just to see what happens. The time you spend doing so can greatly reduce the amount of time you spend fixing problems after you ship your software.

Compile-time bugs

Compile-time bugs are those that occur when you attempt to create your program executable or run the project. Visual Basic can locate compile-time bugs for you if you correctly set up Visual Basic. By default, Visual Basic sets several options for you (see Figure 33-4), which you can change as needed.

Note   Make sure the Background Compile and Compile On Demand options are off (cleared) to ensure that Visual Basic will find all the compile-time bugs.

Visual Basic detects compile-time bugs automatically when you compile using F5 (Start) or Ctrl+F5 (Start With Full Compile). If you do not use the Start With Full Compile options to do a full compile and you have Compile On Demand turned on, you will not find many bugs until the line of code with the bug is actually executed.

Simply running your code by pressing the Run toolbar button or pressing F5 does not guarantee that errors do not exist. Visual Basic does a full compile when it builds an executable — if you miss something, Visual Basic will notify you.

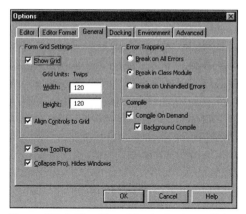

Figure 33-4: The Visual Basic Options dialog and the options for compiling

Runtime bugs

A Visual Basic *runtime error* is the exception generated by Visual Basic when it detects that your code is about to attempt to do something illegal. An illegal function could be something as simple as trying to determine the size of a file that does not exist or attempting to multiply two numbers. For example, the Visual Basic runtime Error 6, overflow, occurs whenever the result of a calculation requires more storage space than the data type can contain. An integer can have values from -32,678 to +32,767. If the results of a calculation are outside this range, Error 6 occurs, as the following code shows:

```
Dim a As Integer
a = 32768 * 32768
```

Over 500 Visual Basic runtime errors exist — hundreds more if you take into account all the custom controls, database drivers, and ActiveX extensions that Visual Basic comprises.

There is no way to turn Visual Basic's error generation off, although Visual Basic does give you several methods of working with the generation of errors. However, to create and deploy robust programs, you must plan how to handle unexpected runtime errors.

Also note that not all errors Visual Basic can generate are bad — you can also use this Visual Basic behavior to your own advantage. For example, to see if a file exists, you can check for it using Visual Basic's Open statement. If the file does not exist, you will get Error 53, as shown in Figure 33-5.

Figure 33-5: The Visual Basic error dialog box for Error 53

However, by using an *error handler*, you can prevent the error dialog box from showing and keep the program from crashing. You can also use your knowledge that Error 53 will be generated to help guide your logic. This sort of "inline" error handling is very powerful. The following code shows how to build an inline error handler that checks for the condition of Error 53 and then does something if the file is not available.

```
Dim f As String
Dim h As Integer
f = "c:\config.bak"
h = FreeFile
On Error Resume Next
Open f For Input As h
If Err.Number = 53 Then
        ' file not there
        MsgBox "Sorry, that filename is incorrect"
Else
        ' file available
End If
```

If you don't use error handling, your application will crash. So what can you do about it when something goes wrong? Well, you start by identifying what caused the error. Next, you reproduce the error and monitor the code to see the location and reason for the error.

Finally, you implement a code change to handle the occurrence so that the problem no longer occurs, or if it does occur, it is handled gracefully, either by returning an error to the caller, or some other acceptable result. You decide to implement an error handler.

Visual Basic has many internal objects, windows, methods, and properties to help you build robust programs and debug those that are less robust.

Error-handling statements and objects

Visual Basic provides a series of intrinsic statements, methods, and objects you can use to handle errors. These include

✦ Err object

✦ Erl

✦ Error$

✦ On Error

✦ On Error Resume Next

✦ Resume

Using these language extensions enables you to control errors in your programs. Note that these commands won't let you write code that doesn't generate runtime errors — they simply enable you to write code that recovers from runtime errors without crashing your program!

Err object

The Err object maintains information about the last error that occurred. It also enables you to generate your own error conditions, in order to test your error handler without actually having to write erroneous code. When an error is generated, Visual Basic populates the Err object. Each error has an associated number and a description. You use the error number to determine the type of error, and handle it based on your application requirements. Err object methods and properties include

✦ Clear

✦ Description

✦ HelpContext

✦ HelpFile

✦ LastDLLError

✦ Number

✦ Raise

✦ Source

Clear

The Clear statement resets the Err object to its default (empty) state. This is handy when you have handled an error and want to reset your Err object so that other procedures don't mistakenly think an error has occurred when they query the Err.Number property. It is easy to get confused as to the exact location of an error because the Err object is persistent. In the following example, Foo generates an error; however, due to the On Error Resume Next statement, you cannot tell if the error comes from Foo or from the rest of the code:

```
On Error Resume Next
Dim X As Double
Foo() X
X = X + 1.1
If Err.Number <> 0 Then
```

```
            ' an error happened
       End If
```

In this example, you don't know whether the error occurred in procedure Foo as a result of code in the procedure itself. Therefore, in Foo, you handle all errors that Foo may generate, and then clear the Err object before exiting. Note, in some cases, the handling of the error may consist of raising the error to the caller. For example, when using ActiveX UserControls or classes, the error may be trapped in a UserControl public property and then raised to the container of the UserControl for handling.

The following example shows how to trap an error in a procedure, handle known or expected local problems locally, and raise any unexpected error back to the caller of Foo.

```
Sub Foo (X As Double)
        On Error Goto MyError
        If X > 10 Then Error vbObjectError + 512
        X = X * .345
myExit:
        Err.Clear 'clear any error info
        Exit Sub
myError:
        Select Case Err.Number
        ' known or expected error
        Case vbObjectError + 512
        ' my own error, so make X = 10
        X = 10
        Resume ' go to next line
        Case Else
        ' unplanned errors so raise with vbObjectError
        Err.Raise vbObjectError + Err.Number
        End Select
End Sub
```

In this way, you can handle the errors you need to, propagate errors to other procedures, and pass on errors coming from other procedures that your procedure called. Note that using Err.Raise as shown in this example caused the procedure to exit at that point. The Err.Clear never executes, as it must if you are to be able to access the Err object in the calling function.

Description

The Description property returns a text message that often provides help in understanding an error. You can use Description with the MsgBox instruction to notify the user of the cause of an error. Description returns the same information as the Error$ keyword. The major difference is that Error$ is read-only, whereas you can create and assign your own help or descriptive text to the Description property.

HelpContext

The HelpContext property returns a value indicating the help context number in an optional help file (indicated by the HelpFile property). A *help context number* is the pointer into a Windows help file that indicates a specific topic to display. Using this help context value, you can then offer F1 help to the user. When you raise an error, you can also set this value to point to your own help file. This is most often done for components such as controls.

HelpFile

The HelpFile property returns a value indicating the help file referenced by the optional HelpContext property. When you raise an error, you may also set this value to point to your own help file. This is most often done for components such as controls.

LastDLLError

The LastDLLError property returns a system error code produced by a dynamic link library. When a DLL that you use causes an error, it will be returned to you through this member of the Err object. If a DLL call fails, check here first to see if you have an error code to work with. This is important because Visual Basic uses many system and runtime DLLs and internal Windows API calls as it operates.

Number

The Number property returns a value indicating a numeric value representing the Visual Basic error code.

Raise

The Raise method lets you create a Visual Basic runtime error. You can also create a runtime error using the Error statement. Most of us don't have time to willingly create erroneous code in our programs. However, in a number of situations you should generate errors — especially if you are creating components or classes that you or others will use. As mentioned previously, when you work with UserControls and classes, raising an error to the host container or caller is the recommended method of reporting errors.

The way Visual Basic indicates the failure of a running instruction is to generate a runtime error. It's okay for your components to raise errors, and in fact that is the expected method of reporting errors from UserControls and classes. If you choose to implement this sort of error handling, be consistent about how your code generates these errors, and document the potential errors and their conditions for the users of your software. For example, if your UserControl raises error vbObjectError + 512 to its host, you should provide a description of the conditions under which this error occurs and how to resolve it.

The Raise method creates an error that can be passed from an OLE component to the container of the component. This is what enables your custom control to generate a runtime error in a Visual Basic program that uses your control. An error that is raised to the host does not terminate the process that raised the error. If your component raises an error, the component continues to execute.

The `Error` statement, on the other hand, synthesizes an error to invoke the Visual Basic error handler that is currently active or, if no error handler is active, the default Visual Basic error handler that terminates the program. The `Error` statement only synthesizes a runtime error in the program that uses it. In other words, using `Error` will only synthesize an error in the current program; it does not generate or raise an error to the host. If you use the `Error` statement to synthesize an error in your component, then your entire component will fail and terminate. This does cause an error in the host, but it does not create a recoverable error that can be managed — not a good thing.

That's why the `Raise` method is available — which is not to say times won't occur when you want to generate an error inside your own class or component that throws an execution back to its caller. For example, consider a nested series of function calls within your component. The key here is that these calls are all within your component.

```
Sub Foo()
    On Error Goto myError
    Foo1
    Exit Sub
    myError:
        'error happened somewhere in Foo1 or Foo2
End sub

Sub Foo1()
    Call Foo2
End Sub

Sub Foo2()
    Error 5
End Sub
```

This example shows three functions: `Foo`, `Foo1`, and `Foo2`. `Foo` calls `Foo1`, which in turn calls `Foo2`. `Foo2` generates an error, and because it has no Visual Basic `On Error` statement, Visual Basic searches its caller (`Foo1`) for an active error handler. `Foo1` has no error handler, so Visual Basic moves up to `Foo`. `Foo` has an error handler, and the error is handled in `Foo`. It is important to note that this use of `Error` is perfectly legitimate, even in a component or class.

However, to generate a trappable error in the component's host, use `Raise`. You create your own errors in an OLE component to allow someone else to handle an error. This is required when writing components with public methods and properties; the host needs to know if the user is using them properly. A component should never pop up message boxes; you should always raise the error to the host.

When you use `Raise` without specifying arguments, any current values in the `Err` object serve as the values for your error. You should therefore invoke the `Clear` method for `Err` before raising your own error. You can specify the exact source module or class that generated the error using the `Source` property of `Err`, and you can specify a link to your help file by using that object's `HelpFile` and `HelpContext` properties.

Always start your errors using 513 as the first error (it's beyond the internal Visual Basic error assignments), and always use the `vbObjectError` constant to define your component errors as coming from a component. For example, Listing 33-1 raises an error to its host unless the error is already been raised.

Listing 33-1 Forwarding a Class-Generated, Programmer-Defined Error to the Code That Invoked That Class

```
Public Sub Foo()
    On Error GoTo myError

    ' your code goes here

    Exit Sub
' error handler that passes on raised errors or raises
' an error if not already raised by another
' procedure.
myError:
    On Error GoTo 0 ' no going back...
    Select Case Err.Number
    Case vbObjectError To vbObjectError + 65536
        ' errors from others in this component, so pass it on
        Err.Raise Err.Number
    Case Else
        ' unknown/unplanned errors so raise with vbObjectError
        Err.Raise vbObjectError + Err.Number
    End Select
End Sub
```

The code can figure out what caused the error by examining the `Number` property of the `Err` object, and determining if the object has been raised using `vbObjectError`. If another procedure generated an error using `vbObjectError` plus an error code, then all the `Foo` procedure must do is pass it on.

The window of possible values for a raised error is from `vbObjectError` to `vbObjectError + 65536`. If the error number is within this window, then the code in Listing 33-1 passes it on without adding it to `vbObjectError`. However, if this is a new error, the code uses `vbObjectError` so that other routines can use the same logic. This way you can propagate errors across many objects, classes, and procedures without losing the error information. Of course, it goes without saying that you must have consistently implemented similar logic wherever needed. Note that in the Visual Basic IDE, you can allow or disallow Visual Basic to raise errors using the General settings dialog box, which is available from the Tools menu.

Source

The Source property is the name of the project that caused the error. If the error is in a class module, Source contains a name in the form of *project.class*. To get detailed source information from one of your forms or modules, you will have to write your own handler or get a third-party tool to do it for you.

Erl

Line numbers are numeric values that precede the line of code. If you have added line numbers in your code, the Erl internal variable will be set to the line number where the error occurred. When it comes to pinpointing hard-to-locate bugs, nothing is more accurate than an error handler that provides the offending line's number.

On Error

The On Error statement directs program execution to the label (or line number) indicated. When you direct program flow this way, you are implementing error handling.

On Error instructs Visual Basic to take some action when Visual Basic generates a trappable runtime error. Note the use of the word *trappable*. Not all errors that a Windows program can create may be recovered; the "blue screen of death" (a system crash) is an example of an error from which a Visual Basic project cannot recover.

However, virtually any VB-generated error is trappable. This includes most errors generated from third-party controls and DLLs. To use On Error, you need to define where program execution should resume when an error occurs. That's how On Error works. You define this location using a label or line number. A *label* is a VB string that terminates with a colon. For example, in the following code, MyError is a label:

```
Public Function Size(lFilehandle As Long) As
    On Error Goto MyError
    Size = LOF(lFilehandle)
MyError:
End Function
```

You can also specify that Visual Basic resume execution at a line number. The following code uses line numbers:

```
Public Function Size(lFilehandle As Long) As

10  On Error Goto MyError

    ' return number of records in a random file
```

```
       ' less header, assuming 512 bytes records
20  Size = (LOF(lFilehandle) \ 512) - 512

myExit:
30  Exit Sub

MyError:
40  MsgBox "Size Function Failed"
60  Resume MyExit

End Function
```

Using line numbers is completely optional; many developers do not care for them. However, if you use line numbers, Visual Basic will indicate the actual line of code where the error occurred. This is quite valuable when you consider what Visual Basic gives you when your *compiled* program crashes. All Visual Basic tells you is that an error — for example, Error 5, `Invalid procedure call or argument`. It does not tell you where the error happened, what the user was doing, or the event trail that led to the error — all the things you really want to know in order to resolve the problem.

If your program is running in the IDE, you receive more information: Visual Basic stops (in most, but not all cases) on the line of code generating the error. Then, using VB's built-in debugging tools, you can view argument values, procedure stack, and other relevant information about the crash.

The following code example shows how to use `On Error` to direct program flow to an error handler:

```
Public Function Size(lFilehandle As Long) As

    On Error Goto MyError

    ' return number of records in a random file
    ' less header, assuming 512 bytes records
    Size = (LOF(lFilehandle) \ 512) - 512

myExit:
    Exit Sub

MyError:
    MsgBox "Size Function Failed"
    Resume MyExit

End Function
```

This simple example directs program execution to the line following the label `myError` if an error occurs.

Note   You need to use the `Exit Function` statement to make sure your code execution does not flow into the error handler if no error occurs.

On Error Resume Next

`On Error Resume Next` tells Visual Basic to ignore any errors that occur. The following sample function, `InLine`, generates an error if the filename contained in the argument to `FileLen` is not found. When using `On Error Resume Next`, the line of code generating an error does not complete execution; instead, further execution of the line of code is aborted, and execution resumes with the line following the offending line of code.

```
Function InLine(sFile As String) As Boolean
    Dim FileSize As Long
    On Error Resume Next
    FileSize = FileLen(sFile)
    If Err.Number <> 0 Then
        ' something bad happended!
        ' deal with it
    End If
End Function
```

Visual Basic follows a stringent set of rules for deciding how to handle the runtime errors your code generates. These rules involve the concept of a *call stack*. VB is an event-driven language — vents such as the loading of a form, the clicking of a mouse, or the expiration of a timer's trigger-code execution. `Function` and `Sub` procedures can call one another, resulting in a complex chain of execution. For example, a `Form_Load` event procedure might call another procedure that loads a database, which in turn triggers an event that in turn loads data into a text box, which in turn triggers the text box's `Change` event:

```
Form_Load
    Data1_Resize
        Textbox_Change
```

If we could freeze the program at the point where the text box `Change` event occurs, three separate procedures would be in various states of execution. You can view such a call stack by using the menu or toolbar, or using Ctrl+L (see Figure 33-6). Often your application will cause an error when a particular sequence of events occurs. If you are running in the IDE, the call stack can tell you how you got to where you are.

Figure 33-6: The Visual Basic call stack

If an error were to occur in the text box's Change event, Visual Basic first looks in that procedure for an On Error statement indicating what to do. If the procedure that generated the error does not have an active error handler, Visual Basic moves up the stack to the caller of the procedure. Figure 33-6, that caller is the Data1_Resize procedure. Again, Visual Basic would look for an active error handler in Data1_Resize; failing to find one, Visual Basic would go back up the stack. Visual Basic continues searching for an active error handler until it runs into one of two walls: a process boundary or an active error handler.

Visual Basic generates runtime errors as an indication of problems in the application. If your component does not implement error handling, any error caused by that component will result in its termination and disabling by Visual Basic for this instance of the host. This means the component and whatever functions it provides are no longer available until the next time the host application starts and initializes the component.

Visual Basic Debugging Tools

The best way to keep bugs out is to prevent them in the first place. Visual Basic gives a programmer several tools, including IDE options and compile directives, to help achieve this goal.

IDE options

Visual Basic offers several IDE options that can help you write better code

- ✦ Auto Syntax Check
- ✦ Require Variable Declaration
- ✦ Auto List Members
- ✦ Auto Quick Info
- ✦ Auto Data Tips
- ✦ Option Explicit
- ✦ Option Compare Text

You can view additional settings and debugging aids from the dialog box shown in Figure 33-7 by using the following steps:

1. Choose the Tools menu.
2. Choose Options.
3. Choose the Editor tab.

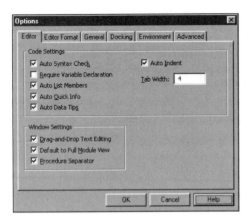

Figure 33-7: The Visual Basic Options dialog with settings for additional debugging and development aids

Require Variable Declaration

The Require Variable Declaration option automatically inserts the `Option Explicit` statement in each new form, module, or class that you create. This statement requires that you explicitly declare all variables for the code that is to use them. You will need to use a `Dim`, `Private`, `Public`, `ReDim`, or `Static` statement to declare a variable before you assign a value to it. If you attempt to use an undeclared variable, an error occurs at compile time.

One of the most significant causes of program errors in Visual Basic is mistyped variable names, as demonstrated in the following example:

```
Function IsEven( iNum As Long) as Boolean
    Dim bTest as Boolean
    bTest = iNum Mod 0
    IsEven = bTst  = 0
End Function
```

Notice the variable mistyped as `bTst`. With no `Option Explicit` in place, this code seems to compile and run fine — except you always get `True` (-1) returned from the function, whether or not the number is even. This is because `bTst = 0` will always return `True` (-1). With `Option Explicit` provided by the Require Variable Declaration option, you get a compile-time error when you attempt to build your project — because the mistyped variable, `bTst`, has not been declared yet.

Figure 33-8 shows the dialog Visual Basic displays if you attempt to use a variable that has not been declared and you have enabled Require Variable Declaration.

Figure 33-8: Using the Require Variable Declaration option generates an error when a variable is mistyped.

Auto Syntax Check

The Auto Syntax Check option forces Visual Basic to check the line of code when you move your cursor off the line. After a while you might find this option annoying, but it can ensure that you are using the proper syntax for VB instructions. For instance, VB generates an error dialog if the cursor is on the middle line and you attempt to move it off that line by pressing Enter or one of the arrow keys consider thsi code:

```
Private Sub Form_Load()
    Open "config.sys" For Input
End Sub
```

Figure 33-9 shows the dialog generated by the Auto syntax option. Visual Basic is telling you that the correct usage of the Open statement requires the use of As.

Figure 33-9: Using the Auto syntax feature generates an error when a method is not declared properly.

Auto List Members

The Auto List Members option instructs Visual Basic to display a list of object members as soon as you type a period after an object name. This enables you to choose which member you want and keeps you from incorrectly choosing or typing a name that is not a member method or property. With the list active, VB locates the closest match and highlights that term as you type. Pressing the Tab key then completes the method name.

Auto Quick Info

The Auto Quick Info option has Visual Basic display any required or optional parameters for methods. VB displays all possible parameters while highlighting the one you're currently entering. Auto Quick Info makes it easier to use methods and properties because you no longer have to remember or look up all the arguments these properties and methods might take.

Stepping

Visual Basic provides several built-in methods for controlling the execution of your program in real time. You can execute your program line-by-line or procedure-by-procedure or a combination of the two. These basic debugging actions are called *stepping*. Because it enables you to walk through your program, examining the variables and logic, stepping is probably the most powerful debugging tool Visual Basic offers. Figure 33-10 shows the Debug menu in the VB IDE during an application's runtime.

Figure 33-10: The Visual Basic Debug menu during debugging of a running project

Step Into

The menu command Debug ➪ Step Into moves program execution to the procedure called by the method or property your cursor is currently on. You can access this option from the Debug menu or by pressing the F8 key. This enables you to see every line of code as it's being executed. You might think you can see this without using the Step command; however, it is often difficult to predict program flow due to the changing values of arguments that often direct program flow. Using the Step commands enables you to "walk" through your code line-by-line, seeing which lines are executed and which are skipped.

Step Over

Step Over moves program execution over the procedure and to the next line of code in the current routine. The procedure you step over does execute, but Visual Basic does not walk through the "stepped over" procedure line-by-line. The procedure represented by its name is executed in full, and then execution halts at the first instruction outside that routine. For example, in the following Foo code example, using Step Over would single-step by executing lines 10, 20, and 30, without actually stepping into the code that Foo1 contains:

```
Public Sub Foo()
    10 X = X + 1
    20 Foo1 X
    30 X = X - 1
End Sub
```

Step Out

Step Out moves program execution back to the calling procedure. This is the functional equivalent of Exit Sub or Exit Function — it simply exits the current procedure without executing any more code in that procedure.

Run To Cursor

Run To Cursor tells Visual Basic to execute all the code between the current execution point and the cursor. Visual Basic provides several optional visual cues as to the location of the execution point. By default Visual Basic displays a yellow arrow in the left margin of a code window, pointing to the active line of code. The entire line of code that is about to execute is also highlighted in yellow. Note that you can change this behavior using the Options dialog available from the Tools menu. This command can be accessed from the toolbar or by using the Ctrl+F8 key combination.

Set Next Statement

Set Next Statement enables you to move program execution to any executable line of code in the current procedure — handy for making changes and then re-executing code blocks until you either understand what the code is really doing or have the code block doing what you want.

Breakpoints

When debugging, you may often want to stop execution at a certain line of code — this is called *breaking*. The point at which you tell Visual Basic to stop is called a *breakpoint*. Visual Basic offers two types of breakpoints — a programmatic breakpoint using the Stop statement, and a nonpersistent breakpoint set using the F9 key. Figure 33-11 shows what happens when you use an F9 breakpoint.

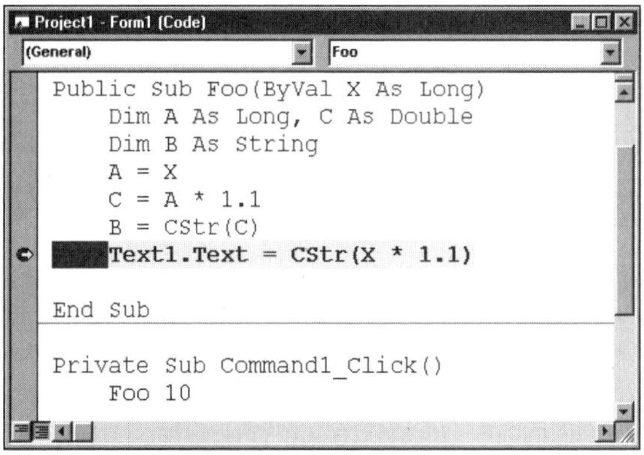

Figure 33-11: A breakpoint in action

Breakpoints are useful when you want to run through all sections of code up to a certain point so you can see what is happening. Due to the event-driven nature of Visual Basic, you often need to be able to run through hundreds or thousands of lines of code and then stop on a certain line. Setting a breakpoint is the way to accomplish this. To set a breakpoint, simply position the mouse cursor over the line of code on which you want execution to stop, and then press F9. You can toggle (add or remove) a breakpoint in two other ways: using the Debug ➪ Toggle Breakpoint option or clicking the right mouse button in the left margin of the code window.

When you use a breakpoint, VB stops program execution but does not terminate the program. When the program is paused, you can then examine variables and data structures to locate the cause of the faulty logic. The Locals window is used with breakpoints for just this purpose.

Stop statement

You may also want to pause execution of the program without using a breakpoint
set using F9. You can use the Stop statement to stop program execution without
terminating the program. You may then continue stepping from the Stop statement.
The following code demonstrates the use of Stop in a conditional If statement:

```
If Err.Number <> 0 then
    ' stop here, then use stepping and variable
    ' watching to see why this happened
    Stop
End If
```

Stop breaks execution in the Visual Basic IDE. Using Stop in a compiled program
terminates the program.

Caution   Using Stop is strictly a development technique; do not leave Stop statements in
your deployed code.

Def statement

Visual Basic has the capability to default any newly created variables, property
results, procedure arguments, and function return types to a given data type. By
default Visual Basic assigns any nontyped variable, argument, property, and so on
to the variant data type. The variant is the largest and slowest data type Visual
Basic offers. Because Visual Basic also attempts automatic translation of the data
stored in a variant as you use the variable, unexpected conversion can occur. For
example, a double-precision integer can lose decimal places when assigned to a
single-precision integer. This mishap is referred to as *evil type cohesion*.

To prevent this use of variant data types and cause all undeclared variables to
default to another data type, Visual Basic gives us the Def statement. Def lets you
define the default data type. You enter the Def statement in the Declarations
section of a module, form, class, or other Visual Basic code window. There are
several Def statements — one for each data type. Using Def, you define the range
of variable names that will use a particular type. For example, the following
statement tells Visual Basic to default any variable, argument function, or property
result to Integer if the variable starts with A through Z.

```
Option Explicit
DefInt A-Z
```

The Def statements include

- ✦ DefBool — default to Boolean
- ✦ DefByte — default to Byte
- ✦ DefInt — default to Integer (16-bit)

✦ DefLng — **default to** Long Integer (32-bit)

✦ DefCur — **default to** Currency

✦ DefSng — **default to** Single **Precision Float**

✦ DefDbl — **default to** Double **Precision Float**

✦ DefDec — **default to** Decimal

✦ DefDate — **default to** Date

✦ DefStr — **default to** String

✦ DefObj — **default to** Object

✦ DefVar — **default to** Variant

You can also use Def to implement automatic typing for your variable notations by using multiple Def statements as follows:

```
Option Explicit
DefInt I ' if starts with I then it's an integer
DefStr S ' if starts with S then it's a string

Private Sub Form_Load()

    Dim iCounter, sName
    Show
    sName = "hank"
    Print iCounter + 1, sName

End Sub
```

Locals window

The Locals window enables you to see the value of every variable, and each member of all objects that are currently in scope. You can view the Locals window, shown in Figure 33-12, by choosing Locals from the View menu. Figure 33-12 shows the Locals window and its contents for a procedure named Foo.

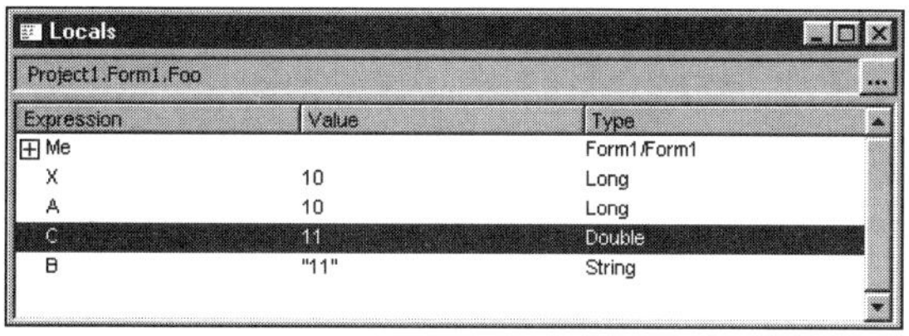

Figure 33-12: The Locals window displays all the variables and their values in a procedure.

Immediate window

You may also need to modify a variable based on the results of your debugging. For example, you might want to force a case to be executed, requiring you to manually change a variable's contents. The Immediate window makes this a snap. This window, shown in Figure 33-13, is a great place for you to modify data or to test functions during development. You can enter any valid expression in the Immediate window, and VB will execute it. If you reference an object outside of the scope of the current code execution, VB will generate an error. However, simple math and other basic VB functions are always available from the Immediate window, even if the program is not loaded or not running.

> **Tip** The Immediate window does not support extended lines using the _ character; nor can you create code blocks that span multiple lines. To enter a complex command that normally requires multiple lines (such as a ForNext loop), use the colon statement separator instead. Using a colon after a statement causes Visual Basic to treat it as another line, even though all the code is on the same physical line.

Figure 33-13: The Immediate window

Debug object

You can also use the Immediate window programmatically to output messages or state variables as your program runs, by referring to it as the Debug object. This object is a great tool for getting information out of your program while you are debugging. There is no penalty for using Debug at design time, because Visual Basic removes the Debug object code when compiling. The object has just two methods: Print and Assert.

Print

The Print method prints the result of any legal expression to the Immediate window. Using this method, you can display data in the Immediate window while your application runs — very handy for debugging Select Case statements. Select Case statements often have many branches and execution possibilities, using Debug.Print you can see which conditions are executing.

You can also use the Print method for *tracing*. Tracing provides a method for physically monitoring the entrance and exit of a procedure.

```
Public Sub Foo( X As Integer)
```

```
        Debug.Print "Foo: X = " & X ' print value of X and let _
            me know we are in Foo
End Sub
```

The `Print` method of the `Debug` object is one of the most useful of all the built-in debugging aids that Visual Basic offers to developers.

Debug.Assert

The `Assert` method takes an expression that returns a Boolean `True` or `False` value and then stops execution if the expression is `False`. The `Assert` method works only in the development environment, but it is very useful. The method takes a little getting used to because you need to think in opposites: It pauses execution only if the expression you pass evaluates to `False` (0). For example, if you want to trap for the case of a variable X less than 0, the following logic is required:

```
Private Sub Form_Load()
    Dim x As Integer
    x = -1
    Debug.Assert Not (x < 0)
End Sub
```

To create a `False` (0) value for `Assert`, use the `Not` operator to invert the truth of the expression to trap for a value of X less than 0. If you choose, you can also invert the expression, `Debug.Assert x >= 0`. It's counterintuitive but manageable.

Watches

At times you might want to monitor the value of a variable for a certain state — for example, to determine whether a flag is set to `True`. You might want program execution to pause on the instruction that sets a certain date. You can use the Watch window for such purposes.

The Watch window is more flexible than the Locals window; you can set a watch expression that causes Visual Basic to break when a variable changes values or when an expression's value is `True`.

To set a watch, use the Debug Add Watch menu dialog shown in Figure 33-14, and enter the expression. The expression may be a simple variable to monitor, or it might be a complex expression.

Figure 33-14: The Add Watch dialog

After setting up the watch, you can view the Watch window, shown in Figure 33-15, where the current values of the expressions or variables you entered are displayed in real time.

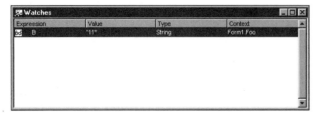

Figure 33-15: The Watch window

You can add, edit, or delete watches at any time during the execution of your program. Select the Watch window option from the View menu if the window is not visible. Visual Basic automatically shows the window at design time when the watch is created, but removes it at runtime if it has not been selected.

Advanced Debugging

This section is provided as a sort of handbook for helping you understand what may be going wrong in your program, and how to resolve it.

Visual Basic has transformed Windows development through the expandable architecture of ActiveX. You can literally use Visual Basic as the glue to create powerful applications in record time. You can even create your own components.

This power comes by masking off Windows's internal details. Using debugging tools such as NuMega SmartCheck, you can watch even the simplest Visual Basic programs generate hundreds and thousands of API calls and memory allocations. It's truly amazing to see how a "simple" Form_Load event generates thousands of low-level system and API calls. The good news is that you don't have to worry about them most of the time!

A methodology for resolving recurrent issues

When you hit a wall at any level of development, try this step-by-step approach for resolving it:

1. Use the Visual Basic IDE to run your program. Visual Basic will usually stop on the instruction generating the error.

2. Try using Visual Basic's built-in help system to search for help on the keywords you are using, and read all the information displayed. Check all the notes and

See Also keywords, as well. Make sure you view the example if one is presented, because the example or its comments often contain valuable information.

3. Pay particular attention to any Readme or extra help sources indicated. Problems are often found and then documented this way.

4. Reduce the complexity of the line of code. It's easy to write sloppy, hard-to-understand code in Visual Basic. When an error occurs, simplify the failing line. Break it into several smaller lines if possible. For example, a line of code with four or five Visual Basic keywords can often be coded instead as several smaller and less complex lines of code. This helps narrow down the keywords to the one that is causing the problem; then go back to Step 2.

5. If you can narrow down your problem to a single keyword or two, then go to the Microsoft Knowledge Base (`http://support.microsoft.com/support`), and do a keyword search. If the problem is known, you will probably find a solution to it.

6. If you cannot find a solution at Microsoft, try checking DejaNews at `http://www.dejanews.com`. DejaNews has a newsgroup search engine that you can use to perform a quick keyword search across a vast amount of indexed messages from other developers. With any luck, one of them has already asked your question, and it has been answered.

7. If all else fails, you can try some newsgroups (`comp.lang.basic.visual.*`), or forums such as those on CompuServe (GO MSBASIC, GO VBPJ), or several good Web sites. Carl & Gary's (`http://www.apexsc.com/vb`) has an excellent listing of related Web sites.

8. If you are still having problems, you can call Microsoft support. They have an awesome database of problems and solutions. From personal experience, I can tell you that you will most likely get an answer that solves your problem if your problem is a bug, anomaly, or known issue. (Note, however, that this option might cost you money.)

9. Of course, you can always purchase tools to locate and describe these bugs automatically for you.

Visual Basic is quite complex; often problems stem from a lack of understanding of how Visual Basic works. Your handling of problems is a function of your experience. Three classes of self-inflicted problems face Visual Basic developers:

✦ **Syntax misuse errors** are the problems you face in using the language, whether they are from misuse of syntax or unexpected results from proper syntax usage. For example, the Visual Basic `Kill` keyword will fail if the file passed as an argument is opened by another process — even when the call is used properly.

✦ **Visual Basic IDE errors** are more complex situations in which it's not the use of the language elements themselves causing the problem, but rather the interaction of Windows and Visual Basicenvironment with your choice of code.

✦ **Operating-system errors** are severe problems — often counterintuitive, not obvious, and possibly resulting from many sources. These problems are often quite tough and take a long time to unravel, understand, and repair.

Syntax misuse errors

When you start programming in Visual Basic, the first thing you notice is the sheer number of keywords, properties, methods, and extensions that make up the language. Even simple VB keywords can do unexpected things.

For example, the Asc() function returns the ASCII code representing the first character in a string. Asc() seems safe enough, but it will generate an error if the string used as an argument is empty (" ").

In complex programs with lots of string parsing or processing, it is easy and common to have crashes. For example, consider the following code:

```
Dim sEmpty As String
Dim iAscii As Integer
sEmpty = "Hello"
iAscii = Asc(sEmpty$)     'sets iAscii to 72, ASCII value of H

sEmpty = ""
iAscii = Asc(sEmpty$)     'Illegal function call
```

Always test to confirm that the string argument passed to Asc is not empty before you use Asc. One possible approach: You could write your own function to replace Asc that would test for the length of the string before calling Asc.

To implement this fix, make a new function called ASCsafe, and use it instead of Asc. The following function returns the ASCII value of a string, as does Asc; unlike Asc, however, it returns 0 for an empty string. It uses Len to test the string's size instead of testing the string for contents, because Len is much faster than accessing the string's contents.

```
' function to return ASC of a string, or 0 if string is
' empty
Function AsciiSafe (sInput As String) As Integer
    If Len(sInput) > 0 Then AsciiSafe = Asc(sInput)
End Function
```

Visual Basic IDE errors

Some errors arise as the result of your use of language keywords and their interaction with the Visual Basic environment, Windows, or both. These are generally tougher to figure out, but Visual Basic's IDE helps you somewhat by generating runtime errors.

A common example problem is how Visual Basic replaces missing controls with picture boxes. If a Visual Basic project uses a custom control (OCX) whose CLSID has changed since the project was last opened, Visual Basic will not be able to display the object. So once the project is opened, all occurrences of the custom control will have been replaced with PictureBox controls. This is quite disheartening but is actually good for you, because this way Visual Basic keeps all the code under the missing controls' event procedures. A CLSID of a custom control changes when any of the following conditions true:

✦ The custom control project's Version Compatibility setting is set to No Compatibility. When No Compatibility is set, a new CLSID is generated for a custom control every time it is compiled.

✦ The custom control project's Version Compatibility setting is set to Project Compatibility or Binary Compatibility, and the control's interface has been modified in such a way that compatibility could not be maintained. This will occur primarily when a property or method definition has changed.

✦ A control is overwritten, and the newer version has a different CLSID.

Operating-system errors

Operating-system errors are the not-so-obvious, counterintuitive problems resulting from many sources. These are often "killer" problems, which take a long time to unravel, understand, and repair. These problems often appear outside of the Visual Basic IDE, making it very hard, if not impossible, to track down what is going on. A great number of these problems are OLE server-, ActiveX-, or control-related. These problems become evident after you create the software and begin testing it outside of Visual Basic.

For example, one of the first things I wanted to do when I got Visual Basic was to create some controls that I could use in other ActiveX hosts beyond Visual Basic itself — for example, Visual Basic 4.0 32-bit and others. Apparently I was not the only person who found out that not all properties would appear in certain ActiveX host property browsers. Here's why.

A public property of an ActiveX control (OCX) created in Visual Basic might not appear in the Properties window when the control is used in certain ActiveX host design environments. This is because, by default, a `Public Property Let` procedure passes its arguments by reference and not by value. When these arguments are passed by reference from an ActiveX control, the property will not be visible in some hosts' Properties windows. To resolve this problem, be sure that all arguments passed by a `Public Property Let` procedure are passed by value. For example, if you have the following property procedure definition:

```
Public Property Let MyProperty(newValue As Boolean)
```

it should be changed to

```
Public Property Let MyProperty(ByVal newValue As Boolean)
```

in order to work correctly. Without the `ByVal` keyword, custom properties just won't appear in the Properties window.

Third-party tools

When all else fails, you can resort to tools that are specifically designed to help you locate and resolve problems in your programs. On the CD that accompanies this book are evaluation copies of NuMega SmartCheck, FailSafe, CodeReview, and TrueTime.

SmartCheck

SmartCheck is the first runtime debugging tool for Visual Basic that provides clear, detailed analysis of program errors. It automatically detects and diagnoses VB runtime errors and translates vague error messages into exact problem descriptions. Its EventDebugging feature provides developers with an easy way to solve the toughest problems.

SmartCheck is one of a trio of NuMega SmartDebugging tools for Visual Basic. At runtime, Visual Basic developers need a debugger that not only traps and finds errors, but also explains why errors occurred and how to fix them. SmartCheck helps VB developers quickly find and solve software problems so that enterprise applications and components can be deployed on time and free of defects. The key features of SmartCheck are discussed in the following sections.

Fatal error analysis

For fatal runtime errors, Visual Basic shows only the error number, error category, and an OK button. The program terminates prematurely with a cryptic error message. Without detailed information, these errors are very hard to diagnose and correct. For example, there are more than 10 reasons why a program could fail and display the message `Error 429—ActiveX component can't create object.` VB leaves the developer with the difficult and time-consuming task of problem diagnosis.

SmartCheck quickly decodes Visual Basic runtime errors and tells you what happened and what to do about it. SmartCheck automates the process of fatal runtime error location and diagnosis. For example, SmartCheck might say `Error 429 - Component creation failure - key 'server.class' was not found in the registry` instead of `Error 429 - ActiveX component can't create object.` This extra information is the key to resolving the problem.

ActiveX control checking

Visual Basic developers use ActiveX components referred to as *custom controls* (OCXs) to provide functions that VB cannot. The VB developer does not write most of these controls and often does not have source code for them, yet they are critical to the ultimate application. Developers need to ensure correct usage of controls within their applications and must be able to locate problems within the controls. SmartCheck pinpoints controls that are leaking or corrupting memory.

With SmartCheck ActiveX control checking, VB developers can develop and use ActiveX controls with confidence. For example, SmartCheck will spot a control written in C/C++ that leaks memory or resources. If source code to the control is available, SmartCheck will pinpoint these problems and point the debugger right to the source line.

Windows API checking

Visual Basic developers often need to use Windows API calls to perform functions that VB can't handle directly. Because API calls are built and documented for C/C++ developers, the VB programmer may pass parameters incorrectly or fail to check return codes. When the API fails, there is no indication of the problem. Developers must ensure correct usage of Windows APIs within their applications and must be able to locate API problems. SmartCheck finds and highlights incorrect usage or the failure of Windows API calls.

With SmartCheck Windows API Checking, VB developers can use the latest API functions with complete confidence. For example, SmartCheck will spot failed API calls in any module, form, class, or control — even those written in other languages such as C/C++. If source code for the control is available, SmartCheck will pinpoint these problems down to the line number.

Visual Basic argument checking

Just as developers must check Windows API calls, they must ensure correct usage of Visual Basic functions. Cryptic error messages such as Error 5, `Invalid procedure call or argument` make it difficult to locate and fix VB function argument errors. This problem is compounded by the fact that the error may be generated on a complex line of VB code with many VB keywords in use, leaving the developer to locate the invalid argument from many VB functions called on the same line.

SmartCheck identifies invalid arguments used with Visual Basic keywords such as `Left$` or `Mid$` that often result in VB runtime errors. With SmartCheck argument checking, VB developers can easily locate and fix problems involving VB functions.

EventDebugging

Not all problems in Visual Basic are runtime or system errors. Many common problems result from unexpected program flow. Without EventDebugging, isolating problems can be quite difficult, if not impossible. Error detection and debugging become even more complicated when simple actions—such as setting the property of a control—trigger other events the programmer is not expecting.

SmartCheck shows properties, methods, and events as they are used in order to isolate event-driven problems. SmartCheck EventDebugging tracks events to simplify error location. For example, SmartCheck shows all methods and properties as they are set or read, along with the form load triggered by these events.

Data value coercion detection

Visual Basic makes it easy to manipulate variables without explicitly specifying their types. This can result in some of the most difficult errors to find, because value coercion occurs without the programmer's knowledge or intention. A *value coercion* occurs when the contents of a variable of one data type is assigned to another variable of another data type — for example, a Boolean True value getting assigned to a string. Program performance can be degraded by too much value coercion. SmartCheck detects data type changes and indicates the old value and the new value. SmartCheck detects and reports data value coercion as it happens.

For example, a programmer might create a Boolean variable and set it to True. However, depending on how the variable is used, its value might be interpreted as the literal string "True" or as -1. Developers can also improve program performance by declaring correct data types to eliminate excessive conversions.

SmartCheck summary

SmartCheck is for Visual Basic developers at all levels. SmartCheck displays information using terms VB developers already know. It enables even an inexperienced developer to find and fix tough problems quickly by indicating why an error happened and what to do about it. Advanced developers can zoom beneath VB to view the runtime, OLE, and Windows APIs that VB creates as it runs.

Developers and testers are the primary users of SmartCheck. In fact, SmartCheck can only be used on compiled applications; thus, it is logical to use SmartCheck after using CodeReview. SmartCheck developers and testers typically use SmartCheck in two scenarios:

✦ **Bug-driven debugging** — When a developer runs into a runtime error while developing, SmartCheck can be used to quickly identify why the error happened. The model is as follows: Encounter a problem, use SmartCheck to figure out why, and then fix it. In other words, developers can use SmartCheck as a debugging tool when a problem arises.

✦ **Testing** — Developers and testers will use SmartCheck to validate Windows API functions, custom controls (OCXs or ActiveXs), DLLs, and other components. The model here is to use SmartCheck as a testing tool at milestones or intervals during development.

FailSafe

FailSafe is an automatic error-recovery system for Visual Basic. It intercepts program errors before they crash a program, which keeps programs running. FailSafe then captures, records, and communicates — to the developer, support organization, or help desk — the critical information needed to locate and resolve the cause of the error. The program is especially valuable for managing unexpected errors on remote user machines.

FailSafe is one of a trio of NuMega SmartDebugging tools for Visual Basic. When an error occurs in a deployed application, the program terminates with a short, cryptic error message that does not indicate where, how, or why the error occurred. Visual Basic developers need a system for automatically capturing important program and system information from these crashed programs, and communicating that information back to the support or help desk. The key features of FailSafe are discussed in the sections that follow.

Error management

You cannot "turn off" Visual Basic runtime errors. Every error must be handled, or the program will terminate. Manually adding an error handler to each procedure is not practical, and coding a centralized error manager is a huge effort. Often error handling does not get implemented, placing the application at risk because any unexpected error will crash the program.

FailSafe automatically crashproofs every program with its unique, customizable global error handler. FailSafe Interceptor pinpoints errors to the line number, details exactly what the user was doing, and documents the state of the program and of the system when the error occurred, even after deployment. FailSafe compiles into your program and works even in compiled programs running on remote machines. Abundant system information helps the developer isolate platform-dependent problems quickly.

Procedure tracing

Not all problems in Visual Basic are runtime or system errors. Many common problems result from unexpected event execution or program flow. It is not possible to obtain a true execution list from Visual Basic, and many events are not triggered during step-tracing in the IDE. A true execution list shows all of the events that occur. For example, in Visual Basic many events are not executed while step-tracing — for example, GetFocus. Visual Basic simply does not fire certain events during the step trace. This leads to maddening problems, such as the code failing when it's run but working fine when it's step-traced. Without a tracing system, isolating problems can be quite difficult, if not impossible. FailSafe Visual Tracer provides unparalleled visibility into program flow.

FailSafe Visual Tracer is ideal for debugging crashes or for developing ActiveX components, add-ins, and OLE servers. FailSafe Visual Tracer graphically displays what the user (or user interface) did, as well as what the program did in response. FailSafe Visual Tracer shows programs executing call-by-call and shows interactions between components. Visual Tracer can also display resources, memory, hits, timings, and user-defined information such as record counts or disk space call-by-call.

Performance profiling

Developers often need to optimize application speed. A profiler is needed to determine timings, hits, and utilization. To be accurate, the profiler must examine the executing EXE and should run on end user machines as well as developer machines. FailSafe Visual Profiler automatically pinpoints performance bottlenecks.

FailSafe Visual Profiler graphically displays your project performance and utilization. Advanced filtering, sorting, and graphing options let you zoom into areas needing optimization, without wasting your time on those that don't.

FailSafe summary

FailSafe is for regular, everyday use. Whenever code is written, FailSafe should be used to add error-handling capability. While you've alpha- and beta-testing software, FailSafe is ready, out of your way, waiting to spring into action. FailSafe Interceptor nails bugs to the line number and provides key information needed to resolve the problem.

FailSafe, working hand-in-hand with SmartCheck, takes the drudgery out of writing error handlers and captures the important information required to resolve tough problems. FailSafe tells you what the user did and where the error occurred. A developer with SmartCheck can use the FailSafe error report to then quickly diagnose why the error happened.

CodeReview

CodeReview is an automated source-code analysis system for Visual Basic. It rigorously examines Visual Basic source code for hundreds of potential problems in application components, logic, Windows, and Visual Basic itself. When CodeReview finds a problem, it recommends a solution. CodeReview also provides coding standards enforcement and statistical quality-control metrics.

The extensibility of Visual Basic introduces the problem of undesirable and unplanned component interactions, resulting in opportunities for programs to corrupt data or crash. These known interaction problems are so numerous that it's difficult and time-consuming to manually examine code for each and every type of problem that Visual Basic is prone to have. The key features of CodeReview are discussed in the sections that follow.

Known bug detection

Visual Basic custom controls, IDE, runtime, and database systems can have many bugs resulting from the interactions of Visual Basic, Windows, ActiveX (OCX), and other add-ons. Visual Basic also has many features that do not perform as the developer might expect, but are not performing incorrectly according to Microsoft.

CodeReview lets you clean up your code. It rigorously examines your project for all known bugs in Visual Basic, Windows, and third-party custom components.

Comprehensive repair recommendations

The CodeReview knowledge base has over 350 events and more than 1,000 triggers. CodeReview reports on six categories of problems, with each category displaying three levels of severity on each problem. Whenever CodeReview finds a problem, it shows the offending code and pinpoints problems by module, procedure, and line number. The categories of problems found by CodeReview are

✦ **Logic** — Known bugs, and common but fatal mistakes.

✦ **Portability** — Conditions that limit a project to specific OS/versions.

✦ **Performance** — Conditions that reduce execution speed and bloated EXE size.

✦ **Windows** — API side-effects, tips, and other issues.

✦ **Standards** — Noncompliant object naming and/or coding styles.

✦ **Usability** — Interface issues such as duplicate or missing accelerator keys and help.

CodeReview not only finds problems, it helps resolve them. CodeReview provides detailed information about the cause of a problem, and then shows available workarounds. It links to Visual Basic help and Microsoft's Internet Knowledge Base to give you exact problem descriptions, references, and details about syntax.

Network-capable

CodeReview uses a knowledge base to store its code review rules. The knowledge base may be updated at any time. This knowledge base may also be stored on a network and shared among workgroups or the enterprise. Corporations can create and enforce code practices and standards across their enterprises.

For example, a corporation might decide to enforce certain coding practices to enable an upcoming application or planned migration. Once the rules are established, the CodeReview knowledge base is updated, and the new rules are immediately applied to all developers.

Standards enforcement

Different organizations may demand specific adherence to certain coding standards. In addition, not all organizations will implement all CodeReview recommendations. The CodeReview knowledge base is available for customizing to the specific needs of an organization whenever needed.

Rules are editable, so you can edit and add custom rules as needed. You can enable, disable, or edit any CodeReview rule, and you can assign any alert message to any event level. This flexibility allows managers and leaders to mold CodeReview for their own specific needs.

CodeReview summary

Team leaders, QA personnel, or developers typically use CodeReview before checking in the source code, or before releasing it for peer or management review. CodeReview examines your source code for problems, potential problems, and hundreds of "known bugs" before VB compiles your project.

A "known bug" is a problem known to NuMega, or a problem whose trouble report, white paper, or workaround is posted on the Microsoft Web site.

Most corporate and professional VB development teams perform peer code review. This is a process in which the source code is reviewed and everyone makes comments about it and checks for problems. Code review meetings can take all day and consume hundreds of hours of developers' time. CodeReview can make code significantly cleaner in a matter of minutes. This reduces the amount of time the peer review takes, and lets the meeting focus on key architectural and functional issues instead of looking for gross mistakes and "fat fingers."

Most organizations have internal standards and requirements for code. CodeReview can automatically ensure most organizations' standards are adhered to, making it easy to write tight, bug-free code.

Summary

The rich depth and breadth of the Visual Basic language leaves lots of room for us to make mistakes. Of course, the best medicine is prevention. Build and implement error handling in all your code, and make sure your components raise errors consistently to their hosts.

✦ Always use `Option Explicit` in each module. The most common, easy-to-find-and-fix problems are absolutely insidious, sneaky things we do to ourselves. Using `Option Explicit` will automatically find incorrect variable names for you, saving you hours or perhaps days (or more) of wasted time. It's free, so use it.

✦ Always define a default type using `Defxxx` in each module. For example, using `DefInt` at the top of each module, form, class, and so on will save you innumerable problems caused by evil type coercion. This type of coercion occurs silently and automatically. You will not even know it happens — unless your program is having strange logic problems, not running the way you want, or crashing at odd times.

✦ Research the types of tools and debugging aids available from Visual Basic and other vendors. Have the required tools on hand that enable you to localize and resolve problems as required. Some problems are so insidious that it's unlikely anyone can figure them out without professional-quality tools.

✦   ✦   ✦

Optimization and Performance Tuning

Generally speaking, developers demand and require
the fastest processors with dozens of megabytes of
memory and huge hard drives. Most of the time, the testing
developers do takes place over high-speed network
connections, to dedicated testing servers. Often these test
servers are not fully loaded with traffic and respond very
quickly. On the other hand, users of the applications you
create probably do not have as capable a computing platform
as you do.

This situation often leads to a common problem: Your
software is speedy, fast, and generally works great on your
machine; but users complain about poor performance, slow
response time, and inability to use more than one application
at a time. Congratulations — you have just experienced the
need for speed. Whether it is to reduce the disk size of the
program, decrease the amount of memory required, improve
network performance, or boost user interface responsiveness,
you need to optimize your application.

This chapter covers development methodologies, tips, and
techniques required to create applications that are not only
usable by end users, but that give above-average
performance.

Defining Optimization

Optimization is examining your application's performance, and then making informed decisions about which parts of the application to modify to enhance that performance. "Performance" refers to

✦ Algorithm performance

✦ Image size (disk space)

✦ Memory utilization

✦ Network performance

✦ User interface performance

Today, no matter what aspect of your application's performance needs to be improved, the act of improvement is referred to as *optimization*. Most of the time you will not be able to optimize for individual performance characteristics. For example, optimizing to reduce the compiled size of an executable (called the *image*) typically reduces execution speed, and optimizing for speed often results in an increase in disk image size. Keep this in mind when you read this chapter, because the techniques given for one area are often in direct opposition to the techniques for optimizing another area.

It is almost impossible to "add on" performance at the end of the development cycle. If you find yourself at the end of the cycle needing to clean up and optimize an application, don't feel disheartened. There are still many things you can do to quickly optimize it.

First, you have to figure out where to optimize. Then you have to know if the optimization even makes sense. And finally, you optimize. Many studies indicate developers can waste an awful lot of precious development time trying to optimize something that either doesn't matter or is inherently optimized as much as possible.

One way to avoid the problem presented earlier, where an application works great on your machine but is unusable by end users, is to make sure you are thinking about optimization at every moment during development. Failure to do this results in an application that is a tangled mass of inefficiency. Thinking about optimization as you code means asking yourself three basic questions as you move through your development cycle:

✦ Where to optimize?

✦ How much to optimize?

✦ What to optimize?

Where to optimize

Where to optimize means finding out where in your program the performance problem originates. Attempting to optimize a problem without locating the source of the problem is a waste of time. Where you will need to focus your optimization efforts depends on the type of optimization you are pursuing. No matter what sort of optimizations you are after, locating the real cause of a performance problem is seldom obvious and requires careful evaluation of your program's current performance — as well as the underlying code and any objects you use to implement program functionality.

Looking into the sources of the performance degradation (for example, memory requirements, disk bloat, slow speed) is crucial to understanding the real problem. For example, if you are optimizing for execution speed, then you must examine your code for complex lines of code, and nested procedures that call other procedures (the largest source of speed penalties). At first blush, it seems like common sense would tell you to "optimize the slow parts" if you are optimizing for speed. However, the most important question to answer is "What makes this code slow?" Once you can locate the poorly performing code, you can then consider alternative coding solutions that execute more swiftly.

If you are optimizing to reduce the size of your program, then you should examine your code for unneeded or unexecuted code that has crept into your program — the most common source of code bloat. The most important question to answer here is "What makes this program too large?" This will guide your analysis towards dead code and pictures and images.

Considering what might cause a performance problem and then checking your hypothesis by testing and observation will indicate where to optimize.

How much to optimize

How much to optimize means knowing when to stop optimizing. You will know when to stop optimizing when your program performs as it should. You can spend forever trying to create the "completely optimized program," so it's important to define in advance what acceptable limits of performance are, and then make the program conform. When the program meets expectations, cease optimization.

As mentioned previously, some things might not need optimizing. Further, some relatively slow things might not require optimization. For example, a Sub procedure might take an average of .25 seconds to complete. Another procedure might take 6 seconds to complete. You might think that the 6-second procedure is the one to optimize, until you realize that the .25 second procedure is called thousands of times by your program, resulting in a dramatic slowdown of all the routines that use it. Often shared routines can be modified, resulting in enough of a performance gain that the calling routines sharing the common routine won't need optimization themselves.

Understanding why the performance is what it is in your application is the key to knowing when to optimize and when to stop optimizing. Most of the time, you should treat performance problems like bugs, especially when there is a known problem — for example, when a form takes too long to load. You should fix the problem and then stop.

What to optimize

What to optimize refers to the aspect of program performance you wish to address. As mentioned previously, the first step in optimizing is to determine just where the problem really is. You can optimize an application for many factors: memory, image size, network performance, user interface, and so on.

Rather than waste a lot of time optimizing the wrong things, you should set your optimization plan based on predefined performance expectations. These expectations should have been developed with the needs of the end user in mind, as well as the other requirements of the program you are developing. For example, it may not make sense to reduce the disk image size of an application distributed via CD-ROM; however, for an Internet component, disk size might be most important.

You need to understand the implications of your optimizations before you begin optimizing. You may often find that as you increase performance in one area, you decrease performance in another area. A classic example of this is speed versus code size. For example, adding a `Show` statement to your `Form_Load` procedure may increase the speed at which the form becomes visible. However, you have added more code, making the application's image on disk larger. It becomes important, then, to determine just what you want to optimize.

Generally, you can optimize your programs for

- ✦ Display speed
- ✦ Execution speed
- ✦ Perceived speed
- ✦ Size in memory
- ✦ Size on disk

Display speed

Display speed refers to the speed with which your forms load and display, graphics load and paint, controls such as list boxes load and navigate, and so on. Display speed is a critical factor in user's acceptance of your application. Even modest optimizations of display speed can make an "unusable" application "usable."

Execution speed

Execution speed is the speed with which your code executes. In general, Visual Basic makes it easy to write sloppy, unoptimized code. Slow code bogs down the entire application. For example, consider a routine to show a status bar as the user navigates your menus. If the code to implement the status bar is unoptimized, users will experience a delay as they navigate the menu, resulting in unhappy users. Consider the following code example that searches a string for a delimiter and then returns a substring:

```
Private Function StatusBar(Byval sMenuText As String) _
    As String
    Dim i As Long
    ' walk through string looking for delimiter
    For i = 1 To Len(sMenuText)
        If Mid$(sMenuText, i, 1) = vbLf Then
            ' now extract string
            tmp = Mid$(sMenuText, i - 1)
            ' exit loop
            Exit For
        End If
    Next
    ' assign status bar text
    StatusBar = tmp
End Function
```

This code is flawless in its logic and implementation. It steps through each character of the source string sMenuText and, when it finds the line feed delimiter, returns a sub string. However, this code can slow down menu navigation in this example because it has to step through every single character looking for the delimiter vbLf. Further, the sub string is assigned to a variable tmp, which in turn is assigned as the result of the function. Every single time the user of this hypothetical program chooses a menu item, this processing delay is imposed.

Thus, the code is slower than it has to be. Examine the following to understand how this code could be optimized:

```
Private Function StatusBar(Byval sMenuText As String) _
    As String
    Dim i As Long
    ' locate delimiter
    i = InStr(sMenuText, vbLf)
    ' assign status bar text
    If i > 0 Then StatusBar = Left$(sMenuText, i - 1)
End Function
```

The improved StatusBar function uses the Visual Basic Instr keyword to locate the delimiter in a single call — many times faster than using the For...Next loop of the original code. Then the substring is parsed directly into the function return without using an intermediate variable, again many times faster. The end result is a fast and efficient procedure.

Just because Visual Basic makes it easy to write sloppy code doesn't mean that all Visual Basic code is slow — quite the opposite. In later sections of the chapter, we will go over the numerous methods available to increase the speed at which your application executes.

Perceived speed

Perceived speed refers to the user's impression of performance, not necessarily poor performance itself. This is an important concept, in view of the fact that Visual Basic by default can make for a poorly perceived application.

For example, any Visual Basic form automatically executes all its contained code and then displays the form last. Therefore, at startup the user might be looking at nothing for several seconds as your form initializes, resulting in the perception that the program is slow. By simply adding a Show method as the first line of code for your application, the user will see the form much sooner, making for a completely different user experience. Of course, the form still takes as much time to actually load as it took before the optimization. The point of perceived speed is to make the user feel that the program is speedier than it is. This psychological impact on users can make a real difference in their perceived value of your program.

Size in memory

Size in memory refers to how much memory will be used as the program runs. Visual Basic can use a lot of memory, especially if you don't take care to minimize the amount of memory used. For example, every form loaded uses memory. You might think that by hiding or unloading the form, the memory used by its graphics and code would be released. Think again.

By default, Visual Basic only releases all used memory as needed (Visual Basic decides) or when the application terminates. However, by unloading and then setting the Form object to Nothing, as shown in the following code, you can recover a form's memory at the moment you unload it:

```
...
Unload Form1
Set Form1 = Nothing
...
```

Size on disk

Size on disk is the size, in bytes, of your compiled executable program. Most of the time you optimize your application for memory size, execution speed, or perceived speed, you increase its size on disk. This is a direct result of adding more code to optimize these areas.

Unfortunately, this is life when optimizing. However, there are still a number of things that you can do to reduce disk size. For example, Visual Basic supports many types of images, including JPG, GIF, and compressed bitmap (RLE) formats. Visual Basic also supports images with many colors, such as TrueColor images with thousands or millions of colors. In many cases you can reduce the size of an image simply by saving it as 16- or 256-color image, dramatically reducing the size of the image. Using JPG, GIF, or RLE and reducing color depth can produce amazing reductions in executable size.

Another simple way you can dramatically reduce the size of your finished program is to compile for p-code (described later as a compiler organization) instead of native code. This alone will often halve the size of the compiled program. Of course, p-code executes slower than native code, so again, there is a performance trade-off.

Measuring Performance

Before you optimize anything at all, you need to locate the source of the performance problem. Figuring out the best response to a performance challenge isn't always easy. Many times you must experiment with a variety of configurations to determine which one is most accurate. This requires some sort of mechanism to accurately measure the amount of time spent in a procedure or function call.

Listing 34-1 presents three procedures that you can use to implement access to the high-resolution system time that Windows exposes in the winmm.dll library and its associated Windows API functions. The first method, ProfStart, initializes the timer and stores a starting value. The second method, ProfStop, stops the counter and stores the difference in time between ProfStart and ProfStop. The third method, ProfTime, returns the amount of time since the call to ProfStart if ProfStop has not been called. If ProfStop has been called, then ProfTime returns the total time elapsed between ProfStart and ProfStop.

Listing 34-1: **A Set of Timekeeping Procedures**

```
Defint A-Z

Option Explicit

Private Declare Function timeBeginPeriod Lib "winmm.dll" _
    (ByVal uPeriod As Long) As Long
Private Declare Function timeEndPeriod Lib "winmm.dll" _
    (ByVal uPeriod As Long) As Long
Private Declare Function timeGetTime Lib "winmm.dll" _
    () As Long

Dim gfProf As Currency 'Timer
```

(continued)

Listing 34-1 *(continued)*

```
Public Sub ProfStart()
    ' stores current time
    gfProf = timeGetTime()
End Sub

Public Sub ProfStop()
    'stores total elapsed time as negative
    'so later we can see if clock is stopped —
    'if negative, clock is stopped, otherwise
    'the clock is running
    gfProf = (timeGetTime() - gfProf) * -1
End Sub

Public Function ProfTime() As String
    On Error Resume Next

    ' if negative then ProfStop was called
    If gfProf < 0 Then
        ' format, flip sign and return
        ProfTime = Format$(Abs(gfProf) / 1000, "###.000")
    Else
        'clokc running, determine elapsed time
        ProfTime = Format$((timeGetTime() - gfProf)_
                    / 1000, "###.000")
    End If
End Function
```

With these functions, you can accurately judge the time duration of a routine. For example, consider an imaginary routine `Foo`:

```
Sub Foo()

    Dim A As Double

    ProfStart ' start timer

    A = Timer
    A = A * A
    ProfStop ' stop timer
End Sub
```

Now, you can use `ProfTime` to return a formatted string indicating the amount of time used, as follows:

```
Debug.Print ProfTime
```

Although this tells you the time a procedure takes, one other important consideration is the number of times a procedure is called. Further, you need to take into account the amount of time consumed by the procedures called by the procedure under study. You need a means to track not only the total time used, but also the time used by contained procedures. The easiest method for doing this is to purchase and use a tool that measures performance speed for you. One such tool is NuMega TrueTime, a trial version of which is included on the CD-ROM.

NuMega TrueTime

TrueTime enables you to spot slow code by gathering timings and statistics for applications, components, source files, procedures, and individual lines of code. TrueTime can determine how your application is affected by all its components. Even if you do not have the source code to a control, you can still get excellent performance information from TrueTime. TrueTime collects and reports many statistics at the module, procedure, and line levels, allowing you to quickly find the slowest component and procedure in your application. For example, at the function and line levels, you can see the percentage relative to the total time spent in the session. You can also make comparisons between successive sessions by examining the average execution time of a procedure.

TrueTime records the number of times every procedure and line were called during a session. It tracks the relationships between callers and called functions. By knowing how often and why a function was executed, you can quickly focus your attention on the slowest path through the code.

The event-driven model of Visual Basic makes it difficult to know which functions are called by other functions. This makes it difficult to determine the performance of many procedures. With the TrueTime Source Tab, it is easy to see which line in a function was the slowest. The Detail Dialog makes this data easy to view and enables you to readily understand exactly what contributed to a function's total time.

Exploring Speed Optimizations

The speed of your program's execution, and the user's impression of your program's performance can make or break an application. Visual Basic by default can make for a poorly perceived application. Therefore, you are often going to make your program execute faster or seem to execute faster. The areas affected by these optimizations are:

✦ **Display speed** — The speed with which forms load and display, graphics load and paint, controls such as list boxes load and navigate, and so forth.

✦ **Perceived speed** — The user's impression of performance, not necessarily poor performance itself

✦ **Code execution speed** — The speed with which your code executes

As mentioned earlier, not all optimizations result in measurable gains, nor should all potential optimization be implemented. Remember to treat optimization problems as bugs — locate and identify the problem, and then fix it.

Optimizing real display speed

Real display speed is the true amount of time it takes to print or update the screen. When you perform optimization for real display speed, the application or procedure is truly faster. This contrasts with *perceived display speed*, in which case the user only perceives that the action is faster.

Most applications today have continued with the trend of providing more graphical feedback and visual queues to the user. Therefore, the speed of graphics and interface display operations is important. The faster your forms appear, the faster your application seems to the end user. Several simple techniques almost always speed up the apparent speed of your application. These include:

- ✦ Hiding controls when changing or setting properties, to avoid multiple repaints
- ✦ Setting the `ClipControls` property of containers to `False` to prevent unwanted redraws of areas that might not need it
- ✦ Using `AutoRedraw` appropriately, which typically means setting `AutoRedraw` to `False`
- ✦ Using Image controls, where appropriate, instead of PictureBoxes, since Image controls use much less system resources
- ✦ Using the `Line` method instead of the `PSet` method, since `PSet` is fairly unoptimized when compared with `Line`
- ✦ Using a single call to the `Move` method, rather than multiple calls setting the `Top` or `Left` properties

Hiding controls

Every time Visual Basic repaints, time is expended. Therefore, the fewer times you application repaints the screen, the faster your application seems.

One common problem with Visual Basic is that when a control updates itself through the change or setting of a property, it often forces a repaint of itself, which may in turn force a repaint of the entire form. List boxes are a great example — simply adding a member to the list forces a repaint of the control.

One method of avoiding this flickering and redrawing is to hide the control before manipulating its property. In the case of a list box, set the `Visible` property to `False`, add all the elements, then set the `Visible` property to `True`. This causes a single repaint instead of one-per item that you add, resulting in much less screen flicker and faster performance.

ClipControls property

The ClipControls property of a form determines whether or not Visual Basic updates the entire screen section affected by a repaint. This includes repainting anything graphical that is underneath the control itself. Most of the time, there is no need to update or repaint the area under a control.

Setting ClipControls to False tells Visual Basic not to paint under the control. This makes VB simply update the control itself, resulting in faster operation. If your forms have many controls, you will see a noticeable improvement using this technique.

Note   The important exception to this rule is when you are using graphics methods such as Circle, Line, or Print to create your own graphics, in which case you must set ClipControls to True in order for Visual Basic to properly draw your custom graphics.

AutoRedraw

The AutoRedraw property of a form or control determines whether or not Visual Basic stores a copy of the form image in memory. When the property is True, VB paints using a static memory "snapshot" of the form or control.

For simple forms, this can make the screen paint more quickly. However, for forms that use graphics methods, this slows down the process considerably because Visual Basic first writes the graphic to the memory image, stores it, and then paints the screen. Not only does this slow down the repaint, it also uses much more memory, because VB has to maintain a bitmap that represents the form.

Image controls

You should always use an Image control instead of a PictureBox, unless you require the extra capabilities of the PictureBox. Image controls don't have an hDC property or the capability to contain other controls, making them much "lighter" with regard to memory used and the amount of time taken to process images. The net result is that pictures draw faster than using an image control.

Line versus PSet

This is an excellent example of counter-intuitive reasoning. To create a point on the screen you would think PSet would be the right choice — however, it's not. The Line method can create very short lines — including lines one pixel long! The Line method is much faster than using the PSet method.

Move versus Left/Top

Another classic optimization is to use the Move method instead of setting the Left and Top properties. Each call to Left or Top results in a series of related calls and a screen paint. Using Move on the other hand, sets the Left and Top properties and then moves the control or object all at once — resulting in significantly higher performance.

For example, the two segments of the following code are equivalent, although the Move instruction is much faster than the two Left and Top instructions:

```
txtLastname.Left = 50
txtLastname.Top = 50

txtLastname.Move 50, 50
```

Optimizing perceived display speed

Other common techniques that improve the perceived speed of an application are

✦ Use the Show method in the Form_Load procedure

✦ Use a splash screen at the start of your application

✦ Do background tasks with timers

✦ Load and hide forms until they're needed

✦ Reduce code in the Form_Load procedure

✦ Lay out code modules by function

Show Method

Visual Basic executes all the code in the Form_Load event procedure occurs before the form is displayed. As mentioned earlier, you can override this default behavior by using the Show method in the Form_Load procedure.

The upside of this technique is that it gives the user something to look at while the application continues to load and the code in Form_Load executes. Therefore, users know the program is loading and working, and they perceive it to be faster. The downside is that they might see the form but won't be able to use any controls it contains, until all code in the Form_Load executes — and all then contained controls load and initialize.

Splash screen

One of the best techniques for making your application seem snappy on load is to create a very simple main form that displays a notice to the user. This gives the user something to look at as your application loads, making the application seem quicker. Combine the Show method with the splash screen for very fast-appearing forms. For example:

```
Private Sub Form_Load
    Show     ' show me
    DoEvents ' force form to show
    ' now load another slower form
    Load Form2
    ...   ' do whatever else is needed
End Sub
```

Visual Basic can automatically add a simple splash screen to your applications if you use the Application Wizard. The Visual Basic splash screen does not implement the previously presented techniques, but it is a good place to start.

The upside to this technique is that the user again has something to look at while the program loads. The downside is that your code will be more complex and disk image size will increase.

Timers

Many times, tasks can be run in the background — for example, printing. Instead of making the user wait while your print routine slowly prints out a line at a time, you can create a snappier user experience by placing the print routine in a Timer event. Then, every time the timer executes, the VB application can print a line of text. Between each Timer event, your program runs as usual; the user gets control back right away and thinks the program is faster.

This method, however, creates a classic problem: complexity versus usability. Generally speaking, as applications become more user friendly and usable, they get more complex. My example with the printer suffers the same fate. Actually, implementing this technique requires shared variables to track how much of the job is printed, and then you must update those variables every time the Timer event fires and you print a line. It also requires logic to stop or cancel the printing; the user may decide to print something else before the first print job is completed.

For example:

```
' array of text to print
Public TextLines() As String

' menu procedure
Private Sub mnuPrint_Click()
    Timer1.Interval = 100 ' print 10 lines/sec.
    Timer1.Enabled = True ' turn on timer
    Timer1.Tag = 0 ' use tag to carry line to print
End Sub

' timer used to print
Private Sub Timer1_Interval()
    ' increment line to print
    Timer1.Tag = Timer1.Tag + 1
    If Timer1.Tag < UBound(TextLines) Then
        ' print line
        Printer.Print TextLines(Timer1.Tag)
    Else
        ' end printing
        Timer1.Enabled = False
    End If
End Sub
```

This code assumes a public string array labeled `TextLines`. When the user chooses the `mnuPrint` menu option, a timer is set up and enabled to fire every 100ms or 10 times per second. When the timer fires, a counter is incremented and used as the index into the string array to print. When the counter increments to a higher value than what the array contains, the timer is disabled.

The upside to this technique is incremental execution of your code — that is, your program remains responsive to the user while doing a large (in this case, print) job. The downside is increased complexity and more code.

Hidden forms

A form that is hidden (that is, one whose `Visible` property is set to `False`) is fully loaded into memory. All its controls and code have loaded and are active in memory. To make the form "pop" onto the screen almost instantly, you set its `Visible` property to `True`.

The upside to this technique is very fast screen display. The downside is that it does use memory. The more forms that are loaded and hidden, the more memory your application requires.

Reduce code in Form_Load

The greater the amount of code in your `Form_Load` event procedure, the longer it takes to load. If you can reduce the amount of code in the `Form_Load` event procedure, the form will load more quickly. Use this technique with the previously mentioned splash screen and timer examples.

For example, you could move some code out of the `Form_Load` event and into a routine called by a timer. In the `Form_Load` event, you enable the timer so that after the `Form_Load` event completes, the timer fires and executes your code.

The upside to this technique is fast loading of forms; the downside is increased complexity and potential changes to your existing logic.

Lay out code modules by function

Visual Basic loads code modules on demand. So if you reference a procedure in a module that is not in memory, Visual Basic has to load the entire module. Therefore, during `Form_Load`, do not access procedures in modules outside of the form itself. This can dramatically reduce the time it takes for a form to appear.

All together, these techniques will let you improve both the real and perceived display speed of your applications. In many cases, these techniques do not require a lot of coding, either; by and large, they are simple modifications that do not affect the logic of the code itself.

The upside of this technique is improved memory management, which in turn results in faster load times. The downside is more work on your part to determine and maintain code by function.

Optimizing code execution speed

When you optimize code that is slow, what you are really doing is finding a way to make it execute in less time. You can improve the execution speed of your code in a number of ways, and not all of them have to do with how you wrote the code.

Visual Basic itself can affect the execution speed of your code, based on your choice of variables and how you implement procedures. You can choose simple options to make your existing code faster. The simple things that control code speed, which typically do not require any modifications to your code itself, include the following:

✦ Avoid using variants

✦ Use long integers

✦ Use integer math

Evil variants

The Visual Basic default data type is the variant. The variant is probably the single most inefficient data structure ever given to any language. Ostensibly, the need for a variant data type is for new users who cannot be concerned with mundane issues such as data typing. In reality, a variant is a structure; it has a descriptor indicating the real type of data it carries. Therefore, the variant can be any common type of data—and therein lies its horrible inefficiency. Every access to a variant requires multiple internal calls by Visual Basic to overhead assignments, and a read to determine the real data type and then process it accordingly. This contrasts with a typed variable, which doesn't require all the overhead to determine type.

Variants use 16 bytes per variable, not counting the actual data. Compare this to 2 bytes per integer variable. Not only do variants consume memory, they also consume a special type of memory called *stack space*. The stack is a fixed amount of memory used by Visual Basic to manage all the variables and arguments in your procedures. As your procedures call other nested procedures, the stack is used to hold intermediate results. Variants can cause the stack to fill up more quickly than typed variables.

The single best thing you can do to improve speed is get into the habit of always starting every single form, module, class, or control with the `DefLng A-Z` statement—which forces the default data type to be a Long integer—and then using `Option Explicit`, which forces you to declare all variables before usage.

Long integers

When your code requires simple math, use long integers and avoid the floating-point mathematics data types of currency, single, and double. Long integers are the fastest variables available to Visual Basic. The slowest variable type is currency (or variant, if you consider nontyped variables).

Integer division

Always use integer division (\) instead of floating-point division (/) if you don't need fractional results. Integer math is always faster than floating-point math because it doesn't require access to a math coprocessor.

For example, the first code line in this pair would be much faster than the second code line:

```
A = B \ C
A = B / C
```

More speed may be achieved by applying these modifications:

✦ Use `ByVal` instead of `ByRef`

✦ Cache properties

✦ Use inline code

✦ Use constants

Use ByVal instead of ByRef

When you create procedures that take arguments, there are two possible ways to pass those arguments: by value (`ByVal`) or reference (`ByRef`). `ByVal` means that Visual Basic passes a copy of the variable to the procedure. This method does not allow the procedure to change the actual contents of the variable in the calling procedure. For example:

```
Dim Arg As String

Arg = "hank"
Foo Arg 'call foo

If Arg = "hank" Then
    MsgBox "The same"
Else
    MsgBox "Changed"
End If

. . .

Sub Foo (ByVal Arg As String)
    Arg = "hank was here"
End Sub
```

In this example, the `Arg` variable would remain "hank" outside of `Sub Foo`, even though it was changed within the procedure. This is because using the `ByVal` keyword did not pass the actual variable `Arg`. It passed a copy instead. On the other hand, by using `ByRef` (or leaving off the modifier), the change to `Arg` within `Sub Foo` would change the data outside of the procedure.

Note

By default (that is, if you don't use `ByVal` or `ByRef`), Visual Basic passes arguments by reference.

Passing arguments by value using `ByVal` is generally faster than passing arguments by reference using `ByRef`. So if your code does not need to change the data type, use `ByVal` for fastest results.

The exception to this rule occurs when passing large string or array arguments. Even if the procedure will not modify them, it's often faster to pass the argument `ByRef` than using `ByVal`. This is because `ByRef` passes a four-byte pointer to your data, not the actual data. If you are passing a large character string or a large array, it's quicker to use `ByRef` instead of `ByVal`.

Cache properties

To *cache* something, in programming parlance, means to store a copy of something. With regard to optimization, this is one of the most powerful methods for improving the speed with which your code executes.

To see the problem, examine the following code:

```
For i = 1 To 10
txtLastName(i).Top = txtLastName(0).Top + 20
Next
```

In this code, an array of text boxes are aligned using the value of a fixed control `txtLastName(0)` plus an offset 20. While not readily apparent, it is somewhat time-consuming to access the properties of a control or object. All sorts of Visual Basic induced hand-holding is involved with each property access. All this extra work takes time.

Since the assignment references a nonvariable value, this code can be optimized by storing or caching the nonchanging value of `txtLastName(0).Top + 20` into a variable, and then using that variable instead of the property.

```
Dim nTop As Long
nTop = txtLastName(0).Top + 20
For i = 1 To 10
        txtLastName(i).Top = nTop
Next
```

This code will execute as much as 20 times faster than the preceding example. This technique also works for common Visual Basic runtime instructions such as `Screen.TwipsPerPixelX`, or other commonly used functions.

Use inline code

Most developers would like their code to be reusable. One popular way to do this is to make any procedure that performs useful and frequently required actions a function. Another technique is to code in a class, just so next time it will be easy to use. These are common practices. These are also common sources of performance hits.

For optimization, it's sometimes simply better to leave some block of code in the procedure that uses it, rather than take the speed-hit by making it a callable method or property. This holds true even if more than one other procedure calls the same code. Of course, the trade-off for this technique is "code bloat"—the disk image size will expand. However, in some optimization scenarios this is quite acceptable. For example, the following code uses a function called Cotan to return the cotangent of a variable:

```
Sub Foo()
    Dim X As Double

    X = .12
    X = Cotan(X)
End Sub

Function Cotan ( Byval X As Long )
    ' return Cotangent of 'X'
    Cotan = 1 / Tan(X)
End Function
```

To rewrite this as inline code and dramatically increase performance, move the code from the function Cotan into Foo, rewriting Foo as follows:

```
Sub Foo()
    Dim X As Double

    X = .12
    X = 1 / Tan(X) ' return Cotangent of 'X'
End Sub
```

Use constants

You can make your code execute faster if you use constants for frequently required static values, rather than variables or function calls. This holds true for intrinsic Visual Basic constants as well. This is because constants are calculated and written directly into your code during compilation, unlike traditional variables that require calculation at runtime to resolve.

Constants also have the added benefit of making your code more easily understood. Finally, any unused constants are removed from your compiled program during compilation—reducing code bloat as a result of unused instructions.

Constants are a powerful resource in optimizing your programs.

Optimizing object usage

Objects are a powerful extension of Visual Basic and you use them all the time. You access objects in your programs via Visual Basic code, and the way you code usage of an object has a direct impact on the performance associated with using the object. Any object usage induces overhead in the form of time. This is due to a process called *binding*.

Binding is the term used to describe the setup and execution of a property or method of an object. The amount of time lost due to binding is mainly due to the overhead required to move arguments to the stack, call the procedure, and return a value to the caller.

The overhead for object access depends on the type of binding Visual Basic uses. This depends on how the author of the object (maybe you, maybe not) has declared that object. Two main types of binding are available in Visual Basic: *early* and *late binding*.

Late binding

When you declare a reference to an object using the `As Object` or `As Variant` syntax, Visual Basic can't possibly know in advance what kind of object the variable will contain. Therefore, VB can only determine this information at runtime when the object is actually loaded into memory and VB can examine it. This is referred to as *late binding*. For example:

```
Dim vRes As Object ' Visual Basic can't
                   ' resolve until object is used
```

Every time you access a property or method of a late-bound object, Visual Basic has to invoke a number of internal processes to locate and set up a call into the object, resulting in significant overhead and speed penalties. For out-of-process objects, this forces an additional, cross-process method call, which essentially doubles the overhead. Late binding is the most inefficient method possible.

This is not to say late binding does not have a place in programming. Late binding is useful for connecting to objects whose properties and methods may vary. For example, you might code two objects with similar functionality but with operating system dependencies. Then, based on operating system, you'd connect to either one or the other. This way you can create and use the "Windows 98" object when your program runs under Windows 98, and the "Windows NT" object when your program runs under Windows NT.

Early binding

When you declare a reference to an object using the `As ObjectName` syntax, Visual Basic can determine the address of the calls you make at compile time. Thus, when the program runs, there is none of the overhead associated with looking up the method found in late binding. For example:

```
Dim vRes As ResourceObject ' Visual Basic resolves
                           'at compile time
```

Early binding dramatically reduces the time required to access methods or properties of that object. It is the most efficient and recommended method of accessing an object.

Of course, at times early binding is not possible or not efficient, such as in remote database programming or when accessing out-of-process ActiveX servers (ActiveX EXEs). However, if you know the type of object you will be accessing in advance and that object will not change, then your highest performance will be delivered using early binding.

Examining Memory Optimizations

Memory refers to both the disk image or size of your application, as well as how much RAM is required for the running program. You can use several techniques to create applications with smaller disk images and that require less RAM to run.

Virtually all of the optimization techniques for memory involve removing unnecessary parts of your application. Don't worry; we're only going to remove the deadwood, not your masterpiece! In previous versions of Visual Basic, the following things caused your EXE file size to bloat:

✦ Labels

✦ Names

✦ Comments

✦ Blank lines

Now Visual Basic automatically removes these when you compile, so there is no need to worry about them. None of these items affect the size of your application in memory when it is running as a compiled program.

However, such things as

✦ Line numbers

✦ Debug info

✦ Variables

✦ Forms

✦ Procedures

do take up memory and can make your program take up more disk space. So our optimizations for memory will address the latter list and ignore the former. Luckily there are many techniques you can use to slim down the memory footprint of your application on disk and in RAM. Techniques that can reduce code size include the following:

✦ Avoid variants

✦ Eliminate dead code

✦ Use resource files

✦ Organize modules by function

✦ Reclaim strings and object memory

✦ Reduce controls count

✦ Reduce loaded forms count

✦ Use Dynamic rather than Static arrays

✦ Use Label controls rather than TextBox controls

Avoid variants

While variants are flexible, they are also the largest and most inefficient data type. To reduce the memory used by your application, replace variants (variables and arrays) with other typed data types.

Variants use 16 bytes per variable, plus the actual data. Compare this to 2 bytes per integer variable. Not only do variants consume memory, they also consume a special type of memory called stack space.

The stack is a fixed amount of memory used by Visual Basic to manage all the variables and arguments in your procedures. As your procedures call other nested procedures, the stack is used to hold intermediate results. Variants can cause the stack to fill up more quickly than typed variables.

Eliminate dead code

In developing a typical application, you write and modify a lot of code. As your application evolves, code is often orphaned. That is, you may include a procedure that is no longer called. Such a procedure is called *dead code*. Although Visual Basic automatically eliminates unused constants, it does not remove any actual code you write. Over time, this dead code can build up and consume considerable amounts of memory — all for nothing. To find this dead code, you will probably require a good tool such as VBCompress from Whippleware.

You can manually search for dead functions by using the Edit ⇨ Find feature of the Visual Basic IDE. This technique works best for functions you have written yourself. Highlight the name of the function and then search for it. If no references to the name of the function are found, it is "dead" and you may safely remove it. Note that some procedures, such as `Sub Main` or Visual Basic-added events, are not typically called by your code and should not be deleted.

Use resource files

When you create an application and assign data to variables such as captions and other properties, that data gets compiled into the application. This not only makes your application larger on disk, it also uses more memory at runtime. You can avoid this by using resource files to contain strings and images, and then loading property values as needed. Unfortunately, this is one of the cases where your EXE file will be smaller, but it will take a bit longer to load and display the string or image data because the resource data need to be read from disk.

Organize modules by function

As mentioned earlier, Visual Basic loads modules on demand. This means the entire module containing a procedure is loaded whenever any procedure in that module is used. Therefore, avoid cross-module calls unless absolutely required. This way only the minimal amount of modules will ever be loaded at any one time. Because only the minimum set of modules are loaded at any one time, memory usage is reduced.

Reclaim strings and object memory

When you create a string variable in a procedure, Visual Basic automatically reclaims its space when you exit the procedure. However, for strings with public (or global) scope, the memory used is not reclaimed automatically. For these sorts of strings, you need to explicitly reclaim the memory used. For example, imagine a procedure that loads a text file into a global string. After processing the text file contents, you should set the string to empty as follows:

```
MyString = "" ' free memory used by string
```

Reduce control count

Controls use memory. Every single control in your form has a definition and gets allocated memory. The more controls in a form, the larger the disk image and the more memory required. A common technique to reduce memory consumed is to use control arrays instead of multiple controls of the same type. Because only a single control is on the form and compiled into the program EXE, memory requirements and disk space requirements are lowered.

At runtime, you dynamically load and display as many instances of the control as you need, and you may dynamically unload instances of controls you no longer need. Instead of having multiple controls in memory at all times, this technique lets you maintain only the number of controls you need at any given time.

Reduce loaded form count

All forms loaded in memory use memory—just how much depends on the code and controls the form contains. As mentioned earlier, you can load and hold forms in memory and then use the form's `Visible` property to make it "pop" onto the screen. While this technique improves the perceived performance of your application, it uses significantly more memory than simply loading forms as needed and unloading when done with them.

Therefore, when memory counts, make sure you always unload all forms when you're done with them. Furthermore, you must also force Visual Basic to release all memory used by the form using this instruction:

```
Set Form = Nothing
```

Here, `Form` refers to the name of the form being released from memory. Failure to use this instruction results in significant amounts of memory remaining in use, even though you unloaded the form.

Labels versus text boxes

Much like the Image-versus-PictureBox discussion, label controls use fewer Windows resources than textboxes. Additionally, TextBox controls have many events that labels don't. These extra events require memory and disk space to define and instantiate. Therefore, you should use a label if you don't need the extra capabilities of a text box.

Dynamic versus static arrays

Visual Basic has two basic types of arrays you can use: dynamic arrays and static arrays. Dynamic arrays are created using the `Dim`, `Public`, or `Private` keywords. Dynamic arrays do not have a preset size and may be expanded or erased at runtime.

If you use a dynamic array, use `Erase` or `ReDim Preserve` to empty that array of unneeded elements and recover the memory used by the unneeded elements. You can recover memory from a dynamic array as follows:

```
Erase MyArray
```

Static arrays cannot be resized, and using `Erase` simply "empties" the contents of the array elements; it does not release the memory used by the array elements.

Comparing Compiler optimizations

Visual Basic 5 brought us a native code compiler, which is probably the most misunderstood addition to Visual Basic ever. The compiler comes with several options, with seductive-sounding options such as "compile for speed" and "compile for size."

Many people are horrified when they port over their Visual Basic application and then "compile for size," only to find out that the disk image size has tripled or worse! The reason that Visual Basic can create programs with tremendous size differences is due to the two very different types of programs that Visual Basic can create. Visual Basic creates interpreted or *p-code executables* as well as native executables. Interpreted code is actually a series of codes that tell the runtime library what to do at runtime.

Native executables, on the other hand, are actual compiled instructions that do not need to be expanded into statements as p-code does. In many cases, compiling to native code can provide substantial gains in speed over interpreted code — however, not always.

Also note that native code executables always are larger with regard to disk image than their p-code cousins, even when using compiler optimizations. This is because p-code is quite efficient and communicates many runtime instructions in a single byte, as opposed to native code, which requires instructions for every single operation.

When to compile to p-code

Generally speaking, you should compile to p-code if you want the smallest possible image size. For example, if your program is a component for Internet download, then p-code is almost always the way to go because of the sheer size difference. Note, however, p-code is not compatible with most debugging tools, including Visual Studio. Therefore, use p-code for your programs that require the smallest size after debugging them.

When to compile to native

Generally speaking, you should compile to native code when you require compatibility with debuggers or when you require highest program execution speed. For example, if your program does a lot of mathematics, native code would be best. Interestingly, for programs that do a lot of Windows API calls or string manipulation, native code will not be much faster than p-code.

In Closing

Visual Basic is so flexible, it's easy to write nonoptimized code — but that's because of you, the developer, and not of the language. I have always said it's not so much the language you use, but how you use the language that counts. It's just as easy to write poor C code as it is to write poor Visual Basic code. For example, the simple line

```
Asc(Mid$(somestring$,1,1))
```

or

```
Asc(Left$(somestring$,1))
```

returns the same result as

```
Asc(somestring$)
```

except the last line operates much faster. `Asc` returns the ASCII code of the first character of a string, so using `Mid$` to isolate the first character is unnecessary and invokes string-management code within Visual Basic that affects performance.

The same logic holds true for conditional loops under Visual Basic. There are no less than eight ways to program a loop in Visual Basic: `Goto`, `Do...Loop`, `Do While...Loop`, `Do Until...Loop`, `Do...Loop While`, `Do...Loop Until`, `While...Wend`, and `For...Next`. Which one is fastest depends on how you implement the loop and the other code in the loop. Only experimentation can tell you which is optimal for your situation.

`Select Case` is another example where we can optimize. Using a string as the compare item for a `Case` statement is much slower than using the `Asc` value.

The same is true as well when testing for greater than, less than, or equality. Only one works best for a given situation, but how many of us take the time to figure it out?

So what's the point? Well, if you apply yourself, and apply sound programming skills, the result using Visual Basic can equal or better the result using another language. If you take the time to write quality code, you will find that in a lot of cases using an OCX or a DLL written in C++ is slower than just using Visual Basic code to do the same job.

You can prove this with a simple test. Use Windows API calls to seek to a file location and return a string a set number of bytes long. Use the API calls `_lread` and `_llseek`. Then use the Visual Basic `Get` call, which does the same job. When run side-by-side, Visual Basic's `Get` is about two times faster than the API calls! In this example, the use of DLL calls to read a disk file is slower than using Visual Basic!

There are many things you can do just as quickly and efficiently in Visual Basic as in any other language. The important thing to understand is that the assumption that a program written in C or C++ must be more efficient, smaller, better, or faster than Visual Basic code is dead wrong.

Summary

Optimization should be treated as an integral part of development. You should have a performance plan that details expected, acceptable, and unacceptable performance. This plan should be developed based on the computing infrastructure available to your users as well as their expectations.

Once you have determined that a performance problem exists, you must locate the cause of the problem and then determine if the problem needs to be addressed through real optimization and execution speed or through managing the users' perceived expectations.

When setting out to optimize your program, remember that optimizing one area will probably impact another — often negatively. Therefore, you need to choose carefully what you are going to optimize.

When you are starting a project, don't let your judgment be clouded about what you assume you can and/or cannot do using Visual Basic. Good programming style, discipline, an in-depth knowledge of the language, and experimentation are the keys to how well any program turns out, regardless of language. Remember, it's not what language you can use, it's how you use the language!

✦   ✦   ✦

Using DHTML in Visual Basic

No longer are your Visual Basic applications confined to a single desktop. Visual Basic 6 introduces the ability to write Visual Basic code that works with Dynamic HTML (DHTML) pages in Microsoft Internet Explorer. As you'll see in this chapter, VB 6 comes with a number of features to make it easy to write Web pages using DHTML. VB includes a graphical editor that allows you to draw your DHTML forms instead of typing them. The editor can also import existing DHTML code. The best part about developing DHTML applications in Visual Basic is that you can use all of VB's capabilities for development, testing and debugging.

What Is DHTML?

Dynamic HTML (DHTML) is not really a new language. All of the traditional HTML elements are present, such as element headings and list tags. Moreover, DHTML is a set of enhancements that allow elements of a page to be changed or manipulated by the browser. In previous versions of HTML, once the page left the server, the browser made no modifications; it parsed precisely the page that it received.

In some cases, the older method worked to a developer's advantage. The developer could craft the page either through code or a template system of some sort and know exactly what the page would look like when it arrived at the user's browser. However, because the server receives no feedback from the client displaying the page, there was no way for the server to respond to the activities going on in the browser. For instance, there would be no way to change the form's appearance based on an event such as the user clicking a radio button, as in VB (Click event). In addition, whenever it was time to proceed to the next page, a new session would have to be started with the server and any information that the server needed would have to be retransmitted. This problem is known as having a stateless connection. In contrast, Visual Basic can keep track of everything, or *maintain state*, while the application is running. In short, DHTML helps solve these problems. The Web page's data can be changed and used in a variety of ways, including via JavaScript or VBScript.

Besides the dynamic nature of the language, DHTML can also be used to help maintain state in the Web application. You can maintain state in the page itself instead of having to rely on the server, cookies, or hidden data in the page. The browser itself becomes the state manager and it provides information to the currently loaded page and to the server to determine what to do next.

For more information about the official dynamic HTML specification, you can visit the W3 Consortium's site at www.w3c.org. The Consortium is the official keeper of all Web protocol and language specifications, including DHTML.

Creating a "Hello World" DHTML Application

This section will show you the new features in Visual Basic to allow you to build applications that use DHTML. This chapter assumes you have a working knowledge of HTML. DHTML is not really that different — it is an extension of HTML.

To get started, open Visual Basic to the New Project window, which is shown in Figure 35-1.

Figure 35-1: DHTML Application is a new entry in the New Project dialog in Visual Basic.

Changes to the VB environment

Visual Basic now supports a special type of project called the *DHTML application*. When you click on the DHTML icon and press OK, you'll be taken to the standard Visual Basic environment that has been slightly modified. The first change is to the Project Explorer window, shown in Figure 35-2.

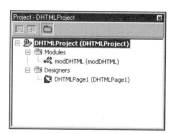

Figure 35-2: DHTML applications add both a code module and a designer to the project — automatically.

Whenever you create a new DHTML application, VB automatically builds a DHTML designer module along with a code module. This code — as VB's own comments at the top of the module states outright — allows you to get and retrieve properties from the Web browser itself. These are custom-built properties that you use in your code for your own purposes. For instance, you may need to track a unique user ID once a user has logged in. The returned value could be stored in a `UserID` property using the `PutProperty` procedure. Your code could later retrieve that value using the `GetProperty` function procedure. After retrieving the value once, you never have to ask the server for it again. This is the best part of DHTML: less network traffic. As slow as the World Wide Wait seems to be sometimes, this feature is one of the most important.

The new type of file added to a DHTML project is the page designer. (You can add another of these yourself by selecting Project ➪ Add DHTML Page.) As with the `WebClass` designer file in the previous chapter, DHTML designer files are saved with the .DSR extension. The designer module includes features allowing you to import HTML/DHTML into VB so that you don't have to start from scratch.

The new DHTML controls

Another difference you should notice about DHTML projects is that the Toolbox has changed. In a new and separate HTML category, new controls have been added, as shown in Figure 35-3.

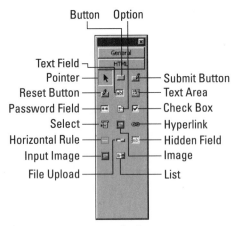

Figure 35-3: DHTML designers use a different palette of controls on the Toolbox.

These new controls are restricted for use within the DHTML designer, and will be unavailable if you attempt to open a standard form. Likewise, the standard controls, while still accessible on the Toolbox, cannot be used with DHTML designers.

Each control maps to a particular type of HTML element, mainly dealing with forms. The controls are documented here, for reference:

✦ **Button** — This represents a button on the page. The buttons common to a standard HTML form either submit the data or clear the form. This new button does not correspond to either of those; instead, it can be used for whatever purpose you like. Since the events generated by it will be received by DHTML, this control will become much more valuable.

✦ **SubmitButton** — This button submits data in a form to the URL specified at the beginning of the `<FORM>` tag. Because this button has a single function and is specified differently in HTML/DHTML, it is a separate control in VB. This button translates to `<INPUT type=submit>` in HTML.

✦ **ResetButton** — This control clears any data in the form in which it is placed. If you have a data entry form in DHTML, it is always a good idea to have a ResetButton so that the user can clear any data that was typed in. This button translates to `<INPUT type=reset>` in HTML.

✦ **TextField** — This is just a standard text box into which a user can type a line of data. It is not designed for more than one line (use TextArea for scrolling text). This control translates to `<INPUT type=text>` in HTML.

✦ **TextArea** — This control is used for multiple lines of standard text with a scroll bar attached, similar to the standard VB list box. It allows you to place unformatted text between the `<TEXTAREA>` and `</TEXTAREA>` tags.

✦ **PasswordField** — This type of text box has a few extra features. First of all, it echoes each character of text you type with an asterisk, indicating that you typed a character but not revealing which one. In addition, the control is always cleared if you leave the page and then use the back button to return to the page. This helps ensure that the data won't be read or copied accidentally or intentionally. This control translates to `<INPUT type=password>` in HTML.

✦ **Option** — This control provides a radio button (known as an option button in VB) on the form. All Option controls with the same `Name` property operate as a group. To make another group, simply choose another `Name` property for the controls in that group. You don't have to place the controls in a container like you do in VB. This control translates to `<INPUT type=radio>` in HTML.

✦ **Checkbox** — This control shows a check box on the DHTML form. Each Checkbox operates independently from any other Checkbox control on the page. This control translates to using an `INPUT type=checkbox` in HTML.

✦ **Select** — The Select control is used to create a drop-down list box. VB has separated this control from a standard list box, even though the two are actually created with the same HTML tag. Normally, this control is represented by a `<SELECT>` tag with a series of embedded `<OPTION>` tags identifying the list items. If the `<HEIGHT>` attribute is set to 1 (or omitted) in the `<SELECT>` tag, a drop-down list (Select control) is shown. Otherwise, a full list is shown of the specified height.

✦ **Image** — This shows an image on the page. Normally, this translates to an `<IMG>` tag, which works well both within or outside of a `<FORM>` element.

✦ **Hyperlink** — This control shows a hyperlink on the page. This translates to the `<A HREF>` tag.

✦ **HorizontalRule** — This control shows an bar on the page, typically used to separate sections of a page. This translates to the `<HR>` tag.

✦ **FileUpload** — Since the latest Web specification includes a way to let users upload files to a server, this feature is supported in DHTML also.

✦ **HiddenField** — This type of field is used to send data to the server without the user having to type it in. This type of data should be low security as anyone who looks at the source of the page can see the data. This translates to an `<INPUT type=hidden>` tag.

✦ **InputImage** — Documentation is pending for this control.

✦ **List** — A standard list box, which translates to a `<SELECT>` control whose `HEIGHT` attribute is set to a value above 1.

The application-building process

With the control definitions out of the way, let's build an application. This application will show a page and change the text on the page to display the message, "Hello World." This is a trivial test, but it will take you through the whole development process.

To build the application, start by double-clicking on the DHTMLPage1 designer entry in the Project Explorer. The designer window, shown in Figure 35-4, will be displayed.

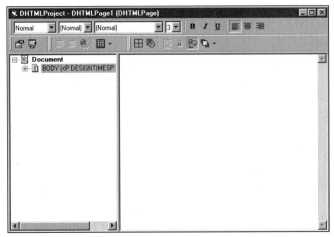

Figure 35-4: The DHTML designer window in VB

The drop-down list on the far left portion of the upper toolbar contains common HTML paragraph styles, which are shown in Table 35-1 next to their corresponding HTML tags.

Table 35-1 HTML Tag List	
List Entry	**HTML Tag**
Normal	None
Formatted	<PRE>
Address	<ADDRESS>
Heading 1	<H1>
Heading 2	<H2>
Heading 3	<H3>
Heading 4	<H4>

(continued)

List Entry	HTML Tag
Heading 5	`<H5>`
Heading 6	`<H6>`
Numbered List	`<OL>`
Bulleted List	`<UL>`
Definition List	`<DL>`
Menu List	`<MENU>`
Definition Term	`<DT>`
Definition	`<DD>`
Paragraph	`<P>`

The next drop-down list box to the right shows any classes you have defined in your style sheet. Classes are a further breakdown of how styles are defined in a Cascading Style Sheet. For instance, you can have one H1 style that uses one set of attributes, and define another H1 style (with a class name) that uses a different set.

Farther to the right, another drop-down list shows you fonts are installed on your system. When you pick fonts, remember that only a few of them are standard to Windows: Times New Roman, Arial, Courier, and a few others. Unless you know that the browser user will have a particular font, stick with the basic ones.

The final drop-down list rightward shows the relative point sizes for the chosen font, which translate to the SIZE attribute as in `<FONT SIZE=4>`. Unfortunately, you can't specify a specific point size in this interface — you can only specify a relative size. If you want to make your text 12 points high, for instance, you'll have to use a style sheet to do that.

Follow these steps to add a simple element of text to your page:

1. With the DHTML Designer window showing, in the right-hand pane, type in any text you wish, such as "Hello World." The text will appear as shown in Figure 35-5.

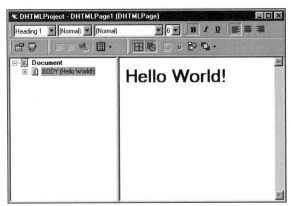

Figure 35-5: The DHTML designer with your text visible

2. Feel free to select other tags from the left-hand list and add more text. When you're done, click Run ➪ Start. The dialog shown in Figure 35-6 will appear. This dialog allows you to pick which DHTML page should be the starting page. You can also specify which browser you wish to use to view your pages. Currently, Internet Explorer 4.0 and 5.0 are the only browsers that support this DHTML specification. Make sure you have it installed on your system. Netscape supports its own version of DHTML that is not compatible with the W3C standard adopted by Microsoft. The options are correct as shown here; click the OK button.

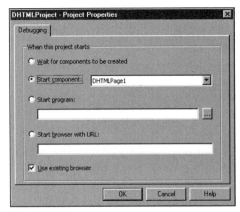

Figure 35-6: DHTML project debugging option dialog

3. At this point, your DHTML page will be shown in Internet Explorer, as seen in Figure 35-7. Not much to look at right now, but this example shows you briefly how to run your DHTML projects in Visual Basic. Click Run ➪ End to shut down your program.

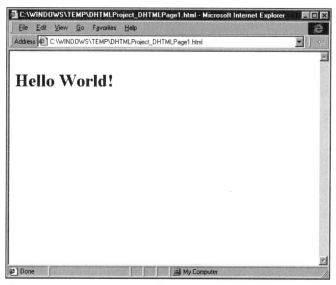

Figure 35-7: Your DHTML project running in Internet Explorer

Note that if you want to see the source in your browser, you have to do it before you stop your program. Visual Basic automatically deletes the temporary source file after you stop your program.

Using Fonts and Colors in DHTML

The DHTML designer allows you to apply a wide variety of fonts and colors to your text. These styles are applied as a style sheet so that repeatedly used styles are given reference names. For instance, all text formatted with <H1> tags appears the same. You won't have to keep duplicating all your font and color tags throughout the page any longer with style sheets.

Designating an external HTML editor

Unfortunately, style sheets are not directly supported in the DHTML editor. However, the editor gives you a way to save the HTML source code generated by VB to an external file, which can then be examined with a text or HTML editor. To do this, follow these steps:

1. From the DHTML Designer toolbar, select the DHTML Page Designer Properties toolbar button. The Properties dialog will be displayed, as shown in Figure 35-8.

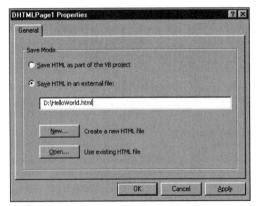

Figure 35-8: Specify the filename to use in this dialog.

2. Select the option labeled *Save HTML in an external file*, and then enter a filename to use.

3. Click on OK. VB will write your HTML source code to an external file.

At this point, you can use any text editor (such as Notepad) to edit your HTML source code. The code for the "Hello World" project should appear as shown in Listing 35-1.

Listing 35-1: **DHTML Code from VB Project**

```
<HTML>
<BODY>
<H1>Hello World!</H1>
</BODY>
</HTML>
```

Cascading Style Sheet modifications

To spice up your text a bit, modify your HTML to include the boldfaced instructions shown in Listing 35-2.

Listing 35-2: **DHTML Code with Style Sheet**

```
<HTML>
<head>
<style>
<!—
H1 {
    font-family: Verdana;
    font-size: large;
    font-weight: bold;
    font-style: normal;
    color: #FF0000;
}
—>
</style>
</head>
<BODY>
<H1>Hello World!</H1>
</BODY>
</HTML>
```

You don't have to worry about capitalization of tags. DHTML is case-insensitive, just like HTML. This style sheet, located between the `<style>` tags, was created using HomeSite, a popular HTML editor that knows how to build style sheets. It specifies that all heading 1 text should be shown in Verdana font, bold, large size, and in bright red.

Save your changes and exit your text editor. When you switch back to Visual Basic, you'll see the message shown in Figure 35-9.

Figure 35-9: Visual Basic detected the file update and wants to reload the file.

Visual Basic detected that the file has been modified. Since you specified that you wanted to use an external file for your DHTML source, VB will watch it and ask to reload it for you when you make changes. Click the Yes button and you'll see some changes in your DHTML designer window, as shown in Figure 35-10.

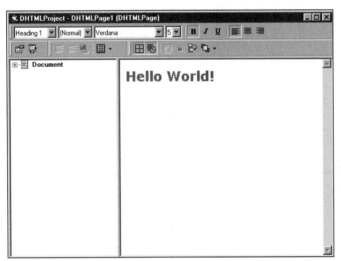

Figure 35-10: Visual Basic reloaded the file and applied your style sheet to the text.

The text is now boldfaced; and although it isn't obvious here, it's now red as well. Visual Basic reloaded the file and applied your style sheet to the text. If you open the tree on the left, you won't see the style sheet anywhere there. The only place it exists and can be edited is in your DHTML source file. If you run your page now, the results of the style sheet will also be visible in Internet Explorer, as shown in Figure 35-11.

Figure 35-11: Your style sheet applied to your text

Many sites are using style sheets to provide better control of text and graphical elements. A good site to view for examples is Microsoft's Site Builder Network site (http://www.microsoft.com/sitebuilder). There are many examples of how to use style sheets there. The W3C Consortium (http://www.w3c.org) has the entire specification for Cascading Style Sheets available online.

Responding to DHTML Events

With that little technique under your belt, it's time to respond to some events in your page. In much the same way a Visual Basic program responds to events from its controls, a DHTML page can respond to events from its elements. For instance, did you ever wonder how some pages can make text change when you move your mouse over it? You'll see how to do that and more in this section.

Mouse events

In the next example, you'll see how the DHTML page responds to mouse movements. We're going to change the color of the text on the page based on several mouse events. In order to respond to events, an element has to have a name for VB's sake. So to name the element and create an event for it, follow these steps:

1. To name the heading 1 text element, click on the text in the Designer window, and then in the Properties window, under the (ID) property, enter an identifier for the element. The example shown here uses txtTitle as the name.

2. To add event code, from VB's View menu, select Code. VB will bring up the Visual Basic (not HTML) code window for this project.

3. Select txtTitle from the left-hand drop-down list, and select onmouseover from the list on the right.

4. Add the boldfaced code in the following segment:

```
Private Sub txtTitle_onmouseover()
   txtTitle.Style.Color = "#0000FF"
End Sub
```

This code will change the text's color to blue whenever the mouse passes over it.

5. Since we only want to change the color when the mouse is actually over the text, we need to change the color back when the mouse leaves the area. Add the following code to the page:

```
Private Sub txtTitle_onmouseout()
   txtTitle.Style.Color = "#FF0000"
End Sub
```

The onmouseout event occurs whenever the mouse is no longer over the piece of text.

By switching the color back to red, the text appears to blink back and forth as the mouse moves over the text. Run your project to try this functionality out. This is a handy function to have for text-based menus and toolbars.

Note   You won't find Visual Basic source code, such as the event procedures listed here, stored in the HTML text file you edited. The code is stored in the .DSR designer file attached to your project. Be sure to remember this if you ever want to reuse your code; don't panic if you don't find it in the HTML file.

Form events

Since data entry forms are a pretty common item on HTML pages, it's important to know how to work with them. This example will show you how to respond to a simple button press on a form. Using your existing page, do the following:

1. Modify your HTML source code to resemble the following:

```
<HTML>
<head>
<style>
<!--
H1 {
    font-family: Verdana;
    font-size: large;
    font-weight: bold;
    font-style: normal;
    color: #FF0000;
}
-->
</style>
</head>
<BODY>
<H1>Hello World!</H1>
<FORM ID="frmInput">
Enter your name: <input type="Text" id="txtUserName"><P>
<input type="button" value="OK" id="cmdOK">
</form>
</BODY>
</HTML>
```

The new HTML code here adds a simple form to the document. The button is added to the form with the name cmdOK and the label OK. Save your text file and allow VB to reload the source. It should resemble Figure 35-12. The important thing here is to make sure that every element has an ID value. This is how you'll use them in the code you're going to write.

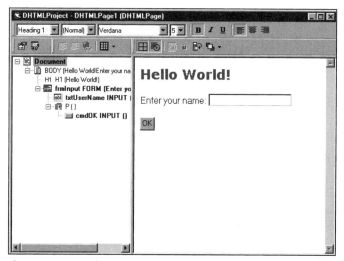

Figure 35-12: A form is now part of your document.

2. With the form added, click View ➪ Code and add the following code to the document:

```
Private Function cmdOK_onclick() As Boolean
    BaseWindow.alert "User's name is " & txtUserName.Value
End Function
```

This event handler responds to a click on the OK button on the form. When clicked, it causes a message to be displayed with the user's name in the message. Note that the Value property has to be explicitly added. Unlike controls such as the standard VB text box, the HTML input box does not have a default property. If the Value property was left off in this case, the output would be incorrect in the message.

As you use the DHTML Designer more, you may find that you like using a plain-text editor instead of the WYSIWYG editor provided in VB. Although that's fine for creating the HTML portion, remember that when you want your code to respond to various events, you have to use VB to add to your code.

Summary

This chapter gave you an introduction to the DHTML capabilities of Visual Basic. DHTML is still evolving; expect to see more changes to Visual Basic in future releases of the product.

✦   ✦   ✦

Certification Requirements and Study Guide

This appendix shows you how to use this book to prepare for the new exams required for the Microsoft Certified Solution Developer certification. Each requirement for each of the two Visual Basic 6.0 exams is listed next to the chapter covering it. Any items without a chapter reference are not covered specifically in this book. The Microsoft Certified Professional Web site (`http://www.microsoft.com/mcp`) provides other references for study material.

Exam 70-176 Designing and Developing Desktop Applications	
Skill Being Measured	**Chapter**
Assess the potential impact of the logical design on performance, maintainability, extensibility, scalability, availability, and security.	All
Design Visual Basic components to access data from a database.	Chapters 9–13
Design the properties, methods, and events of components.	Chapters 19–21, 23–25
Establish the environment for source-code version control.	
Install and configure Visual Basic for developing desktop applications	

(continued)

Exam 70-176 *(continued)*

Skill Being Measured	Chapter
Implement navigational design.	Chapter 4
Dynamically modify the appearance of a menu.	Chapter 7
Add a pop-up menu to an application.	
Create an application that adds and deletes menus at runtime.	
Add controls to forms.	
Set properties for command buttons, text boxes, and labels.	
Assign code to a control to respond to an event.	
Create data input forms and dialog boxes.	Chapter 4
Display and manipulate data by using custom controls. Controls include `ListView`, `ImageList`, `Toolbar`, and `StatusBar`.	Chapter 11
Create an application that adds and deletes controls at runtime.	
Use the `Controls` collection to manipulate controls at runtime.	
Use the `Forms` collection to manipulate forms at runtime.	
Write code that validates user input.	
Create an application that verifies data entered by a user at the field level and the form level.	Chapter 7
Create an application that enables or disables controls based on input in fields.	
Write code that processes data entered on a form.	Various
Given a scenario, add code to the appropriate form event. Events include `Initialize`, `Terminate`, `Load`, `Unload`, `QueryUnload`, `Activate`, and `Deactivate`.	
Add an ActiveX control to the toolbox.	Chapter 6 Chapter 23–24
Use data binding to display and manipulate data from a data source.	Chapter 9
Instantiate and invoke a COM component.	Chapter 19–21
Create a Visual Basic client application that uses a COM component.	

Skill Being Measured	Chapter
Create a Visual Basic application that handles events from a COM component.	
Create call-back procedures to enable asynchronous processing between COM components and Visual Basic client applications.	Chapter 19–21
Implement online user assistance in a distributed application.	
Set appropriate properties to enable user assistance. Help contents include `HelpFile`, `HelpContextID`, and `WhatsThisHelp`.	
Create HTML Help for an application.	
Implement messages from a server component to a user interface.	
Implement error handling for the user interface in desktop applications.	Chapter 33
Identify and trap runtime errors.	
Handle inline errors.	
Use an active document to present information within a Web browser.	Chapter 26
Create a COM component that implements business rules or logic. Components include DLLs, ActiveX controls, and active documents.	Chapters 19–26
Create ActiveX controls.	Chapters 23–25
Create an ActiveX control that exposes properties.	
Use control events to save and load persistent properties.	
Test and debug an ActiveX control.	
Create and enable property pages for an ActiveX control.	
Enable the data-binding capabilities of an ActiveX control.	
Create an ActiveX control that is a data source.	Chapter 26
Create an active document.	
Use code within an active document to interact with a container application.	
Navigate to other active documents.	
Debug a COM client written in Visual Basic.	Chapter 33
Compile a project with class modules into a COM component.	Chapter 19–21

(continued)

Exam 70-176 *(continued)*

Skill Being Measured	Chapter
Implement an object model within a COM component.	
Set properties to control the instancing of a class within a COM component.	
Use Visual Component Manager to manage components.	Chapter 14
Register and unregister a COM component.	Chapter 19–21
Access and manipulate a data source by using ADO and the `ADO Data` control.	Chapter 10
Given a scenario, select the appropriate compiler options.	
Control an application by using conditional compilation.	
Set watch expressions during program execution.	Various
Monitor the values of expressions and variables by using the Debug window.	Various
Use the Immediate window to check or change values.	
Use the Locals window to check or change values.	
Implement project groups to support the development and debugging process.	Chapter 33
Debug DLLs in process.	
Test and debug a control in process.	
Given a scenario, define the scope of a watch variable.	Various
Use the Package and Deployment Wizard to create a setup program that installs a distributed application, registers the COM components, and allows for uninstall.	Chapter 21
Plan and implement floppy disk-based deployment or compact disc-based deployment for a distributed application.	
Plan and implement Web-based deployment for a distributed application.	
Plan and implement network-based deployment for a distributed application.	
Fix errors, and take measures to prevent future errors.	Chapter 33
Deploy application updates for distributed applications.	

Exam 70-175
Designing and Developing Distributed Applications

Skill Being Measured	Chapter
Given a conceptual design, apply the principles of modular design to derive the components and services of the logical design.	Chapter 15
Assess the potential impact of the logical design on performance, maintainability, extensibility, scalability, availability, and security.	
Design Visual Basic components to access data from a database in a multi-tier application.	Chapters 9–13
Design the properties, methods, and events of components.	Chapters 19–21, 23–25
Establish the environment for source-code version control.	
Install and configure Visual Basic for developing distributed applications.	
Configure a server computer to run Microsoft Transaction Server (MTS).	
Install MTS.	
Set up security on a system package.	
Configure a client computer to use an MTS component.	
Create packages that install or update MTS components on a client computer.	
Implement navigational design.	Chapter 4
Dynamically modify the appearance of a menu.	Chapter 11
Add a pop-up menu to an application.	
Create an application that adds and deletes menus at runtime.	
Add controls to forms.	
Set properties for command buttons, text boxes, and labels.	
Assign code to a control to respond to an event.	
Create data input forms and dialog boxes.	Chapter 6
Display and manipulate data by using custom controls. Controls include `ListView`, `ImageList`, `Toolbar`, and `StatusBar`.	Chapter 11
Create an application that adds and deletes controls at runtime.	

(continued)

Exam 70-175 *(continued)*

Skill Being Measured	Chapter
Use the `Controls` collection to manipulate controls at runtime.	
Use the `Forms` collection to manipulate forms at runtime.	
Write code that validates user input.	Chapter 5
Create an application that verifies data entered by a user at the field level and the form level.	Chapter 7
Create an application that enables or disables controls based on input in fields.	Chapter 11
Write code that processes data entered on a form.	Various
Given a scenario, add code to the appropriate form event. Events include `Initialize`, `Terminate`, `Load`, `Unload`, `QueryUnload`, `Activate`, and `Deactivate`.	
Add an ActiveX control to the toolbox.	Chapter 6 Chapter 23–24
Create dynamic Web pages by using Active Server Pages (ASP).	
Use data binding to display and manipulate data from a data source.	Chapter 9
Instantiate and invoke a COM component.	Chapter 19–21
Create a Visual Basic client application that uses a COM component.	
Create a Visual Basic application that handles events from a COM component.	
Create call-back procedures to enable asynchronous processing between COM components and Visual Basic client applications.	Chapter 19–21
Implement online user assistance in a distributed application.	
Set appropriate properties to enable user assistance. Help contents include `HelpFile`, `HelpContextID`, and `WhatsThisHelp`.	
Create HTML Help for an application.	
Implement messages from a server component to a user interface.	
Implement error handling for the user interface in distributed applications.	Chapter 33
Identify and trap runtime errors.	
Handle inline errors.	

Skill Being Measured	Chapter
Determine how to send error information from a COM component to a client computer.	
Use an active document to present information within a Web browser.	Chapter 26
Create a COM component that implements business rules or logic. Components include DLLs, ActiveX controls, and active documents.	Chapters 19–26
Create ActiveX controls.	Chapters 23–25
Create an ActiveX control that exposes properties.	
Use control events to save and load persistent properties.	
Test and debug an ActiveX control.	
Create and enable property pages for an ActiveX control.	
Enable the data-binding capabilities of an ActiveX control.	
Create an ActiveX control that is a data source.	
Create an active document.	Chapter 26
Use code within an active document to interact with a container application.	
Navigate to other active documents.	
Design and create components that will be used with MTS.	
Debug Visual Basic code that uses objects from a COM server.	Chapter 33
Choose the appropriate threading model for a COM component.	Chapter 19
Create a package by using the MTS Explorer.	
Use the Package and Deployment Wizard to create a package.	
Import existing packages.	
Assign names to packages.	
Assign security to packages.	
Add components to an MTS package.	
Set transactional properties of components.	
Set security properties of components.	
Use role-based security to limit use of an MTS package to specific users.	
Create roles.	
Assign roles to components or component interfaces.	

(continued)

Exam 70-175 *(continued)*	
Skill Being Measured	**Chapter**
Add users to roles.	
Compile a project with class modules into a COM component.	Chapter 19–21
Implement an object model within a COM component.	
Set properties to control the instancing of a class within a COM component.	
Use Visual Component Manager to manage components.	Chapter 14
Register and unregister a COM component.	Chapter 19–21
Access and manipulate a data source by using ADO and the `ADO Data` control.	Chapter 10
Access and manipulate data by using the Execute Direct model.	Chapter 10
Access and manipulate data by using the Prepare/Execute model.	Chapter 10
Access and manipulate data by using the Stored Procedures model.	Chapter 10
Use a stored procedure to execute a statement on a database.	
Use a stored procedure to return records to a Visual Basic application.	
Retrieve and manipulate data by using different cursor locations. Cursor locations include client-side and server-side.	Chapter 10
Retrieve and manipulate data by using different cursor types. Cursor types include forward-only, static, dynamic, and keyset.	Chapter 10
Use the ADO `Errors` collection to handle database errors.	Chapter 10
Manage database transactions to ensure data consistency and recoverability.	
Write SQL statements that retrieve and modify data.	Chapter 10
Write SQL statements that use joins to combine data from multiple tables.	Chapter 10
Use appropriate locking strategies to ensure data integrity. Locking strategies include Read-Only, Pessimistic, Optimistic, and Batch Optimistic.	Chapter 10
Given a scenario, select the appropriate compiler options.	
Control an application by using conditional compilation.	

Skill Being Measured	Chapter
Set watch expressions during program execution.	Various
Monitor the values of expressions and variables by using the Debug window.	Various
Use the Immediate window to check or change values.	
Use the Locals window to check or change values.	
Implement project groups to support the development and debugging process.	Chapter 33
Debug DLLs in process.	
Test and debug a control in process.	Various
Given a scenario, define the scope of a watch variable.	
Use the Package and Deployment Wizard to create a setup program that installs a distributed application, registers the COM components, and allows for uninstall.	Chapter 21
Register a component that implements DCOM.	
Configure DCOM on a client computer and on a server computer.	
Plan and implement floppy disk-based deployment or compact disc-based deployment for a distributed application.	
Plan and implement Web-based deployment for a distributed application.	
Plan and implement network-based deployment for a distributed application.	
Implement load balancing.	
Fix errors, and take measures to prevent future errors.	Chapter 33
Deploy application updates for distributed applications.	

✦　　✦　　✦

What's on the CD-ROM

The CD-ROM included with this book provides additional materials with which you can continue learning about Visual Basic. The primary reason a CD-ROM is included is to supply you with all the sample files used throughout the book. These samples are located in the Samples directory on the CD-ROM, and the files are divided into subdirectories by chapter. The files for chapter 4, for instance, are in the \Samples\Ch04 directory.

The other purpose of the CD-ROM is to introduce you to a number of Visual Basic add-on products that provide capabilities that are either limited or nonexistent in Visual Basic itself. Many times, you will find that it is cheaper in time and maintenance to purchase third-party products to solve issues that would be hard or impossible to avoid in your development. The remainder of this appendix lists all the products on the CD-ROM, as well as their vendors' names and addresses. All products are located in the Vendors directory on the CD-ROM. All products are fully functional; however, some are limited in the amount of time that you can use them. Other products will generate a "nag" message if you have not purchased and registered them.

As the book you just purchased may have been on the shelf a while, visit the vendors' Web sites for the latest versions of their products.

Aardvark

Aardvark Software, Inc.
972 Sheffield Road
Teaneck, NJ 07666-5617
Orders: (800) 482-2742
Web site: http://www.aardsoft.com

Polisher

Polisher is a Microsoft Visual Basic add-in application. Polisher formats, comments, and spell-checks Visual Basic code. It helps programmers create better, more reliable, more readable programs. And it takes the grunt work out of keeping code in order, commenting code, and spell checking. Unique among Visual Basic development tools, Polisher can spell-check string literals and comments.

Pretty Printer

Pretty Printer produces professional listings of Visual Basic source code. The product provides a choice of fonts, types sizes, type styles and colors to enhance readability. These options can be set for comments, identifiers, keywords, literals and page headings. Other options include autoindents and connectors. The connectors display the extent of structures such as For/Next, Do/Loop, If/Else/End If. Pretty Printer's options make it easier to find bugs, understand structure, and modify programs. Pretty Printer is compatible with all black-and-white or color printers supported by Windows.

To install Polisher or Pretty Printer, copy each installer to a temporary directory on your hard disk and run it from there.

Advantageware

Advantageware, Inc.
425 Madison Avenue
Suite 1700
New York, NY 10017-1155
Orders: (888) 858-0800
Web site: http://www.advantagewareny.com
To install: run VB Advantage Demo.exe

VB Advantage gives you more than 80 productivity tools (complete with over 10,000 lines of royalty-free source code) and an expanded design-time environment. Get a VBA Compatible macro facility, powerful parser, awesome formatter, and IDE function library. Use tools right out the box. Modify tools and/or create your own. There are also additional libraries located on Advantageware's Web site.

Apex

Apex Software
4516 Henry St.
Pittsburgh, PA 15213
Orders: (800) 858-APEX
Web site: http://www.apexsc.com

True DBGrid 5.0

True DBGrid Pro 5.0 is the official upgrade to the DBGrid included with Microsoft Visual Basic 4.0 and 5.0. True DBGrid Pro 5.0 is a powerful and efficient data-aware ActiveX grid that completely manages all database operations, thereby enabling the developer to concentrate on important application-specific tasks. True DBGrid Pro 5.0 includes many new advanced data presentation and user interface features, and provides 16-bit and 32-bit OCX support.

True DBInput 5.0

True DBInput 5.0 is a suite of high-quality, data-aware, ActiveX input controls specifically designed for 32-bit Visual Basic applications. True DBInput has become popular among even the most demanding developers because of its reliability and extensive functionality.

True DBList 5.0

The power and flexibility of APEX's True DBGrid Pro 5.0 is now available in True DBList Pro 5.0. Patterned after the DBList and DBCombo controls included in Visual Basic, True DBList and True DBCombo were built using award-winning APEX technology. True DBList Pro 5.0 includes all the functionality of the original VB controls and more. Provides 16-bit and 32-bit OCX support.

True DBWizard 5.0

True DBWizard 5.0 is an ActiveX control that will greatly simplify the design effort of your database applications, without compromising software reliability or integrity. Designed for 32-bit applications, True DBWizard 5.0 can operate as an intelligent data mediator between data source controls and data-aware controls, enriching raw data with application logic that would otherwise have to be hard-coded.

VBPartner 5.0

VBPartner 5.0 is an add-in for Microsoft Visual Basic 5.0 that lets developers work more productively with Visual Basic. VBPartner 5.0 offers more than 10 unique tools or partners to assist developers with application design, documentation, error handling, and more, by simplifying routine tasks and offering handy and frequently missed functions.

BeCubed

BeCubed Software Inc.
1750 Marietta Hwy., Suite 240
Canton, GA 30114
Orders: (888) BE-CUBED (232-8233)
Web site: http://www.becubed.com

Basic Constituents

Basic Constituents is a set of 23 constituent controls designed specifically for use in ActiveX control creation. Basic Constituents unlocks the power of the base window classes of the Windows operating system. This gives the Visual Basic programmer the power to do things that would previously have been difficult or impossible to do directly within Visual Basic. Basic Constituents provides access to features of the base window classes not provided by standard controls, access to the objects of the Windows Shell, and access to the Windows System Image List.

OLE Tools

OLETools will save programmers loads of time with its multitude of controls for interface builders. Multimedia, time management and more! Enhanced calendar, list box, wave player, plus new International control, Floating Text, 2D Slider and more!

VBCommander

VBCommander is a practical and powerful Visual Basic productivity tool that commands performance! This essential tool pack assists you by adding over 100 features to the VB IDE with more than 20 productivity tools! Guaranteed to add true functionality and greatly speed your Visual Basic design time, VBCommander is not only fast and easy to use, but it has more practical power!

Catalyst

Catalyst Development Corporation
56925 Yucca Trail
Suite 254
Yucca Valley, CA 92284
Orders: (760) 228-9653
Web site: http://www.catalyst.com

Library Edition

The SocketTools Library Edition consists of 32-bit dynamic link libraries (DLLs), suitable for use with virtually any Windows development environment or scripting tool. A total of 16 libraries provide client interfaces for application protocols such as the File Transfer Protocol, Simple Mail Transfer Protocol, and Telnet protocol. The application program interface for the Library Edition is implemented with a simple elegance that makes it easy to use with any language, not just C or C++.

Visual Edition

The SocketTools Visual Edition consists of 32-bit ActiveX (OCX) controls for use with visual development environments such as Visual Basic, Visual C++ and Delphi. A total of nineteen controls provide client interfaces for the major application protocols such as the File Transfer Protocol, Simple Mail Transfer Protocol, Domain Name Service, and Telnet. All versions of Visual Basic from 2.0 and later are supported, and the ActiveX controls can be used with any 32-bit development tool that supports COM and the ActiveX control specification.

Enterprise Edition

The Enterprise Edition offers the best of both worlds for the corporate developer who needs visual controls for rapid application development, as well as the power and flexibility of dynamic-link libraries for developing core application systems. Including 32-bit ActiveX controls and 32-bit DLLs, the Enterprise Edition is suitable for use with virtually any Windows development environment or scripting tool. A total of 19 controls and 16 libraries provide client interfaces for application protocols such as the File Transfer Protocol, Simple Mail Transfer Protocol, Post Office Protocol, and Telnet Protocol.

Dart

Dart Communications
6647 Old Thompson Rd.
Syracuse, New York 13211
Orders: 315-431-1024
Web site: http://www.dart.com

PowerTCP Toolkit

PowerTCP enables the rapid construction of TCP/IP applications from proven software components. Using high-level PowerTCP ActiveX controls, developers can quickly construct custom networking applications without writing protocol and socket library code. PowerTCP controls provide tested networking code that uses the Windows Sockets interface, so your product will run on any platform with Windows Sockets support (Windows 3.*x*, Windows NT, Windows 95, and third-party TCP/IP kernels). And, since PowerTCP is tested and used in thousands of applications worldwide, you can be assured your application will seamlessly integrate with the Internet or any private intranet.

To install PowerTCP Toolkit, copy the installer to a temporary directory on your hard disk and run it from there.

Data Dynamics

Data Dynamics
2600 Tiller Lane
Columbus, OH 43231
Orders: (614) 895-3142
Web site: http://www.datadynamics.com

ActiveBar

ActiveBar™ gives you *and your users* complete control over toolbar and menu appearance and functionality. ActiveBar™ is an ActiveX control that lets you effortlessly create dockable toolbars, detachable menus, tabbed toolboxes, and sliding tabs. Power your products with the same types of flexible, customizable UI features now appearing in the world's best-selling software applications. You can implement new UI conventions such as Microsoft's Office *97* CommandBars™ and Internet Explorer™ CoolBars, and Delphi's tabbed toolbars, plus a few new varieties not available anywhere else.

ActiveReports

ActiveReports combines the power and ease-of-use of Microsoft Visual Basic ® with advanced ActiveX Designer Component technology to provide the ultimate report designer for Visual Basic Developers. ActiveReports is fully integrated in the Visual Basic programming environment. It feels and works like VB. No more cryptic scripts or workarounds. It provides a fully open architecture that lets you use VB code, ActiveX, and OLE Objects in your reports so you can handle the toughest reports without limits.

DynamiCube

The power of a multidimensional OLAP tool, coupled with the Data Dynamics microCube™ persistent data storage technology (built in), yields astonishingly small, manageable data objects. What happens from your perspective is this: With virtually no coding, you provide users with the SQL query path to any ODBC, DAO, RDO, or BDE data source. DynamiCube builds and displays results at the user's PC. Users perform as much interactive analysis as they need, *locally*, including data filtering, drill-down, roll-up, addition of user data and calculations, data marking, dimensional pivoting, ranking, print/preview, and graphing. You get all this power, without impacting production databases or requiring changes to current relational or multidimensional database systems.

Desaware

Desaware Inc.
1100 E. Hamilton Ave., Suite #4
Campbell, CA 95008-0733
Orders: 408-377-4770
Web site: http://www.desaware.com

Gallimaufry

The Desaware ActiveX Gallimaufry includes a collection of useful, entertaining, and educational ActiveX controls that include complete Visual Basic 5.0 source code. Among them are a MDI Taskbar Control, Hex Edit control, Rotate Picture control, SpiralBox control, Banner control, PerspectiveList control, and a Common Dialog component. These components are worthwhile for the educational value alone, even if you have no use for them in your applications and Web sites.

Spyworks

You CAN do that with Visual Basic! ActiveX extension and OLE Hook technology let you override the default behavior of standard interfaces. You can add new interfaces to your classes and controls, use Dynamic Export Technology™ to export functions from your VB ActiveX DLLs, create Control Panel applets, and export function libraries, ISAPI filters, and NT services! Includes subclassing and hook controls (includes the source code to a commercial-quality subclasser/hook control), sample code and more. SpyWorks Professional is a subscription-based edition that includes SpyWorks 2.1 and Standard and three additional shipments of new features, application notes, and upgrades delivered to you every 3 to 4 months.

StorageTools

The ultimate data storage and file manipulation toolkit for Visual Basic and other OLE clients, StorageTools is your key to the OLE 2.0 Structured Storage Technology. Easily work with OLE 2.0 structured storage files from within your application. Take advantage of the same file-storage system used by Microsoft's own applications. Includes documentation and controls to make it easy to work with the registration database under Windows, Windows NT, and Windows 95. Plus, we include a simple resource compiler (with source) so that you can create your own RES files for use with Visual Basic and more.

VersionStamper

VersionStamper helps eliminate incompatibility problems that occur when distributing component-based applications by embedding into your executable version information about all of the DLLs and custom controls used by that application. Supports the Internet and corporate intranets. Now you can keep an updated list of file dependencies on your Web or FTP site that your application can be programmed to check. If it finds a problem or updated file, it can notify the user, send e-mail back to your company, or even have VersionStamper automatically download the correct components from your Web or FTP site.

DT Software

DT Software
2101 Crystal Plaza Arcade
Suite 231
Arlington, VA 22202
Orders: (800) IT-FINDS (483-4637)
Web site: http://www.dtsoftware.com

dtSearch

dtSearch is able to search through the text of thousands of files in a second, because it builds an index that stores the location of words in your files. Once dtSearch has built an index, search speed is usually less than a second. Indexing is easy — just click on the directories you want dtSearch to index, and dtSearch will do the rest. dtSearch supports all popular file formats and never alters your original files. Since you may sometimes want to search files that dtSearch has not indexed, dtSearch also does unindexed as well as "combination" searches. dtSearch is fully programmable from your Visual Basic applications — no more shelling out to separate programs to find files!

HexaTech

HexaTech
725 Mariposa Avenue
Suite 107
Mountain View, CA 94041
Orders: (650) 254-0610
Web site: http://www.hexatech.com

Ace Toolbar

The Ace of OCX/ActiveX for Visual Basic Toolbar, Visual C++, and Delphi. AceToolbar is an award winning active toolbar OCX/ActiveX control for creating a variety of active toolbars (and menus), including but not limited to Internet Explorer toolbar, Office 97 toolbars, and other innovative toolbars. If you are looking for a versatile toolbar OCX/ActiveX control for Visual Basic, Visual C++, or Delphi, try this one.

ViewPro

ViewPro is a Visual Basic print preview OCX/ActiveX control. It adds powerful print and preview capabilities to your forms, dialog boxes, and other windows. It replaces Visual Basic's printer object for preview support and enhanced capabilities, and replaces Visual C++'s print/preview form for RAD (Rapid Application Development). If you are looking for a Visual Basic print preview OCX/ActiveX control, this is the right one for you. ViewPro can also be used as a lightweight, versatile runtime report generator to replace bulky and inflexible static report writers.

XRosyGUI

XRosyGUI comprises 16- and 32-bit OCX/ActiveX controls for developing versatile, intuitive and great-looking GUIs. An XRosyGUI scene can be many things — such as an office, a shopping center, an instrument control panel, or a beautiful virtual world full of on-screen renderings of objects casting accurate shadows — only imagination is the limit. Conventional Windows GUI elements — such as buttons, check boxes, menu bars, toolbars, and so on — are just special cases of XRosyGUI scenes or objects.

To install XRosyGUI, copy the installer to a temporary directory on your hard disk and run it from there.

Mabry Software

Mabry Software
503 316th Street Northwest
Stanwood, WA 98292
Orders: (800) 99-MABRY (996-2279)
Web site: http://www.mabry.com

Internet Pack

This package contains controls for giving your applications access to the Internet. All of them are VBXs and 32-bit OLE controls (OCXs) ready to run under Windows 3.1, Windows 95 or Windows NT. The controls support ASocket, Finger, FTP, GetHst,

Gopher, Mail (SMTP/POP), News (NNTP), RAS, Time, and WhoIs. There's even a control that gives you direct access to Windows sockets.

Mega Pack

The Mega Pack 2 contains 22 of our custom controls: Alarm, BarCod, BmpLst, DFInfo, FLabel, FMDrop, HiTime, IniCon, JoyStk, LED, MenuEv, MSlot, MSStat, PerCnt, PicBtn, Probe, RoText, SoundX, Tips, Ver, Wave, and ZipInf.

To install Mega Pack, copy the installer to a temporary directory on your hard disk and run it from there.

Modern Software

Modern Software
P.O. Box 14
Putnam, CT 06260
Orders: (860) 963-1071
Web site: http://www.modernsoftware.com

Modern GuardX

Modern GuardX solves your software security problems with powerful, multilevel password protection. You can protect any application, dialog (Form or UserForm), Class, UserControl, Worksheet, Document, menu, or procedure. Just drop our Protection ActiveX Component into your ActiveX, set some properties, respond to some events, and you're done! GuardX lets you quickly implement a powerful password-protection security system in any program.

Numega

NuMega Technologies, Inc.
9 Townsend West
Nashua, NH 03063 USA
Orders: (800) 4-NUMEGA (468-6342)
Web site: http://www.numega.com

CodeReview

CodeReview is the only automated source-code analysis system for Visual Basic. CodeReview rigorously examines Visual Basic source code for hundreds of potential problems in application components, logic, Windows, and Visual Basic itself. When CodeReview finds a problem, it recommends a solution to resolve it.

CodeReview also provides coding standards enforcement and statistical quality-control metrics.

TrueTime

NuMega TrueTime automatically locates performance bottlenecks in applications and components written in Java, Visual C++, and Visual Basic. TrueTime provides a precise analysis code performance, which allows developers to optimize runtime performance and usability. TrueTime helps developers deliver the fastest applications and components for the enterprise and the Internet.

Pinnacle Publishing

Pinnacle Publishing
216 First Ave. S.
Suite 260
Seattle, WA 98104
Orders: (800) 231-1293
Web site: http://www.graphicsserver.com

Graphics Server

Since its release in 1990, Graphics Server has set the industry standard for high-end data analysis and presentation. Because of its ability to provide seamless graphing support across both 16-bit and 32-bit Windows platforms, Graphics Server's graph control is currently being used in software packages from industry leaders including Microsoft, Borland, Novell, Intel, and many others — and is trusted by over one million developers worldwide. With the release of version 5.0, Graphics Server brings statistical power, stylistic control, and ease-of-use to all new levels.

Protoview

Protoview Development Corporation
2540 Route 130
Cranbury, NJ 08512
Orders: (800) 231-8588
Web site: http://www.protoview.com

ActiveX Component Suite

The ProtoView ActiveX Component Suite Version 2.0 contains three of the best-selling ActiveX component products on the market. The ActiveX Component Suite Version 2.0 contains new versions of these three ProtoView ActiveX component products:

✦ Data Explorer — the only ActiveX component that lets developers display and edit data in a Windows Explorer-style UI.

✦ DataTable — the high-speed grid component of choice for developers worldwide.

✦ WinX Component Library — Contains 17 display and editing components.

InterAct

InterAct is a reusable component that allows developers to create a diagramming engine for any application interface. Its open programming model and extended features provide developers with a wide range of deployment possibilities for creating a variety of diagramming UIs. InterAct can be used as a front end for developers to create "real-time" status information charts with custom tool palettes that allow properties to change with the click of a mouse.

Sheridan

Sheridan Software Systems
35 Pinelawn Road
Melville, NY 11747
Orders: (800) 823-4732
Web site: http://www.shersoft.com

Note: All products can be installed by running SETUP.EXE in the Sheridan directory. Because this software is packaged on this CD-ROM, some of the setup options relating to company information or ordering Sheridan's products do not function properly. For information on Sheridan or to order their products, visit their Web site listed above.

ActiveListBar

The Sheridan ActiveListBar is a navigation control that brings the look of Microsoft® Outlook™ to your applications. It incorporates a system of sliding groups, each of which is identified by its header. Clicking a group's header causes the group to become active, slide into view, and display the items it contains. The ActiveListBar adds an advanced yet easy-to-use interface to your applications. You can use it to provide users with the ability to group and categorize a variety of items for quick access. Intuitive and visually appealing, ActiveListBar provides a look familiar to anyone who works with the Microsoft Outlook personal organizer or the Office 97 suite of applications.

ActiveToolBars

The ActiveToolBars control provides an easy way to incorporate the look and feel of Microsoft Office in your applications. Through the implementation of toolbars and menus that remember their position from session to session, as well as the layout of their comprised tools and commands, an application that utilizes ActiveToolBars can easily allow each user to assemble a familiar and comfortable environment, regardless of his or her individual preferences.

ActiveThreed

ActiveThreed is a set of seven 32-bit ActiveX controls that give the most prevalent elements in applications an Internet/intranet look and feel. Features include marquee captions, transparent backgrounds, multiline captions, animated pictures, and multiple button styles. Powerful new features in ActiveThreed include a Splitter control for quickly and easily creating frames, active borders on ribbon and command buttons, and more.

ActiveTreeView

The ActiveTreeView control is an advanced interface for displaying hierarchical data. It provides a superset of the features found in the Microsoft TreeView common control, and can be used as a drop-in replacement for that control. By using the ActiveTreeView in your projects, you gain abilities that go far beyond those of the standard tree control. The ActiveTreeView control consists of a collection of nodes. Each node represents a data item in the tree. Nodes are organized into hierarchical relationships, and are connected by tree lines that represent the "branches" of the tree. Each node has properties that determine its relationship to other nodes in the hierarchy. The control automatically structures the tree based on the interrelationships of the nodes within it.

CalendarWidgets

Calendar Widgets is the perfect set of Sheridan Reusable Components for use in any Windows-based application that needs to visually display, select and manage dates and times. Including versions for 16-bit Visual Basic custom controls and 16-bit and 32-bit ActiveX controls, Calendar Widgets consists of four controls: MonthView, YearView, DateCombo, and DayView. Besides being a great fit for a typical Personal Information Manager (PIM), Calendar Widgets is a natural for data entry, accounting, billing, project management, or any other application referring to and using time and dates.

DataWidgets

The premier set of database controls for developing in Microsoft Visual Basic, C++, or Internet Explorer just got better. Designed with ease-of-use in mind, DataWidgets 3.0 virtually eliminates the need for time-consuming coding when developing applications that involve database operations. What used to take hours of development can now take minutes. And for the ultimate in flexibility and control over data storage, retrieval, and display, Data Widgets Grid, ComboBox, and DropDown Data controls let you choose from three data modes: Bound, Unbound, and AddItem.

DesignerWidgets

DesignerWidgets 2.0, a set of Sheridan Reusable Components, is designed to give your applications interfaces similar to those of today's most popular commercial applications. They are supplied as version 3, 16-bit Visual Basic custom controls (VBX), and 16-bit and 32-bit ActiveX Controls. DesignerWidgets is loaded with the most enhanced interface controls, including Dockable Toolbar, the Notebook Tab Control, the Index Tab Control, and FormFX. There is no other package that combines controls allowing you to program with the style and power of DesignerWidgets 2.0.

spAssist

sp_Assist is a multiuser development tool for SQL Server. It's used to manage the coding process of SQL database objects including stored procedures, triggers, tables, indexes, keys, defaults, and rules. Features include a multiuser SQL coding environment, code generation of both SQL and Visual Basic code, encapsulation of all SQL keywords, executable statements, system stored procedures, database administration tools, and more. sp_Assist is the only tool you'll need for SQL Server to manage and code client/server applications.

VBAssist

VBAssist is a set of 15 major productivity tools that seamlessly integrate into the Visual Basic development environment. VBAssist has been totally re-architected to take maximum advantage of Visual Basic's 32-bit environment. VBAssist's new ActiveX DLL design, in which each tool is an in-process component, provides the best possible overall performance in Visual Basic. Its plug-in architecture will allow future VBAssist components to be created and delivered in the timeliest manner. VBAssist utilizes the `CommandBar` object for seamless integration with the rest of the Visual Basic design IDE.

VideoSoft

VideoSoft
5900-T Hollis Street
Emeryville, CA 94608
Orders: (888) ACTIVE-X (228-4839)
Web site: http://www.videosoft.com

Note: All products can be installed by running SETUP.EXE in the Videosoft directory.

VSDATA

VSDATA is a complete database engine in one ActiveX control! This powerful control gives applications faster access to data. Due to its small footprint, VSDATA is the ideal database system for your Internet or multimedia applications. VSDATA gives you full control of your data access by supporting record locking and multifield indexing. VSDATA is multimedia aware. Store your video and sound files into native database fields. Then you can use any of the built-in playback methods to give life to your applications with sound or video.

VSDIRECT

VideoSoft VSDIRECT is an ActiveX control package that allows Visual Basic developers to exploit the power and speed of Microsoft DirectX technology. VideoSoft VSDIRECT has multiple component features that allow game and multimedia developers to easily integrate sound and drawing capabilities into their applications by leveraging Microsoft's DirectX technology. These components include vsDirectDraw, vsDirectSound, and vsDirectPlay. vsDirectDraw works with various creative interfaces that accelerate animation techniques through direct access to video memory and hardware. vsDirectSound enables hardware and software sound-mixing and playback. vsDirectPlay provides connectivity of games over a modem link or network.

VSDOCX

VSDOCX automatically documents ActiveX controls. Create your controls using Visual Basic 5.0 or Visual C++, and VSDOCX will create the user documentation and help files for you. You can even document controls you download from the Web (no source code is required). VSDOCX is easy to use. Select all ActiveX controls to be documented, click a button, and the control's basic documentation—including a context-sensitive, indexed, cross-linked help file—is done. Of course, you may customize it and update the information at any time using VSDOCX's wizard-style dialogs.

VSFLEX

VSFLEX is a flexible data-analysis tool! Just add your data to the vsFlexArray control, set a couple of properties, and your users will be able to dynamically pivot the data between columns. All the data is automatically sorted, merged, and rearranged. VSFLEX also includes vsFlexString, a powerful control that allows you to find and replace complex string patterns.

VS-OCX 5.0

No more resizing code! Just add a single vsElastic control to your existing form, set a couple of properties and voilà: Your form becomes resolution-independent — EGA, VGA, SVGA — it doesn't matter. The vsElastic control automatically resizes all of the controls on your form. No more switching between forms! Let the vsIndexTab control present several screens' worth of data in the space of one by using notebook-style tabs like those in Word or Excel. Resize the form and watch the contents of each tab automatically resize. No more slow code to parse strings and read files! Let the vsAwk string-parser control slice and dice your strings automatically. It even includes an expression evaluator that supports variables.

Elastic-Light 6.0

VideoSoft ElasticLight is the easiest way to add elasticity to your forms. Just add the new ElasticLight control to your existing applications, and your forms automatically become resolution independent. When you resize your form, the vsElasticLight control automatically resizes all the controls contained in it. No code is required! Version 6.0 has a small footprint, and it doesn't require additional DLLs to be distributed. Add elasticity to your forms without writing a single line of code.

VSREPORTS

VSREPORTS moves you into a new era of reporting! VSREPORTS allows you to print Microsoft Access-created reports without having Access or its runtime DLLs installed on the user's machine. This ActiveX control permits you to use the industry-leading report designer Access to create your reports and then print them using Visual Basic or any ActiveX container. Place a vsReport ActiveX control on your form, set a few properties, and presto! Your Access report is ready to be previewed or printed! VSREPORTS re-creates Access reports, reproducing the exact positioning of fields and page breaks, fonts, colors, sorting, and filtering into groups and sections, just as in the original report.

VSSPELL

VideoSoft VSSPELL is a set of two controls: vsSpell and vsThesaurus. vsSpell allows you to have instant access to its extensive standard American English word dictionary with more than 50,000 entries. A utility is included to easily build and maintain custom dictionaries. vsSpell dictionaries are compatible with those created by Microsoft Word. Built-in dialog boxes allow you to add full-fledged spell checking to your apps, with no code. Quickly customize functionality like automatic or manual correction, generation of suggestions for specific words, and so on vsThesaurus allows access to an American English thesaurus with more than 30,000 entries and has properties and methods that allow you to build and maintain thesaurus files.

VSVIEW

VideoSoft VSVIEW makes printing and reporting intuitive! VSVIEW's vsPrinter control uses a familiar word-processing metaphor to create your output. You can print paragraphs and text that will automatically wrap. You can easily combine paragraphs, graphs, graphics, tables, and columns anywhere on the page. With its rich set of formatting options such as headers, footers, text alignment, text angle, indentation, word-wrapping, "Page 1 of X" functionality, and margins, you can create virtually any document or report you can imagine.

Vivatexte

Vivatexte
112 Bayswater Avenue
Ottawa, Ontario K1Y 2G1
Canada
Information: tshaver@vivatexte.com
Web site: http://www.vivatexte.com

Multipage Browser Control

The Vivatexte Multipage Browser Control is a state of the art ActiveX control that lets you launch and access multiple Web pages in a single browser. You can then switch among pages by clicking on a tab. It is built using Microsoft Internet Explorer® technology, so you know that the browser will support the latest page technologies, such as VBscript, ActiveX controls, ActiveX documents and all the other advanced features inherent in IE3 or better. You also can be assured that fixes and upgrades to IE on your system will automatically be reflected in the multipage browser control.

Wise Solutions

Wise Solutions
2200 North Canton Center Road
Suite 220
Canton, MI 48187
Orders: (800) 554-8565
Web site: http://www.wisesolutions.com

WISE Installation System 6.0

Wise creates installations that easily and quickly install your applications on a variety of destination platforms. Wise automatically compresses and splits your files onto floppy disks, or creates a single EXE file, for online or e-mail distribution. Wise has true multiple language support — a single installation script can contain up to 15 languages, with 10 pre-translated languages available. Wise installations support both 16-bit and 32-bit destination platforms in Windows, as well as the DEC Alpha platform.

✦   ✦   ✦

Index

(continued)

(continued)

(continued)

(continued)

F

(continued)

(continued)

(continued)

(continued)

(continued)

(continiued)

(continued)

Hungry Minds, Inc., End-User License Agreement

contained in the individual license agreements recorded on the Software Media. These limitations may include a requirement that after using the program for a specified period of time, the user must pay a registration fee or discontinue use. By opening the Software packet(s), you will be agreeing to abide by the licenses and restrictions for these individual programs that are detailed in Appendix B "What's on the CD-ROM" and on the Software Media. None of the material on this Software Media or listed in this Book may ever be redistributed, in original or modified form, for commercial purposes.

5. **Limited Warranty.**

   (a) HMI warrants that the Software and Software Media are free from defects in materials and workmanship under normal use for a period of sixty (60) days from the date of purchase of this Book. If HMI receives notification within the warranty period of defects in materials or workmanship, HMI will replace the defective Software Media.

   (b) HMI AND THE AUTHOR OF THE BOOK DISCLAIM ALL OTHER WARRANTIES, EXPRESS OR IMPLIED, INCLUDING WITHOUT LIMITATION IMPLIED WARRANTIES OF MERCHANTABILITY AND FITNESS FOR A PARTICULAR PURPOSE, WITH RESPECT TO THE SOFTWARE, THE PROGRAMS, THE SOURCE CODE CONTAINED THEREIN, AND/OR THE TECHNIQUES DESCRIBED IN THIS BOOK. HMI DOES NOT WARRANT THAT THE FUNCTIONS CONTAINED IN THE SOFTWARE WILL MEET YOUR REQUIREMENTS OR THAT THE OPERATION OF THE SOFTWARE WILL BE ERROR FREE.

   (c) This limited warranty gives you specific legal rights, and you may have other rights that vary from jurisdiction to jurisdiction.

6. **Remedies.**

   (a) HMI's entire liability and your exclusive remedy for defects in materials and workmanship shall be limited to replacement of the Software Media, which may be returned to HMI with a copy of your receipt at the following address: Software Media Fulfillment Department, Attn.: *Visual Basic® 6 Bible,* Hungry Minds, Inc., 10475 Crosspoint Blvd., Indianapolis, IN 46256, or call 1-800-762-2974. Please allow four to six weeks for delivery. This Limited Warranty is void if failure of the Software Media has resulted from accident, abuse, or misapplication. Any replacement Software Media will be warranted for the remainder of the original warranty period or thirty (30) days, whichever is longer.

   (b) In no event shall HMI or the author be liable for any damages whatsoever (including without limitation damages for loss of business profits, business interruption, loss of business information, or any other pecuniary loss) arising from the use of or inability to use the Book or the Software, even if HMI has been advised of the possibility of such damages.

(c) Because some jurisdictions do not allow the exclusion or limitation of liability for consequential or incidental damages, the above limitation or exclusion may not apply to you.

7. **<u>U.S. Government Restricted Rights.</u>** Use, duplication, or disclosure of the Software for or on behalf of the United States of America, its agencies and/or instrumentalities (the "U.S. Government") is subject to restrictions as stated in paragraph (c)(1)(ii) of the Rights in Technical Data and Computer Software clause of DFARS 252.227-7013, and in subparagraphs (a) through (d) of the Commercial Computer — Restricted Rights clause at FAR 52.227-19, and in similar clauses in the NASA FAR supplement, when applicable.

8. **<u>General.</u>** This Agreement constitutes the entire understanding of the parties and revokes and supersedes all prior agreements, oral or written, between them and may not be modified or amended except in a writing signed by both parties hereto that specifically refers to this Agreement. This Agreement shall take precedence over any other documents that may be in conflict herewith. If any one or more provisions contained in this Agreement are held by any court or tribunal to be invalid, illegal, or otherwise unenforceable, each and every other provision shall remain in full force and effect.

CD-ROM
Installation
Instructions

The CD-ROM that accompanies this book contains a complete set of demonstration programs developed in the text, plus a selection of programming tools from several vendors.

- ✦ For the demo programs from the text, simply copy the files into a new folder on your hard disk.

- ✦ For the programming tools, simply double-click each self-extracting installer to install the files.

- ✦ For more details on the content of the CD-ROM and how to use it, see Appendix B.